Mastering
System Center 2012
Configuration Manager

Steve Rachui

Kent Agerlund

Santos Martinez

Peter Daalmans

WILEY

John Wiley & Sons, Inc.

Acquisitions Editor: Agatha Kim

Development Editor: Tom Cirtin

Technical Editor: Brett Bennett

Production Editor: Dassi Zeidel

Copy Editor: Linda Recktenwald

Editorial Manager: Pete Gaughan

Production Manager: Tim Tate

Vice President and Executive Group Publisher: Richard Swadley

Vice President and Publisher: Neil Edde

Book Designers: Maureen Forys, Happenstance Type-O-Rama; Judy Fung

Proofreader: Rebecca Rider

Indexer: Ted Laux

Project Coordinator, Cover: Katherine Crocker

Cover Designer: Ryan Sneed

Cover Image: © Thomas Northcut / Digital Vision/ Getty Images

Dear Reader,

Thank you for choosing *Mastering System Center 2012 Configuration Manager*. This book is part of a family of premium-quality Sybex books, all of which are written by outstanding authors who combine practical experience with a gift for teaching.

Sybex was founded in 1976. More than 30 years later, we're still committed to producing consistently exceptional books. With each of our titles, we're working hard to set a new standard for the industry. From the paper we print on, to the authors we work with, our goal is to bring you the best books available.

I hope you see all that reflected in these pages. I'd be very interested to hear your comments and get your feedback on how we're doing. Feel free to let me know what you think about this or any other Sybex book by sending me an email at nedde@wiley.com. If you think you've found a technical error in this book, please visit http://sybex.custhelp.com. Customer feedback is critical to our efforts at Sybex.

Best regards,

Neil Edde
Vice President and Publisher
Sybex, an Imprint of Wiley

I'd like to dedicate this book first to my beautiful and supportive wife, Sherri. She is a true gem—one I was very lucky to find. I'd like also to dedicate this book to my family—immediate, extended, and acquired by marriage! Their constant support and belief in me are the best gifts they could ever give. Last—and should be first—my Lord. Christ is the true meaning of life. The rest is just filler material.
—Steven Rachui

I dedicate this book to my loving and understanding wife, Susanne, who never seems to stop amazing me. I also want to dedicate this book to my two wonderful children, Nanna and Julie. Thank you for putting up with me while I was writing this book. You are forever in my heart and thoughts—You'll Never Walk Alone!
—Kent Agerlund

I dedicate this book to my wonderful wife, Karla, for helping me achieve all our goals in life; love you in this life and the next one. To my son, Bryan Emir, for being such a great son; keep up with the basketball—you will be an NBA player one day. To my daughter, Naomy Arwen, for all your questions overnight about what I'm doing and why; you are so awesome—keep dancing like you always do; I enjoy watching you and your brother grow.
—Santos Martinez

I dedicate this book to my father; you are still deeply missed. To my mother, for all of your love and support in my life. To my girlfriend, Samantha, and our son, Stef; thanks for putting up with me and for all of your love and support while writing this book.
—Peter Daalmans

Acknowledgments

First and foremost—thanks to God for salvation and providing the true meaning in life. Without Him everything else would be useless. I'd also like to thank my many friends and colleagues across Microsoft—particularly in the product team, Premier Field Engineering, and Customer Support Services—for always keeping me sharp. This is a great product and a milestone achievement for ConfigMgr—it was great to write about it! And, as already stated, my wife. Sherri is an inspiration and a great sounding board even though there isn't a ConfigMgr bone in her body! Lastly, my bichon, Mollie, a constant companion while writing.

—*Steven Rachui*

I want to thank the Microsoft Configuration Management team for giving us a great product to write about. Especially warm thanks go to Wally Mead, Doug Eby, and Carol Bailey for always taking their time to answer my questions. I also want to thank all my colleagues at Coretech for being the best bunch of guys I have ever worked with. I also want to thank my family for allowing me the time required for this book and for being the true inspiration in my life.

—*Kent Agerlund*

The first person I want to thank is God for bringing me into this world and giving me a wonderful mother, Isabel. She always encouraged me to do better when I was a kid. Also I want to thank God for giving me the strength and the clarity of mind to take on this project. I want to truly thank my wife, Karla, for being by my side for the past 14 years. We've learned a lot together, and every goal I have achieved is because of her support.

I also want to thank my MVP lead Fernando Garcia Lorea; during my eight years on the MVP program, he always guided me to be a better MVP and challenged me to do great things for the MVP LATAM community. Fernando, thank you for your support all these years.

To my friend Elias Mereb, thanks for your support; you are like my brother and always will be.

To my manager, David Tolkov, for giving me the opportunity to join Microsoft and the great team of South Central. You are the best manager I have had in many years, and without your support and motivation, this project wouldn't be complete. Thank you.

To my mentor Neil Peterson at Microsoft; you don't really know how much your words have impacted my career and my role as a premier field engineer.

To the PFE ConfigMgr community; you have been there when I needed some advice and have supported me to achieve successful engagements with many customers. Thank you all for being such great peers.

To the Premier customers: you are always friendly and open when I come onsite to guide you, and together we learn about this wonderful product. Thank you for your kind words; your business will be always be appreciated.

To the TechNet Forum users; thank you for all your questions over these past few years. Keep supporting the product and the forums, and you will always find the solutions to your questions from professionals who are as passionate about this product as yourselves. Thank you for your support.

Finally, I want to thank my technical editor, Brett Bennett, for his efforts and work on this book; I will always be grateful to have had you on this team. To my peer authors, Steve, Kent, and Peter; you guys rock as a team, and I'm looking forward to co-authoring more books with you. Also I want to thank the entire Sybex team for their efforts and patience during these months that we have been working together; from the bottom of my heart to all of you, thanks.

—*Santos Martinez*

Special thanks to my family and friends. I had to balance my time with you with my commitment to writing chapters for this book. I couldn't have done this without you guys!

I also want to thank Agatha Kim and Pete Gaughan at Wiley/Sybex for giving me the opportunity to write this book. I never thought I would be writing a book about this great product!

Furthermore, many thanks to the Configuration Manager product team, who created this great product, and to Nicole Pargoff of Microsoft and her splendid Community Evaluation Program team, who allowed me to become familiar and play with the early versions of Configuration Manager 2012, which allowed me to blog about it in the first place.

Also special thanks to my employers, Marco and Koos from IT-Concern, who allowed me to build a real-life Configuration Manager 2012 lab environment, which gave me a good foundation for writing this book.

Finally, many thanks to my coauthors Kent, Santos, and Steve and editors Brett and Tom and the rest of the Sybex team for guiding and supporting me in the writing process.

—*Peter Daalmans*

About the Authors

Steven Rachui, premier field engineer for Microsoft, has supported System Center products—including Configuration Manager and Operations Manager—at Microsoft for 13 years. Steven blogs at `blogs.msdn.com/steverac`. Steven is well known in ConfigMgr circles and has spoken at the Microsoft Management Summit several times. Little known to most is the fact that Steven started his career as a microbiologist. ConfigMgr was quite a change!

Steven has traveled extensively—in the United States and also internationally—training and consulting on ConfigMgr. He and his wife live in the Dallas/Ft. Worth area of Texas, with their bichon, Mollie.

Kent Agerlund is a System Center specialist working as a certified trainer and consultant in the area of Configuration Manager. He started his computer endeavors back in the late eighties working with databases such as dBase, Paradox, and FoxPro. Almost since the beginning of his professional computer career, Kent has been working as a certified trainer and consultant. Today Kent works for Coretech, a Danish System Center house, where he also contributes by writing articles and sharing tips and tricks on `http://blog.coretech.dk`. In recent years Kent has been traveling around the globe delivering Mastering Configuration Manager 2007 training and now 2012 training. Kent also speaks at events around the world.

Over the years, Kent has attained various certifications and achievements such as MCSE+A, MCT, and Configuration Manager MVP. Kent was a co-founder of SCUG.DK, the Danish System Center User Group, in 2009.

Kent resides 10 miles outside Copenhagen, Denmark, with his wife, Susanne (his high school sweetheart), and his daughters, Julie and Nanna. When not working on technical information or solutions, he can be found exploring the local forest or highway in his running shoes or on his bike.

Santos Martinez was born in Caguas, Puerto Rico, in 1982, and grew up in Caguas. Santos has more than 10 years of experience in the IT industry. He has worked on major implementations and in support of ConfigMgr and SMS migrations for financial institutions in the United States and Puerto Rico. Santos was a senior Configuration Manager engineer for a Fortune 500 financial institution and an IT consultant before joining Microsoft. For the Fortune 500 company, he helped with the implementation and support of more than 200 ConfigMgr servers and support of more than 165 clients worldwide. After completing this project he did IT consulting work for many other corporations that were implementing ConfigMgr.

Santos was a SQL Server MVP from 2005 to 2009 and then a ConfigMgr MVP from 2009 to 2011. He is well known in the Microsoft LATAM communities as a mentor for other MVPs and for helping other IT community members. He has also participated in Microsoft Tech Ed and Microsoft MMS as a technical expert for SMS/ConfigMgr. Santos is also a former Puerto Rican martial arts champion and currently holds a fourth-degree black belt in TaiFu Shoi Karate Do.

Santos and Karla (a pastry chef) have been married for 11 years and have two kids, Bryan Emir and Naomy Arwen.

Santos currently is a premier field engineer for Microsoft in the south central region of the United States.

Peter Daalmans is a senior technical consultant at IT-Concern, a Gold Certified Microsoft partner in the Netherlands. Peter worked with deployment tooling from Microsoft competitors since

1998; in 2005 Peter discovered BDD and SMS 2003 deployment tooling and has embraced them since then. In recent years numerous (international) deployment projects have crossed Peter's path.

Peter is an active member of the Community Evaluation Program for Configuration Manager 2012 and the Configuration Manager community, and he shares his experiences on his weblog (`www.systemcenterblog.nl`) and at myITForum.

Peter resides in Breda, in the south of the Netherlands, with his girlfriend, Samantha, and his son, Stef. In addition to his daily work, he is the chairman of the NAC Museum Foundation, which preserves the history of the soccer club NAC Breda. Australia is also a huge passion; he travels Down Under whenever he gets the chance to sniff the outback and the Aussie lifestyle.

About the Contributing Author

Brett Bennett is a senior premier field engineer at Microsoft and has been working with SMS/ConfigMgr since SMS 1.0. Brett lives in Texas with his wife, Rosalie, and their three children. His daughter, Brittany, and his oldest son, Jamie, attend Texas A&M University (gig 'em!) and his youngest son, Justin, is in high school. The Bennetts have three dogs: two black labs (Yogi and Boo Boo) and a golden retriever (Reeses). Brett's hobbies include playing golf, playing the guitar, cycling, and watching movies in his home theater.

Contents at a Glance

Contents

Introduction

Microsoft has accomplished a lot in making System Center 2012 Configuration Manager the product that it is today. It started as a little-known niche product, back when there wasn't even really a name for what it did, and it's now the premier configuration management product on the market.

This book is written by a group of individuals who have endured the growing pains of this product, some even from day one, and who have even helped Microsoft improve Configuration Manager with countless hours of real-world use and testing.

Welcome to *Mastering System Center 2012 Configuration Manager*. We hope that you find this book helpful in learning how to use Configuration Manager to its full potential.

The Mastering Series

The Mastering series from Sybex provides outstanding instruction for readers with intermediate and advanced skills in the form of top-notch training and development for those already working in their field and provides clear, serious education for those aspiring to become pros. Every Mastering book includes the following:

◆ Real-world scenarios, ranging from case studies to interviews that show how the tool, technique, or knowledge presented is applied in actual practice

◆ Skill-based instruction, with chapters organized around real tasks rather than abstract concepts or subjects

◆ Self-review questions, so you can be certain you're equipped to do the job right

What This Book Covers

Mastering System Center 2012 Configuration Manager covers Microsoft's System Center 2012 Configuration Manager. We detail the changes to Configuration Manager since 2007.

These new features include, but are not limited to, the following:

◆ A completely new mechanism for content distribution—focusing on the needs of the user while retaining the ability to distribute to systems as well

◆ A user self-service catalog for content deployment

◆ Updates to software update management and operating system deployment

◆ The ability to manage mobile devices, including Windows Phone, iPhones, iPads, Android, and more

◆ A robust alerting mechanism

◆ A redesigned infrastructure to increase scale and reduce complexity

What You Need to Get the Most Out of This Book

To be able to follow the step-by-step instructions in this book, it is recommended that you have a minimum of Windows Server 2008 R2 x64 and SQL Server 2008 R2 with all the applicable updates installed; read more on this subject in Chapter 2. Also, make sure you have the media for Configuration Manager 2012 RTM, because we will go through installing this software in the first few chapters. Your computer also needs an Internet connection so you can download updates in various parts of the installation process. Evaluation versions of any of this software are fine for our purposes.

How We Structured This Book

To help you understand the features of Configuration Manager, we have structured this book to match the names of features as they are listed in the Configuration Manager administrative console wherever possible, with a few exceptions.

Chapter 1, "Overview of Operations Management," covers general management concepts, such as ITIL and MOF, and how System Center 2012 Configuration Manager supports those concepts.

Chapter 2, "Planning a Configuration Manager Infrastructure," covers site roles, how they are leveraged, and their application in your enterprise.

Chapter 3, "Migrating from Configuration Manager 2007," covers the process of moving from ConfigMgr 2007 to ConfigMgr 2012. Discussions include planning the migration, using the new migration tool, and more.

Chapter 4, "Installation and Site Role Configuration," covers the details of site role installation, configuration, and troubleshooting.

Chapter 5, "Role-Based Administration," covers the new approach to security in ConfigMgr 2012. Role-based security is used to assign the access needed for specific job functions.

Chapter 6, "Client Installation," covers client installation aspects in relation to Configuration Manager 2012, such as the various installation methods found within Configuration Manager 2012.

Chapter 7, "Application Deployment," provides a comprehensive look at planning, configuring, and using the new application deployment model in ConfigMgr 2012, including elements like deployments, deployment types, dependencies, rules, and relationships.

Chapter 8, "Software Updates," gives you a step-by-step guide of this completely redesigned feature that is now based on Windows Server Update Services.

Chapter 9, "Operating System Deployment," gives you an in-depth look at how Configuration Manager 2012 allows an administrator to deploy a single operating system to multiple types of machines.

Chapter 10, "Asset Intelligence," covers the mechanism ConfigMgr 2012 uses for tracking assets, including hardware, software, and licensing.

Chapter 11, "Inventory and Software Metering," focuses on the heart of Configuration Management Server 2012, one of the core features that most other features tie into.

Chapter 12, "Reporting," discusses probably the most used aspect of Configuration Manager by users outside the IT department. It gives other users the ability to report on various parts of Configuration Manager.

Chapter 13, "Compliance Settings," offers an in-depth look at setting up a predefined level of standards for all your devices and how Configuration Manager 2012 will ensure your clients are maintained at that standard.

Chapter 14, "Mobile Device Management," gives you an inside look at mobile devices and how Configuration Manager 2012 can manage these types of devices.

Chapter 15, "Troubleshooting," shows how to ensure your Configuration Manager 2012 environment stays healthy and gives you a baseline of where and what to look for if problems arise.

Chapter 16, "Disaster Recovery," provides the information necessary to protect your Configuration Manager databases by backing them up properly so that you can use those backups to recover from a disaster if it strikes.

Chapter 17, "System Center Endpoint Protection," details the use of ConfigMgr to manage malware protection throughout the computing environment.

Chapter 18, "Client Health," covers the new mechanism ConfigMgr 2012 uses to help ensure clients remain healthy.

Errata

We have done our best to make sure that the content in this book is as accurate as possible at the time it was written. If you discover any mistakes that we have missed in the editing process, please let us know at http://sybex.custhelp.com so we can address them in future versions of this book.

Chapter 1

Overview of Operations Management

System Center 2012 Configuration Manager, like the previous versions of the product, plays a very important role in operations management in the information technology (IT) world. As IT professionals, we are not responsible for every task required to accomplish a key business activity in our environments. However, we are an important piece of the IT systems management process. This is one of the many reasons Microsoft created the Microsoft Operations Framework (MOF), which is based on the IT Infrastructure Library (ITIL).

The idea behind MOF and ITIL is to create a complete team structure with the ultimate goal of service excellence. Numerous groups fall under the IT department tag, but we often see many of them acting as separate departments rather than as one cohesive unit. Desktop support, application developers, server support, storage administrators, and so forth are all members of IT, but they are not always as unified as they should be.

System Center 2012 Configuration Manager was built with MOF and ITIL in mind, so we will start the book by describing these two systems and how they are the basis for the System Center family of products. System Center Configuration Manager, or ConfigMgr, is much more than just a mechanism to deploy software. In this chapter, you will learn how we define IT service management, how ITIL is the foundation, and how MOF expands ITIL, but you will also learn about all of the Microsoft System Center products and new features of the ConfigMgr 2012.

Defining Operations Management

There is often some confusion when it comes to the actual definition of *operations management*. Microsoft's System Center family of products comprises several products that span a wide range of "management" aspects. The most confusing overlap of this area is between systems management and operations management. This section looks at the differences between the two.

Systems Management

Systems management is typically defined as using software to centrally manage large groups of computer systems. This software contains the tools to control and measure the configuration of both hardware and software in the environment.

Microsoft's solution in this arena is a product called System Center 2012 Configuration Manager. Configuration Manager provides remote tools, software update management (otherwise known as patch management), software distribution, hardware and software inventory, software metering, settings management, operating system deployment, and much more. With each capability of Configuration Manager you take advantage of, you can reduce the total administrative effort required to maintain the systems within your environment, thus lowering the total cost of ownership (TCO) of the resources that are being fully managed.

Operations Management

Now that you have an understanding of what falls under the category of systems management, we can explore operations management. *Operations management* is mainly focused on ensuring that business operations are efficient and effective through processes that are aimed at improving the reliability and availability of IT systems and services. You accomplish this by gathering information from your current systems, having the proper people in place to decipher that data, and having proper procedures in place to carry out any tasks that may arise if there is a current or potential problem in your environment.

The System Center solution that addresses this need is System Center Operations Manager. Operations Manager provides you with the information you need (i.e., performance, security, scalability, knowledge, and so on) to help reduce time and effort in managing your IT infrastructure by automating service tasks and giving you a proactive approach to determining possible problems.

Understanding IT Service Management

The IT Infrastructure Library and the Microsoft Operations Framework were introduced as a way to deliver consistent IT service management (ITSM). Some of the key objectives of ITSM are as follows:

◆ To align IT services with current and future needs of the business and its customers

◆ To improve the quality of IT services delivered

◆ To reduce the long-term cost of service provisioning

Think of ITSM as a conduit between the business and the technology that helps run the business. Without a proper conduit in place, one cannot function properly without the other. ITSM is about process, *not* about software products.

Exploring the IT Infrastructure Library

Before we dig into the inner workings of ITIL Version 2, it is important for the ITIL beginner to understand that ITIL, and its counterpart Microsoft Operations Framework Version 4, are not based on technology. Both ITIL and MOF are based on IT processes. This is an important distinction. Readers interested in IT processes and procedures, as well as how the Microsoft System Center family of products fits into these processes, should find the rest of this chapter very interesting.

If you start researching ITIL, you will find that it is a series of books that describe an approach to IT service management. Originally created in the United Kingdom to address strict operations management standards, ITIL has become the accepted standard in IT service management. The library is owned by the UK government's Office of Government Commerce (OGC). If you really want to get cozy with ITIL, be prepared to spend a lot of time reading. In its original form, the ITIL volumes were at a count of 60 books. These books were created by industry leaders of the time and described best practices for IT processes.

There is much more to ITIL than just the books, however. ITIL as a whole includes the books, certification, ITIL consultants and services, and ITIL-based training and user groups. ITIL is mainly updated by its own user group, known as the IT Service Management Forum (itSMF). The last piece of the puzzle, ITIL certification, is administered by the Netherlands Examination Institute for IT (EXIN) and the Information Systems Examination Board (ISEB).

ITIL can be divided into two categories: service support and service delivery. The two categories include numerous processes.

Service Support Service support is described as the practice of disciplines that enable IT services to be provided. Without those disciplines, which we'll outline shortly, any attempt to provide IT services would potentially be unmanaged and possibly chaotic.

Service Delivery Service delivery is described as the management of the IT services themselves, and it involves a number of practices to ensure IT services are provided between the provider and the customer.

Underlying this division is the difference between what is considered a *user* of the system and what is considered a *customer* of the system.

Now you may be thinking, "I run an internal network. Everyone on my network is a user; we don't have any customers who connect into the network." In all actuality, every administrator (admin) has both users and customers on their network, and often the same individual can be both a user and a customer. For example, HallieM is a *user* of the network when she interacts with the service desk. HallieM is also a *customer* of the network when she obtains certain services from another department, such as services that she must pay for or services that have Availability Management in place, as would be the case with email and database services. Table 1.1 shows the breakdown of the differences between service support and service delivery.

TABLE 1.1:　　ITIL service support and service delivery differences

CATEGORY	FOCUS	AREAS
Service support	User focused	Service desk
		Incident management
		Problem management
		Configuration management
		Change management
		Release management
Service delivery	Customer focused	Service-level management
		Financial management
		Capacity management
		IT service continuity management
		Availability management

SERVICE DESK

We will first look at the service desk, because it is unique among the items in Table 1.1. The service desk is a *function*, unlike the other items listed, which are processes. All incident reporting and service requests are routed through the service desk. It is the function that ties the service providers with the users, keeping users informed of service events and actions that may impact their day-to-day activities. The service desk becomes a single point of contact for customers and users to interact with the IT department. This approach helps expedite the call process by managing it in a timely and satisfactory way.

INCIDENT MANAGEMENT

Incident management is the mechanism by which the service desk records, updates, and tracks the enterprise "fires." The incident-management process is mainly concerned with restoring normal service operations as soon as possible. This will help minimize any adverse effects on business operations and will ensure high levels of service quality and availability. Service-level agreements (SLAs) will determine what a "normal" service operation is. Information is collected about the incident to allow changes or enhancements in the environment to prevent future incidents. This information can also be used to compare against SLA compliance metrics and service quality information.

PROBLEM MANAGEMENT

The problem-management process is mainly concerned with minimizing the impact of incidents and problems. The goal is to reduce incident resolution times by providing insights for known errors and removing the underlying causes. This strategy improves IT service quality by helping the service desk resolve incidents at the time of logging. If an incident can be resolved at the time of logging, business impact is reduced, business efficiency is improved, and IT efficiency is improved.

The problem-management process should not be considered a reactive-only approach, however. When dealing with incident management, problem control, or error control, it is very reactive. However, the problem-management process can be viewed as proactive when you consider how it is used for problem prevention.

Problem investigation and diagnosis are used when known errors are created. During this investigation and diagnosis period, insightful details of the known errors are captured and communicated until a fix for the problem is found. This approach helps with the staffing of the incident-management process, thus ensuring there aren't too many IT staff members duplicating work while trying to fix the same issue.

CONFIGURATION MANAGEMENT

The configuration-management process is responsible for keeping an accurate and up-to-date model of the entire IT infrastructure. It uses this information to help support a number of areas by doing the following:

- Allowing for assessment of change or problem-management functions
- Allowing financial information to be gathered to help determine lease, rental, maintenance, and support costs for IT infrastructure components

♦ Supplying information about component performance and reliability to support capacity and availability management

♦ Improving security by identifying the location and details of assets, making it difficult for unauthorized changes to be carried out undetected

♦ Helping with legal obligations by identifying the location of unauthorized software, determined by enabling authenticity checks on software and making sure current, correct versions of the software are being used

Configuration management uses this information to identify relationships between items that are going to be changed and any other components of the infrastructure that an item is tied to. Such a strategy enables the owners of the other components to be notified and involved in the impact-assessment process.

CHANGE MANAGEMENT

The change-management process is used to ensure that standard methods are used when implementing change and for developing and documenting reusable processes. Implementing a change-management system can reduce the possibility that a change in the environment could cause a failure, thus resulting in an incident.

The IT infrastructure is constantly changing. Patches, service packs, updates, firmware, drivers, and so forth are released on an almost daily basis. Having a safe and repeatable process in place is vital to service management.

RELEASE MANAGEMENT

Changes in the environment often result in the need for new iterations of software, hardware, documentation, and so forth. The release-management process works closely with change management and configuration management to produce a secure and managed rollout of the new item. Consequently, physical changes to the environment are taken into account and the transition to live operation is successful—including both hardware and software releases.

The quality of a new software release is identified through this process, along with tests to determine whether patches and updates are going to affect already approved software. In this way, the process guarantees that only the authorized versions of software releases are being installed.

SERVICE LEVEL MANAGEMENT

The service-level management (SLM) process is responsible for creating service-level agreements and making sure operation-level agreements (OLAs) are met at all times. During this process, changes to the environment are assessed to determine the effect on SLAs.

SLAs play an important role in SLM. They help set expectations for IT by determining what the customer's service-level requirements are, and they help customers by having a measurable understanding of what good service is. Both sides can agree on timelines for deliverables for everything from service upgrades to updates to incident resolution. SLAs also provide a clear understanding of what value customers are receiving from IT and can be used as a basis for charging for IT services. This brings us to the Financial Management process.

FINANCIAL MANAGEMENT

The Financial Management process is responsible for determining the costs of IT services as well as calculating the return on IT service investments. It is also a key in the role of recovering costs from customers if you charge for your services. As mentioned earlier, having SLAs in place to manage expectations is very important.

Budgeting can become much more accurate as well because Financial Management is responsible for tracking costs of IT assets and resources. Financial management allows you to break down the money spent on IT services so you can clearly view where IT budget money went. Because budgeting is a more accurate and a much more precise data point, it helps support future business decisions on IT investments.

If you are considering charging for IT services, a fair recovery system is determined by data gathered through the financial-management process. Charging for internal services has its advantages and disadvantages. One advantage to charging for IT services is that it helps customers and users see the value of IT. Customers and users may also behave differently if they are faced with a charge model. Such a model helps the customers decide whether the services they are receiving are cost justified. Using a model could lower the demands on the IT department.

One of the disadvantages of charging for services is that the customer has the ability to take business or services elsewhere, which could have a severe effect on budgeting. Also, charge systems are often expensive, and the cost of such a model could offset the money that is generated by the system.

CAPACITY MANAGEMENT

The capacity-management process involves determining the required service delivery, the current service delivery, and the IT infrastructure and ensuring that all current and future capacity and performance requirements from the business are met. Capacity management also needs to take into account changes in new technology and the improvement in performance that new technology brings to the table. Basically, this process is responsible for identifying the current service delivery as well as the service delivery potential at any given time.

Capacity management is responsible for making sure business requirements for system capacity are met at all times. Again, this does not directly relate to a technical capacity. It is related to the business requirements for the system, not necessarily the performance of the system.

IT SERVICE CONTINUITY MANAGEMENT

The IT service continuity management process ensures that an organization can continue to function with predetermined and agreed-on levels of IT services to support the minimum business requirements following an interruption to the business. The idea behind this process is that the organization will always have a base level of required IT services.

Each IT service is examined to determine the minimum level it can function at to meet the business requirements. A plan is then put in place to guarantee that this level of service can be reached at all times under any circumstances.

AVAILABILITY MANAGEMENT

The availability management process deals with the design, implementation, and management of IT services to guarantee that certain business requirements for availability are obtained. This requires information from both incident management and problem management to determine why an IT service failed and the time it took to resume service. This process can help IT departments meet SLAs that define availability levels. These SLAs cannot be met without a thorough understanding of the availability and reliability of IT components.

Availability management is a high-profile process. Take an accounting server offline during a month-end run and see what kind of attention it gets. Because of this high-profile status, it is beneficial to have a single process owner for all availability issues to ensure that consistent and comprehensive measures are taken for managing and improving availability to IT systems.

Exploring the Microsoft Operations Framework

As stated earlier, the Microsoft Operations Framework is the basis of System Center 2012 Configuration Manager. The MOF was developed by Microsoft and a group of partners to expand on the best practices developed by ITIL. MOF includes a plethora of resources that are available to help you achieve mission-critical system reliability, manageability, supportability, and availability with Microsoft products and technologies. These resources are in the form of white papers, operation guides, assessment tools, best practices, case studies, templates, support tools, courseware, and services. All of these resources are available on the official MOF website at www.microsoft.com/mof.

How MOF Expands ITIL

While ITIL is based on IT operations as a whole, MOF has taken the route of providing a service solution as its core. MOF focuses on the release and life cycle of a service solution, such as an application or infrastructure deployment.

Because ITIL was based on a philosophy of "adopt and adapt," Microsoft leveraged that strategic fundamental basis for the MOF. Although Microsoft supports ITIL from a process perspective, Microsoft decided to make a few changes and add a few things when it built MOF. One of these changes and additions includes moving to a "prescriptive" Process Model. Microsoft defines the ITIL Process Model as "descriptive." It has more of a "why" approach, whereas MOF has more of a "prescriptive," or "how," approach.

MOF also introduced the concept of service management functions (SMFs). As Table 1.2 illustrates, there are now 21 SMFs that describe the series of management functions performed in an IT environment. All of these SMFs map to an ITIL-based best practice for performing each function. Notice that the SMFs are grouped into *quadrants*, a concept we explain shortly in the section "The Microsoft Operations Framework Process Model."

TABLE 1.2: MOF quadrants breakdown

QUADRANT	SMF
Optimizing	Service-Level Management
	Financial Management
	IT Service Continuity Management
	Availability Management

TABLE 1.2:   MOF quadrants breakdown *(CONTINUED)*

QUADRANT	SMF
Optimizing	Capacity Management
	Workforce Management
	Infrastructure Engineering
	Security Management
Changing	Change Management
	Configuration Management
	Release Management
Operating	System Administration
	Security Administration
	Service Monitoring and Control
	Job Scheduling
	Network Administration
	Directory Services Administration
	Storage Management
Supporting	Service Desk
	Incident Management
	Problem Management

MOF also extended many of the existing processes in ITIL and created new processes. These will be discussed later in the chapter.

MOF also introduced the Team Model. This gives the MOF two core models: the Team and Process Models. The Team Model was added to fill a gap in ITIL, which identifies roles for the process owner of each operation process, whereas MOF creates seven distinct role clusters that describe the functional role or team:

Service   Primary responsibility is to make sure all IT services are at a satisfactory level to customers and users. This is done by creating SLAs and ensuring that they are being met on a regular basis.

Infrastructure   Responsible for ensuring that plans are in place to keep networking, tele-communications, hardware, and software running in order to satisfy business requirements.

Support   Maps to the Service Desk, Incident Management, and Problem Management functions in ITIL.

Operations   Responsible for making sure that the day-to-day tasks of running the IT systems are met, according to SLAs.

Partner   This is more of a "virtual" team in the IT department, usually made up of outsource vendors, IT partners, resellers, service providers, consultants, and so forth.

Security   Responsible for data confidentiality, data integrity, and data availability.

Release   Transitions a release between a development or test environment into production. A release could be a new software package, an update, a patch, and so forth. The release role also has the responsibility of maintaining accurate inventory management and asset management.

The risk-management discipline was added to recognize that the management of risk is its own discipline. ITIL only provides discussion about the handling of risk for each IT operations process.

Explicit management review checkpoints are also built into MOF to guarantee that there is involvement by management at each key step in the process. The ITIL books do not include these checkpoints. This is another added value that Microsoft provides with MOF.

THE MICROSOFT OPERATIONS FRAMEWORK PROCESS MODEL

The MOF Process Model breaks down a complex environment into an easy-to-manage and easy-to-understand set of functions, thanks to the numerous SMFs that Microsoft added when they created the MOF. SMFs are just a portion of the overall release cycle that MOF employs.

Microsoft defines a *release* as any change, or set of changes, that is incorporated into a managed environment. A release includes not only changes in applications or operating system updates but also changes in operations processes or in the physical environment. These releases have a defined life cycle. The life cycle is defined by quadrants, operations management reviews (OMRs), and SMFs. The four quadrants are essentially categories, defined by the different SMFs that each quadrant contains. SMFs are groups of best practices; each category explains the activities of an operations environment. These quadrants reflect those found in Table 1.2.

The Changing Quadrant

The Changing quadrant is a group of SMFs that define the proper introduction of approved changes into a well-managed IT environment. This can include changes in applications, hardware, and systems, as well as changes in policies and procedures. The Changing quadrant maps to the ITIL discipline of service support. The three SMFs that reside in the Changing quadrant are Change Management, Configuration Management, and Release Management:

Change Management   The Change Management SMF is intended to place a rigorous process for introducing change into a well-managed IT environment with minimal impact to the operations of that environment. In the most efficient and well-managed enterprises, there are Change Advisory Boards as well as special subcommittees such as the Change Advisory Boards—Emergency committee.

Configuration Management   Configuration Management is all about being able to identify and maintain revisions and track every version of processes, procedures, documentation, hardware, software, or any other component within the enterprise. Once this catalog manifest has been achieved, these attributes can become potential configuration items (CIs), which then build into an overall model with the environment.

Release Management   Release Management is the culmination of Change and Configuration Management to inject or deploy change into the environment. This can be a single change or multiple changes that have been developed, tested, and packaged for a deployment. The goal of Release Management is to record and track changes into an environment with success, accountability, and the least impact possible to the environment.

The Operating Quadrant

The Operating quadrant is a group of SMFs that are used to monitor, control, manage, and administer service solutions to achieve and maintain service levels. All of the SMFs in the Operating quadrant are items that Microsoft has specifically added to expand ITIL:

System Administration   The day-to-day administration of services and systems in an IT infrastructure could include user and group account administration; administration of file, print, database, and applications servers; low-level monitoring; and troubleshooting of the systems in the IT infrastructure.

Security Administration   The administration of security in an IT infrastructure includes monitoring the environment in both a reactive and proactive way, thus ensuring that the environment is safe from attack. This is accomplished in many ways, including identification and authorization control, access control, and auditing.

Service Monitoring and Control   The near real-time monitoring and alerting of the health of an IT environment ensures that SLAs are in place and that business requirements for IT services are being met.

Job Scheduling   This SMF covers the administration and scheduling of jobs and processes so that an efficient sequence is utilized. This could include scheduling batch jobs to maximize system throughput and utilization and to meet SLAs.

Network Administration   Administration of the network ensures that the network operates at an efficient level at all times. This includes the administration of people, processes and procedures, vendors, and service providers, as well as the administration of the network hardware.

Directory Services Administration   This SMF provides for the administration of resources in Active Directory, such as users, applications, servers, printers, and so forth. The goal of this SMF is not only to make sure that directory access is always available but also to ensure that information from the directory is available via a simple and centralized process.

Storage Management   This SMF covers administration and control of data, both electronic and physical, for the purposes of restoration and historical archiving. This includes both onsite and offsite storage. Storage Management was put into place to help guarantee the physical security of backups and archives.

The Supporting Quadrant

The Supporting quadrant is a group of SMFs that identify, assign, diagnose, track, and resolve incidents and problems in a timely manner within SLAs. The Supporting quadrant maps to the

ITIL discipline of service support. The three SMFs that reside in the Supporting quadrant are Service Desk, Incident Management, and Problem Management:

Service Desk   Almost identical to the service desk within ITIL, the service desk should be the primary point of contact for an organization to receive customers' problems, concerns, questions, complaints, or requests. This function can also bridge or broker other technical resources that work independently across multiple geographic locations.

Incident Management   Incident management is the process by which, when an issue or occurrence is detected, the correct support resource can address and resolve the incident as quickly as possible. This process allows an organization to better understand the impact an incident has on the overall SLA, as well as to map recurring issues and potential financial impact.

Problem Management   In conjunction with incident management, problem management leverages the data results from the incident-management process to trend repeating incidences, prioritize, and analyze root causes. Without this important process, IT can be perceived as a "budgetary black hole" as well as impacting customers' productivity by repeating incidences.

The Optimizing Quadrant

The Optimizing quadrant is a group of SMFs that help maintain business and IT alignment by attempting to decrease IT costs while maintaining or improving service levels. The Optimizing quadrant introduces three new SMFs to help expand the base ITIL disciplines:

Workforce Management   This function was added specifically to address staffing issues in the IT infrastructure team. It helps with the process of attracting, developing, and retaining a properly trained and prepared IT staff. It also ensures that the work environment is safe and efficient.

Security Management   This function was created to help an IT infrastructure define and communicate the business's security plans and policies, based on the guidelines and regulations that apply to that business.

Infrastructure Engineering   Infrastructure engineering is the conduit and link between the people, process, and technology of an IT department. The reusable and consistent standards, policies, and procedures in the Infrastructure Engineering SMF could be linked to any other SMF to help coordinate engineering policies and standards.

Service Level Management   The process of service-level management is where the rubber meets the road. This process defines which services are offered and supported and at what cost to the business. Most organizations we have spoken and worked with have unwritten expectations or assumptions ("we expect the application to be available 100 percent of the time," "my email is running slowly," and so on), but few have well-defined, written SLAs. As organizations start defining and agreeing on service levels, along with seeing the cost of doing business, drastic behavior modifications or acceptance will generally result.

Capacity Management   The art and process of capacity management understands what an organization has and how it's performing, knowing its current and future capabilities and optimizing for existing and future needs. The art is bringing together business, services, and appropriate optimized resources, which achieve the agreed SLAs of the customer.

Availability Management   As noted previously, it's an expectation within the service-level management process for an application to be available 100 percent of the time. So it becomes apparent that availability management has become one of the most important aspects with an IT service organization. Availability, or the occurrence of an incident, has a tremendous impact on customer perception of the IT services being provided.

Financial Management   In order for an organization to meet its requirements within the service-level management process, there are business demands for fiscal responsibility from a cost and budgetary perspective. In other words, for every request (action) there is a financial impact (reaction). At the end of the day, there needs to be a cost/benefit analysis.

Service Continuity Management   Another reason you should work toward achieving a well-defined SLA is preparing for the worst to happen: losing a hard drive, having an incorrect network configuration, having a WAN link trunk cut, or having a network administrator accept another job, for example. A customer or consumer of IT services doesn't really care about the "hows" or "whys" of making things happen; they just want their things to happen.

In order to keep things happening, an organization must adopt a service continuity management process. This ensures keeping the business running or documenting risks that the business is willing to accept when managing an incident. This is a fine balance of resilient systems, failover or recovery options, and risk management.

Operations Management Reviews

Because the Microsoft Operations Framework is depicted as a circle, it is a continually evolving set of processes. Along with the distinct processes, continual customer feedback is always a part of the processes in order to further refine them. Along with the four distinct SMF quadrants are the operations management reviews, which are process review assessments that include the appropriate stakeholders.

OMRs are either event based or time based. The Change Initiation and Release Readiness reviews are event based and occur at the initiation and final installation of a review into the target environment.

Change Initiation Review   The Change Initiation Review is triggered when approval has been requested for a proposed change to the environment. This begins the process of actually implementing the release. Investments in money, time, equipment, and staff will now begin to work on the process and get it ready for release.

Release Readiness Review   The Release Readiness Review determines when a release is confirmed as ready for production. The proposed release is checked to ensure standards, policies, and quality; metrics are in place to support the release.

The Operations Review and Service Level Agreement Review occur at regular intervals to assess the internal operations as well as performance against customer service levels.

Operations Review   The Operations Review is a regularly scheduled review to assess and improve IT operations based on business needs and SLAs. Operations reviews use information from operations guides, company policies and procedures, and operating-level agreements to measure and evaluate the performance of the operations staff.

Service Level Agreement Review   The Service Level Agreement Review is a regularly scheduled review to assess and improve the alignment of business needs with IT service delivery defined in SLAs. During this review, the operations staff and service-level management take current information and measure that against published SLAs to determine whether the service has met its service-level requirements.

Within these four quadrants is a collection of 21 SMFs. Each quadrant consists of a group of SMFs that divide the quadrant into logical procedures and tasks. Each SMF is assigned to a home quadrant, but SMFs are by nature cross-functional and cross-quadrant.

ITIL VERSION 3 AND MOF VERSION 4

In April 2008, Microsoft released MOF Version 4, which is based on ITIL Version 3. Although there is somewhat of a realignment of service management functions and the like, the fundamentals remain true. MOF v4 consists of four phases that include 16 SMFs. The four phases and goals are as follows:

Plan   Plan and optimize an IT service strategy to support business goals and objectives.

Deliver   Ensure IT services are developed effectively, deployed successfully, and ready for operations.

Operate   Ensure IT services are operated, maintained, and supported in a way that meets business needs and expectations.

Manage   This is the foundation of the IT service life cycle. This phase provides operating principles and best practices to ensure that the investment in IT delivers expected business value at an acceptable level of risk. This phase focuses on IT governance, risk, compliance, roles and responsibilities, change management, and configuration. Processes in this stage occur during all phases of the life cycle.

Within each phase, service management functions define the people, process, and activities required to align IT services. These functions are shown in Figure 1.1.

FIGURE 1.1
Microsoft Operations
Framework 4.0

MICROSOFT OPERATIONS FRAMEWORK 4.0

- Business/IT Alignment
- Reliability
- Policy
- Financial Management

- Operations
- Service Monitoring and Control
- Customer Service
- Problem Management

- Envision
- Project Planning
- Build
- Stabilize
- Deploy

- Governance, Risk, and Compliance
- Change and Configuration
- Team

Phase
SMF (Service Management Function)
Management Review

WWW.MICROSOFT.COM/MOF

RELIABILITY WORKBOOK FOR CONFIGMGR

This workbook can be found on the MOF Technology Library:

http://technet.microsoft.com/en-us/library/ee923724.aspx

This workbook presents hands-on tasks that you can fine-tune to meet the goals of your organization. The workbook provides knowledge, specific tasks, and schedules needed to keep ConfigMgr running smoothly in your environment. Two documents are contained within the workbook:

♦ The first of these documents is an Excel spreadsheet that has Monitoring Activities, Maintenance Activities, Health Risks, and Standard Changes that can help you understand the task you need to modify or implement to support the MOF quadrant for this technology.

♦ The second is a Word document that is a guide to help you understand this quadrant and how to fine-tune the ConfigMgr servers' daily tasks to achieve a desired compliance state.

 Real World Scenario

WORKBOOK ON REAL IT WORLD

You are the Contoso Pharmaceuticals ConfigMgr administrator and your manager asks you to provide the most common ITIL and MOF associated with ConfigMgr. You find the Reliability Workbook for ConfigMgr and start reading it. After a few moments you find out this workbook will help you identify the tasks and procedures you need to deliver and implement as standard operating procedures for ConfigMgr in your environment. You provide the task lists that are used to monitor and maintain the reliability of your IT environment.

Overview of System Center Configuration Manager

So far you have read about the IT Infrastructure Library and Microsoft Operations Framework and now have a better understanding of the IT process and its quadrants. Now let's look at System Center 2012 Configuration Manager, explore the new features of the product, and examine how the product has developed into an enterprise management tool that provides a total solution for Windows client and server management. ConfigMgr includes the ability to acquire hardware and software inventory in order to identify the assets for the enterprise; provides a wide variety of features that include delivery of new software packages, virtual applications, software updates, and operating systems; and also ensures the systems are protected with the latest antivirus definitions. All of these features are available through a single centralized console. ConfigMgr provides IT administrators with the capability to stay in control of the environment and help configure, manage, and secure the clients and applications.

Configuration Manager Features

Before you can begin planning to deploy Configuration Manager on your network, you need at least a basic understanding of the features that Configuration Manager provides. For veteran

SMS 2003 and Configuration Manager 2007 administrators, these features will not be very different from what you are already familiar with. However, you will find several new features added to Configuration Manager 2012, several features that were feature packs or add-ins in SMS 2003, and others that have been improved from Configuration Manager 2007. Configuration Manager 2012 no longer takes advantage of the Microsoft Management Console (MMC) technology for the administrator console; instead, each administrator console has its own stand-alone application, as shown in Figure 1.2.

FIGURE 1.2

Microsoft
Configuration
Manager 2012
console

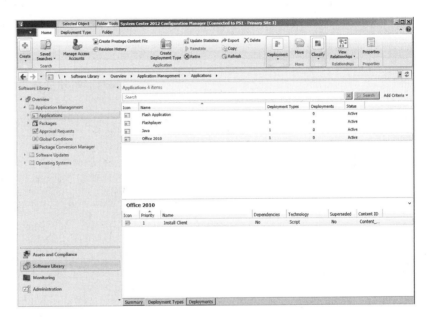

The major features include the following:

Inventory   Configuration Manager offers you the ability to inventory the hardware and software of its client computers. Hardware inventory can gather information from your systems such as processor information, the computer manufacturer, and the amount of installed memory. Software inventory can gather lists of file types and their versions installed on your computers, with EXE files being the default. Combine this with extensive information in the Asset Intelligence (AI) knowledge base, and you can use Configuration Manager to really get a handle on what kind of hardware and software are being used in your environment.

Inventory is the backbone of Configuration Manager; you can run Configuration Manager without enabling inventory, but you really wouldn't be able to do much, since so many other features, such as software updates, require inventory. Inventory is just about the same as it was in SMS 2003 and Configuration Manager 2007. Inventory is a very important piece of the MOF quadrant. Operations management is easy to maintain with a proper inventory of the IT environment; without one it's very hard to maintain detailed information of the infrastructure and the current assets. We will go into more detail about this feature in Chapter 11, "Inventory and Software Metering."

Queries Queries allow you to gather information from the Configuration Manager database through the WBEM query language. This allows you to answer questions quickly or make mini-reports that might not be used often enough to be imported into the reporting interface. You can export these reports from the Configuration Manager console into different file formats and then email them for others to use in programs such as Microsoft Excel. Queries are primarily used to make groups of Configuration Manager resources, called *collections*, that are used by other Configuration Manager features. These queries are a good way to identify resources based on T-SQL. Parameters entered in the queries GUI inside Configuration Manager can simplify the reuse of code within a collection. As you can see, queries are a very important piece of the Capacity Management function in the Optimizing quadrant in ITIL and MOF.

Collections Collections can be the answers or results to a question that involves specifying various resources, such as, "Which resources are running Windows XP Professional Service Pack 2 with more than 2 GB of RAM, with more than 1 GB of free disk space, and with a certain BIOS version?" Collections allow you to organize Configuration Manager resources into logical groups, based on a query. A collection can target Configuration Manager tasks to the resources that you specify. You can make collections based on queries, allowing them to be updated dynamically based on a configurable schedule or by directly assigning resources. Collections can consist of computers, users, user groups, or any discovered resources in the Configuration Manager database. Collections, as a fundamental feature, have not changed much since SMS 2003 or Configuration Manager 2007, but they are now the necessary building blocks used to enable other features such as maintenance windows and collection variables. Collections are a good way to analyze and organize resources; they can also depend on the Capacity Management SMF and the Optimizing quadrant in ITIL and MOF.

Application Management This feature allows Configuration Manager to distribute just about anything to its client computers. This is probably the most-used feature of all the previous versions of Configuration Manager, and it's probably the most dangerous if not used carefully. It is likely that just about all SMS admins have accidentally deployed a piece of software that they shouldn't have (if you haven't, then keep up the great work!). This isn't a fault of this feature but something that can happen if you don't test, test, test, and then test again. Anything you plan on deploying to client computers must be carefully managed, and you must pay close attention to the details of what you are doing.

 Real World Scenario

USING ADMINSTUDIO CONFIGURATION MANAGER EDITION

It is important to note that Configuration Manager is just the method of distribution; it doesn't have any built-in capability to package software before it is distributed. You will have to use another piece of software to do that yourself. Microsoft has licensed AdminStudio Configuration Manager Edition to give administrators a reliable and repeatable tool to assist in creating Windows Installer packages. This, of course, is where the testing comes in. This feature has had numerous improvements since SMS 2003, such as the deployment of not only physical applications but also virtual applications, as well as improvements since Configuration Manager 2007, but overall it works basically the same as it did before. Application management is part of systems management on ITIL and the Changing quadrant of the MOF.

Software Updates This feature of Configuration Manager has to be one of our favorites. Using this feature, you can manage the daunting task of deploying updates to Microsoft applications and operating systems after the perfect storm that is Patch Tuesday blows through once a month (or whenever updates are released for other applications in your environment). Not only does this apply to Microsoft security patches and updates, but having this flexible and extensible environment has allowed partners (such as HP, Dell, IBM, Citrix, and others) to create custom catalogs to update server and desktop BIOS, firmware, and drivers as well as to create internal catalogs. This enables customers to create their own line-of-business application update catalogs and update them through the same streamlined process as Microsoft uses for patch management.

Deploying updates requires a Windows Server Update Services (WSUS) server. Configuration Manager leverages WSUS with its own functionality and provides a higher level of granularity than is available with WSUS alone. Software updates are an important phase in the Incident Management and Operations Management functions of ITIL and MOF. We will cover software updates in more detail in Chapter 8, "Software Updates."

Software Metering Software metering, also covered in Chapter 8, allows you to collect information on software usage to assist in managing software purchases and licensing. Using software metering, you can do the following:

♦ Report on the software that is being used in your environment and on which users are running the software

♦ Report on the number of concurrent users of a software application

♦ Report on software license requirements

♦ Find unnecessary software installs

♦ Find software that is installed but isn't being used

The new twist to software metering is that the metering rules are autopopulated, or created, but disabled by default, based on the software inventory. This allows you to rapidly meter applications and gain insights into usage. SMS 2003 had metering, but it was cumbersome to figure out the appropriate rule setup. This now is a thing of the past. Software metering is part of the Supporting quadrant in ITIL and MOF. Based on the utilization of software, you can measure when applications are properly used in the environment for better inventory of the current assets.

Operating System Deployment (OSD) This feature was originally released as a feature pack for SMS 2003. It was workable but was a minimalist approach that was sometimes difficult to implement and troubleshoot. Configuration Manager not only has this feature fully integrated into the product, but it has become a feature-rich, process-driven way to deploy servers and workstations. It leverages other new technology specifically designed by Microsoft to deploy operating systems to computers with multiple options.

Originally this feature supported the deployment of desktops only, but it now supports deploying servers. With the addition of the task sequencer and driver catalog, you can deploy to bare-metal computers or to ones that already have an operating system installed, as well as deploy software to these computers after they have been configured. This allows you to minimize the number of images for different hardware, and it gives you more granular configuration options. OSD is also part of the Changing quadrant of the ITIL and MOF and an important piece of systems management. We will discuss this robust feature in more detail in Chapter 9, "Operating System Deployment."

Remote Control   This feature allows computer support staff to remotely troubleshoot problems with users' computers just like they were sitting in front of the computer. This feature is still integrated with Remote Assistance and Remote Desktop, and it works pretty much the same as it did in the previous version.

The ability to support the desktops via remote control is a beneficial part of the Service Continuity Management function for ITIL and MOF.

Settings Management   This feature is designed to address configuration drift within the enterprise. Enterprise administrators (for workstations and servers) as well as security teams need a tool that enables them to set configuration baselines (based on SOX, HIPPA, GLBA, or other compliancy regulations), deploy machines to an environment meeting these baselines (for example, with the local guest account disabled, Windows Integrated Security for SQL Server enabled, and so on), and then detect when these changes occur. Microsoft delivers configuration packs that jump-start an organization in the compliancy areas mentioned and allow you to set up a baseline of standards for your workstations and servers and audit your environment against that baseline.

You can configure your own baselines from scratch, or you can use best practices from Microsoft and their partners in the form of Configuration Manager Configuration Packs, which can be modified if needed. The ability to configure, monitor, and remediate the systems based on specific needs is key to System Management on ITIL and MOF. This feature will be covered in Chapter 13, "Compliance Settings."

Mobile Device Management   This feature allows you to manage mobile devices such as Windows Mobile Pocket PC and smartphones. Inventory, file collection, software distribution, and device configuration are all options with this feature. This was an add-on feature in SMS 2003 and is now fully integrated into Configuration Manager. New environments are bringing mobile devices to each environment. There is a need to support mobile devices to ensure that IT is running on the same track as the consumer. This is part of the Supporting, Changing, Operating, and Optimizing quadrants on ITIL and MOF. This feature will be discussed in Chapter 14, "Mobile Device Management."

Network Access Protection   This is a new feature in Configuration Manager. It leverages technology built into Windows Vista and Windows Server 2008 that allows you to protect your network from potential threats by not allowing computers to access your network that do not meet certain system health requirements such as having updated antivirus definitions or security patches installed. With this feature you can also enforce certain network protocols. The ability to secure the environment is one of the tasks on the Supporting and Operating quadrants on ITIL and MOF. Chapter 15, "Troubleshooting," covers this feature.

Wake on LAN   This feature, added to software distribution, was available in SMS 2003 only by purchasing third-party software. It allows you to leverage technology built into computer hardware to wake up computers that have been turned off so they can run assigned deployments. Chapter 7, "Application Deployment," shows how to enable it. This option brings more power to the tasks of the Operating and Supporting quadrants for the ITIL and MOF.

Reporting This feature is great for reviewing the status of the environment, for showing return on investment, and for matching licensing with what is actually installed. It grants visibility into the enterprise with the integration of Asset Intelligence (covered in Chapter 10, "Asset Intelligence"). This allows you to gain an understanding into licensing (Microsoft and third-party licenses), asset age, Client Access License (CAL) utilization, product families/ categories, and much more insightful data. With this feature you can create web-based reports, via Configuration Manager or through SQL Reporting Services, that can show all the data that has been collected by the various other Configuration Manager features, such as software update deployment success or a list of computers of a certain manufacturer.

You can also group together commonly viewed reports into "dashboards" for easy viewing with just one click. Numerous reports are already created out of the box, and you can create your own custom reports with a little knowledge of SQL queries. On ConfigMgr 2012 the only report option we have is based on Reporting Services. This is the most beneficial piece of systems management for ITIL and MOF: being able to report back everything that is going on with the IT resources makes the job of auditing and reporting a simple one. Reporting is discussed in several chapters and is covered fully in Chapter 12, "Reporting."

OUT-OF-BAND MANAGEMENT

A business challenge that has been a struggle for years is the ability for software to communicate directly with hardware. Let's say, for example, that you're supporting a worldwide organization and have a centralized help desk. You have a desktop that is thousands of miles away, and the user has contacted you because of an operating system "blue screen." A typical support remediation from years past would be to create a ticket so that a local technician would be able to physically visit the location.

Intel introduced manageability directly into its chip set with the Intel Active Management Technology (AMT) initiative; the direct result was the Intel vPro desktop processor. Intel and Microsoft worked on a strategic management initiative so that software could communicate directly with hardware. Now, when a user contacts the help desk with that same scenario, a help desk administrator can actively engage and potentially resolve an issue without needing to escalate a ticket to another team.

Configuration Manager leverages four key areas to communicate directly to hardware. These areas may be leveraged holistically within an organization's standard operating procedures for in-band and out-of-band management to provide a streamlined resolution process. In-band management is used when the Configuration Manager client agent is functioning, and out-of-band management occurs when software communicates with hardware because no other means may apply. These are the four areas:

Discovery Discovery is an area of out-of-band management that provides an administrator with the ability to achieve discovery on demand. This can be performed on a single machine or groups of machines via a Configuration Manager collection. It also allows you to schedule a discovery so that if the software does not respond, the hardware still can provide the insight into an asset.

Power Control Power control provides the flexibility to allow both scheduled and on-demand power-on capabilities. From a scheduling perspective, this can potentially improve efficiency and data consistency when used in conjunction with other Configuration Manager features such as software distribution, software update management, or operating system deployment. From an on-demand perspective, this enables administrators to wake up, restart, or shut down a remote machine. One area of efficiency that enterprises are increasingly demanding is power management. Thus, the ability to control hardware and software from a single pane of glass becomes an attractive feature.

Provisioning Provisioning workstations, either as new assets that enter the enterprise or as a means to an end in the remediation process, has become a necessary part of an administrator's role. As the operating system becomes less independent of hardware (that is, the operating system hardware abstraction layer [HAL]), the provisioning process may become more streamlined. With an integrated solution such as AMT and Configuration Manager, a secure, zero-touch setup and provisioning of workstations can be achieved.

Remote Console Remote console for out-of-band management enables administrators to perform advanced abilities such as serial over LAN, IDE redirection, BIOS password bypass, and manual power control. This allows an administrator to remotely mount a bootable, troubleshooting image (ISO image); boot into the BIOS to change the boot order; or turn the targeted machine on or off at will.

To that end, when the user contacts the help desk with a nonfunctioning operating system, the help desk administrator can proactively take the appropriate actions. For example, the standard operating procedure might look starkly different from just creating a ticket and dispatching a desktop support technician. It may be that the help desk administrator reboots into the BIOS, leveraging the serial-over-LAN capabilities, and changes the boot order in the BIOS so that the network card is the first in the boot order. From there, a diagnostic tool is mounted with IDE redirection, which gives the administrator the insight that the operating system has some corrupt DLLs. Thus, the administrator can then provision a role-based operating system image to this user to re-image the workstation. A process or help desk ticket that might have been very expensive or time-consuming now becomes a streamlined process that results in the user having less downtime and a higher degree of satisfaction with their help desk interaction.

Asset Intelligence

Asset Intelligence, which was included within Configuration Manager 2007, now comes with its own node within the Administrator console. This isn't the only new aspect of Asset Intelligence; AI also became part of the Software + Services initiative within Microsoft. The services component of AI is not a fee-based feature but is just another extension of the holistic approach; it includes the following functionality:

- New catalog and license management UI in the Configuration Manager Administrator console

- The ability to customize the local catalog, in other words, create new categories and families

- On-demand or scheduled catalog update synchronization through the Configuration Manager console

- The ability to tap software assets unknown to the catalog and pass them up to the online service for a-sync identification

- The ability to import licensing data from Microsoft and compare it to installed inventory

Asset Inventory is one of the reporting structures used to analyze and ensure every asset on the system is being used properly and report this to management. This ability is part of systems management and configuration management for ITIL and MOF; we'll discuss this further in Chapter 10.

APPLICATION VIRTUALIZATION MANAGEMENT

With the newest release of App-V, Configuration Manager 2012 leverages its existing infrastructure and extends the reach to deliver virtual applications:

- It integrates Microsoft App-V 4.6 with ConfigMgr 2012.

- Application Virtualization Management (AVM) allows you to use Configuration Manager to manage and deploy virtual applications, when possible, to make managing virtual applications for the Configuration Manager admin the same experience as when managing standard or "physical" software.

- AVM has version checking, user-based targeting, and streaming functionality.

OPERATING SYSTEM DEPLOYMENT ENHANCEMENTS

Although Configuration Manager 2007 was good at deploying operating systems, a couple of improvements were needed in order to compete in the marketplace. The following enhancements now round out the offerings of Configuration Manager in the enterprise:

- With ConfigMgr 2012, an unknown machine can now receive a task sequence to install an operating system.

- There is support for multicasting operating system images to a PXE environment—for well-connected LANs leveraging Windows Server 2008 R2 technologies, on the same distribution point.

SQL REPORTING SERVICES INTEGRATION

SQL Reporting Services (SRS) is an evolution of reporting just as previous technologies have been. The Microsoft management team has standardized on SRS for reporting within the System Center family of products. The SRS integration within Configuration Manager 2012 enhancements includes the following:

- The new server role Reporting Services point

- The ability to manage, browse, and run SRS Configuration Manager reports from the Configuration Manager console

CENTRALIZED POWER MANAGEMENT

Saving energy and preserving the environment are important goals for IT professionals and organizations. The ability to control the power-saving settings on workstations is a great achievement for many organizations. Also important are the abilities to monitor the power consumption, create different power plans based on organization need and different operational departments, and check compliance and remediate those workstations that are in noncompliance. It's easy to manage these situations on the SQL Reporting Services.

SYSTEM CENTER ENDPOINT PROTECTION

This feature brings the ability to scan and secure system resources from viruses or malware. System Center Endpoint Protection enables businesses to align security and management to improve endpoint protection while greatly reducing operational cost.

Endpoint Protection is built on three pillars: simplify, integrate, and protect.

Simplify   Creates a single administrator experience for managing and secure endpoints

Improves visibility for identifying and remediating potentially vulnerable endpoints

Integrate   Lowers ownership cost by using a single infrastructure for both endpoint management and security

Deploys effortlessly to hundreds of thousands of endpoints

Protect   Provides highly accurate detection of known and unknown threats

Actively protects against network-level attacks by managing Windows Firewall configurations

Chapter 2

Planning a Configuration Manager Infrastructure

Properly planning a Configuration Manager infrastructure is crucial in utilizing the software to its full potential. This is even more the case with Microsoft System Center 2012 Configuration Manager, with its new and improved features.

The first step is to define a project plan with the phases defined in the Microsoft Solution Framework. The Microsoft Solution Framework will guide you to set up a project plan with the following phases:

◆ Envision: Gather deployment intelligence.

◆ Plan: Plan and design the Configuration Manager environment.

◆ Develop: Build the proof-of-concept and the new environment.

◆ Stabilize: Perform a pilot with multiple key users.

◆ Deploy: Migrate the users to the new infrastructure.

More information about the Microsoft Solution Framework can be found at the Microsoft Technet documentation library.

In this chapter, you will learn to

◆ Plan and design a central administration site.

◆ Plan and design an effective Configuration Manager 2012 infrastructure.

◆ Identify the enhancements on the distribution point site system role.

◆ Prepare your current Configuration Manager 2007 environment for the migration to Configuration Manager 2012.

Gathering Deployment Intelligence

When you want to implement a new Configuration Manager 2012 infrastructure in your environment or you want to migrate from Configuration Manager 2007, you need to write a plan of approach. The installation of Configuration Manager 2012 looks like a Next, Next, and Finish installation, but without a solid plan you will not use most of it. It's crucial to describe your current environment and define a goal you want to reach or make a business case for your project. The following sections describe the process in detail.

THREE PILLARS OF CONFIGURATION MANAGER

Configuration Manager 2012 is built on three pillars:

◆ Empower Users

◆ Unify Infrastructure

◆ Simplify Administration

The Empower Users pillar means that Configuration Manager gives the users the ability to be productive from anywhere on whatever device they choose.

The Unify Infrastructure pillar means that Configuration Manager gives the IT department the ability to reduce the cost of the IT management infrastructure. This is done by the simplified Configuration Manager infrastructure and the integration of other technology in Configuration Manager 2012, for instance, by embedding Forefront Endpoint Protection and most of the features of Microsoft System Center Mobile Device Management.

The Simplify Administration pillar means that Configuration Manager will give Configuration Manager administrators a less complex infrastructure to manage and, with the role-based administration feature, more effectiveness.

Since the positioning of Configuration Manager in the IT environment has changed and has become more important, planning the Configuration Manager environment is essential for an effective implementation of Configuration Manager 2012.

Determining What You Need to Accomplish

Before installing Configuration Manager in your environment, it's wise to define the business case and scope of your project. Ask yourself, "What do we need to accomplish with the implementation of Configuration Manager?" and try to answer this question with the help of your colleagues.

While planning a Configuration Manager environment you can schedule a workshop to define the scope and expectations of your project. You want the results to be accepted by your colleagues or customer. You also need to think from the users' perspective since Configuration Manager 2012 placed the user in the center. User-centricity is new but can be very powerful and well adopted by your organization or customer. During the workshop try to answer the following questions:

◆ Does the Configuration Manager 2012 environment need to have high availability?

◆ How is your IT management organized? Do you need role-based administration, or are all the administrators allowed to perform every task?

◆ How is your organization organized?

◆ Do you need to implement or do you support a full application life cycle model?

◆ What kind of devices are you going to support? Which level of support do you want to provide?

◆ Are there relationships between users and systems?

◆ Do you deploy operating systems? If so, where do you need to deploy them?

◆ Would you like to implement self-service for the end users?

- Are you going to use one set of client settings, or is there a need for client settings based on collections of users or devices?

- Will you need to use the remote management features of Configuration Manager? If so, for what devices?

- Is there a need to use hardware and software inventory and asset intelligence?

- Is there a service-level agreement available that must be met after the implementation?

Describing the Network

When planning a Configuration Manager infrastructure, you want to look at your current network design. Collect as much information as you can about your current Configuration Manager 2007 infrastructure, your Active Directory, and your network design; this can help you make the right design decisions.

Think about the following when describing the network:

- Make a diagram of your network. The diagram must include the following: LAN and WAN infrastructure, network size per location, available bandwidth, network latency, and the use of firewalls.

- Do Configuration Manager clients need to connect to the Configuration Manager site from the Internet?

- Are you allowed to extend Active Directory with the Configuration Manager schema?

- Document your IPv4 and IPv6 number plan.

- Describe your Active Directory forest structure and possible Active Directory trusts.

- Describe your Active Directory organizational unit structure; where are your assets?

- Describe your security demands. Does Configuration Manager need to be configured to support HTTP or HTTPS intranet connections or both? Is a public key infrastructure available?

- Describe your servers and roles; if you want to manage your servers with Configuration Manager 2012, it's good to define different maintenance windows per groups of servers.

- Do you already use Windows Server Update Services in your environment? Can it be replaced by Configuration Manager 2012?

Describing Your Migration Needs

With the Migration feature in Configuration Manager 2012 you need to really think about how you want to migrate the investments you made in Configuration Manager 2007.

There is only one supported scenario for migrating to Configuration Manager 2012; this is a side-by-side scenario. You need to list which collections, applications, software update deployments, operating systems, and other objects you want to migrate.

Define up front how long you want to keep the two environments operational since you need to administer two Configuration Manager infrastructures and possibly re-migrate objects you migrated earlier in the process.

Planning the Configuration Manager Environment

In order to plan, design, and implement a Configuration Manager 2012 environment, you need to take several steps to be able to implement it in the right way for your business. Configuration Manager 2012 can be installed and configured in many different ways, and you must make many design decisions.

Plan a workshop with your Configuration Manager team to make decisions about the following subjects:

◆ System requirements

◆ Active Directory considerations

◆ Hierarchies and sites

◆ Site boundaries and boundary groups

◆ Site system roles

◆ Site communications

◆ Site security

◆ Discovery of your resources

◆ Client settings and client deployment

◆ Content management

◆ Role-based administration

◆ Migration

◆ Disaster recovery

System Requirements

When planning your Configuration Manager 2012 infrastructure, you need to define what kind of hardware and software your infrastructure will use and what kind of devices you want to manage via the Configuration Manager 2012 infrastructure. This section describes the hardware and software requirements for the Configuration Manager 2012 infrastructure.

CONFIGURATION MANAGER CLIENT REQUIREMENTS

Configuration Manager 2012 supports managing various clients with various operating systems. In addition to the Windows operating systems, Configuration Manager now also supports mobile operating systems. In the tables in this section you will find the supported client operating systems.

HARDWARE

The minimum and recommended hardware requirements for the Configuration Manager 2012 clients are shown in Table 2.1.

TABLE 2.1   Hardware requirements/recommended

COMPONENT	REQUIREMENT	RECOMMENDED
Processor	233 MHz	300MHz or faster Intel Pentium/Celeron family or comparable processor
RAM	128 MB	256 MB or more (384 MB required if using operating system deployment)
Free disk space	350 MB for a new installation and minimum 265 MB to upgrade an existing Configuration Manager client	

OPERATING SYSTEM

Configuration Manager 2012 supports various operating systems for desktops, laptops, and mobile devices. Windows versions ranging from Windows XP to Windows 7, plus Windows Server, Windows Mobile, and Nokia Symbian are supported by Configuration Manager 2012. The exact versions and editions are found in the tables of this section.

Windows XP

Windows XP is still a very popular operating system and is well used in a lot of environments. As well as normal operating system versions, the operating systems for tablet and embedded devices are supported. Table 2.2 lists the supported versions.

TABLE 2.2:   Supported Windows XP versions

WINDOWS XP VERSION	X86	X64
Professional Service Pack 3	✓	
Professional for 64-bit Systems Service Pack 2		✓
Windows Embedded Standard 2009 (based on Windows XP SP3)	✓	
Windows XP Embedded SP3 (based on Windows XP SP3)	✓	
Windows Fundamentals for Legacy PCs (WinFLP) (based on Windows XP SP3)	✓	
Windows Embedded POSReady 2009 (based on Windows XP SP3)	✓	
WEPOS 1.1 SP3 (based on Windows XP SP3)	✓	

Windows Vista

Configuration Manager 2012 is able to manage Windows Vista versions as of Service Pack 2. If you still have the RTM version of Windows Vista or earlier Service Pack releases, you first need to install Service Pack 2 before the Configuration Manager 2012 Client can be installed. Table 2.3 shows the supported Windows Vista versions.

TABLE 2.3:   Supported Windows Vista versions

WINDOWS VISTA VERSION	X86	X64
Business Edition Service Pack 2	✓	✓
Enterprise Edition Service Pack 2	✓	✓
Ultimate Edition Service Pack 2	✓	✓

Windows 7

Not all Windows 7 editions are supported; Table 2.4 shows you the Windows 7 editions and whether they are supported by Configuration Manager 2012.

TABLE 2.4:   Supported Windows 7 versions

WINDOWS 7 VERSION	X86	X64
Enterprise Edition	✓	✓
Ultimate Edition	✓	✓
Professional Edition	✓	✓
Enterprise Edition Service Pack 1	✓	✓
Ultimate Edition Service Pack 1	✓	✓
Professional Edition Service Pack 1	✓	✓
Windows Embedded Standard 7	✓	✓
Windows Embedded POSReady 7	✓	✓
Windows Thin PC	✓	✓

Windows Server 2003

Windows Server 2003 is also well used in IT environments. Configuration Manager 2012 supports Windows Server 2003 as of Service Pack 2 and the R2 version. Table 2.5 shows you the complete list of supported versions.

TABLE 2.5: Supported Windows Server 2003 versions

WINDOWS SERVER 2003 VERSION	X86	X64
Web Edition Service Pack 2	✓	
Enterprise Edition Service Pack 2	✓	✓
Datacenter Edition Service Pack 2	✓	✓
R2 Standard Edition	✓	✓
R2 Enterprise Edition	✓	✓
R2 Storage Server Edition	✓	✓

Windows Server 2008

Windows Server 2008 comes in different editions and for different platforms. Table 2.6 provides the complete list of supported versions and editions.

TABLE 2.6: Supported Windows Server 2008 versions

WINDOWS SERVER 2008 VERSION	X86	X64
Standard Edition Service Pack 2	✓	✓
Enterprise Edition Service Pack 2	✓	✓
Datacenter Edition Service Pack 2	✓	✓
R2 Standard Edition (core and full)		✓
R2 Enterprise Edition (core and full)		✓
R2 Datacenter Edition (core and full)		✓
R2 Standard Edition Service Pack 1 (core and full)		✓

TABLE 2.6:   Supported Windows Server 2008 versions   *(CONTINUED)*

WINDOWS SERVER 2008 VERSION	X86	X64
R2 Enterprise Edition Service Pack 1 (core and full)		✓
R2 Datacenter Edition Service Pack 1 (core and full)		✓

DATACENTER RELEASES ARE SUPPORTED BUT NOT CERTIFIED

The Datacenter versions of Windows Server 2003, Windows Server 2008, and Windows Server 2008 R2 are supported but not certified for Configuration Manager 2012.

Operating Systems for Mobile Phones and Handheld Devices

Configuration Manager 2012 supports management for several mobile phones and handheld devices. The level of support and the features vary per platform and client type, but each platform supports inventory, settings management, and software deployment. The support can be divided into two levels:

◆ Depth management

◆ Light management

Devices that are supported through depth management are enrolled in Configuration Manager 2012 and receive a Configuration Manager 2012 client. To be able to support the light management of devices, you need to connect the Configuration Manager 2012 environment to a Microsoft Exchange Server 2010 (SP1) on-premise or online environment. In Table 2.7 you can find the supported features and the supported mobile devices.

TABLE 2.7:   Supported mobile devices

FEATURE	EXCHANGE ACTIVESYNC CONNECTED DEVICES	WINDOWS MOBILE 6.1, WINDOWS PHONE 6.5.X	NOKIA SYMBIAN BELLE (SR1)	WINDOWS MOBILE 6.0, CE 5.0, CE 6.0
Need a Public Key Infrastructure to secure communications		✓	✓	✓
Over-the-air enrollment		✓	✓	

Feature	Exchange ActiveSync Connected Devices	Windows Mobile 6.1, Windows Phone 6.5.x	Nokia Symbian Belle (SR1)	Windows Mobile 6.0, CE 5.0, CE 6.0
Support over the Internet	✓	✓	✓	✓
Hardware Inventory	✓	✓	✓	✓
Software Inventory		✓	✓	✓
Monitor with the fallback status point				✓
Connections to management points		✓	✓	✓
Settings management	✓	✓	✓	
Software distribution		✓	✓	✓
Remote wipe	✓	✓	✓	

Supported platform languages by Configuration Manager for Windows Mobile 6.1, Windows Phone 6.5.x, Windows CE 5.0, and Windows CE 6.0 are the following:

◆ Chinese Simplified

◆ Chinese Traditional

◆ English

◆ French

◆ German

◆ Italian

◆ Japanese

◆ Korean

◆ Portuguese-Brazil

◆ Russian

◆ Spanish

Supported languages by Configuration Manager for the Nokia Symbian Belle (SR1) are the following:

- Arabic
- Basque (Basque)
- Bulgarian
- Catalan
- Chinese (Hong Kong SAR/ Simplified/Traditional)
- Croatian
- Czech
- Danish
- Dutch
- English (UK/US)
- Estonian
- Farsi
- Finnish
- French (Canada/France)
- Galician
- German
- Greek
- Hebrew
- Hungarian
- Icelandic
- Indonesian
- Italian
- Kazakh
- Korean
- Latvian
- Lithuanian
- Malay
- Norwegian
- Polish
- Portuguese (Brazil/ Portugal)
- Portuguese
- Romanian
- Russian
- Serbian (Latin/Cyrillic)
- Slovak
- Slovenian
- Spanish (Latin America/ Spain)
- Swedish
- Tagalog (Filipino)
- Thai
- Turkish
- Ukrainian
- Urdu
- Vietnamese

Examples of Exchange ActiveSync connected devices are

- Blackberry devices

- Apple iPhone, iPad, and iPod Touch devices

- Android devices

- Symbian devices

- Windows Phone 7.X devices

CONFIGURATION MANAGER SITE SERVER REQUIREMENTS

The Configuration Manager Site Server roles can be installed on different kinds of hardware and software platforms. This section will help you to identify the hardware and software options you have when planning your site servers.

HARDWARE

In Table 2.8 you will find the minimum and recommended hardware requirements for Configuration Manager site systems. Be sure that the hardware supports a 64-bit operating system. The only exception is for the distribution point site role; this role can be installed on a limited list of 32-bits operating systems. The following requirements are based on the requirements of Windows 2008 SP2 x64.

TABLE 2.8   Hardware requirements / recommended

COMPONENT	REQUIREMENT	RECOMMENDED
Processor	1.4 GHz processor	2.0 GHz or faster
RAM	4 GB	8 GB
Free disk space	5 GB	15 GB (if using operating system deployment)

In many cases you will need fewer servers than with earlier versions and have less resource waste.

SOFTWARE REQUIREMENTS FOR SITE SYSTEM ROLES

To be able to install and configure Configuration Manager 2012 site system roles on your servers, the operating system must comply with some requirements. Site system roles are roles that can be installed and configured on Configuration Manager 2012 site systems. This section will describe the requirements for installing the different site system roles.

Operating Systems

Depending on the roles you want to install, you can choose which operating system you want to install the site system role on. Every site system role has certain requirements for which operating system it can be installed on. For instance, a management point site system role can only be installed on a 64-bit Windows Server operating system in contrast to the distribution point site system role, which is supported on a large number of operating systems. This section helps you to identify the operating system requirements for site system roles.

Site System Roles with the Same Operating System Requirements

Most site system roles require the same operating systems. The following site server roles have the same OS requirements:

- Central administration site
- Primary site server
- Secondary site server
- Site database server
- SMS provider
- Enrollment point
- Enrollment proxy point
- Fallback status point
- Management point
- Application Catalog webservice point

◆ Application Catalog website point

◆ Asset Intelligence synchronization point

◆ Endpoint Protection point

◆ Out of band service point

◆ Reporting services point

◆ Software update point

◆ State migration point

◆ System Health Validator point

The operating system versions in Table 2.9 support installing the site roles mentioned here.

TABLE 2.9: Supported operating systems

OPERATING SYSTEM	X86	X64
Windows Server 2008 Standard Edition		✓
Windows Server 2008 Enterprise Edition		✓
Windows Server 2008 Datacenter Edition		✓
Windows Server 2008 R2 Standard Edition		✓
Windows Server 2008 R2 Enterprise Edition		✓
Windows Server 2008 R2 Datacenter Edition		✓
Windows Server 2008 R2 SP1 Standard Edition		✓
Windows Server 2008 R2 SP1 Enterprise Edition		✓
Windows Server 2008 R2 SP1 Datacenter Edition		✓

The site system roles are not supported on a Core installation of Windows Server 2008, Windows Server 2008 R2, Windows Server 2008 Foundation, or Windows Server 2008 R2 Foundation editions.

Some of the site server roles can be installed on different operating systems than the ones required for the roles listed previously. The following site server roles can be installed and configured on many more operating systems:

◆ Distribution point

◆ Client status reporting host system

The operating systems that are supported for the distribution points are listed in Table 2.10. The support of distribution points on Windows Server 2003 have some feature limits. For instance, BranchCache will not work with Windows Server 2003.

TABLE 2.10: Supported operating systems for distribution points

OPERATING SYSTEM	X86	X64
Windows Vista Business Edition 64-bit SP1		✓
Windows Vista Enterprise Edition 64-bit SP1		✓
Windows Vista Ultimate Edition 64-bit SP1		✓
Windows Server 2003 Standard Edition R2	✓	✓
Windows Server 2003 Enterprise Edition R2	✓	✓
Windows Server 2003 Web Edition SP2	✓	
Windows Server 2003 Standard Edition SP2	✓	✓
Windows Server 2003 Enterprise Edition SP2	✓	✓
Windows Server 2003 Datacenter Edition SP2	✓	✓
Windows Server 2003 Storage Server Edition SP2	✓	
Windows Server 2008 Standard Edition	✓	✓
Windows Server 2008 Enterprise Edition	✓	✓
Windows Server 2008 Datacenter Edition	✓	✓
Windows Server 2008 R2 Standard Edition	✓	✓
Windows Server 2008 R2 Enterprise Edition	✓	✓
Windows Server 2008 R2 Datacenter Edition	✓	✓
Windows Server 2008 R2 SP1 Standard Edition	✓	✓
Windows Server 2008 R2 SP1 Enterprise Edition	✓	✓
Windows Server 2008 R2 SP1 Datacenter Edition	✓	✓
Windows 7 Professional Edition (with or without SP1)	✓	✓
Windows 7 Enterprise Edition (with or without SP1)	✓	✓
Windows 7 Ultimate Edition (with or without SP1)	✓	✓

For Windows Vista, Windows 7 and Windows Server 2003 R2 counts that only the standard distribution point is supported on this platform. Enhanced features like PXE or Multicast are not supported. For Windows Server 2008 counts that Multicast is not supported.

Prerequisite Software Requirements

The following software must be installed and, if needed, configured before you can install Configuration Manager 2012:

◆ Windows Server Update Services 3.0 SP2

◆ Microsoft .NET Framework 3.5.1

◆ Microsoft .NET Framework 4

◆ Active Directory scheme extended with Configuration Manager 2012 classes

The following SQL Server versions are supported:

◆ SQL Server 2008 SP2 (Standard or Enterprise) with Cumulative Update 7

◆ SQL Server 2008 R2 (Standard or Enterprise) with SP1 and Cumulative Update 4

◆ SQL Server Express 2008 R2 with SP1 and Cumulative Update 4 (secondary sites only)

Like Configuration Manager 2007, several roles and features of Windows Server need to be installed and configured:

◆ Background Intelligent Transfer Service (BITS)

◆ Remote Differential Compression

◆ IIS7 (with IIS6 Management compatibility, ASP.NET, Static Content Compression, and the common IIS and security features)

We'll discuss more on the installation of Configuration Manager 2012 in Chapter 4, "Installation and Site Role Configuration."

Extending Active Directory Schema

When you are migrating from Configuration Manager 2007 and you already have extended the Active Directory Schema, you do not have to extend the Active Directory Schema again. The Active Directory Schema of Configuration Manager 2007 is the same for Configuration Manager 2012. The schema extensions for Configuration Manager 2012 are unchanged.

When planning the extension of the Active Directory schema for Configuration Manager 2012, you need to take into account that several site roles require the extension.

Extending Active Directory is not part of the installation process; when extending you can publish the Configuration Manager site information into Active Directory automatically. Extending the Active Directory schema is done by executing a separate executable; you can find more about this procedure in Chapter 4.

Extending the Active Directory schema is optional, but for some features extending it is required. Table 2.11 provides the list of Configuration Manager 2012 features that require an extended Active Directory schema or need it optionally.

TABLE 2.11:   Configuration Manager 2012 features that require an extended Active Directory schema

FEATURE	SCHEMA EXTENSION	DESCRIPTION
Client installation	Optional	When installing or pushing a new Configuration Manager client, the client will default search Active Directory for information about the Configuration Manager 2012 environment. Searching Active Directory provides such information as where the management point resides, and the Configuration Manager site name.
		If you don't want to extend Active Directory, you can install the client with installation parameters such as SMSMP, or you can publish the management point in DNS and in WINS.
Automatic site assignments/ global roaming	Optional	If you don't want to extend Active Directory, you need to publish the management point in WINS. Otherwise, the Configuration Manager client won't find the management point and cannot communicate with the site servers.
Port configuration for client-to-server communication	Optional	When you install a Configuration Manager client, it is configured with information about the ports that are used to communicate with the site servers.
Network Access Protection	Required	Configuration Manager publishes health state information to Active Directory; this way the system health validator point can validate whether a client is healthy.

Microsoft best practice is to extend Active Directory with the Configuration Manager schema. Also be sure that the primary site servers have access to the Systems Management container in Active Directory.

Hierarchies and Sites

When planning for a Configuration Manager 2012 infrastructure, you need to have a clear understanding of what your global network infrastructure looks like; also, you need to take into account your business needs. The Configuration Manager 2012 architecture is simplified from earlier versions and consists of the following site types:

◆ Central administration site

◆ Primary site

◆ Secondary site

Next to the site types, a distribution point can have an essential role in the Configuration Manager hierarchy. A Configuration Manager hierarchy consists of Configuration Manager sites that are linked directly or indirectly and have a parent-child relationship, as shown in Figure 2.1.

FIGURE 2.1
A Configuration
Manager hierarchy

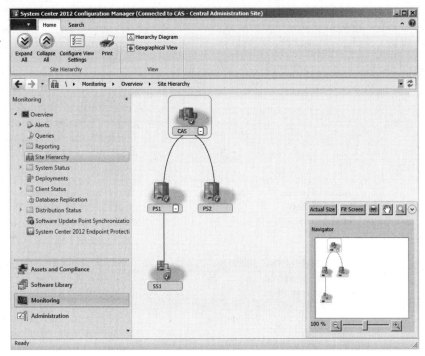

CENTRAL ADMINISTRATION SITE

The central administration site is the top-level site in a Configuration Manager hierarchy and is the recommended location for all administration and reporting for a Configuration Manager 2012 hierarchy. It has limited site roles available, has no clients assigned, and doesn't process client data.

The central administration site supports only primary sites as child sites. When you are using two or more primary sites, a central administration site is always the first site you need to install. A primary site that is installed before implementing a central administration site cannot be attached to the central administration site. A SQL server is needed for data that is gathered from the hierarchy. The data includes such information as inventory data and status messages from the hierarchy. You can configure the discovery of objects in the hierarchy from the central administration site by assigning discovery methods to run in individual sites in the hierarchy.

The following site roles can be configured for central administration sites:

◆ System health validator point

◆ Software update point

◆ Asset intelligence synchronization point

- Reporting Services point
- Endpoint Protection point

A central administration site can support up to 25 child primary sites.

PRIMARY SITE

The primary site serves clients in well-connected networks. A primary site can have a central administration site as its parent tier. A primary site cannot have another primary site as its parent tier. Since role-based administration is a real feature, no separate primary sites are needed for security, administrative, or data-segmentation purposes.

Extra primary sites can be added for the following reasons:

- Managing clients directly.
- Providing a local point for administration.
- Supporting more than 100,000 clients.
- Reducing the effect of a single point of failure by adding a primary site for fault tolerance.

The following are design rules for primary sites:

- Primary sites can be stand-alone or members of a hierarchy.
- A primary site cannot change its parent site relationship after the installation.
- A stand-alone primary site cannot be assigned to a central administration site after the installation.
- Primary sites that are installed as children of a central administration site will configure database replication to the parent site automatically.
- Primary sites use database replication for the communication to their child and parent sites.
- Primary sites can have only a central administration point as a parent site.
- Primary sites can support one or more secondary sites as child sites.
- Primary sites process all client data from their assigned Configuration Manager clients.
- A primary site is able to support up to 10 management points for load balancing.
- A primary site is able to support up to 250 secondary sites.

The following site roles can be configured for primary site servers:

- Management point
- Distribution point
- Software update point
- System health validator point

- State migration point

- Fallback status point

- Out-of-band service point

- Asset intelligence synchronization point (only on stand-alone primary site)

- Reporting Services point

- Application Catalog web service point

- Application Catalog website point

- Enrollment proxy point

- Enrollment point

- Endpoint Protection point (only on stand-alone primary site)

SECONDARY SITE

A secondary site is installed through the Configuration Management console. The site can be used to service clients in remote locations where network control is needed. You can use secondary sites for servicing site roles such as software update points, PXE enabled distribution points, and state migration points and if you need tiered content routing for deep network topologies.

Reassigning a secondary site to another primary site is not possible; you need to delete the secondary site and reinstall it from the Configuration Manager console.

The following are design rules for secondary sites:

- When installing a secondary site, it will automatically install SQL Server Express if a local SQL Server is not available.

- Secondary sites that are installed as children of a primary site will configure database replication to the parent site automatically.

- Secondary sites use database replication for the communication to their parent sites and receive a subset of the Configuration Manager database.

- Secondary sites support the routing of file-based content between secondary sites.

- When installing secondary sites, a management point and a distribution point are installed automatically.

- Upward and downward flow of data is required.

The following site roles can be configured for secondary site servers:

- Management point

- Distribution point

- Software update point

- State migration point

DISTRIBUTION POINTS

Distribution point is the Configuration Manager role that stages packages to clients. The distribution point role is more enhanced than in earlier versions. In Configuration Manager 2012, the old standard, server share, and branch distribution points are merged into one distribution point role.

The following are design rules for distribution points on a remote site without a local primary site or secondary site server present:

◆ The bandwidth of your network is sufficient to communicate and send and receive information such as client inventory, client policies, reporting status, or discovery information to or from a management point.

◆ Background Intelligent Transfer Service does not provide enough bandwidth control for your network environment.

◆ You need to stream virtual applications to clients at a remote location.

◆ You need to use the multicast protocol for deploying operating systems to clients at a remote location.

◆ You need downward flow of data.

If these rules do not apply and a primary site or secondary site is also not needed, your clients can probably use a remote distribution point.

A distribution point cannot be configured on a central administration point; it always communicates with a primary site or a secondary site.

The distribution point role now supports the following:

◆ Scheduling and throttling of data synchronization

◆ PXE

◆ Multicast

◆ Content library

◆ Content validation

◆ State-based distribution point groups

◆ Prestaged content

◆ BranchCache

These are described in detail in the following sections.

Scheduling and Throttling

Whereas in Configuration Manager 2007 you needed a secondary site to be able to manage the synchronization of data on the distribution points, you are now able to control content distribution by using bandwidth, bandwidth throttling, and scheduling options. With scheduling you are able to define periods for restricting synchronization traffic to the distribution point. You can configure synchronizations per day, per hour, and by priority. With throttling you are able to configure options like the following:

Unlimited   When you choose the Unlimited option, the available bandwidth will be used for distribution point synchronization traffic.

Percentage of the Bandwidth   Configure per hour the percentage of the bandwidth that is allowed to be used for distribution point synchronization traffic.

Block Size and the Time between Data Blocks   When you choose this option, you can define the block size of the data that needs to be synchronized and the time between each block that is sent to the distribution point.

Scheduling and throttling are available only on site systems with only the distribution point site role installed.

PXE

To be able to install operating systems in your environment, you need to configure PXE support. PXE support allows you to boot into a boot image that is used to initiate operating system deployment for Configuration Manager 2012 clients. With Configuration Manager 2012, this role is moved from the site server to a server with the distribution point available. Per site, up to 250 PXE enabled distribution points are supported.

Multicast

The multicast support is used to deploy operating systems while conserving network bandwidth by simultaneously sending data to multiple clients instead of sending data to each client using a separate session.

Best practice is that the same distribution point is not used for multicast and unicast distributions at the same time.

Content Library

The way of storing data on the distribution point has changed drastically; where Configuration Manager 2007 stored a lot of duplicate content, Configuration Manager 2012 stores content only once. The content is stored in the content library (SCCMContentLib). This library is divided in three parts:

Data Library (DataLib)   The data library holds INI files with metadata information about each file in the file library.

File Library (FileLib)   The file library holds the actual files of the packages. It provides single-instance storage of files on the site server and distribution point.

Package Library (PkgLib)   The package library stores information about the content in each package.

The content library replaces the compressed content on the Configuration Manager 2007 distribution points and replaces the smspkg$ share, the place where the compressed content was stored.

For site-to-site replication of distribution point content, compressed copies of the content are still used. The compression method is new and has a higher compression rate. A new component called PkgXferMgr performs the distribution.

The location of the distribution point share can be spanned over different drives. Drives will have a priority set for file storage, instead of the drive with the most space being used like in earlier versions.

Content Validation

A new feature in Configuration Manager 2012 is the ability to validate the content on a distribution point (see Figure 2.2). When validating the content on a distribution point, the validation process will check to see if the content on the distribution point is the same as the content in the source of the application or package. Validating the content can be scheduled for the distribution point or done per package.

FIGURE 2.2
Managing the content on the distribution point

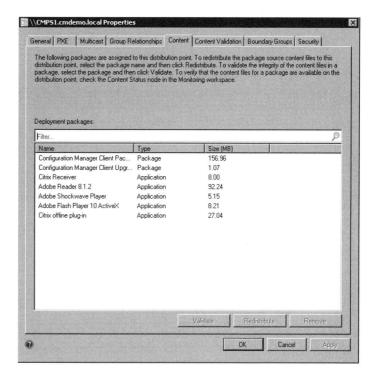

Per application on the distribution point, you are able to validate, redistribute, or remove the content. If the content is not valid, it will then be reported in the Content Status node in the Monitoring workspace of the Configuration Manager console.

State-Based Distribution Point Groups

In Configuration Manager 2007, distribution point groups were just for administrative purposes to easily target software, but in Configuration Manager 2012, the concept has changed. The distribution point groups are *state based*; this means that when you add a distribution point to a group, it will receive all the content that is assigned to the distribution point group.

Content Prestaging

A new feature that replaces the courier senders and the package preload tool used in earlier versions of Configuration Manager is called Content Prestage. The courier sender and the package preload tool were used to provide distribution points with content from a physical medium (DVD, tape, external disk, etc.) instead of synchronizing the content over the WAN. The feature allows you also to deploy a remote distribution point without using the WAN to let it synchronize with the site server in the hierarchy. With Content Prestage you are able to save content to an offline media device and load it locally on the remote distribution point.

BranchCache

Since Configuration Manager 2007 SP2, distribution points also support a feature of Windows Server 2008 R2 called BranchCache. BranchCache is used to reduce WAN utilization and enhance access to content at the central office from branch office locations. When BranchCache is enabled, a copy of content retrieved from a server is cached in the branch office. When someone else wants to retrieve the same content, the client will retrieve the content from the cache available in the branch office; this way the WAN is not used to get the content again from the centrally located server. This BranchCache feature caches HTTP, HTTPS, BITS, or SMB-based content on both distributed cache and local cache locations. A distributed cache is a cache location on a Windows 7 client that is configured to use BranchCache. A local cache location is a location on a Windows 2008 R2 server in the branch office where BranchCache is enabled.

There is no special configuration option in Configuration Manager 2012 to enable BranchCache since it is not a feature of Configuration Manager 2012. The only thing you need to configure is that your deployments are enabled for downloading and running the applications locally.

BranchCache is often used in WAN environments with a lot of latency and WAN environments with slow data links between the sites.

BranchCache works only in a combination of Windows 7 clients and Windows Server 2008 R2.

Site Boundaries and Boundary Groups

In Configuration Manager 2012 you can define one or more network locations called *boundaries*. A boundary in Configuration Manager 2012 can be based on the following types:

IP Subnet   A boundary can be a subnet ID, which is automatically calculated while entering the IP subnet and subnet mask.

Active Directory Site Name   When you are using Active Directory sites in your Active Directory domain, you are able to configure the boundary to use an Active Directory site.

IPv6 Prefix   If you are configuring Configuration Manager 2012 in an IPv6 environment, you can configure a boundary to use an IPv6 prefix. An IPv6 prefix is a fixed part of the IPv6 address or the network ID.

IP Address Range   Instead of using an IP subnet, you can configure the boundary to use an IP address range. The IP address range can be defined according to your needs.

The boundaries can contain devices that you want to manage with Configuration Manager 2012. Each boundary must be a member of one or more boundary group(s), which are collections of boundaries. Boundaries are available for the Configuration Manager 2012 hierarchy, whereas boundaries in Configuration Manager 2007 were site specific.

New for clients is that before clients can identify an assigned site or locate content on a distribution point, a boundary must be associated with a boundary group. The boundary group is used for clients to find their assigned site, and they are used to locate content. In a boundary group you are able to associate system servers that have distribution points or state migration points installed so that the client can find software like applications, operating system images, and software updates. Boundary groups can be added to keep boundaries organized in a logical way.

Boundary creation can be done by hand, but when you enable the Active Directory Forest Discovery feature, you can create Active Directory site boundaries and IP subnet boundaries automatically at the same time. This process can be configured to run periodically. When migrating from Configuration Manager 2007, boundaries and boundary groups are also automatically created during the migration process.

CONFIGURING NETWORK SPEED

In Configuration Manager 2007, you needed to configure the network speed for your location. In Configuration Manager 2012, you need to configure the network speed on the Content Location property per distribution point in a boundary group.

A boundary group can be assigned to a specific site and can have one or more content locations. A distribution point can be added to one or more boundary groups. The boundary groups will provide the clients with a list of distribution points to download the content from. The client will choose the nearest distribution point.

DO NOT OVERLAP BOUNDARIES

When planning boundary groups, avoid overlapping the boundaries. This is allowed in Configuration Manager 2012 and earlier versions, but when you use automatic site assignment, the site that a client will be assigned to is unpredictable. So do not use overlapping in combination with automatic client assignment.

Site System Roles

Site system roles are roles that can be installed on Configuration Manager 2012 site servers. Depending of the size of your site and hardware, you can assign multiple roles to one site system server. Some site system roles are installed while installing Configuration Manager 2012 or when adding a secondary site to the Configuration Manager 2012 infrastructure. Others can be installed in the Configuration Manager console.

The following list provides an overview (in alphabetical order) of all the site roles and what they are used for. More information about the site system roles can be found in Chapter 4.

Application Catalog Web Service Point   The Application Catalog web service point publishes software information from the software library to the Application Catalog website. This site role is available hierarchy wide.

Application Catalog Website Point   The Application Catalog website point publishes the available software for a user, depending on the user rights. The Application Catalog website allows users with mobile devices to remotely wipe their device or request software that is available for distribution but not without approval from the system administrator. This site role is available hierarchy wide.

Asset Intelligence Synchronization Point   The asset intelligence synchronization point synchronizes the Asset Intelligence Catalog information with the System Center online service. This site system role can only be installed on the central administration site server in a hierarchy or a stand-alone primary site server. Synchronization of the asset intelligence information can be scheduled or run manually. This site role is available hierarchy wide.

Component Server   A component server is automatically installed with all site system roles except the distribution point and is used to run Configuration Manager services.

Distribution Point   Distribution point is the Configuration Manager role that stages packages such as application content, software packages, software updates, operating system images, and boot images to clients. The distribution point role in Configuration Manager 2012 also supports PXE, scheduling, bandwidth throttling, multicast, and content validation. This site role is available only in the site.

Endpoint Protection Point   The Endpoint protection role integrates the former Forefront Endpoint Protection with Configuration Manager 2012. The role is configured at the central administration site or a stand-alone primary site. With the System Center Endpoint Protection you are able to secure your clients and servers from viruses and malware. To be able to use the endpoint protection point, you need to accept the license terms and configure the default membership for the Microsoft Active Protection Service.

Fallback Status Point   When a client becomes unmanaged or the management point is unable to communicate with the client, a fallback status point will point out unmanaged clients and helps you monitor the client installation. This site role is available hierarchy wide.

Management Point   The management point provides policy and content location information to Configuration Manager clients. It also receives configuration data from Configuration Manager clients.

The server locator point functionality as known in Configuration Manager 2007 is moved to the management point. If the Configuration Manager client is no longer able to retrieve site information from Active Directory or WINS the management point is used to provide this information.

This site role is available only in the site.

Enrollment Point   When implementing mobile device management or secure out-of-band management, an enrollment point is needed. Public key infrastructure (PKI) certificates are required to complete the enrollment of the mobile device, and the device will provision AMT-based clients. This site role is available only in the site.

Enrollment Proxy Point When implementing mobile device management, an enrollment proxy point is needed to manage enrollment requests from mobile devices. Mobile device enrollment will need a PKI to secure the over-the-air communication with the mobile devices. This site role is available only in the site.

Out-of-Band Service Point The out-of-band service point is used for provisioning and configuring AMT-based computers for out-of-band management. This site role is available only in the site.

Reporting Services Point For reporting you need a reporting services point; this role integrates with SQL Server Reporting Services. You can create and manage reports for Configuration Manager. This site role is available hierarchy wide.

Site Database Server Point The site database server hosts the Microsoft SQL Server database. This database is used to store information about assets and site data.

SMS Provider Point This is installed automatically when you install a central administration site and when you install a primary site. The SMS provider is the interface between the Configuration Manager 2012 console and the Configuration Manager 2012 database. Secondary sites do not install SMS providers.

Software Update Point The software update point is used for integration with Windows Server Update Services, so that software updates can be deployed and managed with Configuration Manager. This site role is available only in the site.

State Migration Point When a computer receives a new operating system, the user state will be stored at the state migration point. The state migration point receives the user state from User State Migration Toolkit 4.0, which is executed in an operating system deployment task sequence. This site role is available only in the site.

System Health Validator Point When implementing Network Access Protection (NAP) a system health validator point validates the Configuration Manager NAP policies. The role needs to be installed on the NAP health policy server. This site role is available hierarchy wide.

Best Practices for Site System Design

When planning and designing a Configuration Manager 2012 site hierarchy, you also need to place your site system roles on the right server. Depending on the role and the size of the site, the role can consist of other roles on one or more site servers. This section will provide information about some best practices for capacity planning of Configuration Manager 2012.

CAPACITY PLANNING OF CONFIGURATION MANAGER 2012

Table 2.12 lists the maximum recommendations for planning and designing your Configuration Manager 2012 infrastructure. The actual figures depend on your available hardware, your network infrastructure, and also on your demands.

TABLE 2.12: Site system planning figures

SITE SYSTEM	NUMBER	DESCRIPTION
Clients	400,000	This is the maximum number of clients supported for the entire Configuration Manager 2012 hierarchy.
Primary site	25	A central administration site supports up to 25 child primary sites.
Primary site	100,000	A primary site supports up to 100,000 clients.
Secondary site	250	There is a maximum of 250 secondary sites per primary site.
Secondary site	2,500	A secondary site can support communications from up to 2,500 clients.
Management point	10	A primary site can support up to 10 management points.
Management point	25,000	One management point can support up to 25,000 clients.
Distribution point	4,000	A distribution point is capable of supporting up to 4,000 clients.
Distribution point	250	A site can hold up to 250 distribution points.
PXE enabled distribution points	250	Up to 250 PXE enabled distribution points are supported per primary site.
Software update point	25,000	If the software update point runs on the WSUS server and other site roles coexist, the software update point supports up to 25,000 clients.
Software update point	100,000	If the software update point runs on the WSUS server and no other site roles coexist, the software update point supports up to 100,000 clients.
System health validation point	100,000	The system health validator point in Configuration Manager 2012 supports up to 100,000 clients or one per hierarchy if less than 100,000 clients.
Fallback status point	100,000	The fallback status point in Configuration Manager 2012 supports up to 100,000 clients or one per site.
Application Catalog website point	400,000	One application catalog website point supports up to 400,000 clients, but for better performance plan for 50,000 clients per point.
Application Catalog web service point	400,000	One application catalog web service point supports up to 400,000 clients. Best practice is to place the website point and web service point on the same server.

HIGH AVAILABILITY/LOAD BALANCING

If there is a need for a highly available Configuration Manager 2012 infrastructure in your environment or you want to load balance some site system roles, there are some options that you can implement. The following high availability options are offered:

Adding Extra Management Points When you add extra management points, you are providing load balancing for the management points but also a form of high availability. When one management point fails, the second management point will take over and provide connectivity.

Adding Extra Distribution Points When you add extra distribution points, you are providing load balancing for the distribution points but also a form of high availability. When one distribution point fails, the second distribution point will take over and provide access to the content.

Adding Extra SMS Providers When you add extra SMS providers, when one SMS provider is unavailable the Configuration Manager 2012 console can still access the Configuration Manager database.

Clustering Configuration Manager 2012 Database Per site you can place your Configuration Manager 2012 database on a Windows 2008 R2 failover cluster.

When you place site system roles such as software update points or distribution points on dedicated servers, you spread the risks and load of the site system servers.

SQL Considerations

While planning the Configuration Manager 2012 infrastructure you also need to plan the SQL environment. The following planning figures in Table 2.13 are valid for your SQL environment.

TABLE 2.13:   Site system planning figures

EDITION	NUMBER	DESCRIPTION
Standard	50,000	The standard edition of SQL supports up to 50,000 clients in the hierarchy when it is collocated with a central administration site server or remote from the site server.
Standard	50,000	The standard edition of SQL supports up to 50,000 clients in the site when it is collocated with a primary site server.
Standard	100,000	The standard edition of SQL supports up to 100,000 clients in the site when it remote from the site server.
Enterprise	400,000	The enterprise edition of SQL supports up to 400,000 clients in the hierarchy when it is collocated with the central administration site server.

Consider the following design rules for you SQL environment:

- If you use a remote database server, ensure that the network between the site server and the remote database server is a high-available and high-bandwidth network connection.

- Each SMS provider computer that connects to the site database increases network bandwidth requirements. The exact bandwidth is unpredictable because of the many different site and client configurations.

- The SQL server must be located in a domain that has a two way trust with the site server and each SMS provider.

- Clustered SQL Server configurations for the site database server when the site database is collocated with the site server are not supported.

Site Communications

The method of replicating data between sites has changed in Configuration Manager 2012. Synchronization of site information between sites is done by database replication, based on SQL replication. The SQL Server Data Replication Service is used to replicate the Configuration Manager 2012 database between the SQL Server databases of other sites in a Configuration Manager 2012 hierarchy. Global and site data are replicated by database replication.

When you install a new site in the hierarchy, a snapshot of the parent site database is taken. The snapshot is transferred by server message blocks (SMB) to the new site, where it is inserted into the local database by bulk copy.

For content, file-based replication is still used, and it uses addresses and senders to transfer data between the sites in the hierarchy. The SMB protocol (TCP/IP port 445) is still used for file-based replication.

Table 2.14 lists the changes regarding the replication of Configuration Manager data.

TABLE 2.14: Site replication of Configuration Manager 2012 data

DATA	EXAMPLES	REPLICATION TYPE	DATA LOCATION
Global data	Collection rules, package meta-data, software update metadata, deployments	SQL	Central administration site, all primary sites, subsets on secondary sites
Site data	Collection membership, inventory, alert messages	SQL	Central administration site and originating primary site
Content	Software package installation sources, software update sources, boot images	File based	Primary sites, secondary sites, and distribution points

Site Security Mode

Configuration Manager 2007 had two security modes: mixed mode and native mode. In Configuration Manager 2007, mixed mode was the default mode, which used port 80 to communicate with the clients. Configuration Manager 2007 in native mode was the more secure mode, which integrated PKI to secure client/server communications. The security mode in Configuration Manager 2007 was site wide.

In Configuration Manager 2012, the concept of native and mixed modes has been replaced. You are now able to decide per individual site system role whether clients can connect through HTTP or HTTPS. Instead of configuring a site role as mixed or native mode, you must configure the site role to use HTTP (port 80), HTTPS (port 443), or both. This way, you are more flexible if you want to implement a PKI to secure intranet client communications.

To allow secure communications between your clients and site servers, a PKI needs to be present in your environment, and certificate templates need to be created to be able to enroll certificates for the Configuration Manager 2012 site systems and the Configuration Manager 2012 clients. The following site roles can be configured in HTTP or HTTPS mode:

◆ Management point

◆ Distribution point

◆ Enrollment point

◆ Enrollment proxy point

◆ Active Management Technology (AMT)

◆ Application Catalog web service point

◆ Application Catalog website point

Internet-based clients and mobile devices always use secure HTTPS connections. For Internet-based clients, you need to install a site system server in a demilitarized zone (DMZ) and configure the Internet-based site roles to accept HTTPS client communications and connections from the Internet. When you configure Configuration Manager 2012 to be accessible from the Internet, you can support your clients from the Internet. If you have a lot of mobile workers, managing your Configuration Manager 2012 clients is essential. Mobile devices communicate over the air via the Internet to your Configuration Manager 2012 environment. For this reason, the communication between the Configuration Manager 2012 environment and mobile devices must be secure.

Discovery of Your Resources

The methods of resource discovery have not changed since Configuration Manager 2007. You can use multiple ways to discover different types of resources in the network. You define which resources you want to discover, how often, and using which scope. The following methods are available:

Heartbeat Discovery   Used to send a discovery data record to the site periodically; it's a method to renew client data in the Configuration Manager database. Heartbeat discovery is available for primary sites.

Active Directory Forest Discovery   Used to discover Active Directory forests from the Active Directory Domain Services. It discovers site server forests plus any trusted forests. It supports boundary creation on demand and automatically. Active Directory forest discovery can be configured on a central administration site and a primary site. Active Directory forest discovery is available for central administration sites and primary sites.

Active Directory Group Discovery   Used to discover group membership of computers and users from the Active Directory Domain Services. Active Directory group discovery is available for primary sites.

Active Directory System Discovery   Used to discover computer accounts from the Active Directory Domain Services. Active Directory system discovery is available for primary sites.

Active Directory User Discovery   Used to discover user accounts from the Active Directory Domain Services. Active Directory user discovery is available for primary sites.

Network Discovery   Used to discover resources on the network such as subnets, SNMP-enabled devices, and DHCP clients. Network discovery is available for primary sites and secondary sites.

Be sure to plan the resource discovery well. For instance, if there is no need to discover the whole Active Directory, plan the resource discovery to discover only resources in dedicated Active Directory organizational units. This way you keep the Configuration Manager environment free of unwanted objects. Discovered resources can be added to collections, which can be used to deploy applications or compliancy settings to the resources, for example. You will find more information about discovering your resources in Chapter 6, "Client Installation."

Client Settings and Client Deployment

With Configuration Manager you are able to create different client user and client device settings packages for different collections. Besides the default client agent settings that are available for the entire hierarchy, you can create custom client settings that you can assign to collections. Custom client settings override the default client settings. The resultant settings can be an aggregation of default and one or more custom settings.

Implementing client settings is the easiest step to reduce the infrastructure; there is no need for primary sites for different client settings.

Depending on the implementation or migration scenario, different ways of deploying the Configuration Manager client to the devices are supported. Configuration Manager 2012 still supports the client push mechanism and pushing clients via the WSUS infrastructure. Deploying the client with a third-party application deployment environment or Active Directory is of course also possible. Read more about installing Configuration Manager clients and client settings in Chapter 6.

Content Management

Managing content in Configuration Manager 2012 can be done on different levels and in different parts of the Configuration Manager 2012 console:

Distribution Points/Distribution Point Groups   Per distribution point or distribution point group you are able to see, redistribute, validate, or remove content easily. Content validation can be done automatically based on a schedule. When adding a new distribution point to a distribution point group, all the applications or packages assigned to a distribution point group will be automatically copied to the new distribution point.

Content-Related Objects   Objects that have content have a Content Locations tab where you can manage the content and see on which distribution point the content is available. From the object you are also able to validate, redistribute, and remove the content from the distribution points. Objects that have content are applications, packages, boot images, driver packages, operating system images, operating system installers, and software update deployment packages.

Monitoring   In the monitoring workspace of the Configuration Manager console you can monitor your applications and packages in the Content Status node. You can also monitor the distribution point group status and distribution point configuration status.

Role-Based Administration

In Configuration Manager 2012, role-based administration is a feature that brings you "Show me what's relevant for me" based on security roles and scopes. Configuration Manager 2012 comes with 14 standard roles, and you can also create custom roles.

Role-based administration is based on the following concepts:

Security Roles   What types of objects can someone see, and what can they do to them?

Security Scope   Which instances can someone see and interact with?

Collections   Which resources can someone interact with?

As part of role-based administration you are able to limit collections; every collection is limited by another. Assigning a collection to an administrator will automatically assign all limited collections.

While planning role-based administration, explore the 14 standard roles and assign the rights to your administrators depending on the part of Configuration Manager they need to manage.

The 14 different roles from which you can choose are these:

◆ Application administrator

◆ Application deployment manager

◆ Application author

◆ Asset manager

◆ Compliance settings manager

◆ Endpoint protection manager

◆ Full administrator

◆ Infrastructure administrator

◆ Operating system deployment manager

◆ Operations administrator

◆ Read-only analyst

◆ Remote tools operator

◆ Security administrator

◆ Software updates manager

Role-based administration allows you to map organizational roles of administrators to security roles. Hierarchy-wide security management is done from a single management console.

You can add Active Directory user accounts to Configuration Manager 2012 in the Configuration Manager 2012 console. In the Administration workspace you will find Administrative Users under Security And Permissions; here you can add the user accounts from your users who need to have access to Configuration Manager 2012. After adding the user accounts you can assign the proper role to the user account.

Migration

In Configuration Manager 2012 the migration feature is used to migrate your Configuration Manager 2007 investments to the new user-centric platform. With the migration feature you are able to migrate the following objects:

◆ Asset Intelligence Catalog

◆ Asset Intelligence hardware requirements

◆ Asset Intelligence software list

◆ Boundaries

◆ Collections

◆ Configuration baselines

◆ Configuration items

◆ Operating system deployment boot images

◆ Operating system deployment driver packages

◆ Operating system deployment drivers

◆ Operating system deployment images

◆ Operating system deployment packages

◆ Software distribution packages

◆ Software metering rules

◆ Software update deployment packages

◆ Software update deployment templates

◆ Software update deployment lists

◆ Task sequences

◆ Virtual application packages

HOW CAN YOU PREPARE YOUR CONFIGURATION MANAGER 2007 ENVIRONMENT?

Before planning for a migration of your Configuration Manager 2007 environment, prepare the environment so it is compliant on the following matters:

◆ Flatten your hierarchy where possible, for instance by removing secondary sites or unnecessary primary sites in the Configuration Manager hierarchy.

◆ Plan for Windows Server 2008 R2, SQL 2008, and 64-bit by acquiring hardware that is compatible with 64-bit software.

◆ Start with the implementation of BranchCache with Configuration Manager 2007.

◆ Move from web reporting to SQL Reporting Services by configuring the reporting site role in Configuration Manager 2007.

◆ Avoid mixing user and device-collection definitions.

◆ Use UNC paths in your packages instead of local paths.

◆ Migrate your Windows XP Branch Distribution Points to Windows 7.

Be sure to always plan your migration, and address the following subjects in your migration plan:

◆ Prepare the Configuration Manager 2007 environment to be able to migrate the objects to Configuration Manager 2012.

◆ Decide how often the data-gathering process needs to be run.

◆ Determine which objects you are going to migrate.

◆ Discover where the objects are that need to be migrated.

◆ Determine how to migrate the distribution point and whether you will use distribution point sharing.

◆ Plan the client migration.

◆ Decide how to remove the Configuration Manager 2007 environment.

You can read more about the migration feature in Chapter 3, "Migrating from Configuration Manager 2007."

Disaster Recovery

When planning a new Configuration Manager 2012 infrastructure, be sure to also make a disaster recovery plan. Since Configuration Manager 2012 is an important part of your IT infrastructure, you will need to be sure that when a disaster occurs, your Configuration Manager 2012 infrastructure will not be affected.

To protect yourself from failure, you can make your environment highly available. This can be done by implementing the following options:

◆ Installing more than one primary site server in a site

◆ Placing the Configuration Manager databases on a SQL cluster

◆ Installing more than one site role per site

It is recommended that you test your disaster recovery plan in a test environment so you can document the disaster recovery process and know what to expect while recovering your Configuration Manager 2012 environment.

You can read more about disaster recovery in Chapter 16, "Disaster Recovery."

Designing Your Configuration Manager Environment

After you've gathered your information about the new Configuration Manager 2012 infrastructure, you can design the new infrastructure. When designing a new Configuration Manager 2012 infrastructure, you need to keep a couple things in mind. Whereas in SMS 2003 and Configuration Manager 2007 you could easily design an infrastructure based on bandwidth, languages, or administrative purposes, in Configuration Manager 2012 the hierarchy is simplified and modernized. For most cases you can do more with less. Of course, you still need to identify your network locations and the bandwidth between your locations. Keep in mind that Configuration Manager 2012 has the goal of simplifying your Configuration Manager infrastructure by flattening the hierarchy and by server consolidation.

NONCRITICAL DESIGN ISSUES

The design of Configuration Manager 2012 was changed; for this reason, the following items are no longer critical decision points for designing a site hierarchy:

◆ Support of multiple languages

◆ Different client settings per region

◆ Decentralized administration of your Configuration Manager infrastructure

◆ Logical data segmentation

◆ Content routing for deep hierarchies

When designing a Configuration Manager 2012 infrastructure, you will need to review your gathered intelligence and translate this into a design. Things you need to take in account are the following:

Physical Locations of Your Environment   As I said, the first step is to translate your network infrastructure information into information that can be used for the design of the Configuration Manager infrastructure. Ask yourself the following questions:

◆ Where are my locations?

Are my locations in the same country? If so, larger locations often are well-connected sites, and smaller locations usually have less bandwidth available.

◆ Are my locations on the same continent?

If your locations are on the same continent, you need to place a management point at your site, and you can create a secondary site for each location. If a location is not on the same continent, it is wise to create a primary site for that location.

◆ What is the available bandwidth?

For well-connected locations it is often unnecessary to create a Configuration Manager site for that location. If there is a need for local content, you can install a distribution point on such locations since the distribution point now has throttling and bandwidth control.

◆ How many users are working at the location?

One primary site can handle 100,000 clients. Depending on your hardware performance and bandwidth, you can implement one primary site for your entire Configuration Manager infrastructure. Consider using for small locations BranchCache or just a distribution point.

◆ What kind of traffic needs to flow down in the network?

Depending on the data that need to flow down for administrative or political reasons, it might be necessary to implement a primary site at a location that should normally not be a primary site because of the size or available bandwidth.

Central Administration Site or Not? When you need more than one primary site in your Configuration Manager infrastructure, you also need a central administration site. The placement of this central administration site can be a design choice, but often you will place this site at the datacenter or the location where the IT department resides. Configuration Manager clients do not connect to a central administration site.

High Availability Considerations If you need a highly available Configuration Manager site or infrastructure, you can install multiple roles (management point, provider, etc.) of the same role in one site without the need for network load balancing. The Configuration Manager 2012 client automatically finds the right management point if one is offline. You also can cluster the SQL database.

Client Settings As I said, client settings are no longer a reason to implement a primary site. Multiple client settings can be assigned to collections of users or computers. While designing, try to define different client settings for the groups of users or computers as needed. Otherwise, just use the default client settings.

Boundary Management Boundaries and boundary groups are fundamentals of your Configuration Manager infrastructure. Be sure to identify all the boundaries so that all the Configuration Manager clients can be managed.

Virtualization Microsoft supports the virtualization of Configuration Manager site servers. Before implementing, always check the Microsoft website for the latest versions and supported third-party virtualization software.

Managing Untrusted Environments In the past you could manage untrusted domains by supplying accounts with rights. With Configuration Manager 2012 you can manage other forests only via two-way trusts.

Another way is to install site roles in an untrusted domain, but it cannot be a primary site role. You can provide some services but not all of them.

Naming the Configuration Manager Sites After determining your sites in your Configuration Manager 2012 infrastructure, you need to name the Configuration Manager sites. Like in earlier versions, you use a three-character-length code. The site code can contain only standard characters (A–Z, a–z, 0–9, and the hyphen, "-") and must be unique for your Configuration Manager infrastructure. In earlier versions of Configuration Manager you were not able to use Microsoft reserved names: SMS, CON, PRN, AUX, NUL, OSD, SRS, or FCS. This is still the case.

Planning the Configuration Manager Hierarchy

When designing your Configuration Manager hierarchy you need to create an implementation plan for where to install which server with what kind of roles. The deployment information you gathered in an earlier stage will give your requirements for where you need to install the central administration site, primary sites, secondary sites, and distribution points. To come up with the right design, follow these design steps:

1. Define a naming convention if one doesn't already exist.

2. Determine whether a central administration site is needed and where to place this site in your environment. The central administration site is the topmost site in your Configuration Manager hierarchy.

3. Define the placement of the primary sites, secondary sites, or just distribution points; remember that tiering primary sites is no longer possible. Look at your WAN and keep the design rules in mind and which roles you need in a specific site.

4. Look at the logical and physical connections between your Configuration Manager sites so you can decide whether addresses need to be configured to manage the traffic between the sites.

5. Assign the boundaries that represent your Configuration Manager sites, and be sure that no boundaries overlap each other.

6. Depending on the Configuration Manager sites, high availability demands, and other requirements, you can place the site system roles where they are needed.

Designing a good Configuration Manager hierarchy is a must for an effective and solid Configuration Manager infrastructure. Always check the proposed design, and if possible let someone else review the design.

Planning Configuration Manager Site Systems

After designing and planning the Configuration Manager hierarchy, the next step is to plan and design your site systems. This is done by analyzing your requirements per site, gathered during the deployment intelligence phase, described in the section "Gathering Deployment Intelligence." Depending on the expected load and the number of connecting users, you can place roles on different servers or group them on one server.

When planning a highly available Configuration Manager infrastructure, you will need to plan several site roles on more than one server. Not all roles can be installed on every site, so be sure that you determine this while planning the hierarchy.

For detailed information on all the Configuration Manager 2012 site system roles and the installation of these roles, see Chapter 4.

Planning Configuration Manager Clients

The clients managed by Configuration Manager 2012 are an essential part of the Configuration Manager infrastructure. You need to plan the deployment of your Configuration Manager 2012 clients while migrating from Configuration Manager 2007 or while building a new Configuration Manager 2012 because the deployment can be carried out in different ways. Planning your Configuration Manager 2012 client agent settings is also essential. In Configuration Manager 2012 you can create more than one client settings package.

Client Installation Planning

Like in earlier versions, you are able to deploy the Configuration Manager 2012 client via different methods. Depending on your scenario, you can choose different ways to deploy the Configuration Manager client to clients.

◆ When clients are managed by a third-party desktop management tool, you can choose to install the client via the current desktop management tool or install it via the supported ways in Configuration Manager 2012, via client push and software updates. Or you can choose to deploy a new operating system to the clients with the operating system deployment feature of Configuration Manager.

◆ When clients are managed with Configuration Manager 2007, you can migrate the clients to the new Configuration Manager 2012 management point.

◆ Unmanaged clients can receive a client via the supported ways in Configuration Manager 2012, via client push and software updates. Or you can choose to deploy a new operating system to the clients with the operating system deployment feature of Configuration Manager.

Every solution has it pros and cons, but try to find out which method is the best for your environment. For instance, installing a Configuration Manager client on an unmanaged client can result in lots of legacy and unmanaged software in your environment. Installing a new operating system on thousands of clients can be a lot of work and very expensive.

You can read more about client installation methods and best practices in Chapter 6.

Client Agent Planning

A Configuration Manager client consists of agents that support several Configuration Manager features. There is one default Client Settings package with settings for all manageable agents. With Configuration Manager 2012 you are able to create custom client settings and deploy them to clients on collection levels to users or devices.

Planning your client (agent) settings is more complex, because you have the ability to assign client settings to collections. For this reason it's important to analyze the needs of groups of devices and the users. You can read more about client settings methods and best practices in Chapter 6.

Determining How to Deploy Configuration Manager

After you have verified your site design in your test lab, you should plan an initial pilot deployment of Configuration Manager on a small section of your network. Monitor the deployment progress and any potential client problems with your first-level support department.

With the lessons that you learn during your pilot deployment, you'll be able to decide which method of Configuration Manager installation to use for your site deployment. Your goal will be to accomplish the deployment as efficiently as possible while preserving the functionality of any previous methods of system management that you already have in place for as long as needed. The deployment method you use will then help you decide whether you will need additional hardware or personnel resources to do that.

There are several starting points for an implementation of the new Configuration Manager 2012 infrastructure. When a Configuration Manager 2007 infrastructure is already in place, you will probably choose to migrate the environment via the side-by-side migration feature, which is available in Configuration Manager 2012. If you have a version older than Configuration Manager 2007, then you have only two options since direct migration of earlier versions is not supported:

◆ Build a *greenfield* (new) Configuration Manager 2012 infrastructure.

◆ Migrate first to Configuration Manager 2007 and then perform a side-by-side migration.

If you don't have any Configuration Manager infrastructure in place, you need of course to build a new environment without migrating any assets. An in-place upgrade like that supported in earlier versions is not supported by Configuration Manager 2012.

In the next chapter you will read more about the migration options and the dos and the don'ts when migrating assets from Configuration Manager 2007.

Building a Proof-of-Concept Environment

After your plan and design phase is finished, you need to verify your design in a test or *proof-of-concept* (POC) environment. In this environment you can test your future Configuration Manager 2012 environment and create, if necessary, a detailed migration plan. The POC environment can also be used to train your Configuration Manager administrators so that they become familiar with the new environment and will accept the new Configuration Manager 2012 environment.

Be sure to create a test plan upfront as a guideline for your proof-of-concept phase of the project. A couple of test steps that you want to take are shown here; depending on your demands, you can shorten or lengthen the list:

◆ Deployment of the Configuration Manager 2012 clients

◆ Deployment of applications, software updates, and settings

◆ Deployment of operating systems

◆ Synchronization of data between sites

◆ Migration of objects from Configuration Manager 2007

If all tests are successful, you can start implementing the new Configuration Manager 2012 infrastructure in the production environment. Be sure to keep the POC environment so that you will have a test lab for testing future changes in the Configuration Manager 2012 environment or for testing your disaster-recovery plan.

Real World Scenario

IMPLEMENTING A NEW CONFIGURATION MANAGER INFRASTRUCTURE

Sports Clothes United Inc. develops and sells sportswear to retailers and their own shops all over the world. The head office is located in San Francisco. The company is growing fast, and they are now using a third-party deployment tool for applications and operating systems.

You as a consultant or Configuration Manager administrator are asked to develop a real desktop management environment where user experience is the key to the success of the project and acceptance.

DEPLOYMENT INTELLIGENCE

As I said, Sports Clothes United is using a third-party deployment tool, and the assets and investments made in the years they have been using it are not compatible for migration. The company has four locations with offices and factories spread over the United States and China, and they are planning to open offices in Europe soon. The proposed Configuration Manager environment must be scalable and support future expansions.

Currently Sports Clothes United has major offices and factories in San Francisco, Houston, Shanghai, and Suzhou. The corporate systems are available from a datacenter in Washington, D.C. The local stores in the United States connect through an MPLS network to the nearest office. In China the offices and plants are connected through a 2-MB fiber connection. The United States and China are connected through a 10-MB fiber connection.

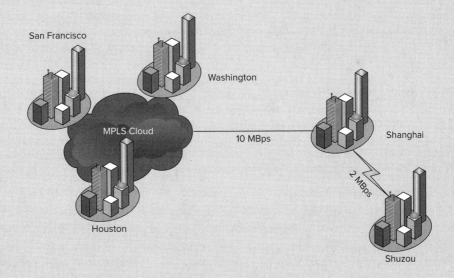

The following locations serve local or remote clients:

◆ Washington, D.C.: no clients connecting

◆ San Francisco: 4000 clients connecting

◆ Houston: 1000 clients connecting

◆ Shanghai: 3000 clients connecting

◆ Suzhou: 100 clients connecting

At this time Sports Clothes United isn't able to support their users at the level they want. The corporate IT department is professionalizing their processes, and they currently cannot service their internal customers according to the service-level agreement. To able to do this they want to have the following features in their new Configuration Manager 2012 infrastructure:

◆ Software inventory

◆ Hardware inventory

◆ Software distribution to any (mobile) workplaces

◆ Zero Touch operating system deployment of Windows 7 Multi-Language

◆ Wake on LAN

◆ User self-service portal to request or install applications

◆ Deployment of software updates

◆ Compliancy settings management to control the workplace

◆ Role-based administration for delegation of tasks

◆ Software metering to control licenses

◆ Remote administration to support internal customers

◆ Support for mobile device management

For software updates in the United States, a local software update point must be present in every major location.

One of the major requirements in managing applications is that the new environment must support people bringing their own devices to work. Supporting this new way of working is the key to success because it will reach internal customer satisfaction. The assets owned by Sports Clothes United must be able to receive a corporate image, and applications installed via Microsoft Installer Package (MSI) and assets that are brought in or are owned by the employees must be able to receive a virtualized version of that same application. Support for Virtual Desktop Infrastructure(VDI)- and Sever Based Computing (SCB)-based environments is also a must-have.

DEPLOYMENT PLANNING

With the information and requirements gathered during the deployment intelligence phase of your project, you now need to translate the information requirements to a design and a deployment plan.

One of the best practices is not to create a primary site that covers more than one continent. Since Sports Clothes United Inc., currently has locations in two continents and is planning one or more in Europe, you will need to place a primary site in North America and Asia.

Because of the fact that the company needs two or more primary sites, a central administration site is needed. The datacenter in Washington, D.C., can be used for the central administration site. No clients will connect to this site.

The locations in San Francisco and Shanghai are chosen as primary sites because of the size of the location in Shanghai and the availability of the corporate IT in San Francisco. The Houston site will be a secondary site because of the requirement that all sites in the United States need a local software update point. The site in Suzhou will receive a local distribution point with PXE, bandwidth control, and throttling enabled and configured.

The basic proposed Configuration Manager hierarchy is shown here.

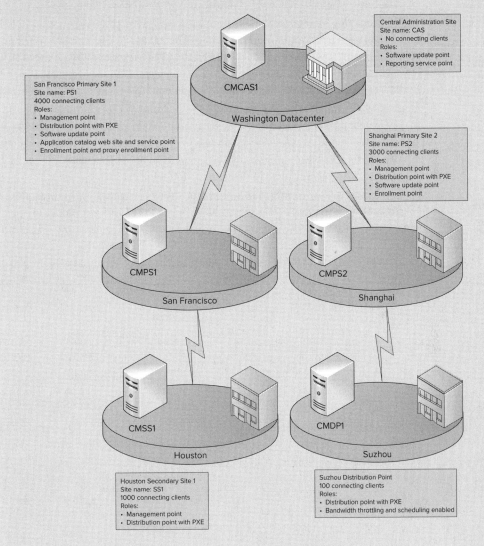

This Configuration Manager 2012 infrastructure can be a greenfield environment, and the transition is done after a pilot phase has proven that the requirements have been met.

The Bottom Line

Plan and design a central administration site.   One of the first questions you will ask yourself while starting to design and plan a new Configuration Manager 2012 hierarchy is "Do I need a central administration site?" The answer to this question is essential for your final design.

> **Master It**   Determine when a central administration site is needed.

Plan and design an effective Configuration Manager 2012 infrastructure.   When planning and designing a new Configuration Manager 2012 infrastructure, it is important to plan your primary sites appropriately. The design rules for primary sites have changed from how they were in Configuration Manager 2007.

> **Master It**   Understand the reasons for *not* needing a primary site implementation.

Identify the enhancements to the distribution point site system role.   Distribution points in older versions were used to provide local points for accessing content and later also for App-V streaming. In Configuration Manager 2012 distribution points do a lot more.

> **Master It**   Distribution points have been enhanced. What roles and components are merged with the new distribution point, and what's new?

Prepare your current Configuration Manager 2007 environment for migration to Configuration Manager 2012.   An in-place upgrade of Configuration Manager 2007 to Configuration Manager 2012 is not supported. Configuration Manager 2012 has a migration feature within the feature set to enable side-by-side migration.

> **Master It**   How can you as a Configuration Manager administrator or consultant prepare a current Configuration Manager 2007 environment for migration to Configuration Manager 2012?

Chapter 3

Migrating from Configuration Manager 2007

In the past an upgrade or migration of Systems Management Server (SMS) to Configuration Manager 2007 was not an easy process. You could migrate the SMS 2003 environment side-by-side manually or by using scripts, but at the end of the process you were not able to monitor the migration of your objects. Very often a *greenfield* (new) environment was created next to the old SMS infrastructure, and the objects that were needed in the new Configuration Manager 2007 infrastructure were re-created by hand.

For Configuration Manager 2012, Microsoft invested a lot of time to create a good, solid migration scenario that is easily managed. The new feature, called a *side-by-side migration*, allows you to migrate your objects to the new Configuration Manager 2012 infrastructure.

The migration feature in Configuration Manager 2012 will assist you with the following goals:

◆ The migration of Configuration Manager 2007 objects

◆ The migration of Configuration Manager 2007 clients

◆ Minimizing WAN impact

◆ Flattening the Configuration Manager infrastructure by reducing the number of primary sites

◆ Maximizing the reusability of x64-bit hardware

Besides the migration feature, you can also wipe and load your Configuration Manager environment when, for instance, still using SMS 2003.

In this chapter you will learn to

◆ Determine what you are able to migrate with the migration feature.

◆ Discover which migration approach is supported.

◆ Ascertain what kind of interoperability is supported during the migration.

◆ Migrate packages and programs to the new application model.

Introducing Migration

The migration feature and the migration concept bring with them some new terminology. In this section you will find out what's covered in the migration feature and where you can find it in Configuration Manager 2012.

Client Information   Client information includes such items as the client globally unique identifier (GUID), the inventory, and the client status information. Every Configuration Manager 2012 client has an ID that is unique in the Configuration Manager 2012 environment.

Client Migration   The process of upgrading the Configuration Manager 2007 client to the new Configuration Manager 2012 client is called client migration. This process can be initiated in different ways, but during the migration process the old Configuration Manager 2007 client will be uninstalled and the new Configuration Manager 2012 client will be installed.

Content   The content consists of the package binaries and files. The source of these packages needs to be accessed via a UNC path. The UNC path must be available for the Configuration Manager 2012 site server.

Data Gathering   One of the first steps in the migration process is discovering all the objects in the Configuration Manager 2007 environment. To be able to discover the objects, you need to configure a data-gathering service that is part of the migration feature.

This data gathering is an ongoing migration process that discovers all the objects or changes in the old infrastructure. During the migration period, this process is scheduled by default to run every four hours.

Migration Jobs   Migration jobs are used to migrate specific objects from Configuration Manager 2007 to the new infrastructure. Migration jobs can be scheduled or started instantly.

Monitoring Migration   While migrating assets from Configuration Manager 2007 to Configuration Manager 2012, it is mandatory to be able to monitor the migration process. Monitoring your migrations can be done from the Configuration Manager 2012 console and can be found on the migration jobs and the migration dashboard. You will be able to see which migrations are completed, which were failed, and which are in progress or need to be done.

Objects   The objects are packages, software update deployments, driver packages, OS images, configuration items, and the like within Configuration Manager.

Server Settings   Server settings are the site role settings and site properties in the Configuration Manager hierarchy.

Shared Distribution Points   Shared distribution points are distribution points that are active in the Configuration Manager 2007 source hierarchy. Enabling shared distribution points enables you to use the Configuration Manager 2007 distribution points in the new Configuration Manager 2012 infrastructure. During the migration process, the Configuration Manager 2012 clients can receive the content from the shared distribution points.

Source Hierarchy   The source hierarchy is the Configuration Manager 2007 hierarchy from which you want to migrate objects to the Configuration Manager 2012 infrastructure. The source hierarchy is always the topmost site of the Configuration Manager 2007 hierarchy.

Source Sites   Source sites are the sites in the active source hierarchy that hold Configuration Manager data that you want to migrate to Configuration Manager 2012. You need to configure account settings per source site to be able to connect to each source site.

Migration Functionality in Configuration Manager 2012

Configuration Manager 2012 comes with a migration feature that allows you to migrate your Configuration Manager 2007 objects to Configuration Manager 2012. Migrating objects is done via migration jobs, but first you need to designate a source hierarchy to be able to gather information from Configuration Manager 2007 and to create migration jobs.

Source Hierarchy

When migrating a Configuration Manager 2007 hierarchy to a new Configuration Manager 2012 hierarchy, you need to specify a source hierarchy. You must use the topmost Configuration Manager 2007 primary site server as the source hierarchy, as shown in Figure 3.1.

FIGURE 3.1

Specifying the Configuration Manager source hierarchy

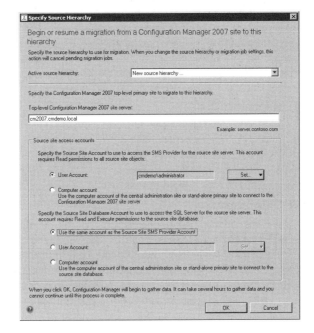

During the creation process you need to supply a user account that has access to the SMS provider of the source site. This account needs read permission to all the objects in the source site. For SQL access you can use the same account, you can specify a different user, or you can use the local system account of the Configuration Manager 2012 central administration site or stand-alone site to connect to the Configuration Manager 2007 site database. The user account needs read and execute permissions.

After you specify the source hierarchy, the data-gathering process take several hours depending on the source hierarchy.

Once the data-gathering process has finished discovering the sites in the hierarchy, you will need to supply credentials with the right permissions per site to be able to access the sites in the hierarchy.

Data-Gathering Process

The initial data-gathering process can take a while depending on your source hierarchy. It will gather all information about the configured site, the object data, and information about other child sites in the hierarchy. It will also set up the connection between the Configuration Manager 2012 site and Configuration Manager 2007 site. The data-gathering process must be complete before you can proceed with creating migration jobs or configuring credentials for other sites. Depending on the size of the source hierarchy, the data-gathering process can run from a couple of minutes to several hours. The more objects you have in the source hierarchy, the longer the data gathering process will take.

The data-gathering process runs every 4 hours by default, but you can change this interval at the source hierarchy object to 1 hour, 2 hours, 4 hours, 8 hours, 12 hours, 18 hours, or 24 hours. The process runs periodically to keep the data accurate for the migration. The gathered information is stored in the Configuration Manager 2012 database for reporting purposes.

The data-gathering process can be stopped by using the Stop Data Gathering action on the Ribbon of the Configuration Manager 2012 console. While gathering data you can check the `migmctrl.log` located in the `Logs` folder in the Configuration Manager 2012 installation path.

Migration Job Types

The migration of Configuration Manager 2007 objects is done by creating migration jobs. Configuration Manager 2012 supports three different kinds of migration jobs, so you can choose how and when you want to migrate your assets. These three kinds of migration jobs are explained in the following sections.

COLLECTION MIGRATION

With the Collection Migration option you can migrate all the objects that are related to the collection, including all objects that are related to members of the collection. When you choose this option, you are able to exclude specific kind of objects.

You are not able to migrate all Configuration Manager 2007 objects via the Collection Migration option since not all objects are related to collections.

With Collection Migration, you can migrate the following related objects:

- Advertisements
- Software distribution packages
- Virtual application packages
- Software update deployments
- Software update deployment packages
- Operating system deployment boot images
- Operating system deployment images
- Operating system deployment packages
- Task sequences
- Configuration baselines
- Configuration items

OBJECT MIGRATION

With the object migration job type you are able to migrate individual objects or object types that you select. This way you can easily migrate your operating system deployment objects, for instance, to test your operating system deployment feature in Configuration Manager 2012.

With object migration, you can migrate the following object types:

◆ Boundaries

◆ Software distribution packages

◆ Virtual application packages

◆ Software update deployment packages

◆ Software update deployment templates

◆ Software update lists

◆ Operating system deployment boot images

◆ Operating system deployment driver packages

◆ Operating system deployment drivers

◆ Operating system deployment images

◆ Operating system deployment packages

◆ Task sequences

◆ Configuration baselines

◆ Configuration items

◆ Asset Intelligence Catalog

◆ Asset Intelligence hardware requirements

◆ Asset Intelligence software list

◆ Software metering rules

PREVIOUSLY MIGRATED OBJECT MIGRATION

With the Previously Migrated Object Migration option you can re-migrate objects from Configuration Manager 2007 that have been migrated before and that have changed over time. The wizard shows you only the objects that have been changed.

With Previously Migrated Object Migration, you can migrate the following object types:

◆ Boundaries

◆ Software distribution packages

◆ Software update deployment packages

◆ Software update deployment templates

- Software update lists
- Operating system deployment boot images
- Operating system deployment driver packages
- Operating system deployment drivers
- Operating system deployment images
- Operating system deployment packages
- Task sequences
- Configuration baselines
- Configuration items
- Asset Intelligence Catalog
- Asset Intelligence hardware requirements
- Asset Intelligence software list
- Software metering rules

To be able to re-migrate virtual application packages, you first need to delete any virtual application packages from the Configuration Manager 2012 infrastructure.

Objects Supported for Migration

The migration feature in Configuration Manager 2012 supports the migration of the following objects:

- Collections
- Advertisements
- Boundaries
- Software distribution packages
- Virtual application packages
- Software updates
  - Deployments
  - Deployment packages
  - Templates
  - Software update lists
- Operating system deployment
  - Boot images
  - Driver packages
  - Drivers

- ◆ Images
- ◆ Packages
- ◆ Task sequences
- ◆ Settings management
  - ◆ Configuration baselines
  - ◆ Configuration items
- ◆ Asset intelligence customizations
- ◆ Software metering rules

These are all described in detail in the following sections.

COLLECTIONS

Collections can be migrated, but there are a couple of things that you need to take into account when migrating collections to the new Configuration Manager 2012 infrastructure.

In the new Configuration Manager infrastructure, subcollections and linked collections no longer exist. Also collections with both users and devices are not supported and will not be migrated to Configuration Manager 2012. In Figure 3.2 the Collections That Cannot Be Migrated dialog box shows that mixed query collections, mixed collection hierarchies, or collections limited to multiple other collections in Configuration Manager 2007 cannot be migrated.

FIGURE 3.2
Collections that cannot be migrated are automatically discovered

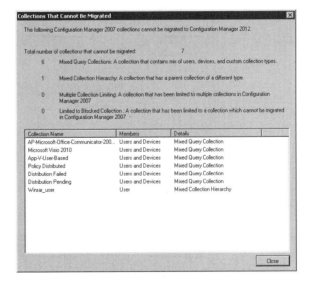

Some rules regarding the migration of collections apply:

- ◆ If you build a hierarchy of collections in Configuration Manager 2007, the related empty collections are migrated to folders. This way your hierarchy is preserved.
- ◆ Empty collections are migrated as folders.

- ◆ Direct membership collections are migrated as is and also when the direct membership is a Configuration Manager 2007 client that has not yet migrated to the new Configuration Manager 2012 site.

- ◆ Underlying collections with a mixed collection in the hierarchy cannot be migrated.

- ◆ By default collections are limited to all users or all systems.

- ◆ Collections that are limited to multiple collections in Configuration Manager 2007 cannot be migrated.

- ◆ Collections that are limited to blocked collections in Configuration Manager cannot be migrated.

In Configuration Manager 2007 the collections were only replicated within the site where the collection was created. This way the collections were limited to the site. In Configuration Manager 2012 the collection definitions are globally replicated. The migration feature in Configuration Manager 2012 will assist you to prevent unintentionally increasing the scope of the migrated collections during the migration process. A dialog box like the one shown in Figure 3.3 will help you to limit the collection scope.

FIGURE 3.3
Limit collections
for which the scope
will be possibly
increased

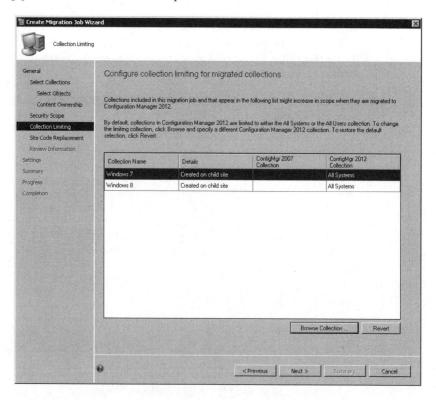

When using site codes in collection query definitions at your source Configuration Manager hierarchy, you will be assisted in replacing the site code during the migration of the collections.

As you know, the Configuration Manager 2012 hierarchy will have new site codes. In Figure 3.4 you can see that site code CM7 is replaced with PS1. With the pull-down option you can choose whatever site code you want to replace.

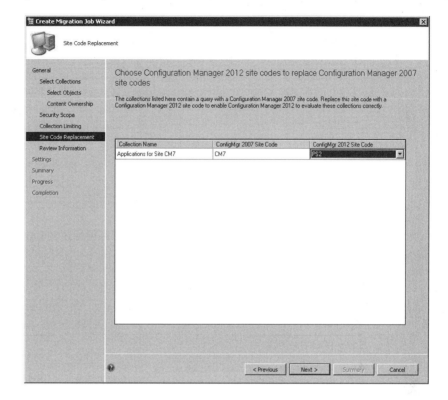

FIGURE 3.4
Replacing the discovered source site code with the new site code

With the collection migration job type, you will be assisted with the migration of the collections and the migration of the related Configuration Manager 2007 objects. The feature will preserve customer investments in collections and advertisements.

ADVERTISEMENTS

Advertisements are migrated and converted to deployments. The settings are preserved. During the collection migration job, you can automatically enable the deployment after the migration; by default the deployment is not enabled.

When an advertisement is migrated and converted, the deployment will *not* deploy the software again to computers or users where the software was already deployed in Configuration Manager 2007. The reason for that is that the GUIDs of the software packages and advertisements are preserved in Configuration Manager 2012.

BOUNDARIES

Boundary groups that are created by the migration process are enabled only for content lookup. This way you will avoid boundary overlap in Active Directory, and it will prevent new

Configuration Manager 2012 clients from getting assigned to the new Configuration Manager 2012 environment.

When Distribution Point Sharing is enabled, boundaries associated with the distribution points in Configuration Manager 2007 are migrated automatically.

SOFTWARE DISTRIBUTION PACKAGES

Software distribution packages are migrated as is. During the migration, packages are not converted to the new application model. To be able to migrate the classic packages, which of course are still supported in Configuration Manager 2012, to the new application model, you need to use Application Conversion Manager. This tool will help you to migrate the classic packages to the new application model. The Application Conversion Manager is discussed further in this chapter.

The central administration site always needs access to the Configuration Manager UNC package source path. For this reason you will need to replace all the local package source paths in Configuration Manager 2007 with UNC paths.

VIRTUAL APPLICATION PACKAGES

Virtual application packages are converted to the new application model. After the migration of the packages you will need to create a deployment. In Chapter 6, "Client Installation," you'll learn how to create deployments for your virtual applications.

To be able to use virtual applications in Configuration Manager 2012, you need to upgrade the App-V client to version 4.6 SP1.

When Distribution Point Sharing is enabled, the streaming of App-V packages is not supported.

SOFTWARE UPDATES

Software updates can be migrated with the three different migration jobs in Configuration Manager 2012. You must be sure that all the updates that are available within Configuration Manager 2007 are also available in Configuration Manager 2012 and ensure that the software update point is configured. Making the same software updates available in Configuration Manager 2012 can be done as follows:

Use Export and Import of Software Updates Use the tool `wsusutil.exe` to export the software updates from Configuration Manager 2007 and to import the software updates in Configuration Manager 2012. This option is the most common option to use when migrating the software update source to Configuration Manager 2012.

To export and import software updates using `wsusutil.exe`, perform the following steps:

1. Start the command line at the Configuration Manager 2007 Software Update site server, and go to

   ```
   C:\Program Files\Update Services\Tools
   ```

2. Start the `wsusutil.exe` export:

   ```
   WSUSUTIL.exe export .\cm2k7updates.cab .\import.log
   ```

3. Check the log file, and copy the exported CAB file to the Configuration Manager 2012 Software Update site server.

4. Start the command line at the Configuration Manager 2012 Software Update site server, and enter

   `C:\Program Files\Update Services\Tools`

5. Start the `wsusutil.exe` import:

   `WSUSUTIL.exe import .\cm2k7updates.cab .\import.log`

After the source is migrated, you may migrate the Configuration Manager 2007 objects to Configuration Manager 2012. For the conversion of the Software Update objects, the following rules apply:

◆ Update lists are converted to update groups.

◆ Software update deployments are migrated to deployments and update groups.

OPERATING SYSTEM DEPLOYMENT

The following operating system deployment–related objects in Configuration Manager 2007 are suitable to be migrated to Configuration Manager 2012:

◆ Boot images

◆ Driver packages

◆ Drivers

◆ Images

◆ Packages

◆ Task sequences

Not all operating system deployment–related objects are supported for migration to Configuration Manager 2012:

◆ Migration of Microsoft Deployment Toolkit task sequences is not supported.

◆ The default Configuration Manager 2007 boot images are not migrated because of the new Windows Automated Installation Kit that is supported in Configuration Manager 2012.

CUSTOMIZED BOOT IMAGES

Boot images that have been customized cannot be migrated. The migration process will replace the customizations made in the boot image with the default settings from Configuration Manager 2012 boot images. A new boot image ID is assigned to each boot image. The newly created boot image can only be accessed from Configuration Manager 2012 distribution points.

When migrating a boot image that has drivers embedded, be sure that the drivers remain available from the Configuration Manager 2007 source location. Configuration Manager 2012 must also be able to access the driver from its specified source location.

Configuration Manager 2012 removes all the references to operating system client packages from the migrated task sequences. After the migration of the task sequence is finished, you are able to edit them in the Configuration Manager 2012 console to restore references to the client installation packages.

When migrating the operating system deployment functionality, you need to be sure that the dependent Configuration Manager 2012 site roles are installed and configured. The state migration point needs to be configured, and the distribution points must support PXE. You can read more about configuring operating system deployment in Chapter 9, "Operating System Deployment."

Settings Management

Configuration baselines and configuration items created by you as an administrator or created by an independent software vendor are supported for migration by the migration feature of Configuration Manager 2012.

When you need to re-migrate configuration items or baselines, any changes to the objects will be added as revisions of the objects.

Existing 2007 configuration packs can also be added to 2012 through the import feature. The Configuration Manager 2012 import feature will automatically convert the 2007 schema to the 2012 schema. Keep in mind the following migration rules when migrating configuration baselines and configuration items:

◆ When migrating a configuration baseline, its assignment will not be migrated at the same time. You must migrate the configuration baseline assignment separately by using the collection migration job type.

◆ Configuration items in Configuration Manager 2007 might have rules that are not supported by Configuration Manager 2012. When you migrate configuration items that have unsupported rule operators, Configuration Manager 2012 will convert them to equivalent values.

◆ If the objects and settings of an imported configuration item are not visible in the Configuration Manager 2007 console, also known as incomplete or uninterpreted configuration items, they are not supported by Configuration Manager 2012. For this reason you are not able to migrate these configuration items.

Asset Intelligence Customizations

You can migrate asset intelligence customizations made for classifications, labels, families, and hardware requirements to Configuration Manager 2012. This is done by using the Object Migration option in the migration feature.

When migrating Asset Intelligence customizations, always assign the Configuration Manager 2012 site that is the closest to the Configuration Manager 2007 site that owns the Asset Intelligence content because of WAN traffic that can occur during the migration. Gathered Asset Intelligence data is not migrated to Configuration Manager 2012.

SOFTWARE METERING RULES

Software metering rules can be migrated with the Object Migration option in the migration feature. All rules that are available in Configuration Manager 2007 can be migrated.

After the migration all software metering rules are disabled by default.

SEARCH AND ADMINISTRATIVE FOLDERS

Administrator-created folders for administrative duties are migrated if chosen while migrating collections or objects. Be sure to enable the "Transfer the organizational folder structure for objects from Configuration Manager 2007 to the destination site" option when migrating objects from Configuration Manager 2007 to Configuration Manager 2012. You can set this option in the process of creating a migration job and scheduling when the migration job is to run.

REPORTS

When you want to migrate reports, the only way to do so is to use SQL Reporting Services in Configuration Manager 2007 instead of the default web reporting of Configuration Manager 2007. With SQL Reporting Services you can export your custom reports (RDL files) from the old SQL Reporting Services and then import them into your new SQL environment in Configuration Manager 2012.

Objects Not Supported for Migration

Not all objects can be migrated by the migration feature from Configuration Manager 2007 to Configuration Manager 2012. You can create workarounds for some objects, but for others you cannot. Table 3.1 shows whether workarounds are available for non-migratable objects.

TABLE 3.1:   Workarounds for non-migratable objects

OBJECT	WORKAROUND
Queries	Export the queries in Configuration Manager 2007 to a MOF file and import the MOF file into Configuration Manager 2012.
Security rights for the site and objects	No workaround available.
Configuration Manager 2007 reports from SQL Server Reporting Services	Export your reports from SQL Server Reporting Services and import them into the new SQL Server Reporting Services servicing the Configuration Manager 2012.
Configuration Manager 2007 web reports	No workaround available.
Client inventory and history data	No workaround available.
AMT client provisioning information	No workaround available.
Files in the client cache	No workaround available.

PRESERVING YOUR CUSTOM *SMS_DEF.MOF* INVESTMENTS

The migration of hardware inventory is not supported, but you can import your custom SMS_DEF .MOF files into the new Configuration Manager 2012 infrastructure. Analyze and test the custom MOF edits before importing them into the production environment of Configuration Manager 2012, and ensure that there are no conflicting data types in Configuration Manager 2012.

Distribution Point Sharing

In the process of migrating your Configuration Manager 2007 objects and clients to Configuration Manager 2012, you can use distribution point sharing. This feature allows Configuration Manager clients to retrieve content for migrated packages that are hosted on Configuration Manager 2007 distribution points.

You need to configure distribution point sharing per site; Figure 3.5 shows the dialog box with the check box for enabling or disabling distribution point sharing. Once you enable distribution point sharing, another data-gathering job will be started.

FIGURE 3.5
Enabling distribution point sharing

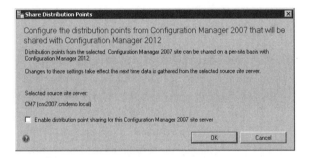

After the data-gathering process is finished, you'll see all the distribution points, including branch distribution points and distribution point shares. Boot images and App-V applications are not supported on shared distribution points. You will need to migrate those objects and make them available on a Configuration Manager 2012 distribution point. As mentioned earlier, associated boundaries are migrated when you enable distribution point sharing.

INTEROPERABILITY WITH CONFIGURATION MANAGER 2007

The migration feature in Configuration Manager 2012 gives you a level of interoperability while migrating your Configuration Manager 2007 infrastructure. Since you have two Configuration Manager hierarchies to maintain, it's a good idea to look at some interoperability possibilities and scenarios.

Once you specify a source hierarchy for the new Configuration Manager 2012 hierarchy, by default every four hours a data-gathering process will run to collect all the information about the source hierarchy. During the migration period the source hierarchy is configured in Configuration Manager 2012, and your two Configuration Manager environments are connected to each other, providing a sort of interoperability.

Re-migrate Updated Objects The migration process doesn't move objects to the Configuration Manager 2012 environment but instead copies, and if necessary, converts the objects to Configuration Manager 2012 standards. The original objects remain in Configuration Manager 2007 and can still be used and changed. If a change is made to an original object, the data-gathering process will detect the change, and you can re-migrate the updated object.

Distribution Point Sharing Enabling distribution point sharing allows you to share a distribution point that's available in a Configuration Manager 2007 site with Configuration Manager 2012. The migrated or new Configuration Manager 2012 clients are able to retrieve content from a shared distribution point.

Content As mentioned earlier, the content is not migrated during the migration process. The source content also stays at the same location if this is a Configuration Manager 2007 site server. Be aware that you may need to migrate the source content also.

Planning a Migration

This section describes the steps required to prepare the migration from Configuration Manager 2007 to Configuration Manager 2012. The newly designed Configuration Manager 2012 infrastructure must be in place. Consult Chapter 4, "Installation and Site Role Configuration," for information on how to install and configure the Configuration Manager 2012 environment that you designed in Chapter 2, "Planning a Configuration Manager Infrastructure."

As you define your project phases and the steps you need to take to migrate your Configuration Manager 2007 infrastructure to the new Configuration Manager 2012 infrastructure, you need to plan your migration.

Preparing Your Migration

Regardless of when you want to migrate to Configuration Manager 2012, you should prepare your Configuration Manager 2007 environment in advance to allow a smooth migration, as follows:

◆ Be sure that your new Configuration Manager 2012 infrastructure is in place.

◆ Be sure that your Configuration Manager 2007 infrastructure is at least using Service Pack 2.

◆ Use UNC paths for the package source path. Avoid using local paths; always use UNC paths to a file share.

◆ Avoid mixing users and devices in collection definitions; mixing users and devices is no longer supported.

◆ Avoid using collections with multiple query rules that limit different collections.

◆ Use different site codes in Configuration Manager 2012 than in Configuration Manager 2007; they must be unique.

Planning Your Migration Strategy

When you want to migrate a Configuration Manager 2007 infrastructure to a new Configuration Manager 2012 infrastructure, you will need to walk through a migration process that can take a long time depending on your source Configuration Manager 2007 infrastructure.

As we said in the introduction of this chapter, Configuration Manager 2012 supports side-by-side migration. This means that you need to build a new Configuration Manager 2012 infrastructure next to your current production Configuration Manager 2007 infrastructure. The best way is to define a project for your migration to the new infrastructure.

As noted in Chapter 1, "Overview of Operations Management," any well-planned migration leverages a well-thought-out project plan. This should be based on a solid foundation or methodology such as the Microsoft Operations Framework (MOF).

The initial steps in any project are a typical gap analysis. They fall into three basic categories; you must ask yourself the following:

◆ Where are we?

◆ Where do we want to be?

◆ How do we get there?

A thorough project plan should include some or all of the following phases as well as work tasks for each phase:

Phase 1: Define and capture phase

◆ Create a project plan.

◆ Document the current environment.

◆ Conduct an initial risk review.

◆ Create business test cases.

◆ Finalize the business proposal.

Phase 2: Build phase

◆ Conduct a planning workshop.

◆ Install a proof-of-concept lab.

◆ Conduct server and workstation testing.

◆ Procure hardware.

Phase 3: Test phase (pilot)

◆ Draft a communication plan for the following groups.

　　◆ Executive/management

　　◆ Project team

　　◆ Site (users)

- Build and deploy hardware and software.

- Implement change control for the pilot phase.

- Perform a pilot with the new environment.

Phase 4: Production deployment phase

- Implement change control for the production development phase.

- Deploy your new environment.

Phase 5: Review phase

- Conduct a lessons learned workshop.

- Conduct a project reflection session (party).

One fundamental part of a project plan that is commonly overlooked is the communication plan. This is generally used in two different ways: first, to inform users of what is changing on their desktops, but more important, as a communication vehicle to show the value that you bring to the business! Use this project to highlight the capabilities of Configuration Manager 2012 as well as the business value and insights of reporting, software updates, and software distribution. Don't be afraid to highlight the hard work of the migration team and the value that a project of this magnitude brings to the business.

Performing the Migration

Two main upgrade strategies are available to deploy Configuration Manager 2012 to an existing infrastructure:

Side-by-Side Migration A side-by-side migration creates a new Configuration Manager 2012 infrastructure that runs alongside the Configuration Manager 2007 infrastructure. This migration allows clients to be managed 100 percent of the time while the migration is being conducted. The migration feature in Configuration Manager 2012 assists you with the migration of Configuration Manager 2007 objects.

Wipe and Load The wipe-and-load approach is useful if the goal is to start over with change and configuration management. Thus, there will be zero data saved or migrated.

In this section, you'll learn both types.

Using the Side-by-Side Migration Strategy

In a side-by-side migration, an existing Configuration Manager 2007 implementation can function while client systems are moved from Configuration Manager 2007 to Configuration Manager 2012. This enables you to do the following:

- Use new hardware.

- Modify your existing hierarchy.

- Retain historical client data.

◆ Redesign the Configuration Manager hierarchy.

◆ Retain custom objects within Configuration Manager 2007.

Migrating Configuration Manager 2007 to Configuration Manager 2012 can take a while, depending on the source and target Configuration Manager hierarchies. In this section the migration process is explained.

UNDERSTANDING THE MIGRATION PROCESS

After preparing the Configuration Manager 2007 infrastructure, as described in the "Planning a Migration" section of this chapter, you can proceed with the migration process. The migration process has several steps, depending on your source infrastructure. The following steps are part of the migration process:

Configure the Migration Feature   You configure the migration feature by creating a source hierarchy in the Configuration Manager 2012 hierarchy. You need to connect the Configuration Manager 2012 infrastructure to the topmost site of the Configuration Manager 2007 SP2 infrastructure.

You must also configure the gathering process. You need to configure the schedule and supply administrative access for the gathering process.

Once the gathering process is complete and other source sites have been discovered, you must configure credentials for each of the additional source sites.

Share Distribution Points   Sharing distribution points allows you to postpone their migration. It also reduces network traffic when you enable this feature on remote locations.

Create Migration Jobs   Migration jobs are used to migrate objects from Configuration Manager 2007 to Configuration Manager 2012. You can create one or more jobs, depending on your source Configuration Manager 2007 infrastructure.

When creating a migration job you can choose to exclude objects, assign content ownership, set the security scope, limit the collections, and change site codes in your query definitions.

The migration job does not migrate the content of your Configuration Manager objects. Configuration Manager 2012 will retrieve the content from the original source file location.

Migrating content can be started instantly but can also be scheduled to start later.

Monitor Migration Jobs   In the process of migrating your Configuration Manager 2007 objects to the Configuration Manager 2012 environment, you must monitor the migration. When you select the migration job, you can monitor the migration by selecting objects in the job. Besides the in-console monitoring, Configuration Manager records migration actions in the migmctrl.log file located in the Logs folder in the Configuration Manager 2012 installation path.

If a migration job fails and other jobs are still running, you should review the details in the migmctrl.log file as soon as possible. Migration actions are continually added to the file and overwrite the old details.

In the Configuration Manager Console, you are able to monitor the migration by looking at the migration dashboard, shown in Figure 3.6.

FIGURE 3.6
The Migration
Dashboard

Reporting Migration results   With the reporting feature within Configuration Manager 2012 you are able to report information about the Migration of the Configuration Manager 2007 objects to Configuration Manager 2012. The following reports are available in the Migration Category:

◆   Clients in exclusion list

◆   Dependency on a Configuration Manager 2007 collection

◆   Migration Job Properties

◆   Migration Jobs

◆   Objects that failed to migrate

You are able to find more information about reporting in Chapter 12, "Reporting."

Upgrade Distribution Points   When upgrading distribution points you want to avoid having a large amount of data flowing through the WAN. For this reason, you can migrate distribution points in two ways: automatic and manual. Configuration Manager 2012 supports upgrading the following distribution points:

◆   Branch Distribution Point

◆   Server Share Distribution Point

◆   Standard Distribution Point

When you choose automatic migration, you need to enable distribution point sharing and upgrade the distribution point from the Configuration Manager 2012 console. During the migration process, the distribution point is removed from the Configuration Manager 2007 database and the new Configuration Manager 2012 distribution point is installed on the server. After the installation, the content of the distribution point is copied to the new content library of Configuration Manager 2012. Be sure to have enough disk space available.

If there is a Secondary Site available, the Secondary Site will automatically be uninstalled before installing the Configuration Manager 2012 Distribution Point. The upgrade job will pause until the next data gathering job to check if the Secondary Site is completely uninstalled.

One distribution point upgrade migration job is performed at the time and each other subsequent job is queued.

After upgrading the Configuration Manager 2007 distribution point, you need to manually delete the old content; be sure to test your deployments first.

START PREPARING NOW

You can prepare distribution point upgrades by preparing your environment by upgrading your Branch Distribution Points to Windows 7. Windows XP is not supported. Use the "Branch Distribution Point management task" to migrate it from Windows XP to Windows 7 without having to redistribute the content. Find more information about the Branch Distribution Point management task, see the online documentation of Configuration Manager 2007.

Upgrade Secondary Sites   Upgrading secondary sites is only possible by uninstalling the Configuration Manager 2007 secondary site and then installing the new secondary site from the Configuration Manager 2012 console.

Migrate Clients   The migration of the clients is done using the same methods as for deploying a new Configuration Manager 2012 client. The first step in the migration is to uninstall the Configuration Manager 2007 client and install the Configuration Manager 2012 client. During this process the Configuration Manager data, for instance, advertisement history and the GUID of the client, are preserved.

Upgrade the Administrative Console   The administrative console can be installed on several servers and workplaces. To be able to manage the new Configuration Manager 2012 infrastructure, you also need to upgrade the administrative console to the Configuration Manager 2012 console.

Perform Post-Migration Tasks   After migrating all the old Configuration Manager 2007 content, you must perform post-migration tasks. The first task is to stop the data-gathering process, clean up the migration data, and remove the source hierarchy. Then you need to remove the old Configuration Manager 2007 infrastructure from your environment.

The step-by-step details of these procedures are provided in the following sections.

CONFIGURING THE MIGRATION FEATURE

Configuring the migration feature can be done with the following steps. First, you will need to specify the source hierarchy:

1. In the Configuration Manager console choose the Administration workspace.

2. Expand Overview ➤ Migration in the Administration workspace, and choose Active Source Hierarchy.

3. After selecting the Active Source Hierarchy, choose the Home tab of the Ribbon and choose Specify Source Hierarchy.

4. In the Specify Migration Source screen, select New Source Hierarchy at the Active Source Hierarchy.

5. Specify the top-level Configuration Manager 2007 site server of your source Configuration Manager 2007 hierarchy by filling in the full qualified domain name of the server.

6. Specify the site access account for the SMS provider of the source site server. Verify the connection of an existing or new account before submitting.

   The account needs read permissions to all source site objects.

7. Specify the site access account for the SQL server of the source site server.

   The account needs read and execute permissions to the site database. This can be the same account as the account that has access to the SMS provider.

8. Click OK to save the configuration and to start the data-gathering process. You'll see the Data Gathering Status dialog box, as shown in Figure 3.7.

FIGURE 3.7
The first data-gathering process is complete

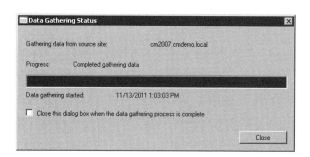

After the first data-gathering process has finished, all other primary sites in the hierarchy are discovered. In Figure 3.8 you see a primary site that has been discovered but the data-gathering process has not run yet. The next step is to configure the credentials for the Configuration Manager 2007 source site to be able to gather the data.

FIGURE 3.8
Additional sources site discovered during the data-gathering process

1. In the Configuration Manager console choose the Administration workspace.

2. Expand Overview ➤ Migration in the Administration workspace, and choose Active Source Hierarchy.

3. Select the site with the status Have Not Gathered Data.

4. On the Home tab of the Ribbon, select Configure Credentials in the Source Site section.

5. Specify the site access account for the SMS provider of the source site server.

   The account needs read permissions to all source site objects.

6. Specify the site access account for the SQL Server of the source site server.

   The account needs read and execute permissions to the site database. This can be the same account as the account that has access to the SMS provider.

7. Click OK to save the configuration and to start the data-gathering process.

After configuring the credentials for the additional sites, the gathering process will start to gather all the objects in the Configuration Manager 2007 source site.

ENABLING DISTRIBUTION POINT SHARING

The distribution points from a selected Configuration Manager 2012 site can be shared on a per-site basis in the Configuration Manager 2012 console:

1. In the Configuration Manager console open the Administration workspace.

2. Expand Overview ➤ Migration in the Administration workspace, and select Active Source Hierarchy.

3. Select the site for which you want to enable distribution point sharing.

4. Go to the Home tab of the Ribbon tab, and choose Share Distribution Points.

5. In the Share Distribution Points dialog box choose the Enable Distribution Point Sharing For This Configuration Manager 2007 Site Server option.

6. Click OK.

After enabling distribution point sharing, the gathering process will start to gather all the objects and distribution point data in the Configuration Manager 2007 source site. Once the site servers are protected, the boundaries related to the site servers of the distribution points are migrated also.

CREATING MIGRATION JOBS

As mentioned earlier, you can create three different migration jobs. Depending on your purpose, you need to follow one of the following three procedures. The purposes of the three different migration jobs are to provide support for migrating collections with all the related objects and to provide support for migrating one or more objects or objects that are changed after being migrated.

Creating a Collection Migration Job

Collection migration jobs can be used to migrate the collections with objects that are associated with the specific collections. To create a collection migration job, follow these steps:

1. In the Configuration Manager console select the Administration workspace.

2. Expand Overview ➤ Migration in the Administration workspace, and chose Migration Jobs.

3. Select the Home tab of the Ribbon, and choose Create Migration Job.

4. Give the migration job a name and description.

5. Select Collection Migration as the job type, and click Next.

6. Select the collections that you want to migrate, as shown in Figure 3.9, and select Migrate Objects That Are Associated With The Specified Collections.

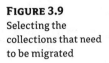

FIGURE 3.9
Selecting the collections that need to be migrated

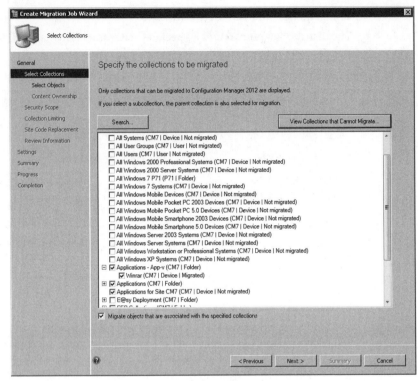

Another option instead of pick and choose is to search for the collection(s) that you want to migrate. This is done by selecting the Search button and searching for the collection based on the collection name, Site Code, Collection ID, or Status.

7. After searching or selecting the collections click Next.

8. Review the objects that will be migrated, and click Next.

9. Select the destination site that will be the owner of the objects, and click Next.

10. Configure the security scope, and click Next.

11. Limit the collection if needed, and click Next.

12. Replace the site code, and click Next.

13. Review the migration job information, save it optionally to a file, and click Next.

14. Select the schedule, configure the conflict handling and additional settings for the migration job, and click Next.

15. Confirm the settings in the summary, and click Next.

16. Click Close to see the migration.

Creating an Object Migration Job

Object migration jobs are used for migrating one or more Configuration Manager 2007 objects to Configuration Manager 2012. To create an object migration job, perform the following steps:

1. In the Configuration Manager console select the Administration workspace.

2. Expand Overview ➢ Migration in the Administration workspace, and choose Migration Jobs.

3. Select the Home tab of the Ribbon, and choose Create Migration Job.

4. Give the migration job a name and description.

5. Select Object Migration as the job type, and click Next.

6. Select the objects that you want to migrate, as shown in Figure 3.10.

FIGURE 3.10
Select the objects that need to be migrated

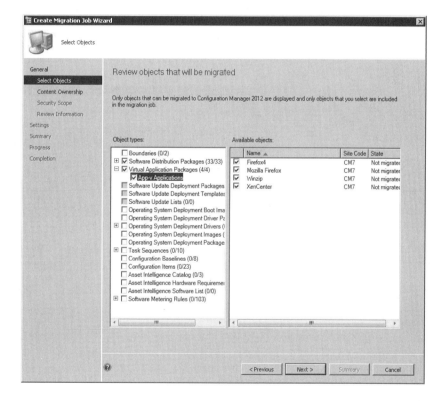

7. Click Next.

8. Select the destination site that is going to be the owner of the objects, and click Next.

9. Configure the security scope, and click Next.

10. Review the migration job information, save it optionally to a file, and click Next.

11. Select the schedule, configure the conflict handling and additional settings for the migration job, and click Next.

12. Confirm the settings in the summary, and click Next.

13. Click Close to see the migration.

Creating an Objects Modified After Migration Job

During a lengthy migration process, objects in the Configuration Manager 2007 infrastructure will change. With the objects modified after migration job, you can re-migrate the changed objects. Follow these steps to create an objects modified after migration job:

1. In the Configuration Manager console open the Administration workspace.

2. Expand Overview ➤ Migration in the Administration workspace and choose Migration Jobs.

3. Select the Home tab of the Ribbon, and choose Create Migration Job.

4. Give the migration job a name and description.

5. Select Object Modified After Migration as the job type, and click Next.

6. Select the objects that you want to re-migrate, as shown in Figure 3.11, and click Next.

FIGURE 3.11
Select the changed objects that need to be re-migrated

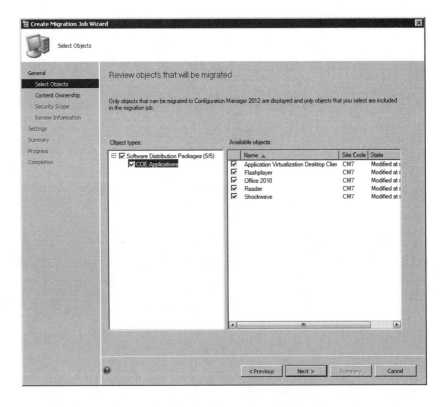

7. Select the destination site that is going to be the owner of the objects, and click Next.

8. Configure the security scope, and click Next.

9. Review the migration job information, save it optionally to a file, and click Next.

10. Select the schedule, and click Next.

11. Confirm the settings in the summary, and click Next.

12. Click Close to see the migration.

UPGRADING DISTRIBUTION POINTS

Migrating distribution points can be done in two ways:

◆ Automatically

◆ Manually

The procedures for both options are described in the following sections.

Migrating Distribution Points Automatically

Migrating a distribution point can be done automatically by removing the distribution point from the source database and adding it to the target database. It is supported only when no other site roles other than a Management Point of a Secondary Site are active. So you must remove the other roles like software update points, PXE service points, or state migration points before proceeding. To be able to migrate the distribution point, you need to enable the site for distribution point sharing.

You can upgrade the distribution point by following this procedure:

1. In the Configuration Manager console, choose the Administration workspace.

2. Expand Overview ➤ Migration in the Administration workspace, and choose Active Source Hierarchy.

3. Select the source site and choose Distribution Points.

4. Select the Configuration Manager 2007 distribution point that you want to migrate.

5. Select the Distribution Point tab of the Ribbon, check if the Distribution Point is eligible for upgrade, and choose Upgrade. If the Distribution Point if not eligible for upgrade, other site roles than described earlier are active on the selected Distribution Point.

6. Choose in the Upgrade Shared Distribution Point wizard the site code where the distribution point must connect to after upgrading. At this point, also configure if the distribution point must be available from the Internet by filling in the fully qualified domain name (FQDN) for the site system for use on the Internet. Click on Next.

7. Configure the distribution point settings by choosing if the setup must install and configure IIS, if the distribution point is available via HTTP or HTTPS, and configure if the distribution point can handle prestaged content. Click on Next.

8. Configure the drive settings for the distribution that is going to be upgraded, and click on Next.

9. Configure PXE support if needed and click on Next to configure content validation for this distribution point. Click on Next to proceed.

10. Configure Boundary group membership for the new Configuration Manager 2012 distribution point and click on Next.

11. Be sure to have enough free space to proceed with the upgrade. Check if the required space, as shown in Figure 3.12, meets the available space on your configured drives. When migrating a Distribution Point the content located at the Distribution Point is copied and converted to the new content library. Click on Next when you are sure that there is enough space available.

FIGURE 3.12
Be sure you have enough disk space for converting packages to the new content library

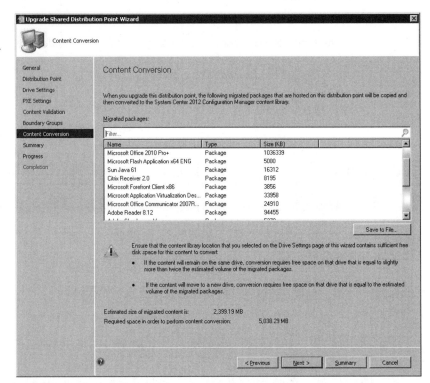

12. Review the summary and click on Next to process the upgrade.

You can monitor the migration process in the `migmctrl.log` file in the `Logs` folder in the Configuration Manager installation folder and in the Application log in the event viewer on the target server. Also on the target server there is a folder called `SMS_DP$\SMS\Logs` and a file called `SMSDPPROV.LOG` where you can find possible errors in the installation of the distribution point. You can also view the status in the Distribution Point Upgrades node, as shown in Figure 3.13. Refreshing the screen will update the status of the upgrade.

FIGURE 3.13
Monitor the upgrade
status

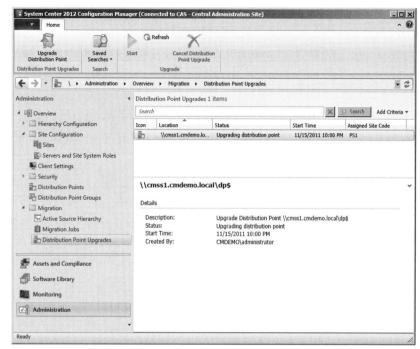

FIGURE 3.13
Monitor the upgrade status

The content is copied and converted to the new content library with the single-instance storage. Be sure to delete the old content from the old Distribution Point since the old content is not removed automatically.

Please go to Chapter 4 for more in-depth information about installing and configuring Distribution Points.

Migrating Distribution Points Manually

The manual migration of a distribution point is done in two general steps:

1. Uninstalling the current distribution point from the Configuration Manager 2007 environment

2. Installing the distribution point with prestaged content in the new Configuration Manager 2012 environment

This scenario can be used for all distribution points, including branch distribution points, distribution point shares, and normal distribution points. For in-depth distribution point installation and configuration instructions, please consult Chapter 4.

To uninstall a distribution point from Configuration Manager 2007, follow these steps:

1. In the Configuration Manager 2007 console, open the site under Site Management, and select the site system with the distribution point.

2. Select the distribution point or distribution point share, and click Delete in the Actions area of the console.

To install a distribution point with prestaged content in Configuration Manager 2012, perform the following procedure:

1. In the Configuration Manager console open the Administration workspace.

2. Expand Overview ➤ Site Configuration in the Administration workspace, and choose Servers and Site System Roles.

3. Select the Home tab of the Ribbon, and choose Create Site System Server.

4. Click Browse, and search for the server on which you want to install the distribution point.

5. Supply the FQDN for use on your intranet.

6. Supply, if needed, the FQDN for use on the Internet.

7. If the server is in a different Active Directory forest, select "Require the site server to initiate connections to this system."

8. Supply the site system installation account, and click Next.

9. Select the Distribution Point option, and click Next.

10. Select "Install and configure IIS if required by Configuration Manager," and configure how the client computers are allowed to communicate with the distribution point.

11. Configure, if necessary, the certificate, or choose the option Create Self-Signed Certificate.

12. Enable the option "Enable this distribution point for prestaged content," and click Next.

13. Configure the drive settings, and click Next.

14. Configure PXE, and click Next.

15. Configure multicast, and click Next.

16. Configure content validation, and click Next.

17. Configure boundary groups, and click Next.

18. Review the summary, and click Next.

19. Click Close.

Since the distribution point is enabled for prestaged content, you can now create prestaged content packages that you need to deploy on the new distribution point. Content that can be prestaged includes the following:

◆ Applications

◆ Packages

◆ Software deployment packages

◆ Driver packages

◆ Operating system images

♦ Operating system installers

♦ Boot images

Creating prestaged content packages can be done up front as follows:

1. In the Configuration Manager console choose the Software Library workspace.

2. Select a content package that needs to be prestaged, and save the PKGX files to an external disk.

The next step is to extract the created PKGX files to the remote distribution point:

1. Open a command prompt in administrative mode on the server that serves as the new distribution point.

2. Copy the `ExtractContent.exe` command-line utility from `<Configuration Manager Source Folder>\Tools` to a location on the server of the distribution point.

3. Navigate to the location where you saved the file `ExtractContent.exe`.

4. Execute the following command, and you will receive results like those shown in Figure 3.14:

```
ExtractContent.exe /p:<location of the prestaged file>\<prestagedfile>.pkgx /c
```

FIGURE 3.14
Extracting the prestage package file to the new distribution point

```
Administrator: Command Prompt
USAGE:
===========================================================================
ExtractContent.exe /P:<path> [/C:] [/S] [/I] [/?]

WHERE:

/P - path to a file or to a folder with one or more files to prestage
/C - validate the content without prestaging
/S - skip content with lower or equal versions from prestaging
/I - print out the metadata info of the content
/? - print out command line parameters of content prestaging tool
===========================================================================

D:\install\ConfigMgr_2012_Beta2_ENU_7561\TOOLS>ExtractContent.exe /p:d:\pre\pre.
pkgx /s

Log file - "C:\Users\ADMINI~1.CMD\AppData\Local\Temp\2\PrestageContent.log"

Prestaging content to content library D:\SCCMContentLib
        uncompress      25 %
        uncompress      50 %
        uncompress      75 %
        uncompress     100 %
        extract         25 %
        extract         50 %
        extract         75 %
        extract        100 %
Content of package PS100002.3 is prestaged and registered.

D:\install\ConfigMgr_2012_Beta2_ENU_7561\TOOLS>
```

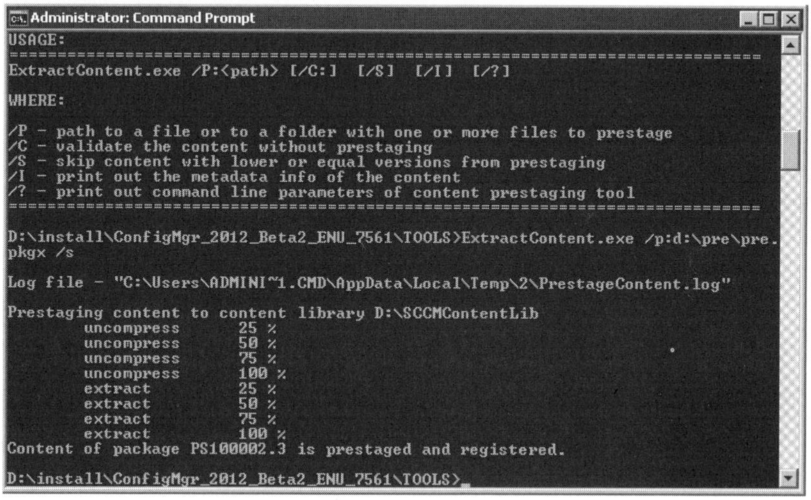

The extraction to the distribution point will be processed in the background. For troubleshooting purposes or to follow the process, you can monitor the `PrestageContent.log` file, which you can find in the `temp` folder of your user account.

UPGRADING SECONDARY SITES

Secondary sites need to be manually uninstalled from the Configuration Manager 2007 environment; there is no upgrade path for the scenario. Consider while planning your Configuration Manager 2012 hierarchy the replacement of a secondary site with just a distribution point. Chapter 2 describes when you can consider replacing a secondary site with a distribution point.

1. Right-click the secondary site and click Delete.

2. Click Next.

3. Select Deinstall the Site, and click Next.

4. Review the information about the secondary site to be deinstalled (Figure 3.15), and click Finish.

FIGURE 3.15
Deinstalling the secondary site from Configuration Manager 2007 SP2

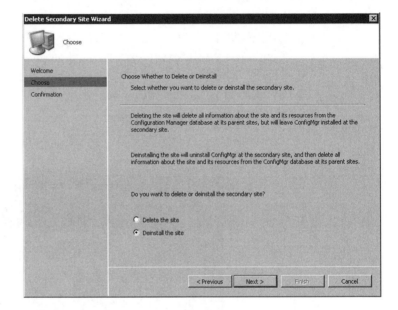

After the deletion process is finished, you can install the Configuration Manager 2012 secondary site server role.

MIGRATING CLIENTS

The Configuration Manager 2007 clients need to be migrated also; the process of client migration consists of uninstalling the Configuration Manager 2007 client and installing the new Configuration Manager 2012 client.

You can migrate the clients via the following methods:

◆ Client push installation

◆ Software distribution

◆ Group Policy

◆ Windows Software Update Services (WSUS)

◆ Manual installation

◆ Integrated with operating system deployment

Chapter 6 offers more information about client installation. The installation of the Configuration Manager 2012 client will automatically uninstall the Configuration Manager 2007 client and install the Configuration Manager 2012 client.

Remember that only the following clients are supported:

◆ Windows XP SP2 (64-bit)

◆ Windows XP SP3 (32-bit)

◆ Windows Server 2003 SP2

◆ Windows Vista SP2

◆ Windows 7 RTM and SP1

◆ Windows Server 2008 SP2

◆ Windows Server 2008 R2 RTM and SP1 (64-bit)

A requirement of all clients is that .NET Framework 4.0 needs to be present. You must deploy this version before migrating to the new Configuration Manager 2012 client.

Using the Wipe-and-Load Strategy

The wipe-and-load strategy is the most basic and straightforward of any of the approaches. Generally speaking, this strategy is intended for environments in which the following apply:

◆ You still use SMS 2003 or Configuration Manager 2007 as a single-server solution.

◆ None of the existing data (i.e., collections, inventories, packages, and so on) needs to be retained.

Although this approach may seem like the path of least resistance, there are a few pitfalls that you need to stay aware of:

Client Manageability   If you take the wipe-and-load approach, the quickest way to accomplish it is to perform a software distribution to run the `ccmclean.exe` Microsoft Resource Kit utility for SMS 2003 or Configuration Manager 2007 on all SMS 2003 or Configuration Manager 2007 clients. This poses the potential problem that the clients will remain unmanaged until the server (current or new future hardware) is rebuilt and Configuration Manager 2012 is installed and configured properly. Depending on the environment, this might be a non-issue. A risk assessment would need to be performed to see if mission-critical application updates or zero-day exploit patches need to be deployed and to assess the potential impact to your enterprise. If the risk can be minimized or negated, then a wipe-and-load operation might be possible.

Implementation Timeframe   Rebuilding a server and installing or configuring all the components that are required to support a Configuration Manager 2012 installation is no small task. Not to mention that if you have a strict change control process, this might hinder your forward momentum significantly. All these factors equate to dollars—money spent rebuilding, installing, configuring, and testing a server that was already up and running in production.

The bottom line is, just because the wipe-and-load option appears to be the path of least resistance, don't be tempted. Weigh your options before coming to a decision that you might regret later.

Upgrading the Configuration Manager Console

As with the Configuration Manager 2012 site server itself, you must consider the upgrade of all the Configuration Manager 2007 Administrator consoles to Configuration Manager 2012 Administrator consoles. This potentially is an area for automation or an unattended installation routine.

Any of the setup functions (Primary Site, Secondary Site, or Administrator Console) can be scripted with an initialization file to answer key questions of a setup routine. In this scenario, we want to automate the Administrator console setup for Configuration Manager 2012.

The following steps will enable you to perform an unattended installation of the Configuration Manager 2012 Administrator Console:

1. Ensure that administrator workstations meet the minimum requirements for the Configuration Manager 2012 Administrator Console. In order to run the Installation Prerequisite Checker to verify the workstation, you can run `prereqchk.exe /ADMINUI` from the command line. You can find this file in the installation source on the DVD (SMSSetup\Bin\x64).

2. Advertise the setup of Configuration Manager 2012 with the following command line, substituting the <*msiexec /I \SMSSETUP\BIN\i386\AdminConsole.msi /qn*> text with the name and location of the file from above:

   ```
   msiexec /I \SMSSETUP\BIN\i386\AdminConsole.msi /qn
   ```

The unattended installation will not remove the old Configuration Manager 2007 console. You can remove the console by uninstalling it via the Programs And Features option in Control Panel.

The following steps enable you to perform a GUI installation of the Configuration Manager 2012 Administrator Console:

1. Ensure that administrator workstations meet the minimum requirements for the Configuration Manager 2012 Administrator Console. In order to run the Installation Prerequisite Checker to verify the workstation, you can run `prereqchk.exe /ADMINUI` from the command line.

2. Insert the System Center 2012 Configuration Manager DVD, browse to the \SMSSETUP\ BIN\i386\ folder, and double-click `AdminConsole.msi`.

   The Welcome to the Microsoft System Center 2012 Configuration Manager Console Setup Wizard appears.

3. Click Next.

4. Supply the site server name, and click Next.

5. Browse to the installation location, and click Next.

6. Click Install.

7. Review any fatal errors, errors, or warnings that are presented (although part of your homework was to run the Installation Prerequisite Checker and address all errors), or review the `ConfigMgrAdminUISetup.log` and the `ConfigMgrPrereq.log` on the root of the system drive to see which errors need to be addressed.

8. Click Finish to start the newly installed Configuration Manager 2012 Administrator Console.

Post-Migration or Installation Considerations

Once you have performed the selected installation, it is imperative to maintain its health moving forward. The obvious choice for performance and availability monitoring is Microsoft System Center 2012 Operations Manager; for this you need to install the Configuration Manager 2012 Management Pack in Operations Manager 2012. More information about support for Operations Manager 2012 can be found in Chapter 1.

1. First, review the site status from within the System Status node in the Monitoring workspace in the Configuration Manager 2012 console.

2. Review all of the site system roles to ensure that they are identified properly as well as the component status.

3. If there are any critical or red components, right-click the targeted component and select Show Messages ➤ Errors.

   This produces all of the error status messages, which highlight the problems within the site.

You'll find more detailed troubleshooting coverage in Chapter 15, "Troubleshooting."

Another area of concentration should be within the site settings. With the new functionality and roles within Configuration Manager, a plethora of settings need to be set up and configured. A more detailed and in-depth view of site settings is covered in Chapter 4.

After you review the new environment, you need to clean up Configuration Manager 2012 by doing the following:

◆ Stop the data-gathering process.

◆ Clean up the migration data.

STOPPING THE DATA-GATHERING PROCESS

You stop the data-gathering process by following the next procedure. You need to first stop the data-gathering processes in all of the child sites in the source hierarchy.

1. In the Configuration Manager console open the Administration workspace.

2. Expand Overview ➤ Migration in the Administration workspace, and choose Active Source Hierarchy.

3. Select the site with data gathering enabled.

4. Select the Home tab of the Ribbon, and choose Stop Data Gathering.

5. Click Yes when the Stop Data Gathering dialog box appears.

6. Repeat this for all sites in the hierarchy.

CLEANING UP MIGRATION DATA

The next step in the post-migration task is to clean up the migration data, as follows:

1. In the Configuration Manager console choose the Administration workspace.

2. Expand Overview ➢ Migration in the Administration workspace, and choose Active Source Hierarchy.

3. Select the topmost source hierarchy site with data gathering disabled.

4. Select the Home tab of the Ribbon, and choose Clean Up Migration Data.

5. Verify that you have the right source hierarchy, and click OK when the Clean Up Migration Data dialog box appears (Figure 3.16).

FIGURE 3.16
Cleaning up the migration data of the source hierarchy

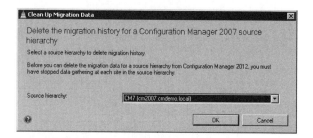

Migrating Packages to the New Application Model

When you migrate your packages to Configuration Manager 2012, the classic packages are migrated as is. Configuration Manager 2012 is built around the new application model, and to get all the features of the new application model you need to convert the package to an application. You can find more information about the new application model in Chapter 7, "Application Deployment."

After migrating the packages from the Configuration Manager 2007 environment to the Configuration Manager 2012 environment, you have a couple of options for what to do with the packages:

Do Nothing   You can leave the package and program as they are, since some packages are best left in the classic packages and programs format, for instance, system maintenance tools like defrag and backup. System maintenance tools are often deployed to systems instead of users. System-based classic packages cannot be converted by Package Conversion Manager since it only supports classic packages.

Convert the Packages Manually   You can manually convert packages and programs to the new application model. This option is not a best practice, and it can be time consuming.

Convert the Packages with Conversion Manager   Package Conversion Manager will lead you through the process of converting packages to the new application model. The conversion process will move the data to the application model.

Best practice is to convert the packages with System Center Configuration Manager Package Conversion Manager; this way you are able to use all features of the application model of Configuration Manager 2012.

What Is Package Conversion Manager?

Package Conversion Manager helps you analyze packages and determines the readiness for the conversion of classic packages to the new application model (see Figure 3.17). After the analysis, Package Conversion Manager will convert the package to the new application model by building applications and deployment types, and it migrates machine collection queries to the application model by building global conditions and requirement rules. The converted global conditions and requirement rules are ANDed with the program requirements. This means that the global conditions and requirement rules are merged with the classic program requirements.

FIGURE 3.17
Configuration Manager console with Package Conversion Manager

While you're in the migration process, the summarization screen of Package Conversion Manager helps you identify the progress of your migration.

Package Conversion Manager is fully integrated with the Configuration Manager 2012 console, but it must be installed separately.

Not all packages are suitable for migration with Package Conversion Manager; the Manager supports the migration of packages that are *user facing,* for instance, packages that users interact with, such as these:

◆ MSI-based applications

◆ App-V-based applications

◆ EXE-based applications

Applications that are not supported or not able to be migrated include the following:

◆ System maintenance tools like defrag or backup

◆ End-of-life packages

The Conversion Process

You will need to go through the process of converting the packages and programs to the new application model. The process consists of the following phases:

◆ Installing Package Conversion Manager

◆ Analyzing the packages

◆ Converting the packages

INSTALLING PACKAGE CONVERSION MANAGER

You need to install Package Conversion Manager on the primary site. Package Conversion Manager is downloadable from the System Center website of Microsoft. Follow the next steps to install the Package Conversion Manager.

1. Close the Configuration Manager Console and double click on the executable (PCMSetup.exe) that you have downloaded from the System Center website.

2. Click on Next in the welcome screen and accept the end-use license agreement before going further by clicking on Next.

3. Select the type of installation and click on Next and Install.

4. Click on Finish after the installation is finished and start the Configuration Manager console.

ANALYZING PACKAGES

Packages need to be analyzed before they can be converted to the new application model. Analysis of packages can done in four ways:

◆ You can analyze a single item.

◆ You can analyze in bulk by selecting additional packages.

◆ You can analyze during the conversion process automatically.

◆ You can schedule bulk analysis during nonpeak hours.

You can run the analysis today to see if the packages are compliant for conversion, but you can migrate the packages at a later stage because while the conversion process is running the packages will be reanalyzed.

CHANGING THE COLUMNS OF THE PACKAGES LIST

If you want to view the status of the packages in the packages list, you are then able to add columns to the packages list. This is done by right clicking on the columns and by selecting the Readiness and Last Analyzed/Converted columns.

The analyzing process can result in the following readiness states of the to-be-converted packages, as shown in Figure 3.18 in the Package Conversion Dashboard.

FIGURE 3.18

Package Conversion Dashboard

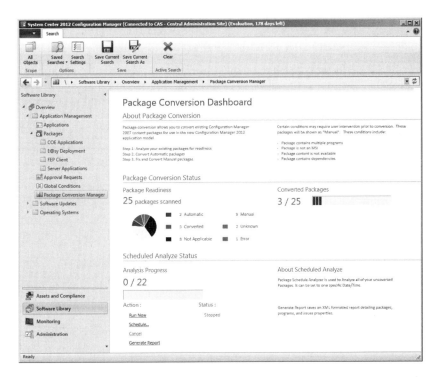

Unknown   Analysis has not been run for this application.

Automatic   The package can be automatically converted to the application model. This is the best state to use for bulk migrations.

Manual   There is not enough data available to convert the package automatically. The administrator needs to supply input for the conversion. You may need to supply information like detection methods and the deployment type preference order through a wizard supplied by Package Conversion Manager.

Not Applicable   The Package Conversion Manager tool is not able to do anything with the package in this state. You may need to modify the source package to be able to convert the package to the new application model.

Converted   The package has been converted to the application model. The application is manageable through the Configuration Manager 2012 console.

Error   If there is an error reported, go to the package, select it, and view the summary to see the readiness issues. For instance, quotes are not supported in the command line of the program.

If you need to convert the package, you need to be sure of the following:

- The content of the package is present.
- It is a software distribution package.
- It contains at least one program.

If one of these three must-haves is not present, then the application is not applicable. If the three are available, you can migrate the application manually. You can use an automatic migration when the three must-haves are present and you have only one MSI per package available, the content is accessible, and there are no unconverted dependencies.

AUTOMATIC CONVERSION

Once you finish the conversion process, the application is ready for testing. The application is not fully ready for deploying yet because you still need to provide detection methods and configure the deployment type preference order.

All packages need to be analyzed before you can convert the packages and programs to the new application model. The option Convert Package is greyed out until the analyzing phase is finished.

To manually analyze packages, perform the following steps:

1. In the Configuration Manager console open the Software Library workspace.

2. Expand Overview ➤ Application Management ➤ Packages, and select one or more classic packages.

3. Select the Home tab of the Ribbon, and choose Analyze Package in the Package Conversion Manager section.

If you want to schedule the analyzer to analyze the packages off peak hours you are able to schedule analyzing the classic packages by following the next steps:

1. In the Configuration Manager console open the Software Library workspace.

2. Expand Overview ➤ Application Management ➤ Package Conversion Manager.

3. In the Package Conversion Dashboard you have the option to click on the Schedule Action. Click on the Action and set the schedule by supplying a date and time before clicking on Ok.

In the notification area of the taskbar you will see an icon for the schedule; by clicking on the icon you are able to cancel the schedule.

CONVERTING THE PACKAGE

When the package is analyzed and the readiness state changes from Unknown to Automatic or Manual, you can convert the packages and programs to the new application model. Packages that have an Automatic readiness state can be converted as follows:

1. In the Configuration Manager console select the Software Library workspace.

2. Expand Overview ➤ Application Management ➤ Packages, and select one or more classic packages that have an Automatic readiness state.

3. Select the Home tab of the Ribbon, and choose Convert Package in the Package Conversion Manager section.

4. Review the programs and confirm the conversion of the selected packages into new application objects. Click OK.

   After the conversion progress dialog box closes, you will see a dialog box with the results of the conversion.

5. Click OK and review the converted packages in the Applications section of the Application Management workspace (Figure 3.19).

FIGURE 3.19
Conversion of
the packages is
complete

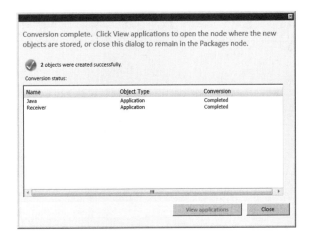

During the conversion process the package is reanalyzed to be sure that the latest information about the package and program is available. The readiness state of the classic package will be changed from Automatic to Converted.

To manually convert packages and programs, follow these steps:

1. In the Configuration Manager console choose the Software Library workspace.

2. Expand Overview ➤ Application Management ➤ Packages, and select one or more classic packages that have a Manual readiness state.

3. Choose Fix And Convert in the Package Conversion Section of the Home Ribbon.

4. Review the items to fix in the Package Selection screen of the Package Conversion Wizard and click on Next.

5. Review dependencies on unconverted packages and possible issues and click on Next.

6. Review the deployment types associated with the new application and fix possible issues.

In Figure 3.20, you see that there is an issue with the detection method. To fix this click on Edit Detection Method and click on Add to configure a detection method. In this case, an MSI product code is missing, so select Windows Installer as Setting Type and browse to the MSI to retrieve its product. Click on OK twice and check if the issue is fixed.

FIGURE 3.20
Deployment type
issue

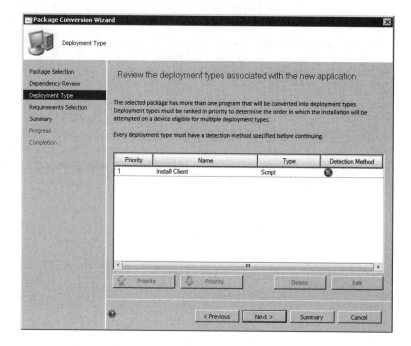

7. Click on Next to review the requirements selection and check the requirements to add to the selected deployment type and, click on Next.

8. Review the summary and click on Next. After the Package Conversion Wizard is completed successfully, click on Close. You will find the converted package in the applications node where all the applications reside.

NOT APPLICABLE CLASSIC PACKAGES

When the readiness state of a classic package is shown as Not Applicable for a migration, you can find out why the package and programs are unable to be migrated by selecting the package and viewing the summary. As mentioned previously, there are several reasons why a package can be tagged Not Applicable.

CONVERTING PACKAGE DEPENDENCIES

Classic packages with an unconverted dependency will have a readiness state of Manual after the first analysis. The reason is that Package Conversion Manager cannot automatically convert a package that is a dependency. You will need to convert any package that is a dependency first before converting the classic package. For instance, if you have a classic package that depends on a classic package with the .NET Framework, you need to convert the .NET Framework classic package. If you reanalyze the classic package with the .NET Framework dependency and there are no other issues, it will be available for conversion.

The Conversion Process Steps

The conversion process does a lot of work to convert and migrate all settings to the new application model. The conversion process converts information like package properties, program properties, and MSI information. Not only such things as application name, deployment type name, or detection method are converted, but also, 28 optional properties of the packages and programs. Investments you made are preserved for the new application model.

Package Conversion Manager Best Practices

For the integration of Package Conversion Manager within Configuration Manager 2012, the following pre-migration and migration best practices are defined.

PRE-MIGRATION

You can prepare the migration of the packages to the new application model by using the following best practices:

Utilize Platform Requirements   In the package program set the platform that the program will run on. The settings are migrated as global conditions and requirements for the application.

Use the UNC Path for Source Location   This is required for migrating the package to an application. Otherwise the new Configuration Manager 2012 site server cannot access the source content.

Use Only MSIs with One Unique PID   The MSIs need to have one unique PID. When creating your own MSI, include only one PID. Otherwise, the detection methods for installation of the applications won't work correctly.

CONVERSION PROCESS

For the conversion process the following best practices are defined:

Convert Any Depended Classic Packages First   Always convert the dependent classic packages first before converting the classic packages that are depended on them. Depended classic packages that have a readiness state of Automatic will optionally be converted automatically.

Concentrate on Your User-Centric Applications   Since Configuration Manager 2012 is user centric, be sure to concentrate on you user-centric applications. Configuration Manager 2007 was designed for system targeting, so try to find the classic packages that can interact with the user and that can be converted with Package Conversion Manager.

Keep Track of Your Efforts   Use the summarization to plan the conversion of the classic packages and to keep track of your conversion process. For instance, you can check to see what percentage has converted.

Once Converted, Check Requirements   Once a package is converted, check the requirements of the application to make sure that they are sufficient for the new application model.

Monitoring Conversion

Besides the Package Conversion Manager Dashboard, shown in Figure 3.18, you are also able to monitor the conversion of your packages, shown in Table 3.2.

TABLE 3.2   Package conversion monitoring features

MONITORING FEATURE	DESCRIPTION
Package Conversion Dashboard	The dashboard shows the overall readiness/conversion state of all of your packages. This is the best way to monitor your package conversion process.
PCMTrace.log	This log file can be found in the temporary directory of the user. This log file consists of all information about the package conversions.
Packages Node	Add the Readiness and the Last Analyzed/Converted columns to packages node view.
Packages properties	You are able to view the package conversion manager status per package. Possible readiness issues are reported here.
Package Scan Report	From the Package Conversion Dashboard you are able to generate a report. This report is saved in the users temp folder (%TEMP%) and is called PackageScanReport.XML, shown in Figure 3.21.

FIGURE 3.21
Package Scan Report

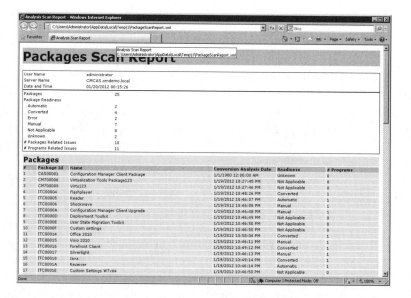

Migrating Branch Offices with the Physical-to-Virtual Migration Toolkit

To achieve the Configuration Manager 2012 migration goals set in the beginning of this chapter, you will need the physical-to-virtual (P2V) Migration Toolkit to take care of the "Maximizing the reusability of x64-bit hardware" goal. This P2V Migration Toolkit can be used when you have a branch office with limited hardware availability to perform a side-by-side upgrade.

The P2V Migration Toolkit eliminates the need for a side-by-side migration of physical servers. It enables you to host the Configuration Manager 2007 site server and the Configuration Manager 2012 site server on the same machine using virtualization with Hyper-V. The P2V Migration Toolkit uses Configuration Manager operating system deployment to create a virtual instance of the Configuration Manager 2007 site server. It uses a virtualization task sequence so that the creation of the P2V virtual machine is simplified and automated.

Requirements

The P2V Migration Toolkit requires Hyper-V to be available on the Windows Server 2008 R2 server. For virtualization with Hyper-V the following are required:

- The server must have an x64 processor.

- The BIOS must support hardware-assisted virtualization and hardware data execution prevention. Virtual machines will not start unless these features are enabled.

The P2V Migration Toolkit requires that the Configuration Manager 2007 SP2 console be installed on the workstation or server where you want to start it from. Further requirements are as follows:

- Windows 7 or Windows Server 2008 R2

- Microsoft .NET Framework 4.0 or Microsoft .NET Framework 4.0 client profile

- Windows Automated Installation Kit for Windows 7

- Desktop experience feature in Windows Server 2008 R2

The source server that needs to be virtualized has the following operating system requirements, shown in Table 3.3.

TABLE 3.3   Operating System requirements for P2V conversions

OPERATING SYSTEM	EDITION	ARCHITECTURE
Windows Server 2003 SP2 or greater	Standard, Enterprise and Datacenter	X86, x64
Windows Server 2003 R2 SP2 or greater	Standard, Enterprise and Datacenter	X86, x64
Windows Server 2008	Standard, Enterprise and Datacenter	X86, x64
Windows Server 2008 R2	Standard, Enterprise and Datacenter	x64

P2V Migration Scenario

The physical-to-virtual migration scenario is primarily used for two types of scenarios:

◆ It can be used for branch offices that are part of your Configuration Manager 2007 hierarchy and where you have only one piece of hardware that can be reused for Configuration Manager 2012 and that can support Hyper-V.

◆ It can be used for a branch office with very slow WAN links that doesn't allow an over-the-wire migration because of costs; the global SQL replication over the WAN is too expensive.

After a P2V migration of an old server is finished, you can migrate Configuration Manager 2007 and Configuration Manager 2012 side by side.

The Task Sequence

The task sequence is a sequence of tasks that are performed, for instance, during an operating system deployment. The task sequence that is used for the P2V migration scenario performs the following list of tasks that result in a virtual machine on a new Windows Server 2008 R2 operating system. (You'll learn more about task sequences and operating system deployment in Chapter 9.)

The task sequence tasks are as follows:

1. Capture the selected physical disk partitions into virtual hard disks.

2. Install Windows Server 2008 R2.

3. Enable the Hyper-V role on the new Windows Server 2008 R2 server.

4. Set up and configure the Windows Server operating system by doing the following:

   a. Install the Configuration Manager 2007 client to be able to connect the Configuration Manager 2007 site server.

   b. Join the domain.

   c. Add predefined local administrators.

5. Prepare and compact virtual hard disks.

6. Create the virtual machine, configure the network, and attach the virtual hard disks.

Steps for Using the P2V Migration Toolkit

The P2V Migration Toolkit helps you create a task sequence that can be used in two different ways:

◆ Create a task sequence with stand-alone media.

◆ Create non-task sequence bootable media.

This way you are flexible in the P2V migration approach.

CREATING A TASK SEQUENCE WITH STAND-ALONE MEDIA

This option is used when you want to automate the entire end-to-end process from operating system rebuild to virtual machine creation. To create the task sequence with stand-alone media, the following four broad steps are required:

1. Create the task sequence.

2. Create a stand-alone media.

3. Boot off the stand-alone media.

4. Run the task sequence.

The first step, though, is to create the task sequence itself:

1. Start the P2V Migration Toolkit, and you will see the screen, shown in Figure 3.22.

FIGURE 3.22
The P2V Migration
Toolkit

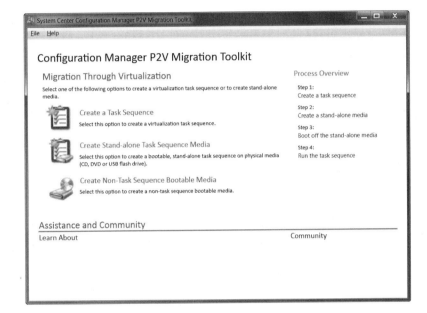

2. Click Create A Task Sequence.

3. Supply the site server name and site code, and click OK.

4. When the Task Sequence Designer launches, supply the name for the task sequence in the Task Sequence Name field.

5. Click Browse, and select an existing 32-bit boot image and click on OK.

6. Click Next.

7. Click Browse, and select the Windows Server 2008 R2 image package, shown in Figure 3.23.

FIGURE 3.23
Specify the
operating system
WIM image

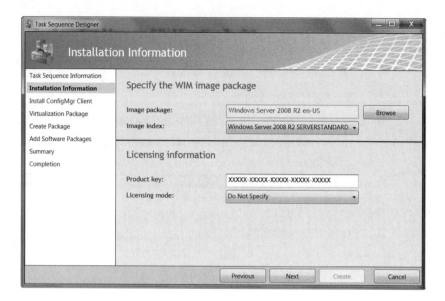

8. Provide the license key and license information, and click Next.

9. Click Browse, and select the Client Installation Package. Click Next.

10. Select Create New Virtualization Tools Package, or select Use An Existing Virtualization Tools Package, and click Browse to select the package. Click Next.

11. If you need to create a new virtualization tools package, supply the package name, specify the deployment share, and select the distribution points where the package need to be placed. Click Next.

12. Select Software Packages that need to be installed during the P2V installation process, and click Next.

13. Review the summary, and click Create.

14. Click Close.

The next step in the process of virtualizing the Configuration Manager 2007 site server is to create a stand-alone media. The stand-alone media can consist of a USB drive or a CD/DVD set. To create a stand-alone USB flash drive, follow this procedure:

1. Start the P2V Migration Toolkit.

2. Select Create Stand-alone Media.

3. Supply the site server name and site code, and click OK.

4. Select USB Flash Drive.

5. Click Yes if you want to format the USB flash drive.

6. Supply a password (optional), and click Next.

7. Click on Browse to select the task sequence you created earlier, and click Next.

8. Select the distribution point(s), and click Next.

9. Review the summary, and click Create.

10. If the wizard has completed successfully, click Close.

To create a stand-alone CD/DVD set, perform the following steps:

1. Start the P2V Migration Toolkit.

2. Select Create Stand-alone Task Sequence Media.

3. Supply the site server name and site code, and click OK.

4. Select CD or DVD.

5. Select the media size (650 MB, 4.7 GB or 8.5 GB).

6. Select Browse to be able to browse to the file location, and supply a name for the ISO file.

7. Supply a password (optional), and click Next.

8. Click on Browse to select the task sequence you created earlier, and click Next.

9. Select the distribution point(s), as shown in Figure 3.24, and click Next.

FIGURE 3.24
Be sure to place all
the content on the
distribution points

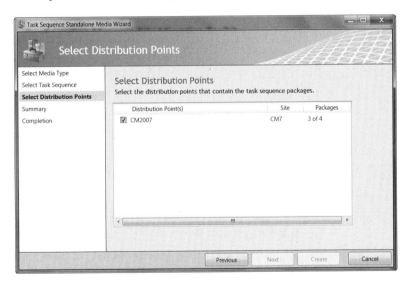

10. Review the summary, and click Create.

11. When the wizard has completed successfully, click Close.

The final phase of the process is to run the task sequence. Do the following:

1. Boot the branch office site server from either USB or CD/DVD.

2. Configure IP settings and supply the password if necessary and click on Next.

3. Click Next when the conformation is displayed after booting.

4. Click Next on the welcome page of the bootable device, shown in Figure 3.25.

FIGURE 3.25
The Physical-to-Virtual Migration Toolkit

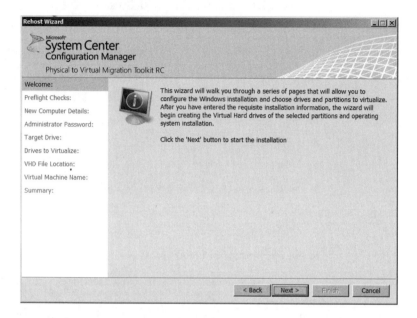

5. Your system will be validated; if the system is okay, click Next.

6. Supply the computer name, domain information, and an account that will have domain join rights. Click Next.

7. Supply the password for the local administrator and a username that must be added to the Local Administrators group. Click Next.

8. Select the target drive that needs to be captured and where the new operating system needs to be installed, and click Next.

9. Select the drives to virtualize, and click Next.

10. Supply a UNC path to a location where the new virtual hard disk (VHD) image can be saved.

11. Supply the credentials of a user who will have permissions to save the virtual hard drive.

12. Click Next.

13. Supply a new name for the virtual machine, the memory, the virtual network name, and the network that will be connected to the virtual machine. Click Next to continue.

14. After reviewing the summary, click Finish, and the process will start.

The task sequence will begin the physical-to-virtual process. Once that is complete, the operating system will be installed and the VHD files will be added to Hyper-V on the new operating system.

CREATE A NON-TASK SEQUENCE BOOTABLE MEDIA

Another option is to create a non-task sequence bootable media; this can also be a CD/DVD set or a USB flash drive. This procedure is just to create a virtual hard disk that can be used in Hyper-V. A non-task sequence bootable media is created with the following procedures.

To create a stand-alone media USB flash drive, do the following:

1. Start the P2V Migration Toolkit.

2. Select Create Windows PE Boot Media. In the next screen of the WinPE Creator Wizard, select the boot image OS architecture type to target in order to create the bootable Windows PE image, and then click on Next.

3. Select USB Flash Drive, as shown in Figure 3.26.

FIGURE 3.26
Selecting the USB
flash drive

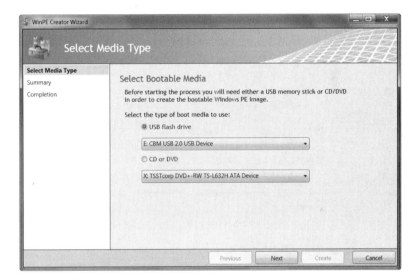

4. Click Yes if you want to format the USB flash drive, and click Next.

5. Review the summary, and click Create.

6. When the wizard has completed successfully, click Close.

To create a stand-alone media CD/DVD set, perform these steps:

1. Start the P2V Migration Toolkit.

2. Select Create Non-Task Sequence Bootable Media.

3. Select CD or DVD, select the CD/DVD drive with an empty CD or DVD, and click Next.

4. Review the summary, and click Create.

5. When the wizard has completed successfully, click Close.

After creating the stand-alone media USB device or DVD/CDs, you can boot the Configuration Manager 2007 site server from that media and start the following process:

1. Boot the branch office site server from either USB or CD/DVD.

2. Click Next on the welcome page of the bootable device.

3. Select the drives to virtualize, and click Next.

4. Supply a local path to a location where the new virtual hard disk (VHD) image can be saved. This can be a USB disk. Click Next.

   The file is created and copied to the defined location.

5. Once the creation is complete, click Finish.

When finished, copy the VHD image to a Windows Server 2008 R2 server and configure a virtual machine in Hyper-V to use the VHD image.

 Real World Scenario

MIGRATING TO CONFIGURATION MANAGER 2012

Sports Clothes United Inc. is a company that develops and sells sports clothing to retailers and their own shops all over the world. The head office is located in San Francisco. The company is growing so fast that they acquire a new company called Fit Clothes. Fit Clothes has their own Configuration Manager 2007 R3 SP2 environment.

You as a consultant or Configuration Manager administrator are asked to migrate the Fit Clothes Configuration Manager 2007 R2 SP2 environment to the new Configuration Manager 2012 infrastructure and deploy the corporate standard of Sports Clothes United.

MIGRATION SCOPE

The Corporate IT department investigated the Configuration Manager 2007 R3 SP2 environment of Fit Clothes and came to the conclusion that only the classic packages, advertisements, and collections need to be migrated to the Configuration Manager 2012 environment of Sport Clothes United. After the classic packages are migrated, they must be converted to the new application model.

Your assignment is to migrate these assets.

MIGRATION APPROACH

Because the corporate IT department decided that the assets needs to be migrated, you need to use the migration feature of Configuration Manager 2012. You always need to test your migration approach in your test lab and define and crystallize your steps while testing your approach. The following steps should be used:

1. Define the topmost source site as the source hierarchy.

2. Configure credentials to be able to gather data from the source site(s).

3. Use the collection migration to migrate your collections with the associated applications and advertisements.

4. After successfully migrating the classic packages to Configuration Manager, analyze the packages to discover the readiness level for the new application model.

5. Convert the classic packages with a readiness level of Automatic.

6. Fix and convert the packages with a readiness level of Manual.

7. Stop the data-gathering process, and clean up the migration data.

8. Uninstall Configuration Manager 2007.

Once you have completed those steps, you have migrated the required Configuration Manager 2007 assets to Configuration Manager 2012.

The Bottom Line

Determine what you are able to migrate with the migration feature. The new migration feature in Configuration Manager 2012 allows you to migrate the old Configuration Manager 2007 investments to Configuration Manager 2012 side by side. In earlier versions you were able to migrate the server in place or side by side by replicating data, but no real manageable migration feature was available.

Master It With the migration feature you cannot migrate things like the following:

◆ Queries

◆ Security rights for the site and objects

◆ Configuration Manager 2007 reports from SQL Server Reporting Services

◆ Configuration Manager 2007 web reports

◆ Client inventory and history data

◆ AMT client-provisioning information

◆ Files in the client cache

To keep it positive, identify what objects you are able to migrate with the migration feature of Configuration Manager 2012.

Discover which migration approach is supported. Configuration Manager 2012 provides migration features that can be used for your migration of Configuration Manager 2007 to Configuration Manager 2012.

Master It With the earlier upgrades or migrations of Configuration Manager in your mind, what migration approaches are supported when migrating from Configuration Manager 2007 to Configuration Manager 2012?

Ascertain what kind of interoperability is supported during the migration. Interoperability like that supported in earlier versions is no longer supported; nevertheless, the migration feature of Configuration Manager 2012 supports some kinds of interoperability during the migration process. Depending on the size of your Configuration Manager 2007 source hierarchy, this can take some time.

> **Master It** Interoperability like you were used to in SMS 2003 and Configuration Manager 2007 is no longer supported. Give two examples of interoperability features in Configuration Manager 2012.

Migrate packages and programs to the new application model. The classic packages just migrated to Configuration Manager 2012 can be used and targeted to collections of users and computers, but Configuration Manager is built around a new application model that allows you to implement user-centricity in your Configuration Manager 2012 environment.

> **Master It** Converting classic packages to the application model is not a feature of Configuration Manager, but with extra software it can be done from the Configuration Manager 2012 console in a couple of different ways. What is the name of the tool that you use to convert the classic packages, and what are the steps to convert a classic package?

Chapter 4

Installation and Site Role Configuration

Previous chapters have already begun pulling back the covers on the changes in Configuration Manager 2012. This chapter is focused on discussing Configuration Manager 2012 sites, hierarchies, and site system roles along with a walkthrough of building a sample hierarchy.

A major design pillar for Configuration Manager 2012 was hierarchy simplification. In previous versions of Configuration Manager it was not uncommon to find hierarchies with dozens of sites and in some cases thousands of sites, and often hierarchies would be built four to five or more layers deep. Both the number of sites in a hierarchy and the depth of the hierarchy bring with them configuration complexity, potential delays, and sometimes errors, when transmitting data from the top level of the hierarchy to the bottom tier sites.

Configuration Manager 2012 changes potential hierarchy design significantly in a few ways.

Because of the numerous changes and efficiencies—not the least of which is enhancements in the security model—in many cases, organizations with fewer than 100,000 client systems won't need to implement a hierarchy at all. A single site server and its associated "helper" servers will be all that is necessary to provide a robust Configuration Manager 2012 experience.

A hierarchy will be required by organizations that manage more than 100,000 clients or have other nontechnical reasons that require a hierarchy to be implemented, such as legal or political requirements. In those cases, the efficiencies gained in Configuration Manager 2012 should often result in far fewer numbers of installed sites and, as a result, a simpler hierarchy.

A couple of interesting facts about hierarchy changes in Configuration Manager 2012 will serve to whet the appetite for what is to come. A Configuration Manager 2012 hierarchy supports only a single tier of primary sites. A tier of secondary sites may be added if absolutely necessary, but in most cases, as detailed in the chapter, there is no reason for secondary sites any longer.

In this chapter, you will learn to

- Understand Configuration Manager 2012 sites and the new approach to hierarchy design.

- Construct a Configuration Manager 2012 hierarchy.

- Determine when to expand a hierarchy and when to simply add a site system role for additional service.

- Deploy and configure the various site system roles available per site.

Understanding Configuration Manager 2012 Site Types

It doesn't take long when working with any of the versions of Systems Management Server or Configuration Manager to be introduced to the concept of a site server. Site servers exist to provide service to Configuration Manager clients. Site servers understand which clients they should serve by defining management boundaries, which may be AD sites, IP subnets, or IP address ranges. Depending on the size and organization of the Configuration Manager environment, there may be a need to have more than a single site to manage all of the clients in the enterprise. When more than one site is needed, it is common to establish a site hierarchy, which will facilitate centralized management of all Configuration Manager clients.

A specific design goal of Configuration Manager 2012 is to reduce the number of sites that are needed in a hierarchy and also to reduce complexity. More discussion of this will come shortly.

Site servers historically have fallen into one of two categories, either a *primary site server* or a *secondary site server*, and now a third type is part of Configuration Manager 2012, the *Central Administration Site*.

Primary Site Server   A primary site server has historically been identified as having a few characteristics:

◆ It has its own database hosted on a SQL Server to maintain configurations.

◆ It is the only site type where clients can be directly assigned.

◆ It has the ability to host child sites—either other primary sites or secondary sites.

Both the first and last characteristics are no longer items that distinguish a primary site. In Configuration Manager 2012 primary site servers *do* still have their own copy of SQL running, but secondary sites do as well. Further, a primary site *can* have child sites, but those child sites can *only* be secondary sites. Introduced in Configuration Manager 2012 is the fact that only primary sites can be assigned to the Central Administration Site—secondaries need not apply!

Secondary Site Server   A secondary site server has historically been identified by a few characteristics:

◆ It does not make use of a SQL database.

◆ There is no way to directly administer a secondary site; all administration would have to come from an administration console connected to a primary site somewhere above the secondary.

The former condition is no longer true—secondary sites now *do* have a database. When installing a secondary site, you have a choice of either using an existing instance of SQL or, if SQL is not present on the target server, you can install and use SQL Express. The latter observation remains true—secondary sites cannot be administered directly through the console.

Also, the historical justification for secondary sites has primarily been to provide local content access for clients residing in or roaming into its defined boundaries and to help control network traffic for content moving between the secondary site and its assigned parent primary site. Secondary sites are still used for that purpose today (although the argument is far less compelling).

So, secondary sites still are available in Configuration Manager 2012, but before you plan to install one, check out the various bandwidth-control features of Configuration Manager 2012. One key addition is that it is now possible to control, or throttle, network bandwidth between a site and its remote distribution points within the site. This one addition in Configuration Manager 2012 makes it at least worth considering whether secondary sites really are necessary. If secondary sites were in use in an environment for the sole purpose of controlling network bandwidth for content distribution (some content is *huge*), then the ability to throttle content delivery between a site and a remote distribution point introduced in Configuration Manager 2012 will be of interest. We'll cover this shortly.

Other reasons for having a secondary site include the ability to throttle non-content site-to-site communications. This is a much reduced data size compared to content, but if throttling is still of concern to you, then a secondary site may be justified. (In previous versions of Configuration Manager this content would be files that contained status information, site configuration information, client information, and so on. In Configuration Manager 2012 this content is still transferred between sites but is split between traditional file-based transfer and SQL replication.)

When it comes to secondary sites—or any other site type for that matter—*think* before following the same old pattern for a hierarchy. Configuration Manager 2012 *is* about hierarchy simplification after all and really does a nice job of increasing site efficiency!

Central Administration Site   Another type of site that has been around in previous versions of ConfigMgr is the central site server. A central site server is the one at the top of a hierarchy and is used to centrally administer the entire Configuration Manager implementation. Because of its role in hierarchy-wide management, a central site typically should not have clients directly assigned (although it is possible). Further, because all information in the hierarchy resides at the central site, this is typically the key site in the hierarchy where reporting is configured.

The central site server is no longer present in Configuration Manager 2012. It has been replaced by a new type of site server known as a Central Administration Site (CAS). The CAS is much like the central site server except that it cannot have any clients assigned (not even an option), some site functions are not available at the CAS (such as most of the discovery options), and the CAS must be installed as the first site of the hierarchy. There is no option to install a CAS later or migrate a stand-alone primary site to a new CAS.

As we mentioned, sites manage clients. To facilitate client management and depending on the services being delivered, several different functional roles must be in place at the site. These functional roles are either added to the site server itself or configured on external servers. Either way, the servers that host these support roles are known as site systems. The option for distributed site servers to fulfill various functions allows for very flexible and scalable designs. Ultimately, the decision on where to place these site systems or whether to use external site systems at all is up to the administrator. And, if these roles need to be moved to other servers after installation, or other servers need to be added, that is easy to do. This work is performed in the Site Systems node of the Configuration Manager console, as shown in Figure 4.1.

FIGURE 4.1
The Site Systems
node within the
Configuration Manager
2012 console

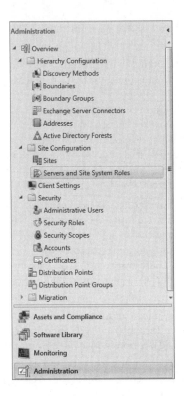

 Real World Scenario

HIERARCHY DESIGN AND IMPLEMENTATION

Now that we've discussed the types of sites available in Configuration Manager 2012, it's natural to begin thinking about implementation details. Hopefully it is clear that Configuration Manager 2012 introduces significant changes in terms of site and hierarchy design. Administrators who have experience with previous versions of Configuration Manager might be tempted to set up Configuration Manager 2012 in the same design that is currently being used. That approach might work, but it would be a mistake and would likely mask many of the features for simplified management that are available in Configuration Manager 2012.

One of the major design pillars for Configuration Manager 2012 was hierarchy simplification. With that in mind, during the design phase remember that each primary site is capable of supporting 100,000 client systems, and the hierarchy as a whole is able to support 400,000 clients. This means that for many organizations the total Configuration Manager 2012 design might be handled with only a single primary site along with additional servers to support various roles in the environment. It's interesting to note that even in Configuration Manager 2007 a primary site was also able to support 100,000 clients. That type of scale often was not realized because of the need for additional sites for political or load reasons. The design of Configuration Manager 2012 removes virtually all technical reasons for adding additional site servers unless the addition is driven by scale.

Implementing Site Servers

The terms *site* and *site server* are often used interchangeably. In reality this shouldn't be the case. A Configuration Manager 2012 site encompasses all servers that are used to deliver the services offered by the site. Said another way, a Configuration Manager 2012 site can consist of one to several servers. The size of the site will dictate how many servers are needed to deliver service to clients. In smaller environments it may be that only a single server is needed to host all components needed to deliver the site's services. In larger environments multiple servers may be needed. With the new design of Configuration Manager 2012 the expectation is that the number of total sites needed for an environment will decrease, but the number of supporting servers for a site might increase.

A site server is the one server in a site that orchestrates delivery of service to clients. This server will interact with any other servers that are in place supporting the site's ability to deliver services. These additional servers are known as site systems. (A site server is also a *site system*.)

As services are added to a site and assigned to a server, the list of site system roles will increase. A quick glance at the Configuration Manager console will reveal the site systems that are in use to support a site and also what services those site systems are delivering on behalf of the site. An example is shown in Figure 4.2. Note that two systems are shown related to site code PS1. One is the site server itself and the other is a site system server providing service for the site.

FIGURE 4.2
Site systems
and roles

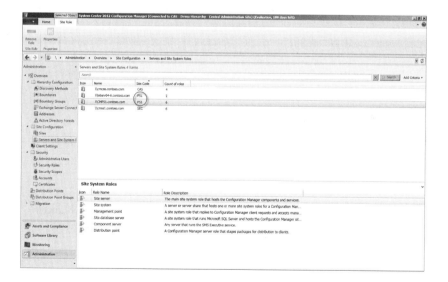

Software Requirements

Before further discussing Configuration Manager 2012 it is beneficial to install the software. There are a few prerequisites for installing a site server. For a full list of these prerequisites, go to

```
http://technet.microsoft.com/en-us/library/gg682077.aspx
```

These prerequisites may also apply to site systems that may be installed depending on the services those servers will offer:

◆ All site servers must be members of a Windows 2008 or Windows 2008 R2 Active Directory domain (server edition Standard or above).

◆ The site servers must be deployed on 64-bit hardware. Configuration Manager 2012 is a native 64-bit application, and there is no version that can be installed on 32-bit systems. (32-bit systems are supported as Configuration Manager clients.)

◆ .NET Framework 3.5 SP1 and 4.0 must be installed.

◆ Microsoft XML Core Services 6.0 or greater must be installed.

◆ Microsoft Remote Differential Compression must be installed.

◆ SQL Server 2008 or 2008 R2 is required to host the ConfigMgr database.

And don't worry; if a required configuration happens to be missed along the way, the Configuration Manager 2012 prerequisite checker, which runs as part of the install wizard, will let you know. The details of the checks that are performed during prerequisite validation are recorded in the `ConfigMgrPrereq.log`, located in the root of the `C:` drive of the server where Configuration Manager 2012 is being installed. If it would be helpful to run the prerequisite checker outside of the Configuration Manager 2012 setup wizard, it is available as a separate executable located in the `\SMSSETUP\BIN\<platform>` folder of the installation media. The filename is `PREREQCHK.EXE`. The following list documents the prerequisite checks that are done as part of the install or as part of independently running the Prerequisite Wizard. The list of prerequisite checks is detailed for the Central Administration Site. Any additional checks performed are detailed for other site types.

Central Administration Site

◆ Confirm targeted server is a Windows server.

◆ Confirm operating system is a supported version.

◆ Verify targeted server is a domain member.

◆ Check to ensure schema extension has been completed and is correct.

◆ Verify short filename (8.3) support is enabled.

◆ Confirm disk space is sufficient for installation.

◆ Confirm disk size for installation.

◆ Verify MSXML 6.0 is installed.

◆ Verify Remote Differential Compression is installed.

◆ Confirm the correct version of MSI is installed.

◆ Confirm .NET Framework Version 3.5 is installed.

◆ Verify SQL SysAdmin rights are configured.

- Verify site server computer account has administrative rights.

- Confirm SQL Server security mode.

- Verify SQL Agent logon.

- Verify SQL Agent service status.

- Confirm version of SQL Server is as required.

- Verify firewall settings for SQL Server access.

- Confirm SQL hotfix 977443 is installed.

- Confirm SQL Server is configured as not case sensitive.

- Verify connectivity to SQL Server.

- Confirm WIM filter driver is installed.

- Verify sufficient disk space for installing the Windows Automated Installation Kit.

- Confirm ConfigMgr is not already installed.

- Verify sufficient disk space for SDK server.

Primary Site

- Confirm the user installing the primary site has administrative rights on site system and CAS (if applicable).

- Verify connectivity to CAS (if applicable).

- Confirm disk is *not* formatted with FAT partition.

- Check to see if WSUS is installed on the site server and, if so, whether it is of the proper version.

- Verify Windows Server 2003 sChannel hotfix is installed.

- Verify Windows Remote Management 1.1 is installed.

- Confirm MMC updates are installed.

- Confirm .NET update for Configuration Manager is installed.

- Verify PowerShell 2.0 is installed on the site server.

Some prerequisite checks may fail, but if they aren't critical for a successful site installation, the installation process is allowed to proceed.

Implementing a Central Administration Site

Installing Configuration Manager 2012 begins by installing the first site. A very important question should be answered before launching the Setup Wizard: Is it expected that more than a single primary site will need to be included in the deployment? If the answer is *yes*, then the very first site that needs to be installed is a Central Administration Site. The CAS is the top site in the hierarchy and is used solely for administration of the entire hierarchy. No clients or client-related functions are possible at the CAS. This is critical to understand. If there is any expectation of joining multiple primary sites in a hierarchy relationship, then the CAS must be the first server installed. If this is not done, then there is no ability to create a hierarchy later without a full reinstall!

For those of you who have worked with previous versions of Configuration Manager, your initial reaction may be that multiple sites *are* needed because they were needed in the current implementation (whatever version that is) of Configuration Manager. Not so fast! Remember that one of the design goals of Configuration Manager 2012 is hierarchy simplification. A Configuration Manager 2012 site is more efficient in many ways, not the least of which is the ability to throttle traffic to remote distribution points (thus often eliminating the need for secondary sites). This one tweak by itself will go a long way to reducing the number of sites. Further, a single site has been able to scale to support 100,000 clients for some time now. Often, this kind of scale for a single site was not realized because of the need for additional sites due to network conditions, security considerations, and the like. With Configuration Manager 2012 and hierarchy simplification along with other improvements, expect to see primaries carrying much more of a client load than might have been seen in previous versions.

For the examples given here, installation will proceed assuming a three-site hierarchy is to be built. The hierarchy will consist of a single CAS, a single primary site, and a single secondary site.

With the decision made as to how many sites are needed for the hierarchy, the first site to be installed is the CAS. Before starting the Setup Wizard, make sure SQL is installed and available.

 Real World Scenario

CHOOSING LOCAL OR REMOTE INSTALLATION

A SQL Server installation can be either local or remote. Arguments rage about the best approach. This argument is helped in Configuration Manager 2012 by some support boundaries. A single primary site server on appropriate hardware is able to support 100,000 clients, but if SQL is collocated, that same primary site server is only supported with up to 50,000 clients. This is mostly due to the load that SQL replication introduces. Still, while the performance differences between a remote versus local SQL server when properly configured are slight, if a site will host less than 50,000 clients, using collocated SQL is still preferred and is considered most efficient. One reason for this is that when SQL is running on the same system, it is possible to take advantage of the shared memory protocol. One consideration for local SQL, however, is the default memory settings. SQL by default is configured to consume all available RAM. This is a good configuration for standalone SQL because RAM is more efficient than disk memory.

When sharing a server, setting a maximum amount of RAM for SQL consumption and thereby reserving the rest for Configuration Manager, the operating system, and other applications such as virus scanners, is an optimal configuration. SQL does a very good job of managing RAM and not over-consuming and starving other applications, but there is a cost, however slight, because SQL pages information out of RAM to make room for the needs of other applications. Setting a maximum from the beginning avoids this problem, and with the amount of RAM available on servers today, there really shouldn't be an issue with specifying a maximum RAM value for SQL.

Finally, it's time for installation! The installation process is wizard driven and does a good job of keeping you on track. The most difficult part of the installation is knowing what options to choose. The example will explain how to configure the various options and what they mean. Let's get started:

1. Insert the installation media, and autorun should cause the initial installation screen to be displayed.

   If this is not the case, or if you're running from a location other than the supplied media, simply double-click the `splash.hta` file, which will display the initial installation screen.

   The splash screen provides options for accessing various documentation and assistance, even links to the Configuration Manager community. There are also links to access server readiness components and links to download Configuration Manager updates that are required during the installation process. These latter links are really nice additions to Configuration Manager 2012, providing a very easy way to download updates and move them to a server that is being installed that may not have Internet access to download the updates during setup. Other links include options to just install the Configuration Manager 2012 console and to download System Center Updates Publisher—a tool that anyone using software updates should take a look at! Clicking the Install link at the top left of the screen launches the Setup Wizard and opens the Setup Wizard Welcome Page.

2. Review the information on the Setup Wizard Welcome page, and click Next to continue to the Getting Started page.

   On the Getting Started page the various install options are presented. The options available here will be based on the state of the system where the install is being run. If a system already has Configuration Manager 2012 installed, only the options to uninstall or perform a site reset may be available. If you're running the wizard on a system without Configuration Manager 2012, the options will be as shown in Figure 4.3.

FIGURE 4.3
Setup Wizard: Getting Started page, when installing on a system without ConfigMgr

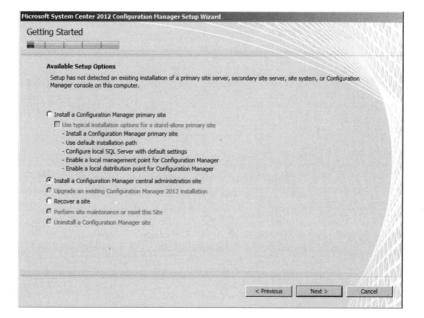

This is the point in the wizard where the decision you made earlier is configured—whether to install a stand-alone primary site or to install a Central Administration Site. This installation will be for a Central Administration Site.

3. With that option selected, click Next to continue to the Product Key page. Decide whether to install as an evaluation or to supply a product key. Once the key is entered, click Next to continue to the Microsoft Software License Terms page.

4. On the Microsoft Software License Terms page, review the information. If you agree, select "I accept these license terms" and click Next to proceed to the Prerequisite Licenses page.

5. On the Prerequisite Licenses page, review the information. This page requires you to accept the license terms for SQL Server 2008 R2 Express, SQL Server 2008 Native Client, and Microsoft Silverlight 4. If you agree, select the appropriate box to accept the terms for each and click Next to proceed to the Prerequisite Downloads page, shown in Figure 4.4.

FIGURE 4.4
Setup Wizard:
Prerequisite
Downloads page

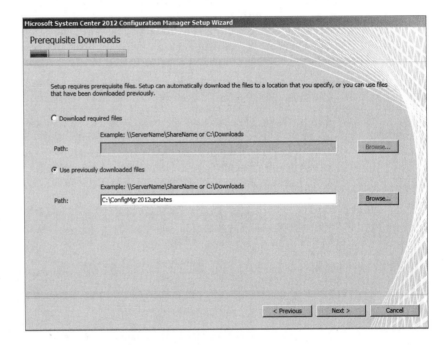

6. On the Prerequisite Downloads page, decide whether to download the updates or, if the updates have been previously downloaded—either from another site installation or using the link on the initial splash page—select the second option.

In both cases, a path for the updates should be specified. For the example, the updates have been previously download and will be installed from the path shown.

7. Once you've completed this screen, click Next, which, depending on the selection made, will initiate the update download process or update evaluation. Once complete the wizard moves on to the Server Language Selection page.

   When migrating from a previous version of Configuration Manager to Configuration Manager 2012, it might be useful to have both consoles installed on a system. Doing so is fully supported.

8. Choose the languages you want to support. The default is English. Once complete, click Next to the Client Language Selection page. On the Client Language Selection page configure additional languages that should be supported from a client perspective. The default here is English. Once complete, click Next to proceed to the Site and Installation Settings page, shown in Figure 4.5.

FIGURE 4.5
Setup Wizard: Site and Installation Settings page

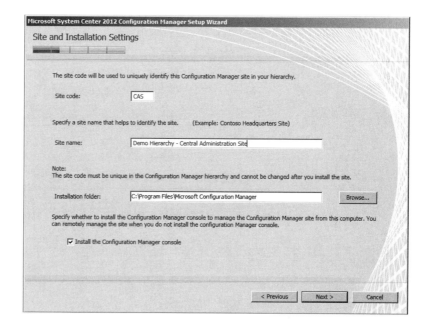

On the Site and Installation Settings page several options are available. The first required option is the Site Code field. The site code can be any three-character alphanumeric code but cannot contain any special character such as a dash or ampersand. In fact, to ensure no mistake is made here, the wizard won't even accept special characters for the site code. Next is the Site Name field. Choose a descriptive name and enter it into this box. Finally, input the Installation path where ConfigMgr should be installed.

Setting the correct path is a critical part of installing Configuration Manager 2012. The default path is on the C: drive, and for the example, that is the path being used.

SELECTING A DISK FOR INSTALLATION

In production environments it is not recommended to install Configuration Manager on a disk shared by other disk-intensive applications, including the operating system, SQL databases, or the page file. Doing so may degrade Configuration Manager performance.

The last option is a choice of whether to include the Configuration Manager 2012 console as part of the installation. This option is commonly used and is checked by default. If you don't want this option, remove the check mark. If you need the administrative console at a later time, it is easily added.

9. Click Next to proceed to the Database Information page, as shown in Figure 4.6.

FIGURE 4.6
Setup Wizard:
Database
Information page

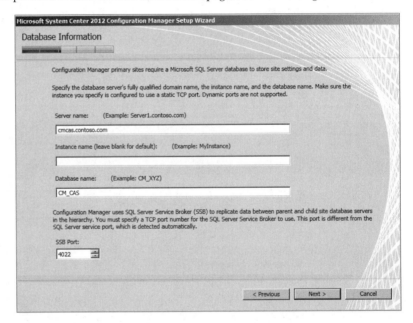

10. On the Database Information page configure the SQL Server information.

For the example, SQL is installed on the same server where the Setup Wizard is being run, so the default location that shows up for SQL Server is the local server. If you're installing SQL on a remote server, enter the name of that remote server in the SQL Server box.

An option to name the database is also provided. If a different database name is preferred, modify the default entry as needed.

11. Click Next to proceed to the SMS Provider Settings page where an option is given to specify where the SMS Provider should be installed.

You may ask, what is the SMS Provider? Detailed information on the SMS Provider can be found at

`http://technet.microsoft.com/en-us/library/bb680613.aspx`

but in short, the SMS Provider is the resource the Configuration Manager 2012 console uses for most of its access to data residing in the Configuration Manager 2012 database.

In the example, the Central Administration Site and SQL are installed on the same server, so it only makes sense that the SMS Provider be colocated on that same server. If the SQL Server being used for the Central Administration Site were remote, then you'd need to choose whether to place the SMS Provider on the Central Administration Site or on the SQL Server. Typically the provider would be placed on the SQL Server in that configuration for best performance. It is also possible that the SMS Provider could be placed on a totally separate server. In practice, I've never seen a condition where using a separate server to host the SMS Provider is warranted. More information regarding SMS Provider placement is available in the About SMS Provider Locations section of the Planning for Site Systems in Configuration Manager document available at

`http://technet.microsoft.com/en-us/library/gg712282.aspx`

12. Configure the location, and then click Next to proceed to the Customer Experience Improvement Program Configuration page. Review the information and decide whether or not to participate in the program.

13. With the selection made, click Next to proceed to the Settings Summary page, as shown in Figure 4.7.

FIGURE 4.7
Setup Wizard:
Settings
Summary page

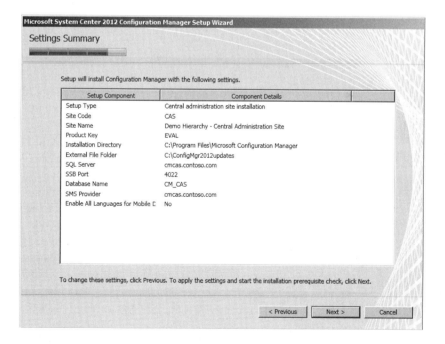

14. On the Setting Summary page, review the configured settings, and if corrections are needed, use the Previous button to move backward in the wizard and correct any mistakes.

15. Once all settings are as desired, click Next to proceed to the Prerequisite Check page, shown in Figure 4.8.

FIGURE 4.8
Setup Wizard: Prerequisite Check page

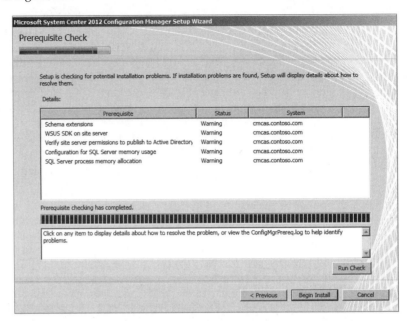

On the Prerequisite Check page, the wizard immediately starts the Prerequisite Wizard to verify that all components required for a successful installation are present. Note that in the figure five items are flagged with a Warning status. Missing prerequisites that are not vital to successful installation will be listed with a warning to raise awareness of their absence. In this case, the conditions listed are as follows:

Scheme extensions   This warning alerts administrators to the possibility that Active Directory schema extensions may not be installed. In most cases, extending the Active Directory schema is advantageous but in some corner cases it can cause confusion.

WSUS SDK on site server   This warning alerts administrators to the fact that there is no installation of Windows Server Update Services (WSUS) on the CAS. In most environments ConfigMgr is used to deploy software updates. Software update functionality requires WSUS components to be installed. When they aren't the warning results.

AD permissions   In order to publish to Active Directory the site server must have permissions. This warning is an alert to administrators that required permissions may not be in place.

SQL memory usage   By default SQL Server is configured to consume all available memory and to manage the memory so that other applications have what they need and SQL has the rest. While good in theory, and where a server is dedicated to SQL, when other Enterprise applications share a system, which is the case when ConfigMgr is collocated with SQL Server, there can be some performance degradation due to memory management. It is recommended in such cases to place a maximum on the amount of memory available to SQL. This is done directly in the SQL interface.

SQL Server process memory allocation   This warning alerts administrators that on the CAS it is recommended that SQL Server be allocated no less than 8 GB of memory.

Having the listed components installed may or may not be appropriate for a specific scenario depending on the ultimate configuration of the server. If only warning messages are listed then it is OK to proceed with the install. These warning scenarios can be fixed later if needed. If any critical prerequisites are missing, then setup cannot proceed.

16. Fix anything that shows a Critical status, and run the prerequisite check again by clicking Run Check. If more information is needed about a particular prerequisite, click any specific item to see more detail.

17. Once all prerequisite issue are resolved, click Begin Install to proceed to the Install page and being installation. Figure 4.9 shows the page after installation is finished.

FIGURE 4.9
Setup Wizard: Install page: installation complete

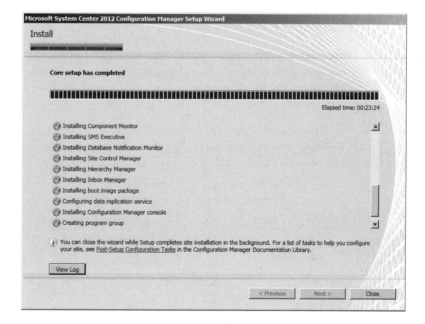

The wizard will remain on the same page, and each phase of the installation will be listed, along with its status, as the installation proceeds. Depending on hardware the installation will take several minutes or longer. One of the longest steps is installing the boot image package used for operating system deployment (OSD).

18. Once the install completes, scroll through the list of installed components, verifying that each has completed successfully.

19. Also, review the details of the installation procedure by clicking View Log.

The setup process is recorded in two logs, the `ConfigMgrSetup.log` and the `ConfigMgrPrereq.log`. If you're installing the administrative console, that portion will be recorded in the `ConfigMgr AdminUISetup.log`. Lastly, the wizard progress is recorded in the `ConfigMgrSetupWizard.log`. All of these logs are located in the root of the drive where ConfigMgr was installed.

20. When you're ready, click Close to exit the wizard.

And that's it; the Central Administration Site is now installed. Feel free to explore the console at this stage if you like. The next step is to install a primary child site and attach it to the Central Administration Site. Proceed to the next section when ready.

Implementing a Primary Site

The next step in building out a hierarchy is to install a primary site. Remember that primary sites can exist either stand-alone or in association with other sites in a structure known as the site hierarchy. As a reminder, if you're installing a primary site in a stand-alone configuration, it can never be joined to a CAS without a reinstall. If you're planning a primary site as part of a hierarchy, which is the case for our example, that primary site must be installed and joined to the Central Administration Site. Said another way, a primary site in Configuration Manager 2012 must be a child site of the Central Administration Site. This implies that there can only be a single tier of primary sites in the hierarchy. That implication is correct. Unlike previous versions of Configuration Manager, where it was possible to build hierarchies multiple layers deep with primary sites, Configuration Manager 2012 allows only a single tier of primary sites. This change was made specifically to help simplify hierarchies and increase the efficiency and speed of data moving from one site to another. With Configuration Manager 2012, it is possible to have up to four tiers of hierarchy if secondary sites are used. More on that soon, but for now, let's install the primary child.

The Setup Wizard is very similar when installing a primary child site. There really are only a few differences. Since we've already discussed the setup process for a Central Administration Site, we'll examine only the specific steps that are different for installing a primary site.

1. As before, ensure that the server where the primary site will be installed meets all prerequisites and is ready to receive the installation.

2. When you're ready, launch the splash page, choose to install, and move through the wizard using the information we've already discussed until arriving at the Getting Started page, shown in Figure 4.10.

FIGURE 4.10
Setup Wizard:
Getting Started
page for a
primary site

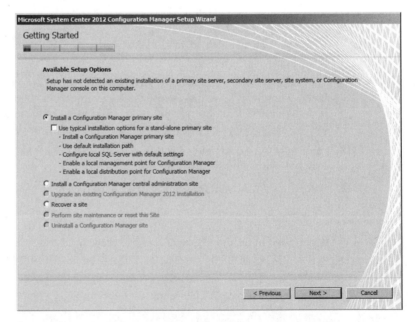

INSTALLING STAND-ALONE VS. INCLUSION IN A HIERARCHY

If you're installing a stand-alone primary site and if the option Use Typical Installation Options For A Single Server installation is selected, then certain pages of the Setup Wizard will be skipped, including the ability to change the directory in which Configuration Manager is installed. This option would be similar to the simple install option available with Configuration Manager 2007. While this option exists, my experience is that most Configuration Manager administrators prefer to see each option as the wizard proceeds to ensure nothing is configured in error.

It is possible to select the option Use Typical Installation Options For A Single Server Installation even when the intent is to join the new primary site to a hierarchy. At this stage of the installation process, setup doesn't have sufficient information to know the intent. If the option is selected, there will be no option to join to a Central Administration server.

This is the first place where the setup process will differ from what has already been described.

3. On this page, ensure that the option Install A Configuration Manager Primary Site Server is selected, but do *not* choose Use Typical Installation Options For A Single Server Installation because this installation isn't for a stand-alone primary site. Click Next, and proceed through the wizard as before until arriving at the Prerequisite Components page.

4. On the Updated Prerequisite Components page, select the option Use Previously Downloaded Updates From The Following Location, and specify the update folder used when installing the Central Administration Site.

   Since the updates are already downloaded and local, this setting should prevent any download delays. Click Next to continue.

5. Continue through the wizard until arriving at the Primary Site Installation page. There, you can choose to install the primary site in a stand-alone configuration or join it to the Central Administration Site.

6. The example installation is to be part of a hierarchy, so do the following:

   a. Select the Primary Site Will Be Joined To An Existing Hierarchy option.

   b. Specify the name of the Central Administration Site server.

   c. Click Next to proceed to the Database Information page, shown in Figure 4.11.

FIGURE 4.11
Setup Wizard:
Database
Information page
for a primary site

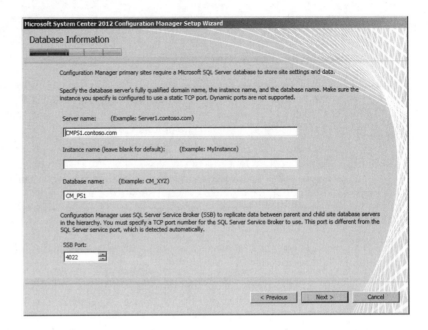

If you had selected the Use Typical Installation Options For A Single Server Installation option on the Getting Started page, this screen of the wizard would have been suppressed.

7. Configure the settings on Database Server page as before.

8. Continue through the wizard as before until you arrive at the Client Computer Communication Settings page, shown in Figure 4.12.

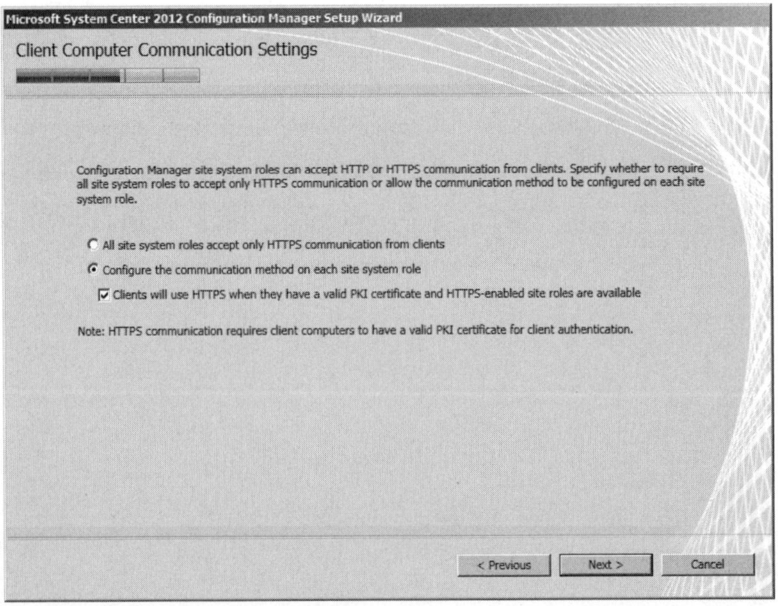

FIGURE 4.12
Setup Wizard:
Client Computer
Communication
Settings page for a
primary site

9. On the Client Computer Communication Settings page, decide whether clients will require secure HTTP communications or whether they can use either secure or non-secure HTTP communication.

   For the example, choose the latter option, and ensure that the box for Clients Will Use HTTPS When They Have A Valid PKI Client Certificate And HTTPS-Enabled Site Roles Are Available is selected. Setting this option ensures that when secure communications are possible, they are used.

10. Click Next to proceed to the Site System Roles page, shown in Figure 4.13.

FIGURE 4.13
Setup Wizard: Site System Roles page for a primary site

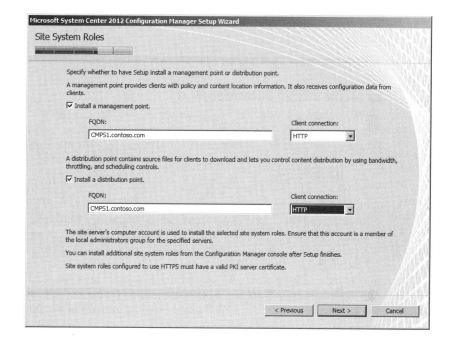

11. On the Site System Roles page, configure whether or not setup should attempt to install a management point and/or a distribution point and, if so, on what server they should be installed and what communication protocol they should be using—either HTTP or HTTPS.

    Remember, site system roles do not have to be configured on the site server itself. Often the management point role is configured on the site server and the distribution point role is configured on both the site server and remote servers. For our example the management point and distribution point will be configured on the site server to use HTTP communication.

FURTHER INDICATION OF CENTRAL ADMINISTRATION SITE UNIQUENESS

Notice that the option to specify a management point and a distribution point was not a part of the Central Administration Site Setup Wizard. This is another aspect of the fact that the Central Administration Site is different from a standard primary site. As already mentioned, the Central Administration Site cannot host clients, and therefore there is no need for a management point or distribution point.

12. Once this is configured, click Next and complete the wizard as previously described and allow the primary site server to complete installation. Be sure to fix any relevant prerequisite failures!

If all goes well, the site should be installed. It's time to move to our next type of site: the secondary site.

Implementing a Secondary Site

Secondary sites historically have been used to allow local access to distribution points across slower WAN links. The secondary site installation allowed communication of content from its primary parent site to be compressed and the sender to throttle communication across sensitive or slow WAN links. Such a configuration was the most compelling reason for a secondary site installation in the past.

There are other reasons to maintain secondary sites in a hierarchy. One such reason would be if WAN links are too fragile to tolerate client traffic as policy data is retrieved from the management point and discovery and inventory data is uploaded to the management point. An example of such a condition would be a facility, such as a cruise ship, relying on unstable satellite connections for communications. In such a case a secondary site may still be needed.

The procedure for installing a secondary site in previous versions has been to either push the secondary site installation across the network or install the secondary site from installation media. You may have noticed that the Setup Wizard has no option to allow for installing a secondary site from media, which leaves only the first option—remote install of the secondary site—available in Configuration Manager 2012. A remote install does *not* mean that media will need to be pushed to the target server. If media is available locally, then it can be used, or if not available locally, the needed content can be pushed. For our example, a secondary site will be installed as a child of the primary site just completed.

Initiate the secondary site from the Configuration Manager 2012 administrative console. The installation can be initiated from either the Central Administration Server or the primary server. For the example, and since central administration is most commonly used, you'll start the installation from the Central Administration Site.

1. If the administrative console is not open on the Central Administration Site, open it by selecting Start ➤ All Programs ➤ Microsoft System Center 2012 ➤ Configuration Manager ➤ Configuration Manager Console.

2. Once it is open, select the Administration node, and then expand Site Configuration ➤ Sites.

3. Select the primary site you just installed, and from the Home tab of the Ribbon, choose Create Secondary Site, as shown in Figure 4.14. This action launches the Create Secondary Site Wizard.

FIGURE 4.14
Secondary site installation: Administration node

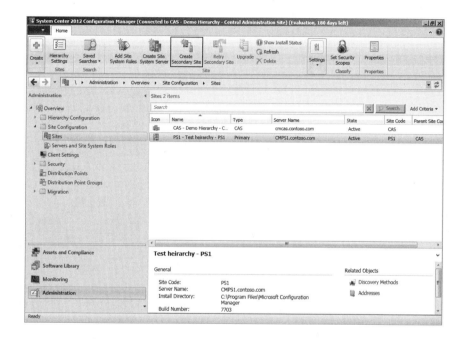

Note in the wizard that a management point and a distribution point will be installed on the secondary site. This is an important distinction because with previous versions administrators had a choice of whether to install a management point, known as a proxy management point at a secondary site, or not. In Configuration Manager 2012 there is no choice. As already mentioned, if you choose a secondary site configuration, it is assumed the WAN is too fragile to tolerate any unthrottled traffic and that local access to policy is required.

4. Review the remaining information on this page, and click Next to proceed to the General page, shown in Figure 4.15.

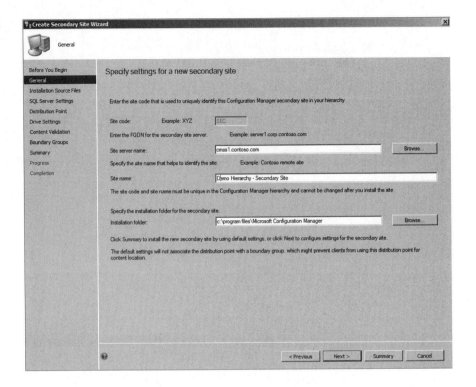

5. On the General page, provide information for the site code and the site name as well as the name of the site server where the secondary site will be installed and a path for the installation.

6. Click Next to proceed to the Installation Source Files page. Select whether to transfer the source files over the network, to use source files at a given network location or to use source files already staged on or near to the remote system being selected for the secondary site installation.

   The latter option allows for scenarios where the network link is insufficient or too unstable to reliably transfer data. For our example, data will be transferred across the network.

7. With that option selected, click Next to proceed to the SQL Server Settings page, shown in Figure 4.16.

FIGURE 4.16
Create Secondary
Site Wizard:
SQL Server
Settings page

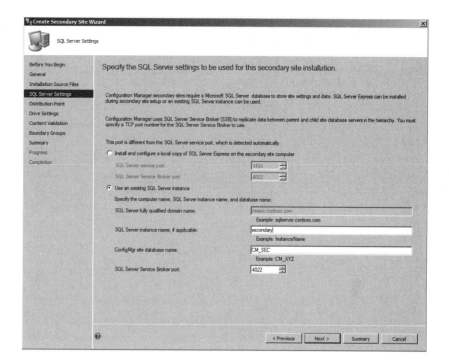

8. On the SQL Server Settings page, either choose to install and configure SQL Express for the secondary server or, if an instance of SQL Server already exists on the destination server, choose the second option and enter details to configure the secondary site accordingly.

SQL AND SECONDARY SITE SERVERS

SQL may already be installed on the secondary site to support other applications, or it may be installed to support components needed by Configuration Manager, such as Windows Server Update Services. If it is, you may choose to install the secondary site database to the existing instance of SQL or choose to install SQL Express instead. If a full version of SQL is already installed, choosing to install SQL Express will result in another instance of SQL running.

Administrators with experience using previous versions of Configuration Manager may see the option to provide a database name and wonder whether they need to take manual action on the destination secondary site server to manually create the database. There's no need for concern. The installer will take the supplied database name and create the required database automatically.

For our example, SQL is already installed on the destination server, so follow these steps:

a. Select Use An Existing SQL Server Database.

b. Supply SQL connection details.

c. Click Next to proceed to the Distribution Point page, shown in Figure 4.17.

FIGURE 4.17
Create
Secondary
Site Wizard:
Distribution
Point page

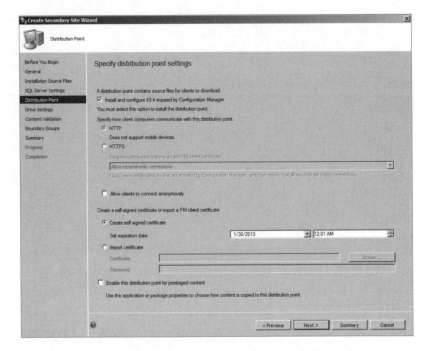

9. On the Distribution Point choose the security options for how clients will communicate and also whether the distribution point will be enabled for prestaged content.

10. Click Next to proceed to the Drive Settings page, shown in Figure 4.18.

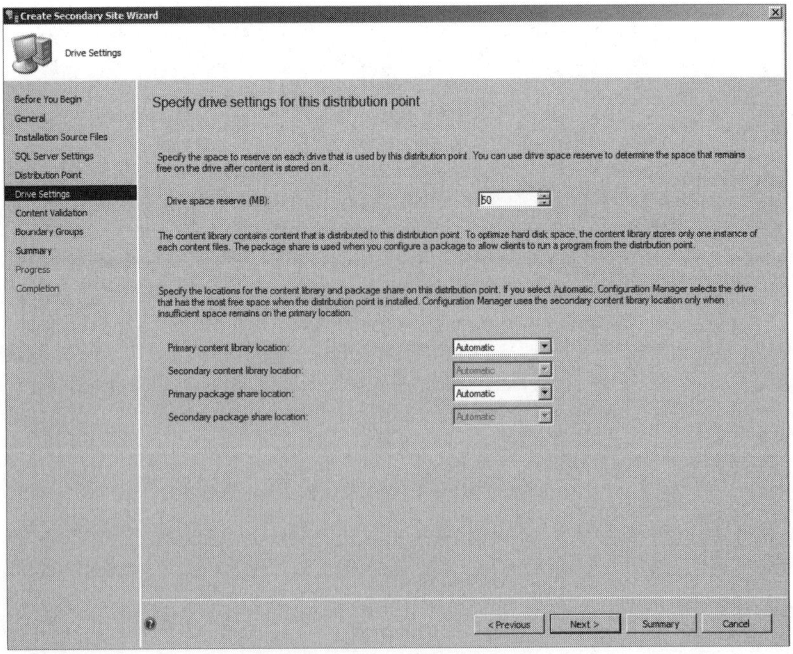

FIGURE 4.18
Create
Secondary Site
Wizard: Drive
Settings page

On the Drive settings page configure how you would like your disk drives to be configured for use by the distribution point.

Click Next to proceed to the Content Validation page, shown in Figure 4.19.

FIGURE 4.19
Create
Secondary Site
Wizard: Content
Validation page

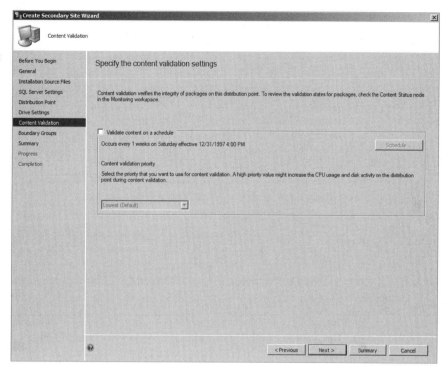

On the Content Validation page configure whether validation should take place and on what schedule and priority. Content Validation is discussed in more detail in the Distribution Point site system role section later in this chapter.

11. Click Next to proceed to the Boundary Groups page. This page provides an opportunity to choose which boundary group the secondary site distribution point should join. There is no requirement to join a boundary group at this stage, and since none have yet been created during the install and further discussion of boundary groups is beyond our focus at the moment, we'll bypass configuring any options on this page.

12. Click Next to proceed to the Summary page shown in Figure 4.20. This page displays the choices made in the Create Secondary Site Wizard.

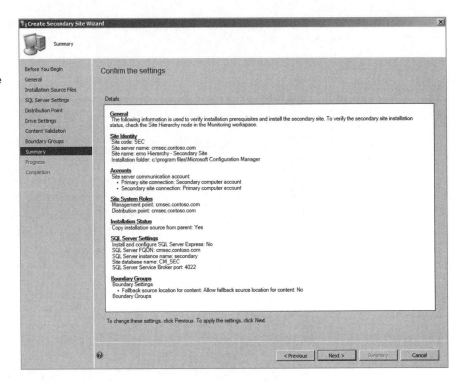

13. Review the summary, and click Previous if you need to make any corrections. When finished, click Next to begin the secondary site installation.

A progress page will come up while the secondary site installation job is being submitted, followed by the Completion page, which shows the installation details in roughly the same way as they appeared on the Summary page.

Installing a secondary site requires checking for prerequisites. This is done behind the scenes as a part of the installation. It is possible to review the prerequisite checks during secondary site installation in the console. Simply right-click on the pending secondary site and select to Show Install Status.

To check the status of the installation select Show Install Status from the right-click menu of the secondary site as shown in Figure 4.21.

FIGURE 4.21
Right-click the secondary site and choose
Show Install Status

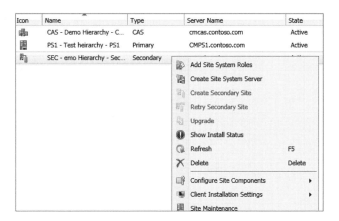

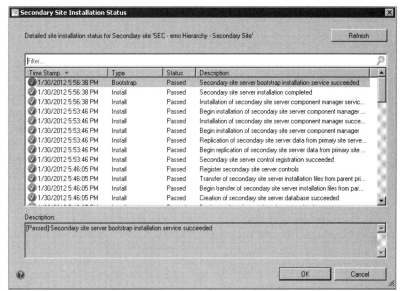

Finally, a hierarchy is born! All that's left is to double-check the installations.

Verifying Proper Site Installation

It seems that all sites in our example installed successfully. The Administration console for the Central Administration Site shows all sites listed as expected and in an active state, as shown in Figure 4.22.

FIGURE 4.22
Administration
console showing
the Sites node

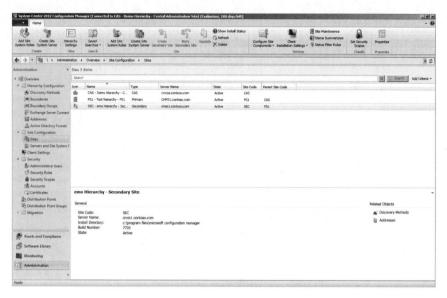

Based on this view alone everything appears healthy. To make sure that this is truly the case, it's worth taking a look at a few key locations to verify. The locations to check may differ depending on the type of site being installed and the associated services chosen. The primary site will be used as an example, but the topics generally apply to all types of sites. The areas discussed next are being presented to help with site installation validation. Providing the information in no way infers that it is OK to modify the described settings. In many cases Microsoft doesn't support modifying the settings, and doing so can result in a damaged site.

REGISTRY VALIDATION

A couple of registry locations are important for validating proper site installation. The list provided below is not exhaustive of all registry keys that are added as part of site installation but rather is intended for use in spot-checking installation success.

```
HKEY_LOCAL_MACHINE\SOFTWARE\Microsoft\SMS
```

It may be obvious but the SMS registry key is created as a result of site installation and should appear similar to Figure 4.23. The `Identification` key is selected to show some of the details about the site.

The CCM registry key is a shared key and will be present when either the management point component of a site server is installed or when a Configuration Manager 2012 client is present on the system. If both are present, then the registry key is shared. The CCM key in this case is present because the installed site is a primary site, and the management point was installed as part of installing the site. If the management point is remote, the key won't necessarily be present on the site server. Note also that the client elements are missing from the registry key since the client is not yet installed at the site. This is shown in Figure 4.24.

FIGURE 4.23

Post-installation
Identification
key

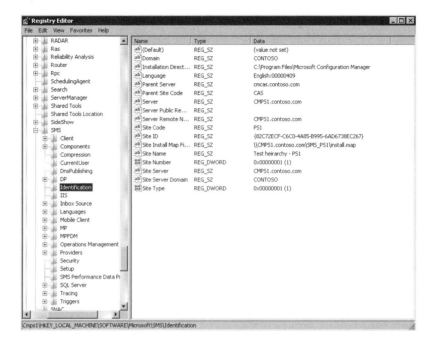

FIGURE 4.24

Post-installation
CCM key

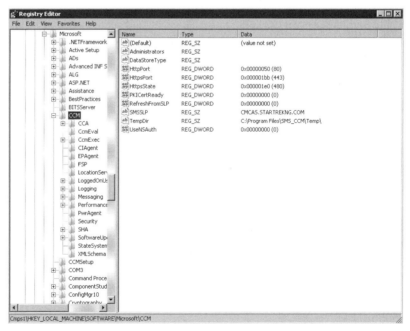

The Central Administration server will not have the CCM key unless a client is installed on the system. The Central Administration server cannot host any clients and therefore cannot have a management point installed.

```
HKEY_LOCAL_MACHINE\SOFTWARE\Microsoft\CCM
```

The ConfigMgr 10 registry key results from the console installation. Installing the console as part of the installation is optional, so this key may not be present. The key is shown in Figure 4.25.

```
HKEY_CURRENT_USER\Software\Microsoft\ConfigMgr 10
```

FIGURE 4.25
Post-installation
ConfigMgr
10 key

The Services registry key is host to an abundance of keys for the various services running on the system. There will be a number of keys beginning with SMS_ after a successful install. The number and type will depend on the type of site in question. This key is shown in Figure 4.26.

```
HKEY_LOCAL_MACHINE\SYSTEM\CurrentControlSet\Services
```

FIGURE 4.26
Post-installation
Services key

FILE SYSTEM VALIDATION

Site installation files are located in a couple of different file locations. Pick the disk where Configuration Manager 2012 was installed and navigate to Program Files\Microsoft Configuration Manager. The folder will look similar to Figure 4.27. In addition, for sites with management points navigate to Program Files\SMS_CCM. The folder will look similar to Figure 4.28.

FIGURE 4.27
Microsoft
Configuration
Manager installa-
tion folder

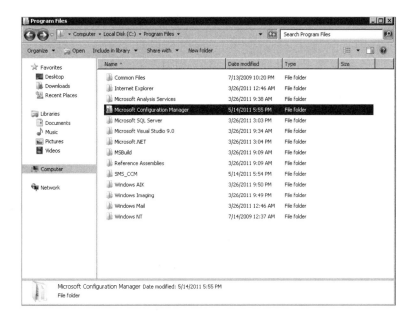

FIGURE 4.28
Management
point SMS_CCM
installation folder

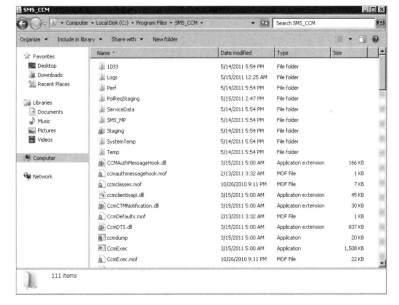

GROUP VALIDATION

The idea of a site hierarchy has been mentioned several times. In order to have a site hierarchy, the individual sites must be able to communicate. Detailed discussion about how this is done is beyond the scope of this chapter except to mention one thing: communication between sites requires a security context. In Configuration Manager 2012 such configuration is facilitated using groups configured on the site servers during installation. There are several groups created during site installation but only a single group, the SMS_SitetoSiteConnection_<site code> group, is used to configure the security context for site-to-site communication. When sites attempt communication, the default option is to do so with computer accounts. In the example hierarchy this would mean that when the Central Administration Site attempts to communicate with the primary site, it will attempt a connection using the computer account of the Central Administration account. This communication will fail unless the Central Administration Site's computer account is part of the SMS_SiteToSite_Connection_PRI group. Said another way, any site that needs to communicate with the primary site must have its computer account as a part of the SMS_SiteToSite _Connection_PRI group. This group is shown in Figure 4.29.

FIGURE 4.29
SMS_ groups
added as part of
installation

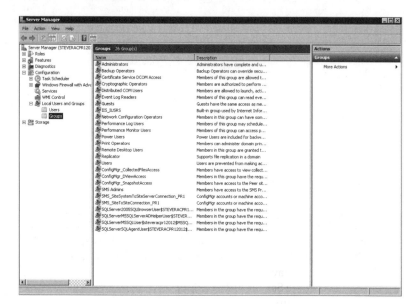

ADDING COMPUTER ACCOUNTS AS ADMINISTRATORS

OK, it's not really true to say that the computer accounts must be members of the SMS_SiteToSite_Connection_<site code> group. Simply adding the computer accounts as administrators of the various servers would achieve the same purpose and is not uncommonly done. Taking this approach grants more rights than are necessary to the computer accounts and is not a recommended method.

If you prefer not to use the computer accounts as administrators, then it is possible to configure specific credentials to facilitate site-to-site communication. Simply substitute those credentials for the computer account in the same group.

WINDOWS MANAGEMENT INSTRUMENTATION VALIDATION

We've already mentioned the idea of the SMS Provider. The SMS Provider is used to interact with the site server database, so ensuring that the installation created information in Windows Management Instrumentation (WMI) as required is important. The current discussion is not intended to be a detailed WMI discussion; simply ensuring the namespaces were created as required is enough. To verify, follow these steps:

1. Open Computer Management.

2. Select Configuration and then WMI Control.

3. Right-click WMI Control and select Properties.

4. Select the Security tab and expand Root.

A successful installation will result in the SMS namespace being created along with the child namespace site_<site code>, as shown in Figure 4.30.

FIGURE 4.30
WMI namespace
validation

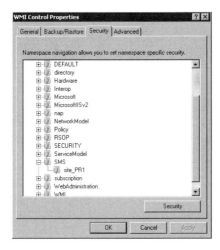

SERVICES VALIDATION

The services have already been validated in the registry, but it's also a good idea to take a look at them in the Services list to ensure all are present and in the proper state of operation. This is shown in Figure 4.31.

FIGURE 4.31
Services
validation

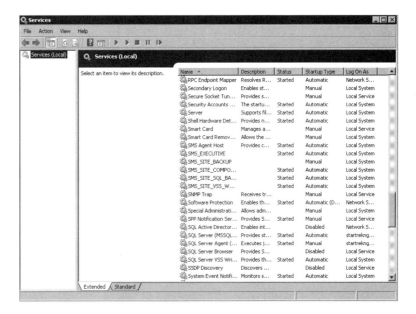

Database Validation

A site can't work without its database, so it stands to reason that the site couldn't be installed successfully without the database being installed successfully. Very true, but it's still worth a look for familiarity if nothing else. To view the database, launch SQL Management Studio and follow the steps listed. In our example, SQL is located on the same server as the site.

1. Connect to the database.

2. Open the server.

3. Expand Databases, and the CM_PRI example database should be present. This is shown in Figure 4.32.

FIGURE 4.32
Database
validation

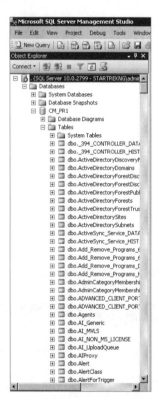

Troubleshooting a Configuration Manager 2012 Site Installation

We've validated the hierarchy installation, but that doesn't guarantee the site is working properly. Configuration Manager has many moving parts, and at times problems will surface. Understanding how to troubleshoot those problems is important to maintaining a healthy Configuration Manager hierarchy. So where should you look to troubleshoot issues with a site? Let me first say that this chapter is not an exhaustive troubleshooting chapter. Troubleshooting is covered in some depth in Chapter 15, "Troubleshooting." Still, it's helpful to know how things have progressed for a site installation. Fortunately, Configuration Manager is not lacking in information to help administrators check for problems and ascertain the nature of the problems. As with validation, this brief troubleshooting discussion will focus on the primary site that was installed.

The key component in place at a site, whether that site is the Central Administration Site, a primary site, or a secondary site, is the SMS_Executive component. This one service orchestrates most every activity at a site, and the list of SMS_Executive threads is extensive. Figure 4.33 is a screenshot of the various threads that run as part of the SMS_Executive component.

FIGURE 4.33

SMS_Executive threads

Since this is such a key service for all sites, it's a good idea to check the status of the Executive service in general to make sure all is well. Details on the various threads of the SMS_Executive component will mostly be left for later.

There are several ways to view details on the status of SMS_Executive. First, Configuration Manager provides a robust status message system so administrators can tell at a glance if all is good with a particular component. Taking a look at the Monitoring ➢ Component Status node of the administrative console; the SMS_Executive component, along with all of the other threads, is visible. A quick look shows that the status of this thread is OK, as shown in Figure 4.34. Note that the SMS_Executive component from all three sites is displayed here.

FIGURE 4.34

SMS_Executive component status

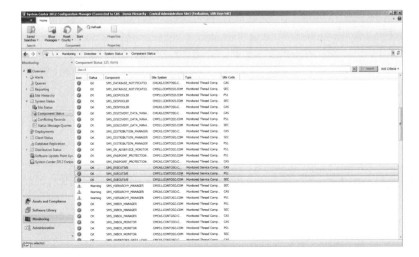

Status messages are not shown in real time, and there may be some short lag in reporting an error condition or reverting back to an OK condition if a component is again running healthy.

If the status is not OK or you need more details about this component, you can see them by right-clicking, selecting Show Messages, and selecting what kind of messages are of interest. On the context menu is also the Reset Counts option, which will reset any error counts being held for the various types of messages, errors, and warnings, back to 0. You can take this action after resolving an issue and to restart tracking of a component.

Another way to view the status of a component, and the method preferred by many administrators, is to take advantage of the extensive logging system provided in Configuration Manager. The logs are located in the Microsoft Configuration Manager ➤ Logs directory on the site server. Just as the status system showed the various components, there are logs representing them as well. The names aren't identical to the component names, but they are very similar and generally easy to correlate. In the case of the `SMS_Executive` component, the corresponding log is `smsexec.log`, as shown in Figure 4.35.

FIGURE 4.35
Smsexec log file

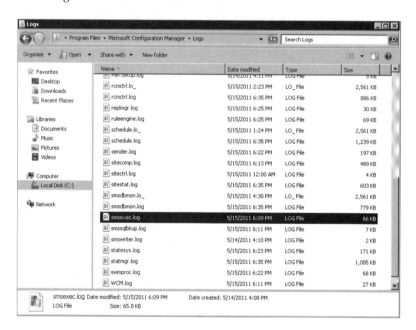

These log files can be viewed directly in Notepad, but the native Trace32 log viewer utility is preferred because it formats the logs nicely and also allows monitoring logs in real time as they are written.

GOOD OLD TRACE32

Configuration Manager 2012 introduces an updated version of Trace32. The new name is CMTrace. Previous versions of the Trace32 utility may have problems if used in Configuration Manager 2012. The updated utility is available in the Tools folder on the Configuration Manager 2012 media.

Line Trace32, the CMTrace utility, is very flexible, and administrators will find it to be useful for examining logs other than those from Configuration Manager.

Another critical component of the site is the site server database. Without the database, the site fails to function. To that end, you must understand how to at least begin an investigation of the database should problems arise. The database status can be seen in the Monitoring node of the Configuration Manager console as well. In terms of the database, isolating specific components to troubleshoot is difficult because it really does depend on the problem at hand. However, two components are fairly important for interaction with the database: the SMS Database Monitor and the SMS Provider.

SMS Database Monitor The SMS Database Monitor, represented in the Monitoring node as `SMS_Database_Notification_Monitor` and in the logs as `smsdbmon.log`, is responsible for monitoring actions that are taken by the administrator in the console and taking steps to implement those changes by notifying the various components of the `SMS_Executive` component that work is waiting to be done.

SMS Provider The SMS Provider is important because it is the conduit between most console actions and making those actions effective in the database. As an example, when an administrator selects a site to view in the console or makes changes to a console setting, the SMS Provider interacts with the SMS Database via WMI to retrieve needed data or make changes to data. Without the SMS Provider the site cannot function.

Another useful location for quickly checking the status of the database and more is again in the Monitoring node but this time under Site Status. In this node it's quick to see the amount of disk space available for various components that make up a site. This node is shown in Figure 4.36.

FIGURE 4.36
Site Status
Monitoring node

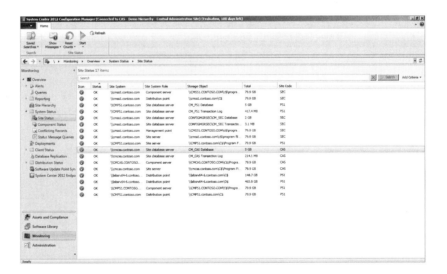

Unattended Installation

In some cases it may be of interest to perform a scripted install of Configuration Manager. This chapter won't go into depth about how this process works, but suffice it to say that the most difficult part of installing a site often is the *answer file* used during installation. Configuration Manager 2012 makes this easier by the fact that when a site is installed through the UI, an unattended installation file is created as part of the process. This unattended file is called `ConfigMgrAutoSave.ini` and is located in the `temp` directory for the user installing the product. The file is easily modified to perform scripted installs of other sites.

The unattended files generated in the example are shown to give an idea of how these are constructed based on different site types. When you're using the unattended file to initiate a site installation, a command line similar to the following should be used:

```
Setupwpf.exe /script <path to script>\ConfigMgrAutoSave.ini
```

This command line should be initiated from within this directory:

```
<Configuration Manager Source>\SMSSetup\BIN\x64
```

The content of the unattended files are shown in Listing 4.1 and Listing 4.2.

LISTING 4.1:   Central administration site unattended file

```
[Identification]
Action=InstallCCAR

[Options]
ProductID=
SiteCode=CAS
SiteName=Demo Hierarchy - Central Administration Site
SMSInstallDir=C:\Program Files\Microsoft Configuration Manager
SDKServer=cmcas.contoso.com
PrerequisiteComp=0
PrerequisitePath=C:\SCCM2012Updates
AdminConsole=1
JoinCEIP=0

[SQLConfigOptions]
SQLServerName=cmcas.contoso.COM
DatabaseName=CM_CAS
SQLSSBPort=4022

[HierarchyExpansionOption]
```

LISTING 4.2:   Primary site unattended file

```
[Identification]
Action=InstallPrimarySite

[Options]
ProductID=
SiteCode=PS1
SiteName=Test Hierarchy - PS1
SMSInstallDir=C:\Program Files\Microsoft Configuration Manager
```

```
SDKServer=cmps1.contoso.com
RoleCommunicationProtocol=HTTPorHTTPS
ClientsUsePKICertificate=1
PrerequisiteComp=1
PrerequisitePath=\\cmcas\c$\sccm2012updates
MobileDeviceLanguage=0
ManagementPoint=cmps1.contoso.com
ManagementPointProtocol=HTTP
DistributionPoint=cmps1.contoso.com DistributionPointProtocol=HTTP
DistributionPointInstallIIS=0
AdminConsole=1
JoinCEIP=0

[SQLConfigOptions]
SQLServerName=cmps1.contoso.com
DatabaseName=CM_PS1
SQLSSBPort=4022

[HeirarchyExpansionOption]
CCARSiteServer=cmcas.contoso.com
```

Installing Site System Roles

The process just discussed has resulted in a hierarchy with three sites: a Central Administration Site, a primary child site, and a secondary site. But just installing the sites doesn't mean that installation is complete. In order to provide service to clients that will be *interacting* with these sites, you must first decide what services will be provided and then configure the additional site components that facilitate providing the needed services. These site components are also known as *site system roles*. The site system roles available for a given site will depend on the site type:

Central Administration Site

◆ Asset Intelligence synchronization point

◆ Software update point

◆ System Health Validator point

Primary site

◆ Application Catalog Web Service point

◆ Application Catalog Website point

◆ Enrollment point

◆ Enrollment proxy point

◆ Fallback status point

- Out of band service point
- Reporting services point
- State migration point
- System Health Validator point

Secondary site

- State migration point

Notice that the term *interacting* was used in regard to clients and site servers. Administrators familiar with Configuration Manager may have expected the term *assigned* to be used instead. This term was used on purpose because in Configuration Manager clients can only be assigned to primary sites but are able to interact with any site their boundaries match. This concept is known as *roaming* and describes how clients are able to interact with secondary sites and other primary sites if they're within defined boundaries for those sites. Roaming is beyond the scope of discussion for this section.

A common element in installing all site system roles is the Add Site System Roles Wizard. Before launching the wizard to add the role, you must first decide whether the role will be added to an existing server or a new server. In the example hierarchy just built, that means a choice of adding the new role to a site server itself or creating a new server on which to add the role (both are shown in Figure 4.37).

FIGURE 4.37
Use the Create Site System Server button on the ribbon to create a new server; use the context menu to assign a new role on an existing server

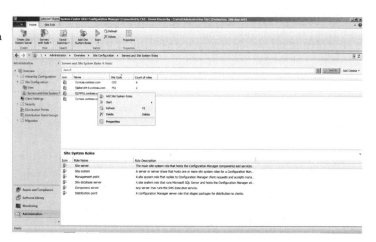

- If you're adding to an existing server, simply right-click that server under the Servers And Site Systems node of the console, and choose Add Site System Role.
- If you're adding a new server to host a site system role, that process is initiated by selecting the Create Site System Server action from Home tab of the ribbon.

A single remote site system server cannot host roles from multiple sites!

Both methods will result in the Add Site System Roles Wizard being launched. The only difference is whether the server name field will be populated and grayed out, and there is no option to specify the site code that the new server should support since it is already part of a site. For the example, site system roles are being added to the primary site, which already exists. The first page of the wizard is shown in Figure 4.38.

FIGURE 4.38
Add Site System
Roles Wizard:
General page

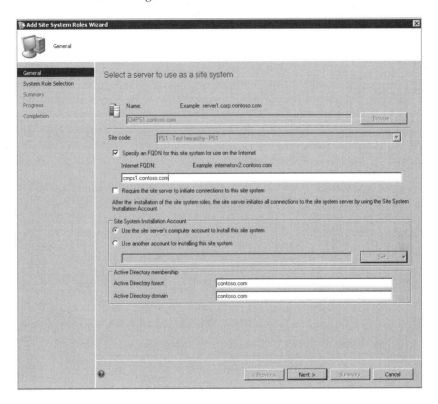

On this page of the wizard you have the opportunity to provide a server name. This option will be available only if you're creating a new site system server. In addition options are available to supply the FQDN of the server if it will be addressable from the Web. This option was also available in Configuration Manager 2007, but this brings up an interesting point of discussion. Configuration Manager 2007 supported two security modes: standard security and native mode security. Native mode security was required when specific functions were to be used, such as Internet-based client management and mobile device management. Native mode as a security option in Configuration Manager 2012 is gone and has been replaced by the ability to designate site system servers as those that will participate on the Internet or serve other functions that require certificate-based security. In this way the additional security afforded by certificates can be applied just where it's needed—to the site system itself.

The option "Require the site server to initiate connections to the site system" appears new but is actually just a relabeling of the Configuration Manager 2007 option that was on this page: "Allow only site server initiated data transfers from this site system." The goal of this option, as the wizard states in Configuration Manager 2012, is to designate that communication to site systems should be initiated from the site server itself rather than the site system pushing data back to the site server. This adds additional security and also accommodates scenarios where trusts aren't in place to accommodate cross-forest authentication.

Administrators accustomed to previous versions of Configuration Manager may note that the option to set the site system as a protected site system is no longer available on the first page of the Add Site System Roles Wizard. Site system protection only ever applied to distribution points and state migration points. Based on the new design of Configuration Manager 2012, meaning distribution points and state migration points are protected by default (more on that shortly), the option to do so was not needed on the Site System Wizard.

Clicking Next on the wizard will move you to the node to allow you to select which site system roles should be added to the target server. Once the roles are selected and movement through the wizard continues, you must configure the various options for the role-specific pages that will be displayed. Those pages will be discussed shortly for each type of site system.

As previously stated, the available site system roles for a given server depend on the type of server being configured. Each available site system role is described next.

Understanding Configuration Manager 2012 Site System Roles

The various site system roles available for each site type can be seen using the administrative console and focusing on the site in question. The list of available site systems that might be installed at the Central Administration Site, for example, can be obtained by doing this:

1. Open the console and navigate to Administration ➢ Site Operations ➢ Servers And Site System Roles.

2. Select the site type of interest, right-click, and choose Add Site System Roles.

3. In the wizard, move to the System Role Selection page.

4. Compare the roles available on this page to the roles already installed for the site, as shown in the console.

5. Then, generate a full list of available roles for a given site.

You can use the same approach for obtaining lists of available site systems for a primary site and a secondary site. Table 4.1 shows the available sites for each site type.

TABLE 4.1:   Available site system roles by site type

SITE SYSTEM ROLES	CENTRAL ADMINISTRATION SITE	PRIMARY SITE	SECONDARY SITE
Component server	X	X	X
Distribution point		X	X
Management point		X	X
Site database server	X	X	X

SITE SYSTEM ROLES	CENTRAL ADMINISTRATION SITE	PRIMARY SITE	SECONDARY SITE
Site server	X	X	X
Site system	X	X	X
System Health Validator point	X	X	
State migration point		X	X
Fallback status point	X	X	
Out of band service point		X	
Reporting Services point	X	X	
Application Catalog Web Service Point		X	
Application Catalog Web Site Point		X	
Mobile device enrollment proxy point		X	
Mobile device and AMT enrollment point		X	
Asset intelligence synchronization point	X		
Endpoint protection point	X		
Software Update point	X		

Notably missing from the list of roles at the Central Administration Site is the Management point role and the Distribution point role. This might seem strange at first until you again factor in that a Central Administration Site is not intended to support any clients; it is solely for the purpose of administration.

Also notably missing are the PXE Service Point role for operating system deployment and the Server Locator Point role used to help clients during site assignment and management point lookup. Don't worry, neither role is gone. The PXE Service Point is now available as a component of the Distribution Point role and the Server Locator Point has been merged into the management point role.

Another interesting aspect is that one of the site system roles listed for each site is the site server itself. That may seem odd, but in truth the site server function is but one role, albeit the key one, for a site. Note also that these roles can be placed on the same server or they can be placed on dedicated servers. The decision is driven by client count and load on a given role. For some site systems types such as distribution points (discussed shortly), it's quite possible that the same role will be needed on multiple servers to support a single site.

Now, let's discuss what each site system role does, the services it delivers, how it can be used, and some tips on troubleshooting each role.

Component Server

A *component server* is a unique site system role in Configuration Manager. This role cannot be manually added, nor can it be manually removed. This role is managed by the site server itself and will exist on any server that is running the SMS_Executive service within the hierarchy. This service runs specified threads that support other roles such as a management point.

TROUBLESHOOTING A CONFIGURATION MANAGER COMPONENT SERVER

This role manages the threads of the SMS_Executive service. It maintains which roles are local and remote for a given site. The overall health of the site server role can be reviewed in the Monitoring node. You can review the following logs to gain insight into the component server health:

sitecomp.log   This log shows all the site roles and where they're configured to be running.

compmon.log   This log records the status of all the threads of the SMS_Executive service and writes that status to the system registry under HKEY_LOCAL_MACHINE\SOFTWARE\ Microsoft\SMS\Operations Management. This information is used to keep track of component status and is also used as a resource for System Center Operations Manager in monitoring the status of Configuration Manager.

Distribution Point

The *distribution point* role has been expanded in Configuration Manager 2012. In previous versions this site system was nothing more than a glorified file server, storing files for access by clients requiring content.

The role of the distribution point is still to store file content and make it available to clients, but the way in which it does this has been updated. The first thing that we should mention is that the distribution point is designed to support both classic package distribution and the new application distribution mechanism introduced in Configuration Manager 2012. The legacy style distribution point, which is noted by a file folder named SMSPKG<*driveletter*>$, still remains but is used only for packages set to Run From Distribution Point and this is the only deployment mechanism that bypasses the requirement to use Background Intelligent Transfer Service (BITS). Beyond that, the updated distribution point structure is used universally. While the function of the distribution point in Configuration Manager 2012 remains the same, making content available to clients, the structure and function of the distribution point to provide it's service has been substantially updated.

- ◆ There is no option to use the distribution point without making use of BITS.

- ◆ The distribution point structure is no longer just a file store. Now, files are stored in a cache that takes advantage of single-instance storage, supports automated integrity checks, and more.

◆ The branch distribution points are gone and replaced with the fact that a standard distribution point is now fully supported on a supported Windows 7 workstation system, no client required. The workstation system is still subject to the connection limitation for a given operating system. In Windows XP administrators were accustomed to a 10 connection. In Windows 7 the connection limit has increased to 20.

Bottom line, this isn't your grandpa's distribution point anymore! First things first—the distribution point must be installed.

It may be that the distribution point role is already installed. One of the default settings when installing a primary or secondary site is to also add the distribution point and management point roles. If the role has not yet been added or if an additional distribution point is needed, then this component won't yet be present on the server and will need to be added.

1. In the Add Site System Roles Wizard, and as shown in Figure 4.39, select the distribution point role, and click Next to proceed to the Distribution Point page of the wizard, as shown in Figure 4.40.

FIGURE 4.39
Add Site System
Roles Wizard:
Distribution point
selected

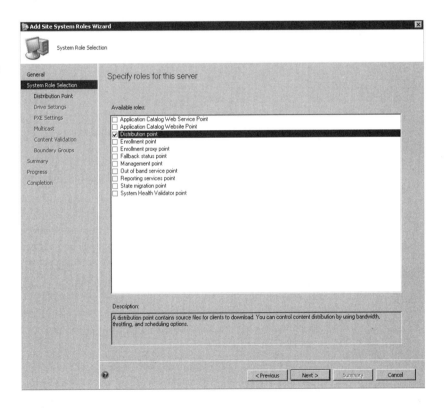

FIGURE 4.40
Add Site System
Roles Wizard:
Distribution
Point page

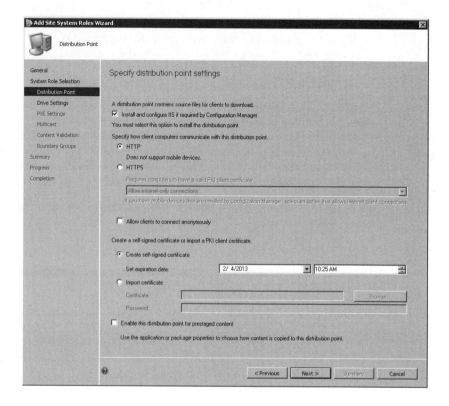

2. On the Distribution Point page of the wizard, configure a few options that are available:

- The first option, Install And Configure IIS If Required By Configuration Manager, is not selected by default, but you must select this option prior to proceeding. This option highlights the fact that with Configuration Manager 2012 it is not possible to create a non-BITS-enabled distribution point. This fact may influence distribution point placement but is a welcome modification for sure.

- Next on the page is the choice of whether clients should communicate with the distribution point using HTTP or HTTPS traffic. When clients use BITS to pull information from the distribution point, as is required by Configuration Manager 2012, the clients do not directly connect to the distribution point structure but rather initiate a BITS session through IIS.

- Other options on this page allow the administrator to decide whether the distribution point will use self-signed certificates or certificates imported from a different source, such as a Certificate Authority. If supporting Internet scenarios, a certificate would be imported at this step.

- The last option on the page allows configuration of a distribution point to support prestaged media. Prestaged media is a new feature of Configuration Manager 2012 and addresses scenarios where administrators would prefer to deliver content in bulk to a distribution point rather than having it copied over the network. In previous versions of Configuration Manager this was not supported natively, although there were tools available to help at least partially address this need, such as PreLoadPkgOnSite.

3. Once you've configured all options on this page as needed, click Next to proceed to the Drive Settings page, shown in Figure 4.41.

FIGURE 4.41
Add Site System
Roles Wizard:
Drive Settings page

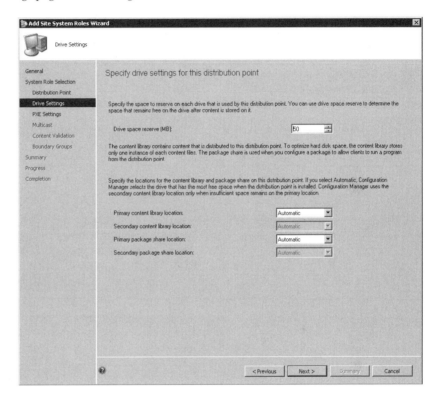

Also new to Configuration Manager 2012 is the ability to control distribution point drive selection and allocate reserved storage when configuring the distribution point. Mechanisms did exist in previous versions of Configuration Manager to make similar configurations effective, notably the use of the no_sms_on_drive flag file, but having these options in the console allows more effective and granular administrator control. A couple of options are presented here:

◆ First is the ability to preconfigure the amount of drive space that should be reserved for the distribution point.

◆ The next set of options, which are perhaps more important, let you choose which drives should be used for the content libraries and package share locations. In our example, there is only a single drive on the site server, so leaving the option set to Automatic makes sense.

Also, since there is only a single drive on the server, it doesn't make sense to set a secondary content location, so that option is grayed out as well. If multiple drives are available and the setting is left at Automatic, then the system will pick the drives to use the same way it has done historically—using the NTFS drive with the most available space as a first choice and so on.

4. Once the settings are configured as needed, click Next to proceed to the PXE page of the wizard, shown in Figure 4.42.

FIGURE 4.42
Add Site System Roles Wizard:
PXE page

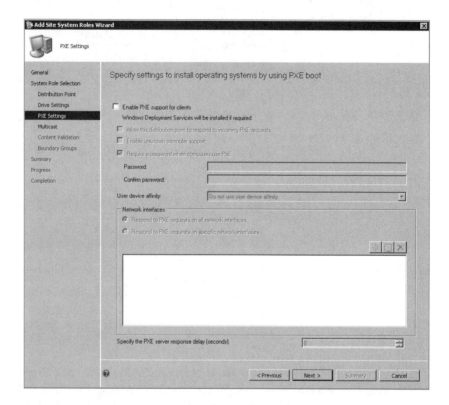

The PXE page of the wizard lets you choose whether the distribution point being configured should also act as a PXE server for operating system deployment. Because of the dependency the PXE server has on the distribution point to deliver boot images, having this setting as part of the distribution point makes sense. For the example we won't install a PXE point; it can be added later as needed.

5. Review the settings on this page and click Next to proceed to the Multicast page of the wizard, shown in Figure 4.43.

FIGURE 4.43

Add Site System Roles Wizard: Multicast page

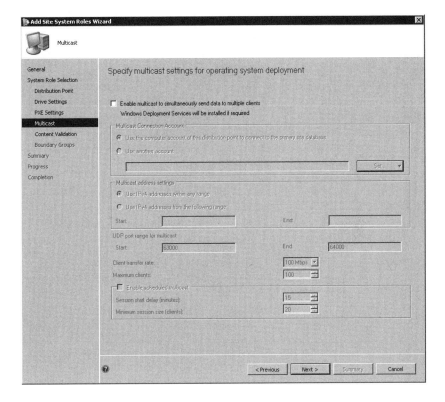

The Multicast page of the wizard allows administrators to specify whether the distribution point being configured should support multicast or not. Multicast is used with operating system deployment and is a very efficient protocol for delivering images to multiple systems simultaneously. The example distribution point will not be used for multicast support for now, so this option will not be selected. It can be added later as needed.

6. Review the settings on this page, and click Next to proceed to the Content Validation page, shown in Figure 4.44.

FIGURE 4.44
Add Site
System Roles
Wizard: Content
Validation page

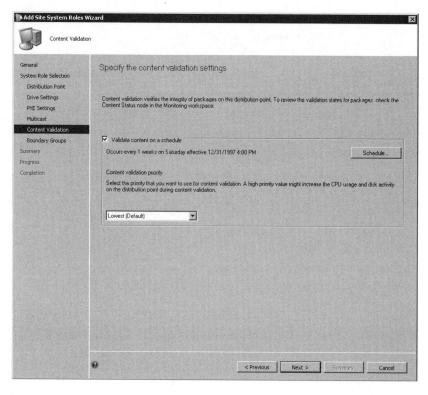

The Content Validation page of the wizard allows administrators to specify whether or not content should be periodically validated on the distribution point and, if so, on what schedule and at what priority. When Validate Content On A Schedule is selected, the default evaluation period is once per week and at a low priority, to ensure other activities on the server are not disrupted.

This is a significant feature update for Configuration Manager! Most readers who have used distribution points in previous versions of Configuration Manager will have encountered the scenario where content will be distributed to distribution points, work fine for a period of time, and then start to show errors, typically a hash mismatch problem. This might happen for several reasons, often due to on-demand virus scanning of the distribution points, but when encountered, the problem is disruptive until fixed. The ability to do content validation and proactively identify problems is a welcome change indeed! Further, the updated structure of the distribution point should help keep content in a good state as well. More on the distribution point structure shortly.

7. Once you've configured these settings, click Next to proceed to the Boundary Groups page of the wizard, which allows the administrator to choose the boundary group(s) in which the distribution point should be a member. While it is not a strict requirement that a distribution point be a member of any boundary group in order to be created, the distribution point may not be accessible by any client until it is added to the appropriate boundary group(s). Detailed discussion of boundary groups is beyond the focus of this chapter, but based on the tight dependency between distribution point function and boundary groups, a bit of discussion is appropriate here.

Boundary groups are new in Configuration Manager 2012 and serve two purposes: client assignment and content access. The latter item is the one of concern for distribution point access. We mentioned earlier that on the Add Site System Roles Wizard—General page, the option to specify a site system as protected was removed. In Configuration Manager 2012, when a distribution point (or state migration point in operating system deployment) is added to a boundary group, by definition the distribution point is protected and only those clients that are within the boundaries defined by the boundary group are able to retrieve content from the distribution points that have membership in the boundary group. Further, a distribution point is able to have membership in multiple boundary groups. By taking this new approach, administrators are afforded additional control to easily specify which distribution points are available to service clients depending on which subnets the clients happen to be located near.

But what if a client requires access to content but is not within boundaries defined by any boundary group, such as a laptop in a hotel room? That scenario is also addressed. Boundary groups can be flagged as accessible to systems when the system is in a location where no other distribution point can be resolved. This is known as *fallback* and is enabled by default for the boundary group, as noted at the bottom of the Boundary Groups page. For the example, the distribution point has been added to a boundary group that was previously created for the example primary site.

8. Once the boundary group configuration is complete, click Next to review the Summary page of the wizard.

9. After confirming all settings, click Next to finish the wizard and implement the distribution point deployment. The successful completion is shown in Figure 4.45.

FIGURE 4.45
Add Site System
Roles Wizard:
Completion page

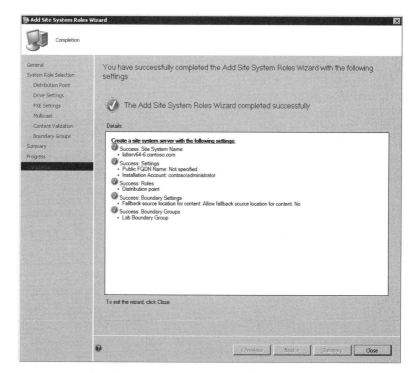

As mentioned earlier, the Configuration Manager 2012 distribution point structure has changed. After installation is complete and after a couple of applications have been deployed, open the drive hosting the distribution point and check for a few folders, shown in Figure 4.46.

FIGURE 4.46
Distribution point structure

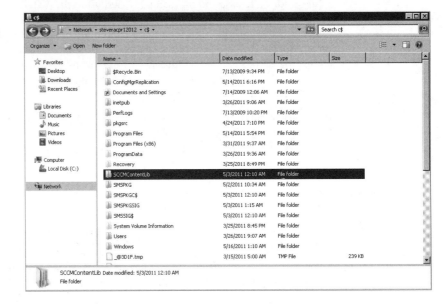

The same folders you might expect from previous versions are still present to support distribution of classic software packages configured to Run from Distribution Point: SMSPKG, SMSPKG<*driveletter*>$, SMSSIG$, and SMSPKGSIG. In addition to these folders another is present called SCCMContentLib. This folder contains the new structure for the distribution point and is worth further discussion.

Historically, opening the distribution point folder will reveal a list of folders named with package IDs and, within the folder, the contents of the package. That still is the case, but the structure is far different. Remember that the new distribution point structure in Configuration Manager 2012 is designed to take advantage of single-instance storage and also to be a bit more stable. Looking inside the SCCMContentLib folder reveals three additional folders, DataLib, FileLib, and PkgLib, shown in Figure 4.47.

FIGURE 4.47
SCCMContentLib
structure

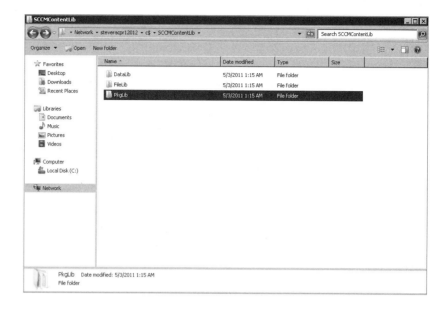

The PkgLib folder is the starting place to examine the new structure, and it contains files with names that match the package ID from the site, shown in Figure 4.48.

FIGURE 4.48
PkgLib folder
structure and INI
files

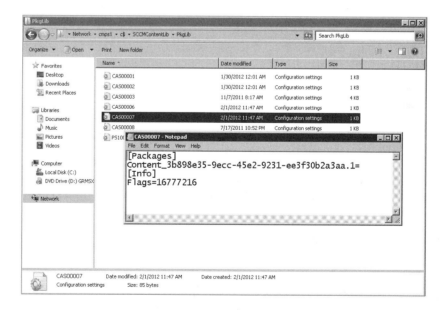

Note that these files are INI files. Looking inside reveals the packages that are associated with the package ID. From here, copy and paste the two Content_ GUIDs and navigate to the

DataLib folder, shown in Figure 4.49. For the example, use `Content_3b898e35-9ecc-45e2-9231-ee3f30b2a3aa.1`.

FIGURE 4.49
DataLib folder
structure, GUID
folder, and configu-
ration file

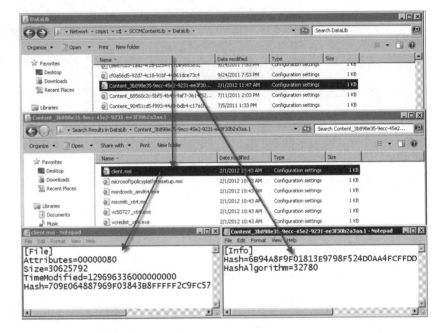

In the DataLib folder there are two entries that match; the first is a folder and the second is a configuration file. Looking at the GUID folder first, it looks like the location of the package content! But not so fast. The filenames here will match the filenames from the source file folder, but a quick glance at the file sizes and file extension will show that these are just configuration files. Taking a look at a the `client.msi` file reveals details about the actual file, including file size, in this case 30625792 bytes, and the hash value for the file. The first four characters of the hash value here are key to finding the actual file. In the example, the hash value of interest is 709E. More on this shortly.

In addition to the source file structure there is another configuration file matching the GUID in question; it is at the root of `DataLib`. Opening it shows a hash value for the folder itself.

Armed with information gained from this folder, it's time to visit the `FileLib` folder, shown in Figure 4.50.

FIGURE 4.50
FileLib folder
structure

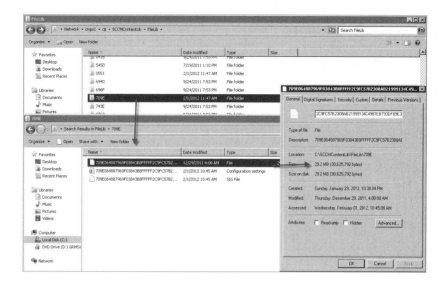

Within the FileLib folder is a series of other folders with names that at first appear cryptic—only four characters. Aha! Remember that we just mentioned that the first four characters of the hash value for the `client.msi` file were important. In this folder there is a subfolder named 709E. A quick look inside that folder reveals a file with the exact size of the `client.msi` file—30,626,792 bytes. Bingo! This is the location of the actual `client.msi` file, simply renamed and placed into this single-instance storage format.

Software Requirements

Configuration Manager 2012 distribution points require the following:

♦ All site servers must be members of a Windows 2003 or Windows 2008 Active Directory domain.

♦ Distribution points require Background Intelligent Transfer Service (BITS) version 2.0 or higher and cannot be installed or used without it.

♦ Distribution points may be installed on any supported server or client operating system.

♦ All Configuration Manager distribution point systems using BITS bandwidth throttling require BITS 2 or higher.

Troubleshooting a Configuration Manager 2007 Distribution Point

Without the packages being staged on the distribution points, content deployment (packages, applications, operating systems, and software updates) in the environment cannot be completed. Providing insight into the process and health of the hierarchy distribution points, status messages, and log files can be an administrator's best friend.

The Monitoring node of the administrative console, shown in Figure 4.51, will give insight into the health of the distribution points.

FIGURE 4.51
Monitoring node,
distribution point
focus

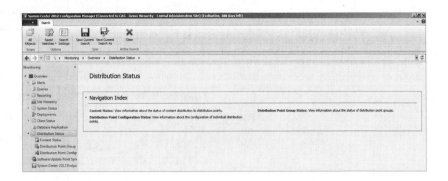

There is a specific folder for the distribution points, called `Distribution Status`, that provides insight into the status of content, distribution groups, and distribution point configuration. There is also the `Component Status` folder, where you can review the health of `SMS_DISTRIBUTION_MANAGER`, the key component for deploying content to distribution points.

In addition to status messages, `distmgr.log` provides insight into the distribution points for troubleshooting purposes: It tracks the different packages by package ID, size, and location where they are to be stored.

Management Point

A *management point* is the primary point of contact between the Configuration Manager 2012 clients and the site server. All site servers that host clients must have at least one management point installed; this includes primary site servers and secondary site servers. A management point installed at a secondary site server is known as a proxy management point. Clients use the management point to retrieve and send all data to and from their assigned site server; this includes retrieving settings and configuration via the policy and forwarding operational data such as inventory, state messages, status messages, discovery information, and more. In addition, clients will send requests to the management point requesting help locating content they may need, such as finding which distribution points are available to the client and contain needed software update or software package content or even the location of a software update point used in software update scanning.

Once a management point receives data from the client, it will be further analyzed and converted into a form acceptable by the site server and then forwarded to the site server for further processing. This also includes content location requests, but in these cases there is no data to forward to the site server. Instead, the management point will execute queries against the site database and return that information to requesting clients.

Here are a few things to remember about management points:

◆ Every primary and secondary site must have a management point specified.

◆ The Central Administration Site cannot host a management point.

◆ Management points require access to the site database for certain operations.

◆ Management points require a local installation of IIS to be installed.

◆ Management points make use of BITS when moving content, depending on size, to help avoid impacting network utilization.

Also of interest for management points is that they no longer have a dependency on WebDav. Add to this that management points are now treated similarly to distribution points in that they can be placed where needed to support clients. In previous releases of Configuration Manager, the only way to host multiple management points at a site was by using a network load balancer as a front end. Now management points are simply looked up by clients—similar to distribution points—and the best choice at a site is returned to the client. This statement may cause you to ask how exactly clients learn about possible management points. There are a couple of ways. It's possible to specify a single or multiple management points on the command line when installing the client using the SMSMP switch. If Active Directory publishing is enabled, then clients will be able to look up the management point list from there as well. During client installation, and during ongoing client operation, they will learn which management point is optimum for their use through boundary groups—again, much the same as distribution points.

Another big shift for management points is that now the server locator point functionality is included in this role.

It may be that the management point role is already installed. One of the default settings when installing a primary or secondary site is to also add the management point role. If the role was not yet added as part of setup, then you will need to add it.

1. In the Add Site System Roles Wizard, select to add the management point role, and click Next to proceed to the Management Point page, as shown in Figure 4.52.

FIGURE 4.52
Add Site System
Roles Wizard:
Management
Point page

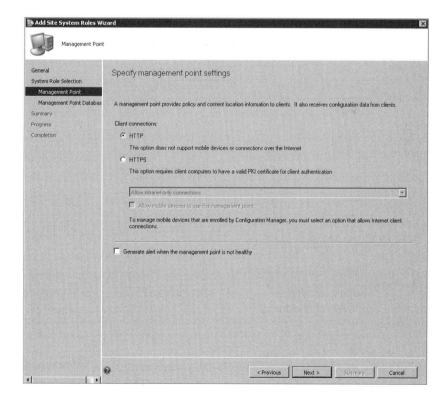

♦ The first choice on this page allows administrators to choose how clients should communicate with this management point, either by HTTP or by HTTPS.

♦ Administrators are also able to specify whether they want to receive an alert in the console indicating when the management point is unhealthy.

This is a new option for Configuration Manager 2012, and it points to the basic monitoring capability that has been added. If this option is selected, administrators can find alerts generated in the Monitoring node of the console.

2. Click Next to continue to the Management Point Database page shown in Figure 4.53.

FIGURE 4.53
Add Site System Roles Wizard: Management Point Database page

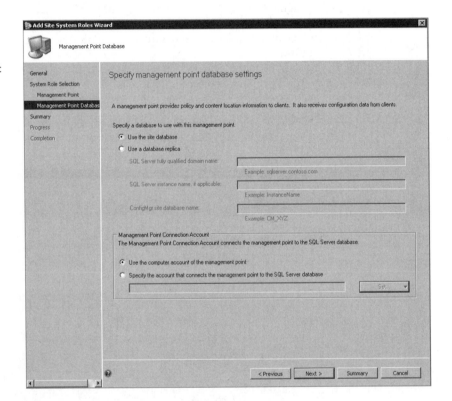

PROXY MANAGEMENT POINTS

Proxy management points are the same as standard management points except that they are located at a secondary site. In previous versions of Configuration Manager it was the administrator's choice whether to include a proxy management point at secondary sites. In Configuration Manager 2012 there is no choice; proxy management points are automatically installed on every secondary site server.

Proxy management points exist to help reduce the impact on the WAN when clients are operating outside the boundaries of their assigned primary site but within the boundaries of a secondary site that is a child of their assigned primary site. A client in this configuration will consider the proxy management point to be its local management point but will always consider the management point from its assigned primary site to be the assigned management point. The difference between the two is that the client is able to use the local management point to find local distribution points via content location requests and also as a point for offloading data, such as inventory and state messages, on its way to the parent site's database. The client will still use its assigned management point to retrieve all policy changes.

Proxy management points can significantly reduce the load on WAN traffic by processing data from and providing client policy to those clients that fall within their roaming boundaries. Data flow between Configuration Manager clients and the Configuration Manager 2012 hierarchy is as follows:

1. Clients send discovery data, inventory data, status data, and software-metering data to the proxy management point in XML format.

2. The proxy management point processes the submitted XML file, converts it into the appropriate file type, and places it in the associated Inbox directory on the secondary site server.

3. The secondary site server processes the data as it would under normal circumstances and forwards it up the hierarchy to its parent site.

Proxy management points also retrieve policy information from the database of the primary site and forward the data to Configuration Manager clients. Proxy management points allow the client to function locally when roaming to a secondary site, while further allowing administrators to control the replication of client data from the secondary site to the primary parent by means of standard sender throttling.

HOW CLIENTS FIND MANAGEMENT POINTS

During installation and general operation, Configuration Manager 2012 clients obtain management point locations in much the same way as they look up distribution points. Configuration Manager 2012 allows for multiple management points per site. Periodically, clients will poll for which management point they should be using. The determination is made by evaluating boundary groups in relation to the client, very similar to the mechanism used to find distribution points. If a client roams outside of its assigned sites boundaries, then the lookup is a bit more complex but is needed to allow clients to access local management point servers where possible. There is also a lookup mechanism for management points in Active Directory.

LOCATING MANAGEMENT POINTS IN AD

In an environment that provides Active Directory services, Configuration Manager 2012 clients locate management points as follows:

1. The client searches the Active Directory global catalog for a local site code with a matching Active Directory site name, IP network, or IP address range that has been previously registered by a site server.

2. If a match is not found or if required content is not available at the local site, then the client uses the site code of its assigned site.

3. The client then queries Active Directory again to find the appropriate management point for the site code identified in the previous steps.

For this reason, management points should be installed prior to Configuration Manager client deployment, but the client will be able to access the management point once it becomes available.

4. If there is only one management point for the site, the client gets the name of that management point from Active Directory and then connects to it.

OVERLAPPING BOUNDARIES AND MANAGEMENT POINT LOCATION

The fact that the client will always query Active Directory first when attempting to locate management points is one of many reasons why overlapping site boundaries is unsupported and will wreak havoc on an environment. When sites publish their information to Active Directory and that information is inconsistent, as in the case of overlaps, the client may not choose the correct management points for use when looking up content locations. The result may be failed software deployment in the environment, not to mention the implications for proper client assignment if installing clients.

AUTOMATIC MP QUERY

When installing the Configuration Manager client, you must either set it to determine the SMS site automatically or specify site assignment as part of the command line for the installation. During installation and after assigned to a site, the client will look up the appropriate management point it should be using. The client gets this list either by command line during installation, querying Active Directory, or learning about additional management points and adjusting after installation.

In addition, a new option has been added to Configuration Manager 2012 to specify a default site a client should be assigned to if it is unable to find a site by normal lookup mechanisms. This fallback ability helps ensure clients do not get installed and immediately orphaned because they cannot find a site.

You can see this in the `LocationServices.Log` file of the Configuration Manager client, located at `%Windir%\System32\CCM\Logs`.

SERVER LOCATOR POINT FUNCTIONALITY

As mentioned, the server locator point functionality has been merged into the management point role. But what is a server locator point used for? Server locator points (SLPs) are used within a Configuration Manager 2012 hierarchy to provide services for client site assignment, location of client installation files, and location of management points when clients cannot access that information within Active Directory. Thus, merging this role with the management point role is a natural fit.

LOGGING

Logs of management point activity can exist in one of two locations, depending on which was installed first: the Configuration Manager client or the management point. The management point and the client share a common framework and thus both run under the SMS Agent Host service or the short name of CCMExec. This is potentially confusing at first because it is possible to have just a management point installed without the client component, but the service name will still be SMS Agent Host.

If the management point is installed on a server first, the logs will be located in the SMS_CCM\ Logs directory. When the Configuration Manager client has already been installed on the server, the logs are located in the %Windir%\System32\CCM\Logs directory along with the client-side logs.

Default logging is good for both the client and the management point, but there are some log details that won't be seen unless verbose and debug logging are enabled. Some of the information that is accessible with this extra level of logging is so useful that it is common practice to configure verbose and debug logging as a standard across the environment. There is additional overhead because more data is written to the logs, but it is minimal and should cause no impact to the operation of the system.

Enabling verbose and debug logging requires two registry changes. First, you enable verbose logging by navigating to

    key_local_machine\software\microsoft\ccm\logging\@global

and changing the value LogLevel to 0 (which will require a permissions change on the @GLOBAL key). To enable debug logging, create a registry key called DebugLogging directly under

    HKEY_LOCAL_MACHINE\SOFTWARE\Microsoft\CCM\Logging

Inside this registry key create a string value named Enabled and set its value to True.

Software Requirements

Configuration Manager 2012 management points require the following:

- All site servers must be members of a Windows 2003 or Windows 2008 Active Directory domain.

- IIS 6.0 or higher must be installed.

Troubleshooting a Configuration Manager 2012 Management Point

The Configuration Manager management point is the entry point into a Configuration Manager hierarchy from a client perspective. The client receives its Configuration Manager policies and advertisements from the MP and places its inventories and status there. As with all components, administrators have a choice of using status messages and/or log files to verify management point function.

You can view management point status in the Monitoring node of the console by checking components such as SMS_MP_CONTROL_MANAGER or SMS_MP_FILE_DISPATCH_MANAGER. If you prefer using logs, then the following logs are key to verifying proper management point installation and function:

mpMSI.log This is the Microsoft Installer (MSI) log for the management point installation.

mpSetup.log This is the site-specific management point log, which shows which site and server the management point is configured to use.

mpcontrol.log This log maintains the management point by reviewing and checking the management point availability and status.

Site Database Server

Every Configuration Manager 2012 implementation will have at least one server running the site database server role. The simplest implementation will have a single server running all the

Configuration Manager 2012 roles as well as Microsoft SQL Server 2008 Service Pack 1 or higher. As noted earlier, at least one database repository is required to store all the client information and site configurations.

A Configuration Manager 2012 site database server requires the following:

◆ All site servers must be members of a Windows 2003 or Windows 2008 Active Directory domain.

◆ Microsoft SQL Server 2008 Service Pack 1 or higher is the only version of SQL Server supported for hosting the Configuration Manager 2012 database.

◆ The SQL database service is the only SQL Server component required to be installed to host the site database.

TROUBLESHOOTING A CONFIGURATION MANAGER SITE DATABASE SERVER

This is the database server that hosts the Microsoft SQL Server 2008 Service Pack 1 database. There is one database that holds all information about inventory, packages, status, and all the other pertinent data of System Center Configuration Manager 2012. The following logs provide insight into the health of the database server:

smsdbmon.log   This log shows all activities such as inserts, updates, drops, and deletes from the Configuration Manager 2012 database.

smsprov.log   This log shows the SQL transaction calls made from the Configuration Manager console or automation scripts via the SDK.

Site Server

A *site server* is a unique site system role in Configuration Manager. This role cannot be manually added, nor can it be manually removed. This role is managed by the site server itself and will exist on any server that is serving as a site server in the hierarchy. When a site is installed, whether a Central Administration Site, primary site, or secondary site, it will be shown as having the site server role.

This role manages all functions of the site and interacts with all remote systems hosting site system roles for the site. The overall health of the site server role can be reviewed in the Monitoring node of the console and also by examining the site server logs generated.

Site System

A *site system* is a unique site system role in Configuration Manager. This role cannot be manually added nor can it be manually removed. This role is managed by the site server itself and will exist on any server that is serving as a as a site system in the hierarchy. The site server itself will always be a site system as will any remote servers that are deployed to host various roles to provide services needed by the site.

The overall health of the site system server can be reviewed in the Monitoring node of the console. The specific nodes to review as well as the specific log files will be dictated by the specific functions being performed by the site system server.

System Health Validator Point

The System Health Validator point is the Configuration Manager 2012 site system role that runs on Windows Server 2008 and Windows 2008 R2 servers with the Network Policy Server role enabled.

Network Policy Servers evaluate clients as they attempt to come on the network and either grant access or deny access depending on whether clients comply with configured policy. The System Health Validator point is the Configuration Manager add-on to the Network Policy Server that provides the ability to judge whether a given client complies with required patch levels.

In brief,

1. Client health state evaluation proceeds by the client producing a statement of health locally and sending this to the Network Policy Server.

2. When received, the statement of health is evaluated against configured conditions and a resulting client health state is determined. The state may be

   ◆ Compliant, resulting in network access

   ◆ Noncompliant, resulting in network access being denied until the detected problem is remediated

An error condition may be returned that prevents evaluation.

The System Health Validator point validates a statement of health using a sequential series of checks. These include the following:

◆ Time validation when the statement of health was created

◆ Validation against the health state reference

◆ Compliance status and failures

The System Health Validator point never communicates directly with Configuration Manager 2012 site servers to validate client statements of health. When a Configuration Manager Network Access Policy is created or modified or inherited from a parent site, the site server writes a health state reference to Active Directory Domain Services. The System Health Validator point periodically retrieves the health state references for all Configuration Manager primary sites that are enabled for Network Access Protection (NAP).

Because Active Directory Domain Services is used to store the health state references, the Active Directory schema must be extended with the Configuration Manager 2012 extensions. The health state reference is published to a System Management container in Active Directory, which requires that Configuration Manager 2012 publish site information to Active Directory Domain Services. When there is more than one Active Directory forest and your Configuration Manager site servers and System Health Validator points are not in the same forest, you must designate which forest and domain will store the health state references.

If the System Health Validator point role has not yet been added, it will need to be selected. Until now components have been installed on just the site server system. In production it is unlikely that the site server will also act as a Network Policy server, so configuring this role will likely require creating a new site system server to host the role. The new site system server should be the server hosting the Network Policy server components in the environment.

1. In the Add Site System Roles Wizard select to add the System Health Validator point role.

2. Click Next to proceed to the System Health Validator page of the wizard. There are no properties to configure on this page.

3. Simply complete the wizard to install the component.

SOFTWARE REQUIREMENTS

Configuration Manager 2012 System Health Validator points require that all site servers be members of a Windows 2003 or Windows 2008 Active Directory domain.

TROUBLESHOOTING A CONFIGURATION MANAGER 2012 SYSTEM HEALTH VALIDATOR POINT

Within the entire Network Access Protection scenario, this role allows the infrastructure to validate the statement of health from a NAP-capable Configuration Manager client. For troubleshooting, use the SMSSHVSetup.log file, which documents the prerequisite and installation progress.

State Migration Point

Think of the state migration point role as a reverse distribution point. The state migration point is a Configuration Manager site system role that provides a secure location to store user state information as part of an operating system deployment. User state is stored on the state migration point while the operating system deployment proceeds and is then restored from the state migration point to the new computer at the appropriate time during imaging. Each state migration point site server can be a member of only one Configuration Manager 2012 site, but each site may have multiple state migration points if needed.

If the state migration point role has not yet been added, you will need to select it, as shown in Figure 4.54.

FIGURE 4.54
Add Site System Roles Wizard: State migration point selected

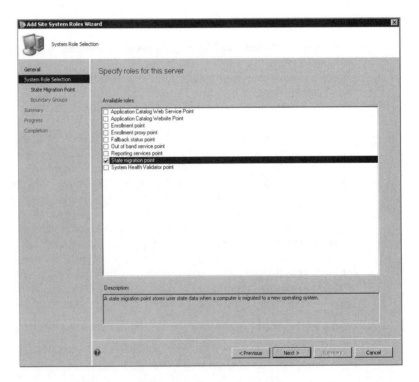

1. Choose the site where the state migration point will be located, and select the role in the Add Site System Roles Wizard.

2. Click Next to proceed to the State Migration Point page of the wizard, shown in Figure 4.55.

FIGURE 4.55
Add Site System
Roles Wizard:
State Migration
Point page

This page allows configuration of the state migration point.

3. First, choose the folder that will host user data sent to the state migration point.

This includes choosing the drive, the folder name, the maximum number of clients that may be served by the state migration point, and also the minimum amount of disk space that should be reserved.

4. Configure the Deletion Policy to show how long user state data is held following a successful operating system deployment before being deleted.

This raises an important point. When user state data is stored on the state migration point, it is with the intention that the state data will be restored to either the same system or a different system as imaging nears completion. If the state data is never restored, it is never marked as eligible for deletion because there might have been problems during the imaging process, and allowing deletion would remove potentially needed data from the system. This is particularly true if the deletion settings specify to remove data immediately.

5. Finally, flag the state migration point as being in restore-only mode.

This special setting, disabled by default, allows administrators to configure a state migration point so that it doesn't receive new state data but is available for use in already stored state data. Typically you would set this option if you have a state migration point server that is scheduled for maintenance or replacement; you could also use this option if you are building a new state migration point but you don't want it to go into service yet.

6. Once the configuration settings are complete, click Next to proceed to the Boundary Groups page of the wizard, shown in Figure 4.56.

FIGURE 4.56
Add Site System
Roles Wizard:
Boundary
Groups page

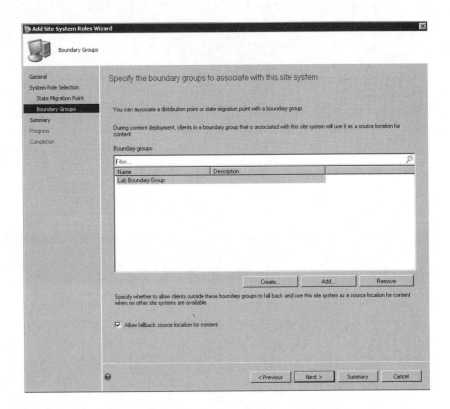

Like the distribution point, the state migration point needs to be added to an appropriate boundary group to make it available for use by clients. If the state migration point is being installed on a server that already hosts the distribution point role, then the boundary group may be prepopulated.

7. Make any needed changes and click Next to continue through the wizard and finish up.

SOFTWARE REQUIREMENTS

Configuration Manager 2012 state migration points must be members of a Windows 2003 or Windows 2008 Active Directory domain.

Troubleshooting a Configuration Manager 2012 Migration Point

This role is leveraged during the operating system deployment. In particular, it is used to store user data for migration back onto their machine that was just reimaged or replaced. The health of the state migration point is visible in the Monitoring node of the console and also by reviewing the following logs.

smssmpsetup.log   This log documents the appropriate prerequisites and logs the initialization of the smp.msi file and installation completion.

smpmsi.log   This log documents the installation setup progress of the smp.msi file.

Fallback Status Point

The fallback status point role helps address today's greater security requirements while enabling a mechanism to catch clients that are not communicating properly. When deploying clients it is critical to know if problems are being encountered. Typically these problems are reported to the management point in the form of status or state messages. When installing the client there is a time when it is not possible to send data to the management point. In addition, there may be problems reaching the management point even after install. In such cases, if the client does not have a mechanism to notify the site of problems, it will become orphaned and unusable. The fallback status point role provides an administrator with insight into the installation and management of a client and works well because the location of the fallback status point is configurable on the command line when client installation is initiated.

A fallback status point is similar to a proxy server that proxies client status messages up to the site server. Two types of messages may occur: the normal messages that appear during client installation and assignment or those identifying unhealthy Configuration Manager 2012. In either scenario, the fallback status point fills the gap and shows the administrator that there are client issues that need to be addressed.

Because of the potential security threat of an unknown client or client status, it is recommended that the fallback status point be placed outside a physical site server. It can be a low-end server, because of the relatively small number of potential requests it should receive. As in any design decision, the criteria of scale versus risk should be investigated before a decision is made.

Through detailed reporting, an administrator can gain knowledge and take proactive measures to ensure that availability remains in its highest state. These reports include detailed client information on capable and incapable client communication.

Installation of a fallback status point is not a requirement for a site but it is recommended. Typically there is one fallback status point installed per site that hosts clients.

If the fallback status point role has not yet added, you will need to select it.

1. Choose the site where the fallback status point will be located, and select the status point in the Add Site System Roles Wizard.

2. Click Next to proceed to the Fallback Status Point page of the wizard, shown in Figure 4.57.

FIGURE 4.57
Add Site System
Roles Wizard:
Fallback Status
Point page

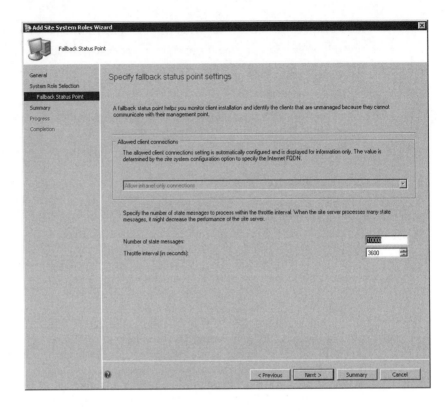

There is little configuration to be done for the fallback status point. The only option is to configure the number of state messages that are allowed to be processed during the given time window. Typically the default values are fine.

3. Make any needed changes, and click Next to complete the wizard.

SOFTWARE REQUIREMENTS

Configuration Manager 2012 fallback status points require that all site servers be members of a Windows 2003 or Windows 2008 Active Directory domain.

TROUBLESHOOTING THE FALLBACK STATUS POINT

The fallback status point is meant for clients that are having difficulties communicating with a Native mode Configuration Manager hierarchy. To provide insights into the proper configuration of this role, the component status is available in the Monitoring node of the console and also by reviewing the following logs:

SMSFSPSetup.log This log documents the prerequisites and kicks off the `fsp.msi` installation.

fspMSI.log This log provides the installation status of the fallback status point role.

Out-of-Band Service Point

The out-of-band service point is the site system role that serves as the management interface between Configuration Manager and client systems that are operating with Intel's Active Management Technology (AMT) vPro chipset, a technology available in workstation-class systems.

Intel is the first hardware vendor to provide direct hardware interactions to leverage Windows Remote Management capabilities. These capabilities include remote boot control, forced PXE boots, remote network boots, and direct inspection of the hardware inventory and power state. AMT is even able to wake a machine from sleep state if needed! A goal of this technology is to empower full system management without the expense of desktop visits. These capabilities become very attractive when addressing geographically dispersed branch offices where there is little or no support staff to physically remediate workstations. Since Configuration Manager is the world-class systems management suite, the inclusion of AMT as a capability just makes sense.

Before a system is able to be managed it must be *provisioned*. In Configuration Manager 2007, a provisioning process known as out-of-band provision was supported, a process that allowed a workstation to be configured even without an installed operating system. Configuration Manager 2012 supports in-band provisioning only—meaning that a Configuration Manager 2012 client needs to be installed and assigned to a site. Provisioning also requires the use of certificates. The out-of-band service point is the focus of activity during provisioning because it connects to and interacts with AMT-capable systems.

Setting up Configuration Manager/AMT integration and management requires several steps. One of the first steps in the process is to install an out-of-band service point.
One out-of-band service point will be needed at each primary site that provides AMT management. If the role has not yet been added, you will need to select it in the Add Site System Roles Wizard.

1. Choose the site where the out-of-band service point will be located, and select the service point in the Add Site System Roles Wizard.

2. Click Next to proceed to the AMT Service Point page of the wizard, shown in Figure 4.58.

FIGURE 4.58

Add Site System
Roles Wizard: AMT
Service Point page

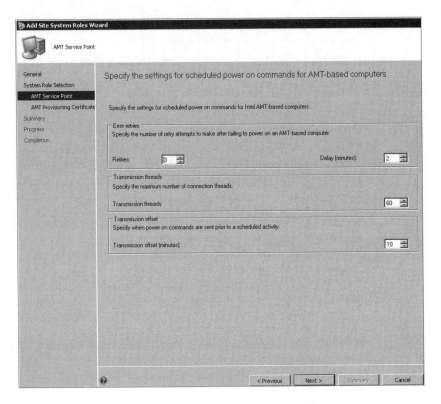

3. On the AMT Service Point page, configure the number of retry attempts that should be made, along with the delay between retries, when attempting to connect to an unresponsive AMT system.

   You can also specify the maximum number of transmission threads between the out-of-band service point and AMT-equipped systems on this page. If AMT is heavily utilized, it may be appropriate to change the default settings. If you make changes, however, take care to ensure the performance of the host system is not adversely affected.

   The transmission offset is the last setting on this page and defines how long before any scheduled activity, such as scheduled software distribution, an AMT system wake-up command should be sent. This is an important feature of AMT and should be considered along with Configuration Manager Wake On LAN capabilities.

4. Adjust configurations as needed, and click Next to proceed to the AMT Provisioning Certificate page, shown in Figure 4.59.

Figure 4.59

Add Site System
Roles Wizard:
AMT Provisioning
Certificate page

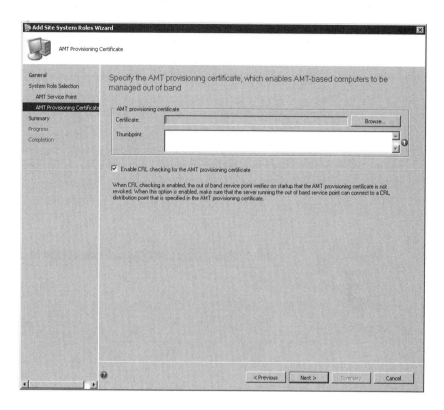

5. On the AMT Provisioning Certificate page, browse to the provisioning certificate that will
be used and import it.

A provisioning certificate will be used for validation when connecting to AMT-enabled
systems and initializing the provisioning process.

6. Choose whether to enable CRL checking for the AMT provisioning certificate, and then
click Next.

Configuration Manager 2012 out-of-band service points require that all site servers must be
members of a Windows 2003 or Windows 2008 Active Directory domain.

Reporting Services Point

The Reporting Services point provides integration between Configuration Manager and SQL
Server Reporting Services (SSRS) to facilitate report publishing and rendering. This is a big
change in Configuration Manager 2012; the reporting engine available in previous versions
of Configuration Manager, classic reporting, is gone. SSRS integration was first introduced in
Configuration Manager 2007 R2 and was available in parallel to classic reporting, providing customers time to adjust to the new (and long overdue!) approach to reporting.

SSRS integration just makes sense. Most people don't enjoy reading through line after line of tabular reports and would prefer to encapsulate that same data in a graphical format. SSRS can handle most any reporting scenario with ease.

If the SSRS role has not yet been added, you will need to select it in the Add Site System Roles Wizard.

1. Choose the site and server where the Reporting Services point will be located.

   If a Central Administration Site is in place, then it is a good choice as a site to host this site system role. It is also possible to install this role on a primary site or to install it in multiple locations. Which options you choose depends on the overall configuration of the hierarchy and reporting needs.

2. Select the role in the Add Site System Roles Wizard. Click Next to proceed to the Reporting Service Point page of the wizard, shown in Figure 4.60.

FIGURE 4.60
Add Site System Roles Wizard: Reporting Services Point page

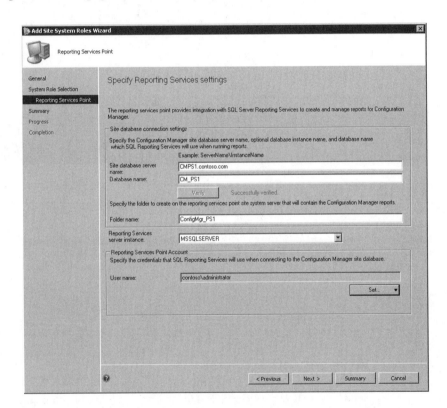

3. On the Reporting Services Point page, provide the server name that is hosting the Configuration Manager database instance and also the database name.

   The server listed here can be the same server hosting the Reporting Services server instance or a remote server.

4. Click Verify to confirm connectivity.

5. Then configure the reporting server component by providing the folder name where the reports will be stored along with the specific SQL Server instance hosting the Reporting Services and the authentication method that will be used for security validation.

Note that for this section there is no option to specify a server name because it is assumed the site system where the role is being configured is the server hosting the SSRS instance.

6. Once these configurations are complete, click Next.

SOFTWARE REQUIREMENTS

The Configuration Manager 2012 Reporting Services point requires that all site servers be members of a Windows 2003 or Windows 2008 Active Directory domain.

TROUBLESHOOTING THE REPORTING SERVICES POINT

The reporting services point is the reporting engine for Configuration Manager 2012 and is a key role for most users. Ensuring this role installs and functions correctly is also critical. To provide insight into the proper configuration for this role the component status is available in the Monitoring node of the console and also by reviewing associated log files.

srsrpsetup.log   This log tracks the setup status of the reporting point.

srsrpMSI   This log provides detail status of the reporting point setup process.

srsrp.log   This log tracks ongoing operational health of the reporting point.

Application Catalog Web Service Point and Application Catalog Website Point

A significant change in Configuration Manager 2012 is its user-centric focus. One component of user-centric focus, and a feature that has been much anticipated, is the ability for users to browse a web page–hosted catalog of published applications available for installation in the environment. These published applications may either be available without restriction to users or configured to require administrative approval prior to installation. Only software deployed to users will appear in the Application Catalog.

Two site system roles work in tandem to provide the Application Catalog service: the Application Catalog Web Service Point and the Application Catalog Website Point. At first glance, the difference between these two site system roles may not be apparent.

Application Catalog Website Point   The Application Catalog Website Point is the site system providing the software catalog service to users.

Application Catalog Web Service Point   The Application Catalog Web Service Point is the site system role that serves as a connection point between the Application Catalog Web Service Point site systems and the Configuration Manager site, providing software information to the website for presentation to users.

ABOUT THE EXAMPLE

For the example, both the Application Catalog Web Service Point and Application Catalog Website Point are presented together. It should not be implied, however, that these site system roles will necessarily be configured on the same server in all cases. While both site system roles are required to facilitate software catalog services, they are not required to be configured together.

If the Application Catalog Website Point and Application Catalog Web Service Point roles have not yet been added, you will need to select them in the Add Site System Roles Wizard, as shown in Figure 4.61.

FIGURE 4.61
Add Site System
Roles Wizard:
Application Catalog
Website Point and
Application Catalog
Web Service Point
selected

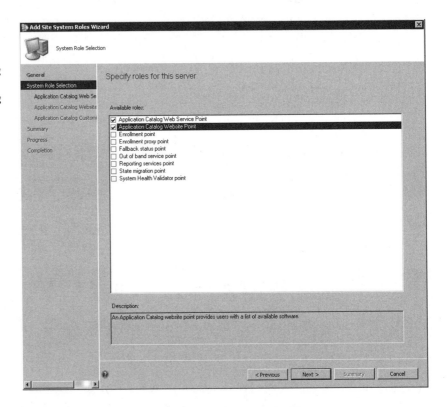

1. Choose the site and server where the Application Catalog Website Point and Application Catalog Web Service Point will be located.

   The exact servers chosen depend on the overall configuration of the hierarchy and mobile management needs.

2. Select the roles in the Add Site System Roles Wizard. Note that the order of the next couple of figures could be different depending on how you choose to install the roles. The net result is the same.

3. Click Next to proceed to the Application Catalog Website Point page of the wizard, as shown in Figure 4.62.

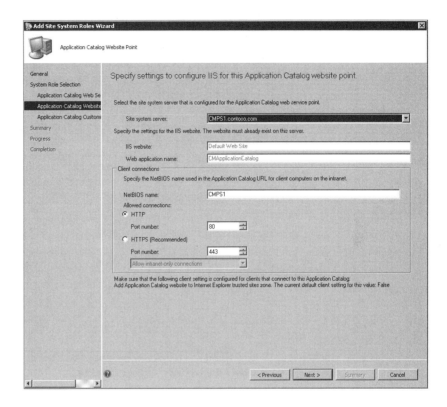

4. On the Application Catalog Website Point page, configure the name for the website to be used.

Also note the web service URL suggested. If the name of the web application is modified on the Application Catalog Web Service Point page, this URL will need to be modified accordingly.

5. Also on this page, choose whether the website will support HTTP or HTTPS traffic and, if HTTPS is selected, whether the website will allow only intranet-connected clients or also allow Internet-connected clients.

Supporting Internet clients requires the use of certificates. In addition, if mobile devices will be supported in the environment, enabling the website to support HTTPS-connected clients is required.

6. Include an organization name to be displayed to users, and also note the warning that the setting to add the default application catalog website to the trusted sites zone is not enabled.

7. Once all configuration is complete, click Next to proceed to the Application Catalog Web Service Point page, as shown in Figure 4.63.

FIGURE 4.63
Add Site System
Roles Wizard:
Application Catalog
Web Service Point
page

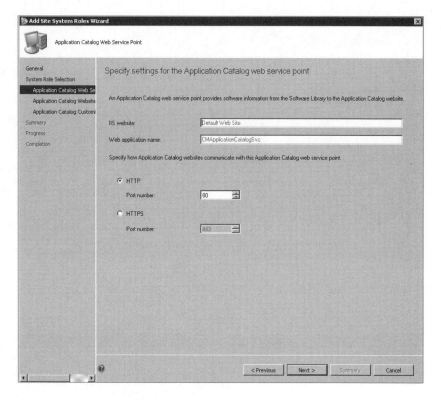

1. On the Application Catalog Web Service Point page, configure the name for the website to be used and whether the website will support SSL.

2. Once all configuration is complete, click Next to proceed to the Application Catalog Customizations page. Here administrators are able to provide some minor customization as to the presentation of the catalog (organization name and website theme). Make any modifications desired and click Next to complete the wizard.

SOFTWARE REQUIREMENTS

The Configuration Manager 2012 Application Catalog Website Point and Application Catalog Web Service Point require the following:

◆ All site servers must be members of a Windows 2003 or Windows 2008 Active Directory domain.

◆ .NET 4.0 must be installed.

TROUBLESHOOTING THE APPLICATION CATALOG WEBSITE POINT AND APPLICATION CATALOG WEB SERVICE POINT

The Application catalog roles are key interfaces to enable user self-provisioning of content. Thus, ensuring these roles are functional is critical. As with all roles, the Monitoring node of the console can provide insight into overall health. In addition, log files are useful to track ongoing operation as well.

smsawebsvcsetup.log   log to track installation of application web service.

smsportwebsetup.log   log to track installation of application web portal.

awebsvcMSI   detailed MSI log to track installation of application web service.

portalwebMSI   detailed MSI log to track installation of application web portal.

awebsctrl.log   This log tracks the ongoing operation of the application web service.

portlctl.log   This log tracks ongoing operation of the application web portal.

Enrollment Proxy Point and Mobile Device and AMT Enrollment Point

Mobile devices have become commonplace in IT environments. With the increase in device number and increasing power and function of these devices, providing management capabilities in the enterprise is becoming more of a focal point for administrators. Configuration Manager 2012 provides two types of management for mobile devices: lite management and depth management.

Lite Management   Lite management is provided to any device that is capable of interfacing with Exchange through the ActiveSync connector. Such devices include Windows Phone 7 and iPhone and Android devices. Configuration Manager 2012 provides an Exchange connector that works with Exchange ActiveSync–connected devices and facilitates settings management, general inventory, and remote wipe capabilities.

Depth Management   Depth management is available for legacy Windows phone platforms, such as Windows Mobile 6.1 and 6.5 as well as Nokia Symbian devices, and allows for a more robust management experience, including the ability to install a native Configuration Manager 2012 client on a device. Depth-managed devices provide all of the features of lite management (though not through Exchange ActiveSync) but also include support for software distribution and over-the-air enrollment. Further, inventory options available for depth-managed clients are more extensive and flexible than those provided through lite management.

Depth-managed devices require a client to be installed, along with certificates to provide access to the various Configuration Manager 2012 systems. Once the client is installed, the device acts similar to a PC, looking up and making use of management points for retrieving policy, sending data such as inventory, and also making use of distribution points for software deployments.

SITE SYSTEMS AND MOBILE DEVICES

Site systems that will interact with mobile devices must be configured to support HTTPS communication. Mobile devices use certificates for authentication and must be able to use these certificates to validate against management points and distribution points (and optionally, Application Catalog servers).

The process of placing the client and certificates on the mobile device, known as enrollment, requires the use of two site system roles: the mobile device enrollment proxy point and the mobile device and AMT enrollment point. These site systems work in tandem to facilitate enrollment, provisioning, and management of mobile devices. At first glance, the difference between these two site system roles may not be apparent.

Mobile Device Enrollment Proxy Point   This is the site system role typically placed in the DMZ and is the initial point of communication for devices. It is also the location where mobile devices find and download the mobile version of the Configuration Manager client. Once the client is installed, and as a part of enrollment, the mobile device enrollment proxy point will communicate with the mobile device and AMT enrollment point, typically located inside the protected network, to retrieve needed certificates and present them to the device being enrolled.

Configuring multiple mobile device enrollment proxy points at a single site to support multiple DMZ configurations is supported.

Mobile Device and AMT Enrollment Point   This is a site system role typically installed inside the protected network, and it serves as an interface between the mobile device enrollment proxy point and the Enterprise Certificate Authority as certificate requests are presented from mobile devices and generated certificates are sent back to mobile devices.

Certificates are also required for provisioning AMT-capable devices. This site system role also serves as the interface between AMT devices requesting certificates and the Enterprise Certificate Authority.

TIDBITS ABOUT SITE SYSTEM ROLES

It is *not* required that these site system roles exist on the same site system server. If you're using lite management of mobile devices, neither of these site system roles is required.

ABOUT THE EXAMPLE

For the example, the mobile device enrollment proxy point and mobile device and AMT enrollment point are presented together. It should not be implied, however, that these site system roles will necessarily be configured on the same server in all cases. While both site system roles are required to facilitate depth management of mobile devices, they are not required to be configured together.

If the mobile device enrollment proxy point or the mobile device and AMT enrollment point roles have not yet been added, you will need to select them in the Add Site System Roles Wizard.

1. Choose the site and server where the mobile device enrollment proxy point and mobile device and AMT enrollment point will be located.

   The exact servers chosen depend on the overall configuration of the hierarchy and mobile management needs.

2. Select the roles in the Add Site System Roles Wizard. Note, the order in which the next pages of the wizard are presented may differ depending on configuration. Click Next to proceed to the Enrollment Proxy Point page of the wizard.

3. On the Enrollment Proxy Point page, configure the name for the website to be used, as shown in Figure 4.64.

FIGURE 4.64
Add Site System
Roles Wizard:
Mobile Device
Enrollment Proxy
Point page

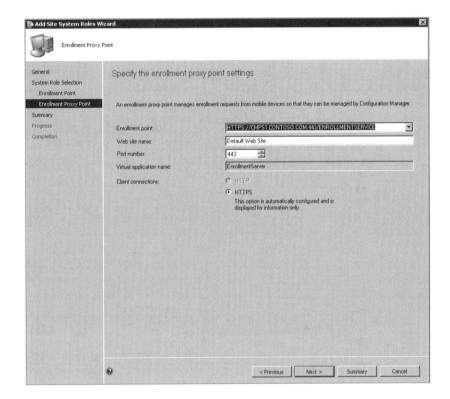

Note that the website must support SSL communication and that a default URL pointing to the mobile device and AMT enrollment point is already present. This URL is configurable and will need to point to whichever location is chosen to host the mobile device and AMT enrollment point role. Note also that the end of the URL refers to the EnrollmentService virtual directory. This is the default name. If a non-default name is chosen for the virtual directory, the URL will need to match accordingly.

Note also that there is a virtual application name listed on the current page that is similar in name. Don't be confused by the similarity; the virtual directory name here is the one used to configure the mobile device enrollment proxy point and is not changeable.

4. Once all configuration is complete, click Next to proceed to the Enrollment Point page, shown in Figure 4.65.

FIGURE 4.65
Add Site System
Roles Wizard:
Enrollment
Point page

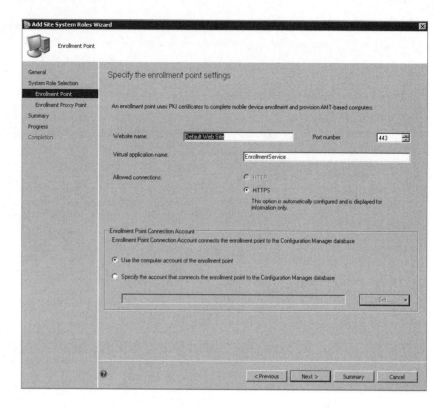

5. On the Mobile Device and AMT Enrollment Point Settings page, configure the name for the website to be used.

   If you make any changes, then the virtual directory name in the URL configured for the mobile device enrollment proxy point must be updated as well. You can also specify which account will be used for database communication. Of the two site system roles, this is the only one that needs to access the database directly.

6. Once all configuration is complete, click Next.

SOFTWARE REQUIREMENTS

The Configuration Manager 2012 mobile device enrollment proxy point and mobile device and AMT enrollment point require that all site servers must be members of a Windows 2003 or Windows 2008 Active Directory domain.

TROUBLESHOOTING THE ENROLLMENT PROXY POINT AND ENROLLMENT POINT

Enrollment points are the key roles to enable mobile devices and AMT-enabled systems entrance into the ConfigMgr world. To provide insights into the proper configuration of this role, the component status is available in the monitoring node of the console and also by reviewing the following logs:

Smsenrollwebsetup.log   This log tracks the installation of the enrollment web proxy point.

Smsenrollsrvsetup.log   This log tracks the installation of the enrollment web point.

Enrollwebmsi   This log tracks the installation of the enrollment web proxy point in detail.

Enrollsrvmsi This log tracks the installation of the enrollment web service point in detail.

Enrollweb.log This log tracks the ongoing operation of the enrollment web point.

Enrollsvc.log This log tracks the ongoing operation of the enrollment web proxy point.

Click Next to proceed to the Summary page of the Add Site System Roles Wizard. Review the settings. If all are correct, click Next to proceed with installation and to finish the wizard.

Software Update Point

The Software Update Point role is integral to the software update mechanism and is responsible for synchronizing all patches from Microsoft Update and making them available in the Configuration Manager 2012 interface for deployment. The Software Update Point requires that Windows Software Update Services 3.0 SP2 be installed on the same server where the Software Update Point is being installed and requires that the instance of WSUS be dedicated to interfacing with the Software Update Point and providing service to Configuration Manager. No sharing allowed! Also, administrators should not perform any administrative work on the WSUS server itself. All administrative work should be applied through the Configuration Manager console and you will find that the options available in the Configuration Manager console are very similar to what is found in WSUS itself.

If the software Update Point has not yet been added, you will need to select it in the Add Site System Roles Wizard as shown in Figure 4.66.

FIGURE 4.66
Add Site System Roles Wizard: System Role Selection Page with Software Update Point selected

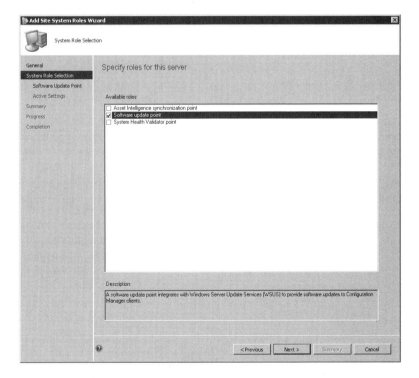

1. Choose the server where the WSUS component is installed.

2. Select the role in the Add Site System Roles Wizard.

3. Click Next to proceed to the Software Update Point page of the wizard.

4. On the Software Update Point page of the wizard, configure whether a proxy server should be used when synchronizing software updates and also whether a proxy server should be used when downloading content with Auto Deployment Rules. If a proxy server is needed, supply the needed information for the proxy server. This is shown in Figure 4.67.

FIGURE 4.67
Add Site System
Roles Wizard:
Software Update
Point page

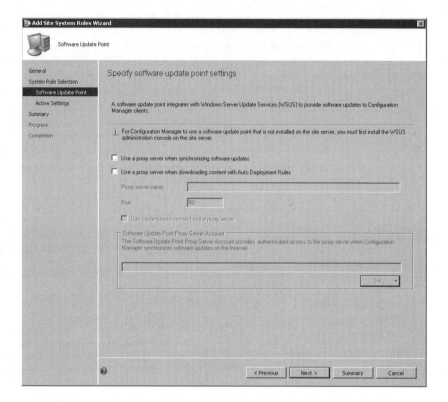

5. Once all configuration is complete, click Next to proceed to the Active Settings page. Here, choose whether or not this software update point is the active software update point. If software update services will be used in Configuration Manager, an active Software Update point is required. Note that a single software update point on properly sized hardware is capable of supporting 100,000 clients in Configuration Manager 2012. If this Software Update Point will be active, decide whether it should be installed to the default website on the associated IIS server or the ConfigMgr custom website. Setting to use a custom website causes Configuration Manager 2012 to look for a website named SMSWEB to be used in place of the default web site.

6. Once all configuration is compete and if this Software Update Point has been configured as active, click Next to proceed to the Synchronization Source page shown in Figure 4.68.

FIGURE 4.68
Add Site System
Roles Wizard:
Synchronization
Source page

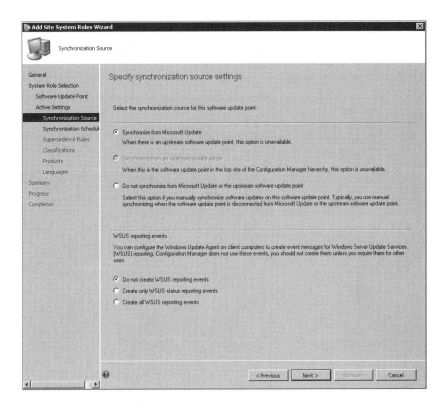

7. On the Synchronization Source page, configure the location that the software update point will use for obtaining update information. Typically this setting will be to Synchronize with Microsoft Updates from the Internet.

   If this software update point is installed at a child site in a hierarchy, then the option to choose here will be to Synchronize from an upstream update point. In this case the CAS would host the top level software update point and the primary site would synchronize from it.

   If the software update point is on the CAS and the CAS does not have access to the Internet, then it's possible to synchronize manually. If this is the case choose the option "Do not synchronize from Microsoft Update or the upstream software update point."

8. On the WSUS reporting event section choose whether or not to create any or all WSUS reporting events.

9. Once all configuration is compete, click Next to proceed to the Synchronization Schedule page. Choose whether or not synchronization should proceed on a schedule. It is not required that the Software Update point be configured to synchronize automatically, but in most environments it is. The schedule is up to you; just remember that Microsoft publishes new patches the second Tuesday of every month and from time to time will have out-of-band patch releases. If you are using EndPoint protection in Configuration Manager, it is recommended to perform synchronization no less than daily.

10. If you would like an alert when synchronization fails (a good idea), select that option as well.

11. Once all configuration is complete, click Next to proceed to the Supersedence Rules page shown in Figure 4.69.

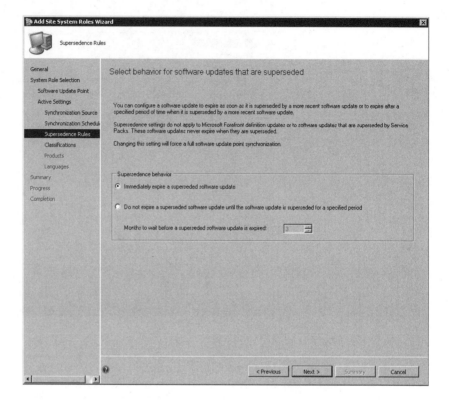

12. On the Supersedence Rules page, choose the behavior that happens when a new update is available and synchronized that replaces an existing update. This option is new to Configuration Manager 2012. The first option, "Immediately expire a superseded software update," is the default and this was the only option in Configuration Manager 2007. This option caused frustration in many environments—not because an update was superseded, but because the action of superseding also caused an update to be expired. When an update is expired it can no longer be deployed. While it is a good idea to stop deploying a superseded update when it has been replaced, the truth is that testing cycles in many environments do not allow for this kind of rapid change easily. For that reason, the second choice ("Months to wait before a superseded software update is expired") was made available in Configuration Manager 2012. Note that the superseded update is still superseded, it just isn't expired and can still be deployed.

13. Once all configuration is complete, click Next to proceed to the Classifications page shown in Figure 4.70.

FIGURE 4.70
Add Site System
Roles Wizard:
Classifications page

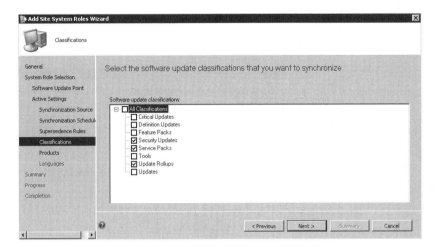

14. On the Classifications page, choose the classifications of updates that should be retrieved from Microsoft Update and made available in Configuration Manager 2012 for deployment.

15. Once all configuration is complete, click Next to proceed to the Products page shown in Figure 4.71.

FIGURE 4.71
Add Site System
Roles Wizard:
Products page

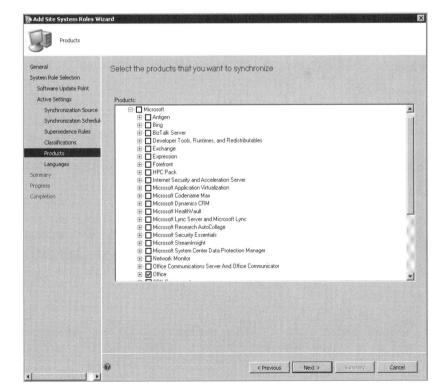

16. On the Products page, choose the products or product families that should be included when retrieving updates from the categories just configured. The expanded list is shown in the figure.

17. Once all configuration is complete, click Next to proceed to the Languages page. Here, choose all languages that are in use in an environment. This will ensure the appropriate language-specific patches are included during synchronization as well.

18. Once all configuration is complete, click Next and proceed through the remaining wizard pages to complete configuration.

SOFTWARE REQUIREMENTS

The Configuration Manager 2012 Software Update point requires that all site servers must be members of a Windows 2003 or Windows 2008 Active Directory domain. In addition, the Software Update Point requires WSUS 3.0 SP2 and Internet Information Services to be installed.

TROUBLESHOOTING THE SOFTWARE UPDATE POINT

The proper installation of the Software Update Point is key to delivering updates through Configuration Manager 2012 in your environment. To provide insights into the proper configuration of this role, the component status is available in the monitoring node of the console and also by reviewing the following logs:

Supsetup.log   This log tracks the installation of the Software Update Point.

WCM.log   This log tracks connections to the WSUS server for subscribed update categories, languages, and classifications.

WSUSCtrl.log   This log tracks connectivity to the database and the general health of WSUS for the site.

WSYNCMGR.log   This log records all synchronization operations for the site.

EndPoint Protection Point

If you will be using Configuration Manager 2012 for EndPoint protection services then you must install the EndPoint Protection Point role. This role is only available at the CAS and requires that separate licensing be in place. Installing this role is very easy and simply enables the use of EndPoint protection in the hierarchy.

If the EndPoint Protection Point has not yet been added you will need to select it in the Add Site System Roles Wizard.

1. Choose the server where the EndPoint Protection Point will be located.

2. Select the role in the Add Site System Roles Wizard. Note that when you attempt to place a check mark in the role, you will see a popup notifying you of default configurations that will be set.

3. On the EndPoint Protection page, accept the license agreement.

4. Once all configuration is complete, click Next to proceed to the Microsoft Active Protection Service page shown in Figure 4.72.

FIGURE 4.72

Add Site System
Roles Wizard:
Microsoft Active
Protection
Service page

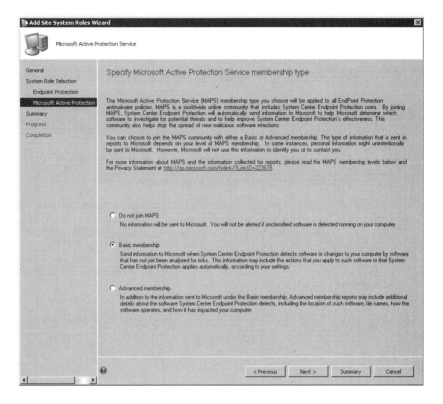

5. On the Microsoft Active Protection Service page, read the description of the Active Protection Service membership and choose what type of membership you would like, if any.

6. Once all configuration is complete, click Next through the wizard to complete installation.

SOFTWARE REQUIREMENTS

The Configuration Manager 2012 Software Update point requires that all site servers must be members of a Windows 2003 or Windows 2008 Active Directory domain.

TROUBLESHOOTING THE ENDPOINT PROTECTION POINT

The proper installation of the EndPoint Protection Point is key to managing malware and firewall settings through Configuration Manager 2012 in your environment. To provide insights into the proper configuration of this role, the component status is available in the monitoring node of the console and also by reviewing the following logs:

EPsetup.log This log tracks the installation of the EndPoint Protection Point.

EPCtrlmgr.log This log details the synchronization of malware threat information from the EndPoint Protection role server to the Configuration Manager 2012 database.

EPMgr.log This log monitors the status of the EndPoint Protection site system role.

Asset Intelligence Synchronization Point

If you will be using Configuration Manager 2012 for Asset Intelligence Information, then you will likely want to install the Asset Intelligence Synchronization Point role. This role is only available at the CAS and is not required but is beneficial. Installing this role enables synchronizing of catalog updates from the Internet and also allows you to upload custom catalog requests and categorization information to Microsoft.

If the Asset Intelligence Synchronization Point has not yet been added, you will need to select it in the Add Site System Roles Wizard.

1. Choose the server where the Asset Intelligence Synchronization Point will be located.

2. Select the role in the Add Site System Roles Wizard.

3. On the Asset Intelligence Synchronization Point Settings page, select whether to use this system as the active system and, if you have a certificate, the UNC path where it can be found. Note that the use of a certificate is not required. This is shown in Figure 4.73.

FIGURE 4.73
Add Site System
Roles Wizard:
Asset Intelligence
Synchronization
Point Settings page

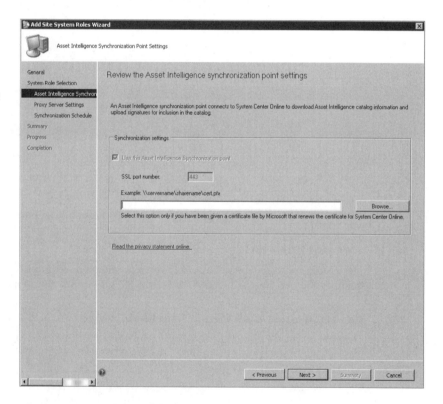

4. Once all configuration is complete, click Next to proceed to the Proxy Server Settings page. On the Proxy Server Settings page, select to add a proxy server if needed and supply any related configuration information.

5. Once all configuration is complete, click Next to proceed the Synchronization Schedule page. Here, configure the schedule you would like to use for synchronizing the catalog and also sending your update requests for the catalog to Microsoft. Typically, the default schedule is appropriate.

6. Once all configuration is complete, click Next through the wizard to complete installation.

SOFTWARE REQUIREMENTS

The Configuration Manager 2012 Software Update point requires that all site servers must be members of a Windows 2003 or Windows 2008 Active Directory domain.

TROUBLESHOOTING THE ASSET INTELLIGENCE SYNCHRONIZATION POINT

The proper installation of the Asset Intelligence Synchronization Point is key to keeping your Asset Intelligence catalog up to date for use in Configuration Manager 2012. This is also critical to communicate your requested updates to the catalog to Microsoft. To provide insights into the proper configuration of this role, the component status is available in the monitoring node of the console and also by reviewing the following logs:

AIUSsetup.log   This log tracks the installation of the Asset Intelligence Synchronization Point.

AIUSMSI.log   This log tracks the specific MSI installation process detail for the Asset Intelligence Synchronization Point.

AIUpdateSvc.log   This log tracks the ongoing operation of the Asset Intelligence Synchronization Point.

The Bottom Line

Understand Configuration Manager 2012 sites and the new approach to hierarchy design.   Configuration Manager 2012 has three types of sites: the Central Administration Site, which is new, and the primary and secondary sites, which are familiar. Although two of the three site types are familiar, their use and approach to hierarchy design—or whether a hierarchy is needed at all—are quite different now.

Master It   Describe the purpose of each site type and map each to specific management needs.

Construct a Configuration Manager 2012 hierarchy.   The site hierarchy in Configuration Manager 2012 consists of the site types just described. The approach to design is very different from the previous version, with the number of primary sites being limited to a single tier. The chapter walked through configuring a hierarchy with all three site types.

Master It   Describe a Configuration Manager 2012 site hierarchy. Detail components needed for site-to-site communication and security settings.

Determine when to expand a hierarchy and when to simply add a site system role for additional service.   A major design goal of Configuration Manager 2012 is simplified hierarchy design. Administrators familiar with previous versions of Configuration Manager may be tempted to retain old hierarchy approaches when designing Configuration Manager 2012. Taking such an approach will often lead to inefficient designs and additional server cost and in some cases simply won't work.

Master It   Understand the changes in sites and site components that lend themselves to hierarchy simplification and enable parity management with fewer site servers.

Deploy and configure the various site system roles available per site.   There are many roles available to enable management at a site. Understanding each role and the service it delivers is critical to getting the most out of an investment in Configuration Manager 2012.

Master It   Review critical system roles and understand the services that are enabled through each.

Chapter 5

Role-Based Administration

Ask a System Center Configuration Manager administrator about one of the more challenging aspects of administering ConfigMgr in their environment, and they might answer "Security!" The class and instance model that was used in SMS and ConfigMgr 2007 to assign users varying levels of access and privileges was somewhat cumbersome and confusing.

System Center Operations Manager 2007 introduced the concept of role-based security administration to the System Center suite. Under the Role-Based Access Control (RBAC) model, administrators are able to use security roles and security scopes to define access to resources for the administrative users in the environment. System Center 2012 Configuration Manager adopts the RBAC security model and, as a result, greatly simplifies the administration of security in ConfigMgr 2012.

In this chapter you will learn to

◆ Understand the role-based administration model in ConfigMgr 2012.

◆ Distinguish security roles from security scopes.

◆ Understand which objects in ConfigMgr 2012 define an administrative user.

Overview of Role-Based Administration

Configuration Manager 2012 uses the Role-Based Access Control model to define access to ConfigMgr features and functions. Under the RBAC model, the ConfigMgr 2012 administrator uses security roles, security scopes, and collections to define the administrative scope for the ConfigMgr administrative users. This provides the ConfigMgr administrator with the ability to define the security configuration for an administrative user in such a way that the only features of ConfigMgr 2012 that the user is able to view and interact with in the console are those that are part of their responsibility. All other items are essentially hidden and not available to the administrative user. This behavior is sometimes referred to as "Show Me" behavior.

For example, consider a help desk analyst who needs the ability to deploy an application to computers in one geographic location but should not have the ability to deploy applications to computers in any other locations. Using the role-based administration model, the ConfigMgr administrator could easily create security roles, security scopes, and collections to satisfy those requirements. We will take a look at a sample scenario later.

Using Security Roles and Security Scopes

Security roles are used to organize tasks or functions, while security scopes are used to define access to objects. ConfigMgr 2012 provides some default roles and scopes, and the ConfigMgr administrator can also create their own to meet specific business needs. By using combinations of security roles, security scopes, and collections, the ConfigMgr administrator can easily control access to the environment and define what the ConfigMgr administrative users can view and manage.

As stated previously, this is sometimes referred to as "Show Me" behavior and basically means that the administrative user will only see what is relevant to them and what they have access to in the ConfigMgr 2012 console. Console objects that the administrative user has access to are visible in the console, while all others are hidden. This greatly simplifies the console experience for the administrative user and helps reduce confusion.

Managing with Flat Hierarchies

One of the design goals for ConfigMgr 2012 is that organizations should have flat ConfigMgr 2012 hierarchies. In fact, many companies may find they need only a single ConfigMgr primary site (and possibly a Central Administration Site) to manage the entire enterprise. One common reason for multiple SMS or ConfigMgr sites in previous versions of the product was to completely segregate the environment based on roles or functions. For example, one ConfigMgr 2007 primary site may manage only desktops and laptops, while another ConfigMgr 2007 primary site may manage only servers. Separating the sites completely ensured that the administrators for the desktop and laptop site could not manage the servers in any way and vice versa.

With the ability to designate control based on security roles, security scopes, and collections in ConfigMgr 2012, segregating the environment through the use of multiple primary sites is unnecessary. In ConfigMgr 2012, the ConfigMgr administrator could have all devices report to a single primary site and then use role-based security to define the required access for the administrative users. The desktop support team could be configured to see and manage only desktop computers, and the server team could be configured to see and manage only servers. Another benefit of the new security model in ConfigMgr 2012 is that the administrative objects (security roles, security scopes, and collections) need to be created only once in the ConfigMgr 2012 hierarchy because that information is sent throughout the hierarchy as globally replicated data.

Security Roles

ConfigMgr 2012 uses security roles to define access to resources for administrative users. Security roles can be configured to provide administrative users with as much or as little access as they need in ConfigMgr to perform their job.

ConfigMgr 2012 includes several built-in security roles that handle many common ConfigMgr administrative task scenarios. Figure 5.1 shows the security roles that are included in ConfigMgr 2012. The following list provides a brief description of the built-in roles:

FIGURE 5.1
Built-in security roles

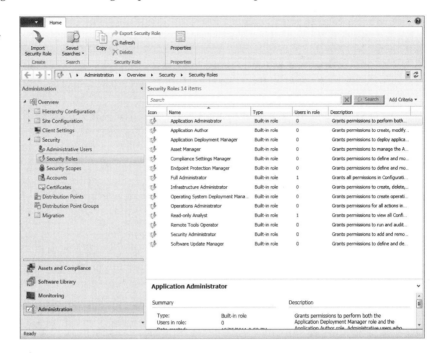

Application Administrator This role provides the permissions to perform both the application Deployment Manager role and the Application Author role. This role also provides the ability to manage queries, view site settings, manage collections, and edit settings for user device affinity.

Application Author This role provides the ability to create, modify, and delete applications. This role also provides the ability to manage packages and programs, manage alerts, and also view status messages.

Application Deployment Manager This role provides the ability to distribute applications. Application deployment managers can view the list of applications and can manage other items related to applications, including alerts, templates, packages, and programs. They can view collections and collection membership and can also view status messages, queries, and conditional delivery rules.

Asset Manager This role provides the ability to manage the Asset Intelligence synchronization point, the Asset Intelligence reporting classes, hardware and software inventory, and software metering settings.

Compliance Settings Manager This role provides permissions to manage the Compliance Settings feature. Compliance Settings managers can create, modify, and delete configuration items and baselines. They can also deploy configuration baselines to collections, initiate compliance evaluation, and initiate remediation for noncompliant computers.

Endpoint Protection Manager   This role provides the ability to manage and monitor Endpoint Protection security policies. Administrative users with this role can create, modify, and delete Endpoint Protection policies. They can also deploy Endpoint Protection policies to collections, create and modify alerts, and monitor Endpoint Protection status.

Full Administrator   This role provides access to all objects. The administrator who installs ConfigMgr 2012 is automatically granted this security role.

Infrastructure Administrator   This role allows the administrative user to create, delete, and modify the Configuration Manager server infrastructure and also provides access to the site migration tasks.

Operating System Deployment Manager   This role provides the ability to create operating system images and to deploy them to computers. Administrative users with this role can manage many aspects of the operating system deployment process, including the operating system installation packages and images, task sequences, drivers, boot images, and state migration settings.

Operations Administrator   This role provides permissions for all actions in ConfigMgr 2012 except for the ability to manage security (managing administrative users, security roles, collections, and security scopes).

Read-only Analyst   This role provides the ability to read all objects in ConfigMgr 2012.

Remote Tools Operator   This role grants permissions to run and audit the remote administration tools. Administrative users with this role can use the ConfigMgr console to run the out-of-band management console and can use remote control, Windows Remote Assistance, and Remote Desktop Services.

Security Administrator   This role provides the ability to add and remove administrative users and to associate administrative users with security roles, collections, and security scopes.

Software Update Manager   This role provides ability to define and deploy software updates. Administrative users with this role can create collections, software update groups, deployments, and templates and can enable software updates for Network Access Protection.

FULL ADMINISTRATOR? OH MY!

As shown in the list, the Full Administrator role in ConfigMgr 2012 provides access to all objects in the environment. Users (or groups) who are assigned to this security role hold all the keys to all of the castles in the ConfigMgr 2012 environment. As a result, the number of users or groups who have this security role should be *very* limited. Because of the power that this role holds, the fewer the administrative users who have this role the better! Also, the organization should periodically review the access requirements for administrative users who hold this role and determine if they can be provided with a less-powerful security role.

As you can see in the preceding list, each security role provides specific permissions for various object types. If you want to see the permissions that a specific security role holds, you can view that information in the ConfigMgr 2012 console. For example, if you wanted to examine the permissions for the Application Administrator role, you would perform the following steps:

1. In the Configuration Manager administrative console, select Administration ➢ Security ➢ Security Roles.

2. Select the role that you want to inspect. In this case it is the Application Administrator role.

3. Click Properties in the Ribbon.

   This will open the Application Administrator Properties window.

4. Select the Permissions tab.

5. Now you can view the permissions for the role (Figure 5.2).

FIGURE 5.2
Application Administrator Properties

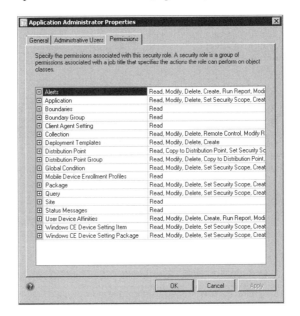

It is worth noting that you cannot change the permissions for the built-in security roles. You also cannot delete the built-in roles or export them. If you need to customize a built-in security role, then you should choose an existing role that is similar to the new role and make a copy of it. You will then have the ability to modify or delete the copied role. You can also export and import copied security roles. This import/export ability may be useful in a test or pilot ConfigMgr 2012 environment and would provide you with the ability to fine-tune the required security roles and permissions in the test site before deploying them to the production ConfigMgr 2012 site.

Also, if administrative users will perform multiple functions in ConfigMgr 2012 (such as deploy applications *and* use remote tools), the ConfigMgr administrator should assign multiple security roles to the administrative user instead of creating a new security role that combines a variety of tasks into a single role.

Security Scopes

ConfigMgr 2012 uses security scopes (Figure 5.3) to provide administrative users with access to secured objects. All secured objects must be assigned to at least one security scope. The association between the object and the security scope is managed from the object itself, not from the security scope.

FIGURE 5.3

Security scopes

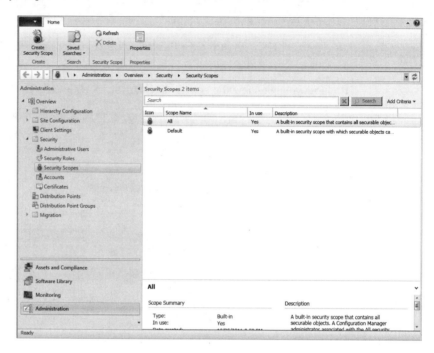

As shown in Figure 5.3, ConfigMgr 2012 includes two built-in security scopes: All and Default.

All The All security scope grants access to all scopes. Objects cannot be assigned to this security scope.

Default All objects are assigned to the All security scope when ConfigMgr 2012 is installed. As new objects are added to ConfigMgr 2012, they are also automatically added to the default scope.

The ConfigMgr administrator can also create custom security scopes that are based on the needs of the environment and add the objects to the custom scopes.

Creating a Custom Security Scope

The following are the steps to create a custom security scope:

1. In the Configuration Manager administrative console, select the Administration workspace ➢ Security ➢ Security Scopes.

2. In the Ribbon select Create Security Scope.

3. Provide a descriptive name for the security scope in the security scope Name field. In this case we will name our new scope Custom Security Scope.

You can add a description and make changes to the administrative assignments if needed.

4. Once the changes have been completed, click OK.

The new security scope should now be visible in the console, as shown in Figure 5.4.

FIGURE 5.4
New security scope

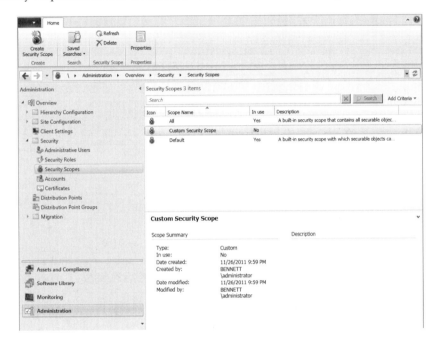

Security scopes can contain one or more object types, which include the following:

◆ Applications

◆ Packages

◆ Boot images

◆ Sites

◆ Custom client settings

◆ Distribution points and distribution point groups

◆ Software update groups

Several object types cannot be included in security scopes and must be secured via security roles. These objects include the following:

◆ Administrative users

◆ Security roles

◆ Security scopes

◆ Default client settings

◆ Boundaries

◆ Exchange Server connector

◆ Site addresses

◆ Active Directory forests

◆ Site system roles

Assigning Resources to a Security Scope

Now that you understand how to create a security scope and you know which object types can be included, we will assign a resource to the new security scope we just created.

1. In the Configuration Manager administrative console, select the resource that will be added to the Custom Security Scope we created previously.

   Remember that only certain types of objects can be added to security scopes.

2. For this example select the application called XML Notepad, which was previously configured.

3. Select Software Library ➢ Application Management ➢ Applications in the ConfigMgr 2012 console, and choose the application that you want to manage.

4. Now choose Classify in the Ribbon and then select Set Security Scopes.

   You could also right-click the application and select Set Security Scopes there.

5. In the Set Security Scopes window select the desired scope or scopes for this object and click OK.

   For this scenario we will select only our new security scope, which we named Custom Security Scope in the previous exercise.

The new security scope should now be visible in the console (Figure 5.5).

FIGURE 5.5
New security
scope and
application

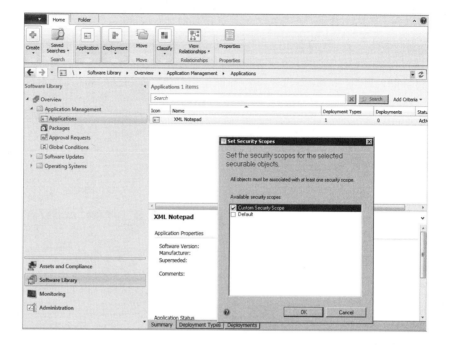

6. Once the setting is applied, view the security scope and see that the In Use value is now set to Yes, as shown in Figure 5.6.

FIGURE 5.6
New security
scope

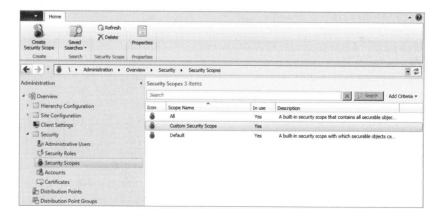

Viewing Security Scope Objects

If you want to view all of the objects that are associated with a given security scope, a built-in report in ConfigMgr 2012 will provide that information.

1. In the Configuration Manager administrative console choose Monitoring ➢ Overview ➢ Reporting ➢ Reports.

There are a few reports related to security scopes. The report we will run is titled "Objects Secured by a Single Security Scope."

2. Right-click the report and select Run.

You can have the report use all values for the Object Type field, but here just select the value for the Security Scope field. You can either select the Values option to have all known values for that field (security scopes in this case) listed or you can simply enter the desired value in the field.

3. For this scenario use Custom Security Scope because this was the name we gave the security scope when it was created.

4. Once the values have been set, click View Report (Figure 5.7).

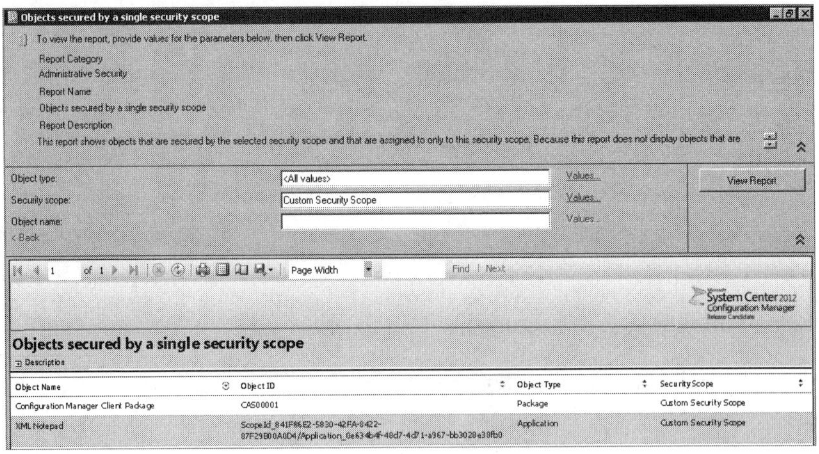

FIGURE 5.7
Objects Secured
By A Single
Security Scope
report

This report is designed to show objects that are secured by only the specified security scope, which is Custom Security Scope in this scenario. If an object is secured by two or more security scopes (the Custom Security Scope and the default security scope, for example), then the object will not be displayed in this report.

Collections

We have discussed how security roles and security scopes are used in the role-based administration model in ConfigMgr 2012. In order for an administrative user to perform functions (for example, deploy an application) on a resource, the user must have access to a collection that contains the resource. We can use collections, along with security roles and security scopes, to tightly control what objects in the ConfigMgr console an administrative user can access.

Collections are probably not a new concept to the SMS and ConfigMgr veterans reading this book, but there are some changes to how collections work in ConfigMgr 2012. This chapter does not perform an exhaustive examination of those changes, but it does highlight some of the changes and differences.

Using Collections

As a bit of background, collections are a way to logically group resources, such as devices or users, and collections can be created to meet various manageability and targeting requirements. The following are just a few examples:

◆ Use collections to separate servers from workstations or laptops.

◆ Use collections to separate pilot users or devices from production resources.

◆ Use collections based on departments, business units, or geographical location for targeting or administrative purposes.

Once the requirements for the collection have been defined and the collection has been created, the collection can be assigned to a ConfigMgr administrative user.

Collections in ConfigMgr 2012 contain one or more rules that control the membership of the collection. There are four rule types:

Direct Rule   This rule type allows the administrator to explicitly define the users or computers that should be members of the collection. The membership of this collection does not change unless the administrator removes the explicit entry in the collection properties or the resource is removed from ConfigMgr. You may think of this approach as hard-coding machine names into the collection membership properties.

Query Rule   This rule type dynamically updates the membership of the collection based on a query that is run on a schedule by ConfigMgr. ConfigMgr uses query-based collections for the built-in collections. Query-based collections are very useful because they routinely evaluate the specified criteria and identify matching devices or users.

Include Collections Rule   This new rule type allows the administrator to include members of another collection in a ConfigMgr collection. The membership of the current collection will be updated on a schedule when members of the included collection change.

Exclude Collections Rule   This is another new rule type, and it allows the administrator to exclude the members of another collection from a ConfigMgr collection. The membership of the current collection will be updated on a schedule when members of the collection change.

Understanding the Default Collections

ConfigMgr 2012 includes a number of default collections. Some of these can be modified if needed, but none can be deleted. The following are the default collections:

All User Groups   Contains user groups discovered during Active Directory Security Group Discovery.

All Users   Contains users discovered during Active Directory User Discovery.

All Users and User Groups   Contains the All Users and the All User Groups collections. This collection cannot be modified and contains the largest scope of user resources.

All Desktop and Server Clients   Contains server and desktop devices that have the ConfigMgr 2012 client installed. Membership is determined by Heartbeat Discovery.

All Mobile Devices Contains mobile devices that are managed by ConfigMgr 2012. Membership is restricted to mobile devices that are successfully assigned to a site or discovered by the Exchange Server connector.

All Systems Contains the All Desktop and Server Clients, the All Mobile Devices, and All Unknown Computers collections. This collection cannot be modified and contains the largest scope of device resources.

All Unknown Computers Contains generic computer records for multiple computer platforms. It's typically used to deploy an operating system via PXE boot, bootable media, or prestaged media.

For more information about collections, see `http://technet.microsoft.com/en-us/library/gg682169.aspx`.

Administrative Users

An *administrative user* is an individual or group that will manage resources in the ConfigMgr 2012 infrastructure. The administrative user may have very limited access to resources in the environment (for example, a help desk analyst who can only deploy Adobe Reader X to computers in a specific office location) or may have complete access to all objects in the ConfigMgr environment (the ConfigMgr administrator).

The administrative user consists of a Windows user account (or a group) and at least one security role and one security scope. If needed, a collection could be used to limit the administrative scope of the administrative user (Figure 5.8). These items are configured when the administrative user is created and can be changed later if needed.

FIGURE 5.8
Assigned security scopes and collections

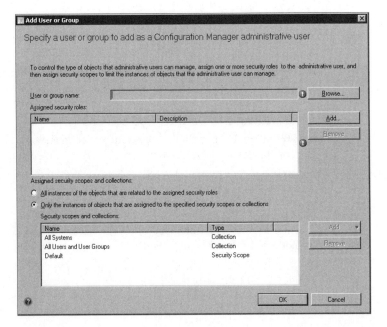

"ASSIGNED SECURITY SCOPES AND COLLECTIONS"—WHAT DOES THAT MEAN?

One issue that comes up during the administrative user creation process requires a bit more explanation. When you create a new administrative user, two options appear when you define the assigned security scope and collection for the user. See Figure 5.8.

The first choice is All Instances Of The Objects That Are Related To The Assigned Security Roles. If this option is selected, the administrative user will be associated with the All security scope and all collections.

The second choice is Only The Instances Of The Objects That Are Assigned To The Specified Security Scopes Or Collections. This option allows the ConfigMgr administrator to add or remove security scopes and/or collections in order to provide a customized administrative scope for the user.

If you modify an administrative user, a third option is available called Associate Assigned Security Roles With Specific Security Scopes And Collections. As the wording of the option implies, this option allows the administrator to create associations between security roles, security scopes, and collections for the user.

We will use the remainder of the chapter to apply what you have learned and walk through a real-world scenario.

 **Real World Scenario**

HELPING THE HELP DESK ANALYST

You are the ConfigMgr 2012 administrator and have been asked to provide ConfigMgr access to an administrative user. A help desk analyst needs the ability to deploy Adobe Reader X to all computers in the Dallas location. The analyst should also have the ability to use remote tools on the computers in the Dallas location. The analyst should not be able to deploy any other software to or interact in any way with the other computers in the infrastructure.

WHICH SECURITY ROLE(S) TO USE?

As the ConfigMgr administrator you first need to identify whether any of the existing security roles meet the needs of the scenario. In the ConfigMgr 2012 console, select Administration ➤ Overview ➤ Security ➤ Security Roles to view the roles that have been defined. The built-in Application Deployment Manager role appears to meet the requirements for the application delivery portion of the requirements. The built-in Remote Tools Operator role appears to meet the requirements for the remote tools functionality. So, you appear to have two existing security roles that will meet your needs.

YOU NEED A SECURITY SCOPE

The next step is to define the required security scope for the help desk analyst. The requirements stated that this user should only be able to deploy Adobe Reader X, so you need to create a security scope. You will use the process defined earlier in this chapter to create the security scope, and you will call the security scope Apps Help Desk Can Deploy. (See the following illustration.)

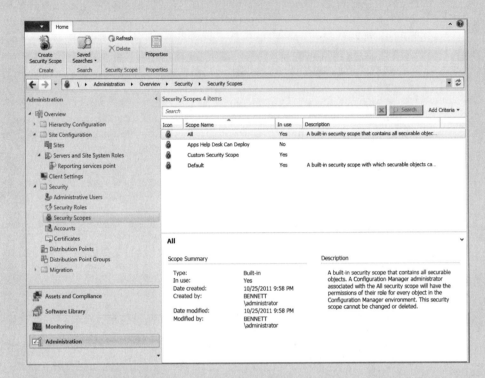

Remember that the In Use column value will be No until the security scope is associated with at least one object.

You may remember that the association between an object and the security scope is managed from the object, not from the security scope. So, you need to associate the security scope you just created with the Adobe Reader X application by performing the following steps:

1. In the ConfigMgr 2012 console, select the Adobe Reader X application in the Software Library workspace (Software Library ➢ Overview ➢ Application Management ➢ Applications).

   For the purposes of this scenario, assume that an administrator has already created and configured the Adobe Reader X application installation in ConfigMgr 2012 and it is ready for deployment.

2. Right-click the Adobe Reader X application and select Set Security Scopes.

3. Uncheck the Default security scope, and check the Apps Help Desk Can Deploy security scope.

4. Click OK. (See the following illustration.)

Note: You may also need to include a distribution point or a distribution point group in the security scope in order for the Deploy Software Wizard to complete when executed under the administrative user's credentials.

If you go back and view the status of the Apps Help Desk Can Deploy security scope in the ConfigMgr console, it should now show a value of Yes in the In Use column.

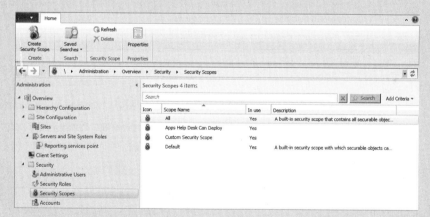

AND NOW YOU NEED A COLLECTION

There are several ways to create the collection for this scenario. In fact, someone else may have already built a collection that includes the Dallas computer devices and you could use that collection for your scenario.

However, let's assume you don't already have a collection that meets your needs and you need to create one. You may already know the names of the computers in the Dallas location and you could simply create a direct membership collection and directly add the computer names to the collection. Or, you could create a query-based collection and use data that is unique to the Dallas site to find computers that match the criteria. Examples of the data could be an Active Directory site, an

Active Directory organization unit, certain TCP/IP subnet ranges, a certain naming standard in the computer names, and so on. For now, assume that you were provided a list of computers in Dallas, and you're going to add them to a direct-membership device collection called Dallas Computers.

FINALLY: CREATING THE ADMINISTRATIVE USER

You have gone through several steps to prepare the required access in ConfigMgr. This may seem rather labor intensive at first, but you created several items that may be used multiple times in future security configuration requests. Let's take a moment to review what you will be using to create the administrative user.

You are going to use two built-in security roles for this scenario: Application Deployment Manager (so the analyst can deploy Adobe Reader X to the Dallas computers) and Remote Tools Operator (so the analyst can use remote tools on the Dallas computers).

You created a security scope called Apps Help Desk Can Deploy and associated the scope with the Adobe Reader X application. This limits the help desk analyst to the Adobe Reader X application.

You created a direct-membership collection that contains the computers in the Dallas location.

The next step is to create the actual administrative user:

1. In the ConfigMgr 2012 console, select Administration ➤ Overview ➤ Security ➤ Administrative Users.

2. Either select the Add User Or Group option in the Ribbon or right-click the Administrative Users option and select Add User Or Group.

   You need to designate the user or group that is being configured as an administrative user. In this scenario you are managing a single user.

3. Select the user's domain account (named hdanalyst).

4. In the Assigned Security Roles section, select the security roles that you decided to use for this scenario: Application Deployment Manager and Remote Tools Operator.

5. In the Assigned Security Scopes And Collections section, use your predefined collection and security scope to limit what the help desk analyst has access to in the console. (See the following illustration.)

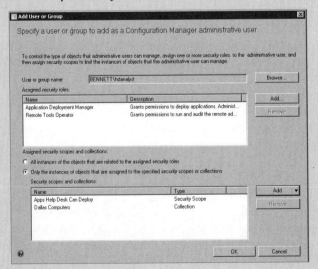

6. After adding the entries, click OK.

If there were several help desk analysts who needed the same configuration, you would probably create a group in Active Directory, add the users to that group, and then configure that group as an administrative user and avoid having to repeat these steps for each user individually.

At this point you have completed your work and are ready for the help desk analyst to test their ConfigMgr 2012 console with their logon credentials and make sure they can perform the required functions.

If you performed the configuration properly, then the administrative user hdanalyst should be able to open the ConfigMgr 2012 console and do the following:

◆ View only the Dallas Computers collection in the Assets and Compliance ➢ Overview ➢ Device Collections view. (See the following illustration.)

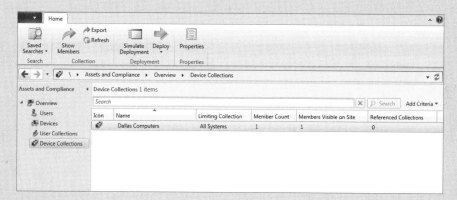

◆ See only the Dallas devices in the Assets and Compliance ➢ Overview ➢ Devices view. Also since the user can see only the Dallas devices, they can also use only remote tools against those computers. (See the following illustration.)

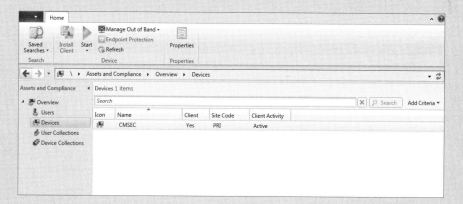

◆ View only the Adobe Reader X application in Software Library ➢ Overview ➢ Application Manager ➢ Applications, and when they deploy it they should only be able to select the Dallas Computers collection. (See the following illustrations.)

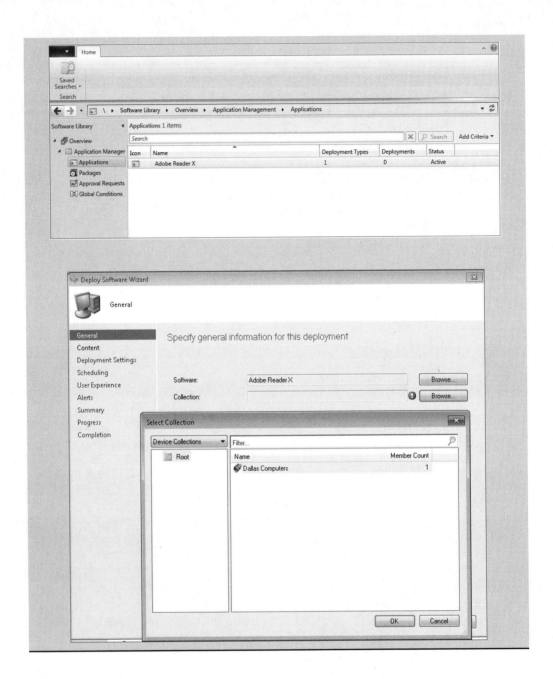

The Bottom Line

Understand the role-based administration model in ConfigMgr 2012.   SMS and ConfigMgr 2007 used a class and instance security model, which could be confusing at times. ConfigMgr 2012 adopts the RBAC model, thereby making the administration of security in ConfigMgr 2012 a less-daunting task.

Master It   What does the acronym RBAC stand for? And what does role-based administration mean?

Distinguish security roles from security scopes.   Security roles and security scopes are important components of the role-based security model in ConfigMgr 2012.

Master It   Can you identify the key differences between a security role and a security scope?

Understand which objects in ConfigMgr 2012 define an administrative user.   The administrative user consists of the security role, the security scope, and collections. In this chapter you learned the differences between a security role and a security scope, and you know that collections can be used to control the objects that an administrative user can access.

Master It   As the ConfigMgr 2012 administrator, do you need to create a custom ConfigMgr 2012 console so that the administrative user can see only what you want them to see?

Chapter 6

Client Installation

Once you have the Configuration Manager site and systems installed and configured, the next logical step is to plan the client deployment. The client deployment success rate very much depends on your knowledge of the internal network infrastructure combined with the ability to understand the components involved in the process. Once you fully understand the process, installing a thousand clients over a short period of time will be no problem. On the other hand, if you do not truly understand the process, installing a single client can be a very time-consuming experience.

No one solution fits all organizations. Most likely you will find yourself using a mix of the different installation techniques described in this chapter.

This chapter covers the prerequisites for installing clients, a walk-through of the different client installation methods, and information needed for troubleshooting the installation process.

In this chapter you will learn to

- ◆ Configure boundaries and boundary groups
- ◆ Select the relevant discovery methods
- ◆ Employ the correct client installation methods
- ◆ Ensure client health

Creating Client Settings

In order to manage a device with Configuration Manager you must first have the client software installed. Regardless of the device and operating system on that device, we always use the term *client*. A client consists of different agents that you can switch on or off. During the installation the full client is always installed. From the console you can control the agents using the Client Settings section of the Administration workspace. In Configuration Manager 2012, client settings are global data and thus no longer controlled by each primary site. Furthermore, you can create multiple custom client settings and assign them to individual collections. By design you should only configure custom client settings as exceptions to the default client settings. There can be several reasons why you'd want to configure multiple client settings, for example:

- ◆ You want to control who can initiate a remote session against servers.
- ◆ You want to disable the remote tools agent on all computers in the HR department.
- ◆ You want different inventory frequencies on servers and desktops.

A set of default client settings is always configured when you install Configuration Manager. In Figure 6.1 you can see an example of where two custom client settings have been created and assigned to two different collections. Notice the number in the Assignments column; it indicates the number of collections that are affected by the custom client settings. Figure 6.2 shows the new client settings interface. You can assign your own custom client settings to any user or device collection. The same settings can be assigned to multiple collections, and one collection can have multiple assignments. In the event of a conflict, the custom setting with the lowest Order number will be assigned.

FIGURE 6.1

Client settings

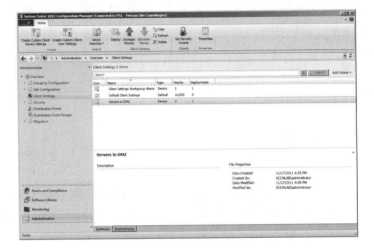

FIGURE 6.2

Creating custom client settings

Real World Scenario

CONFIGURE DIFFERENT CUSTOM CLIENT SETTINGS FOR ALL SERVERS

As the Configuration Manager administrator, you have been requested to ensure that only members of the global group Server Administrators can use Remote Tools on servers. Follow these steps to do so:

1. Open the Configuration Manager 2012 administrative console.
2. Select the Administration workspace and browse to Client Settings.
3. On the Home tab of the Ribbon, click Create Custom Client Device Settings.
4. Type **Remote settings for servers** in the Name column.
5. From the list of custom settings, select Remote Tools.
6. In the left column, select the Remote Tools settings and click Set Viewers.
7. Click the yellow starburst, Browse and type the name of the group in the form of domain\group name, for example, **Contoso\Server Administrators**.
8. Click OK three times.

   Notice the number shown under Permitted Viewers.
9. Click OK to save the custom client settings.
10. Back in the administrative console, select the newly created custom settings, and click Deploy on the Ribbon.
11. Select the All Servers device collection, and click OK.

The individual client agent settings will be discussed in detail in later chapters. Here is a short description of each of the agent settings:

Background Intelligent Transfer   This setting allows you to control the BITS protocol. BITS is the protocol being used by the client when it is downloading and uploading information to the management point and also when it is downloading packages from the distribution points.

Client Policy   The Client Policy settings control how often the client agent will contact the management point for a policy refresh:

- Client Policy Polling Interval (Minutes) defines how often the client will request a new machine policy. It can be any value between 3 minutes and 1440 minutes. Best practice by many is 60 minutes. Notice that unlike previous versions, Configuration Manager 2012 does not use policies when offering new applications to end users.

- Allow User Policy Request From Internet Clients: Use this setting if you have any Internet-facing site systems and you want to support user-centric scenarios for Internet-based clients.

Compliance Settings   This option is used to enable the settings management feature formerly known as Desired Configuration Management in Configuration Manager 2007.

Computer Agent   Here you define most of the basic Configuration Manager client settings:

◆ Deployment Deadline settings are used to control when users will be reminded about future deployments.

◆ Default Application Catalog Website Point: Use this setting to define how clients will connect to the Application Catalog. It can either be automatic, a specific server, or a specific website. If you select Automatic, the management point will supply the client with a random catalog, which is not guaranteed to be the one nearest the user.

◆ Add Application Catalog Website To Internet Explorer Trusted Sites Zone will add the selected website to the trusted site zone.

◆ Organization Name is the name that will be displayed in the Software Center.

◆ Install Permissions can be configured to control the permissions required to start any deployment on the client. You can choose from All Users, Administrators, Primary Users, or No Users. This setting is particularly valuable when you are controlling terminal servers.

◆ Suspend BitLocker PIN Entry Or Restart is used to control whether you want to suspend the PIN requirements after running a deployment that requires a system restart.

◆ Agent Extensions Manage The Deployment Of Applications And Software Updates: Enable this setting only if required by a vendor or if you use the SDK to manage client agent notifications.

◆ PowerShell Execution Policy: By default PowerShell scripts will run in the context of a service. If you want to run a PowerShell script within a task sequence, you should select Bypass, which is the same as running the PowerShell script unrestricted.

◆ Show Notifications For New Deployments controls the default UI experience for the logged on user when a deployment is received or about to start.

Computer Restart   This setting allows you to control when restart notifications are shown.

Endpoint Protection   Here you enable or disable the System Center Endpoint Protection agent. The settings are only configurable once you have enabled the Endpoint Protection Site System role:

◆ Manage Endpoint Protection Client On Client Computers. Configure this setting to True to start managing Endpoint Protection in the hierarchy.

◆ Install Endpoint Protection Client In Client Computers. When this setting is True, the Endpoint Protection client will automatically be installed. Notice that the client is already deployed during the initial Configuration Manager client installation.

◆ Automatically Remove Previously Installed Antimalware Software Before Endpoint Protection Client Is Installed. When this is True, an attempt to uninstall some predefined antimalware application will be performed.

◆ Suppress Any Required Computer Restart After The Endpoint Protection Client Is Installed. If configured to True no restart will be performed, not even if a previously antimalware application is uninstalled first.

- Allowed Period Of Time Users Can Postpone A Required Restart To Complete The Endpoint Protection Installation (hours). This option is only configurable if the setting to suppress computer restart is False. The number of hours will be the maximum number of hours a restart can be postponed by the user before a restart of the computer will be forced.

- Disable Alternate Sources (such as Microsoft Windows Update, Microsoft Windows Server Update Services, or UNS share) For The Initial Definition Update On Client Computers. Configure this setting to False if you want to allow multiple update sources to be considered for the first definition update.

Hardware Inventory   This option is used to scan for and report hardware installed on the computer. You can specify custom agent settings for different collections but only define hardware to collect in the default client settings. Unlike Configuration Manager 2007, there is no unique `sms_def.mof` file per site; instead you use the Custom Client Settings interface to specify the inventory data classes.

Mobile Devices   This controls how often mobile devices will poll for new policies.

Network Access Protection Client Agent   Use this option to enable Network Access Protection compliance on systems as well as to schedule when scans will occur. Notice that NAP requires that you have installed and configured Network Policy and Access Services in Windows Server 2008.

Power Management   This setting enables power management for all clients in the hierarchy and allows you to control whether end users can exclude their own devices from being part of a power management configuration. You configure each of the Power Management settings by collection.

Remote Tools   This is used to control the Remote Tools and Remote Assistance settings for Windows XP and later systems.

Software Deployment   Use this option to configure whether notifications should be shown when deployments are about to run. Schedule Re-evaluation For Deployments determines how often the Configuration Manager client will trigger the re-evaluation process. The process will automatically install required software that is not already installed and remove software that is supposed to be uninstalled.

Software Inventory   This option is used to discover what software is installed on the computer. You can control which file types the agent will scan for and where. Furthermore, you can use the settings to collect software files. Collected files are not stored in the database but will be stored on the site server. Even though it might be tempting to collect files, you should think twice before enabling this feature because it can easily lead to network congestion.

Software Metering   This option enables software metering and controls how often clients will upload the software-metering data from WMI to the management point.

Software Updates   This setting enables software updates, controls how often clients will perform a scan for software updates, and determines whether or not all required updates should be installed upon the deployment deadline.

State Messaging   This setting controls how often state messages are forwarded from the client to the management point.

User And Device Affinity   This setting controls the calculations that are being used to determine when a user(s) is being considered a primary user(s) for a device.

Supported Operating Systems

These are the minimum operating system requirements to install the Configuration Manager client agent. (Mobile devices will be discussed in detail in Chapter 14, "Mobile Device Management.")

- Windows XP Professional Service Pack 3, X86

- Windows XP Tablet SP3

- Windows Vista Business/Enterprise/Ultimate Edition SP2

- Windows Server 2003 Web Edition SP2, X86

- Windows Server 2003 Standard/Enterprise/Datacenter Edition SP2

- Windows 7 Enterprise/Ultimate

- Windows Embedded Standard 2009 X86

- Windows Embedded POS Ready 2009 X86

- WEPOS 1.1 SP3 X86

- Windows XP Embedded SP3 X86

- Windows Fundamentals for Legacy PCs X86

- Windows Embedded Standard 7 X86 and X64

The following are the prerequisites for clients:

- Users who use the Application Catalog must configure Internet Explorer to exclude the ActiveX control `Microsoft.ConfigurationManager.SoftwareCatalog.Website` `.ClientBridgeControl.dll` from ActiveX filtering and allow it to run in the browser.

- Microsoft Windows Installer version 3.1.4000.2435 or later

- Microsoft Background Intelligent Transfer Service (BITS) version 2.5

The following are the prerequisites for clients downloaded during the client installation:

- Microsoft Windows Update Agent version 7.0.6000.363 or later

- Microsoft WMI Redistributable Components version 5.2.3790.1830 or later

- Microsoft Core XML Services (MSXML) version 6.20.5002 or later

- Microsoft Remote Differential Compression (RDC)

- Microsoft .NET Framework 4.0 Client Profile

◆ Microsoft Silverlight 4.0.50524.0

◆ Microsoft Visual C++ 2005 Redistributable version 8.0.50727.42

◆ Microsoft Visual C++ 2008 Redistributable version 9.0.30729.4148

◆ Windows Imaging APIs 6.0.6001.18000

◆ Microsoft Policy Platform 1.2.3514.0

◆ Microsoft SQL Server Compact 3.5 SP2 components

Discovering Network Objects

Discovery is the process by which Configuration Manager finds objects on your network and keeps them up to date in the database. Objects can be users, groups, and computers. All discovery processes will generate one data discovery record (DDR) for each discovered object. For an administrator it is nice to know how many computers you have (and where) before you start deploying clients. To find out you must know the different discovery methods. Discovery also plays an important part in creating those collections that will support features like application deployment, updates deployment, and operating system deployment.

The only discovery method enabled by default is Heartbeat Discovery, described in a later section. Before configuring any other discovery method, you must ask yourself a few basic questions:

◆ What is being discovered by the method?

This is essential knowledge before configuring any of the methods. If you do not understand what's being discovered, chances are that you discover the wrong information.

◆ Why do you need the data?

If you can't answer this question, most likely you do not need to configure the discovery method.

◆ How often do you need to refresh the discovery data?

Configuration Manager 2012 natively supports Delta Discovery, which eliminates the reason for running frequent full discovery processes.

◆ What is the duration of the discovery process?

Not knowing the duration of each discovery method has often resulted in backlogs and incorrect discovery schedules. Having knowledge about the log files generated by each discovery process can give you precise data and help you configure the correct schedules.

◆ What is the impact of configuring the method?

The discovery methods use different techniques to gather a data discovery record (DDR). Active Directory methods will query the nearest domain controller, whereas Network Discovery uses protocols like RIP and OSPF to get the information.

To configure discovery methods, perform the following steps:

1. Open the Configuration Manager administrative console.

2. Select the Administration workspace, navigate to Hierarchy Configuration, and choose Discovery Methods.

3. You can modify each of the discovery methods by selecting the discovery method and choosing Properties from the Ribbon.

Active Directory Discovery Methods

Each of the Active Directory discovery methods requires a target and a schedule. The target can be a single object, an organizational unit (OU), a Security/Distribution group, or an entire domain. While it might not make much sense to search for a single object, specifying individual OUs or groups versus the entire domain is often considered best practice. Especially in the pilot phase, it is an easy way to limit the number of objects you are working with. A new feature in Configuration Manager 2012 allows you to specify the account being used to run in the discovery process. If none is specified, the process will run under the security context of the site server. In order to run a successful discovery, the account you specify must have Read permission on the object.

Figure 6.3 shows the Active Directory Container field that you use to define the locations where you want to search. When you click Browse, you will see the dialog shown in Figure 6.4. This dialog allows you to select the criteria for the LDAP query. You can select any container or OU within the tree view. Unlike with previous versions of Configuration Manager, you can now browse to other domains and forests.

FIGURE 6.3
New Active Directory Container search criteria

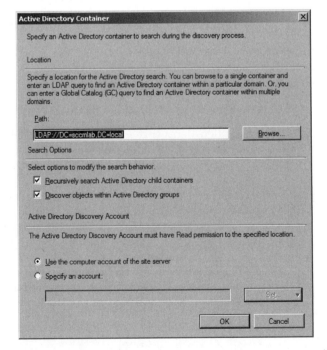

FIGURE 6.4

The Select New
Container
dialog box

DISCOVERY PATHS AND ACTIVE DIRECTORY ORGANIZATIONAL UNITS

It is important to know that Configuration Manager will query all objects in the specified paths every time. If you delete an old computer object from the Configuration Manager database but not from Active Directory, the same computer object will be added to the Configuration Manager database after the next discovery process unless you configure the option to exclude computers from discovery based on when the computer object last logged on to the domain or you changed the password. Failure to exclude computers can have an effect on the automatic client push installation attempts because Configuration Manager will initiate a client push attempt on computers that do not have the client installed. These might be the most important reasons why you should plan the discovery processes carefully; make sure that you have an OU structure in Active Directory where you can store objects that are no longer active and exclude those OUs from the specified LDAP path. Failure to do so might lead to errors related to failed client push installation attempts and discovery of unwanted objects.

Once you choose the start location for the query, the default behavior of the query is to search all of the child objects beneath the starting point. If you do not want to search through the child OUs, you can clear the check box labeled Recursively Search Active Directory Child Containers. This is a good way to limit the data returned from the query.

Discover Active Directory Objects Within Groups is especially useful in scenarios where you want the Active Directory System Group Discovery method to find computer objects within Active Directory groups. Many organizations have a unique OU where they store computer groups.

Figure 6.5 shows all discovery methods available in a primary site. Let's look at each of these methods in detail.

FIGURE 6.5
Discovery
methods

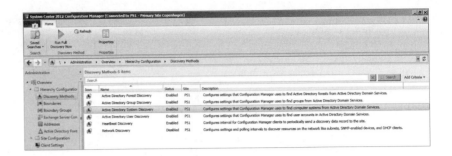

ACTIVE DIRECTORY FOREST DISCOVERY

This discovery method is new to Configuration Manager 2012 and can be very helpful in environments where the Configuration Manager administrator is not always informed about IP infrastructure changes. The method returns information about domains, IP ranges, and Active Directory sites. Furthermore, as shown in Figure 6.6, you can configure the method to automatically create boundaries for the objects being discovered (IP ranges or Active Directory sites only), thus saving yourself hours of work.

FIGURE 6.6
Configuring Active
Directory Forest
Discovery

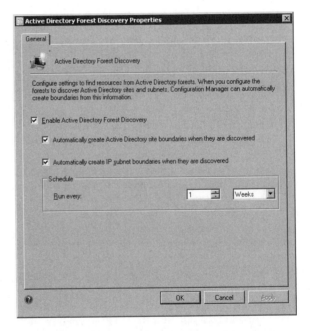

By default the discovery process runs once a week and will only discover those forests that are created as Active Directory Forest objects in the Administration workspace. The local forest is automatically created as part of the site installation process. Figure 6.7 shows how you can specify a new forest using an account from the target forest.

You can monitor this discovery process by reading the ADForestDisc.log on the site server.

FIGURE 6.7

Defining a new Active
Directory forest

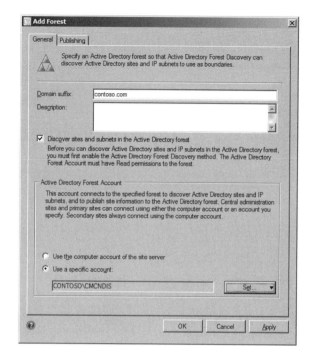

ACTIVE DIRECTORY SYSTEM DISCOVERY

This is the key discovery method for finding devices. In essence you configure one or more LDAP paths to Active Directory and query a domain controller for all objects in those paths. The device attributes returned by the domain controller depend on what you have configured. By default these attributes will be returned:

- ObjectGuid
- Name
- SAMAccountname
- Operating System
- Domain
- ObjectSID
- PrimaryGroupID
- DNSHostName
- UserAccountControl
- OperatingSystemVersion
- Organizational Unit

In Figure 6.8 you see an example where custom attributes have been specified. Attributes can be specified for AD System Discovery and AD User Discovery. The information you specify will be added to the discovery data and used in queries and reports like any other discovery information. You can monitor this discovery process by reading the ADsysdis.log on the site server.

FIGURE 6.8
Custom Active Directory system attributes

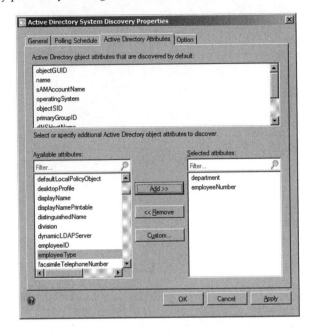

ACTIVE DIRECTORY USER DISCOVERY

This discovery method is not used at all in the client deployment process but plays an important part of the user-centric application model. With the method enabled you will get a list of users to whom you can target different deployments such as applications. By default these attributes will be returned:

- ◆ Distinguished Name
- ◆ Full User Name
- ◆ Mail
- ◆ Name
- ◆ UserAccountControl
- ◆ Domain
- ◆ MemberOf
- ◆ SID
- ◆ PrimaryGroupID
- ◆ Orgazational Unit

You can monitor this discovery process by reading the ADusrdis.log on the site server.

ACTIVE DIRECTORY GROUP DISCOVERY

This discovery method will discover any local groups, global groups, and universal security groups. You can search for objects within a specific group or perform the search for all groups in a specific location. The information is not really used in a client installation scenario. But once you have the client deployed, you will find the Active Directory security group very useful, especially in user target deployments. You can limit the number of computer objects returned in the discovery process by configuring the values on the Option tab, as shown in Figure 6.9. Notice that discovering only computers that have logged on to a domain within a specified number of days requires that the domain function level be at least Windows 2003.

FIGURE 6.9
Option tab for group discovery

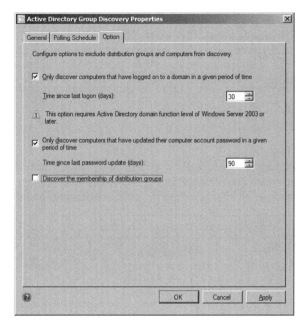

You can monitor this discovery process by reading the ADsgdis.log on the site server.

HEARTBEAT DISCOVERY

This discovery method is enabled by default and differs from the other methods. It is the responsibility of the client to initiate the discovery process. Failure to do can result in unwanted client installation attempts and cause the client to be marked as inactive in the Configuration Manager console. The discovery process will not discover any new objects; instead it rediscovers existing objects. You can look at this method as a way to send a keepalive package from the client to the management point. The heartbeat record is used for the following purposes:

◆ Determine whether a client is marked active or inactive.

◆ Update the Client column from No to Yes in the console when the client is installed.

◆ Re-create the client in a database if you accidently deleted the object.

◆ Has an impact when the "Clear Install Flag" site maintenance task will delete the client install flag in the database. If the install flag is removed and automatic client push is enabled, a new client installation attempt will begin.

How often should you run the discovery method? By default clients will send an updated DDR to the management point every 7 days. Personally I configure the discovery method to run daily. These are some of the attributes that will be returned:

- ClientInstalled
- ClientType
- ClientID
- ClientVersion
- NetBIOSName
- CodePage
- IPSubnet
- Domain
- ADSiteName
- IPSubnet
- IPAddress
- MACAddress

You can monitor this discovery process by reading the `InventoryAgent.log` on the client.

HEARTBEAT DISCOVERY AND MODIFYING COMPUTER NAMES

The Heartbeat Discovery process is responsible for updating changes in the computer name to the database. If you are starting a process where you need to rename a large number of computers, consider modifying the default schedule from 7 days to a more frequent interval.

NETWORK DISCOVERY

Let me start by saying this: run the Network Discovery method only when no other discovery method can find the needed resources. It is considered to be the "noisiest" method and will use protocols like RIP or OSPF to discover objects. Most often you'll need to use this method only if you have a number of workgroup clients in your environment. Network Discovery is used to discover many different types of objects. Not only can you find computers that are on the network, but you can discover any device that has an IP address as well.

You can monitor the Network Discovery process by reading the `Netdisc.log` on the server.

DISCOVERY SCHEDULING OPTIONS

Each method also has a way of scheduling when the discovery will run. For the Active Directory discovery methods, the Polling Schedule tab resembles Figure 6.10 (in this case Active Directory System Group Discovery). The schedule determines when the site server will initiate a full discovery. You can also configure delta discovery. Delta discovery runs by default every 5 minutes and will only discover any changes made to the objects. Unlike in Configuration Manager 2007 R3, the process will discover when you modify existing objects, such as adding an existing computer account to an existing group. Using delta discovery along with the collection property Update This Collection Incrementally, all changes will be reflected in the collection within 10 minutes: 5 minutes for the delta discovery and 5 more minutes for the incremental collection update.

FIGURE 6.10
Polling Schedule tab for a discovery method

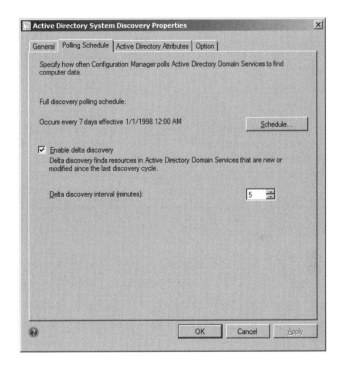

If you need to modify the schedule, click the Schedule button to display the Custom Schedule window.

The Heartbeat Discovery method schedule is found on the General tab, as shown in Figure 6.11. Notice that you can set only a simple schedule for the Heartbeat; your options are much more limited than with the Active Directory methods.

FIGURE 6.11
The Heartbeat
Discovery General tab

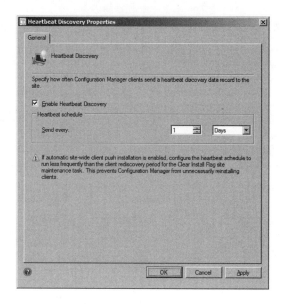

You can create multiple schedules for the Network Discovery method, as shown in Figure 6.12. Configuring the options in the Custom Schedule dialog shown in Figure 6.13, you have a lot of control over scheduling the Network Discovery agent. Because of the time required for the network searches, you may want to configure a maximum runtime.

FIGURE 6.12
The Network Discovery
Schedule tab

FIGURE 6.13
The Custom
Schedule dialog
for Network
Discovery

FIGURE 6.13
The Custom
Schedule dialog
for Network
Discovery

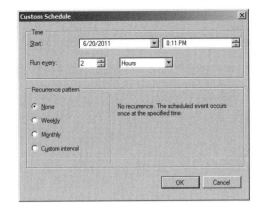

Configuring Boundaries and Boundary Groups

After a client has been installed, it must be assigned to a Configuration Manager 2012 site before it can be managed. Once assigned the client will start receiving the default client policies, using the local resources of the site such as management points, distribution points, and software update points. During the installation, you can configure command-line properties to automatically assign the client a fixed site code or let an auto-assignment process begin. Note that clients will never be assigned to secondary sites, only primary sites.

Configuring boundaries has long been the way you assigned a client to a Configuration Manager/ SMS client site. This has changed in Configuration Manager 2012, where a new feature has been introduced to control the assignments: boundary groups. In essence you still use boundaries, but they have no real value until they have been added to a boundary group. A boundary group is basically a collection of individual boundaries grouped together for one or two purposes:

Site Assignment Used to control which sites clients are assigned to

Content Lookup Used to control which distribution points will be used by the client

Figure 6.14 and Figure 6.15 shows two boundaries added to a boundary group that is configured for site assignment.

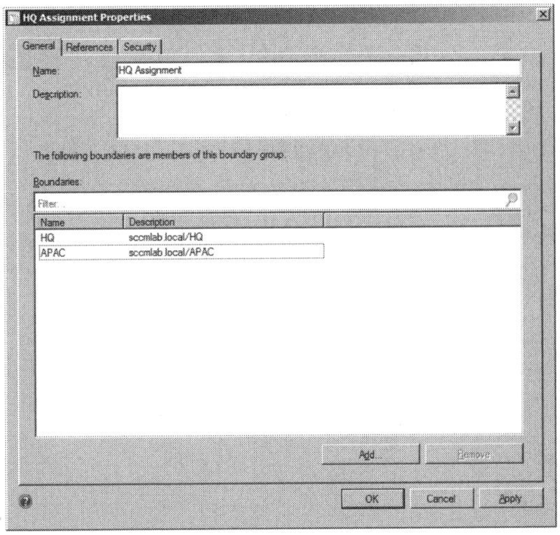

FIGURE 6.14
Boundary
group
with a list of
boundaries

FIGURE 6.15
Boundary group
configured for site
assignment

Boundaries are basically address ranges; the following range types are supported:

◆ IP range

◆ IP subnet

◆ Active Directory site name

◆ IPv6 prefix

Even though all four boundary types are supported, there will be scenarios where one or more of the types will not work correctly. There are known issues with IP subnets and network IDs that might cause clients not to be assigned even if they fall within the boundary defined. Furthermore, AD site boundaries are not supported in IP supernetting environments. If you experience problems, you can always configure IP ranges.

 Real World Scenario

CONFIGURING A BOUNDARY AND A BOUNDARY GROUP

As the Configuration Manager administrator, you have been requested to create an AD boundary and ensure it is used to assign clients to the primary site. Follow these steps:

1. Open the Configuration Manager 2012 administrative console.

2. Select the Administration workspace and browse to Hierarchy Configuration ➢ Boundaries.

3. On the Ribbon click Create Boundary.

4. Type **HQ** in the Description field, and under Type select Active Directory Site.

5. Click Browse, select the Active Directory site, and click OK.

6. Click OK to create the boundary.

7. Navigate to Boundary Groups, and on the Ribbon click Create Boundary Group.

8. In the Name field type **HQ**, click Add, select the newly created boundary, and click OK.

9. Select the References tab.

10. Check the box Use This Boundary Group For Site Assignment. Select the primary site and click OK.

Client Installation Methods

As an important part of your client deployment planning, you need to ask yourself a few questions:

◆ How are you going to deploy the client?

Basically you can choose between a manual installation and an automatic installation. The automatic installation method comes in different flavors.

◆ Where are you deploying the client?

You need to know which environments need a client. Many organizations only plan for client support in the local domain just to realize later in the process that they also need to support workgroup clients, clients in DMZ, and clients in other forests.

◆ When do you want to deploy the client?

You need to decide whether you want to deploy all clients at once or in a controlled manner.

You have several different deployment methods to choose from; most organizations find themselves using a mix of different methods. It is important to know that there is no right or wrong method, but methods used in different scenarios have different requirements. Regardless of the installation method, you need to know the different command-line properties and when to use them. Gaining knowledge about the command-line properties will ensure that you can install clients in different environments such as workgroups, other forests, and DMZs.

Command-Line Properties

Several command-line properties are used to control the installation. Before you start the deployment, you will need to know two things:

◆ What command-line properties are you going to use?

◆ How are you going to provision the command-line properties?

The installation process will always run `ccmsetup.exe` and `client.msi`; both of these processes can be controlled using command lines. Any needed prerequisites will be installed and controlled by `ccmsetup.exe`. When you specify command-line properties, you should do so like this:

```
CCMSetup.exe [CCMsetup properties] [client.msi setup properties]
```

For an updated list of command-line properties, you should look at the TechNet article at this URL:

`http://technet.microsoft.com/en-us/library/gg699356.aspx`

The following are `ccmsetup.exe` command-line properties:

/source   The `/source` switch is used to identify the location of the `client.msi` installer file. You can specify the switch multiple times to provide additional source file locations to provide for redundancy. Usage: `ccmsetup.exe /source:folderpath`.

/MP   The /MP switch is used to specify the management point that will be used as a source location. As with the `/source` switch, you can specify multiple management points by including the switch multiple times. The setting is not used to control the management point that will be used during the site assignment process. Usage: `ccmsetup.exe /MP:Server`.

/retry:<minutes>   The `/retry` switch is used to retry values used to determine how often a client will try to download the installation files. The client will attempt to download the files until it reaches the values specified in the `downloadtimeout`. Usage: `ccmsetup.exe /retry:30`.

/downloadtimeout:<minutes>   The `/downloadtimeout` switch controls the number of minutes the `ccmsetup` process attempts to download the needed client installation files. By default the ccmsetup process will try downloading files for 1 day Usage: `ccmsetup / downloadtimeout:120`.

/noservice   The `/noservice` switch is used to specify that the logged-in user's account is the service account for the installation of the client. For this switch to work, the user account will need to have rights to install software; otherwise the installation will fail. Usage: `ccmsetup /noservice`.

/Service   The `/Service` switch is used to install the client software using the security context of the local system account. For this to work, Active Directory has to be in use within your network, and the computer's Active Directory account must have access to the installation directory where the client installation files are stored. Usage: `ccmsetup /Service`.

/Logon   The `/Logon` switch is used to determine if a Configuration Manager client exists on the system. If a Configuration Manager 2012 client is already installed, the installation process will stop. Usage: `ccmsetup.exe /Logon`.

/forcereboot   The `/forecereboot` switch is used to determine if the `ccmsetup` process needs to perform a restart of the computer in order to finish the installation. Usage: `ccmsetup.exe /forcereboot`.

/BITSPriority:<Priority>   The `/BITSPriority` switch controls the bits download priority when downloading the client installation files. You can specify these values:

- Foreground

- High

◆ Normal

◆ Low

◆ Usage: `ccmsetup.exe /BITSPriority:FOREGROUND`

/Uninstall   The `/Uninstall` switch is used to silently uninstall the Configuration Manager client. Usage: `ccmsetup.exe /Uninstall`.

/UsePKICert   The `/UsePKICert` switch is used to specify that the client will use a PKI certificate that uses client authentication for communication. If no certifiacte can be found the client will use a self-signed certificate and communicate using HTTP. Usage: `ccmsetup.exe /UsePKICert`.

/NoCRLCheck   The `/NoCRLCheck` switch is used to specify that the client will not check the certificate revocation list before establishing HTTPS communication. This example will enable HTTPS communication and not check for any revocation lists. Usage: `ccmsetup.exe /UsePKICert /NoCRLcheck`.

/config:<configuration file>   The `/config` switch is used to specify the name of a user defined configuration file. The configuration file replaces the default `mobileclient.tcf` file. It is a very good idea to modifying an existing `mobileclient.tcf` file whenever you want to create a custom configuration file. That way you ensure that the syntax used in the file is correct. Usage: `ccmsetup.exe /config:C:\Windows\ccmsetup\mysettings.txt`.

The following are `Client.msi` command-line properties:

Patch   This property allows you to apply client patches during the installation. At the time of writing, there are no Configuration Manager 2012 client patches. Usage: *patch=\\Server\ Share\clientpatch.msp*.

CCMALWAYSINF   This property with a value of 1 allows you to control if the client will always be Internet-based, thus never connecting to the intranet. Usage: CCMALWAYSINF=1.

CCMCERTISSUERS   This property specifies the list of certificate issuers trusted by the Configuration Manage site. Notice that the list is case-sensitive Usage: CCMCERTISSUERS= ="CN=CM Root CA; OU=SRV; O=CM, Inc; C=US".

CCMCERTSEL   This property allows you to control the certificate selection criteria used when the client has more than one certificate to choose from. When specifying the criteria you can search for the exact Subject Name (type subject: prior to the SN) or a partial match in the Subject Name (type subjectstr: prior to part of the Subject Name, Object Identifier or distinguished name). Usage: *CCMCERTSEL="subject:Server1.CM2012.COM"*.

CCMCERTSTORE   This property allows you to specify an alternative certificate store. You should only use the command line if the certificate is not found in the default store. Usage: *CCMCERTSTORE="CM2012CERT"*.

CCMFIRSTCERT   With this property configured to 1 the client will automatically select the certificate with longest validity period. Usage: *CCMFIRSTCERT=1*.

CCMHOSTNAME   This property is used to specify the Management Point for Internet-based managed clients. Usage: *CCMHOSTNAME="MPServer.CM2012.COM"*.

SMSPUBLICROOTKEY This property allows you to specify the trusted root key if, for some reason, it cannot be retrieved from Active Directory. You can open the `mobileclient.tcf` file and copy the trusted root key. Usage: *SMSPUBLICROOTKEY= 02000000A40000525341310 0080000010001008186332BF592B793C8B7F7C01FB32CB811465DEB71095C4442DE45661CE-25031FE2B6F8D9C1C71C6C0BB335C3B5747035E028C43C35E4F8DF1E0CB8B42289A8B-9F9A3143964817DCC50F0D5DB9A879705AD0F4063F4F30242472A933FE8B452BEE608147D9E-CED79CA9422D5441894D152C54B0ABB920741BA0B5582482EA1231FAB0BD67AAAB-82DEC50BDCE7D91FCCFB2C3F6C03C8C67C31B5F083A98860389E8D2FD93C4C5BAE-6124A4977EA76B5A89AE2917687782783E003C5F215C767782C0F79A1C1E1F4D14E8B693-25C8CC33C574BE774CEA9579AD765A864DB0FBBBBB854D4390473E72014111EFD-FC11DDDF46EF7B1F03EF1D60A3ABDAA52E8868A0.*

SMSROOTKEYPATH This property allows you to reinstall the trusted root key from a file. Usage: *SMSROOTKEYPATH="D:\NewRootKey\Rootkey.txt"*.

RESETKEYINFORMATION This property allows you to remove the old trusted root key. This is often used when you move clients from one Configuration Manager site hierarchy to another. Usage: ***RESETKEYINFORMATION=TRUE***.

CCMAdmins This property allows you to configure which admin accounts are for the client. If there is more than one account, separate the accounts with a semicolon. Usage: *CCMAdmins=account1;account2;...*

CCMAllowSilentReboot After the installation is complete, if a reboot is required, this property will cause the machine to reboot without saving any user changes. It needs to be specified only if the silent reboot is to be used. A value of 1 forces the reboot if required. Usage: CCMAllowSilentReboot.

CCMDebugLogging This property enables or disables debug logging. A value of 1 enables logging; a value of 0 disables logging. Usage: CCMDebugLogging=0 | 1.

CCMEnableLogging This property turns logging on or off. If this property is not included, then logging is disabled. Usage: CCMEnableLogging=True.

CCMInstallDir This is the directory where the client software will be installed. Usage: CCMInstallDir=*installationfolder*.

CCMLogLevel This property is used to control the amount of logging activity. A value of 0 is verbose logging. A level of 1 logs all information, warning, and error conditions. A level of 2 logs warning and error conditions. A value of 3 logs error conditions only. When included, you must also use CCMEnableLogging. Usage: CCMLogLevel=0 | 1 | 2 | 3.

CCMLogMaxHistory This property controls the total number of previous log files within the Logs directory. When included, you must also use CCMEnableLogging. Usage: CCMLogMaxHistory=*NumberOfLogFilesToKeep*.

CCMLoxMaxSize This property controls the maximum log file size. When included, you must also use CCMEnableLogging. Usage: CCMLogMaxSize=*LogSizeBytes*.

DisableCacheOpt When this property is included in the text box, it disables the Cache configuration setting within the Systems Management properties in Control Panel. Users will not be able to manipulate the settings—only administrators will be allowed to. Usage: DisableCacheOpt=True.

DisableSiteOpt   When this property is included in the text box, it disables the Site Code configuration setting within the Systems Management properties in Control Panel. Users will not be able to manipulate the settings—only administrators will be allowed to. Usage: DisableSiteOpt=True.

SMSCacheDir   This property controls the directory where the cache is created. Usage: SMSCacheDir=*directorypath*.

SMSCacheFlags   This property can be used to control how much space the cache can occupy and the location where the cache will be stored. When used in conjunction with the SMSCacheDir property, you have control over where the cache is stored. The flags are as follows:

SMSCacheFlags=PercentDiskSpace   Used to control the size of the cache by allocating the total cache size as a percentage of the disk size. Cannot be used with PercentFreeDiskSpace.

SMSCacheFlags=PercentFreeDiskSpace   Used to control the size of the cache file by allocating the total cache size as a percentage of the free space on the disk. Cannot be used with PercentDiskSpace.

SMSCacheFlags=MaxDrive   Used to place the cache on the largest drive in the system. Cannot be used with MaxDriveSpace.

SMSCacheFlags=MaxDriveSpace   Used to place the cache on the drive with the most free space. Cannot be used with MaxDrive.

SMSCacheFlags=NTFSOnly   Used to control the placement of the cache drive on volumes formatted with NTFS.

SMSCacheFlags=Compress   Used to compress the files within the cache.

SMSCacheFlags=FailIfNoSpace   Used to stop installation of the client if there is not enough space on the drive for the cache.

SMSCacheSize   This property controls the amount of space in megabytes that the cache will consume or in percentage if used in combination with the PERCENTDISKPACE or PERCENTFREEDISKSPACE. Usage: SMSCacheSize=*CacheSizeInMB*.

SMSConfigSource   This property controls where the configuration source files are stored. Usage: SMSConfigSource=R | P | M | U.

SMSDIRECTORYLOOKUP   This property controls whether WINS lookup is allowed when the client is trying to locate the management point and the site code. Usage: SMSDIRECTORYLOOKUP=NOWINS.

CCMHTTPPort   This is the HTTP port used by the client to communicate with the Site Systems. Usage: CCMHTTPPort=80.

CCMHTTPSPort   This is the HTTPS port used by the client to communicate with the Site Systems. Usage: CCMHTTPSPort=443.

SMSMP   This property is used to configure the initial Management Point that the client communicates with. Usage: SMSMP=Server1.CM2012.COM.

FSP   This property specifies that a Fallback Status Point is used. Usage: FSP=Server1.CM2012.COM.

DNSSUFIX   This property specifies the DNS domain of the Management Point. With this option clients will search DNS for the `.srv` record that includes the DNS suffix of the Management Point. Usage: `DNSSUFFIX=CM2012.COM`.

SMSSiteCode   This property controls the site code that is assigned to the client. Usage: `SMSSiteCode=Auto | SiteCode`.

CCMEVALINTERVAL   This property controls how often in minutes the client evaluation process runs. By default the process is configured to run once a day. Usage: `CCMEVALINTERVAL=2880`.

CCMEVALHOUR   This property controls when the client evaluation process runs (by the hour). By default the process is configured to run at midnight. Usage: `CCMEVALHOUR=14`.

For example, suppose you wanted to push the client to systems, using the following options:

◆ Install the cache in the `\Cache` directory on the largest drive.

◆ Enable verbose logging.

◆ Keep five log files.

◆ Automatically discover the site code.

Your entry within the Property text box would look like this:

```
SMSSITECODE=AUTO SMSCACHEDIR=CACHE SMSCACHEFLAGS=MAXDRIVE SMSENABLELOGGING=TRUE
CCMLOGLEVEL=0 CCMLOGMAXHISTORY =5
```

Provisioning Command Lines

You can provision command lines in three different ways:

◆ Manually type the command lines during the installation.

◆ Publish them to Active Directory.

◆ Configure a Group Policy with the `ConfigMgrInstallation.adm` template.

If the AD schema is extended, you can type the command lines in the Installation Properties for the client push installation method. All properties you enter here will be published to Active Directory and used by any client that can access Active Directory during the installation. Notice this only applies if you start the installation using `ccmsetup.exe` with no other command lines.

For those scenarios where clients cannot access the information in Active Directory, you can provision the command lines using a Group Policy with the `ConfigMgrInstallation.adm` template. The template is found on the Configuration Manager 2012 installation media in `.\TOOLS\ConfigMgrADMTemplates`.

Manually Installing the Client

This installation method might sound like a very time-consuming method; however, you will find yourself installing clients manually for several reasons. You can manually install the client by running `CCMSetup.exe` from the site server or from any management point. The file is located in the `Program Files\Microsoft Configuration Manager\Client` folder on the Site Servers and Management Points node within your Configuration Manager infrastructure.

To manually install a client in an environment where the AD schema has been extended, do the following: From Start ➤ Run, type **\\ConfigMgr Server\SMS_<sitecode>\Client\ ccmsetup.exe**.

To manually install a client on a workgroup computer, follow these steps:

1. Make sure you can access the client installation files or copy them to the local client.

2. Open a command prompt as administrator.

3. Run `ccmsetup.exe smssitecode=PS1 /Source:C:\CM2012Client smsmp=SCCM4 .SCCMLAB.Local fsp=SCCM4.SCCMLAB.Local DNSSUFIX=SCCMLAB.Local`.

This will install the Configuration Manager client from the local source `C:\CM2012Client` and assign it to primary site PS1 using SCCM4 as the Managment Point and fallback status point. The client must be able to resolve the site system names; otherwise the installation will fail. You can use the Hosts and LMHOSTS files to provide the needed naming resolution support.

To support a DMZ installation where the client is not able to resolve the needed hostnames, you configure these settings in the LMHOSTS and Hosts files (in the example the site server is named SCCM4.SCCMLAB.LOCAL with 192.168.1.2 as the IP address). You can find the files in `%windir%\System32\drivers\etc\`. There must be exactly 15 characters between the first " and the \ in the LMHOSTS file.

Add these entries to the LMHOSTS file:

```
192.168.1.2 SCCM4 #PRE
192.168.1.2 "SMS_MP          \0x1A" #PRE
```

Add this entry to the Hosts file:

```
192.168.1.2 SCCM4.SCCMLAB.local
```

Client Push

Client push is one of the most used installation methods because it requires very little work. All you need to do is to specify one or more client push installation accounts along with some client push installation settings. Before you use client push you need to understand the preinstallation phase.

◆ When one of the discovery processes is running, a client configuration request (CCR record) will be generated for each object that does not have a client installed.

◆ Using the client push account, the Client Configuration Manager (CCM) component will make a connection to the client and copy the two files `ccmsetup.exe` and `mobileclient .tcf` to `\\Client\Admin$\CCMSetup`.

◆ Once the files have been successfully copied to the client, the server will verify that the CCMsetup service is starting successfully on the client before it disconnects.

◆ From this point on, the local client is responsible for installing the Configuration Manager agent.

All this information from the pre-installation phase is recorded in the `CCM.log` file on the site server. It is not uncommon to see errors in the log file for reasons like these:

◆ A local firewall is running on the client and no firewall rules have been created. This will generate an error message like this: `---> Failed to connect to \\Client\admin$ using machine account (67)`

◆ The client push account does not have the correct permissions to access IPC$ and Admin$. This will generate an error message like this: `Unable to connect to remote registry for machine name "client ", error 5.`

◆ The client is not running. This will generate an error message like this: `---> Failed to connect to \\Client\admin$ using machine account (67).`

◆ Configuration Manager is unable to locate the client because of naming resolution errors. This will generate an error message like this: `The network path was not found (53).`

If the client Configuration Manager component fails to start the installation on the client, it will retry the installation once an hour for seven days. All retry attempts are stored in `\Program Files\Microsoft Configuration Manager\inboxes\ccrretry.box`.

To configure the client firewall correctly you need to enable

◆ File and Printer Sharing

◆ Windows Management Instrumentation (WMI)

To configure the client push installation account correctly you need to assign it local administrative permissions on the client.

When you create the account, make sure you add it to the group within your Active Directory structure that has the proper security rights on each machine within the site. Once the account(s) are created, you can configure them as client push installation accounts in the Configuration Manager console. If none of the specified client push accounts are able to connect to the client, the site server will attempt to connect using the site server computer account. With that in mind, you can also assign the correct permissions to the site server computer account, thus eliminating the need for multiple client push accounts.

Configuring Client Push Settings

Once the discovery methods have been configured, you will need to configure the client push settings. In the Configuration Manager Administrator console, follow these steps:

1. Select the Administrator workspace.

2. Browse to Site Operations ➢ Sites.

3. Choose Client Installation Settings ➢ Client Push Installation on the Ribbon.

Selecting the check box Enable Automatic Site-wide Client Push Installation means that whenever a computer is discovered within a defined site boundary group, the client will be automatically installed.

Figure 6.16 shows a site where automatic client push is enabled for all computers. It is important to know that client push comes in several flavors. The General tab is only used to configure fully automated client push. For a collection-based or client-based client push, you only need to configure settings on the Accounts and Installation Properties tabs.

FIGURE 6.16
The General tab
of Client Push
Installation
Properties

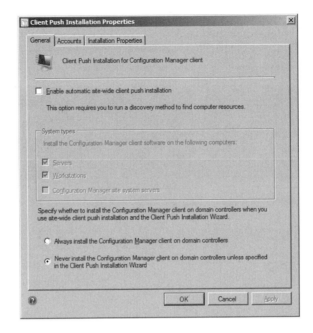

The Accounts tab, shown in Figure 6.17, allows you to specify the accounts to use to install the Configuration Manager client. Configuration Manager will try the accounts in order until it finds an account with administrative rights on the destination computer. It will always try using the sites server's computer account last if one or more accounts are listed and only try the site server's computer account if no accounts are listed. In the figure you will notice that two different accounts, a domain account and a local account, have been specified.

FIGURE 6.17
The Accounts tab
of Client Push
Installation
Properties

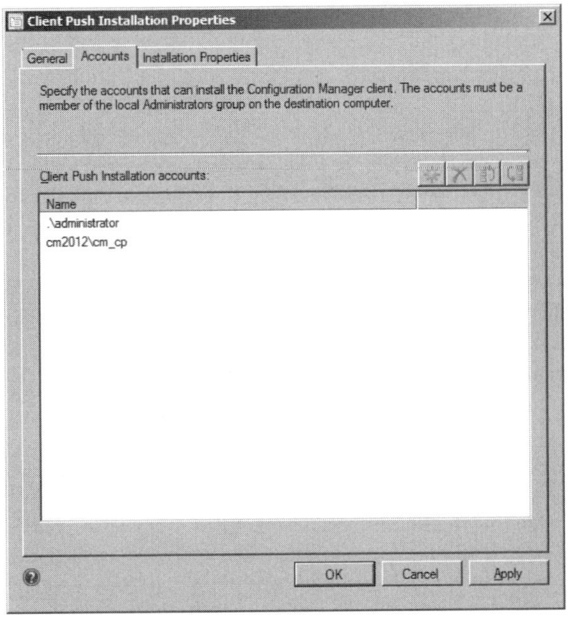

In the Installation Properties tab of Client Push Installation Properties, shown in Figure 6.18, you control how the client is installed by entering installation properties within the text box. The properties that you enter here will be published as command lines in Active Directory. You can enter all available `client.msi` command lines.

FIGURE 6.18
The Installation
Properties tab of
Client Push
Installation
Properties

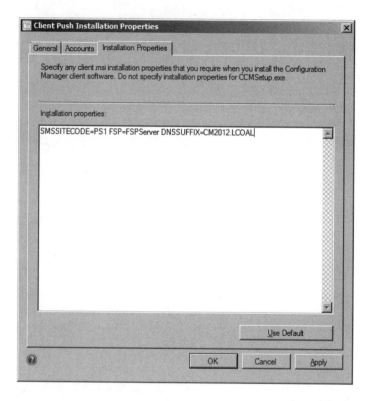

In order to manually push the client install out from within the Configuration Manager administrative console, the target client system(s) needs to be discovered and visible in the Assets and Compliance workspace. Once a system is available, you can push the client to the individual system, or you can push the client to all of the systems within the collection. The simplest way to do this is with the Install Client Wizard. To initiate the wizard, select a discovered system or collection and choose Install Client from the Ribbon. This will open the Install Client Wizard.

Although the properties and the installation account cannot be modified from the wizard, as Figure 6.19 shows, you can change some of the client push installation options on an individual basis. Especially notice that you can select which site you want to use to install the client. The site choice also affects from which server the client will download the needed software.

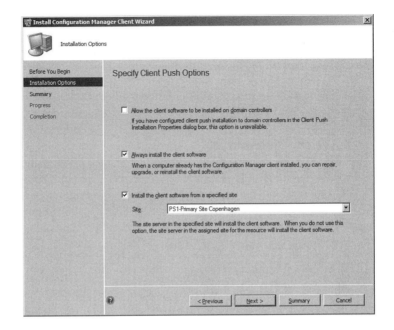

FIGURE 6.19
Client Push Install
Client Wizard
settings

From this page you can also choose to always install the client software. This will force the installation of the client, even if another client is already installed.

You can use the canned reports in the Client Push category to monitor the client push attempts. The reports will provide you with information about all client push attempts divided into days and installation status.

Group Policy

You can use a software installation GPO to install the client. For GPO installations you must use the `ccmsetup.msi` file. This file can be found in the folder `.\Program Files\Microsoft Configuration Manager\bin\i386` on the site server. You cannot specify any command-line properties when publishing the client; instead the command lines that are published to Active Directory will be used. If you are installing the client in another forest, you can use a Group Policy based on the `ConfigMgrInstallation.adm` template to provision the command lines locally on the client in the registry before installing the client.

Software Update

This installation method requires that you have an existing WSUS server in the environment and that it is also configured as the software update point. (A Windows client can only be configured with a single WSUS server. For that reason you need to make sure that the WSUS server specified in the GPO is the same as the one being used as the software update point.) Once you enable this method, the Configuration Manager client will be published to WSUS as a required infrastructure update. You cannot specify any command-line properties when publishing the client; instead the command lines that are published to Active Directory will be used. If you are installing the client in another forest, you can use a Group Policy based on the `ConfigMgrInstallation.adm` template to provision the command lines in the registry before installing the client. You can monitor publishing between the site server and WSUS server by reading the `wcm.log` file on the site server.

Note that if you ever need to uninstall Configuration Manager for any reason, make sure you have disabled this client installation method. Failure to do so will leave the Configuration Manager client in WSUS as a required infrastructure update.

Software Distribution

You can deploy the client using the Software Deployment feature. This method is often used when upgrading the client to a new service pack. You will notice that a new installation of Configuration Manager already ships with a Configuration Manager client package and a Configuration Manager client Upgrade package. If you want to create your own Configuration Manager client software package, follow these steps:

1. Open the Configuration Manager console and navigate to the Software workspace.

2. Select Application Management ➤ Packages and click Create Package From Definition on the Ribbon.

3. Click Next.

4. Under Package Definition, select Configuration Manager Client Upgrade and click Next.

   If you do not see the definition, verify that you have selected Microsoft as the publisher.

5. Select Always Obtain Files From A Source Directory and click Next.

6. In the source directory type **\\<Server>\sms_<Sitecode>\Client** where **<Server>** is the name of the Configuration Manager site server and **<sitecode>** is the site code.

7. Click Next and finish the guide.

You have now created a software package containing the client software that you can deploy using the deployment methods described in later chapters.

Logon Script Installation

Logon scripts have been used by companies for many years to apply settings to users and their systems. The parameters that you can use are the same as those described earlier in this chapter. When installing the client using this method, remember to add the `/Logon` command line to `ccmsetup.exe`; otherwise, the client installation will begin every time the user logs on to a system.

Imaging

This shouldn't be a problem because you are most likely going to use the Operating System Deployment feature to install all your clients. The task sequence step "Set up Windows and ConfigMgr" is a required step and will install the Configuration Manager client correctly in both the reference image and the real image. If you are using another imaging solution and need the Configuration Manager client installed in the reference image, follow these steps:

1. Manually install the client.

2. Stop the SMS Agent Host service by running **NET STOP CCMEXEC**.

3. Remove the trusted root key and any other unique certificates. Removing the trusted root key by running `CCMSetup RESETKEYINFORMATION = TRUE`.

4. Capture the image.

Keeping Clients Up to Date

One of the many challenges of being a ConfigMgr. administrator is keeping the ConfigMgr. client agent up-to-date. The preferred method to upgrade clients is by using the application deployment feature. If for whatever reason you do not manage to upgrade all clients, then ConfigMgr. 2012 allows you to configure the Site settings to automatically update the remaining clients. The feature will make use of a hidden software package and deployment that targets the new client version to the All Systems collection. Targeting anything against the All Systems collection is very rarely a good idea, especially not in a production environment. For that sake, and the lack of control I do not recommend using this client update feature.

To configure ConfigMgr. to automatically update the client to a new version follow these steps:

1. Open the ConfigMgr. Administrator console, select the Administration workspace.

2. Select the Site Configuration, sites and click Hierarchy Settings from the ribbon.

3. From the Site Settings Properties, select the Client Installation Settings, as shown in Figure 6.20.

4. Enable Upgrade client automatically when new client updates are available and click OK in the warning dialog. Notice that this is a somewhat uncontrolled upgrade.

FIGURE 6.20

Enabling site wide automatic client upgrade

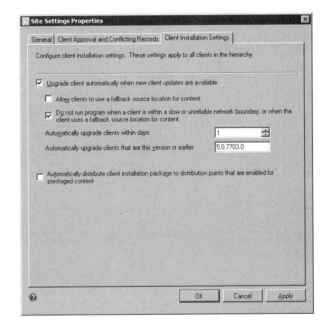

STARTUP SCRIPT

A non-official installation method is to install the client using a startup script. Numerous Configuration Manager forums have example scripts that can be downloaded and customized to your environment. The benefit of using this method is that you will not experience any problems related to local firewalls or installation accounts because the installation will start using the local system account.

Verifying Client Installation

While the installation is in progress, you can view the installation program running within Task Manager or monitor the installation by reading the log files. In Task Manager you will see `ccmsetup.exe` running. As it completes, you will see `ccmsetup.exe` replaced by the agent host program `ccmexec.exe`.

You can also verify that the client has obtained the correct site code and is communicating with the management point, as follows:

1. Open Control Panel, and you will find a new icon named Configuration Manager.

2. Double-click this icon, and the Configuration Manager Properties screen will appear.

3. Click the Site tab to find the site code within the Currently Assigned To Site Code box, as shown in Figure 6.21.

FIGURE 6.21
Verifying that the site code has been obtained

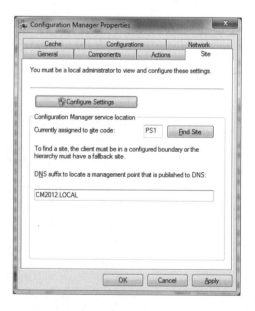

Within the Actions tab of the Configuration Manager Properties screen, you should also find several actions listed by default; other actions will appear in this list as the client agents are enabled. The default actions are Peer DP Maintenance, Discovery Data Collection Cycle, Machine Policy Retrieval & Evaluation Cycle, User Policy Retrieval & Evaluation Cycle, and

Windows Installer Source List Update Cycle. Each of these actions will be covered when we discuss the related components.

Now, unless you have a very small environment, you will not be able to manually verify the installation of each client. Instead you will use the following reports in the SMS Site - Client Information category.

- ◆ Client Deployment Success Report

- ◆ Client Deployment Status Details

- ◆ Client Assignment Status Details Report

- ◆ Client Assignment Success Report

The reports require that you have specified a fallback status point in the command line.

Troubleshooting a Client Installation

To troubleshoot a client installation you will need to understand the three phases in the process. You can troubleshoot each of the phases in real time by reading the correct log files with CMtrace.exe.

The Pre-installation Phase   This phase is described in the "Client Push" section of this chapter. A useful log file in this phase is ccm.log on the site server.

The Installation Phase   This phase begins when ccmsetup.exe reads the mobileclient .tcf file and starts downloading the required files needed to complete the installation. Useful log files in this phase are ccmsetup.log and client.msi.log, both found in the %windir%\ccmsetup folder on the client.

The Post-installation Phase   This phase is also known as the assignment phase, where the client is being added as a managed client to a primary site. Useful log files in this phase are clientidstartupmanager.log, clientlocation.log, and locationservices.log, all found in the %windir%\ccm\logs folder on the client.

Once you have identified where the problem is, you will be able to select the correct log file for further troubleshooting.

Ensuring Client Health

Client Status, and automatic client remediation, are some of the new features in Configuration Manager 2012. In previous versions of Configuration Manager/Systems Management Server, organizations were forced to spend numerous hours creating custom client health solutions, and even more organizations did not even implement a client health process. In Configuration Manager an automatic remediation process runs daily on every client, and reports and alerts tell you if the number of active clients is dropping to a number below the defined SLAs for the company.

Automatic Client Remediation

During the client installation a schedule remediation task is created in Windows. Figure 6.22 shows the scheduled task in Task Scheduler. The process ccmeval will run daily and perform all the checks that are specified in the `ccmeval.xml` file found in the `%windir%\ccm` folder. There are more than 20 different checks. If the evaluation process fails, the client will automatically be reinstalled. All ccmeval status messages will be forwarded to the management point. You can monitor the process by reading the `ccmeval.log` and `CcmEvalTask.log` files found in `%windir%\ccm\logs` and the `ccmsetup-ccmeval.log` file found in `%windir%\ccmsetup\`.

FIGURE 6.22
CCM evaluation task

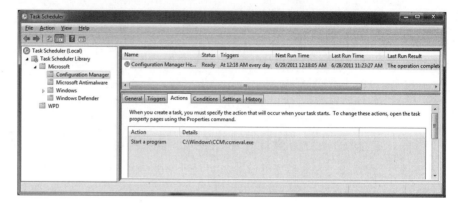

You can monitor the client remediation process in the Configuration Manager console. Navigate to the Monitoring workspace and select Client Status ➢ Client Check.

Determining Client Health

To determine the overall client health Configuration Manager uses multiple objects such as these:

- Discover records

- Hardware inventory

- Software inventory

- Status messages

- Policy requests

- Active Directory integration

As the administrator, you will define when a client goes from being considered active to inactive. To configure the client activity settings, follow these steps:

1. Navigate to the Monitoring workspace.

2. Select Client Status.

3. From the Ribbon click Status Reporting Settings to open the window shown in Figure 6.23.

FIGURE 6.23
Client Status
Settings Properties—
General tab

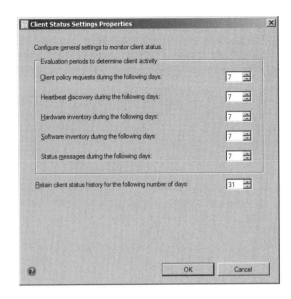

There are no correct or incorrect settings; it all depends on the client behavior in your network. Do you have only workstations that are supposed to be started daily, or do you have a large number of laptops that are infrequently connected to the network? Don't be too aggressive when configuring the settings. If you configure the wrong values, you might find yourself chasing ghosts and trying to troubleshoot clients that for obvious reasons are not connected to the network.

Monitoring Client Status

The client status data is displayed in the Monitoring workspace. When you click the Client Status node, you will see both the client activity and the client Check data. If you click any of the different states you will be taken to the Assets and Compliance workspace, where you will see all the devices that are in the selected state.

You can also use the canned reports in the Client Health category. They will provide you with valuable information about the overall health status and the client agility.

Client Status Summary Can be used as the main client health report. It will give an overview of the client health and client activity data.

Inactive Client Details Will list all inactive clients along with information about the last health check.

Unhealthy Client Details Will display a number and list of all unhealthy clients.

Client Status History Will provide a very good historic view for the last 30–90 days.

Client Time to Request Policy Will display how many clients have requested policies during the last 30 days.

Configuring Alerts

Having a mixed environment with laptops, desktops, and servers often means that you have different activity requirements. You can configure individual thresholds per collection and that way have different settings for the unique computer roles in your environment. Figure 6.24 shows the alerts settings that are configured for a collection containing all servers. Because you can use Configuration Manager to keep the servers compliant with software updates, it is unacceptable to have a server running without a healthy client.

FIGURE 6.24
Configuring
alerts settings
on a collection

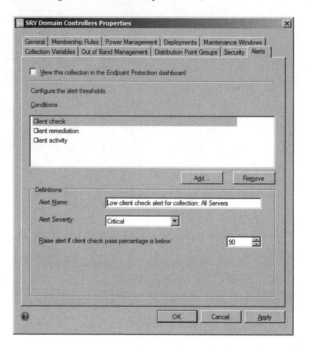

🌐 **Real World Scenario**

CONFIGURING CLIENT HEALTH ALARMS FOR THE ALL SERVERS COLLECTION

As the Configuration Manager administrator, you have been requested to ensure that alerts are generated if any servers become unhealthy. To do so, follow these steps:

1. Open the Configuration Manager 2012 administrative console.

2. Select the Assets and Compliance workspace, and browse to Device Collections.

3. Select the All Servers collection, and click Properties on the Ribbon.

4. Select the Alerts tab, click Add and select each of the three Client Status checks.

5. Click OK.

6. In Conditions select each of the Client Status checks and configure threshold and Alert serverity.

7. Click OK to save the settings.

To monitor the alerts, do the following:

1. Navigate to the Monitoring workspace.

2. Select Alerts.

3. In the Search field, type **Client** and click Search.

You will now see a list of all client remediation, client health, and client activity alerts.

The Bottom Line

Configure boundaries and boundary groups.   Before starting any client installation, verify that you have configured a boundary group for site assignment.

> **Master It**   Let Configuration Manager Forest Discovery automatically create the boundaries and add them to the correct boundary groups.

Select the relevant discovery methods.   You configure discovery methods in the Configuration Manager console. The Active Directory discovery methods all require a schedule and an LDAP path. There are schedules for delta and full discovery. In Configuration Manager 2012, delta discovery will also find changes to existing objects; this eliminates the need to run a full discovery more than once a week.

> **Master It**   Always know what you want to discover and where. Based on that knowledge, configure the needed discovery methods.

Employ the correct client installation methods.   When configuring the client installation methods, make sure you know the pros and cons for each method. Some require firewall settings; others require local administrative permissions. You need to make sure that all the required settings are in place. Do not start any installation until you have the needed site systems, boundary groups, and command lines specified.

> **Master It**   Configure the correct command-line properties and ensure they will work for all environments (local forest, workgroup, and DMZ). Create multiple client push installation accounts, and ensure that you have a good understanding of the three phases (pre-installation, installation, and post-installation).

Ensure client health.   Client Status might not be the first task you think about when implementing a system like Configuration Manager. But it is crucial to the daily administration that you can trust the numbers you see in the reports and in the console. One way to ensure that is by making certain that all clients are healthy and are providing the server with up-to-date status messages and discovery information.

> **Master It**   Discuss the different environment that exists in your organization, and use that information when configuring client health alerts. Make sure that you know the client activity during a normal period and that you have a set of defined SLAs for each of the environments (laptops, road warriors, servers, call center, and so on).

Chapter 7

Application Deployment

The ability to deploy applications has long been a primary function of Configuration Manager. The Application Deployment feature of Configuration Manager 2012 is the new approach for software deployment and allows administrators to deploy most any kind of content to Configuration Manager clients, affecting potentially thousands of systems or users.

The list of content deployable through Application Deployment includes virtually anything—from full applications (i.e., Office) to scripts and batch files. Beyond simply specifying *what* to deploy is also the ability to detail *how* to deploy, including whether an application should be delivered to systems versus users or whether the application should be a full installation on the target system versus a virtualized version using App-V.

With so much flexibility and power comes a great amount of responsibility. Configuration Manager provides robust ability to define and control Application Deployment to systems and users. When properly used, the experience with Application Deployment will be very positive, but it is also possible to make mistakes with this feature and deliver the mistakes to potentially thousands of systems or users. This underscores the need to completely understand the feature and its various options and also the need for proper testing before introducing a change to such a potentially large number of systems or users. This need for proper understanding and testing is not unique to Configuration Manager but applies to any product of enterprise scale.

This chapter will detail the various options and features of Application Deployment in Configuration Manager 2012. In this chapter you will learn to

- ◆ Explain the options available for Application Deployment.

- ◆ Detail the various components required for Application Deployment.

- ◆ Understand the role of and manage distribution points.

What's New in Application Deployment?

The label *Application Deployment* describes the new approach being taken in Configuration Manager 2012 for deploying content. Software Distribution, as it has been historically known, has not been removed from the product; it is still present in the console and represented by the Packages node of Application Management. Also note the Applications node, which is where configurations using the new approach are centered. This is shown in Figure 7.1.

FIGURE 7.1
Applications and
Packages nodes

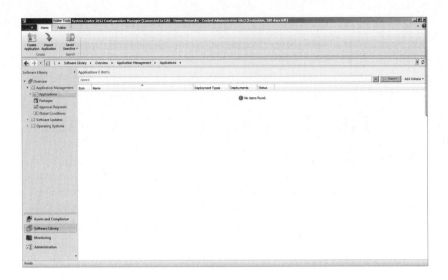

Classic Software Distribution works very much the same way as it did in Configuration Manager 2007. Classic Software Distribution might be seen as available only to facilitate migration and to allow administrators the ability to deploy content the old way while learning the new approach in Configuration Manager 2012. Classic Software Distribution actually remains very useful in certain scenarios. Remember that the new Application Deployment approach is designed to deploy applications, and it offers very rich configurations. The Application Deployment model, however, may not be a good option for every potential deployment. Consider a scenario where an administrator simply needs to deploy a command line to systems. The Application Deployment model isn't well suited for such a task, and instead administrators should use either Classic Software Distribution or a task sequence.

With proper deference given to classic Software Distribution, it is much the same as it was in Configuration Manager 2007, so the discussion in this chapter will be solely focused on the new Application Deployment features.

If you need a full review of the classic Software Distribution model, an excellent discussion is available in the book *Mastering Microsoft System Center Configuration Manager 2007 R2* (Sybex, 2009).

Note the difference in terminology, as shown in Table 7.1.

TABLE 7.1: Terminology differences

APPLICATION DEPLOYMENT	CLASSIC SOFTWARE DISTRIBUTION
Application	Package
Deployment type	Program
Deployment	Advertisement

Because Application Deployment is such a paradigm shift from classic Software Distribution, a bit of discussion about what exactly has changed is warranted.

Distribution Point Changes

Distribution points are key components for any kind of content delivery in Configuration Manager. Understanding the changes to and optimizations of this role will directly relate to the efficiency of your design and satisfaction with the product.

Workstations as Distribution Points   Branch distribution points were first introduced in Configuration Manager 2007, and as of Configuration Manager 2012 they are gone again! Don't worry though; they have been replaced with the ability to directly configure any Windows 7 workstation as a distribution point. This may seem like simply a cosmetic difference—and in some ways that is true, but not totally—there are some significant differences.

The ability to specify a workstation as a distribution point directly means that instead of having a client component to fill the distribution point role, as was the case with Configuration Manager 2007 branch distribution points, now the client doesn't even have to be present!

One limitation of distribution points located on workstation systems is the limit of 20 simultaneous connections. This is a workstation operating system limitation rather than a limit imposed by Configuration Manager.

Single Instance Storage   The traditional distribution point structure and function are still available for very specific classic Software Distribution scenarios, namely, if a legacy package is configured to run from a distribution point. For every other kind of content deployment, whether classic Software Distribution or the new Application Deployment model, the distribution point engine is completely new. The change does also bring some changes in administration, but they are well worth it!

Content storage on traditional distribution points often requires substantial hard drive space. The new distribution point model takes advantage of single-instance storage, which will result in less hard drive space required for content. There are a couple of things to note as a result of this change:

◆ Administrators or users are no longer able to connect to a known distribution point and execute an install remotely.

◆ The Run From Distribution Point option is not available for Application Deployment (but is still available with classic Software Deployment).

◆ The single-instance storage change increases security by obscuring the content and making it difficult for the content to be downloaded and used for other than the intended purpose.

Distribution Point Content Validation   Many Configuration Manager administrators have faced the problem where content initially deploys to distribution points but later becomes corrupt, preventing further deployment until the corruption is resolved. Often the only way administrators have known about the corruption is through failed deployments. Configuration Manager 2012 offers the ability to proactively check content for corruption on both classic and new distribution points and, when found, notify the administrator so proactive corrective action may be taken.

Remote Distribution Point Throttling A common reason for maintaining secondary sites in a Configuration Manager hierarchy is to support locations where it is important to ensure that network bandwidth usage is tightly controlled when sending content to locations with slow, overloaded, or unreliable WAN connections.

Configuration Manager 2012 allows throttling of bandwidth directly between a site and its remote distribution points, helping eliminate the need for secondary sites to achieve this goal.

Hierarchy simplification was a design goal for Configuration Manager 2012. This one added feature helps achieve the simplification goal by drastically reducing the need for secondary sites in most Configuration Manager 2012 hierarchies.

Distribution Point Selection The ability to specify which distribution points are available to clients, an option known as protected distribution points, has been available in previous versions of Configuration Manager.

In Configuration Manager 2012, all distribution points are protected by default. The only way clients are able to access a distribution point is if the distribution point is part of a boundary group that matches the client's current boundary. There is a fallback mechanism to allow clients to access distribution points when the client is in an unknown boundary. Allowing fallback is configured per distribution point and per deployment.

Prestaged Content Managing content in bulk on distribution points has historically been challenging for Configuration Manager administrators. When replacing a distribution point server or even simply renaming, replacing, or modifying hard disks, administrators were faced with the need to redistribute all content to the new server. If connectivity to the server in question was either unreliable or slow, the challenge was even more pronounced.

An initial thought to solve the problem might be to simply copy content from the current to the replacement server. A quick evaluation of this option reveals that it is not a workable choice as a simple file copy does not result in the needed database and other adjustments to reflect the new location of the content. Because of this, administrators either had to use external tools, such as preloadpkgonsite, or suffer through overloading the network while copying potentially gigabytes of content.

Configuration Manager 2012 introduces an option allowing content to be prestaged on distribution points. There is a specific wizard used to accomplish this—as will be seen later in the chapter—but the net effect is that in situations where bandwidth is challenging, content can now be natively staged locally on systems without such strain on network links.

Distribution Point Groups The process of either adding or replacing a distribution point in Configuration Manager is fairly straightforward, but what about the content? If the distribution point being replaced is the storage point for many applications, administrators historically have been faced with either constructing a script to parse through applications and adding them to the new distribution point in bulk or working through applications one by one and enabling the new distribution point. Either task is time consuming!

The use of distribution point groups was possible in Configuration Manager 2007 but was not often used by administrators. Configuration Manager 2012 revamps the use of distribution point groups, and they now take center stage and offer very easy management of distribution points by allowing distribution points that should store similar content to be treated collectively. Simply choose a distribution point group when deploying or removing content, and all distribution points within that group will receive or remove the content. Better still, when a new distribution point is added to the group or removed, then all applicable content targeted to the group will also be added or removed.

User-Centric Focus   In previous versions of Configuration Manager it was possible to target a deployment to users, but this ability was not robust and seemed like an afterthought. In Configuration Manager 2012, the user is the focus—or at least can be!

Yes, it is still possible to target deployments to systems, and many administrators will continue to do this because, in many cases such as server management, that is the best approach. Plus, the ability to target users for deployments and to do so with great specificity is a paradigm shift for Configuration Manager. Don't overlook this feature though, because it offers the ability to significantly enhance a user's experience with and impression of Configuration Manager!

User-centric focus allows administrators to define deployments that function differently based on the location of the user. Consider, for example, a user who is logged onto and using their main computer (known as a primary device in Configuration Manager terminology). Deployments can be configured to recognize this and, in such cases, install software directly onto the user's device, including mobile devices if depth managed—more on that in Chapter 14, "Mobile Device Management." Conversely, if the user happens to be logged onto a device in another location, such as in a remote office, this can be recognized and the deployment delivered automatically as a virtualized application instead, allowing the deployment to be made available quickly and without persisting the installation. This allows the user the same experience regardless of which system they are actually logged onto and using, and it's all seamless to the user!

Software Center   The Configuration Manager Software Center is an updated replacement to the Run Advertised Program option available in previous versions of Configuration Manager. The Software Center is the central location where users are able to view available or required deployments targeted for their system and to also make their own custom changes such as to specify working hours or whether Configuration Manager operations should be suppressed while presentations are taking place, or even whether their computer should honor assigned power management settings.

The only required deployments visible in Software Center will be those that are configured with the ability for users to interact.

Software Catalog   This often-requested and long-awaited feature is finally here! Configuration Manager 2012 allows administrators an option to publish deployments into a web-based Software Catalog. The Software Catalog web page is accessible to any user and is filtered to list only deployments specifically targeted to the given users. Through the catalog, users are able to request available software that is of interest. Entries in the Software Catalog can be configured as freely available or as requiring approval. Note the Approval Requests node under Application Management in Figure 7.1. When software is configured to require approval, the user is able to request the software, but administrators will need to manually approve the request before deployment will continue. Administrators approve pending requests in the Approval Requests node.

Applications: Application References

The Application References mechanism allows administrators to view what dependency and supersedence relationships are associated with a given application. The best way to describe this is by example.

Dependency Assume two applications, RichCopy and .NET Framework 2.0. It is possible to specify a dependency so that RichCopy requires that .NET Framework 2.0 be present on a target device. If .NET Framework 2.0 isn't present on the device when you attempt to deploy RichCopy, you can configure it to automatically deploy as part of the RichCopy deployment. If not, RichCopy will fail to install until .NET Framework 2.0 is present.

The dependencies themselves are configured on the Dependency tab of the application deployment type. The References node simply displays the information for the application as a whole.

Supersedence Assume two applications, RichCopy and Robocopy. It is possible to specify a supersedence relationship to define that RichCopy supersedes RoboCopy. Doing so effectively links the two applications and establishes a path for replacing one application with another, either by upgrade or by uninstalling the superseded application and replacing it with the current application.

 Real World Scenario

Be careful when building relationships between applications. Relationships will prevent an application from being deleted and excessive numbers of relationships will increase complexity and potential confusion.

Deployments

Deployments in Configuration Manager 2012 directly influence the flow of application deployment. There are a number of new options available to help control this flow, as described here:

Deployment Types Deployment types specify how a particular application should be deployed. As shown in Table 7.1 previously, think of deployment types as similar to programs in classic Software Distribution but with much greater flexibility and specificity. There are multiple deployment types including predefined paths for deploying MSI-based applications, App-V versions of the application, mobile device CAB file versions of an application, and also scripts. Beyond these predefined types it is possible to manually define whatever other type of deployment may be needed.

Native Uninstall Support Previous versions of Configuration Manager allowed for software deployment but no native support for software uninstall. Uninstall was possible but required a separate program definition. Configuration Manager 2012 allows specifying options for both install and uninstall within a single deployment type. There is no requirement to use both, but they are available. When creating an application using the wizard, some deployment types— such as MSI-based deployments—will automatically create the uninstall option.

Detection Method Previous versions of Configuration Manager allowed administrators to define a deployment but no mechanism to determine if that deployment had already taken place by another mechanism. The result was that software could get reinstalled even if it was already present. Configuration Manager 2012 allows administrators the ability to define rules to determine if the deployment is already in place on a system and, if so, to simply exit without triggering a reinstall. This mechanism may seem similar to what historically has been seen with software patching. The two mechanisms are very similar.

Requirements   In previous versions of Configuration Manager it was common practice to build collections of systems matching specific criteria or filters and then to target advertisement(s) to those collections. In Configuration Manager 2012, collections remain a requirement for deployment targeting, but the need to build a new collection or multiple new collections to provide filtering for a single deployment should be reduced. Administrators now have the ability to specify deployment requirements per deployment type. These requirements ensure a specific deployment type is not executed unless specific criteria are met. Once defined, Requirement rules are reusable.

TARGETING

Historically it has been recommended to avoid targeting the All Systems collection when deploying software. Doing so meant that the software would be received and executed by every device that is part of the All Systems collection, which is every device at a site and potentially every device in the hierarchy! It is still a good idea to avoid targeting the All Systems collection, but with deployment type requirements properly configured, it would be possible to safely do so if needed.

Dependencies   The ability to specify dependencies between different deployments has been available since the release of SMS 2.0. Until Configuration Manager 2012, however, these dependencies were not so straightforward and creating multiple dependencies often resulted in confusion.

Dependencies in Configuration Manager 2012 are a much more elegant solution and allow administrators to configure other applications on which the one being configured depends. Single dependencies may be specified or multiple. When adding dependencies it is possible also to select whether a given dependency will be automatically installed in the event it is absent. Setting Auto Install for a dependency is not a requirement but can help ensure deployments execute error free.

Adding dependencies essentially joins the current application with whatever dependency is being specified, so later, if a dependent application is removed, a warning will be displayed about potentially breaking a dependency relationship.

While dependencies are a big step forward for controlling and predicting application deployment results there is still no way to define order of installation for dependencies. Typically this fact isn't a big deal but, if multiple dependencies are configured for an application, it could be a concern. If it is required to know the exact order of execution for a deployment and if its related dependencies consider using a task sequence instead.

Return Codes   A successful install of most applications will result in a return code of either 0 or 3010 being generated. These return codes mean success or success pending reboot, respectively. In previous versions of Configuration Manager, if a return code other than these two is returned, then the application deployment is considered to have failed. Depending on the software manufacturer, a return code other than 0 or 3010 may actually be informative about the state of a deployment other than simply indicating success or failure. The number of such applications is relatively small, but when encountered they can be frustrating because a successful install will appear to have failed. The task sequence engine in Configuration Manager 2007 was the first place where administrators were able to account for exit code variations. In Configuration Manager 2012 this ability has been brought forward to Application Deployment as well, fully allowing administrators to define what specific exit codes from an application actually mean and responding accordingly when reporting status.

Deployment Settings Action   Previous versions of Configuration Manager allowed deployments to be built that would be installed on clients. Configuration Manager 2012 also allows for that but introduces the ability to force an application uninstall on clients. This action will cause the uninstall command line configured on the deployment type to be executed.

Deployment Settings Purpose   The deployment purpose can be configured as either available or required These options are similar to specifying a deployment as optional or mandatory in previous versions of Configuration Manager but with a twist. When a deployment is configured as required, the application will be forced onto the client. This is the same behavior as previous versions when selecting a mandatory deployment. The twist is that on a schedule, the deployment is reevaluated, and if the application is found to be missing, it is forced back onto the client system.

Alerts   New to Configuration Manager 2012 is the ability to specify alerts when deployments fail to reach a certain threshold of success, specified as a percentage. The next question that often is asked when discussing this new alerting functionality is whether this ability is intended to replace monitoring by the System Center Operations Manager Configuration Manager 2012 management pack. The answer is a resounding no. The scope of the Configuration Manager 2012 management pack is more encompassing than what can be achieved by native Configuration Manager 2012 alerting. The alerting feature in Configuration Manager 2012 is introduced to allow administrators some ability to raise awareness of issues independently without System Center Operations Manager. In environments with System Center Operations Manager, the Configuration Manager 2012 management pack should be the primary monitoring resource, with the internal Configuration Manager alerting engine acting as a supplement.

Dependencies for Application Deployment

The Application Deployment feature makes use of several different dependencies. These dependencies must all be configured correctly for application deployment to be successful.

Management Point

The management point is the key interface between clients and their assigned site. Through management point policy updates, clients learn about assigned settings and activity requested by the site and also return data to the site, such as inventory or discovery data. It is through management point policies that clients are made aware of pending application deployments and associated settings, and it is through the management point that clients return status after attempting to run an application deployment. It is also through the management point that clients look up which distribution points are available when it comes time to execute an application deployment.

Thus, having a functioning management point is crucial not only for proper client operation but also for proper application deployment. Chapter 4, "Installation and Site Roll Configuration," includes full discussion of management point setup and configuration.

Distribution Point

The distribution point role is crucial for application deployment in that it is the location where all remote content that should be accessed and used during application deployment is stored. If a distribution point is not available to clients when you attempt to initiate an application deployment, the deployment will fail. Multiple distribution points may be present per primary site, including workstation-class machines running Windows 7 or greater. Distribution points installed for a site but on servers other than the site server, also known as remote distribution points, may be configured for content throttling in the distribution point's properties. Chapter 4 includes full discussion of distribution point setup and configuration.

APPLICATION DEPLOYMENT FAILURE

It is possible that an application deployment may fail even if content is available on some or all of the distribution points. In such cases verify that at least one distribution point within the client's boundary is configured with content and, if the distribution point is running on a workstation system, ensure that it is not exceeding its connection limit. In addition, validate whether errors have been encountered when staging content to distribution points.

BITS-ENABLED IIS

In previous releases of Configuration Manager it was optional to enable Background Intelligent Transfer Service (BITS) for a distribution point. In Configuration Manager 2012 BITS is required.

Default Client Settings

A word about client settings: the default list of client settings applies to all clients in the Configuration Manager 2012 hierarchy. It is possible to override the default settings and specify different values for specific sites or specific systems via collection targeting.

This flexibility allows administrators complete control of which settings apply to devices and removes the technical limitation that often resulted in multiple sites or hierarchies, such as scenarios where servers and workstations needed separate management settings. The flexibility offered with client settings applies generically throughout Configuration Manager, but several settings available have specific impact with Application Deployment, as discussed below.

BACKGROUND INTELLIGENT TRANSFER

BITS settings are part of the default client settings and are shown in Figure 7.2. In some environments clients are installed and managed across slow or heavily utilized WAN links. In such cases it may be important to ensure clients are able to sense a heavy load on the network and, during critical times, respond by reducing the amount of data that is being transferred, a process also known as throttling. Throttling controls are found throughout Configuration Manager 2012 to help reduce WAN impact. The BITS client settings specifically allow administrators to configure clients to limit the amount of network bandwidth they utilize when transferring content. This content includes application deployment data, along with several other types of information.

Real World Scenario

Configuring BITS settings through the client settings mechanism is very flexible and gives administrators good options for bandwidth control. These settings alone will work to achieve the desired result in most environments. Where these settings by themselves are not sufficient it is also possible to introduce throttling directly through controls in Internet Information Server. While throttling through IIS is useful and easy to configure, it universally impacts traffic to and from IIS and should be considered only after other options have been exhausted.

FIGURE 7.2
BITS settings

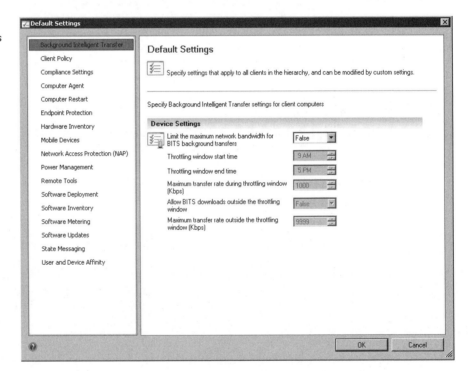

COMPUTER AGENT

Computer Agent settings are part of the default client settings and are shown in Figure 7.3. These settings apply to all deployments, including software updates and operating system deployments, and allow the administrator control over the user experience while deploying content.

FIGURE 7.3
Computer Agent settings

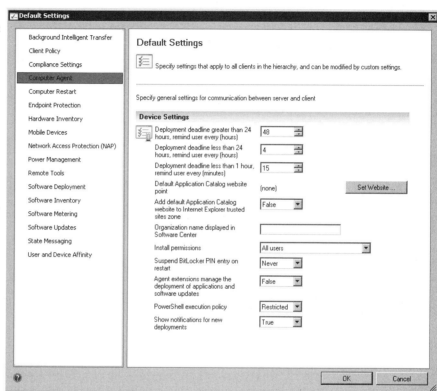

COMPUTER RESTART

Computer Restart settings are part of the default client settings and are shown in Figure 7.4. These settings apply to all deployments, including software updates and operating system deployments and allow administrators to define countdown settings to be used in the event a computer must be restarted as a result of application deployment.

FIGURE 7.4
Computer
Restart
settings

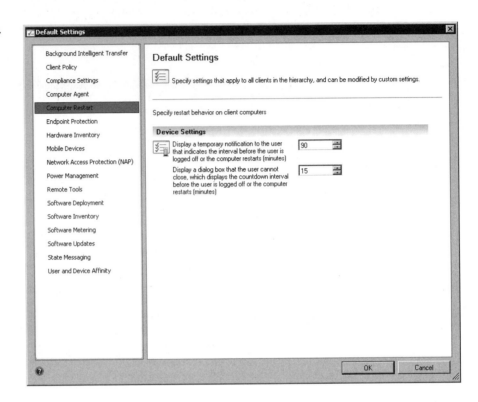

SOFTWARE DEPLOYMENT

The Software Deployment settings are also part of the default client settings and are shown in Figure 7.5. The only option here allows administrators to determine what schedule should be used for reevaluating deployments.

FIGURE 7.5
Software
Deployment
settings

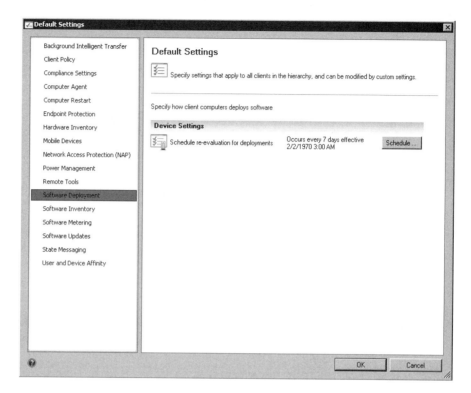

USER AND DEVICE AFFINITY

The User and Device Affinity settings are also part of the default client settings and are shown in Figure 7.6. These settings specify options that Configuration Manager 2012 will use when attempting to determine whether a user is logged onto a primary device or logged on elsewhere.

FIGURE 7.6
User and Device
Affinity settings

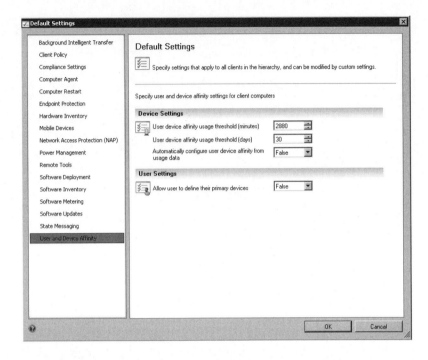

SOFTWARE DISTRIBUTION PROPERTIES

Software Distribution properties, shown in Figure 7.7, are accessible from the Administrative node by selecting Site Configuration ➢ Sites and then selecting a site server hosting distribution points. From the ribbon select Configure Site Components and then Software Distribution Components. This option allows administrators to configure concurrent package distribution settings and also retry settings if a failure is encountered. These settings are the same as what was available in previous versions of Configuration Manager.

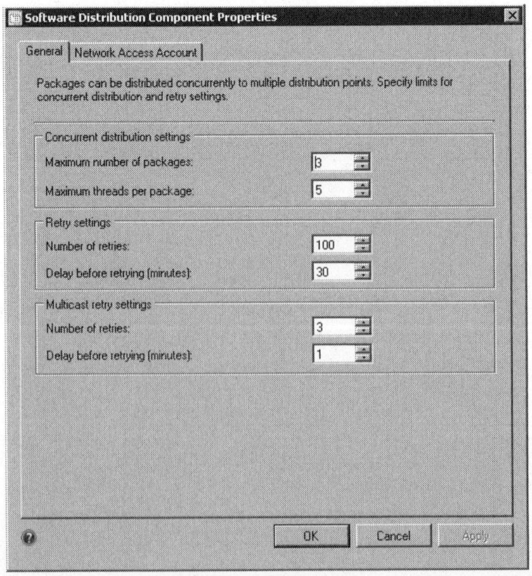

FIGURE 7.7
Software Distribution
Properties

The Network Access Account setting is used to define an account that can be used for network access when content is needed during deployment from a network location other than the Configuration Manager distribution point. The network access account also is used in scenarios where clients are installed in an untrusted scenario, such as workgroup systems or machines in an untrusted forest. This account is also key for use in Operating System Deployment. The network access account in Configuration Manager 2012 is used the same way as it was in previous versions. The only difference is that the location where it is configured has changed. In previous versions this option was part of the computer client agent settings.

SQL REPLICATION

Previous versions of Configuration Manager made use of standard site-to-site communications for sending all data between sites. Configuration Manager 2012 still uses site-to-site communications for some data, but for configuration data, such as application deployment configurations, that data is replicated between sites using SQL replication. Thus, ensuring the SQL replication structure for Configuration Manager 2012 is healthy is key to ensuring consistent data throughout the hierarchy.

SITE-TO-SITE COMMUNICATIONS

The mechanism for site-to-site communications has been part of Configuration Manager for many versions. This mechanism is much the same in Configuration Manager 2012, but its scope is limited to only sending data such as application deployment content. SQL replication is used for transferring site settings information.

COLLECTIONS

Collections remain integral to application deployment. Collections are the ultimate target for all deployments, and so the proper use of collections, including dynamic versus static collections, and the proper replication of collection data between sites via SQL replication are key to successful application deployment.

Proper use of collections is crucial for successful application deployment, but collections are necessary to many functions in Configuration Manager 2012 beyond just application deployment. For that reason, collection management and strategy are not discussed in this chapter, but are discussed in more detail in Chapter 5, "Role-Based Administration."

BOUNDARIES/BOUNDARY GROUPS

Boundaries and boundary groups are the mechanisms Configuration Manager 2012 clients use to locate available distribution points for content access. Configuring these settings correctly will allow for efficient application deployment. Boundaries and boundary groups are detailed in Chapter 2, " Planning a Configuration Manager Infrastructure."

Elements of Application Deployment

Several components are integral to successful configuration of Application Deployment in Configuration Manager 2012. Some of these components are specific to Application Deployment and others apply more generally. In either case, a proper understanding and configuration of these components are important.

Applications

Administrators build applications in Configuration Manager 2012 to describe software that is to be deployed. Administrators create an application to specify details regarding the application, such as the manufacturer, an internal contact for support, information that should appear in the Software Catalog, details regarding the action an application will take, or whether the application being built supersedes a previous version.

A sample application is shown in Figure 7.8. The process of building an application will be detailed shortly.

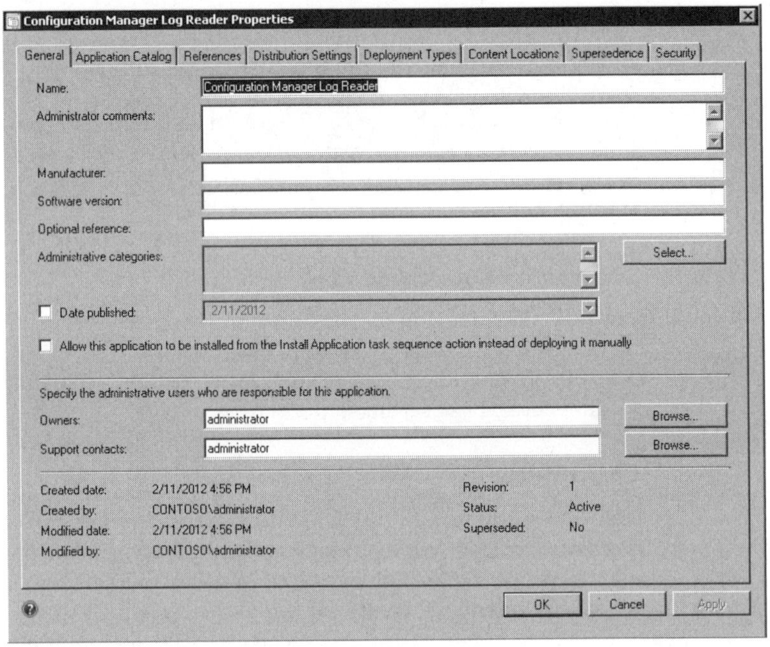

FIGURE 7.8

Sample application properties

Deployment Types

The act of creating an application by itself does not specify sufficient instruction for carrying out deployment of the application. Deployment types provide additional detail for how a given application should be handled in various situations, such as what type of action to take when the application is being deployed to various types of devices or users. In addition, a deployment type also will describe mechanisms to detect whether an application is already installed or command lines needed to remove an application. The deployment type is created when building an application through the Create Application Wizard, so the difference between the application itself and the deployment type may not be clear. Figure 7.8 shows the General tab for the application definition. The Deployment Types tab, which will list all configured Deployment Types for the Application, is also visible in Figure 7.8. Figure 7.9 shows the properties of a sample deployment type. The process of building deployment types will be detailed further shortly.

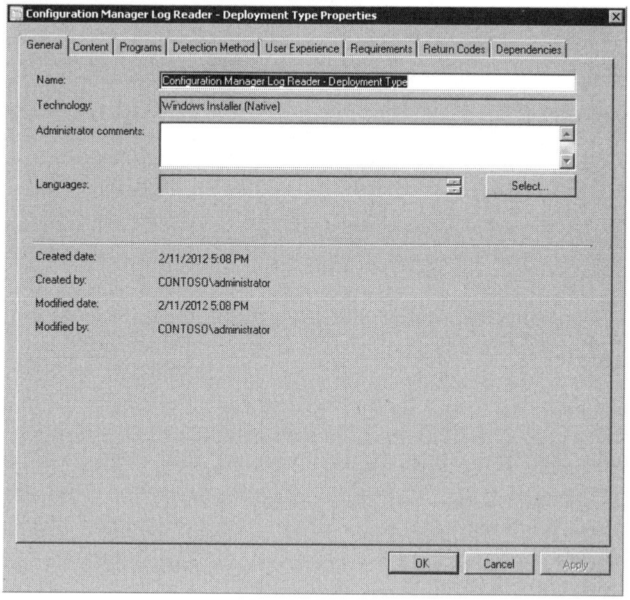

FIGURE 7.9

Sample deployment
type properties

Deployments

A deployment in Configuration Manager 2012 is the mechanism that associates applications and deployment types with a collection of devices or users so that the deployment may proceed. The deployment is not created as part of building the application and deployment type. Deployments are created by selecting the Deploy option from the Ribbon when focused on a particular application in the console. Figure 7.10 shows the properties of a sample deployment. The process of building deployments will be detailed further shortly.

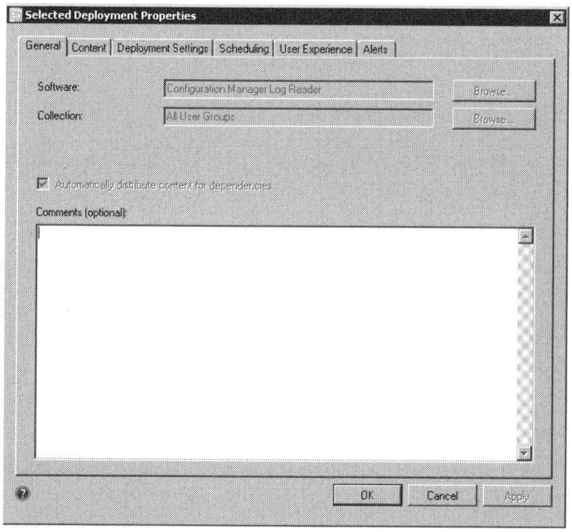

FIGURE 7.10

Sample deployment
properties

The Application Deployment Process

The process of deploying applications in Configuration Manager 2012 has some similarity to previous versions but also has significant differences and additional options. One such example is the use of collections. It remains a requirement to have an application deployed to a collection in order for deployment to begin, but the use of collections is much changed from previous versions. In the past, application-specific collections of systems, and rarely users, would be created ahead of creating the package, program, and advertisement (classic Software Distribution terminology). The collections would be built according to specific criteria to define the scope of the distribution.

Configuration Manager 2012 application deployment introduces the concept of requirements. With requirements it is possible to define the rules of deployment within the deployment itself rather than build specific collections to do the same thing. When requirements are used instead of collections to specify deployment rules the load of evaluation is effectively moved from the site server to individual client systems. Add to this that once a requirement rule is defined it is retained and reusable for other deployments!

The use of requirements is optional but they are both effective and efficient ways to validate deployment requirements. Administrators should consider strongly whether the old style collection sprawl, which tends to junk up the console over time and can get fairly confusing to look at, really continues to be justified.

The best way to discuss the application deployment process is to create a sample application, deployment type, and deployment and then to demonstrate its execution in the environment. To start, a view of the Application Management ➢ Applications node of the console is instructive, as shown in Figure 7.11.

FIGURE 7.11
Application
Management ➢
Applications node

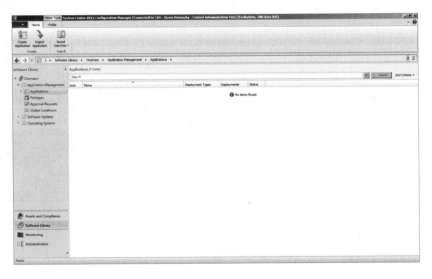

Create Application Wizard

The Create Application Wizard creates an application and the first of potentially several deployment types.

When you're first getting started with Application Deployment in Configuration Manager 2012, the console will be not be populated with any deployments.

A WORD ABOUT PACKAGES

If you're migrating from Configuration Manager 2007, any packages are considered legacy (but still fully functional) in Configuration Manager 2012 and are migrated to the Packages node.

To get started with Application Deployment, you can either import an application from another Configuration Manager 2012 hierarchy by clicking the Import Application button or click Create Application. Both options are on the Ribbon.

To build the sample application deployment, click Create Application to launch the Create Application Wizard. The general page of the Create Application Wizard is shown in Figure 7.12.

FIGURE 7.12
General page of the Create Application Wizard

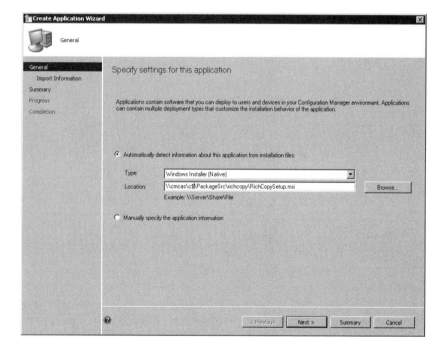

The General page lets you choose either Automatically Detect This Information Using Existing Content or Manually Define The Information. The quickest mechanism for configuring the sample application is to allow information to be automatically detected. This is particularly efficient when deploying an .MSI file. The option you choose on this page is dictated by preference and the type of application being defined. Using the option to manually define the information may be more appropriate depending on the type of content being deployed. Choosing this option simply requires manual entry of data that is otherwise supplied by the automatic option. In either case, reviewing all settings after they're initially configured with the wizard is a good idea.

For the sample application deployment, select the automatic option and choose Windows Installer (Native) as the Type. Then click Next to proceed to the Import Information page of the wizard, shown in Figure 7.13. This page of the wizard is displayed while information is being gathered from the specified source, in this case the RichCopySetup.MSI file. Once the collection is complete, the Import Succeeded page of the wizard will be displayed, as shown in Figure 7.14.

FIGURE 7.13
Import Information
page of Create
Application
Wizard

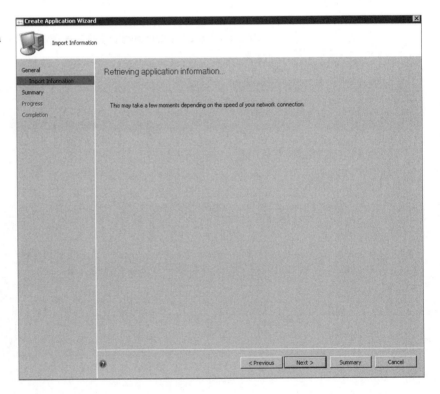

FIGURE 7.14

Import Succeeded page of Create Application Wizard

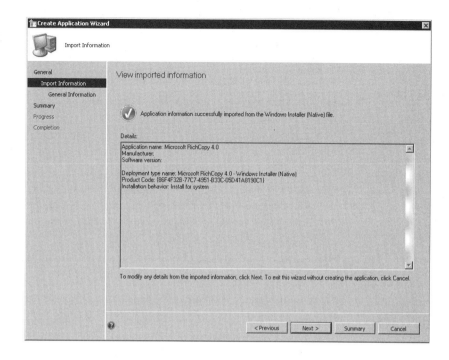

Once the Next option becomes available, click it to proceed to the General Information page of the wizard, shown in Figure 7.15.

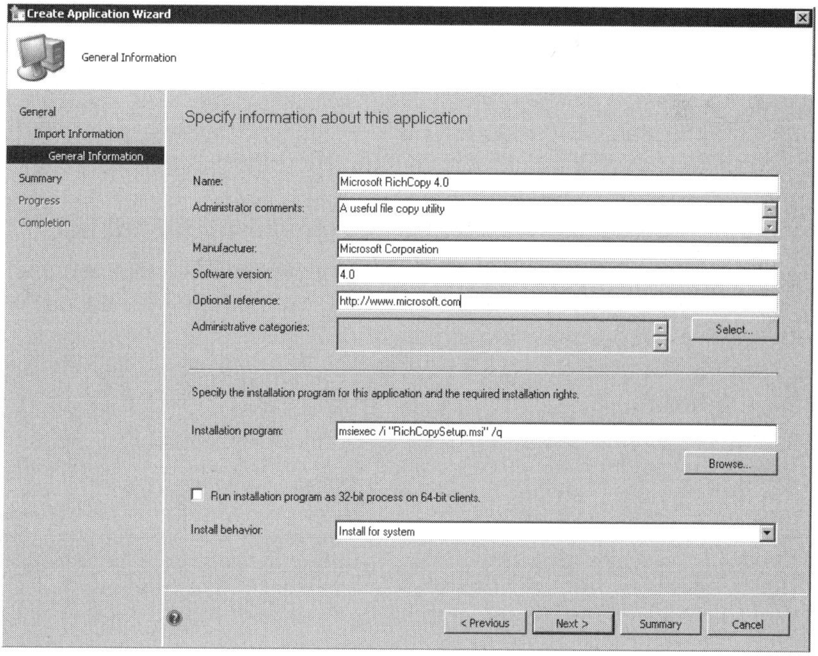

FIGURE 7.15

General Information page of Create Application Wizard

On the General Information page specify the requested information as follows:

Required Information The import process should have completed the required fields of the General Information page leaving only the optional fields to be completed.

> **Name** The name of the application being created.
>
> **Installation Program** The command line of the program to initiate application installation.
>
> **Install Behavior** Options for this setting allow administrators to specify whether the deployment will be targeted to Install For User, Install For System, or Install For System If Resource Is Device, Otherwise Install As User.

Optional Information The information supplied as part of the optional fields is available for user review when applications are published in the Software Center or Application Catalog.

> **Administrator Comments** Allows you to include any comments to further describe or detail the application.
>
> **Manufacturer** Allows you to specify the software manufacturer.
>
> **Software Version** Allows you to specify the software version.
>
> **Optional Reference** Allows you to specify additional reference information for the application.
>
> **Administrative Categories** Allows administrators to group applications together by user-defined categories that make sense in a given organization. Multiple categories may be specified.
>
> There are two types of categories: administrative and user. The dialog here allows specification of administrative categories. Specifying user categories is done on the Catalog node of the application.

When you've finished entering information, click the Next button to proceed to the Summary page of the wizard. Review the summary information, and if it's correct, click Next to create the application. If errors are encountered the wizard will display them. If the application is created successfully, exit the Create Application Wizard and return to the main console.

Options for Application Deployment: the Ribbon

Now that an application is defined in the console, additional options appear on the Ribbon. Let's take a quick pause to explore the options, as shown in Figure 7.16.

FIGURE 7.16
Ribbon options for
application
deployment

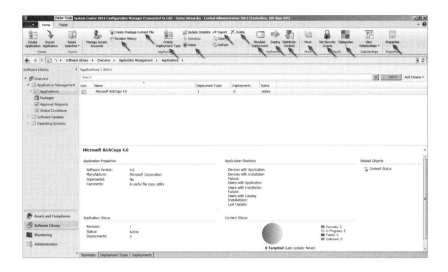

Wow, that's a lot of new options! Yes, and this is the first place that we start to see some of the new choices available for applications in Configuration Manager 2012.

Revision History   The Revision History option tracks all changes that have been made to an application. This tracking not only creates a record of changes but also allows you to revert to a previous version if you've made a mistake. For the sample RichCopy application, we made a simple change to the administrator comments text, resulting in a new version being created. You can view the change by selecting the revision of interest, selecting the record, and clicking View. Notice in Figure 7.17 that the word *very* has been added to the administrator comments. If for some reason you don't want this change, you can simply pick the revision that is correct and click Restore to revert the application.

FIGURE 7.17
Viewing revision
history

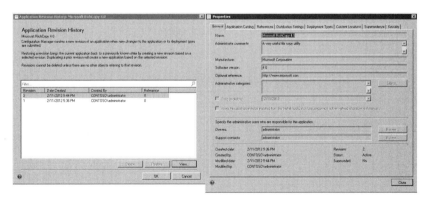

While this example is of a minor change, it does illustrate the power of revision tracking!

Create Prestage Content File   We've already discussed the challenges of managing distribution point content when replacing or adding distribution points in previous versions of Configuration Manager. The challenges are made worse when the distribution points are

positioned across a slow or busy WAN connection from the site server. Historically, solutions for staging content in bulk without saturating such a WAN connection included utilities such as preloadpkgonsite, scripts, or other third-party tools. But all of these tools came with their limitations and challenges. Configuration Manager 2012 introduces Prestaged Content as a mechanism to manage this type of scenario natively. When a distribution point supports Prestaged Content, administrators are able to choose applications that should be made available in a Prestaged Content file, along with all dependencies, which can then be copied locally onto the remote distribution point without the need for substantial WAN communication. Configuring Prestaged Content support requires setting the option on the distribution point and then using the Create Prestaged Content File Wizard to generate a file containing the content of
interest. The Create Prestaged Content File Wizard is shown in Figure 7.18.

FIGURE 7.18
Create Prestaged
Content File Wizard

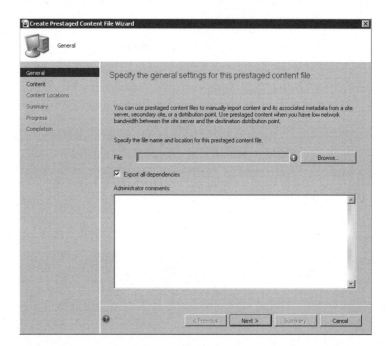

Create Deployment Type   A deployment type for the sample RichCopy application has already been created by the Create Application Wizard. We'll review this shortly. For a given application it is possible to create multiple deployment types. Selecting this button from the Ribbon launches a wizard that walks through the configurations needed for creating new deployment types to augment deployment of the selected application.

Retire/Reinstate   The option to retire an application allows administrators to effectively mark an application as no longer deployable without deleting it from the console. There are a couple of advantages to this approach:

◆ The application deployment status is not removed.

◆ If questions arise about the application configuration, the configuration may easily be reviewed.

◆ If it becomes necessary to reinstate the application to an active status, it is possible to do so by simply selecting the Reinstate option.

Delete Its pretty obvious what this option does but it's still worth a bit of discussion. As we will see shortly, it is possible (and likely) that applications will be tied to each other through dependencies and supercedence relationships. When these relationships exist, or when there is a deployment defined for an application, the deletion option will fail to work. This prevents potentially removing an application that is critical to the function of another. While this is good it is important to understand and be able to resolve these relationships. The View Relationships option helps detail all configured links for a given application.

Simulate Deployment This is a really cool option in Configuration Manager 2012 that allows administrators to perform a test deployment of a configured application which will function only to validate associated relationships and report back on what kind of success might be expected. The Simulate Deployment option is shown in Figure 7.19.

FIGURE 7.19
Simulate Application
Deployment Wizard

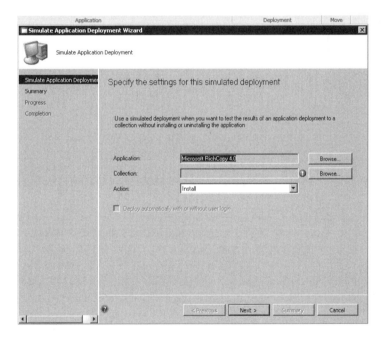

Export A welcome addition to Configuration Manager 2012 is the ability to share almost any configuration, including application definitions, between Configuration Manager 2012 hierarchies. The Export Application button on the Ribbon launches a wizard to walk through steps to complete the export. The wizard is shown in Figure 7.20.

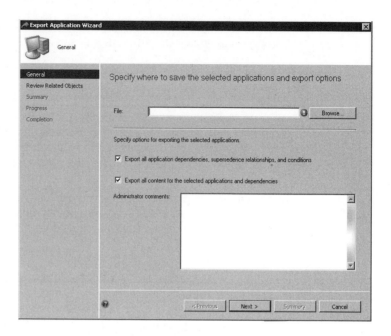

The content created by the Export Application Wizard is available for import into another Configuration Manager 2012 hierarchy using the Import Application button from the Ribbon.

Another potentially interesting use of this functionality is as an extra level of backup for data configured in the site. Consider retiring an application as an example. It could be that the application is ready to be purged from the console but you would like to keep a copy around for those scenarios where it might be needed again. Exporting before deletion is the perfect answer!

Deploy   Creating an application and associated deployment type(s) does not result in any action taking place. To trigger action a deployment is needed. Deployments are *not* created as part of the Create Application Wizard and must be configured through the Deploy Wizard, as will be shown for the RichCopy sample application shortly.

Distribute Content   Deploying applications requires that content needed for the application be distributed to target systems/users. To make content available to clients it must be staged on a distribution point. We'll review the options to distribute content for the RichCopy sample application shortly.

At this stage we will just say that, while this option is useful to stage content to distribution points, using it isn't strictly required. By defining distribution point groups to include collection mappings, when a collection is targeted with a deployment the content needed will automatically deploy to the defined distribution points. A nice option to save a couple of extra mouse clicks!

Move   This option allows administrators to move applications between defined folders. This helps keep things organized as the number of defined applications increases.

Set Security Scope   Security scopes are more of a topic for security, covered in detail in Chapter 5. The role security scopes play with applications is interesting, though, and merits a brief discussion.

A significant change in Configuration Manager 2012 is in how security is handled, both in terms of assignment of user roles and the ability to mark certain objects, such as applications, as being part of one or more defined security scopes. Configuration Manager 2012 console users may also be assigned to one or more security scopes; by so doing, you limit the users' visibility of the Configuration Manager 2012 environment, including applications, to just those items that are part of their assigned scope(s).

Categorize   As already noted when creating the sample RichCopy application, it is possible to create and assign categories to applications for the purposes of organization or grouping. Managing categories can be done as part of the application creation, but that is cumbersome so the Categorize option on the Ribbon is available to enable easier category management.

Properties   This option will open the Properties dialog for selected objects in the console and is useful for editing settings made through the various wizards.

Exploring the Sample Application

The wizard operations are complete. The result? An application and an associated deployment type. That was easy! But what options did the wizard actually set for these items, and what options are available? To take a look, select the application, and from the Ribbon, select Properties. The Microsoft RichCopy 4.0 application property screen opens to the General tab, as shown in Figure 7.21.

FIGURE 7.21
Microsoft RichCopy 4.0
Properties—General tab

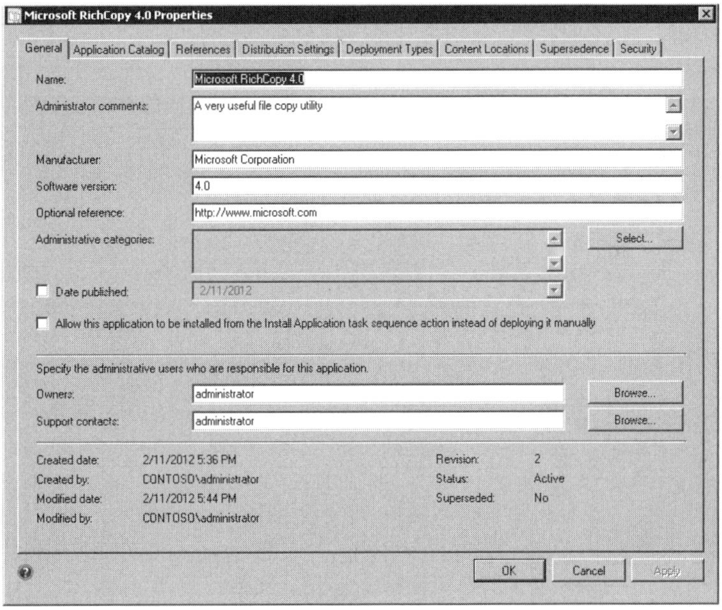

Most of the options on the General tab have already been discussed. In addition to those already mentioned, a few additional options are available:

Date Published   The published date allows administrators to note when the application was published. This date defaults to the current date if not selected and modified.

Allow this application to be installed from the install application task sequence action instead of deploying it manually.   This option is not selected by default. If the application should be deployable via task sequence, you must select this box. If it isn't selected, the task sequence will fail or, when building a task sequence, applications configured without this option will not be available for selection.

Owners   This option allows administrators to define who the owner is for the given application. This information is then displayed in Software Center and also in the Application Catalog.

Support Contacts   This option allows administrators to define who users should contact if problems are encountered with the application. This information is then displayed in Software Center and also in the Application Catalog. The Browse button allows you to select users from Active Directory if desired, or you may enter users manually.

The bottom section of the General tab provides summary information for the application, including its status, whether it is superseded by another application, and the current revision number.

Selecting the Catalog tab details options related to publishing the application in the Application Catalog. Some options here will be provided already. If you're publishing in the catalog, you'll likely need to modify or supply some of the default options. Remember, publishing in the Application Catalog is not actually accomplished on this tab. Rather, this tab collects information to be used *if* the application is published in the catalog. Associating your deployment, described soon, with a collection of users or user groups will result in the application showing up in the catalog. Options for the RichCopy sample are shown in Figure 7.22.

FIGURE 7.22
Microsoft RichCopy 4.0
Properties—Catalog tab

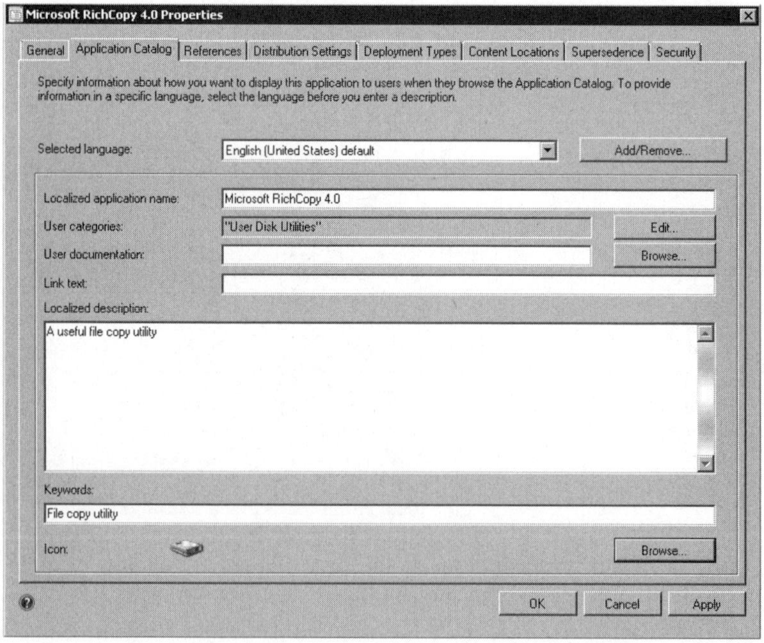

Selected Language   This option allows administrators to add or remove languages that should be supported by the application in the catalog and also to specify which language should be displayed.

Localized Application Name   This option presents the application name localized by the current language selected.

User Categories   User-targeted applications and device-targeted applications maintain separate category lists for grouping purposes. If publishing this application for users, administrators have the option to select an existing user category for describing the application or to create a new one.

User Documentation   With this option, administrators are allowed to specify a path that is available to the user for additional information on the application. This path may be a web page that the user might visit or a link to an online document.

Link Text   This option allows administrators to specify what specific text is displayed in the catalog instructing users how to obtain additional documentation.

Localized Description   This section allows users to specify text, localized to the language selected, to be displayed as the application description in the catalog.

Keywords   When multiple applications and categories are present in the catalog, locating specific content may be difficult. To help with the location process, administrators have the option to specify search keywords for an application that will aid users in finding its location.

Icon   Administrators can choose from a substantial list of custom icons that might be associated with the application.

Selecting the References tab, as shown in Figure 7.23, will display any other defined applications that either depend on the one being configured or any applications that supersede the one being configured. In the case of the sample RichCopy application, no dependency or superseding application is defined.

FIGURE 7.23
Microsoft RichCopy
4.0 Properties—
References tab

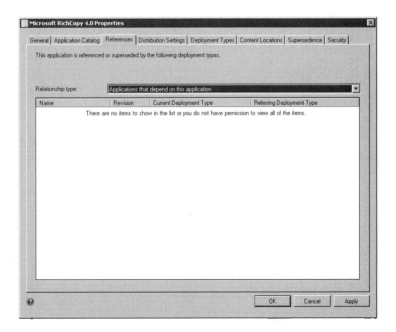

The Deployment Types tab, as shown in Figure 7.24, lists all defined deployment types for the application. It is possible to configure multiple deployment types to cover all potential deployment scenarios for the application. Deployment types will be discussed in detail shortly.

FIGURE 7.24
Microsoft RichCopy
4.0 Properties—
Deployment Types tab

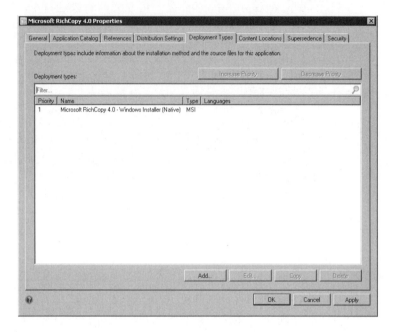

The Content Location tab, as shown in Figure 7.25, will list all distribution points or distribution point groups that have been configured to host the content. In the sample RichCopy application, distribution points have not yet been defined but will be shortly.

FIGURE 7.25
Microsoft RichCopy 4.0
Properties—Content
Location tab

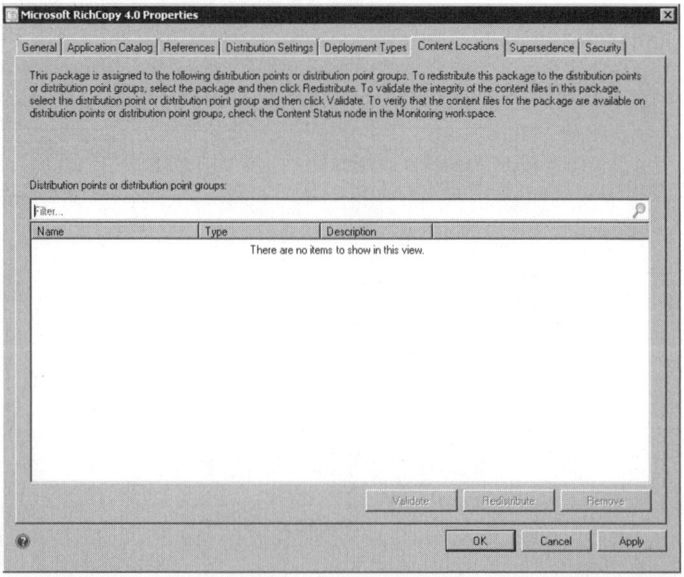

The Supersedence tab, as shown in Figure 7.26, lists any application that the current one supersedes. The ability to build links between applications that supersede each other is much like the experience that is seen with patches and brings significant benefit. (This is discussed in detail in the section "Supersedence" later in this chapter.) The sample RichCopy application does not currently have any superseding relationships defined. By clicking Add on this page it is possible to define the application that is superseded by the one being configured and also to specify the new deployment type to use and whether the previous application should be uninstalled prior to installing the current version. This allows administrators great flexibility in controlling how deployments take place, especially when upgrading from previous versions.

FIGURE 7.26

Microsoft RichCopy 4.0 Properties— Supersedence tab

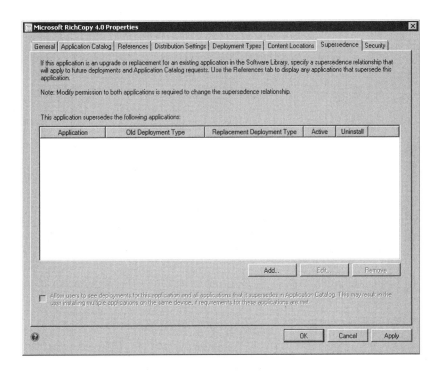

The Security tab, as shown in Figure 7.27, allows administrators to specify users who are able to access the application and their effective rights to the application.

FIGURE 7.27

Microsoft RichCopy 4.0
Properties—Security
tab

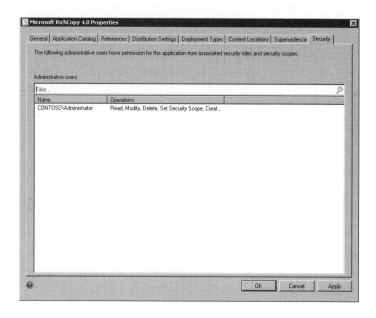

Exploring the Deployment Type

In addition to creating the sample application, the Create Application Wizard also created one deployment type. This was already noted briefly and is shown in Figure 7.24.

The current sample application has only a single deployment type configured. This is shown in Figure 7.28. Note from this same figure that deployment types have as part of their definition an assigned priority. When multiple deployment types are present, it is possible to rank how they should be evaluated in relationship to each other using the Priority option. The priority for a deployment type may be increased or decreased from either the context menu brought up by right-clicking the deployment type or from the Deployment Type option on the Ribbon, which is also identified in Figure 7.28.

FIGURE 7.28

Displaying
deployment type
properties

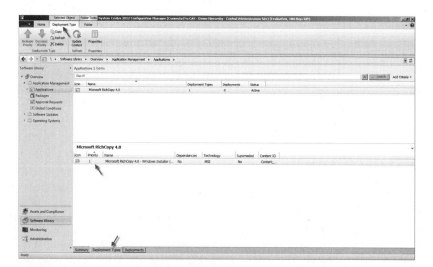

There are several options when creating a deployment type. To access the sample deployment type, either navigate to it through the properties of the application and click Edit or simply select the sample RichCopy application, and in the bottom half of the screen select the Deployment Types tab. This is also shown in Figure 7.28. Right-click the only deployment type available and select Properties.

Selecting Properties will display the properties for the deployment type with the General tab showing, as seen in Figure 7.29. All of the information displayed on the General tab except for the Administrator Comments text was supplied by the Create Application Wizard.

FIGURE 7.29

Sample deployment type properties— General tab

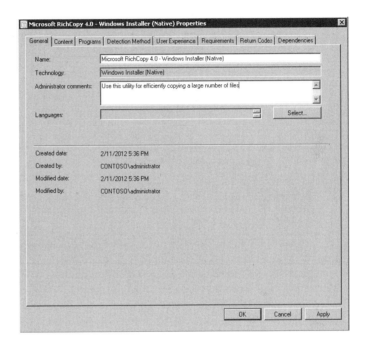

Name   This is the name of the deployment type. Supplying a descriptive name for each deployment type helps administrators know the intended use of each deployment type configured.

Technology   This describes what type of item is being deployed and will change based on whether an MSI (as in this case), script, or executable is being deployed.

Administrator Comments   This field allows administrators to provide any needed additional information regarding the deployment type.

Languages   This field allows administrators to optionally select the specific language for the deployment type.

The bottom section of the General tab provides additional information as to the creation and modified dates for the deployment type.

Selecting the Content tab of the deployment type properties, as shown in Figure 7.30, lists various options specific to configuring content.

FIGURE 7.30
Sample deployment
type properties—
Content tab

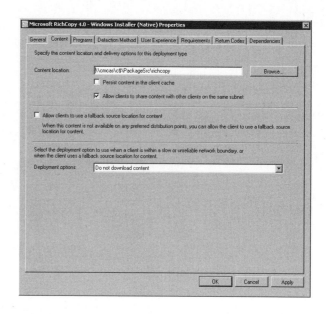

Content Location   The Content Location option allows administrators to specify the location on the network where Configuration Manager 2012 can find the content to be deployed. The path listed for this option must be specified in UNC format.

Persist Content In The Client Cache   This option, disabled by default, flags that the content being deployed should remain in the client cache rather than being marked eligible for deletion. You should consider this option if the content being deployed will be reused. An example might be a script that runs periodically against clients. In such a case it is more efficient and predictable to persist the script in the client cache so it is available locally each time it is scheduled to run. If this option is not selected, after the script content runs successfully the first time, it will be eligible for deletion from the client cache if space is needed and will need to be downloaded again at the next runtime.

Allow clients to share content with other clients on the same subnet.   This option, enabled by default, allows clients (Windows Vista forward) on the network segment to leverage BranchCache capabilities of the Operating System and act as a location cache for content that other clients on the same network segment may need. When a local peer client is detected that already has content available, clients needing the content will simply download it locally rather than from a distribution point.

There are multiple scenarios where this type of configuration is helpful. Consider the following:

◆ Clients reside in a small office with no local distribution point and limited bandwidth. When applications are configured to support shared content, when a single client in the office has downloaded the content, either in total or in part, then it will be possible for other clients in the same office to access the content locally rather than traversing the network.

◆ Clients reside in a small office with a local distribution point hosted on a workstation system and limited bandwidth. In this scenario a local distribution point exists. Depending on the total number of workstations acting as distribution points and the total number of clients, it may still be useful to enable shared content distribution. When a distribution point is configured on a workstation, there is a limit of 20 simultaneous connections possible. If this small office had 100 Configuration Manager clients all needing to run an application at the same time, connections to the distribution point may be exceeded. Having content persisted in the cache of various client systems would present another option for content download.

When an administrator is planning the Configuration Manager 2012 implementation, having the ability to factor in shared content distribution as an option may allow fewer distribution points to be installed at a given location.

Allow clients to use a fallback source location for content.   In Configuration Manager 2012 and with the introduction of boundary groups, protected distribution points will be common. When clients are connected to the corporate network directly, and if Configuration Manager 2012 distribution point access is properly configured, there should be little problem finding a distribution point that is available for use. If a client connects remotely from a boundary not configured in Configuration Manager boundary groups, the client may not be able to find a distribution point that is accessible to it because of boundaries. Setting this option, disabled by default, to allow those clients to communicate with an unprotected distribution point is important to successful application deployment. It probably goes without saying, but to be clear, setting this option by itself is only part of the equation. Distribution points themselves must be configured to be used for fallback, which is not enabled by default.

Deployment Options   When configuring boundary groups in Configuration Manager 2012, administrators are able to designate each included distribution point which is part of the boundary group as being across either a fast or slow connection. This option allows administrators to define how application deployment will proceed. The default option is set to Do Not Download, which means the client will delay content download until it moves inside a boundary noted as being fast. The other option is to Download Content From Distribution Point And Run Locally, which will allow content to be downloaded regardless of connection quality. Remember that clients attempt to download content using BITS, which works to ensure transfers complete successfully even across unreliable or slow network conditions.

Selecting the Programs tab of the deployment type properties, as shown in Figure 7.31, lists program installation and uninstallation options.

FIGURE 7.31
Sample deployment type properties— Programs tab

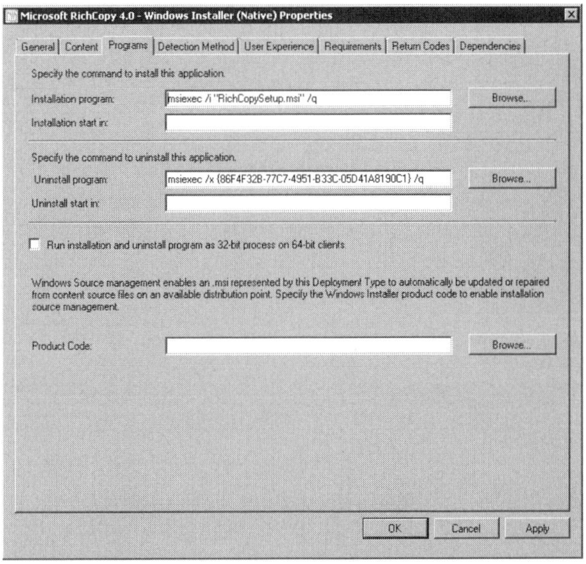

Installation Program   This option allows administrators to specify the command line to be used for program installation. This command line will be initated from the source content downloaded from the distribution point as specified earlier.

Installation Start In   This option allows administrators to specify a specific directory that installation should be initiated from. This option is useful when the root of the content folder on the distribution point does not contain the files needed to initiate an installation. In such a case it would be possible to specify which folder within the content does contain the needed information.

Uninstall Program   This option allows administrators to specify a command that is useful to uninstall the given application. If you're using an MSI, as in the example, the uninstall command is straightforward. It would also be possible to include a script to automate removal of any type of application install.

Uninstall Start In   This option is the same as for Installation Start In discussed previously.

Run Installation and Uninstall Programs in 32-Bit Process on 64-Bit Clients   This option allows administrators to toggle that 43-bit applications should be handled within their own 32-bit process when running on a 64-bit system.

Product Code   This option is specifically for use when deploying MSI applications. The design of MSIs allows for application self-repair and also installation of additional features if the application user selects functions that require them. In order for MSIs to work properly, they must be configured to know where the original source files are located. This option serves that purpose.

Selecting the Detection Method tab of the deployment type's properties, as shown in Figure 7.32, lists options for use in detecting whether an application being deployed is already present on the target device.

FIGURE 7.32
Sample deployment type properties— Detection Method tab

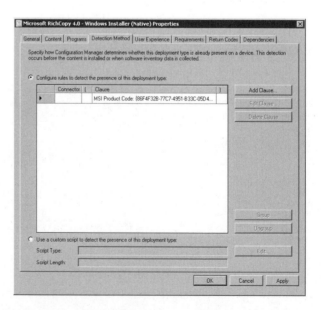

A new feature for application deployment in Configuration Manager 2012 is the ability to configure detection logic to determine if an application is already present on the target device before simply installing it again. This option is much like what is already part of software update deployment but has been brought into the Application Deployment feature! Properly configuring this option will avoid application reinstallations and is also pivotal to verifying dependencies and other configured relationships. When you're using an MSI, as in the example RichCopy application, this information is supplied automatically and is straightforward. Regardless of the type of application being installed, it is possible to configure a useful detection mechanism. Clicking Add Clause starts the Detection Rule Wizard, which is used to add criteria needed to detect if the application is already installed. We'll more fully explore this wizard later in the chapter. Also note the option to execute a custom script to detect an already installed application. In most cases, the available options for detection will suffice, but if not, the script option allows almost any scenario for detection to be handled.

Selecting the User Experience tab of the deployment type's properties, as shown in Figure 7.33, lists options that allow administrators to define the experience users will have during application deployment.

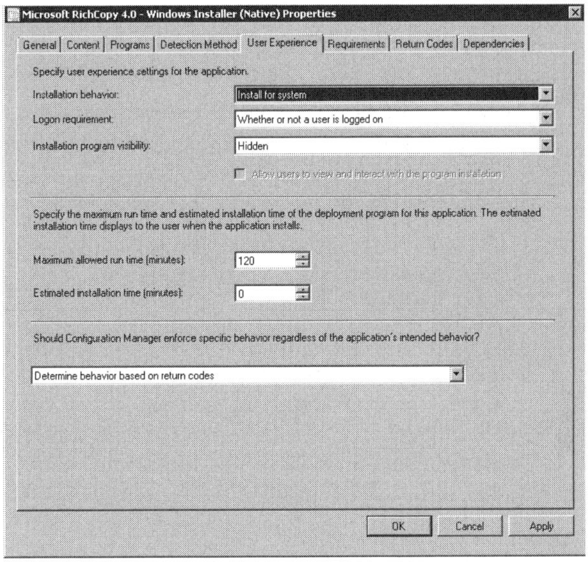

FIGURE 7.33
Sample deployment
type's properties—User
Experience tab

Installation Behavior   This option allows administrators to define whether the application will be a deployment for a system or a user. A third choice allows administrators to define the deployment for a system if the resource is a device but for a user otherwise. Selecting a deployment to a user will gray out the next option so that a deployment can only be executed when a user is logged on.

When a deployment is configured for a system, this indicates that the deployment will take place under the security context of the local system account. When a deployment is configured for a user, this indicates the deployment will take place under the security context of the logged-on user.

Logon Requirement   This option allows administrators to configure whether a user needs to be present during a deployment or not. When a deployment is identified as being for a user, this option is gray. When a deployment is are identified as being for a system, there are three available choices.

Only When A User Is Logged On This option requires a user to be logged onto the client system before a deployment will proceed, even when the deployment is identified as being for a system.

Whether Or Not A User Is Logged On This is by far the most commonly used option because it allows a deployment to proceed without the user being present.

Only When No User Is Logged On This option ensures no application deployment takes place when a user is logged onto the system. This option would be very useful in a scenario where it is crucial to ensure users are not disrupted for application deployment, such as when a retail kiosk system is in use by a customer.

Installation program visibility: Options here allow administrators to configure whether the program will run Maximized, Normal, Minimized, or Hidden. The default option is Hidden. Ultimately these choices really only come into play if an application is deployed to a user or if deployed to a system and the option to "Allow users to view and interact with the program installation" is chosen. Deployments targeted to a system execute in the context of the local system account, so without the "Allow users to view and interact with the program installation" option, users wouldn't be aware of any information displayed on the screen during installation since it is not happening in their logged on context.

Allow Users To Interact With This Program This option, only available when Only When A User Is Logged On is selected for the Logon Requirement, is enabled by default and cannot be disabled when the installation is identified as being for a user, but it can also be enabled when the installation is identified as being for a System.

User When an application is being deployed to a user, the installation proceeds under that user's credentials, and thus the user is able to interact with the application unless it is being deployed silently.

System When the application is being deployed to a system, the install proceeds under the local system's credentials. Since the user's credentials aren't in use, this effectively hides any interaction from the user. Setting the option to Allow Users To Interact With This Program causes the system to pass the local system's interactive experience through to the logged-on user. While this option is not often used in production environments, it can be a useful troubleshooting option so that administrators are able to watch an application as it installs and identify any problems that might occur.

Maximum Allowed Run Time (Minutes) This option allows administrators to configure a maximum amount of time that an application install is able to run before being forcibly terminated. Typically the default setting of 120 minutes is more than sufficient, but in some cases application deployment errors may cause a deployment to appear hung, which will cause the installation to run past the configured window and be terminated. An example of such a situation would be if the application requires user input but is hidden from the user either because of the settings just discussed or because the application was set to run silently. In such cases, using the option Allow Users To Interact With This Program would help identify the problem.

In many environments administrators didn't think to adjust this setting, and in many cases this presented no issue. With the introduction of maintenance windows in Configuration Manager 2007, however, this setting takes on great importance. If maintenance windows are defined for the environment, the Configuration Manager client will first check to see if it is in a maintenance window before attempting to execute the application. If the client is within a maintenance window, then the amount of time configured for the install (this setting) will be compared against the time remaining in the maintenance window. If insufficient time remains, the application deployment is canceled and attempted at the next opportunity. From this alone it is clear that configuring a realistic value for this setting is critical when making use of maintenance windows in the environment.

Estimated Install Time (Minutes)   This option allows administrators to specify how long they anticipate that an application will take, at most, to complete the install. This setting has been an option in previous versions of Configuration Manager.

The bottom part of the User Experience tab allows administrators to configure how the Configuration Manager 2012 client should respond after the application deployment is complete. There are four options available:

Determine Behavior Based On Return Codes   This is the default option and likely makes the most sense in most scenarios. When this option is selected, the action taken by the Configuration Manager 2012 client will be determined by application return codes. Some return codes indicate that the application was successful, while others indicate the application was successful but requires a reboot. Still others may indicate some sort of failure. Administrators are able to specify custom return codes, discussed next, for applications that do not adhere to standards.

No Action   This option simply allows the Configuration Manager 2012 client to exit after the application install is complete, without any further action.

Deployment Program Always Forces A Reboot   This option indicates to the Configuration Manager 2012 client that once the application deployment completes, the application itself will force a reboot.

Force A Mandatory Device Restart   This option causes the Configuration Manager 2012 client to force the device to reboot following an application installation.

Selecting the Requirements tab of the deployment type's properties, as shown in Figure 7.34, lists options that administrators can use to define requirements that must be met before the application installation is attempted. This page is a starting point allowing administrators to review requirements already configured or add additional requirements.

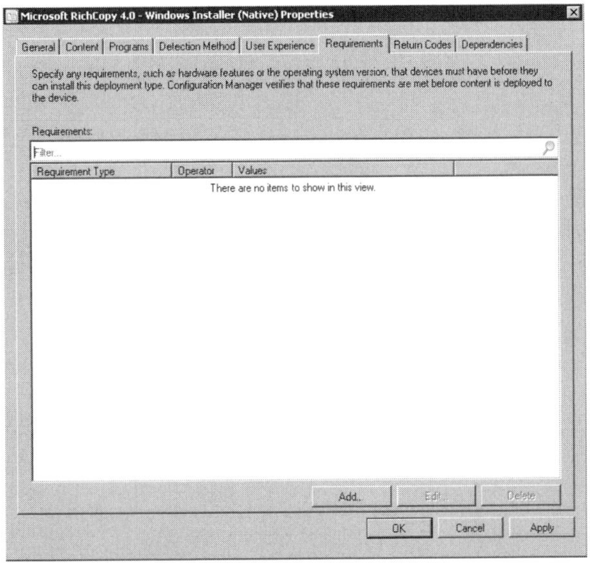

FIGURE 7.34

Sample deployment type's properties—The Requirements tab

The addition of deployment rules is a significant modification in Configuration Manager 2012 and will be detailed later in the chapter. For now, suffice it to say that rules are intended to either take the place of building unique collections with criteria per deployment that need to be managed by the site server or move the responsibility for rules checking to the client system instead. This practice will allow administrators to shift their thinking about how many collections they need to maintain, but they will need some learning time to fully acclimate to this change!

Selecting the Return Codes tab of the deployment type's properties, as shown in Figure 7.35, allows administrators to define possible return codes for the application and how they should be interpreted by the Configuration Manager 2012 client. The default values are shown in the figure. Administrators choose whether the default values are sufficient or they need to augment them.

FIGURE 7.35
Sample deployment type's properties—
Return Codes tab

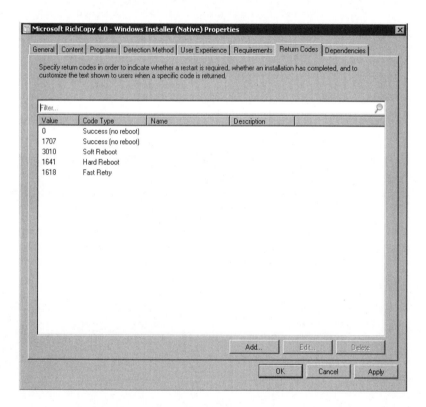

In most cases, the default return codes will be sufficient, but in some cases, applications introduce their own return codes in an effort to help identify certain conditions that may exist at deployment time. A return code of 1, for example, may indicate a successful deployment but one that needs some sort of post-deployment action. If a return code of 1 was not added to this list, then the Configuration Manager 2012 client would interpret it as a failed deployment.

Selecting the Dependencies tab of the deployment type's properties, as shown in Figure 7.36, allows administrators to define any software items that must be installed prior to the current application being installed.

FIGURE 7.36

Sample deployment type's properties— Dependencies tab

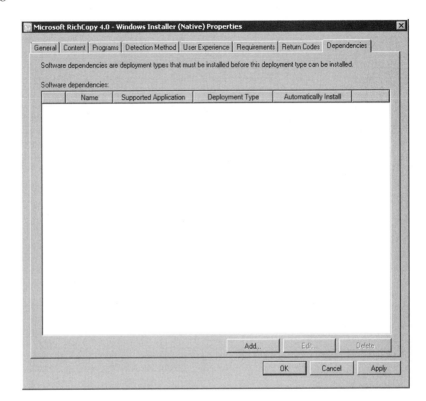

Dependencies will be detailed later in the chapter, but a quick look at the column headers reveals that along with specifying dependencies, administrators are also able to specify whether a given dependency, if absent, should be automatically installed as part of the application deployment.

Create Deployment Wizard

The Create Application Wizard worked to build the sample RichCopy application and deployment type but did nothing to build an actual deployment. To build the deployment, click Deploy from the Ribbon to launch the Deploy Software Wizard. The General page of the Deploy Software Wizard is shown in Figure 7.37.

FIGURE 7.37
Deploy Software
Wizard—General
page

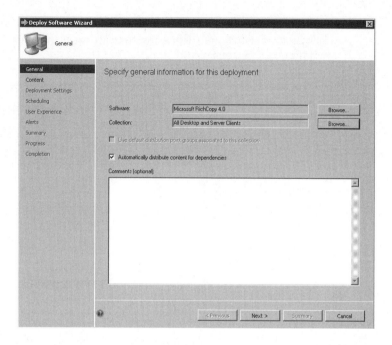

Software   On the General page of the Deploy Software Wizard the software to be deployed likely is already specified, in this case Microsoft RichCopy 4.0. If the provided selection is incorrect or is missing, clicking the Browse button will allow you to select the correct application.

Collection   A deployment must be associated with a collection. A collection is a group of devices or users where the deployment should be made available. Administrators familiar with previous versions of Configuration Manager are accustomed to building collections specific to a given deployment. This can still be done in Configuration Manager 2012, or it is possible to target a generic collection and rely on the requirement rules, mentioned earlier and discussed in more detail later in this chapter, to determine which systems actually run the deployment. In practice, a hybrid approach will likely be used, where a collection is built containing systems that should be targeted with an application but without the various deployment criteria such as minimum disk space, minimum processor, minimum software version, and so on. These latter options will be managed as part of the application's Requirements settings.

Use default distribution point groups associated to this collection.   In Configuration Manager 2012 it is possible to associate collections with a distribution point group. If this is done, the option shown would be available for selection and would result in the deployment being automatically distributed to distribution points based on collections chosen. The benefit of being able to link a collection with a distribution point group allows administrators additional flexibility. As an example, it would be possible to build collections per machine type per a given geography or office location. Then, when building distribution groups, the relevant collections and distribution points that serve those collections could be grouped together, facilitating more efficient management.

Automatically Distribute Content For Dependencies   If dependencies are defined for an application and if those dependencies have not been deployed to the distribution points selected for the deployment being configured, selecting this option will ensure that the content for the dependency is made available in the event it is needed.

Comments   The Comments section allows administrators to optionally add any information that may be pertinent for the deployment.

The content page is shown in Figure 7.38. On the Content page, administrators are able view currently assigned distribution points and distribution point groups and/or select additional distribution points or distribution point groups are appropriate locations to stage the content for client access.

FIGURE 7.38
Deploy Software
Wizard – Content page

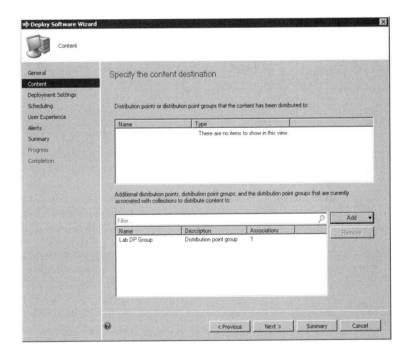

When you've finished with the settings on the Content page, click next to continue to the Deployment settings page, as shown in Figure 7.39:

FIGURE 7.39
Deploy Software
Wizard—Deployment
Settings page

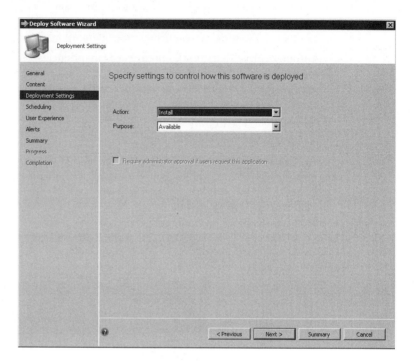

Action This setting is where administrators choose whether the deployment will act to install or uninstall the application.

Purpose This setting is where administrators choose whether the application simply is made available to manual installation, such as through the Software Center or the Web Catalog, or whether the application installation will be required.

If set to required, the application will be enforced on targeted systems/users on the schedule specified. A change in Configuration Manager 2012, with the required setting in place the Configuration Manager 2012 client, will periodically check to see if the application remains installed. If the application has been removed it will be deployed again. As seen when discussing client settings earlier, the default detection cycle is weekly.

Require Administrator Approval if Users Request this Application If this application is targeted to a collection of users or user groups, this option becomes available and allows administrators to flag this application as one that will be listed as needing approval in the Application Catalog.

When you've finished with the settings on the Deployment Settings page, click Next to continue to the Scheduling page, shown in Figure 7.40.

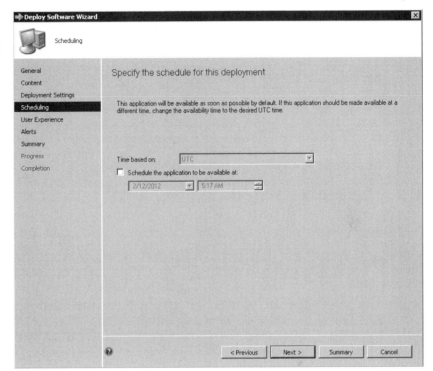

The options available on the Scheduling page will be dependent on the setting chosen for Purpose on the Deployment Settings page:

- When Purpose is set to Available, then the only scheduling option available will be one that allows administrators to schedule application availability.

- When Purpose is set to Required, then the administrator will additionally be able to schedule the deadline for installation, either as soon as possible or for a specific time.

When you've finished with the settings on the Scheduling page, click Next to continue to the User Experience page, shown in Figure 7.41.

FIGURE 7.41
Deploy Software
Wizard—User
Experience page

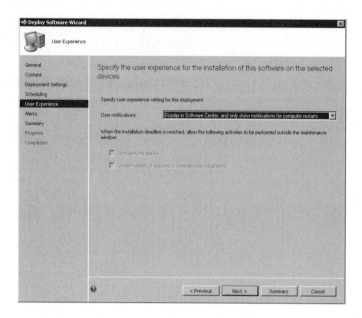

The User Experience page allows administrators to configure user notifications. Available options are Display in Software Center and Show All Notifications or Display in Software Center, and only show notifications for computer restarts. These options are self-explanatory.

The options for specifying activity to allow when an installation deadline has been reached are gray when the deployment is set with a Purpose of Available. When the deployment is set with a Purpose of Required, the options Software Installation and System Restart are configurable.

When you've finished with the settings on the User Experience page, click Next to continue to the Alerts page, shown in Figure 7.42.

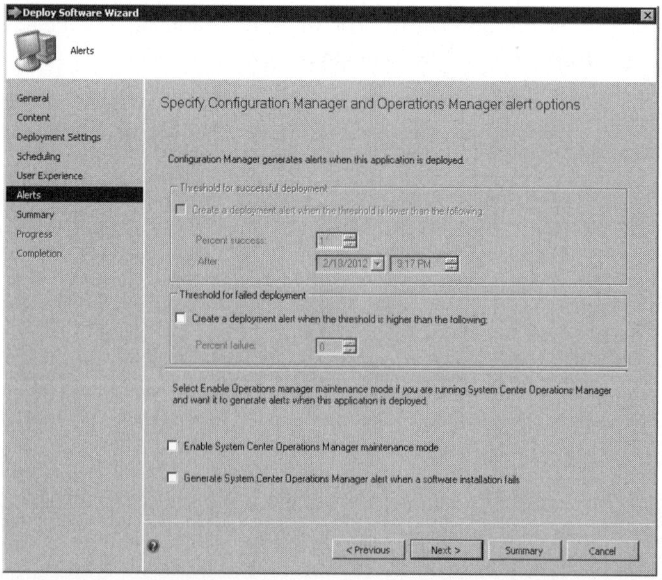

FIGURE 7.42
Deploy Software
Wizard—Alerts page

The Alerts page allows administrators to configure criteria for when to generate alerts in response to deployment status. The alerting ability provided in Configuration Manager 2012 is new and provides an additional mechanism for awareness of deployment health.

Create a deployment alert when the threshold is lower than the following. This option allows administrators to specify a threshold of expected deployment success for a given deployment within a specific time frame. If the deployment success has not met or exceeded the configured threshold within the configured time, an alert will be generated to notify the administrator.

Create a deployment alert when the threshold is higher than the following. This option allows administrators to specify a threshold for a deployment that, if exceeded, will cause an alert to be triggered. This option would be useful in a scenario where a certain number of licenses have been purchased for an application. If a sufficient number of users install the application to cause the number of available licenses to near depletion, the administrator would be alerted and have the opportunity to either order additional licenses or scale back the usage of the application.

Enable System Center Operations Manager Maintenance Mode This option allows integration between Configuration Manager 2012 and Operations Manager. By selecting this option, when a deployment begins on a client and if the client is also an Operations Manager agent, the agent will be placed in maintenance mode. After the deployment completes, the Operations Manager agent will be triggered to exit maintenance mode.

 Real World Scenario

While Operations Manager maintenance mode is beyond the scope of our discussion one thing does need to be mentioned. This option does not cause true Operations Manager maintenance mode to start. Instead, the Health Service on the Operations Manager agent is simply paused for the duration of the application deployment. Once deployment completes the health service resumes from that point in time without accounting for any problems that might have happened during application deployment, such as a system reboot. This is an effective approach to suppress noise in Operations Manager but will not be reflected as maintenance mode in the Operations Manager console.

UPDATED INTEGRATION FEATURE

In Configuration Manager 2007, this integration was not reliable. Configuration Manager 2012 has been updated so that this integration works as intended, regardless of platform.

Generate System Center Operations Manager Alert When A Software Installation Fails This option causes an alert be generated in Operations Manager to raise immediate awareness when the installation of an application fails.

When you've finished with the settings on the Alerts page, click Next to continue to the Summary page. Review the settings on the Summary page. If they're all acceptable, click Next to save the configuration and then exit the wizard.

Application Deployment—Client Experience

The ultimate goal of Application Deployment is to take action on Configuration Manager 2012 clients. The work described so far has built an application deployment, a deployment type, and a deployment. The current sample was configured to be available and was targeted to a collection of devices. The current configurations will simply make the application available for install in the Software Center on all targeted clients.

As configured, the application will *not* show up in the user-centric Application Catalog. Inclusion in the Application Catalog requires that the application be deployed to a collection of users or user groups. To make the sample RichCopy application also show as available in the Software Catalog, a second deployment needs to be added. The only difference for this deployment is that a collection of users will be chosen rather than systems. The new deployment is shown in Figure 7.43.

FIGURE 7.43
Second deployment added targeted to a user collection

With the second deployment added, the application now shows as available in both the Software Center and the Application Catalog. Take a look at the way the applications are presented in both and the descriptive information that is available. Figure 7.44, Figure 7.45, and Figure 7.46 show the settings in the sample RichCopy application side by side with the same information in the Software Center and the Software Catalog. It's good to understand how these configurations map between the different components so that when you configure an application, the user will have meaningful and descriptive information to review.

FIGURE 7.44
Mapping application settings to Software Center and Software Catalog

FIGURE 7.45
Mapping application settings to Software Center and Software Catalog

FIGURE 7.46
Mapping application settings to Software Center and Software Catalog (final)

CLIENT APPLICATION INSTALLATION

When an application is configured to be required, it will be installed regardless of whether the user requests it in the Software Center or selects it in the Application Catalog. In some cases, applications may be marked as required but also as visible in the Software Center and Application Catalog, but that is not automatic. For applications that should be optional for the user, simply mark them as being available and, depending on other configurations, such as requirements, they will appear for the user in the Software Center. If the application is targeted to a user collection, it will also appear in the Software Catalog.

Bottom line, the Software Center is available on each Configuration Manager 2012 client and allows the user to have control over at least some of their own experience with Configuration Manager 2012. As the name implies and as already discussed, the Software Center presents a list of applications to the user that are available for install, along with a good amount of potential detail to help the user understand the application. But the Software Center is more than just an application chooser. Click the Installed Software node, and you'll see that it is also useful for tracking software that has been installed on the system historically.

The Options node, also part of Software Center and shown in Figure 7.47, allows users to specify their own work information and maintenance settings. Think of these settings as a user-controlled maintenance window. By users specifying business hours, they are configuring their system so that they are not disrupted by application installs or system reboots in the middle of the day. Maintenance settings work with Work Information settings to specify when the computer will be available for software installations. Ultimately, the Configuration Manager 2012 administrator retains full control even at this level because, when necessary, application deployment can be configured to proceed regardless of the settings specified.

FIGURE 7.47
Software Center
Options tab

Also available on the Options tab is the ability to configure local remote control settings and whether power management policy will apply to the system, but those topics are beyond the scope of software distribution, so we won't discuss them here.

 Real World Scenario

APPLICATION DEPLOYMENT—BEYOND THE LAB

Stepping through creation of the sample application is enough to start the wheels turning about ways this new model could be used in production. There is tremendous flexibility in the new Application Deployment model, but don't jump too far too fast. Spend time with the model and understand how things work before spinning up deployments in production. Remember, a lab environment is *much* more forgiving—and doesn't result in the need to explain problems to management!

In addition, there are many layers to the Application Deployment model. Explore each layer completely—from the rules-based Requirements engine to the ability to link applications together, known as references, creating a tie between applications that is useful for application upgrade. There is also the ability to verify that prerequisites are in place before deploying a given application. And don't forget a real gem of the new model, the ability to create multiple deployment types that can work with each other to detect information about the environment for the current deployment and deliver a version of the application best suited for each scenario; this includes deployments to devices, users, or both!

Application Deployment—Advanced Configurations

The steps just discussed demonstrated how to configure a basic application, deployment type, and deployment. These building blocks are pivotal to understanding the Configuration Manager 2012 Application Deployment model but in some ways just scratch the surface of what is possible. We've already mentioned several additional and more complex configurations but have not discussed them in any detail. This section takes a step back and reviews these additional configurations. With Application Deployment, all of the various configurations and options that are possible are simply too numerous to cover individually, but the hope is that with the discussion provided you will be able to see the possibilities, flexibility, and power available.

SUPERSEDENCE

This example builds on the previous work by adding an additional deployment that is configured to deploy RoboCopy. In the test environment it is OK to have RoboCopy on Windows 2003/XP systems, but if it exists on Windows 2008/Vista/7 systems, it should be replaced by the RichCopy application. This introduces the first point of discussion: *supersedence*. In the definition of the application it is possible to configure a relationship where one application supersedes another application. This type of relationship is extremely valuable to maintain control of the application upgrade process and also to define how one application should operate during the upgrade process—but that's jumping a bit too far ahead.

Configuring a supersedence relationship is easy. Simply do the following:

1. Open the properties of the application where a supersedence relationship is to be defined.

2. Click Browse.

3. Select the application that the current one should supersede, and then click OK.

The result is shown in Figure 7.48.

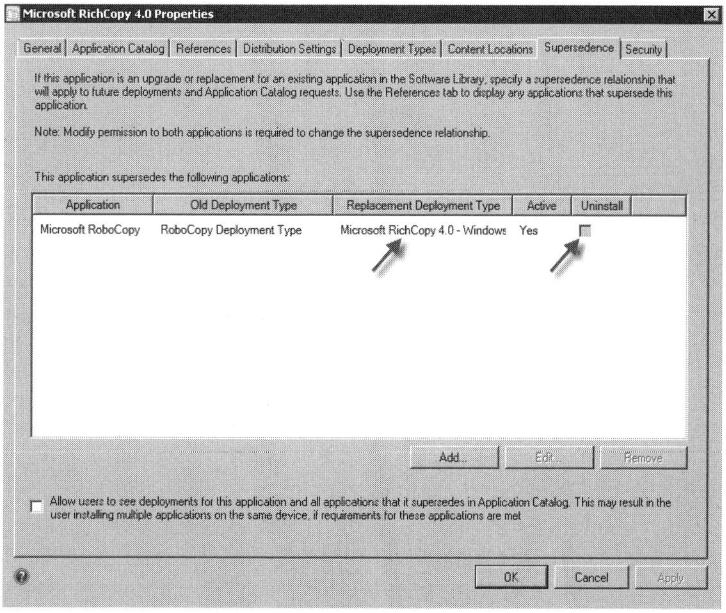

FIGURE 7.48
Supersedence
relationship
added to RichCopy
application

Notice that when defining a supersedence relationship it is possible to specify whether the application being replaced should first be uninstalled. Selecting to uninstall an application, requires that the uninstall command line setting for the previous application has been configured properly to accommodate the uninstall. A further configuration allows specifying which deployment type from the current application will be used during deployment.

To see the results of creating the supersedence relationship, simply look at the properties for the RoboCopy application and select the References tab. There are two options for viewing data on this tab: Applications That Depend On This Application or Applications That Supersede This Application. For the current purpose, select the second option, which will show that the RichCopy application now supersedes the RoboCopy application. This is shown in Figure 7.49.

FIGURE 7.49
Supersedence reference

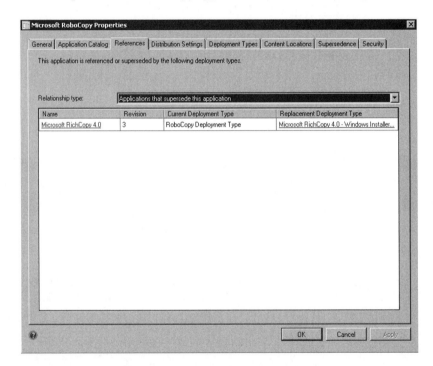

DEPENDENCIES

Going back to the deployment type for the sample RichCopy application, it's time to configure a dependency. The dependency option specifically allows administrators to define software that must be installed before the current application can be deployed. The dependency option is not a vehicle to specify any other kind of requirement. As shown in Figure 7.50, the sample RichCopy application is configured to require that .NET Framework 2.0 be installed first. If this requirement isn't met, and depending on the setting for the Auto Install option, either the application installation will fail or the application installation will pause while .NET Framework installation is completing.

FIGURE 7.50
Dependency
configuration

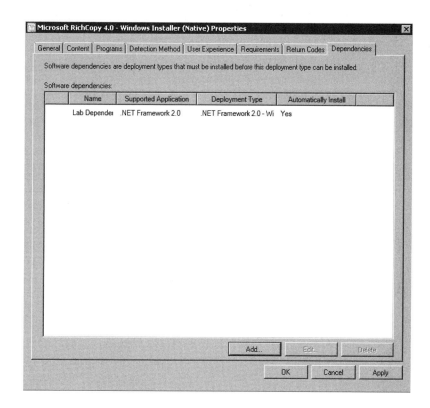

FIGURE 7.50
Dependency
configuration

DETECTION METHOD

The ability to detect whether a dependency is installed or not depends on whether settings to do so are specified in the Detection Method tab for an application. Dependencies also allow administrators to configure potentially complex dependency relationships to ensure all needed applications are present before proceeding with a deployment.

Detections methods are also useful to determine whether a given application has already been deployed to a target system. If so, there is no need to deploy it again, and the application deployment will simply exit.

You can create detection configurations to check the filesystem, a registry location, an MSI GUID, or a combination of these settings to determine if a given application is present. When you use the wizard to build an application deployment based on an MSI, as in the RichCopy example, the detection information is supplied by default. Figure 7.32, shown earlier, is a view of the Detection Method tab.

REQUIREMENTS

When deploying an application, administrators may wish to specify rules to govern the application install. The Requirements tab of the deployment type allows deployment rules to be configured, from simple to complex. You can build rules to check attributes related to the device or user being targeted or build custom rules to cover most any scenario. The conditions that are available for both device and user-targeted applications are shown in Table 7.2.

TABLE 7.2: Rule options

DEVICE	USER
Active Directory site	Primary device*
Configuration Manager site	
CPU speed	
Disk space	
Number of processors	
Operating system	
Operating system language	
Organizational init (OU)	
Total physical memory	

The primary device and its use for application deployment will be discussed along with user affinity.

The mechanisms available for building custom rules are as follows:

Active Directory query

Assembly

Filesystem

IIS Metabase

Registry key

Registry value

Script

SQL query

XPath query

As is noted by the combination of options shown, literally any possible scenario can be covered by specifying the right type of rule.

For the sample RichCopy application, the only systems that should install the applications are those that run Windows 2008 or better and already have the superseded application, RoboCopy, installed. Figure 7.51 shows the completed Requirements node, which details the checks that must pass before proceeding with application deployment.

FIGURE 7.51
Requirements node completed

It's interesting to note regarding the Requirements tab that when Configuration Manager 2012 clients receive notification of a new application and if that application has a list of requirements, those requirements will be evaluated upon receipt, and if the requirements for deployment are not met, the application will not be displayed as available for deployment on the target system. Applications are evaluated periodically to determine if the conditions specified by the requirements have changed.

The rules available for use in the Requirements tab are visible in the Application Management ➤ Global Conditions node of the console. The list will also include any custom requirements that may be created. This is shown in Figure 7.52. Note that the custom global condition just created is stored in the list and selected.

FIGURE 7.52
Global Conditions
node

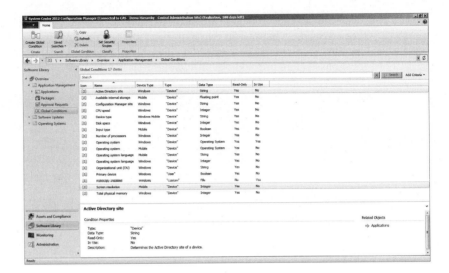

User Device Affinity

As already described, the Application Deployment model in Configuration Manager 2012 is extremely flexible and provides administrators many options for delivering content. A focus for Configuration Manager 2012 is flexibility around delivering applications to users so that a user, regardless of what device they are using, will have a consistent experience. As an example, if a user is logged onto their primary device, then an application may be configured to be installed on the target system, whereas if a user is simply logged onto a shared computer, they may instead receive a virtualized copy of the application. If the user is logged onto a mobile device and a mobile version of an application is available, further options to accommodate software deployment are available there as well. Whatever the case, the user's experience is that their needed software is available, but the administrator has control over how the software is provided.

In order for a user to be properly detected as logged onto their primary device rather than a shared device, a mechanism must be in place to guide that decision. User Device Affinity settings provide that mechanism.

User Device Affinity allows a user to be associated with their primary device(s). User Device Affinity associations are configured in one of several ways:

◆ The user can configure that a device should be considered a primary device in the Software Catalog.

◆ The administrator can configure the My Devices option in the Application Catalog, shown in Figure 7.53. This is the first look we have had at the Application Catalog. Though not directly related, it's worth stopping here and showing the Application Catalog portion of this web page as well, shown in Figure 7.54.

FIGURE 7.53
User Configurable
Device Affinity Option

FIGURE 7.54
Application catalog page

◆ You can use a file to map a user to their primary device(s) and then import this file to Configuration Manager 2012.

◆ You can choose the option Import User Device Affinity settings, which is available in the Assets and Compliance node of the console and is shown in Figure 7.55.

FIGURE 7.55
Import User Device
Affinity console
option

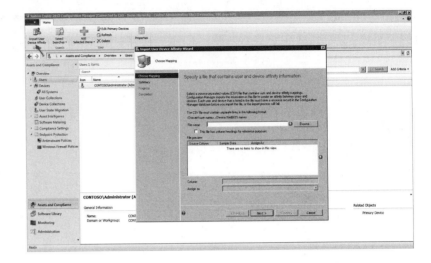

◆ You can configure Configuration Manager 2012 to automatically build user-to-primary device mappings based on information collected about devices used by a user. With this method administrators retain control over whether or not to automatically accept the detected settings or not.

◆ Configuration Manager 2012 is configured to automatically detect primary device mappings through Asset Intelligence, as shown in Figure 7.56. Note that the required inventory class, SMS_SystemConsoleUsage, is enabled by default.

FIGURE 7.56
Configuring
automatic user
device affinity
detection

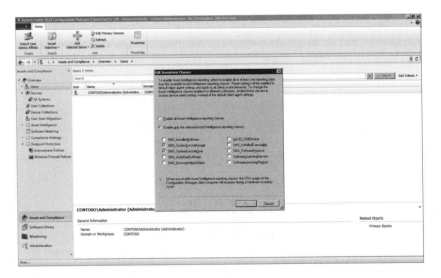

◆ The Configuration Manager 2012 administrator can manually create relationships between user and device(s) by using the Edit Primary Devices node in the console. This is shown in Figure 7.57.

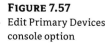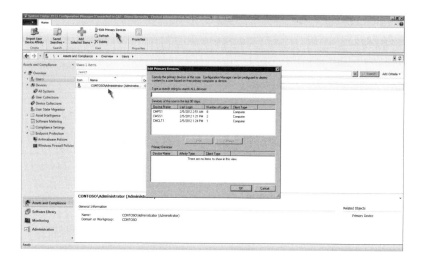

FIGURE 7.57
Edit Primary Devices
console option

◆ Specific to mobile devices, when a user enrolls a device a relationship is automatically created between the user and the mobile device.

Also note that User Device Affinity settings are not limited to specifying one primary device per user. Very often a single user may have more than one primary device, such as a computer, as well as a mobile device. It's also possible that a given device will be the primary device for multiple users, such as in a shared workstation scenario. Configuration Manager 2012 handles any of these device-to-user mapping scenarios.

Troubleshooting Application Deployment

With any product, in-depth troubleshooting requires a good understanding of the overall system to know where to look and common things that might go wrong. Configuration Manager 2012 is a large product with many moving parts, so understanding how to troubleshoot effectively comes with experience. The depth of troubleshooting attempted will depend on available time and your experience level with the system. The latter will grow over time. Chapter 15, "Troubleshooting," discusses the troubleshooting options for Configuration Manager 2012 in general. It is useful to spend a few paragraphs discussing troubleshooting as it relates to Application Deployment. The intention here will be to augment the troubleshooting discussion from Chapter 15.

MONITORING

Configuration Manager 2012 is built to help administrators stay updated on the progress of various work and to flag when a problem is encountered; the Monitoring section of the console is designed specifically with that purpose in mind. Figure 7.58 shows the Deployments node of the Monitoring section.

FIGURE 7.58
Deployments node of
the Monitoring section

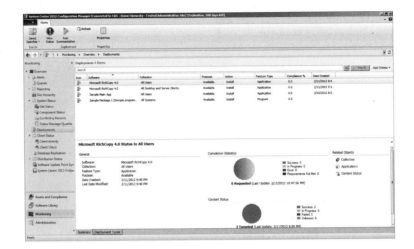

The Deployments node allows administrators to see at a glance the progress of deployments in the environment. The top section of the screen is just a summary. Note that the sample RichCopy deployment is listed twice, one instance being the deployment targeted to users and the other instance targeted to systems. In this node it might be possible that a given deployment is shown as 100 percent compliant, yet no systems may have attempted to run the RichCopy application yet. Why might that be the case? In this case, compliance will reflects that 100 percent of the targeted systems have accepted the deployment and reported back with a status.

This would mean that the systems reporting back have evaluated the deployment and found it to fail the deployment validation—so status is reported back but no install is attempted. Take this type of logic further—consider if this application had been delivered to a collection with six systems—yet we only receive status back for two. Does that mean the other four are having issues? Maybe but not necessarily. If the application requirements exclude deployment to the other four systems then they won't even show up. Remember what was mentioned earlier about how it is feasible to deploy everything to the All Systems collection provided sufficient requirements are in place for an application? This is an example of how that would work. To restate, deploying to the All Systems collection is not recommended but it would be possible.

FIGURE 7.59
Deployment Status

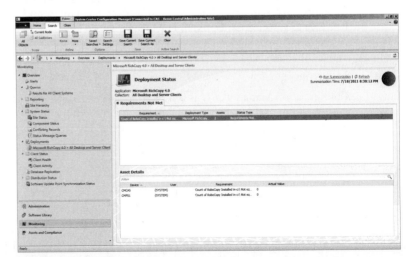

From the Summary view it is also possible to review the target collection, the state of the software, and the status of deployed content.

DEPLOYMENT STATUS

The information available here is critical for understanding the actual state of a deployment. If a deployment has been configured but is not showing up on targeted systems, your initial thought might be that something isn't working right. That may be, but more likely the problem is not with the system but with some configuration. In this case, the deployment arrived at the client, failed requirement evaluation, and simply wasn't made available. The pie chart and detail data lead right to the problem. Without them, an administrator would need to look elsewhere for the source of the problem.

LOG FILES

Configuration Manager 2012 provides an extensive set of log files to aid administrators in troubleshooting scenarios. The information provided by the log files is significant, but even more detail is possible if you configure verbose or debug logging (covered in Chapter 15).

Logs in Configuration Manager 2012 are very beneficial for experienced administrators to quickly pinpoint a problem. For beginning administrators, though, the logs may be intimidating. Experience will help increase your comfort level with logs. A few suggestions will help keep things on track:

◆ Determine which logs to review.

Configuration Manager 2012 processes generally can be broken into processing that happens on the server and processing that happens on the client. The management point is in the middle and can have elements that interact with both the server and client. The place to start reviewing log information depends on where the processing problem seems to be happening: server side or client side.

◆ Be patient.

The logging system in Configuration Manager 2012 is extensive, and finding the right log to review at first might be challenging. Many different Configuration Manager 2012 client components are required when trying to process an application deployment. These components pass information back and forth as the work gets done. With experience it becomes easier to know which log to start with, and it's well worth learning. Never fear though; if it gets too time consuming to dig through the information provided, Microsoft support is just a phone call away.

◆ Watch the time stamp.

Following data in the log files boils down to following the time stamps. As logs update, their time stamps do too. A quick look at which logs have been active recently will help you identify logs that might be good candidates for review after an action is attempted and a failure encountered.

◆   Use Trace.

The log files are viewable with Notepad, but it's definitely not the best environment. The Trace utility (formerly known as Trace32) available in Configuration Manager is perfect for viewing Configuration Manager logs—and many other types of text logs as well. Trace includes an error-lookup capability, the ability to filter by keyword or processing thread, the ability to merge log files to view the entire conversation between components (remember the time stamp discussion?), and so on. The utility has been updated for Configuration Manager 2012.

The Bottom Line

Explain the options available for Application Deployment.   The new Application Deployment model is a significant and welcome change for deploying software in the enterprise. There are many new components including a rules-based Requirements engine, the ability to detect whether the application is already installed, the option to configure application dependencies and relationships, and more.

Master It   List several configuration options available for applications and deployment types.

Detail the various components required for Application Deployment.   Success with Application Deployment requires that several other Configuration Manager 2012 components be available and properly configured. The list includes management point(s), distribution point(s), IIS, BITS, the client itself, and possibly more.

Master It   List the components required for configuring an application deployment.

Understand the role of and manage distribution points.   The role of distribution points has not changed significantly in that this is the role that makes content available to Configuration Manager 2012 devices and users. The options available for implementing the role have changed significantly with the inclusion of throttling control content flow from site server to remote distribution points, the single-instance storage approach for placing content on distribution points, the ability to detect content corruption, and the requirement that all distribution points be BITS enabled.

Master It   Discuss the differences between implementing a distribution point role on the site server locally and remotely.

Chapter 8

Software Updates

Ever since the I Love You (ILoveyou) worm hit the Internet in May 2000 and the Nimda worm hit the Internet in September 2001, patch management has become a very important part of maintaining network security. Those worms revealed the importance of patch management because it was vulnerabilities in Windows that had allowed the worm to spread so fast around the world, and Microsoft had released patches for these vulnerabilities several months earlier.

At the time, patching an operating system was a very labor-intensive task. Windows Update was available, but you still had to run it manually on each machine that needed updates. This meant connecting to the Internet, which was really too dangerous for corporate networks while ILoveyou and Nimda were spreading. As a result, network administrators and PC support staff ended up traveling to all their computers with a CD full of updates to get them patched up and safe again.

Microsoft released Software Update Services in 2002, and System Management Server (SMS) 2.0 got some patch-management functionality through an add-on feature pack. However, it wasn't really until SMS 2003 that there was a truly functional patch-management solution for the corporate enterprise. SMS 2003 used Microsoft Update technology to detect and install its updates, and it allowed reporting to show the progress. This was not without its problems; as more and more patches became available for Microsoft's operating systems and applications, this patch solution became more taxing on server and workstation resources.

The Software Updates feature in Configuration Manager 2007 was rewritten from the ground up and made the software update process even more effective by leveraging the Windows Server Update Services (WSUS) product and incorporating its capabilities into patch management and also by taking some of the load off Configuration Manager clients in the process. With the introduction of Configuration Manager 2012, Microsoft made configuring, deploying, and maintaining the software update role much easier than before.

In this chapter you learn to

◆ Plan to use Software Updates.

◆ Configure Software Updates.

◆ Use the Software Updates feature to manage software updates.

◆ Use automatic update deployment to deploy software updates.

What's New in Software Updates

After integrating Windows Server Update Services in Configuration Manager 2007 as the Software Updates feature, Microsoft further enhanced the feature in Configuration Manager 2012.

With Configuration Manager 2012 you can manage your software updates more easily and quickly. The following changes and enhancements are available in Configuration Manager 2012:

Software Update Groups New in Configuration Manager 2012 are the software update groups; these replace the update lists that were available in Configuration Manager 2007. When you want to organize your software updates in your environment effectively, you need to use software update groups. With Automatic Deployment Rules you can add new updates automatically, or you can add them yourself manually. The deployment of software update groups can also be done automatically or manually.

With software update groups you are also able to retrieve compliance information from devices for the software updates without deploying them.

Automatic Deployment Rules Software update administrators will have a ball with this new feature. With Automatic Deployment Rules you can automatically approve and deploy software updates. You can specify criteria for software updates, and the software updates are automatically added to the software update group. When creating an automatic deployment rule, you can, for instance, use all Windows 7 updates released since the last Patch Tuesday; this way the Windows 7 updates will be automatically added to the software update group. When a deployment for the software update group is available, the software updates will be automatically rolled out to your clients.

Software Update Filtering The new Configuration Manager 2012 console has a good search engine; this search engine is also used for searching or filtering software updates. While defining a search, you can add a set of criteria that makes it easy to filter and find the updates you need. You can save the defined criteria when you are finished and use the criteria at a later stage.

With the results of the search you can select those software updates and add them to an existing or new software update group. You can also see the compliance information about the selected updates.

Software Update Monitoring The in-console monitoring feature is also implemented in the Software Updates feature. The Configuration Manager 2012 console provides real-time monitoring information about software updates and running processes. For instance, you can view the following information:

- Compliance and deployment information about key software updates
- Detailed state messages for the deployments and software update assets
- Error codes with additional information for software updates
- State messages for software update synchronizations
- Alerts for software update issues

Besides real-time information in the Configuration Manager 2012 console, you can also use the software update reports that are available out of the box.

Managing Superseded Software Updates In Configuration Manager 2007 software updates automatically expired after being superseded. This was done in the full software update synchronization process. You could not deploy superseded software updates because they were expired, and Configuration Manager 2007 doesn't allow you to deploy expired software updates.

Configuration Manager 2012 lets you choose to manage superseded software updates. You can also choose to configure a specific period of time in which the software update doesn't automatically expire after being superseded. This way you can deploy superseded software updates if necessary.

HOW TO MANAGE EXPIRED UPDATES

If software updates are expired, you can easily identify them and remove the membership of the software update groups. After you remove the membership, the maintenance cycle will remove the expired updates from the distribution points. This allows you to remove the expired updates from your distribution points in the Configuration Manager hierarchy.

Increased User Control over Installation of Software Updates   The Empower Users pillar of Configuration Manager 2012 fits perfectly in the Software Updates feature. Configuration Manager 2012 allows users to have more control over when software updates are installed on their devices (Figure 8.1). Users can schedule or reschedule software installations or updates via the Software Center during non-working hours.

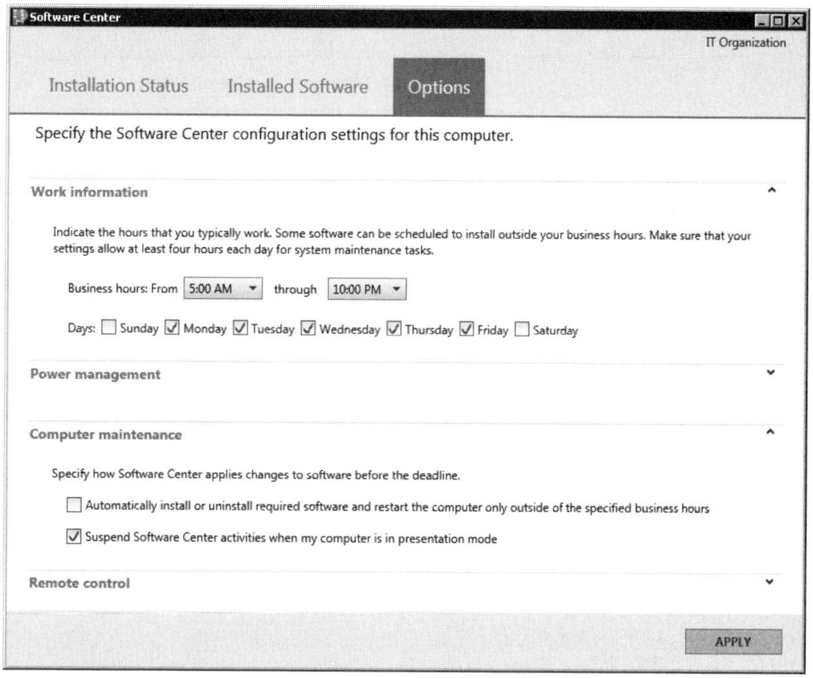

FIGURE 8.1
Defining business hours in the Software Center

Software Update Files Are Stored in the Content Library The content of software updates is also stored in the new content library of Configuration Manager 2012. The single-instance storage of the content library is also used for software updates. Before content files are downloaded, Configuration Manager 2012 checks to see if the content file is already in the content library. If the content file is available, it will use that file for the new software update.

Administrative Access Especially for the Software Update features, a role for software update management is defined in role-based administration. You can now delegate the deployment of software updates to your systems to the security officer, for instance. Or you can delegate it to a local administrator by limiting the scope of the role assignment.

Software Update Deployment Template Software update deployment templates could be created in the Configuration Manager 2007 console, but in Configuration Manager 2012 you can only create deployment templates with the Automatic Deployment Rules Wizard or the Deploy Software Updates Wizard. The deployment template stores many of the deployment properties that will not change when you create new deployments.

Besides the new or enhanced features in the Software Updates feature, some others have been removed from Configuration Manager. Table 8.1 lists the removed features.

TABLE 8.1: Removed features

FEATURE	DESCRIPTION
Update lists	The update lists have been replaced by the new software update groups.
Deployments	Of course you can still deploy software updates. But now the deployment is nested in the software update group.

Prerequisites for Software Updates

Before you can plan and set up the Software Updates feature, you need to be familiar with its components, so you can determine which ones to install and configure for your environment. Table 8.2 provides a list of these components.

TABLE 8.2: External prerequisites to the Configuration Manager Software Updates feature

PREREQUISITE	DESCRIPTION
Windows Server Update Services (WSUS) 3.0 SP1 or later	Software Updates requires WSUS 3.0 or later to be installed before setting up the software update point site system role because it is used for update synchronization and compliance assessment on clients.
WSUS 3.0 Administrator Console or later	The WSUS 3.0 Administrator Console or later is required on the Configuration Manager site server when WSUS is not on the site server itself. The console is required in order to communicate with a remote WSUS server.

PREREQUISITE	DESCRIPTION
Windows Update Agent (WUA) 3.0 or later	The WUA 3.0 client or later is required, in addition to the Configuration Manager client, to connect to the WSUS server so it can retrieve the list of software updates that need to be scanned for.
Network load balancing (NLB)	A software update point can support up to 25,000 clients, but if you expect to have more clients connecting to the active software update point, you can configure it to use an NLB cluster. If a software update point is installed on Windows Server with WSUS 3.0 SP2 installed, the software update point can service up to 100,000 clients. For more information see the Capacity Planning for Software Updates chapter in the WSUS online documentation on TechNet.
Background Intelligent Transfer Service (BITS) 2.5	Microsoft highly recommends that BITS be enabled and configured for a Configuration Manager site and that distribution points also be BITS enabled. Because software updates are downloaded to the local client cache before they are installed, having BITS enabled will allow clients to continue a download of updates if a client is disconnected from a distribution point.
Windows Installer 3.1	Certain updates, such as ones for Microsoft Office, require Windows Installer 3.1 or they will not be detected during a scan for compliance. If you were using the ITMU tool for SMS 2003, this requirement has probably already been met.
Site server communication to the active software update point (SUP)	There may be configuration settings that need to be examined depending on your software update point infrastructure and Configuration Manager settings. We will go into that in more detail in the section on planning the software update point installation.

Of course, you will also need to configure a SQL Reporting Services (SRS) reporting point before you can use the Software Updates reports. We'll go into more detail on configuring a reporting point in Chapter 12, "Reporting."

Elements of Software Updates

Before you can plan to implement the Software Update process, you need to become familiar with the various elements of the process and their roles in the overall picture.

Software Update Point

As discussed in Chapter 4, "Installation and Site Role Configuration," the *software update point* is a site system role that is required for managing software updates in Configuration Manager. Each Configuration Manager site must have at least one active software update point before it can deploy software updates to Configuration Manager clients. The software update point role can only be configured on a server that already has Windows Server Update Services (WSUS) 3.0 SP2 installed. The software update point software provides the bridge between the WSUS components and Configuration Manager. It allows synchronization with the WSUS database to download the latest software update information from Microsoft Update and locally published updates.

When the software update point site system role is created and configured as the active software update point, the software update point components are installed and enabled. The WSUS Control Manager component configures the associated WSUS server with the settings that were chosen when you set up the software update point site system role.

When you are deploying a Central Administration Site (CAS), you need to install the software update point in the CAS first. The software update point can be active or passive.

The software update point settings can be changed from the Software Update Component Properties window via the Configuration Manager console:

1. Choose the System Center 2012 Configuration Manager console ➢ Administration ➢ Overview ➢ Site Operations ➢ Sites.

2. Select the site for which you want to change properties.

3. Choose Configure Site Components ➢ Software Update Point.

The software update point settings can modify the active software update point site system server, the active Internet-based software update point site system if one is needed, the synchronization source, the schedule, and the products, classifications, and languages for which software updates will be synced with the database. You will find more details on these settings later in the chapter.

The first time the software update point completes its synchronization; the Software Updates client agent components are activated from a dormant state and will connect on a schedule to WSUS on the active software update point server to start a scan for update scan compliance, as described earlier in the chapter.

Software Updates Client Agent

The Software Updates Client Agent is part of the Configuration Manager 2012 client. You can configure the Software Updates Client Agent with the client settings. With Configuration Manager 2012 you can create different client agent settings for groups of computers, so you are able to assign different settings for different groups of computers and servers. For instance, you can configure client settings for computers in such a way that all mandatory software updates that reach their deadline are installed immediately. For servers you can configure a different setting.

Software Updates Metadata

A software update has two parts: the software update file(s) and the metadata. The metadata is contained in the Configuration Manager database and provides information about the software update, including its name, description, products supported, update class, size, article ID, download URL, rules that apply, and so on.

Most important, the metadata for each software update defines what products are applicable to the update. A product (for example, Windows 7) is a specific edition of an OS or application. A product family (for example, Microsoft Windows) is a base OS or application from which single products come. You can select a product family or individual products when choosing what will be synced by Configuration Manager.

MULTIPLE PRODUCT UPDATES

If an update is applicable to many products, and at least a few of those products from a product family have been chosen for synchronization, then all the updates will appear in the Configuration Manager console.

The metadata for each update also defines the update's *classification*. This represents the type of software an update will modify on clients. There can be many different classifications for any given product family, which we will go over in the "Planning to Use Software Updates in Configuration Manager" section of this chapter. The metadata also defines what languages the update file is applicable to, and it provides a summary of the software update in one or more languages.

Software Update Files

The software update files are the actual files that the client downloads, such as an .exe, a Windows Installer file (.msi), a Microsoft Update Standalone Package (.msu), or a Windows Installer patch (.msp), and then installs to update a component or application. The software update file might be stored on a WSUS 3.0 server that is configured to be an active software update point, but it is always stored on distribution points for the site when the software update is downloaded or deployed. The process is as follows:

1. Software update files are retrieved from either the upstream server or Microsoft Update.

   An upstream server is a software update point higher in the Configuration Manager 2012 hierarchy.

2. The updates are then copied to distribution points when the software update is downloaded using the Download Updates Wizard or deployed to clients using the Deploy Software Updates Wizard.

   Both methods are covered in detail later in this chapter.

3. Both methods download the software update files to a temporary location on the site server hard drive.

4. The site server creates and stores a compressed package file containing the software update.

5. It decompresses the package file.

6. Then it copies the update file to the content library on the distribution point.

Software Update Objects

The Software Updates node in the Configuration Manager 2012 console is divided into four nodes, as shown in Figure 8.2.

FIGURE 8.2

The Configuration Manager Console with the software update node

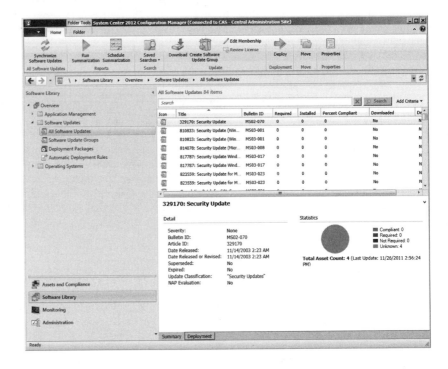

In these sections you will find the items that are related to the Software Updates feature. Table 8.3 lists the items that are related to Software Updates.

TABLE 8.3: Software Updates related items

OBJECT	DESCRIPTION
All software updates	Every software update has a configuration item object that is created during the software update sync cycle.
Software update groups	These are fixed sets of software updates that can be used for delegated administration and creating software update deployments.
Deployment packages	These host the software update source files.
Automatic Deployment Rules	Automatic Deployment Rules give you the ability to automatically approve and deploy software updates.
Deployment template	This stores many of the deployment properties that may not change from one deployment to the next and are used to save time and ensure consistency when creating deployments. The deployment template is stored within the Configuration Manager database and is only accessible when creating a deployment or an automatic deployment rule.
Search	This feature provides an easy way to retrieve a set of software updates that meet the search criteria; the searches can be saved in the Configuration Manager database.

As noted in some of the preceding descriptions, software update deployment and deployment package objects are replicated from the site where they were created to all child sites in the Configuration Manager hierarchy. The objects replicated to a child site will be read-only. Even though the properties for these objects must be modified at the site where they were created, the actions available for deployments at child sites are the same as those at the site where they were created. Also, deployment packages can be used to host the software updates that are deployed on the child sites.

Software Update Groups

A software update group in Configuration Manager contains a set of software updates. Software update groups offer several benefits for deploying and monitoring software updates and are part of Microsoft's recommended Software Updates workflow.

Using a software update group allows you to automate the process of approving and deploying software updates with Automatic Deployment Rules. Tracking the compliance state for the software updates in deployments is an important task for Configuration Manager admins. If deployments are made without update groups, it's very hard to get the overall compliance state for the same set of software updates that have been sent out with multiple deployments. When update groups are used instead, you can use the Compliance 1 - Overall Compliance report for the set of updates in the software update group or the Compliance 3 - Update Group (Per Update) report to get a list of the updates in an update group and the overall compliance of each. This is a great reason to use software update groups as a part of your software update procedure.

Deployment Templates

Deployment templates can store many of the software update deployment properties, and they can be created for consistency, to save time, or to fit your software update procedures. You can create a deployment template in the process of creating a deployment or automatic deployment rule and save the settings in a template. Table 8.4 shows the deployment properties that are saved in a deployment template.

TABLE 8.4:   Deployment template properties

SETTING	DESCRIPTION
Collection	Indicates the collection that will be targeted for the software update deployment. This setting is optional when you make a deployment template.
Deployment Settings	Configured deployment settings such as send wake-up packets or verbosity level are saved in the deployment template.
Deployment Schedule	Sets whether the user will be notified of pending updates, the installation progress for updates, whether the client evaluates the deployment schedule in local or Coordinated Universal Time (UTC), and the time frame between when an update is available and when it is mandatory on clients.
User Experience	Hides software update installation and notifications. Sets the system restart behavior when an update installs on a client and needs to restart to finish. Also allows a system restart to be completed outside a maintenance window.

TABLE 8.4:   Deployment template properties *(CONTINUED)*

SETTING	DESCRIPTION
Alerts	Sets if alerts are generated for the in-console alerting feature. Sets whether Operations Manager alerts are disabled while updates install and/or send an alert if the install fails.
Download Settings	Sets how clients will interact with the distribution points when they get a software update deployment.
Deployment Location	Sets whether to download the software updates from the Internet or a network file share.
Language Settings	Sets the language of the software updates that need to be downloaded and deployed.

Creating deployment templates in advance for typical deployment scenarios in your environment allows you to create deployments using templates that populate many of the properties that are most often static for the particular deployment scenario. Using the deployment template also reduces the number of wizard pages to work through in the Deploy Software Updates Wizard by up to seven pages, depending on what information you have already populated. This not only saves time but also helps to prevent mistakes when setting up a deployment.

Deployment Packages

A *deployment package* is the method used to download software updates (either one or several) to a network shared folder, which must be manually created before it is used, and copy the software updates source file to distribution points defined in the deployment.

Software updates can be downloaded and added to deployment packages prior to deploying them by using the Download Updates Wizard. This wizard provides admins with the capability to provision software updates on distribution points and verify that this part of the deployment process works properly.

When downloaded software updates are deployed using the Deploy Software Updates Wizard, the deployment automatically uses the deployment package that contains each software update. When software updates are selected that haven't been downloaded or deployed, a new or existing deployment package must be specified in the Deploy Software Updates Wizard, and the updates are downloaded to the package when the wizard is finished.

There is no hard link between a deployment and a specific deployment package. Clients will install software updates in a deployment by using any distribution point that has the software updates, regardless of the deployment package. Even if a deployment package is deleted for an active deployment, clients will still be able to install the software updates in the deployment—as long as each update has been defined in at least one other deployment package and is present on a distribution point that the client can get to. To help prevent software update deployment failures, you should make sure that deployment packages are sent to a group of distribution points that can be accessed by all the clients you are targeting.

Deployment package access accounts allow you to set permissions to specify users and user groups who can access a deployment package folder on distribution points. Configuration Manager makes these folders available to everyone by default, but you can modify this access if required for a specific security need.

Configuration Manager 2012 client computers also have the option of selective download: a deployment package might contain both updates that are required for a client and some that are not, but the client can determine which software updates are applicable and retrieve only those files. This allows admins to have multiple updates in a single deployment package and use it to target clients that might need only some of those updates.

Deployments

While it is deployment packages that host the update files, it is *software update deployments* that actually deliver software updates to clients. The Deploy Software Updates Wizard is used to create deployments and can be started using several methods, which we will detail later in the chapter. Table 8.5 lists all the pages in this wizard and describes the settings that can be configured in each one to create a software update deployment.

TABLE 8.5:   Deploy Software Updates Wizard settings

PAGE	DESCRIPTION
General	Provides the name of and comments about the deployment; the update or update group and collection also need to be supplied.
Deployment Settings	Defines if the deployment is required or optional and sets the verbosity level. Also configures whether to send wake-up packets.
Scheduling Settings	Sets whether the user will be notified of pending updates and/or the installation progress for updates, if the client evaluates the deployment schedule in local or Coordinated Universal Time, and the time frame between when an update is available and when it is mandatory on clients.
User Experience Settings	Defines if users will receive notice of installations of software updates and what happens when an installation deadline is reached. Defines the system restart behavior when an update installs on a client and needs to restart to finish.
Alerts	Sets the in-console alert handling of Configuration Manager and sets if System Center Operations Manager (SCOM) alerts are disabled while updates install and whether to send an alert if the install fails.
Download Settings	Sets how clients will interact with the distribution points when they get a software update deployment.
Deployment Package	Shows the deployment package that will host the software updates for the deployment. This setting won't appear if the updates have already been downloaded to a package.
Download Location	Lets you choose to download the updates from the Internet or from a source on the local network.
Languages Selection	Lets you select the languages for which the software updates that will be in the deployment are downloaded.
NAP Evaluation	Indicates whether the software update in this deployment will be added in a Network Access Protection (NAP) evaluation.
Save As Template	Lets you save the deployment settings to a deployment template. This template can only be created when you are creating a deployment.

If an update in a deployment has Microsoft Software License Terms that have not been accepted yet, then a Review/Accept License Terms dialog box will appear before the Deploy Software Updates Wizard and give you a chance to review and accept the license terms. When you accept the terms, then you can deploy the updates. If you don't accept the terms, the process is canceled.

Automatic Deployment Rules

A new Software Updates feature in Configuration Manager 2012 is Automatic Deployment Rules. This feature lets you define rules for specific types of software updates that can be downloaded and added to a software update group automatically. If a software update group is enabled for deployment, the updates are automatically deployed to your workstations. The Automatic Deployment Rules feature can be used for two common scenarios, namely:

◆ Automatically deploying Forefront Endpoint Protection definition and engine updates

◆ Patch Tuesday security patches

When you create an automatic deployment rule, you need to define whether you want to add the updates to an existing software update group or to automatically create a software update group.

When you deploy Forefront Endpoint Protection definition and engine updates, you can add these updates to an existing software update group. The reason for this is that only four definition updates are available per agent for Forefront Endpoint Protection. Three of them are superseded, and only one is active. Every fifth definition update will be expired and fall out of the software update group.

If you want to deploy the Tuesday patches automatically, it is recommended that you create a new software update group every Patch Tuesday. This keeps your software updates organized.

You can automatically select software updates based on the following parameters:

◆ Article ID

◆ Bulletin ID

◆ Custom severity

◆ Date released

◆ Date revised

◆ Expired

◆ Language

◆ Product

◆ Required

◆ Severity

◆ Superseded

◆ Title

◆ Update classification

◆ Vendor

AUTOMATIC DEPLOYMENT OF PATCH TUESDAY SOFTWARE UPDATES

The Automatic Deployment Rules feature allows you to automate the deployment of software updates. You can use it to automatically deploy the Patch Tuesday Software updates for test purposes or prepare the deployment in production. Depending on your requirements, you can configure an automatic deployment rule for Windows 7 Patch Tuesday updates by creating an automatic deployment rule with the following settings:

1. Enable Create a new software update group each time the rule runs.

2. Select Enable The Deployment after this rule has run.

3. Select a collection with your test systems where you want to automatically test the Patch Tuesday patches.

4. Supply the following search criteria for the rule:

   ◆ Product: **Windows 7**

   ◆ Date Released for Revised: **Last 1 day**

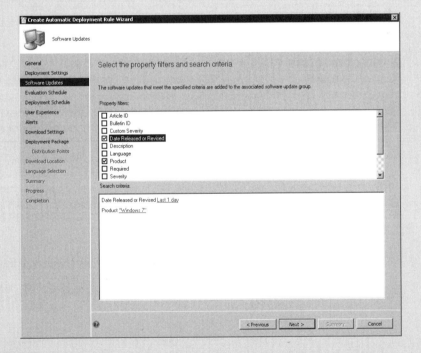

5. Evaluation Schedule: Be sure the evaluation runs after the Software Update Synchronization Schedule on the second Tuesday of every month.

6. Deployment Schedule: Enable the availability of the deployment for four hours after the deployment is created so that you are sure that the deployment has been distributed throughout your Configuration Manager hierarchy. Configure if you want the deadline for the deployment.

After you configure the rest of the automatic deployment rule, the rule will create a software update deployment every second Tuesday of the month.

System Center Updates Publisher

The System Center Updates Publisher was built on the custom updates framework that was introduced in Systems Management Server 2003 R2. Updates Publisher is a standalone tool that enables independent software vendors or line-of-business developers to import custom software update catalogs, create and modify software update definitions, export update definitions to catalogs, and publish software update information to a configured WSUS server. By using Updates Publisher to define software updates and publish them to the WSUS server, the Software Updates feature in Configuration Manager is able to synchronize the custom update from the WSUS server database to the site server database. This will allow you to enable client computers to scan for custom update compliance and to provide administrators with the ability to deploy the custom updates to client computers.

The Software Update Process in Configuration Manager

As you'll see throughout the hands-on portions of this chapter, the biggest parts of the software update process are planning and configuration. After you've completed those, Configuration Manager itself performs three main operational phases: synchronization, scanning for compliance, and deployment.

Synchronization

Synchronization is the process of retrieving the metadata for software updates that meet the configured criteria; it can be retrieved from either the upstream Windows Server Update Services (WSUS) 3.0 SP2 server or Microsoft Update. The WSUS Synchronization Manager component on the software update point works with WSUS to complete the synchronization process. The highest site (Central Administration Site) in the Configuration Manager hierarchy that has an active software update point synchronizes with Microsoft Update; this is done either on a schedule you set up or manually by using the Synchronize Software Updates action on the All Software Updates node in the Configuration Manager console. (We go into more detail on how to do that later in the chapter.) When a sync cycle is started at the CAS, the WSUS Synchronization Manager makes a request to the WSUS service to start a sync cycle. The software update's metadata is then synchronized from Microsoft Update, and any changes are inserted into the WSUS database.

When WSUS finishes its sync cycle, WSUS Synchronization Manager starts syncing with the WSUS database and inserts any changes into the site server database. When that process is finished, the WSUS Synchronization Manager component (SMS_WSUS_SYNC_MANAGER) creates a status message with an ID of 6702.

DIFFERENCE BETWEEN SCHEDULED AND MANUAL SYNCHRONIZATION

A scheduled synchronization does a full sync, but the Run Synchronization action does only a delta sync. Updates are marked as expired if they are superseded by another software update or marked as expired in the update catalog. They are only marked as expired during the scheduled synchronization.

When a sync is run on a schedule, all changes to the software update metadata since the last scheduled sync are put into the site database. This includes metadata that is new (products, languages, and so on), modified, or removed. A manually run sync will be faster than a scheduled one because it only downloads delta changes to what already exists in the database.

When a software update sync finishes at the CAS, a sync request is sent out to all of its child sites. When a child site gets that request, it will first sync itself from its parent site and then send out a request to any child sites that are configured as software update points. This continues on down the hierarchy until all child sites have been synchronized.

With an active Internet-based software update point (which is used in Network Access Protection scenarios), a sync request is sent to it right after the active software update point is finished with its syncing request. The process for both is the same except that the upstream server of the Internet-based software update point is automatically configured to be the active software update point for the site, and the site server database is not updated when the Internet-based software update point finishes its sync cycle.

If the synchronization fails, there is a retry interval of 60 minutes. The WSUS Synchronization Manager component will schedule the sync to run again 60 minutes after the process fails and start over. WSUS Synchronization Manager will create a status message with an ID of 6703 in the case of a sync failure.

Compliance

When software update synchronization completes at each site, a sitewide machine policy is created that allows client computers to retrieve the location of the WSUS server and to start a scan for software update compliance. When a client receives that machine policy, a compliance assessment scan is scheduled to start at a random time within the next two hours. When the scan runs, a component of the Software Updates Client Agent clears the previous scan history, sends a request to find the WSUS server that should be used for the scan, and then updates the local Group Policy with the WSUS server location.

The scan request is then passed to the Windows Update Agent (WUA). The WUA then connects to the WSUS server that it just got information about, downloads a list of the software updates that have been synced with the WSUS server, and scans the client computer for the updates in the list. A component of the Software Updates Client Agent then sees that the scan for compliance is finished and sends a state message for each software update that had a change in compliance state since the last scan. Those state messages are then sent to the client's management point in bulk every five minutes. The management point will then forward the state messages to the site server, where they are inserted into the site server database.

Supersedence occurs when a new software update has the same fixes as a previous update but may have fixed issues with the update and/or added new fixes. In SMS 2003, when new software updates supersede ones that had the same fixes, they may both be marked as needed when only the new one was necessary. In Configuration Manager 2012 Software Updates, you can now configure the supersedence behavior; you can either choose to expire a superseded update or choose to expire the update after a configurable number of months at the software update point. When new software updates are released that supersede others, Microsoft Update is refreshed with that information. When client computers are scanned for compliance, the new updates produce a compliance state by the client, but the older updates do not. The only time this is not the case is when a service pack contains a required update. The WUA will then return a compliance state on both, which allows admins to deploy individual updates or service packs as needed. Table 8.6 shows details on the four states of compliance for Software Updates.

TABLE 8.6: Software Updates compliance states

STATE	DESCRIPTION
Required	The software update is applicable to the client, which means any of the following conditions could be true: ◆ The update has not been deployed to the client. ◆ The update has been installed, but the state of the update hasn't been updated in the database yet. ◆ The update has been installed, but the client requires a reboot before it finishes. ◆ The update has been deployed but is not yet installed.
Not Required	The update isn't applicable on the client.
Installed	The update is applicable on the client, and it has already been installed.
Unknown	This state usually means that the software update has been synced to the site server, but the client hasn't been scanned for compliance for that update.

Deployment

The compliance assessment data is then used to determine which software updates are required on client computers. When you create a software update deployment with the Deploy Software Updates Wizard, as described later in this chapter, the software updates in the deployment are downloaded from the location specified on the Download Location page of the wizard to the configured package source, if they haven't been downloaded already. When the wizard finishes, a deployment policy is added to the machine policy for the site. The updates are then copied from the package source to the shared folders on the distribution points set up in the package, where they will be available for clients.

When a client in the target collection of the deployment receives the machine policy, the software update client component starts an evaluation scan. Updates that are still required on the client are then added to a class in Windows Management Instrumentation (WMI). Any updates that are mandatory deployments are downloaded as soon as possible from the distribution point to the local cache on the client. The updates in the optional deployment category are not downloaded until they are manually started. If an optional deployment has a deadline that makes it mandatory, the client will download the update as soon as it registers the change in deployment status.

> **SOFTWARE UPDATES IN CONFIGURATION MANAGER ARE ALWAYS DOWNLOADED TO THE CLIENT**
>
> Software updates are always downloaded to the local client cache before they are run in Configuration Manager. You no longer have the option to have them run from a distribution point as you did in SMS 2003.

If the client can't find the location of the distribution point through Location Services (embedded in the Management Point), it will keep trying for up to 5 days before it stops. If the client can't connect to the distribution point to download the updates, it will try for up to 10 days before it stops trying. When you start updates manually, the client will try every hour for each distribution point for up to 4 hours before it fails.

When an update deployment has a deadline that becomes available for deployment on a client, the Available Software Update icon will show up in the notification area to tell a user that the deadline is coming up. By default, these display notifications will show up on a periodic basis until all mandatory updates have been installed. They will be displayed every 3 hours for deadlines more than 24 hours away, every hour for deadlines less than 24 hours away, and every 15 minutes for deadlines less than an hour away.

Just imagine the phone calls you'd get if you left things that way! Fortunately, Microsoft has given you the option to turn that off with the client agent settings that let you hide all software update deployments from users. This setting doesn't affect regular Software Deployment settings, but it will keep display notifications, notification area icons, and software update installation progress boxes from appearing at all. However, this will also mean that you can send out only mandatory software update deployments to your clients. We recommend doing that anyway because users would more than likely delay deployments until they become mandatory.

Unless you hide your update deployments, users will be able to open the Express/Advanced dialog box to start up the installation of all mandatory software updates at once. They will also be able to open the Available Software Updates dialog box, where they can choose to install whatever is available.

When the deadline passes on a mandatory update, a scan will start on the client to make sure that the update is still required; the local client cache will be checked to make sure the update is still available, and then the update will be started. When that is done, another scan will start to make sure that the update is no longer required on the client. Finally, a state message is sent to the management point saying that the update is now installed.

Planning to Use Software Updates in Configuration Manager

Now that you have seen what is new in Configuration Manager Software Updates, the prerequisites, and the major components of the process, you can plan the use of Software Updates in your environment.

To plan the implementation of Software Updates in Configuration Manager, you can use the same process of deployment intelligence that we used to plan the deployment of Configuration Manager itself in Chapter 2, "Planning a Configuration Manager Infrastructure." Using this method will help you ensure that you get everything out of Software Updates that your company requires to keep your computer resources up to date with the latest software upgrades and patches.

Deployment intelligence for Software Updates has three parts:

◆ Determine what needs to be accomplished with Software Updates.

◆ Determine what is on the network now and what has been used in the past.

◆ Test in an isolated lab.

Determining What Needs to Be Accomplished

This may seem like a no-brainer, because the first thing that probably comes to mind is "deploy patches," but with Configuration Manager you can do a lot more than just deploy security patches, as you will soon learn.

This part of the planning will also let you decide how you want to configure your test environment, your software update point infrastructure, and the settings for the Software Update Servers and Client Agent.

PLANNING FOR SOFTWARE UPDATE POINT INFRASTRUCTURE

When you have a Configuration Manager 2012 hierarchy, the Central Administration Site server is at the top of the Configuration Manager hierarchy. An active software update point is configured on the Central Administration Site so that software updates can be managed. Most of the synchronization settings are configured there and propagated down to the rest of the sites in the hierarchy. The active software update point on the central site is what syncs with Microsoft Update. When you have only a single primary site, the software update point needs to be configured on the primary site server, and it will sync with Microsoft Update.

All primary sites in Configuration Manager must have an active software update point. The child sites sync with the active software update point that is set up on the parent site. Secondary sites can be set up with an active software update point, or clients at the secondary site can connect directly to the active software update point on the parent primary site.

When your site is in secure (HTTPS) mode, you have the option to configure the active software update point to accept connections from clients on both the intranet and the Internet or from only clients on the intranet. When Internet-based client connectivity is not accepted on the active software update point, you can set up separate active Internet-based software update points if needed.

This site system server role must be assigned to a site system server that is remote from the site server and the active software update point. When the active Internet-based software update point doesn't have connectivity to the active software update point for the site, you will have to use the export and import functions of the WSUSUtil tool to sync the software update metadata.

If you are going to have more than 25,000 clients connecting to WSUS on the active software update point, a network load balancing (NLB) cluster must be configured on the WSUS server and then configured for the Configuration Manager site so that the NLB cluster is used as the active software update point.

PLANNING FOR THE SOFTWARE UPDATE POINT INSTALL

Before setting up the active software update point site system role in Configuration Manager, you must consider several requirements depending on your Configuration Manager infrastructure, such as when the Configuration Manager active software update point will be configured to communicate using SSL, or when the site server is in secure mode, and so on. You must take additional steps before the software update point in the hierarchy will work properly.

As discussed earlier in the chapter, Software Updates requires that Windows Server Update Services (WSUS) 3.0 SP2 be installed on all site systems servers that will be configured for the software update point site system role. There can be many site systems with the software update point role, but only one site system can be configured as the active SUP. Also, when the active software update point is not on the site server itself, the WSUS 3.0 administrative console is required on the site server, which lets the site server communicate with the WSUS components on the active software update point. If you are going to use an NLB cluster, the full install of WSUS 3.0 is required on all site systems that will be in the cluster.

During the WSUS install, you can choose to use the default or a custom website to host the WSUS components. If WSUS is going to be installed on a primary Configuration Manager site system, Microsoft recommends that you choose a custom website so that IIS hosts the WSUS 3.0 services in a dedicated website instead of sharing the site with Configuration Manager site systems or other applications.

You can use a WSUS server that was active in your environment before Configuration Manager was implemented. When the WSUS server is configured as the active software update point, the sync settings are then specified. All of the software update metadata from the WSUS server will be synced to the Configuration Manager database regardless of the sync settings for the active software update point. Be sure to disable the Group Policies that point the clients to the WSUS server.

When your Configuration Manager site server is in secure mode or when the active software update point is configured to use SSL, a web server signing certificate must be assigned to the website used by WSUS. When you use a custom website for WSUS, per Microsoft's recommendation, the WSUS website must be assigned a web server certificate where the Subject Name or Subject Alternate Name field contains the Internet fully qualified domain name (FQDN). The upstream WSUS server must be set with the same certificate, or SSL communication will fail between the servers. The certificate must also reside in Trusted Root Certification Authorities in the Computer certificate store on each client computer, or it will fail to scan for software update compliance.

When the site server is in secure mode, the web server certificate that is used for the Configuration Manager site systems can also be used by the WSUS website. Also, when the WSUS uses the same website as the Configuration Manager site server, and the site is in secure mode, the default website might already be assigned the right web server certificate. The certificate would still need to be configured on the upstream WSUS server, but it should already be configured on Configuration Manager clients.

If there is a firewall between the Configuration Manager active software update point and the Internet, an active software update point and its upstream server, or an active Internet-based software update point and the active software update point for the site, the firewall might have to be configured to accept the HTTP and HTTPS ports used for the WSUS website. By default, a WSUS server that is configured for the default website uses port 80 for HTTP and 443 for HTTPS communication, while one configured for a custom website uses port 8530 for HTTP and 8531 for HTTPS communication.

If your company doesn't allow these ports and protocols to be open for all addresses on the firewall between the active software update point and the Internet, you can restrict access to the following URLs so that WSUS and Automatic Updates can communicate with Microsoft Update.

```
http://windowsupdate.microsoft.com

http://*.windowsupdate.microsoft.com

https://*.windowsupdate.microsoft.com

http://*.update.microsoft.com

https://*.update.microsoft.com
```

```
http://*.windowsupdate.com

http://download.windowsupdate.com

http://download.microsoft.com

http://*.download.windowsupdate.com

http://test.stats.update.microsoft.com

http://ntservicepack.microsoft.com
```

If there is an active Internet-based software update point, or there are child sites with an active software update point, these addresses might also need to be added to a firewall between the servers:

```
http://<FQDN for active software update point on child site>

https://<FQDN for active software update point on child site>

http://<FQDN for active software update point on parent site>

https://<FQDN for active software update point on parent site>
```

PLANNING THE SOFTWARE UPDATE SERVER SETTINGS

There are software update point settings and general site settings that have an impact on software updates in Configuration Manager. These settings configure the active software update point and determine which updates are synchronized, whether there are maintenance windows for installing updates, how much time software updates have to complete, and so on.

The software update point settings configure which site system server is the active software update point, which site system server is the active Internet-based software update point if one is specified at the site, the sync source, the sync schedule, the products, the classifications, and the languages for which software updates will be synchronized.

General Settings

These settings in the Create Role Wizard and the software update point properties control whether the active software update point is a local server or a remote server and if it uses an NLB cluster. They also set which port settings are used for connectivity to the site system server that is assigned the software update point role, whether a software update point connection account should be used instead of the computer account, whether Internet-based clients are allowed to connect the software update point when the site is in secure mode, and whether SSL is used when synchronizing data from the active software update point and when clients connect to the WSUS server on the active software update point.

Internet-Based Settings

When the Configuration Manager site server is in secure mode and the active software update point is configured with Do Not Allow Access From Internet-Based Clients, a software update point site system role must be created (but not configured as the active software update point) and then configured to be the active Internet-based software update point from the Internet-Based tab in the

Software Update Point Component Properties dialog box. You can then set if the active Internet-based software update point is a remote server or uses an NLB cluster, which port settings are used for connectivity to the software update point server, and so on. If synchronization is not configured, the export/import function for the WSUSUtil tool will have to be used to sync update metadata.

Synchronization Settings

The sync settings for the active software update point specify the sync source and whether WSUS reporting events are created during the sync process.

Synchronization Source   The sync source for the active software update point at the central site is configured to use Microsoft Updates. The active software update point on child sites is automatically configured to use the active software update point on its parent site as the sync source. When there is an active Internet-based software update point, the active software update point for the site is automatically set to be the sync source. Also, the active software update point or active Internet-based software update point can be configured not to sync with the configured sync source, and you can use the export and import functions of the WSUSUtil tool instead.

WSUS Reporting Events   The Windows Update Agent (WUA) on clients can create event messages that are used for WSUS reporting. These events are not used in Configuration Manager, so the Do Not Create WSUS Reporting Events setting is checked by default. When these events are not created, the only time clients should connect to the WSUS server is during software update evaluation and compliance scans. If these events are needed outside of the Configuration Manager reporting for software updates for some reason, then you will need to modify this setting for your specific needs.

Synchronization Schedule   The sync schedule can be configured only at the active software update point on the central Configuration Manager site. When this schedule is configured, the active software update point on the central site will start syncing with Microsoft Update at the scheduled date and time. The custom schedule allows you to sync software updates on a date and time when the demands from the WSUS server, site server, and the network are low and less likely to interfere with regular network traffic. You can also run a sync cycle manually from the central site from the Update Repository using the Run Synchronization action in the Configuration Manager console.

After the active software update point successfully syncs with Microsoft Update, a sync request is sent to the active Internet-based software update point, if there is one, and to the active software update point on child sites. This process repeats throughout the hierarchy until it is successful.

Supersedence Rules

You can configure a software update to expire as soon as it is superseded by a more recent software update. You also can set an update to expire that is superseded after a specific period of time.

Supersedence settings are not applicable for Forefront definition updates. Definition files are automatically expired after four newer definition updates are released. Supersedence settings are also not applicable for software updates that are superseded by a service pack; these software updates will never expire after they are superseded.

Update Classifications

Updates are defined with classifications that help to organize the different types of updates. During the sync process, the software updates metadata for the specified classification will be synchronized. Table 8.7 shows the classifications of updates that can be synced with Configuration Manager.

TABLE 8.7: Update classes

UPDATE CLASS	DESCRIPTION
Critical updates	Broadly released fixes for specific problems addressing bugs that are critical but not security related.
Definition updates	Updates to virus or other definition files.
Drivers	Software components designed to support new hardware.
Feature packs	Feature packs will often bring more functionality to a product; they are also deployed via software updates.
Security updates	Broadly released fixes for specific products, addressing security issues.
Service packs	Cumulative sets of all hotfixes, security updates, and updates created since the release of the product. Service packs might also contain a limited number of customer-requested design changes or features.
Tools	Utilities of features that aid in accomplishing a task or set of tasks.
Update rollups	Cumulative set of hotfixes, security updates, critical updates, and updates packaged together for easy deployment. A rollup generally targets a specific area, such as security, or a specific component, such as IIS.
Updates	Broadly released fixes for specific problems addressing non-critical, non–security-related bugs.

You will need to decide if you are going to deploy some or all of these categories or even pick and choose specific updates from each category in your environment. The update classification settings are configured only on the active software update point highest in the Configuration Manager hierarchy. They are not configured anywhere else because they synchronize the metadata from the upstream sync source using the class settings from the central site. When you choose update classes to sync, remember that the more classes you choose, the longer it will take to sync the software update metadata.

Products

The metadata for each update sets the product or products for which the update is applicable. A *product* is a specific edition of an operating system (such as Windows 7) or application, while a product family is the base operating system or application to which the individual products belong (such as Microsoft Windows). You can choose a product family or individual products within a product family.

When updates are applicable to several products and at least one of the products is one you have chosen to update, all of the products will appear in the Configuration Manager console even if they haven't been selected.

The Products settings, like other software update settings, are configured only on the active software update point highest in the Configuration Manager hierarchy.

Languages

This setting allows you to configure the languages for which the summary details will be synced for a software update and the update file languages that will be downloaded for the software update.

Update File

The languages configured for the Update File setting provide the default set of languages that will be available when downloading updates at the site server. When you're on the Language Selection page of the Deploy Software Updates Wizard or Download Software Updates Wizard, the languages configured for the active software update point are automatically selected, but they can be modified each time updates are downloaded or deployed. When the wizard finishes, the software update files for the configured languages are downloaded, if they are available, to the deployment package source location and copied to the distribution points configured for the package.

The Update File language settings should be configured with the languages that are most often used in your environment. For example, if your clients use English and Spanish for the operating systems or applications and not much else, then select those languages in the Update File column and clear the others. This will allow you to use the default settings on the Language Selection page of the wizards most of the time, and it also prevents unneeded update files from being downloaded. This setting is configured at each software update point in the Configuration Manager hierarchy.

Summary Details

During the sync process, the Summary Details information (Software Updates metadata) is updated for the languages selected. The metadata provides information about the software update, such as name, description, products supported, update class, article ID, download URL, applicability rules, and so on.

When selecting the Summary Details languages, you should select only the languages needed in your environment. The more languages that are selected, the longer it will take to sync the software update metadata. The metadata is displayed in the location of the operating system where the Configuration Manager console is running. If localized properties for the software are not available, the information displays in English.

Maintenance Windows

Maintenance windows provide admins with a way to define a period of time that limits when changes can be made on the systems that are members of a collection. Maintenance windows restrict when the software updates in deployments can be installed on client computers, as well as restrict operating system and software distribution advertisements.

Client computers determine whether there is enough time to start a software update install through the following settings:

Restart Countdown   The length of the client restart notification (in minutes) for computers in the site. The default setting is 5 minutes, and it is a global site setting that can be changed in the Computer Client Agent Properties dialog box.

System Restart Turnaround Time   The length of time given for computers to restart and reload the operating system. This setting is in the site control file and has a default of 10 minutes.

Maximum Run Time   The amount of time estimated for a software update to install on a client. The default is 20 minutes for updates and 60 minutes for a service pack. This time frame can be changed for each software update on the Maximum Run Time tab of the properties of a software update.

When you use these setting to determine the available time in a maintenance window, each software update has a default of 35 minutes. For service packs, the default is 75 minutes. When you plan for maintenance windows in your deployments, take these defaults into consideration. When planning software update deployments, be aware of the collection's maintenance window and how many updates are in a deployment, so you can calculate whether clients will be able to install all the updates within the maintenance window or the installation of updates will span multiple maintenance windows.

When a software update installation completes but there is not enough time left in the maintenance window for a restart, the computer will wait until the next maintenance window and restart before starting any more update installs.

If more than one update is to be installed on a client during a maintenance window, the update with the lowest maximum run time installs first, then next lowest installs, and so on. Before installing each update, the client will verify that the available maintenance window is long enough to install the update. Once an update starts installing, it will continue to install even if the install goes beyond the maintenance window.

When you create a software update deployment, there are two settings that can allow maintenance windows to be ignored.

Allow System Restart Outside Of Maintenance Windows   You can set this option to indicate whether you want to allow system restarts for both workstations and servers outside configured maintenance windows. By default, this setting is disabled. This setting comes in handy when you want your software update install to complete on clients as soon as possible. When this setting is not enabled, a system restart will not be triggered if the maintenance window ends in 10 minutes or less. This could prevent the install from completing and leave the client in a vulnerable state until the next maintenance window. This setting is available on the Restart Settings page of the Create Automatic Deployment Rule Wizard or the Deploy Software Updates Wizard.

Ignore Maintenance Windows And Install Immediately At Deadline   This setting determines whether software updates in the deployment are installed at the deadline regardless of a configured maintenance window. It is disabled by default and is available only when a deadline is set up for a deployment. This setting comes in handy when you have software updates that must be installed on clients as soon as possible, such as security patches to fix a vulnerability that is being exploited on the Internet. This setting is available on the Schedule page of the Deploy Software Updates Wizard.

Software Update Properties

Each software update has a properties box with three tabs that provide configuration settings to enable software updates and configure the update settings on clients.

Maximum Run Time Tab This tab allows you to set the maximum amount of time a software update has to complete installing on clients, in minutes. If the maximum runtime value has been reached, a status messages is created and the deployment is no longer monitored. This setting is also used to determine whether the update should be started within a configured maintenance window. If the maximum runtime value is greater than the time left in the maintenance window, the software update installation is not initiated until the start of the next maintenance window.

Keep in mind that if a maximum runtime value is set for more time than the configured maintenance window of a collection it targets, it will never run on those clients. This setting can be configured only on the site synchronized with Microsoft Update, which is more than likely the Central Administration Site, and the default is 60 minutes for service packs and 20 minutes for all other types. Values can range from 5 to 9999 minutes.

NAP Evaluation Tab This tab is used to set whether the software update is required for compliance when using Network Access Protection. Enable NAP evaluation to include the software update in a NAP policy that will become effective on NAP-capable clients based on the configured schedule. When the policy becomes effective, NAP-capable clients might have restricted network access until they comply with the selected software update. Network restriction and remediation depend on how the policies are configured on the Windows Network Policy server.

Custom Severity Tab This is a nice addition to Software Updates that allows you to assign custom severity values for software updates if the default value doesn't meet your organization's needs. The custom values are listed in the Custom Severity column in the Configuration Manager console. The software updates can be sorted by custom severity values, the search criteria can be created based on these values, queries and reports can be made that filter on these values—whatever suits your needs. This setting can only be configured on the site that syncs with Microsoft Update.

PLANNING FOR SOFTWARE UPDATE CLIENT SETTINGS

The software update client settings in Configuration Manager can be configured sitewide (by default), and you can configure client settings for specific collections. There are Software Updates Client Agent settings and general settings that affect when updates are scanned for compliance and how and when updates are installed on clients. The client agent settings specific to software updates are configured in the Software Updates Client Agent properties, and the sitewide general or collection-based settings related to software updates are configured within the Computer Client Agent properties. The software update installation schedule can be modified from Configuration Manager Software Center on the client. You may also need to configure Group Policy settings on the client computer depending on your environment.

COMPUTER CLIENT AGENT SETTINGS

The properties for this client agent are found in various sections that provide configuration settings that affect the software update reminders and the customization for software update deployments on clients. In Figure 8.3, you see the relevant custom settings categories.

FIGURE 8.3
Computer client
agent settings for
software update
deployment

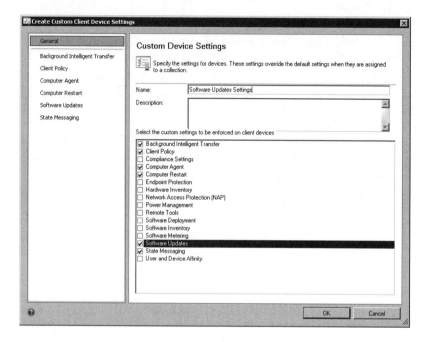

Background Intelligent Transfer Section

The settings in this section specify if bandwidth throttling is configured for the site. These settings apply to Configuration Manager clients when they use BITS to download software update files from distribution points.

Client Policy Section

In the Client Policy section you can specify a polling interval and a reporting cycle for state messages. The Policy Polling Interval (Minutes) setting controls how often clients retrieve the machine policy. This setting is relevant to software updates in that when new deployments are created, the machine policy is updated with the deployment information. Clients can take up to the policy polling interval to get those changes, depending on when they last got the policy. The default for this setting is 60 minutes.

Computer Agent Section

On this tab you can provide custom information about the update that will appear on clients.

Reminder Settings   The settings specify how often notifications are displayed on client computers when a deployment deadline is approaching for software updates. The reminder intervals can be configured for when the deadline is more than 24 hours away, when the deadline is less than 24 hours away, and when the deadline is less than an hour away.

Default Application Catalog Website Point You can configure the default application catalog website point so that the users can define their own working hours when going to the default application catalog website.

Organization Name This setting specifies the name of the organization authoring the software update install. By default this text box displays "IT Organization." The organization name appears in software update display notifications, the Available Software Updates dialog box, and the Restart Countdown dialog box on clients that are deployed software updates. Microsoft recommends that you customize this field with something related to your organization.

Computer Restart Section

These settings configure the start countdown time frame and restart final notification when a software update is installed on client computers, and they use BITS to download software update files from distribution points. By default, the initial countdown is 90 minutes, and a final notification is displayed when 15 minutes remain before the restart will occur.

State Messaging Section

In the State Messaging section you can specify a reporting cycle for state messages. The State Message Reporting Cycle (Minutes) setting specifies how often clients send state messages to the management point. The software update client creates state messages for scan, software updates compliance, deployment evaluation, and deployment enforcement. The default setting for this is 5 minutes.

CLIENT CONFIGURATION MANAGER PROPERTIES

The Configuration Manager Properties box in the Control Panel of a Configuration Manager client provides software update actions and configuration settings. When you browse to the Actions tab, you are able to choose the following actions that are applicable for software updates, shown in Figure 8.4:

Software Updates Deployment Evaluation Cycle When this action is started, active deployments will be evaluated.

Software Updates Scan Cycle This starts a software updates scan when run.

FIGURE 8.4
The Actions tab of the Configuration Manager client properties

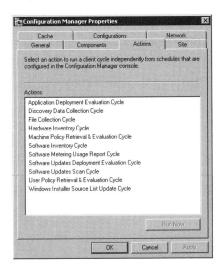

SOFTWARE SETTINGS OPTIONS

New in Configuration Manager 2012 is the Software Center, which is part of the Configuration Manager 2012 client. With the Software Center users can install or request software, but the users are also able to configure some settings that allow users to manage your software update deployment. A user is able to configure the work information and computer maintenance settings, shown in Figure 8.1.

In the Software Center users can configure the following options that are related to software updates:

Work Information   You can configure your business hours and business days. Once you define the hours and days, the software updates will be installed outside your work hours. Users can define business hours per hour from 12 a.m. until 11 p.m. and all hours in between, and they can choose the days by selecting a check box per day. You must reserve at least four hours each day for system maintenance tasks.

Computer Maintenance   For software update installations users are able to choose to automatically install required software after business hours and restart the computer if necessary or suspend Software Center activities when the computer is in a presentation mode.

GROUP POLICY SETTINGS

These settings in Group Policy are required for the Windows Update Agent (WUA) on client computers to connect to WSUS on the active software update point and successfully scan for software update compliance.

Specify Intranet Microsoft Update Service Location   When the active software update point is created for a site, clients receive a machine policy that provides the active software update point server name and configures the Specify Intranet Microsoft Update Server Location local policy on the computer. The WUA retrieves the server name set with Set The Intranet Update Service For Detecting Updates and then connects to that server when it scans for software update compliance. When a domain policy has been created for the Specify Intranet Microsoft Update Service Location setting, it will override local policy, and the WUA might connect to a server other than the active software update point. If that happens, the client computer might scan for software update compliance based on different products, classes, and languages. Microsoft recommends that this domain policy not be configured for Configuration Manager clients; as mentioned earlier, you should disable the Group Policy settings when you already use a WSUS infrastructure in your environment.

Allow Signed Content From Intranet Microsoft Update Service Location   Before the WUA on clients will scan for updates that were created and published with the System Center Updates Publisher, the Allow Signed Content From Intranet Microsoft Update Service Location Group Policy setting must be enabled. When the policy setting is enabled, the WUA will accept updates received through an Internet location if the updates are signed in the Trusted Publishers certificate store on the local computer.

Configure Automatic Updates   The Automatic Updates feature allows clients to receive security updates and other important downloads. It is configured through the Configure Automatic Updates Group Policy setting of Control Panel on the local computer. When Automatic Updates is enabled, clients will receive update notifications (if you have notifications enabled) and download and install required updates. When Automatic Updates coexists with Software

Updates, each might display notification icons and pop-up display notifications for the same update. Also, when a restart is required, each might display a Restart dialog box for the same reason.

Self-Update During a Configuration Manager client install, the Windows Update Agent is installed on a client computer if it is not already installed. When Automatic Updates is enabled, the WUA on each client automatically does a self-update when a newer version becomes available or when there are problems with the component. When Automatic Updates is not configured or is disabled, the WUA is still installed during Configuration Manager client installs. If the WUA install fails or becomes corrupt, or a new version of WUA is available, you must create a software distribution to update the agent on clients. If the WUA fails on a client, the scan for software update compliance also fails until it is fixed.

Role-Based Administration

For administering software update deployment, a special role is defined in the Role-Based Administration feature within Configuration Manager. An administrator who is added to the Software Update Manager role has the permissions delegated that are shown in Table 8.8.

TABLE 8.8:   Permissions of the Software Update Manager role

OBJECT	PERMISSION
Alerts	Read, Modify, Delete, Create, Run Report, Modify Report
Boundary	Read
Boundary groups	Read
Client Agent Settings	Read
Collection	Read, Read Resource, Deploy Client Settings, Deploy Software Updates, Modify Client Status Alert
Deployment template	Read, Modify, Delete, Create
Distribution point	Read, Copy to Distribution Point
Distribution point group	Read, Copy to Distribution Point, Create Association to Collection
Query	Read
Site	Read
Software update groups	Read, Modify, Delete, Set Security Scope, Create
Software update package	Read, Modify, Delete, Set Security Scope, Create
Software updates	Read, Modify, Delete, Create, Move Objects, Modify Folders, Network Access, Run Report, Modify Report

Depending on whether the scope is limited or not, you can deploy the software updates to all Configuration Manager clients or a limited group of Configuration Manager clients. With Role-Based Administration, an administrator who is added to the Software Update Manager role sees only the objects that are related to the role.

System Center Updates Publisher

When planning to implement the current version of System Center Updates Publisher 2011, you need to be able to identify the following items.

COMPONENTS OF SYSTEM CENTER UPDATES PUBLISHER

System Center Updates Publisher 2011 consists of the following components:

Software Update Catalog   Software Update Catalogs are used to import collections of related software updates into the System Center Updates Publisher repository.

Software Update   The repository in the System Center Updates Publisher contains software updates that you can publish or export. You can import them via the update catalogs, or you can create them yourself.

Publications   When publishing a software update to Configuration Manager 2012, you can publish either the full content of the software update or the metadata that describes the software update.

Rules   When you publish software updates in System Center Updates Publisher, the applicability rules are used to check to see if the computer meets the prerequisites for the software update. It also checks to see if the software update is already installed on the computer or not.

WHICH VENDOR UPDATES TO DEPLOY

Currently three third-party custom software update partners publish catalogs that can be used via System Center Updates Publisher. You can import Software Update Catalogs from the following third-party hardware and software vendors: Adobe, Dell, and HP. Check this website for an up-to-date partner list:

```
http://technet.microsoft.com/en-us/systemcenter/cm/bb892875.aspx
```

THE SYSTEM REQUIREMENTS

To be able to install the System Center Updates Publisher you need to be sure that the operating system complies with the following requirements:

- ◆ Windows Server Update Services 3.0 Service Pack 2 (WSUS 3.0 SP2)
- ◆ Windows Server Update Services 3.0 Service Pack 2 hotfix (KB2530678)
- ◆ Microsoft .NET Framework 4

Supported operating systems are these:

♦ Windows Vista

♦ Windows 7

♦ Windows Server 2008

♦ Windows Server 2008 R2

Testing in an Isolated Lab

It is important to understand how software updates will work in your environment, and one way you can do that is to set up a test lab that is as close to your production environment as possible. This section describes a minimum setup of Configuration Manager to use while you are testing or evaluating the software update components and other deployments like applications and operating systems; always test your deployment in a test environment before deploying it in the production environment.

To start, you will need at least one computer for each operating system that you use in your environment. Also, you will need computers that have other crucial line-of-business applications running on them as well.

A single client is adequate for minimum test purposes, but if you want to have a representative sample of how software updates will work with all computers used in your enterprise, then you will need to have a representative of each client configuration in your environment. For example, if you are using Windows XP SP3, Windows Server 2008 R2 SP1, and Windows 7 SP1 in your organization, then you should have at least one client with each of those operating systems on it for testing. If you can't get that many machines together, at least try to get one beefed-up computer with lots of RAM. That way, you can use Windows Server 2008 Hyper-V or Windows 7 Virtual PC to set up virtual representations of the computers that you couldn't procure physically.

By doing this, you will become familiar with how the Software Updates components and the actual software update executables work with the operating systems on your network before you use Software Updates enterprise-wide. By using more than one operating system in your testing you will be able to do the following:

♦ Review the specific software updates that Microsoft has published for those operating systems.

♦ Start becoming familiar with software update management practices for each type of computer.

♦ Learn how software updates work with different operating systems in a controlled environment.

♦ Learn how to find information about specific software updates for a specific OS when you need it.

REQUIREMENTS FOR TESTING SOFTWARE UPDATE POINTS

When you test software updates, create the software update point site role as it would be in your production site. You will need to decide if a single active software update point will be created or if there will be an active software update point for connectivity from client computers on the Internet, and if the active software update point will be set up with an NLB cluster. The deployment intelligence that you have gathered up to this point will be crucial to helping you plan your test environment.

Configuring Software Updates

Now that we have taken the time to look at the components of Software Updates and how they fit together, and you have taken that information with your deployment intelligence and put together a plan as to how you want to set up Software Updates in your environment, we can examine how to get everything working.

Before Software Updates data can be displayed in the Configuration Manager 2012 console and software updates can be deployed to clients, you must set up and configure the software update point, as well as the rest of the components of Software Updates.

Configuring the Software Updates Client Agent

The Software Updates Client Agent is enabled in Configuration Manager by default, but you still have to configure the other settings of this client agent to match your plans for using Software Updates in your environment.

To configure the Software Updates Client Agent, follow these steps:

1. In the Configuration Manager console, choose the Administration Workspace ➢ Overview ➢ Client Settings, and select the Default Client Agent Settings package.

2. Select the Home tab of the Ribbon, and then click Properties.

3. Select Software Updates, and (shown in Figure 8.5) configure the following settings:

FIGURE 8.5
The Default Settings of the Software Updates Client Agent

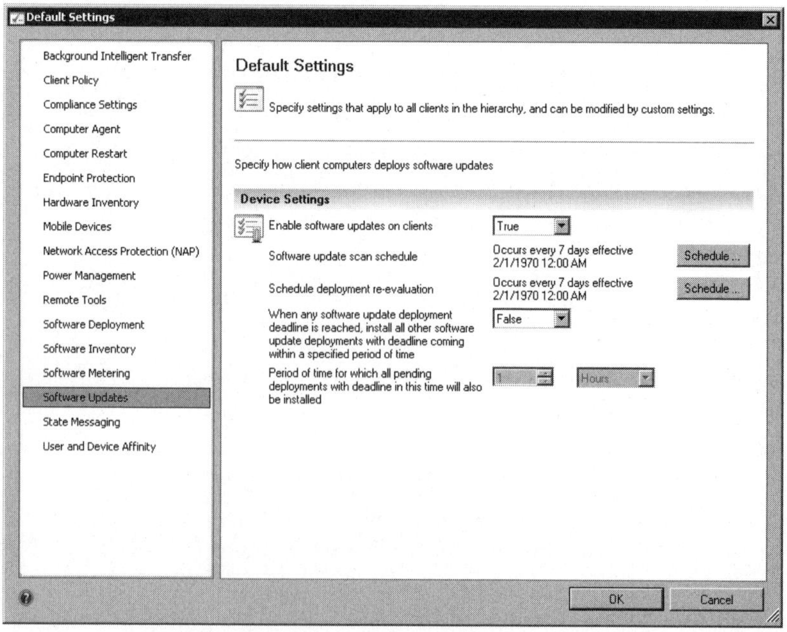

Enable Software Updates On Clients This setting defines whether the Software Updates Client Agent is enabled for the site; this agent is installed and enabled on Configuration Manager clients by default. Make sure that this setting is enabled. If the client agent is disabled, the client agent components are put into a dormant state but not uninstalled, and existing deployment policies will be removed from clients as well. Re-enabling the client agent starts a policy request that the components on clients be enabled and the deployment metadata be downloaded. With Configuration Manager 2012 you can configure more than one Client Agent settings package. Chapter 6, "Client Installation." has more information about client agent settings.

Software Update Scan Schedule This setting specifies how often the client computer scans for software update compliance. By default, a simple schedule is configured to run the scan every 7 days, and the site database is updated with any changes since the last scan. The minimum value for the scan is 1 minute and the maximum value is 31 days. This setting can be configured only after an active software update point site role has been installed on a site system in the site. When a custom schedule is configured, the actual start time on client computers is the start time plus a random amount of time up to 2 hours. This keeps all the clients from starting a scan and connecting to WSUS at the same time.

Schedule Deployment Re-evaluation You can configure how often the Software Updates Client Agent re-evaluates software updates for installation status. When software updates that have been installed are no longer found on client computers and are still required, they will be reinstalled. This re-evaluation schedule will need to be adjusted based on company policy for update compliance, whether users have the ability to uninstall updates, and similar considerations. You also have to consider that every re-evaluation cycle results in some network and client computer activity. The minimum value allowed for the deployment re-evaluation schedule is 1 minute and the maximum is one month. A simple schedule of every 7 days is set by default.

Install All Required Software Updates When Deadline Occurs This setting indicates whether to enforce all mandatory software update deployments that have deadlines within a certain time frame. When a deadline is reached for a mandatory software update deployment, an installation is started on the clients that have been targeted for the mandatory deployment. It also indicates whether to start the install for updates defined in other mandatory deployments that have a configured deadline within a specified time frame. The benefits of this setting are that it expedites software update installs for mandatory updates and that it might increase security, decrease display notifications, and decrease system restarts on clients. This setting is disabled by default.

Set period of time to install Software Updates with a deadline This sets the time frame for the software updates with a deadline to be installed if the deadline is coming within a specified period of time. The minimum value allowed is 1 to 23 hours, and the maximum is 1 to 365 days. By default, this setting is configured for 1 hour.

4. When you have finished setting things the way you want them, click OK to finish.

Installing Windows Server Update Services 3.0 Server

Windows Server Update Services 3.0 Server (WSUS) SP1 or later is required in order to use Software Updates in Configuration Manager 2012. Installing WSUS for use with Configuration

Manager is different from a standard install of WSUS without the Configuration Manager infrastructure.

The WSUS installation procedure that we're going to use can be used for both active software update points (the main software update point installed on the Central Administration Site) and inactive software update points (those for any other primary Configuration Manager sites) or for installing WSUS on a remote server that is not a Configuration Manager site server. The decision to install WSUS on the same server as your site servers or on another remote server will depend on your server resources and your plans for the software update infrastructure.

Next, you have to go through a series of steps to make a software update point the active one for the Configuration Manager hierarchy. We will detail those steps later on in the chapter.

Depending on the version of your operating system, you need to either add the Windows Server Update Services role though the Server Manager of Windows Server 2008 R2 or make sure that you have downloaded the latest version of WSUS at the WSUS home page:

```
http://technet.microsoft.com/windowsserver/bb332157.aspx
```

INSTALLING WSUS ON WINDOWS SERVER 2008 R2

To add the WSUS role to Windows Server 2008 R2, perform the following steps:

1. Start the Windows Server 2008 R2 Server Manager from the Administrative Tools section of the console.

2. Click Roles and select Add Roles, and then click Next at the Before You Begin page.

3. Select Windows Server Update Services, and click Next.

4. Read the introduction to WSUS, and click Next.

5. Confirm the settings, and click Install.

    Once the download is finished, you will see the welcome screen of the WSUS 3.0 SP2 Setup Wizard.

6. Click Next.

7. Click the I Accept The Terms Of The License Agreement check box, and then click Next.

    If the Microsoft Report Viewer 2008 Redistributable is not installed, the Setup Wizard gives you a warning about it.

8. Click Next.

9. The next screen, will ask you to choose if and where you want updates to be stored on the WSUS server. Click Next.

10. The next page lets you choose your database options.

- If you are not installing WSUS on a Configuration Manager site, the default of Install Windows Internal Database On This Computer is probably your best option, because it installs Microsoft SQL Server 2005 Embedded Edition just for the purpose of managing WSUS. This will save you from having to purchase another full SQL Server license for WSUS and managing another instance of SQL as well.

- If you are installing WSUS on a Configuration Manager central administration site or a primary site server and it has the resources to handle it, then we recommend going ahead and using the instance of the SQL Server that is already installed. (If it doesn't have enough resources, you probably shouldn't be installing WSUS on this server anyway.) Having two versions of SQL installed on the same server could cause problems in the long run, and they would be competing for the same resources.

Depending on what you choose, WSUS will either create the Windows Internal Database or test the connection to the existing SQL Server instance.

11. After that is done, click Next.

12. On the next page of the wizard, shown in Figure 8.6, choose how to configure the WSUS website.

Microsoft recommends that you choose to make a custom website if you are using WSUS as a software update point, even if the WSUS server is remote from the Configuration Manager site system. You should definitely use the custom site option if you are installing WSUS on a Configuration Manager site so that the install will not interfere with the other Configuration Manager components that use IIS. By default, the custom WSUS website uses HTTP port 8530 and HTTPS 8531.

13. Click Next.

FIGURE 8.6
The Web Site Selection page of the wizard

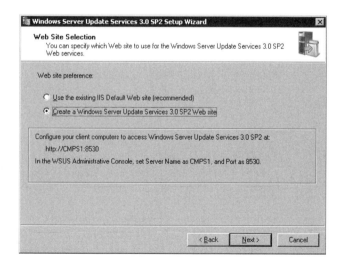

13. Review the settings, and click Next to install WSUS 3.0 SP2.

14. Click Finish and then Close after the installation.

15. The WSUS configuration wizard will start up after that, but you should close it, because Configuration Manager 2012 will take care of configuring all of the settings for WSUS.

NEVER CONFIGURE WSUS USING THE WSUS CONSOLE

When you use WSUS in combination with the software update point role, you should never use the WSUS console to configure WSUS. Always use the Configuration Manager 2012 console to configure the software update point.

INSTALLING THE DOWNLOADED WSUS VERSION

To install the downloaded version of WSUS, perform the following steps:

1. Double-click the WSUS install file that you downloaded, `WSUSSetup_30SP2_x86.exe` (or `WSUSSetup_30SP2_x64.exe` for the 64-bit version of Windows Server 2003), and you will see the opening page of the Windows Server Update Server 3.0 Setup Wizard.

2. Click Next, and then select Full Server Installation Including Administration Console and click Next again.

3. Click the I Accept The Terms Of The License Agreement check box, and then click Next.

   The next screen will ask you to choose if you want updates to be stored on the WSUS server and where you want to store them. You must accept the default and store a copy of these updates locally.

4. Choose where you want to keep these files, and then click Next.

   The next page lets you choose your database options.

   ◆ If you are not installing WSUS on a Configuration Manager site, the default of Install Windows Internal Database On This Computer is probably your best option, because it installs Microsoft SQL Server 2005 Embedded Edition just for the purpose of managing WSUS. This will save you from having to purchase another full SQL Server license for WSUS and managing another instance of SQL as well.

   ◆ If you are installing WSUS on a Configuration Manager primary site server and it has the resources to handle it, then we recommend going ahead and using the instance of the SQL Server that is already installed. (If it doesn't have the resources, you probably shouldn't be installing WSUS on this server anyway.) Having two versions of SQL installed on the same server could cause problems in the long run, and they would be competing for the same resources.

   Depending on what you choose, WSUS will either create the Windows Internal Database or test the connection to the existing SQL Server instance.

5. Once that is done, click Next.

6. The next page of the wizard, shown in Figure 8.6, lets you choose how to configure the WSUS website.

   Microsoft recommends that you choose to make a custom website if you are using WSUS as a software update point, even if the WSUS server is remote from the Configuration Manager site system. You should definitely use the custom site option if you are installing WSUS on a Configuration Manager site, so that the install will not interfere with the other Configuration Manager components that use IIS. By default, the custom WSUS website uses HTTP port 8530 and HTTPS 8531. Click Next.

7. Review the settings and click Next. When the wizard is done, click Finish. The WSUS configuration wizard will start up after that, but you should close it, because Configuration Manager will take care of configuring all of the settings for WSUS.

Installing the Windows Server Update Services 3.0 SP2 Administrative Console

The Windows Server Update Services (WSUS) 3.0 SP2 Administrative Console is required on the Configuration Manager 2012 site server, if WSUS is installed on a remote server, to allow it to communicate with WSUS so it can configure and synchronize software update points. The WSUS Administrative Console can be installed using the WSUS 3.0 Setup Wizard or installed silently from a command line.

To install the WSUS on a Configuration Manager site server, follow one of the procedures discussed in the sections that follow.

INSTALLING THE WSUS ADMINISTRATIVE CONSOLE USING THE SETUP WIZARD

Take the following steps to install the administrative console using the wizard:

1. Double-click the WSUSSetup_30SP2_x86.exe setup file that you downloaded earlier.

2. Click Next to get past the first page of the wizard, and then select Administrator Console Only. Click Next again.

3. Click I Accept The Terms Of The License Agreement, and click Next.

4. If you see the Required Components To Use Administration UI page, click Next.

   The Microsoft Report Viewer 2005 redistributable will have to be installed, because it is required to open the WSUS console. It isn't needed when you are using WSUS with Configuration Manager, however.

5. When the wizard is done, click Finish.

6. To verify that the install completed, click Start ➢ All Programs ➢ Administrative Tools, and then choose Windows Server Update Services. To verify that connectivity, connect to the WSUS server that you are going to use with Configuration Manager.

INSTALLING THE WSUS 3.0 ADMINISTRATIVE CONSOLE FROM THE COMMAND PROMPT

Take the following steps to install the administrative console using the command line:

1. In the folder where you have already downloaded the WSUS installer file, open a command prompt.

2. In the command prompt window, type the following command:

   ```
   WSUS3Setupx86.exe /q CONSOLE_INSTALL=1
   ```

   The WSUS 3.0 SP2 administrative console will then install silently.

3. Verify the install as in step 6 of the previous procedure.

Setting Up the Active Software Update Point

There can be several Configuration Manager site systems with the software update point system role, but there can be only one site system sever configured as the *active* software update point (the one configured to get updates from Microsoft Update) in a Configuration Manager site. When your Configuration Manager site is in HTTPS mode, you can have an active Internet-based software update point assigned to a remote site system server that allows communication from only Internet-based client computers. Also, if the active software update point is on a Network Load Balancing cluster, there should be a software update point installed on every server that is in the NLB cluster. When you have a Central Administration Site in your Configuration Manager 2012 hierarchy, you first need to install and configure a software update point at one of the site servers in your Central Administration Site.

SETTING UP THE SOFTWARE UPDATE POINT IN THE CENTRAL ADMINISTRATION SITE

To set up an active software update point in the Central Administration Site, you need to follow these steps.

1. In the Configuration Manager console, choose the Administration Workspace ➢ Overview ➢ Site Configuration ➢ Server And Site System Roles.

2. Decide whether to create a new site system server or add the software update point role to an existing site system. Depending on which you choose, take the next step:

   ◆ To create a new site system with a software update point, click Create Site System Server on the Home tab of the Ribbon.

   ◆ To add the software update point role to an existing server, do the following:

      a. Select the site server on which you want to install the software update point role.

      b. Choose Add Site System Role in the Home tab of the Ribbon.

3. Configure the server that is to be used for a site server, and click Next.

   See Figure 8.7 to see the options for this choice.

FIGURE 8.7
Configure the
active software
update point
settings

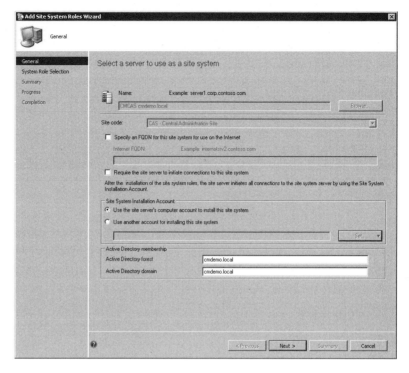

Specify An FQDN For This Site System For Use On The Internet   You will have to configure this setting for an active software update point when the site server is in secure mode or when it is in mixed mode and using Secure Sockets Layer (SSL). By default, you must configure this setting.

Specify An FQDN For This Site System For Use On The Internet   You must configure this setting if you are setting up an active software update point that accepts Internet-based client connections or for the active Internet-based software update point.

Require The Site Server To Initiate Connections To This Site System   This setting must be used when the remote software update point doesn't have access to the inboxes on the site server. This will let a site system from a different domain or forest place files that need to be transferred to the site server. The site server will connect to the remote site system and get the files periodically. The Internet-based software update point might need this setting to be enabled to work.

Site System Installation Account   This setting is configured when the computer account for the site server doesn't have access to the remote site system being set up as a software update point.

Active Directory Membership   Configure the site system membership by supplying the Forest and Domain FQDN.

4. Select Software Update Point and click Next.

5. If you need to go through a proxy server to go to the Internet, you will need to configure the proxy server and the possible credentials. If you have Internet access without a proxy server, just click Next.

6. In the Active Settings page (see Figure 8.8), choose whether the software update point you are setting up will be the active software update point for your site, and specify the port settings that are used by the WSUS you are connecting to. Click Next.

   By default, the port settings for a WSUS custom website (the recommended settings) are HTTP port 8530 and HTTPS port 8531. If you installed WSUS on the default website, the ports are HTTP port 80 and HTTPS port 443.

FIGURE 8.8
Configure the active software update point port settings

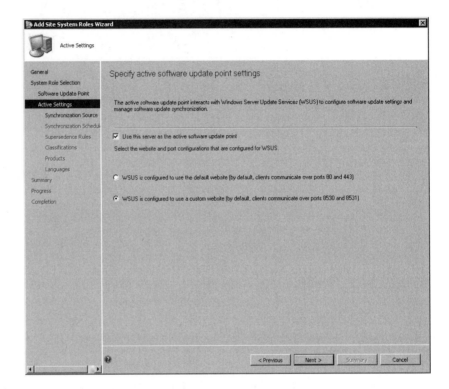

7. Choose the synchronization source for the active software update point by selecting one of the following options and click on Next:

   Synchronize From Microsoft Update   The software update point that is highest in the Configuration Manager hierarchy (usually the Central Administration Site) must use this setting.

   Synchronize From An Upstream Update Server   This option is grayed out and not available when installing a software update server on a site server in the Center Administration Site or stand-alone primary site.

   Do Not Synchronize From Microsoft Update Or The Upstream Update Server   Use this setting when the active software update point can't connect to the upstream update server. This will usually be used by an active Internet-based software update point that doesn't have access to the active software update point. The active software update point on the CAS can't use this setting. Synchronizing a software update point through importing and exporting updates is covered later in the chapter.

8. Configure the synchronization behavior of the software update role by selecting Enable Synchronization on a schedule.

This is disabled by default, and you can start a manual sync by running the Run Synchronization action in the Configuration Manager console. We recommend that you enable a schedule, because scheduled syncs perform full synchronizations, and manual syncs only do delta synchronizations of software updates.

9. Click Next after configuring the synchronization schedule.

10. Configure the supersedence behavior for updates that are about to expire, as shown in Figure 8.9. Choose one of the following:

   ◆ Immediately Expire A Superseded Update

   ◆ Do Not Expire A Superseded Software Update Until The Software Update Is Superseded For A Specified Period

FIGURE 8.9
Configure behavior for software updates that are superseded

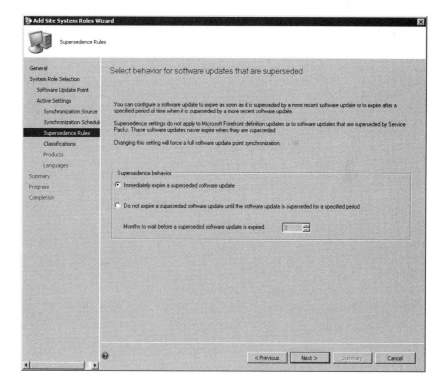

11. Click Next.

12. Choose the update classifications that you want to deploy with software updates, and then click Next. You are able to change the classifications in a later stage.

13. Choose the products that you want to synchronize with software updates; you are able to change the products in a later stage. The number of products will change after the first synchronization with Microsoft Update has finished.

14. Select all the languages that you will be supporting with software updates, and then click Next.

15. Click Next again after reviewing the summary, and click Close after the installation is finished.

SETTING UP THE SOFTWARE UPDATE POINT IN A PRIMARY SITE THAT IS A CHILD OF A CAS

To set up an active software update point in a primary site that is a child of a Central Administration Site, follow these steps.

1. In the Configuration Manager console, choose the Administration Workspace ➢ Overview ➢ Site Configuration ➢ Server And Site System Roles.

2. Decide whether to create a new site system server or add the software update point role to an existing site system. Depending on which you choose, take the next step:

   ◆ To create a new site system with software update point, click Create Site System Server on the Home tab of the Ribbon.

   ◆ To add the software update point role to an existing server, do the following:

      a. Select the site server on which you want to install the software update point role.

      b. Click Add Site System Role on the Home tab of the Ribbon.

   What you do next will depend on your site settings. By default, the computer account for the site server will connect to the site system computer (if you're installing on a separate site) and install the necessary components. If the computer account of the site server has access to the site system server and the Configuration Manager site is in HTTPS mode, the settings shown previously in Figure 8.7 are optional.

3. When the computer account does not have access to the site system server or when the site is in secure mode, you will have to configure the following settings on the New Site Role page:

   a. Specify A Fully Qualified Domain Name (FQDN) For This Site System On The Intranet.

      By default, you will have to configure this setting for an active software update point when the site server is in secure mode or when it is in mixed mode and using Secure Sockets Layer (SSL).

   b. Specify An Internet-Based FQDN For This Site System.

      You must configure this setting if you are setting up an active software update point that accepts Internet-based client connections or for the active Internet-based software update point.

   c. Require The Site Server To Initiate Connections To This Site System.

      This setting must be used when the remote software update point doesn't have access to the inboxes on the site server. This will let a site system from a different domain or forest add files that need to be transferred to the site server. The site server will connect to the remote site system and get the files every so often. The Internet-based software update point might need this setting to be enabled to work.

   d. Site System Installation Account.

   This setting is configured when the computer account for the site server doesn't have access to the remote site system being set up as a software update point.

   e. Active Directory Membership.

   Configure the site system membership by supplying the Forest and Domain FQDN.

4. After you have configured what you need, click Next.

5. Select Software Update Point from the list of available site roles, and then click Next.

6. If you are going to be using a proxy server to connect to the software update point, enter those settings and click Next. Otherwise, just click Next.

7. In the Active Settings page (see Figure 8.8), choose whether the software update point you are setting up will be the active software update point for your site, and specify the port settings that are used by the WSUS you are connecting to. Click Next after configuring the server as the active software update point.

   By default, the port settings for a WSUS custom website (the recommended settings) are HTTP port 8530 and HTTPS port 8531. If you installed WSUS on the default website, the ports are HTTP port 80 and HTTPS port 443. Since the software update point is installed in a primary site that is a child of a Central Administration Site, the synchronization option is automatically set to Synchronize From An Upstream Update Server, as shown in Figure 8.10.

FIGURE 8.10
The Synchronization Source page of the Create Roles Wizard

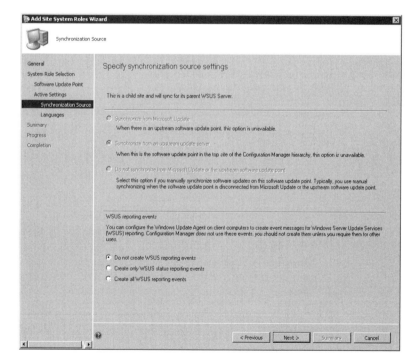

8. On that same page, accept the default of Do Not Create WSUS Reporting Events, and then click Next.

9. Select all the languages that you will be supporting with software updates, and click Next.

10. Review the summary, and click Next to start the installation of the software update point.

11. Click Close when the installation has finished.

SETTING UP THE SOFTWARE UPDATE POINT IN A STAND-ALONE PRIMARY SITE

1. In the Configuration Manager console, choose the Administration Workspace ➢ Overview ➢ Site Configuration ➢ Server And Site System Roles.

2. Decide whether to create a new site system server or add the software update point role to an existing site system. Depending on which you choose, take the next step:

    ◆ To create a new site system with a software update point, click Create Site System Server on the Home tab of the Ribbon.

    ◆ To add the software update point role to an existing server, do the following:

        a. Select the site server on which you want to install the software update point role.

        b. Click Add Site System Role on the Home tab of the Ribbon.

   What you do next will depend on your site settings. By default, the computer account for the site server will connect to the site system computer (if you're installing on a separate site) and install the necessary components. If the computer account of the site server has access to the site system server and the Configuration Manager site is in HTTPS mode, the settings shown in Figure 8.7 are optional.

3. When the computer account does not have access to the site system server or when the site is in secure mode, you will have to configure the following settings on the New Site Role page:

    a. Specify An FQDN For This Site System On The Intranet.

       By default, you will have to configure this setting for an active software update point when the site server is in secure mode or when it is in mixed mode and using SSL.

    b. Specify An Internet-Based FQDN For This Site System.

       You must configure this setting if you are setting up an active software update point that accepts Internet-based client connections or for the active Internet-based software update point.

    c. Require The Site Server To Initiate Connections To This Site System.

       This setting must be used when the remote software update point doesn't have access to the inboxes on the site server. This will let a site system from a different domain or forest add files that need to be transferred to the site server. The site server will connect to the remote site system and get the files every so often. The Internet-based software update point might need this setting to be enabled to work.

    d. Site System Installation Account.

       This setting is configured when the computer account for the site server doesn't have access to the remote site system being set up as a software update point.

    e. Active Directory Membership.

       Configure the site system membership by supplying the Forest and Domain FQDN.

4. When you have configured what you need, click Next.

5. Select Software Update Point from the list of available site roles, and then click Next.

6. If you are going to be using a proxy server to connect to the software update point, enter those settings and click Next. Otherwise, just click Next.

7. In the Active Settings page (see Figure 8.8), choose whether the software update point you are setting up will be the active software update point for your site, and specify the port settings that are used by the WSUS you are connecting to. Click Next after configuring the server as the active software update point.

   By default, the port settings for a WSUS custom website (the recommended settings) are HTTP port 8530 and HTTPS port 8531. If you installed WSUS on the default website, the ports are HTTP port 80 and HTTPS port 443.

FINDING THE PORTS USED BY WINDOWS SERVER UPDATE SERVICES

If someone else installed the WSUS server that is being used for a software update point, you may not know what ports were used during setup. If you input the wrong ports on this page of the wizard, the setup will fail. You can find the ports used by WSUS by following these steps:

1. Under Administrative Tools, click Internet Information Services (IIS) Manager.

2. Expand Web Sites, right-click the website that is being used for WSUS, and click Properties. A custom WSUS site is recommended, but the default website might have been used instead.

3. Look at the Browse Web Site list in the Actions section of the Management console.

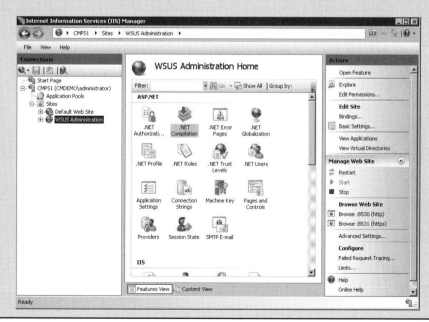

8. Choose the synchronization source for the active software update point by selecting one of these options:

   Synchronize From Microsoft Update   The software update point that is highest in the Configuration Manager hierarchy (usually the Central Administration Site) must use this setting.

   Synchronize From An Upstream Update Server   The active software update point on all child secondary sites and on all Internet-based software update points should use this setting. The wizard will select this option as the default if the software update point meets the criteria (as shown in Figure 8.10). For the primary site this option is disabled.

   Do Not Synchronize From Microsoft Update Or The Upstream Software Update Point   Use this setting when the active software update point can't connect to the upstream update server. This will usually be used by an active Internet-based software update point that doesn't have access to the active software update point. The active software update point on the CAS can't use this setting. Synchronizing a software update point through importing and exporting updates is covered later in the chapter.

9. On that same page, accept the default of Do Not Create WSUS Reporting Events, and then click Next.

10. Choose whether to synchronize software updates on a schedule, by selecting Enable Synchronization On A Schedule.

    This is disabled by default, you can start a manual sync by running the Run Synchronization action in the Configuration Manager console. We recommend that you enable a schedule, because scheduled syncs perform full synchronizations and manual syncs only do delta synchronizations of software updates.

11. Once you have made your choice, click Next.

12. Configure the supersedence behavior for updates that are about to expire, as shown previously in Figure 8.9. Choose one of the following:

    ◆ Immediately Expire A Superseded Update

    ◆ Do Not Expire A Superseded Software Update Until The Software Update Is Superseded For A Specified Period

13. Click Next.

14. Choose the update classifications that you want to deploy with software updates, and then click Next. You are able to change the update classifications in a later stage.

15. Choose the products that you want to synchronize, and then click Next. You are able to change the products in a later stage. The number of products will change after the first synchronization with Microsoft Update has finished.

16. Select all the languages that you will be supporting with software updates, and then click Next. You are able to change the supporting languages in a later stage.

17. Click Next again on the following page, and click Close.

Checking the Installation of the Software Update Point

After the installation of the software update point(s) it is a good idea to check some log files to be sure that the software update point(s) are installed correctly.

1. To monitor the install of the software update point, open the SUPSetup.log in the `<Configuration Manager Install Path>`\Logs folder.

   When the install has finished, you will see the text "Installation Was Successful."

2. Open the WCM.log in the same directory to verify that the connection to the WSUS server worked.

   When the connection to the WSUS server is made and the WSUS components are checked, you will see

   `There are no unhealthy WSUS Server components on WSUS Server servername`

   and

   `Successfully checked database connection on WSUS server servername`

   in the log file.

In this procedure, the only difference between making an active software update point and a non-active software update point is not checking the Use This Server As The Active Software Update Server setting in the previous procedure. If you don't select that option, the wizard will end. Otherwise, everything else is the same as described, depending on what kind of software update point you are trying to set up.

Configuring Software Updates Settings and Synchronization

Software Updates in Configuration Manager 2012 must be synchronized with Microsoft Update before information on those updates will be available to view in the Configuration Manager console. Synchronization starts at the highest level in the hierarchy that has an active software update point and either has a configured schedule or is started manually using the Run Synchronization action.

When synchronization is started on a configured schedule, all changes to the Software Updates metadata since the last scheduled sync are inserted into the site database. This will include metadata for new software updates or metadata that has been modified or deleted. When a sync is started manually, only new Software Updates metadata since the last sync is inserted into the database. The manual sync process is faster since it is not pulling as much Software Updates metadata. A manual sync action is only available on parent sites.

To manually sync the software update point, do the following:

1. In the Configuration Manager console, choose the Software Library workspace ➢ Overview ➢ Software Updates ➢ All Software Updates.

2. Select the Home tab of the Ribbon and click Synchronize Software Updates. Click on Yes to initiate a site-wide synchronization of software updates.

The synchronization process might take longer than an hour to finish, depending on several factors, including whether a synchronization has been run before and what languages, products, and update classifications have been configured to be synchronized. You can monitor the

synchronization process by looking at the log file for WSUS Synchronization Manager, `wsyncmgr`
`.log`. This is located by default at `%Program Files%/Microsoft Configuration Manager/Logs`.

When the synchronization is complete, you will see a 6702 status message from
SMS_WSUS_SYNC_MANAGER.

New in Configuration Manager 2012 is that you also can monitor the synchronization in the
Configuration Manager console.

To monitor the synchronization in the hierarchy do the following:

1. In the Configuration Manager console, choose the Monitoring workspace ➤ Overview ➤
   Software Update Point Synchronization Status.

2. Look at the synchronization status, the link state, and the catalog versions.

When the synchronization with Microsoft Update is complete (either from a schedule or
started manually) at the highest site in the hierarchy, sync requests are sent to all child sites, and
they in turn start synchronization with their configured upstream WSUS servers as soon as the
request has finished processing.

The Software Updates metadata that is synced from Microsoft Update is based on the update
classes, products, and languages that were selected when the active software update point was first
configured. A child site will synchronize whatever updates have been configured on its parent site.

Although all of the settings for update classes, products, and so on were configured at the
setup of the software update point, you can still reconfigure these options if needed. To configure the update properties for software updates, follow these steps.

1. In the Configuration Manager console, choose the Administration workspace ➤ Overview ➤
   Site Configuration ➤ Sites, and select the site that is the highest in the hierarchy.

2. Choose Configure Site Components on the Settings section of the Home tab of the
   Ribbon, and click Software Update Point.

3. To configure Update Classifications, click the Classifications tab, as in Figure 8.11.

FIGURE 8.11
Software Update
Point Component
Properties:
Classifications tab

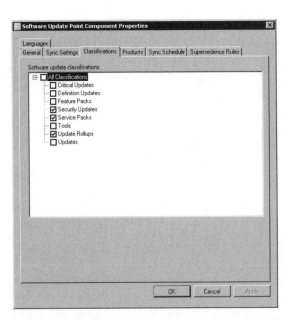

4. To configure products that are being synced, click the Products tab, shown in Figure 8.12.

FIGURE 8.12
Software Update Point
Component Properties:
Products tab

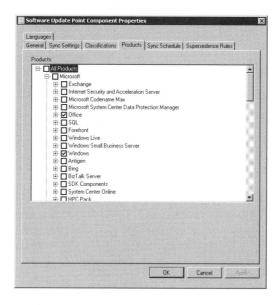

5. To configure languages that are being synced, click the Languages tab shown in Figure 8.13.

FIGURE 8.13
Software Update Point
Component Properties:
Languages tab

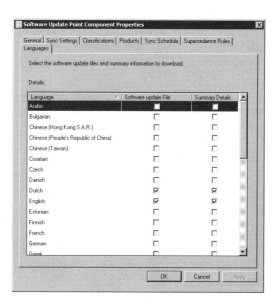

6. To reconfigure the supersedence settings, click the Supersedence Rules tab shown in Figure 8.14.

FIGURE 8.14

Software Update Point
Component Properties:
Supersedence Rules tab

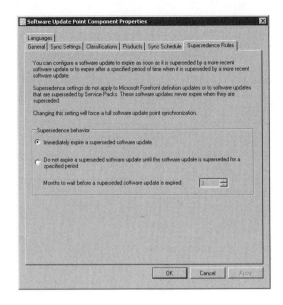

To configure the software updates synchronization schedule, follow these steps:

1. In the Configuration Manager console choose the Administration workspace ➤ Overview ➤ Site Configuration ➤ Sites, and select the site that is the highest in the hierarchy.

2. Choose Configure Site Components on the Settings section of the Home tab of the ribbon, and click Software Update Point.

3. To configure the synchronization schedule, click the Sync Schedule tab, shown in Figure 8.15.

FIGURE 8.15

Software Update Point
Component Properties:
Sync Schedule tab

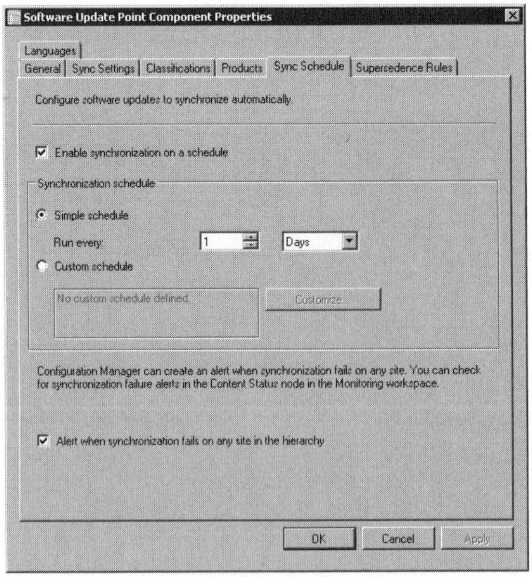

4. To enable synchronization on a schedule, select Enable Synchronization On A Schedule, and set the schedule as you want it.

5. When you have finished, click OK to save the schedule.

Unless you change the Start value in the custom schedule, synchronization will be started as soon as possible and will repeat based on the schedule that you configured.

6. If you want alerts to be reported in the Alerts node of the Configuration Manager 2012 console, enable the Generate An Alert When Synchronization Fails In Any Site In The Hierarchy option.

Synchronizing Updates with Export and Import

When a software update point is not configured or cannot synchronize with its upstream server in the Configuration Manager 2012 hierarchy, the export and import functions of the WSUSUtil tool can be used to synchronize Software Updates metadata manually. The user who performs the export/import must be a member of the local Administrators group on the WSUS server, and the tool must be run locally on the WSUS server itself.

The files found in the `WSUSContent` folder (by default located in `<WSUSInstallDrive>\WSUS\WSUSContent`) must also be copied from the upstream update server to the software update point so that locally stored updates and the license terms for the updates are available to the import server. This procedure can also be used for migrating the software update content from Configuration Manager 2007 to Configuration Manager 2012.

To export and import software updates from the export WSUS server to the import WSUS server, follow these steps:

1. Copy files from the export server to the import server:

   a. On the export server, go to the folder where software updates and the license terms for those software updates are stored. By default, this will be `<WSUSInstallDrive>\WSUS\WSUSContent`.

   b. Copy all of these files to the same folder on the import server.

2. Export metadata from the database of the export server:

   a. At a command prompt on the export WSUS server, go to the folder that contains `WSUSUtil.exe`. By default, this will be located at `%ProgramFiles%\Update Service\Tools`.

   b. Then enter the following:

   `WSUSUTIL.exe export packagename logfile`

   The name of *packagename* doesn't really matter, as long as it and the log file are unique in that folder. This command will export the Software Updates metadata into a file called `packagename.cab`.

   c. Move the export package that you just made to the folder that contains `WSUSUtil.exe` on the import WSUS server.

3. Import metadata to the database of the import server:

a. At a command prompt on the WSUS server that you are importing the updates to, go to the folder that contains `WSUSUtil.exe`, which is `%Program Files%\Update Services\Tools`.

b. Enter this command:

`WSUSUTIL.exe import packagename logfile`

with `packagename` being the name of the export file that you exported in step 2.

This will import all the metadata from the exporting server and create a log file that you can use to review the status.

Preparing Software Updates for Deployment

So far in this chapter, we have planned our implementation of Software Updates and set up and configured Software Updates, and now we are finally ready to deploy software updates to Configuration Manager 2012 clients. Well, nearly ready. We still need to find the updates to be deployed (using any of several methods), download them, and optionally create a software update group and/or an automatic deployment rule. These tasks can be done in the sequence shown here or independently of each other.

Before we get into that process, there are a few things you should keep in mind after you have set up all of the Software Updates components.

Give the process a little time to work. Don't expect to set up everything we have discussed so far and think you are going to be able to do a couple of clicks and deploy updates to your clients. You are going to have a little bit of lead time as updates are synced with Microsoft Update, the metadata is synced with the rest of the Configuration Manager hierarchy, and clients get requests for scans. Depending on the size of your hierarchy and the number and kind of clients you need to be scanned, this might take a while; after all, this is a process.

If you click the Software Updates node in the Configuration Manager console and don't see any results in your compliance summary, then your clients either haven't been scanned or they haven't sent their scan results. Until you see something in those reports, you don't have enough to work with to do any update deployments.

With that said, we can continue preparing for software update deployment.

Finding the Software Updates to Be Deployed

Before you can deploy any software updates to clients, you will need to figure out which ones you want or need to deploy to your clients. Configuration Manager provides several ways to do that, and each allows you to find clients that need the updates you want to focus on installed.

When you are looking for updates to deploy, avoid updates that show up in the Configuration Manager console with a yellow arrow icon. These are updates that have been superseded by another update that contains the same fixes. To avoid installing outdated components to your clients, do not include these updates in your deployments. They are no longer needed.

There are basically three methods to find needed software updates:

◆ Software Updates reports

◆ Software Updates search

◆ All Software Updates node

USING SOFTWARE UPDATES REPORTS TO FIND UPDATES

You can gather compliance information on your clients by running reports under the Software Updates - A Compliance category, because they are designed specifically for this purpose.

To use web reports from the Configuration Manager console to find required updates, follow these steps.

1. In the Configuration Manager console, choose the Monitoring workspace ➤ Overview ➤ Reporting, expand Reports and open the Software Updates - A Compliance folder.

   This will give you a list of all reports in the right pane of the console.

2. Find the report Compliance 4 - Updates By Vendor Month Year, select it, and click Run on the Home tab of the Ribbon.

3. To get an idea of what update data you have collected already, do the following:

   a. Click Values for the collection All Systems.

   b. Click Values for the vendor Microsoft.

   c. Click Values for the update class Security Updates.

   d. Click Values for the current year (2012).

   e. Click View Report.

   You should see a report like the one shown in Figure 8.16.

FIGURE 8.16

A sample compliance report with values entered for Collection ID, Vendor, Update Class, and Year

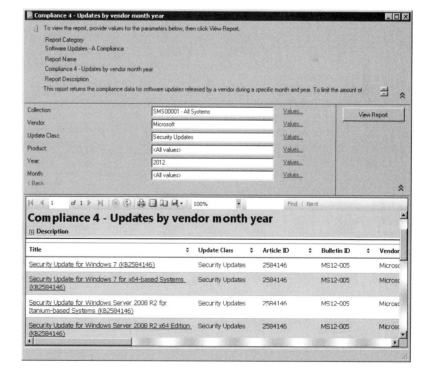

Any software updates that meet those criteria will be displayed in the report. The Required column gives the number of clients that require each software update in the list. The report also shows all of the updates that have been deployed by listing an asterisk (*) in the Approved column. To get more information about any of the updates, click the information link on the far right of the report (you may have to do some side scrolling to see it), and this will pull up the latest information from Microsoft on this update.

4. To get more details click the drill-down link in the first column of the report.

    This will open the Compliance 6 - Specific Software Update States (Secondary) report, and you will see a count of computers for each compliance state for that particular update.

USING THE SEARCH OPTION IN THE CONFIGURATION MANAGER CONSOLE

With the new Configuration Manager 2012 console you also have the ability to use a powerful search engine that comes with the console. Just under the Ribbon, you will find the search option. To use the search option to show software updates, follow these steps:

1. In the Configuration Manager console, choose Software Library ➢ Overview ➢ Software Updates ➢ All Software Updates.

2. Click Add Criteria next to the Search button.

    You will then see the Criteria list box, as shown in Figure 8.17.

FIGURE 8.17
Search criteria

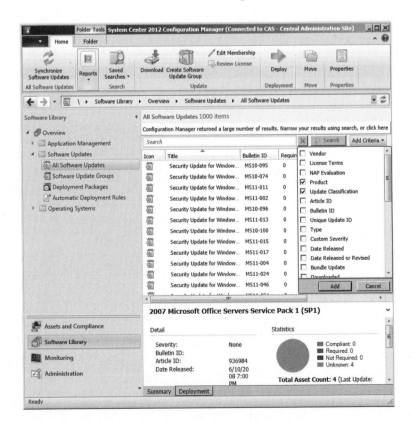

3. You want to search for all security updates for Windows Server 2008 R2. So first you scroll down and look for Update Classification (for Security Updates) and Product (for Windows Server 2008 R2).

4. Click Add to add the criteria to the search box.

5. To select the right product, click the URL next to Product and select Windows Server 2008 R2.

6. To select the right Update Classification, click the URL next to Update Classification and select Security Updates, as shown in Figure 8.18.

FIGURE 8.18
Adding search criteria to the search

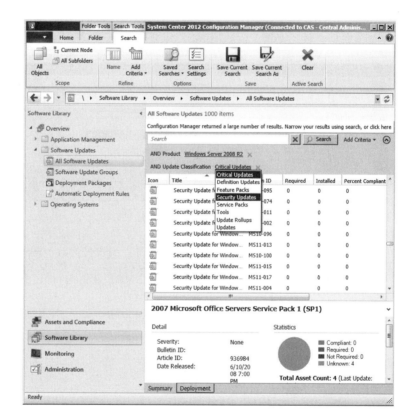

7. Click Search to activate the criteria.

8. To save the search for future use, you can click either Save Current Search or Save Current Search As in the Home tab of the Ribbon of the Configuration Manager console.

You can find all the updates that need to be deployed to Windows Server 2008 R2 computers in this search by looking at the column labeled Required. You can sort by any column by clicking that column. From here you can download these updates, add them to an update group, or deploy them to client computers.

To manage and access saved searches, do the following:

1. In the Configuration Manager console, choose Software Library ➤ Overview ➤ Software Updates ➤ All Software Updates.

2. Choose Saved Searches in the Search or Home tab of the Ribbon of the Configuration Manager console, and click Manager Searches for Current Node.

3. Select the search you need, as shown in Figure 8.19, and click OK to make the search active. You are also able to rename or delete a saved search.

FIGURE 8.19
Selecting the
search you need

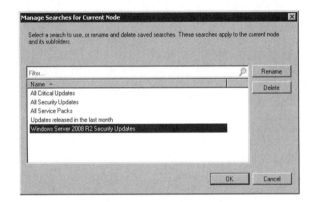

Using the All Software Updates Node

When you browse in the Configuration Manager console to the All Software Updates node, you are also able to select the software updates you want without using the Search option.

To select the updates you want, do the following:

1. In the Configuration Manager console, choose Software Library ➤ Overview ➤ Software Updates ➤ All Software Updates.

2. Browse to the update you want to deploy, or use the search option without the criteria to filter the updates.

Downloading Software Updates

As you saw in the last section, there are several ways to search for software updates that you want to download in Configuration Manager. The Download Updates Wizard allows you to download selected software updates to a deployment package prior to deploying updates to clients.

Software updates are downloaded from the Internet or from a shared folder on the network that the site server has access to and that can be added to new or existing deployment packages.

To download software updates to a deployment package, follow these steps:

1. In the Configuration Manager console, choose Software Library ➤ Overview ➤ Software Updates ➤ All Software Updates.

2. Choose Saved Searches in the Search section of the Home Ribbon of the Configuration Manager console and click Manage Searches for Current Node.

3. Select the created Windows Server 2008 R2 Security Updates Search, and click OK.

4. Sort the updates in the list so that the updates required by the most clients are at the top by clicking the Required column twice.

5. Hold down the Shift key and select all the updates that have at least one client requiring that update.

6. Choose the Home tab of the Ribbon, and click Download.

   This will start up the Download Software Updates Wizard, shown in Figure 8.20.

FIGURE 8.20
The Deployment Package page of the Download Software Updates Wizard

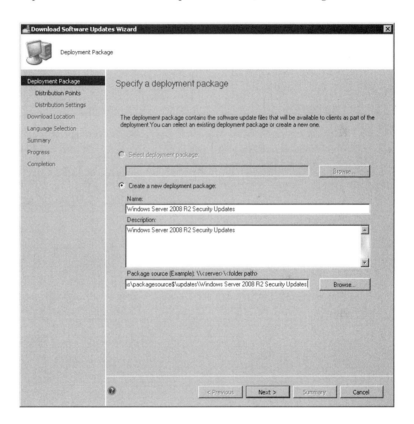

If you already have deployment packages created (as described later in the chapter), you can add these updates to one of them in the first field, by selecting Select Deployment Package. Then click Browse to open a dialog box that will allow you to select a package that is only for hosting software updates, and select one from the list. Otherwise this option will be grayed out, as in our example.

7. The other option on this first page of the wizard is Create A New Deployment Package. There are three fields to fill out:

   Name   The name of the deployment package. You should pick a unique name that describes the content and limit it to 50 characters or less.

Description   The description of the package contents up to 512 characters.

Package Source   The location of the software update source files. You should manually create this share before going any further. When the deployment is created, the source files are compressed and copied to the distribution points that are associated with the deployment package. This location must be entered as a network path (such as *server**sharename*\ *path*), or you can click the Browse button to find the location on the network. This location should not be used by any other deployment or software distribution package.

8. After choosing the deployment package or supplying information for a new deployment package, click Next.

   The next step is the Distribution Points page. The Browse button allows you to select from the available distribution points or distribution point groups on your site that you want to use for this software update package. You can leave this blank for now, and the software update files will be downloaded to the source folder. However, the updates will not be available to deploy to clients until you add at least one distribution point.

9. After adding the distribution point(s), click Next.

10. After configuring on which distribution point the software update package is stored, click Next to proceed with the Download Software Updates Wizard.

    Next is the Distribution Settings page, shown in Figure 8.21. Its options are as follows:

FIGURE 8.21
The Distribution Settings page of the Download Software Updates Wizard

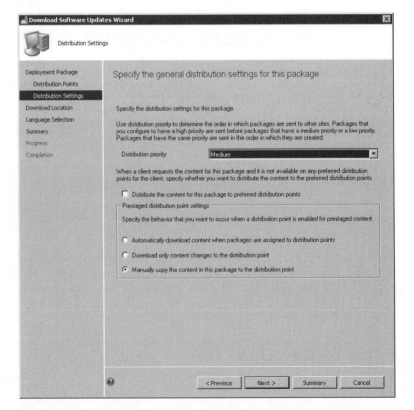

Distribution Priority The distribution priority is used for the deployment package when it is sent to distribution points at child sites. Packages are sent in priority order of High, Medium, or Low. Packages with the same priority are sent in the order in which they are created. Unless there is a backlog, packages should process immediately no matter their priority. Medium is the default priority.

Distribute The Content For This Package To Preferred Distribution Point When a client requests the content for this package and it is not available on any preferred distribution points for the client, specify if you want to distribute the content to the preferred distribution points.

When you enabled content prestaging on your distribution points, because the scheduling synchronization and throttling of your bandwidth do not work for you, you also need to look at the following settings:

Automatically Download Content When Packages Are Assigned To Distribution Points Use this option when smaller software update packages are used and scheduling and throttling settings provide enough control for the distribution of the content.

Download Only Content Changes To The Distribution Point This option should be used when you have an initial package that is possibly large but you want to add future software updates to the content of this package.

Manually Copy The Content In This Package To The Distribution Point Use this option when you have large packages and you don't want to use the network for distribution of the content to the distribution point. You need to prestage the content on the distribution point.

11. Click Next when you've finished configuring the distribution settings.

    Next is the Download Location page, with the following options:

    The Internet This will download the updates from the location on the Internet that is defined in the software update definition. This is the default setting.

    A Network Location The software updates are downloaded from a local directory or shared folder that you set in the box. Use this setting when the site server doesn't have Internet access. The software updates can be downloaded from any computer that does have Internet access and stored in a location on the local network that the site server has access to.

    After configuring the download location, click on Next. The Language Selection page shows the languages in which the software update files will be downloaded. By default, the languages that are configured for the software update point are selected. Adding a selection here does not add it to the software update point settings.

12. Click Next.

13. Review the settings and click Next; the updates will be downloaded.

When the wizard is done, the software updates will show up under Software Updates ➤ Deployment Packages ➤ *<deployment package name>* in the Software Library workspace of the Configuration Manager console.

Creating a Software Update Group

As stated earlier in the chapter, a software update group in Configuration Manager contains a set of software updates. A software update group offers several benefits when deploying and monitoring software updates and is part of Microsoft's recommended Software Updates workflow.

Tracking the compliance state for the software updates in deployments is an important task for Configuration Manager admins. When update groups are used, you can use the Compliance 1 - Overall Compliance report for the set of updates in the update group or the Compliance 3 - Update Group (Per Update) report to get a list of the updates in an update group and the overall compliance of each. This is a great reason to use the update groups as a part of your software update procedure.

To create a software update group, follow these steps:

1. In the Configuration Manager console, choose Software Library ➤ Overview ➤ Software Updates ➤ All Software Updates.

2. Choose Saved Searches in the Search area of the Ribbon of the Configuration Manager console, and click More or use the Recent Searches option.

3. Select the created Windows Server 2008 R2 Security Updates Search and click OK.

4. Sort the updates in the list so that the updates required by the most clients are at the top by clicking the Required column twice.

5. Hold down the Shift key and select all the updates that have at least one client requiring that update.

6. Click Create Software Update Group, and fill in the name and description of the software update group.

7. Click Create, and the software update group will be created.

Your new software update group will appear in the Software Update Group node under Software Updates in the Configuration Manager console.

Deploying Software Updates with the Deploy Software Updates Wizard

Now that all the setup and preparation tasks have been done, you are ready to run the deployment. Before deploying software updates, make sure you've considered things like whether the maintenance windows and client restart settings will work for the different clients in your environment, how you are going to handle servers differently than workstations, and which deployments will be delegated.

To ensure the most successful software update deployments, utilize software update groups that fit the needs of your organization, and keep software updates organized so they are easier to keep track of and deploy.

The Deploy Software Updates Wizard in Configuration Manager allows you to create or modify software update deployments. You can select software updates that you want to deploy from several locations, as discussed earlier in this chapter, and you can start the deployment wizard in different ways as well.

To deploy software updates using the Deploy Software Updates Wizard, use the following steps:

1. In the Configuration Manager console, choose Software Library ➤ Overview ➤ Software Updates ➤ Software Update Groups.

2. Decide what updates you want to deploy.

You can use any of the methods that were described in the "Finding the Software Updates to Be Deployed" section earlier in the chapter, or you can just select several updates from any of the Update Repository sections by Ctrl-clicking the updates that you want.

3. Start the Deploy Software Updates Wizard using either of the following methods:

- ◆ Right-click some selected updates or a software update group, and then click Deploy Software Updates.

- ◆ Click Deploy on the Home tab of the Ribbon of the Configuration Manager console after selecting some updates or a software update group.

For this example, some updates that were not already downloaded were selected before clicking on Deploy.

The first page of the Deploy Software Updates Wizard is shown in Figure 8.22.

FIGURE 8.22
The General page

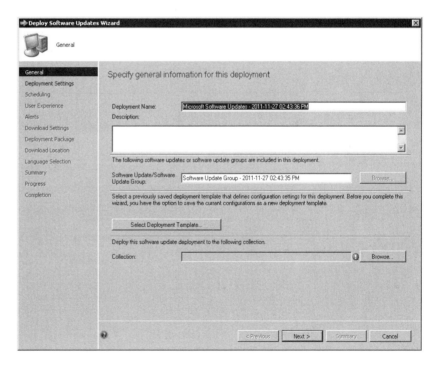

4. Configure the following options.

Select Deployment Template If you have already saved a deployment template, you can select a saved deployment template. This template holds the most common settings.

Deployment Name Give the deployment a name.

Update/Update group This option is active only when you select one or more updates instead of an update group.

Collection Select the collection for which the deployment must deploy software updates to.

5. Click Next.

The next step in creating a deployment for deploying software updates is to configure the deployment settings. The configurable settings are as follows:

Type of Deployment Choose whether the deployment is available or required for installation. If the deployment is required, the installation of the software updates will start automatically, depending on the maintenance windows. If a deployment is available, the user is able to install the software updates. For software update deployments it is common practice to configure the deployment as required.

Use Wake-on-LAN to Wake up Clients for Required Deployments Disabled by default, this option specifies whether at deadline Wake On LAN will be used to send wake-up packets to computers that require updates in the deployment. Be sure to configure the support of Wake On LAN in the Configuration Manager environment, your devices, and your network. See Chapter 4 for more information about configuring the support for sending wake-up packets.

State Message Detail Level The detail level configures the state-message details that are returned by the clients for deployments. There are two levels that you can configure, Normal and Minimal. The Normal option returns all state messages related to the deployment; this option is the best to use while deploying software updates. The Minimum option returns only enforcement success and critical errors.

6. Configure the settings and click Next.

The Scheduling page is next and is shown in Figure 8.23. This page has three sections:

FIGURE 8.23
The Scheduling page

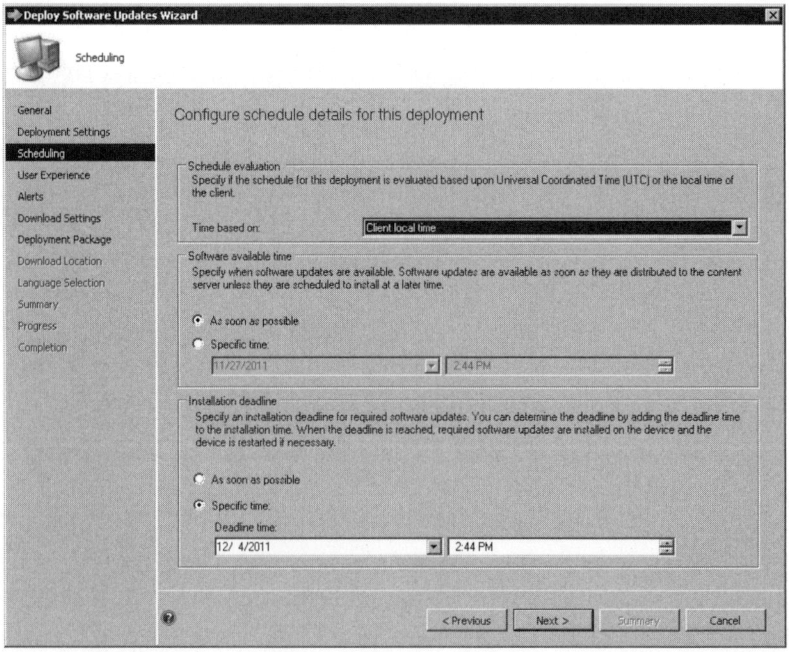

Schedule Evaluation   Select what the scheduled time must be based on: Client Local Time (the default) or UTC.

Software Available Time   Select the date and time when software updates will be made available to clients: As Soon As Possible (the default) or Specific Date, which allows you to set a specific date and time when clients will be able to see the deployment.

Installation Deadline   Specify whether the software updates should automatically install on clients at a configured deployment deadline:

◆ As Soon As Possible

◆ Specific Date: Enabled by default, this allows you to set a date and time as a deadline for this deployment to be installed on clients.

7. Once you have made your choices on this page, click Next.

The software updates will be available as soon as they have been distributed to the distribution points.

The next step that you need to take is to configure the user experience; the options shown in Figure 8.24 can be configured.

FIGURE 8.24
The User
Experience page

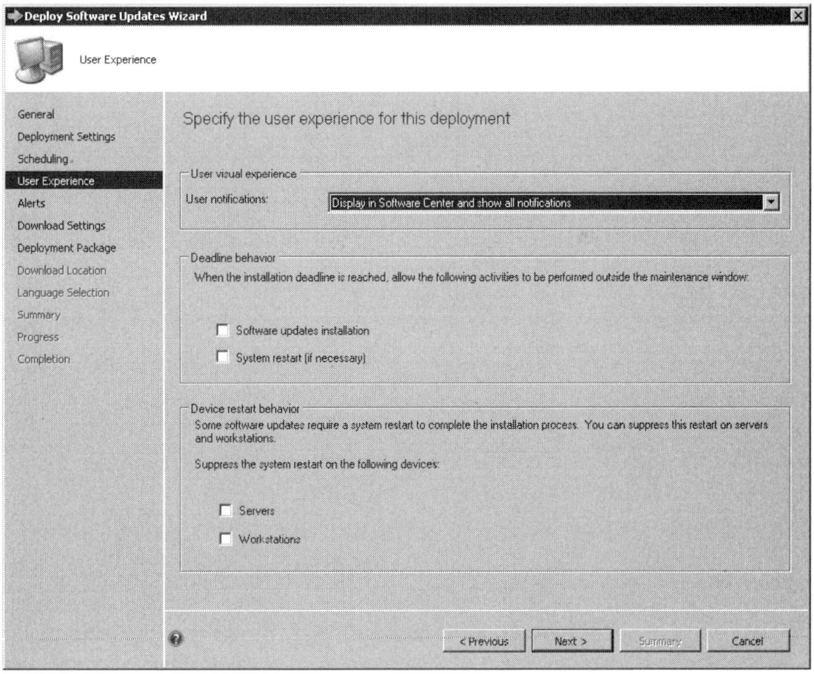

User visual experience   You can set several options to configure the user experience when the software updates are deployed. You can hide software update installations and notifications from your users by selecting "Hide in Software Center and all notifications" or choose "Display in Software Center and show all notifications" or "Display in

Software Center, and only show notifications for computer restarts" if you wany notifications shown to your users.

Deadline behavior   When an installation deadline is reached, the installation can be performed outside the maintenance window, if you want. You can configure the actions by allowing an update installation and a system restart (if necessary) outside the maintenance window.

Device Restart Behavior   Installing software updates on workstations or servers can initiate a system restart. With this setting you can suppress a system restart on workstations and servers.

8. Click Next when you have finished configuring the user experience.

   With the new alerting feature in Configuration Manager 2012, you are able to retrieve alerts in the Configuration Manager console and take actions when required.

9. Configure the options shown in Figure 8.25 for your organizational needs, and click Next.

FIGURE 8.25
The Alerts page

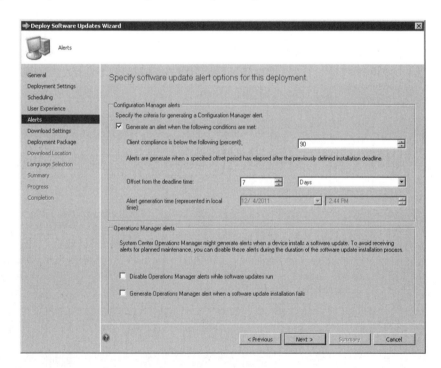

Configuration Manager Alert   This option is disabled by default, but it is recommended that you enable this option to get more control over the compliance level of your Configuration Manager clients. When you receive an alert that your compliancy level is below a selected percentage, you can proactively take action to get the compliance at the right level.

Operations Manager Alert   Besides handling the alerting in the Configuration Manager console, you can retrieve your alerts by using Operations Manager. In this page you can disable the alerts for the duration of the software update installation.

10. Specify the download settings for your deployment. The page is divided into three sections.

    Download Settings For Slow Or Unreliable Network Define what to do if the Configuration Manager client is connected via a slow or unreliable network boundary. You can choose not to install the software updates or to download them from the distribution point and install them after downloading.

    Download Settings For Unprotected Distribution Points Define what to do if the Configuration Manager client is connected via a network boundary with an unprotected distribution point. You can choose not to install the software updates or to download them from the unprotected distribution point and install them after downloading.

    Allow Clients To Share Content With Other Clients On The Same Subnet Select this option if you want to reduce the load on the WAN by allowing clients to download the Software Update content from other clients in the same subnet that already have downloaded and cached the content. This option uses Windows BranchCache.

11. Click Next after configuring the download settings for the deployment.

    The next step is to select an existing deployment package to add the software update to or create a new software update package.

12. Click the first Browse button on the Deployment Package page and select one of the existing packages, or create a new deployment package. Then configure the settings that you need for creating a new deployment package.

    Name Supply the name of the deployment package; be sure it is descriptive so you can identify the deployment package when you want to add other software updates to it.

    Description Supply the description of the deployment; be sure it is descriptive so you can identify the deployment package when you want to add other software updates to it.

    Package Source The package source is a UNC path to a location where the source of the deployment package will be stored. The UNC path must be available for the Configuration Manager site servers.

    Sending Priority The sending priority is used for the deployment package when it is sent to distribution points at child sites. Packages are sent in priority order from High, Medium, or Low. Packages with the same priority are sent in the order in which they were created. Unless there is a backlog, packages should process immediately no matter their priority. Medium is the default priority.

13. After configuring the deployment package, click Next, add the distribution point from which the deployment package must be available from, and click Next again.

    Next is the Download Location page, with the following options:

    The Internet This will download the updates from the location on the Internet that is defined in the software update definition. This is the default setting.

    A Network Location The software updates are downloaded from a local directory or shared folder that you set here. Use this setting when the site server doesn't have Internet access. The software updates can be downloaded from any computer that does have Internet access and stored in a location on the local network that the site server has access to.

14. Configure where you want to retrieve the software updates from and click Next.

The Language Selection page shows the languages in which the software update files will be downloaded. By default, the languages that are configured for the software update point are selected. Adding a selection here does not add it to the software update point settings.

15. Click Next.

16. On the Summary page shown in Figure 8.26, review the options you selected.

FIGURE 8. 26
The Summary page

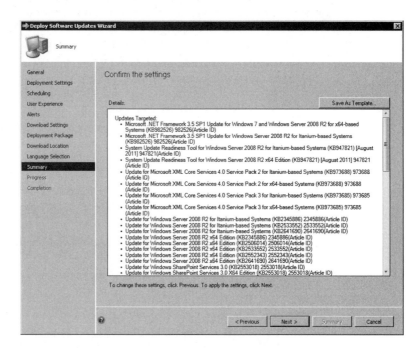

17. You can save all settings in a deployment template by clicking Save As Template.

A dialog with all the settings will appear, as shown in Figure 8.27.

FIGURE 8.27
Name the deployment template

18. Name the deployment template and click Save.

19. After you have finished reviewing the Summary, click Next, and when the progress bar is done, click Close.

Using System Center Updates Publisher

With System Center Updates Publisher you can deploy software updates from third-party manufactures. This section describes how to install and use System Center Updates Publisher.

Installing the System Center Updates Publisher

After downloading the System Center Updates Publisher software and complying with the requirements, you need to install System Center Updates Publisher. This section describes the installation process.

1. Go to the installation source of the System Center Updates Publisher and start SystemCenterUpdatesPublisher.MSI.

2. Click Next when the Setup Wizard starts.

3. If you did not install the WSUS 3.0 hotfix (KB2530678), click the Install Microsoft Windows Server Update Services 3.0 SP2 Hotfix button, and download and install the hotfix, as shown in Figure 8.28.

4. Click Next.

FIGURE 8. 28
Download the
WSUS 3.0 SP2 hotfix

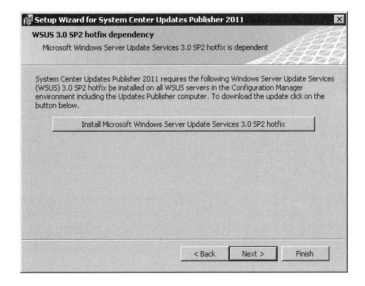

5. Select I Accept The License Agreement, and click Next.

6. Define the installation location, and click Next twice.

7. Click Finish when the installation is complete.

Configuring System Center Updates Publisher

Next you must configure System Center Updates Publisher so that it's able to publish software updates to the WSUS 3.0 SP2 server.

1. Start the System Center Updates Publisher 2011 console from the Start menu within Windows.

   The console will start, as shown in Figure 8.29.

FIGURE 8.29
The System Center Updates Publisher 2011 console

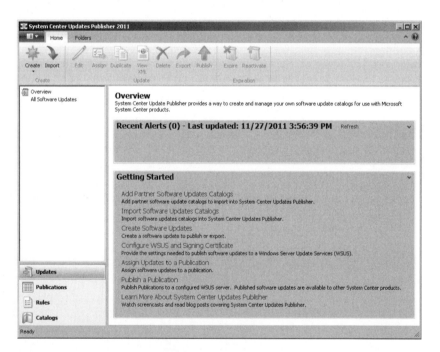

2. Click Configure WSUS And Signing Certificate to configure the System Center Updates Publisher options, shown in the right column of the console.

   Update Server Configure an update server by choosing Enable Publishing To An Update Server. Whether your WSUS server is installed locally or remotely, select the appropriate option to configure the WSUS server, as shown in Figure 8.30. Supply a signing certificate or create a self-signed certificate. Be sure that your computers also trust the certificates that are used to sign the software updates.

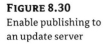

FIGURE 8.30
Enable publishing to
an update server

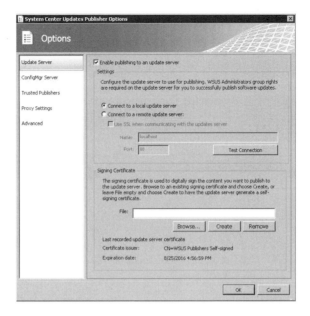

ConfigMgr Server   Configure the connection with your Configuration Manager 2012 server. If you have installed System Center Updates Publisher on a remote server, also configure the thresholds.

Trusted Publishers   If you accept the certificates of the publishers while importing catalogs, you can remove or view them here.

Proxy Settings   Configure the proxy settings if you need to use a proxy to connect to the Internet.

Advanced   If you are signing updates, you need to choose the Enable Add Timestamp When Signing Updates option. You also are able to configure security and local source publishing settings.

Using System Center Updates Publisher

When using System Center Updates Publisher you need to go through the following steps:

1. Add partner software updates catalogs.

2. Import updates.

3. Create rules.

4. Publish updates.

ADDING PARTNER SOFTWARE UPDATES CATALOGS

After configuring System Center Updates Publisher, the next step is to add partner software updates catalogs.

1. Start the System Center Updates Publisher 2011 console from the Start menu within Windows.

2. Click Add Partner Software Updates Catalogs.

3. Select the partner catalogs you want to use, and add them to the Selected Partner Catalogs list, as shown in Figure 8.31.

4. Click OK.

FIGURE 8.31
Adding partner catalogs

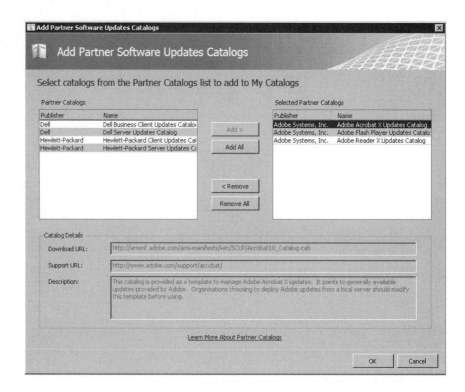

IMPORTING UPDATES

The next step after adding the partner software updates catalogs is importing the updates to System Center Updates Publisher.

1. Start the System Center Updates Publisher 2011 console from the Start menu within Windows.

2. Click Import Software Updates Catalogs, select the update catalogs, as shown in Figure 8.32, and click Next.

FIGURE 8.32
Importing the
update catalogs

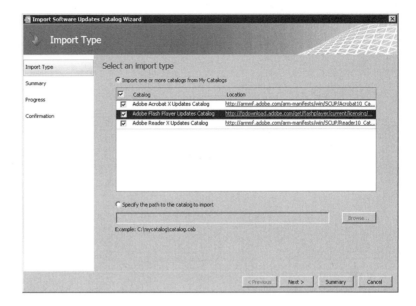

3. Confirm the settings and click Next.

While downloading the catalogs you will see a security warning, as shown in Figure 8.33.

FIGURE 8.33
Accept the catalogs

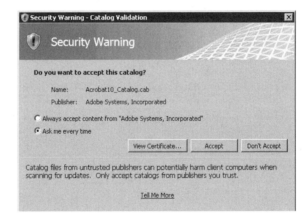

4. Review the certificate, select Always Accept Content From *"Publisher,"* and click Accept.

5. Click Close once the import is ready.

CREATING RULES

With applicability rules you can define which updates can be deployed on what kind of
operating system.

1. Start the System Center Updates Publisher 2011 console from the Start menu within Windows.

2. Click Create on the Home tab of the ribbon in the Rules workspace.

3. Supply a rule name, and click the yellow star icon to add a rule.

   You can configure different kinds of rules based on file, registry, system, or Windows Installer properties.

4. Configure the rule like the example shown in Figure 8.34.

FIGURE 8.34
Configure the rule like you want

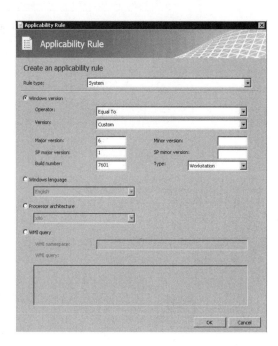

You can add AND or OR operators to the statement, as shown in Figure 8.35, and click OK.

FIGURE 8.35
Combined rule statement

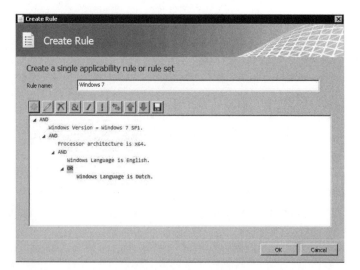

PUBLISHING UPDATES

After assigning the update catalogs, importing them, and creating rules, the next step is to publish the updates to Configuration Manager 2012 so that you can deploy the updates.

1. Start the System Center Updates Publisher 2011 console from the Start menu within Windows.

2. Choose the Updates workspace, and select the updates you want to publish.

3. Click Publish on the Home tab of the Ribbon.

4. Select the publish option you want, as shown in Figure 8.36.

FIGURE 8.36
Select the appropriate publish option

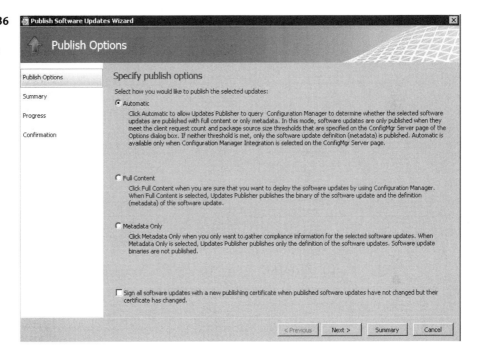

Automatic This option lets Configuration Manager determine whether the selected software updates are published with full content or metadata only. When you select this option, software updates are published only when they meet the client request count and package source size thresholds that are configured at the Configuration Manager Server section while configuring the connection. If the thresholds are not met, metadata will be published.

Full Content When this option is selected, Updates Publisher publishes the binary and the metadata of the software update.

Metadata Only When this option is selected, Updates Publisher publishes the metadata of the software update.

5. Select Sign All Software Updates With A New Published Certificate When Published Software Updates Have Not Changed But The Certificate Has Changed, and click Next.

6. Confirm the settings and click Next.

7. After the updates are published, as shown in Figure 8.37, click Close.

FIGURE 8.37
Confirmation page of the Publish Software Updates Wizard

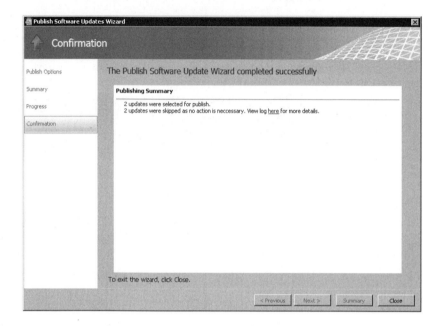

Third-Party Updates in Configuration Manager

To be able to deploy the third-party software updates with Configuration Manager, you need to configure the software update point component to also synchronize the software updates.

1. In the Configuration Manager console choose the Administration workspace ➢ Overview ➢ Site Configuration ➢ Sites and select the highest site in the hierarchy.

2. Choose Configure Site Components on the Settings section of the Home tab of the Ribbon, and click Software Update Point.

3. To configure the third-party software updates, click the Products tab, as shown in Figure 8.38. If the third-party updates are not yet available, manually synchronize the software updates.

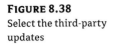

FIGURE 8.38
Select the third-party updates

4. After you synchronize the software updates, the third-party updates will come available in Configuration Manager, as shown in Figure 8.39.

FIGURE 8.39
The third-party updates are available in Configuration Manager

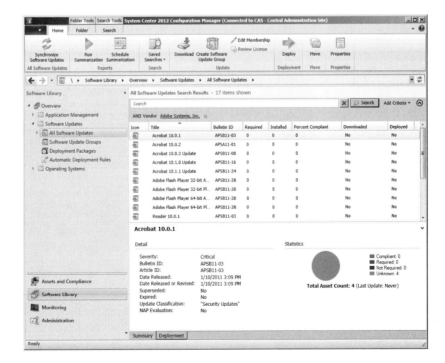

These updates can be deployed like every other software update in the Software Updates feature.

Monitoring Software Update Deployments

Configuration Manager 2012 offers in-console monitoring. You can see the compliancy level per deployment.

In-Console Monitoring

You can find in-console monitoring of software update deployment in the Configuration Manager 2012 console at several places. The error codes are explained, so you can find the solution instantly.

MONITORING PER SOFTWARE UPDATE

When you select a software update in the All Software Updates repository, the statistics of the software update appear. In the Statistics part of the summary in Figure 8.40, you are able to see how many systems are compliant, how many systems don't need the update, where the update is required, and where the status is unknown.

FIGURE 8.40
In-console
statistics per
update

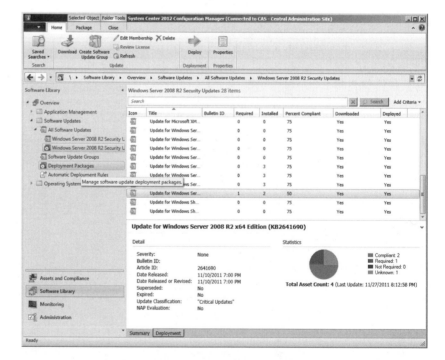

Monitoring per Deployment

When you deploy the updates, you can see the deployment status per deployment. The deployment status contains the following categories and subcategories. The deployment status in Figure 8.41 shows how many systems are compliant, how many systems are in the process of installing the updates, how many systems have an error, and where the status is unknown.

FIGURE 8.41
In-console statistics per update

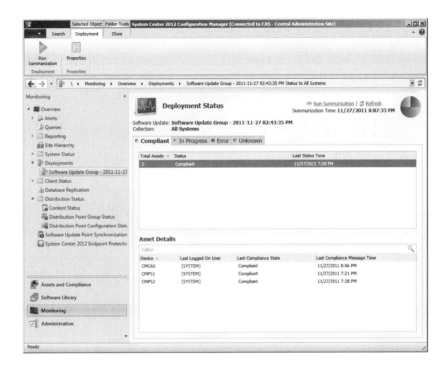

Status: Unknown This status says that the status messages of the Configuration Manager clients have not yet been received by the management point of the primary site. The following subcategories are available:

- Devices Unhealthy/Active
- Devices Healthy/Inactive
- Devices Healthy/Active

Status: Error Errors can occur when you deploy software updates. This category shows all the devices that have had an error while deploying the software updates. The following subcategories and error descriptions are available:

- Scan Tool Policy not found.
- Network connection: Windows Update Agent encountered an error.
- Policy Platform Client: Data is invalid.

◆ Fatal error during installation.

◆ Pre install scan failed.

◆ Software update still detected as actionable after apply.

◆ Unknown error (-2147012744).

◆ Class not registered.

◆ Access is denied.

◆ Unspecified error.

Status: In Progress   The in-progress status displays all devices that are preparing for the deployment of a software update or are currently receiving a deployment.

The following subcategories are available:

◆ Downloading update(s)

◆ Downloaded update(s)

◆ Installing update(s)

Compliant   When the devices are compliant, you will see all the assets that are compliant.

When selecting a system in the Asset Details part of the Deployment Status screen you are able to retrieve more details about the system by right-clicking the system and choosing More Details. In the dialog shown in Figure 8.42 you are able to view the information about the deployment.

FIGURE 8.42
Details about the
Software Update
Deployment

SOFTWARE UPDATE POINT SYNCHRONIZATION STATUS

Besides examining the log files as described earlier, you can monitor the software update point synchronization status from the console.

To monitor the synchronization in the hierarchy, do the following:

1. In the Configuration Manager console, choose the Software Monitoring workspace ➤ Overview ➤ Software Update Point Synchronization Status.

2. Examine the synchronization status, the link state, and the catalog version, as shown in Figure 8.43.

FIGURE 8.43
Software Update Point Synchronization Status

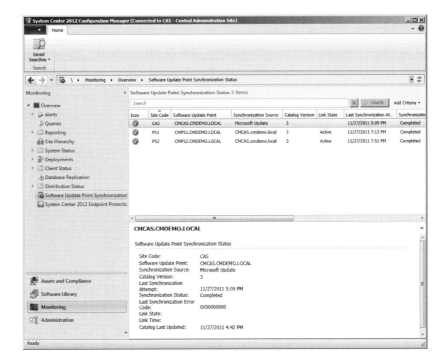

Reporting

The Configuration Manager client software performs two main phases of the software deployment process:

Evaluation   Configuration Manager clients determine if the software updates in a deployment are required.

Enforcement   Clients report their compliance state for the deployment.

Microsoft provides excellent reports to monitor the phases of software update deployments in Configuration Manager 2012, and these reports are considered the best way to monitor the software update deployments. Those reports can be found in the Software Updates - C. Deployment States category in the Reports node in the Configuration Manager console.

To monitor the evaluation phase of software update deployments, you should use the following three main reports:

States 2 - Evaluation States For A Deployment   This report will give you a summary of the evaluation state of clients for a selected deployment and will provide information as to whether clients were able to evaluate a deployment successfully.

States 4 - Computers In A Specific State For A Deployment (Secondary)   You can drill down into this report to get more information about clients in a specified deployment state.

States 7 - Error Status Messages For A Computer (Secondary)   You can use this report to get all error message information for a deployment on a specific computer.

To monitor client enforcement for software update deployments, there are also three main reports that you should use:

States 1 - Enforcement States For A Deployment   This report gives a summary of the enforcement state of clients for a specific deployment. This report shows information on the state for installing the updates in the deployment, such as downloading the update, installing the update, successfully installing the update, and so on.

States 4 - Computers In A Specific State For A Deployment (Secondary)   You can drill down into this report to get more information about clients in a specified deployment state.

States 7 - Error Status Messages For A Computer (Secondary)   You can use this report to get all error message information for a deployment on a specific computer.

 **Real World Scenario**

CONDITION CRITICAL

Now that you have deployed Configuration Manager and have Software Updates up and running, your manager wants you to make a concentrated effort to get clients up to date with critical security patches. He has made it clear that these are to be given priority over other updates until the numbers of required patches are down to a reasonable level, which is not the case now.

To accomplish your new software update initiative, you must first figure out what patches need to be installed on which computers.

One way to do this is to set up search criteria for each operating system that you support, listing all the critical security patches. With those search criteria, you highlight all the security patches that are required by your clients and make an update group out of them.

Once you have done that, you can either download all the updates and put them on your distribution points, or you can start a deployment directly from the update group and configure downloading those updates as part of that update.

The procedures that we have detailed earlier in the chapter for configuring the different elements of Software Updates were made with that method of organization in mind.

The Bottom Line

Plan to use Software Updates.   You can use the same method of deployment intelligence that was used in Chapter 2 to gather information for planning to implement Software Updates. This will be very helpful in making sure that you get the most out of the Software Updates feature for your organization.

> **Master It**   What is the first step in gathering deployment intelligence for planning to implement Software Updates?

Configure Software Updates.   Before you can utilize Software Updates in your environment, you must set up and configure the various components of this feature.

> **Master It**   What is the first thing you have to install before you can use Software Updates?

Use the Software Updates feature to manage software updates.   The hardest thing to do in SMS 2003 relating to patch management was to programmatically prioritize software updates that are critical so they can be deployed with a higher priority than other updates.

> **Master It**   What does Configuration Manager provide that can help with prioritizing software updates?

Use automatic update deployment to deploy software updates.   When you deployed software in Configuration Manager 2007, you deployed software updates through a procedure that consumed a lot of time.

> **Master It**   Configuration Manager has a new feature called Automatic Deployment Rules. What kinds of updates are suitable to deploy via the Automatic Deployment Rules?

Chapter 9

Operating System Deployment

Most IT administrators want to automate as many functions as possible in order to reproduce the same outcome consistently and quickly to as many devices as possible, and setting up a basic computer build is no exception.

In Configuration Manager 2007 the operating system deployment (OSD) feature became one of the most important features of Configuration Manager. With Configuration Manager 2012 are you able to install Windows operating systems without any user intervention. We call this Zero-Touch deployment. When a Windows deployment is finished, the user is able to log into the network and able to start working with the new operating systems and the available applications.

In Configuration Manager 2012 the operating system deployment feature became more mature with added features such as offline servicing. We will walk you through several Windows deployment scenarios without and with the use of the Microsoft Deployment Toolkit 2012.

In this chapter, you will learn to

◆ Specify a Network Access account.

◆ Enable PXE support.

◆ Update the driver catalog package.

◆ Update an image from the console.

What's New in Operating System Deployment

The operating system deployment feature in Configuration Manager 2012 was not significantly changed from Configuration Manager 2007. Nevertheless some parts are enhanced, changed, or new to the feature. The following list shows the changes since Configuration Manager 2007.

◆ The PXE (Preboot Execution Environment) role was moved from the primary site server to the distribution point. This way scalability is increased since it is easier to deploy an extra distribution point.

◆ Updating a WIM image with the latest approved software updates is done from the Configuration Manager console.

◆ You can use task sequence media to deploy operating systems anywhere in your Configuration Manager hierarchy.

◆ A boot image is available throughout the Configuration Manager hierarchy instead of needing to deploy a boot image in every site.

◆ The Create Task Sequence Media Wizard provides the option to add prestart command files to prestage media, stand-alone media, and bootable media.

◆ You can configure the task sequence media to become unattended installation media by suppressing the Configuration Manager Boot Media Wizard during the installation.

◆ In the task sequence, a capture user state or restore user state task supports the new features of the User State Migration Tool (USMT) version 4.

◆ From the task sequence you can install applications from the new application model.

Planning for OSD with Configuration Manager 2012

Before you configure the feature, you should plan your operating system deployment, since you can deploy different kinds of operating systems in numerous ways. To deploy your operating systems in an effective and cost-efficient way, you need to address the following items when planning your operating system deployment:

◆ Deployment scenarios

◆ The kind of images to deploy

◆ The kind of components to use

Deployment Scenarios

You can deploy the operating system in different ways. In Configuration Manager 2012 you can deploy an operating system in two kinds of scenarios:

Bare-Metal Scenario   Installing an operating system to a new out-of-the-box client computer

Refresh Computer Scenario   Deploying an image to an existing Windows installation to perform an upgrade or reinstall while migrating the user state to the new Windows installation

The Kind of Images to Deploy

Configuration Manager 2012 supports, as did the previous version of Configuration Manager, the deployment of two kinds of operating system installations. You can install images, based on the Windows Imaging (WIM) format, or just install operating systems by using the source of an operating system installation. Using the source of an operating system is an unattended installation and is normally used to create a WIM image with a build-and-capture task sequence. The source can be a copy of the DVD of Windows 7, Windows Vista, Windows XP SP3, Windows Server 2003, or Windows Server 2008 (R2).

Operating System Images   Operating images are often custom images that are built with the build-and-capture task sequence. This task sequence allows you to install and create an image of a customized reference operating system image.

Operating System Installer   An installer source is used as the source for a build and capture to perform an unattended installation of the operating system before capturing it to a WIM image.

Operating System Deployment Components

The operating system deployment feature uses different kinds of components within Configuration Manager 2012. We'll look at each of them.

BOOT IMAGES

Configuration Manager 2012 comes with two default boot images. These images are available for all sites in the hierarchy. There is no need to create and deploy boot images for each Configuration Manager site in the hierarchy.

When you access a standard boot image, you can configure several settings in various tabs. To access the boot image browse to the Software Library workspace ➤ Overview ➤ Operating Systems ➤ Boot Images. The tabs shown in Figure 9.1 are available.

FIGURE 9.1

Boot Image properties

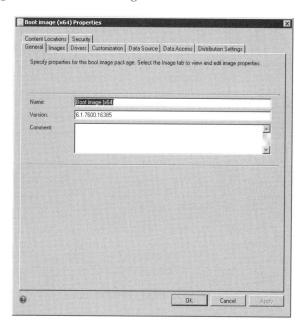

General Tab   In the General tab, you can enter or change the name, version, or comments of the boot image that's already available in Configuration Manager 2012.

Images Tab   The Images tab provides information about the boot image. If you changed the image properties with an external tool, you can reload the original properties.

Drivers Tab   The Drivers tab provides an overview of the drivers that are injected into the boot image. You can also add drivers from the driver store to the boot image. Common drivers to add to boot images are network and SATA/SCSI drivers and any other critical drivers.

Customizations Tab   If you want to customize the selected boot image, you can find some options on the Customizations tab. When you're in the plan and build phases of your project and you want to test the deployment of images, you can enable command support in the Windows Preinstallation Environment (WinPE) phase of your deployment. Pressing F8 opens a command prompt that allows you to access the filesystem and log files that are located in the _SMSTaskSequence\Logs\Smstslog directory. There is also an option to change the background that is shown during the WinPE phase.

If you want to add a prestart command hook and supporting files, you can add the command line here.

Data Source Tab The Data Source tab supplies the path to the boot WIM image that is used for the boot image package. The Data Source tab is also the place to enable or disable the ability to boot the image from PXE.

Data Access Tab With settings in the Data Access tab you can configure how the package is stored on the distribution points.

Distribution Settings Tab Here you can define how the boot image package is distributed to the distribution points and set the priority.

Content Location Tab On the Content Location tab you can see on which distribution points or distribution points groups the image package is available. Selecting a distribution point or distribution point group allows you to validate the copy on the location, redistribute the boot image package to the location, or remove the boot image package from the location.

Security Tab The Security tab shows you the users who have administrative permissions to the boot image object.

DECIDING WHEN TO USE WHICH BOOT IMAGE

There are two different versions of boot images to support two kinds of platforms, namely an x86 version and an x64 version.

You can use the x86 boot image version to deploy the following:

- 32-bit operating system image
- 64-bit operating system image
- 32-bit operating system install package

You can use the x64 boot image version to deploy the following:

- 64-bit operating system image
- 64-bit operating system install package
- You can define per task sequence which boot image to use.

STATE MIGRATION POINT

The state migration point stores the user data that is gathered by USMT 4.0 when a computer is being refreshed by a new Windows operating system. The component can be configured to store user data on different storage folders, depending on the deletion policy.

DISTRIBUTION POINTS

The distribution point is used to store the content that is related to the operating system deployment. But in Configuration Manager 2012 two very important features have been moved to the distribution point, namely PXE and multicast.

When configuring a distribution point for operating system deployment, you can adjust the following settings:

PXE Tab   As mentioned earlier, the PXE feature has been moved to the distribution point. The PXE tab allows you to enable or disable support for PXE, but a Windows Deployment Services service must be present. As in earlier versions, you can configure PXE to respond to incoming PXE requests and unknown computer support. New is the ability to enable Primary User Assignment, which is discussed later in this chapter. If you want to secure PXE with a password, you can configure one. When you enable a boot image for PXE and the boot image is available on the distribution point, the boot image is also copied into the `RemoteInstall\SMSBoot` folder of Windows Deployment Services. Enabling the PXE feature will also install the Windows Deployment Services feature if the feature is not yet available.

Multicast Tab   The Multicast feature has also been moved to the distribution point via PXE. You configure the options per distribution point.

OPERATING SYSTEM IMAGES

The operating system images are the WIM images that can be deployed to workstations or servers. An operating system image can be a captured operating system. When you access an operating system image, you can configure several settings in various tabs. To access an operating system image go to the Software Library workspace ➤ Overview ➤ Operating Systems ➤ Operating System Image.

General Tab   The General Tab is used to supply information about the operating system image, like name, version, and comments.

Images   The Images tab gives you information about the WIM image. Information like OS version, architecture, creation date, and more is shared. If you changed the image properties using an external tool you are able to reload the information from the WIM image.

Data Source Tab   The Data Source tab supplies the UNC path to the WIM image that is used for the operating system image package.

Data Access Tab   With settings in the Data Access tab you can configure how the package is stored on the distribution points.

Distribution Settings Tab   Here you can define how the operating system image package is distributed to the distribution points and set the priority.

Servicing   In the Servicing tab you are able to see or change the offline servicing schedule if offline servicing for an image is scheduled.

Installed Updates   The installed updates tab gives you a list with installed updates that have been installed with offline servicing.

Content Location Tab   On the Content Location tab you can see on which distribution points or distribution points groups the operating system image package is available. Selecting a distribution point or distribution point group allows you to validate the copy on the location, redistribute the operating system image package to the location, or remove the operating system image package from the location.

Security Tab   The Security tab shows you the users who have administrative permissions to the operating system image object.

OPERATING SYSTEM INSTALLERS

The operating system installers are the install source of an operating system. With the operating system installers you are able to install operating systems unattended. Operating system installers are for instance used while building and capturing an operating system image. When you access an operating system installer, you can configure several settings in various tabs. To access an operating system installer package go to the Software Library workspace ➤ Overview➤Operating Systems ➤ Operating System Installers.

General Tab　The General Tab is used to supply information about the operating system installer, like name, version, and comments.

Editions　The Editions tab allows you to see information about the selected edition in the installation source. For instance a Windows Server 2008 R2 install source does have more editions available, editions can be Standard, Enterprise, or Datacenter.

Data Source Tab　The Data Source tab supplies the UNC path to the install source of the operating system installer that is used for the operating system installer package.

Data Access Tab　With settings in the Data Access tab you can configure how the package is stored on the distribution points.

Distribution Settings Tab　Here you can define how the operating system installer package is distributed to the distribution points and set the priority.

Content Location Tab　On the Content Location tab you can see on which distribution points or distribution points groups the operating system installer package is available. Selecting a distribution point or distribution point group allows you to validate the copy on the location, redistribute the operating system installer package to the location, or remove the operating system installer package from the location.

Security Tab　The Security tab shows you the users who have administrative permissions to the operating system installer object.

Task Sequences

Task sequences provide a mechanism to perform a series of tasks on a client computer without any user intervention. Using task sequences, you can deploy operating systems but also distribute software, configure client settings, update drivers, edit user states, and perform other tasks in support of operating system deployment. Task sequences are global data and are available for all Configuration Manager sites in the hierarchy.

With Configuration Manager 2012, you can create three different kinds of task sequences:

Install An Existing Image Package　This task sequence will install an existing WIM image to a computer via the normal distribution method or PXE. This option uses a predefined sequence of steps. The steps will take care of wiping or formatting the disk, installing the operating system, installing software updates, installing applications, and setting the user state.

Build And Capture A Reference Operating System Image　This task sequence will build and capture a Windows operating system in a new WIM image. You can use this WIM image to deploy to the client computers. This option uses a predefined sequence of steps.

Create A New Custom Task Sequence　A custom task sequence is an empty task sequence for which you define your own steps.

A task sequence consists of tasks or steps grouped into the following categories:

General　In the General category the following tasks can be configured for the task sequence:

- Run Command Line
- Install Application

- Install Package
- Install Software Updates
- Join Domain Or Workgroup
- Connect To Network Folder
- Restart Computer
- Set Task Sequence Variable

Disks   In the Disks category the following tasks can be configured for the task sequence:

- Format And Partition Disk
- Convert Disk To Dynamic
- Enable BitLocker
- Disable BitLocker

User State   In the User State category the following tasks can be configured for the task sequence.

- Request State Store
- Capture User State
- Restore User State
- Release State Store

Images   In the Images category the following tasks can be configured for the task sequence:

- Apply Operating System Image
- Apply Data Image
- Setup Windows And ConfigMgr
- Install Deployment Tools
- Prepare ConfigMgr Client For Capture
- Prepare Windows For Capture
- Capture Operating System Image

Drivers   In the Drivers category the following tasks can be configured for the task sequence.

- Auto Apply Drivers
- Apply Driver Package

Settings   In the Settings category the following tasks can be configured for the task sequence:

- Capture Network Settings
- Capture Windows Settings
- Apply Network Settings
- Apply Windows Settings

TASK SEQUENCE MEDIA

When you use task sequence media, you can create a CD, DVD, or USB containing the files required for deploying or capturing an operating system with Configuration Manager. You can select the following kinds of media:

Stand-alone Media   Use this type of media to deploy an operating system without network access.

Bootable Media   Use this type of media to access the Configuration Manager 2012 infrastructure to deploy an operating system across the network.

Capture Media   Use this type of media to capture a WIM image of an operating system on a reference computer.

Prestaged Media   Use this type of media to create a file for operating system deployment that contains an operating system image and bootable media that can be prestaged on a hard disk.

DRIVER CATALOG

The driver catalog is the place to store device drivers that need to be added during a Windows deployment or to a boot image. Normally not all the device drivers need to be added, because Windows 7 supports many hardware platforms and devices. When you deploy an operating system, you can include a driver package or let WinPE discover the drivers through WMI.

You can organize your driver structure by adding the drivers for each make and model to folders or categories. This way you can clean up old drivers in the future.

User Device Affinity

User device affinity helps you create relationships between users and devices. You create relationships by either adding primary devices to users or by adding primary users to devices. When you deploy a new operating system to a device, Configuration Manager 2012 will check the user's collection memberships and predeploy the user-targeted applications. The user's primary device will attempt to install the application that is targeted to the user whether or not the user is logged on.

Configuration Manager 2012 allows you to create the following relationships:

◆ Single primary user to primary device

◆ Multiple primary devices per user

◆ Multiple primary users per device

Deployment Process

When you deploy a Windows operating system using the task sequences of Configuration Manager, you need to follow certain steps to be sure that the deployment will succeed. Generally speaking, there are three major steps to deploy an operating system: prepare, build and capture, and deploy.

Prepare for Operating System Deployment

The first step is preparing the Configuration Manager environment so that you can deploy the operating system. Gather the information that you need to create an image of an operating system and deploy it to client computers. Essential information includes the makes and models of the computers and the devices that need drivers. You also need to incorporate whether you want to add applications to the image or not.

Build and Capture an Operating System

After your design for the operating system is finished, you need to translate the design into a task sequence that will build and capture your operating system.

The build-and-capture task sequence creates a fully unattended installation of a Windows operating system. Depending on your design, the task sequence can take care of installing the available software updates and, if you like, applications that are part of the common operating environment. Incorporating applications into your WIM image is not a best practice, but there are situations where you'll want to add some applications to your image.

Another option is to use a reference computer and capture the reference operating system, which is created manually, using a capture media task sequence.

FAT VS. THIN IMAGES

When you deploy Windows images in your environment, think about how to deploy your common operating environment, operating system, and standard applications. You can choose to deploy your operating system and applications in an image (fat image) or just the operating system in an image (thin image) and the applications during the deployment process. A thin image is easier to maintain because you don't have to recapture your image when an application needs to be updated. However, a fat image may be quicker to deploy.

Deploy an Operating System

After capturing an operating system image, you can deploy it to one or more computers in your environment. The task sequence that you create can be used for bare-metal deployment or to refresh or upgrade a computer that is a member of an existing Configuration Manager 2012 environment. After creating a task sequence to deploy your Windows image, you can change and add tasks to suit your needs. You can also add or change the software updates, installation of applications, disk layout, domain, network settings, and much more.

MAINTAINING IMAGES

Configuration Manager 2012 supports maintaining your Windows images with software updates from the console. You can schedule offline servicing of the Windows image by adding the latest software updates and redeploying the images to your distribution points periodically. This is described in the section "Servicing Your Operating System Images Offline," later in this chapter.

Preparing Configuration Manager 2012 for Operating System Deployment

You need to configure Configuration Manager 2012 for deploying an operating system image. The first step in preparing for OSD is to configure the Network Access account. After that you need to create a Configuration Manager 2012 client package and a user state migration package.

Then you need to install and configure the state migration point role and enable the PXE feature on the distribution points.

Configuring the Network Access Account

The first step is to set up an Active Directory user as the Network Access account. A general rule for this account is to give it an easily identifiable name. For example, a domain administrator would create an account called svc-sccm-na (or whatever fits your environment's naming conventions).

Next, you will need to configure Configuration Manager 2012 to use the Network Access account. Take the following steps:

1. Open the Configuration Manager 2012 console, choose the Administration workspace, and expand Overview ➤ Site Configuration ➤ Sites.

2. Select one of the sites for which you want to configure the Network Access account, and click Configure Site Components in the settings section on the Home tab of the Ribbon.

3. Select Software Distribution.

4. Select the Network Access Account tab, and set the Network Access account to the account created earlier, as shown in Figure 9.2.

5. Click OK.

FIGURE 9.2
Software Distribution
Properties dialog box

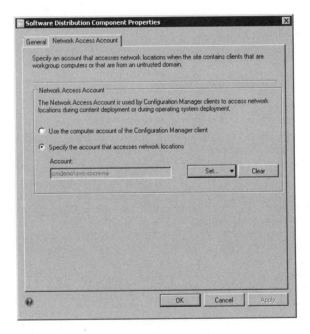

The Network Access account must have access to the computer that is deployed and the content on the distribution points. Normally a Network Access account has permission if it's a member of the Domain Users Active Directory group.

Creating the Configuration Manager Client Install Package

The next step is to configure a package in order for the Configuration Manager 2012 client to be installed once the new operating system has been deployed to a new machine. This will ensure that the new machine gets the Configuration Manager client as soon as the machine comes online. There is nothing out of the ordinary about creating the package for the client:

1. Open the Configuration Manager 2012 console, choose the Software Library workspace, and expand Overview ➤ Application Management ➤ Packages.

2. Select Packages, and select Create Package From Definition on the Home tab of the Ribbon.

   This opens the Package Definition page of the Create Package From Definition Wizard, shown in Figure 9.3.

FIGURE 9.3
Create Package
From Definition
Wizard—Package
Definition page

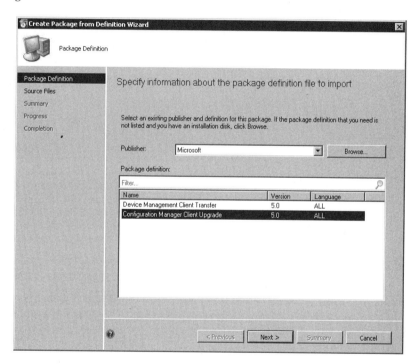

This allows you to select the Configuration Manager Client Upgrade package definition.

3. After selecting the package definition, click Next.

4. On the Source Files page, select Always Obtain Files From A Source Directory, and click Next.

   This opens the Source Directory page, shown in Figure 9.4, allowing you to designate the source file directory.

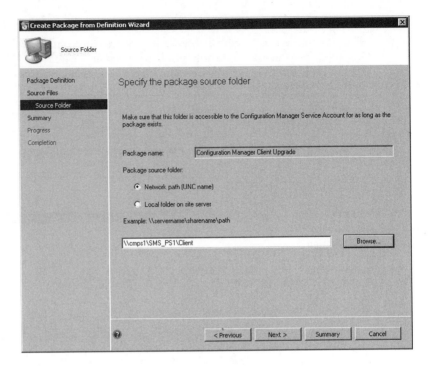

5. In this dialog box, select Network Path, and fill in or browse to the source directory. This source folder called Client is located in a shared folder on your primary site server called SMS_<*sitename*> (for instance, SMS_PS1). Click Next.

6. On the Summary page, click Next, and Configuration Manager 2012 will create the client upgrade package.

7. Click Close to exit the wizard.

This package contains only one program, which is a silent upgrade install of the Configuration Manager 2012 client. You will need to specify a distribution point so you can deploy this package within your organization. Select the Configuration Manager Client Upgrade package, click Distribute Content on the Home tab of the Ribbon, and select the distribution point where you want to deploy the package from.

Creating a USMT Package

You will also need to create a package that OSD will use to gather the entire user state and migrate it to the new environment. This is known as *user state migration*. The following procedures will demonstrate not only how to set up the USMT package but also how to set up the state migration point within Configuration Manager 2012. OSD will use the USMT to capture the user's settings as well as the user's state at the time in which the package runs. This capture is known as the *scan state*. Configuration Manager then migrates this scan state and restores those settings, known as the *load state*, to the new system.

HARD-LINKING INSTEAD OF COPYING FILES

Older versions of USMT were able to copy your files and settings to network shares. Depending on the amount of data and network bandwidth, this could take a while to complete. USMT version 4 offers a new feature called hard-link migration. Hard-link migration in USMT scans the computer for user files and settings and creates a directory of hard links to those files. The hard links are remapped into the appropriate locations in the new operating system. The process takes a few minutes to complete.

The steps for creating a USMT package are similar to those for creating packages that we have discussed earlier in this book:

1. Open the Configuration Manager 2012 console, choose the Software Library workspace, and expand Overview ➢ Application Management ➢ Packages.

2. Select Packages, and select Create Package on the Home tab of the Ribbon.

3. The Package page, shown in Figure 9.5, appears; fill in the name and other information as you see fit.

FIGURE 9.5
Create Package and Program Wizard—Package page

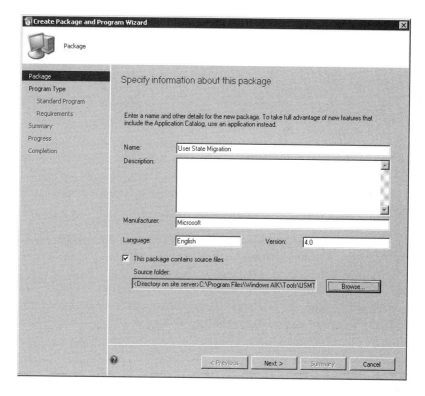

4. Select the This Package Contains Source Files option, and browse to the location where the USMT source is located.

   The default location for the USMT source is `C:\Program Files\Windows AIK\ Tools\USMT`.

5. Click Next.

6. Select Do Not Create A Program For This Package, and click Next.

7. Click Next on the Summary page, and then click Close on the Wizard Completed page.

Remember that you will need to assign a distribution point for this package. There is nothing different about assigning a distribution point for this package.

USER STATE MIGRATION TOOL DOCUMENTATION

You can find the User State Migration Tool documentation here:

   `http://technet.microsoft.com/en-us/library/dd560801(WS.10).aspx`

Configuring the State Migration Point Role

The next step in preparing Configuration Manager 2012 for OSD is to set up a state migration point. The state migration point is used to store the migrated settings and data during the operating system image deployment. This state migration point is a site system role within Configuration Manager 2012, and it will need to be assigned to a server. Follow these few steps to set up the state migration point role:

1. Open the Configuration Manager 2012 console, select the Administration workspace, and expand Overview ➤ Site Configuration ➤ Servers And Site System Roles.

2. Select the site server for which you want to install and configure the state migration point, and click Add Site System Role on the Home tab of the Ribbon.

3. On the Create Roles Wizard's General page, click Next.

4. You will be presented with the System Role Selection page; select State Migration Point, and click Next.

5. On the State Migration Point page, shown in Figure 9.6, click the starburst icon to create a new storage folder.

FIGURE 9.6

Create Roles
Wizard—State
Migration
Point page

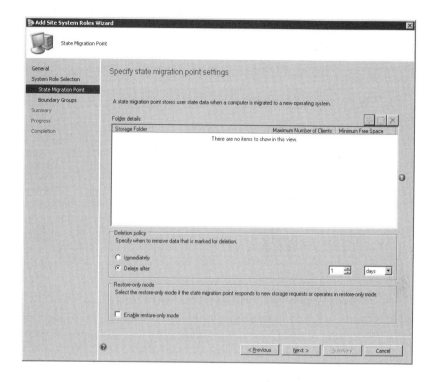

6. Create a new storage folder on the Storage Folder Settings page, shown in Figure 9.7.

FIGURE 9.7

Designating a
storage folder

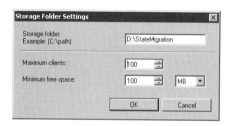

This allows you to enter the path to use when storing state migration data.

7. Under the storage location you also need to configure the maximum number of clients that are allowed to store the data and the minimum required free space on the disk.

A way to determine the size for your state migration point is to identify the number of deployments that must take place, the average size of the user state, and how long the user state must be stored.

8. Click OK to return to the State Migration Point page.

You can change the Deletion Policy setting if you think one day is too long or not long enough until the user data is removed from the state migration point.

Enabling the restore-only mode option will result in the state migration point responding only to restore requests.

9. Click Next to configure boundary groups for the site system.

10. Click Next, and you will be taken to the Summary page.

11. Click Next to allow Configuration Manager to create the new site role.

    This brings up the Wizard Completed page.

12. Click Close.

Don't Configure the Deletion Policy to Delete User State Immediately

A best practice from Microsoft is to not set the deletion policy to delete a user state immediately that is marked for deletion. If an attacker is able to retrieve the user state before a valid computer does, the user state would be deleted before that time. Set the deletion interval to long enough to verify the successful restore of the user state data.

Configuring PXE on Distribution Points

To allow Configuration Manager 2012 to use OSD for deploying to bare-metal devices, you need to configure PXE on the distribution points, for which you will need to set up the Network Access account, which you did earlier in this chapter. You will also need to ensure that the Configuration Manager client upgrade package has been configured and is ready for deployment, as you also did earlier in this chapter. Finally, you need to ensure that the boot image is set up as a package.

To be able to use PXE on a distribution point site server, you also need to install Windows Deployment Services (WDS) on that server.

Installing Windows Deployment Services

You can install Windows Deployment Services through Add Or Remove Programs on Windows 2003 SP2 or higher machines.

The next stage in preparing Configuration Manager 2012 for OSD is to set up PXE support. Configuration Manager no longer has a PXE service point; the PXE feature is embedded in the distribution point role. You need to enable and configure the PXE feature per distribution point.

Follow these few steps to set up the PXE feature:

1. Open the Configuration Manager 2012 console, select the Administration workspace, and expand Overview ➢ Distribution Points.

2. Select the site server on which the distribution point resides, and click Properties on the Site Role tab of the Ribbon.

3. Select the PXE tab and click Enable PXE Service Point.

    When you enable the feature, you will see the PXE Service Point Configuration dialog box, shown in Figure 9.8. This dialog box informs you that Configuration Manager 2012 must have some UDP ports opened on the server.

4. Click Yes to continue enabling a PXE service point.

FIGURE 9.8

PXE Service
Point Configuration
dialog box

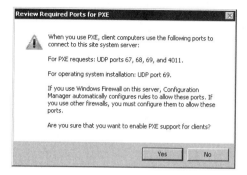

5. After enabling the feature, you can configure how Configuration Manager will allow incoming PXE requests, as shown in Figure 9.9. Click OK when you've finished.

FIGURE 9.9

PXE settings page

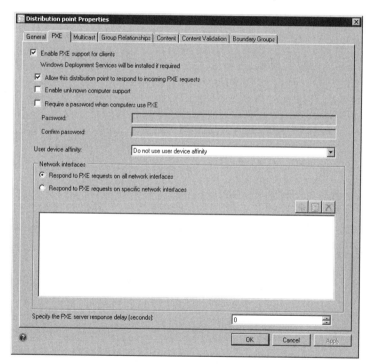

It will take some time for the PXE feature to successfully install on the system. You can monitor the progress of the installation by checking the distmgr.log and smspxe.log files. The Windows Deployment Services wil be installed if it is not already installed.

> **DHCP AND PXE ON THE SAME SERVER**
>
> You'll need to set up some DHCP options for PXE to boot properly. Specifically, you'll need to specify options 60, 66, and 67 when the DHCP server is on the same server as your Windows deployment server. Option 60 needs to be set to PXEClient, which is only used in this scenario, option 66 is the FQDN of the Configuration Manager server, and option 67 should be the path to SMSBoot\<platform>\pxeboot.com.

Distributing the Boot Image Package

The next part of preparing Configuration Manager 2012 for operating system deployment is to distribute the boot image package to a distribution point. This boot image is used to start the computer in the Windows Preinstallation Environment (WinPE) for capturing, prior to deploying the operating system image. This procedure, because of the size of the images, will take some time to complete:

1. From within the Configuration Manager console, choose the Software Library workspace, expand Overview ➤ Operating Systems, and select Boot Images.

   You will notice two boot images for various platforms: one for x64—Boot Image (x64)— and the other for x86 devices. For the purpose of this book, we will concentrate on the x86 boot images, but there is basically no difference in configuring one or the other. The images are configured during the installation of Configuration Manager 2012. However, there are no distribution points assigned for either of the boot images. You need to add both Boot Image Packages to the distribution points.

2. To configure a distribution point, select Boot Images ➤ Boot Image (x86), and click Distribute Content on the Home tab of the Ribbon.

3. This opens the New Distribution Points Wizard's Welcome page; click Next to continue.

4. Select the distribution point you want to use on the Specify The Content Destination page by clicking Add ➤ Distribution Point.

5. Select the distribution points you want to deploy the boot image to, and click OK.

6. Click Next to review the summary.

7. After reviewing the summary, click Next. Then on the Wizard Completed page, click Close.

   It will take some time to copy the boot image package to the distribution point.

Enabling Boot Images for PXE

The last part of preparing Configuration Manager 2012 for OSD is enabling both of the boot images to be available for PXE:

1. From within the Configuration Manager console, choose the Software Library workspace, expand Overview ➤ Operating Systems, and select Boot Images.

2. Select the boot image for which you want to enable PXE support, and click Properties on the Home tab of the Ribbon.

3. Click the Data Source tab, and enable the Deploy This Boot Image From The PXE Service Point option, as shown in Figure 9.10.

4. Click OK.

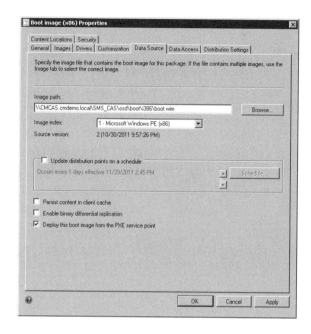

Configuration Manager will process the change and configure the Windows Deployment Services server to use the boot image from Configuration Manager 2012. Configuration Manager 2012 will place the boot image in the `<drive>\RemoteInstall\SMSImages` folder.

Let's review the steps briefly for configuring Configuration Manager 2012 for OSD:

1. First, you configured the Network Access account, and then you created the client install package.

2. After creating the client install package, you set up a package for USMT and then set up the state migration point and PXE for Configuration Manager 2012.

3. Finally, you deployed the boot images to the distribution points and PXE.

Adding Operating System Installers

The next step after preparing Configuration Manager 2012 for OSD is to add the source content of the operating systems. The operating system install packages are used to build and capture a reference image that you can deploy with Configuration Manager 2012.

You can add an operating system install source by following the next procedure:

1. From within the Configuration Manager console, choose the Software Library workspace, expand Overview ➢ Operating Systems, and select Operating System Installers.

2. Click Add Operating System Installer on the Home tab of the Ribbon, and fill in the UNC path to the install source of the operating system, as shown in Figure 9.11.

3. Click Next.

FIGURE 9.11
Create an operating system install package

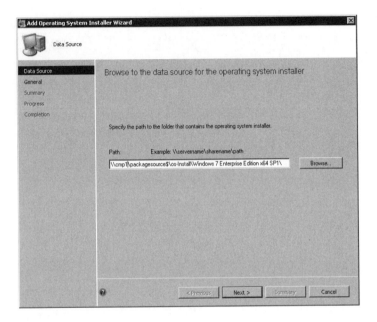

4. Supply the operating system install package with a name, version, and comments, and click Next.

5. Review the summary, and click Next.

6. When finished, click Close.

After creating the operating system installer package, distribute the package to the distribution points in your hierarchy. The source of an operating system install package can be one of the following operating systems:

♦ Windows XP SP3

♦ Windows Vista

♦ Windows 7

♦ Windows Server 2003

♦ Windows Server 2008

♦ Windows Server 2008 R2

Developing a Task Sequence for Creating a Capture Image

Now we will show how to create a task sequence that will be used to capture an image of a workstation. A *task sequence* is a way for Configuration Manager 2012 to perform one or more steps or tasks on a client computer without requiring user intervention, Zero-Touch deployment. A task sequence can consist of a single step or multiple tasks grouped together to perform functions. The tasks can depend on other tasks to complete successfully or be independent of each other.

There are two options for creating task sequences for OSD:

◆ Task sequences used with PXE boot

◆ Task sequences used with media boot

Task Sequences Used with PXE Boot

When you enable PXE on the distribution points, you can simply create a build-and-capture task sequence that will take care of the build-and-capture process. Take the following steps to create a task sequence for creating an image:

1. From within the Configuration Manager console, select the Software Library workspace, expand Overview ➢ Operating Systems, and select Task Sequences.

2. Click Create Task Sequence on the Home tab of the Ribbon, and select the Build And Capture A Reference System Image option.

3. Give the task sequence a name (for instance "Build and Capture Windows 7 Enterprise x64"), select a boot image that will support your operating system version and platform, and click Next.

4. Select the operating system install package, and supply a password that you will remember if you need to troubleshoot.

   The local administrator account will be disabled if you do not supply a password. Do not supply a product key if you are building and capturing Windows 7 or Windows Server 2008 images, as shown in Figure 9.12. Supplying a product key while building and capturing will cause the process to fail.

FIGURE 9.12
Define which Windows operating system will be captured

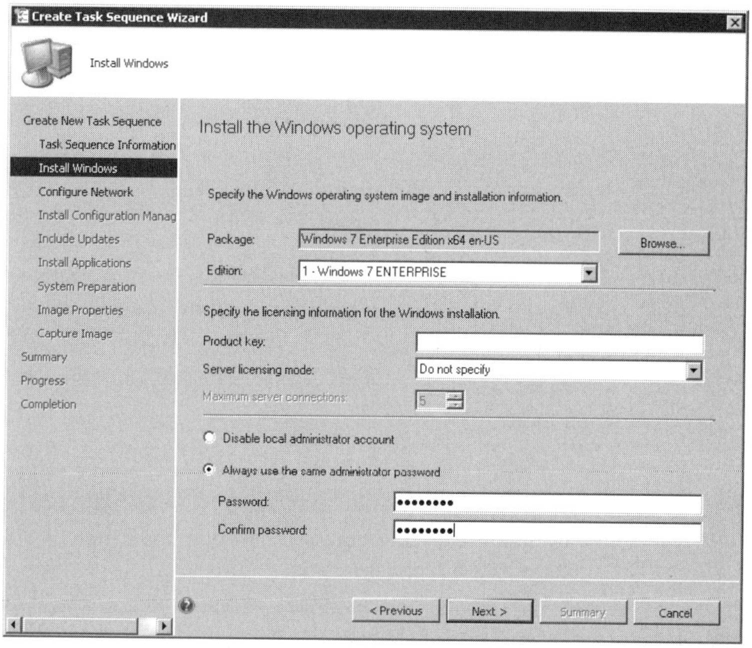

5. Click Next to move to the next page of the wizard.

6. Supply a name for the workgroup that you want to join while building and capturing your operating system.

   Be sure to join a workgroup so that no Group Policies are applied while building and capturing your reference image.

7. Click Next after supplying the name of the workgroup.

8. Select the Configuration Manager 2012 client package, and supply the following installation properties: SMSMP=<siteservername>, as shown in Figure 9.13.

FIGURE 9.13
Install the Configuration Manager 2012 client task

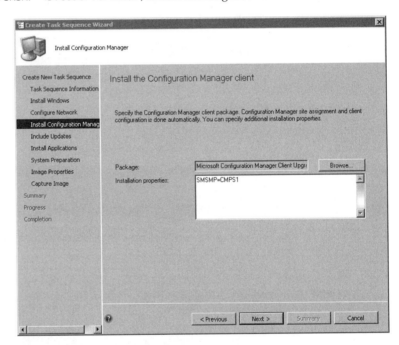

Supplying the installation properties allows you to install approved software updates via the Software Updates feature while the operating system is part of a workgroup.

9. Click Next.

10. Decide whether you want to install software updates during the build-and-capture process.

    Best practice is that you install all software updates that are approved in the Software Updates feature in Configuration Manager.

11. Click Next to be able to select the application that you want to install while building and capturing your reference operating system image, click Next.

12. Depending on the source of your operating system, you may need to supply a system preparation tool; click Next.

When deploying Windows XP SP3, you need to use Sysprep to seal and make the operating system anonymous before capturing. Windows 7 and Windows Server 2008 have a built-in system preparation tool.

13. Supply information about the image, such as creator, version, and description, and click Next.

14. Supply a UNC path and a filename for the captured operating system image, as shown in Figure 9.14, and click Next.

FIGURE 9.14
Captured image
path and filename

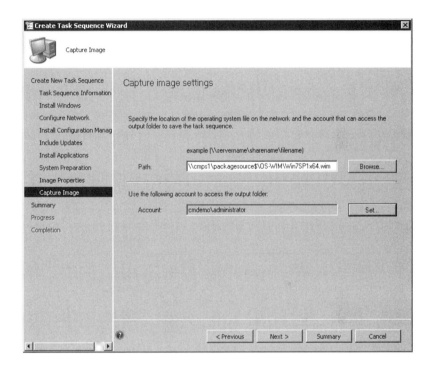

15. Supply an account with Write permission to the share where the image will be captured.

16. Click Next to see the summary.

17. After reviewing the summary, click Next to create the task sequence.

18. When finished, click Close.

Task Sequences Used with Media Boot

If you do not want to enable PXE support on your distribution points or you want to capture a custom reference computer, you are also able to create a build-and-capture task sequence that runs from media. Follow these steps to create a task sequence for creating a capture image:

1. From within the Configuration Manager console, choose the Software Library workspace, expand Overview ➤ Operating Systems, and select Task Sequences.

2. From the Home tab of the Ribbon, click Create Task Sequence Media. This opens the Select Media Type page, shown in Figure 9.15.

FIGURE 9.15
Create Task Sequence Media Wizard— Select Media Type page

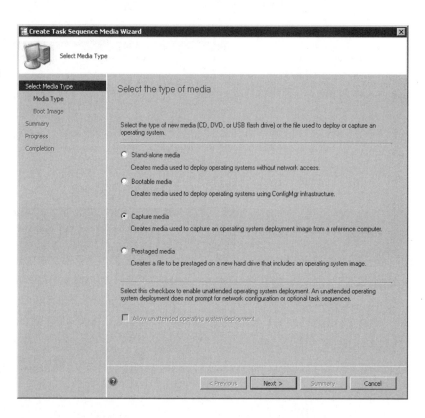

3. On the Select Media Type page, select Capture Media, and then click Next.

   By selecting Capture Media, you will be creating the capture media that will be used to capture the operating system image.

   On the wizard's Media Type page, shown in Figure 9.16, you can select the type of media to create.

FIGURE 9.16

Create Task Sequence
Media Wizard—Media
Type page

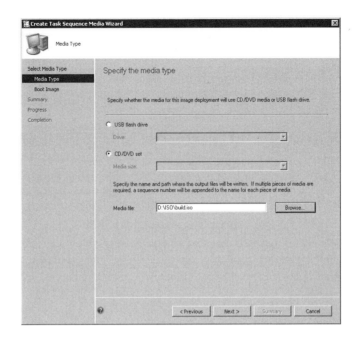

4. For this example, select CD/DVD Set, specify the media file location, and click Next.

5. On the Boot Image page, shown in Figure 9.17, specify the boot image and distribution point you want to use. Click Browse, and select the boot image and click Browse to select the distribution point. Click Next to continue.

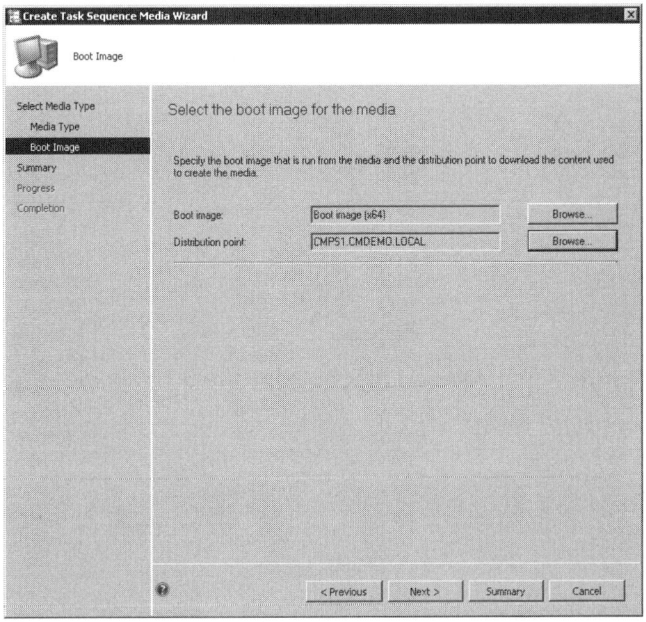

FIGURE 9.17

Create Task Sequence
Media Wizard—Boot
Image page

6. Click Next on the Summary page, and Configuration Manager 2012 will begin creating the capture media ISO file.

7. Finally, you will be presented with the Wizard Completed page; click Close.

You can now burn that ISO file to a CD and use that CD to boot up the computers in which you will be building your operating system image.

Capturing an Operating System Image

Configuration Manager 2012 supports two different ways of capturing an operating system image. You can use the fully automatic way, by using the build-and-capture task sequence, or you can capture a custom reference computer, by using the capture media created earlier.

Building and Capturing Automatically

When building and capturing an operating system image with the specially designed build-and-capture task sequence, you can fully automate the build-and-capture process. This way you know that the result of a task sequence is always the same, and no user intervention is necessary.

To be able to use the build-and-capture task sequence created earlier, you need to make the task sequence available for deployment, as follows:

1. From within the Configuration Manager console, choose the Software Library workspace, expand Overview ➤ Operating Systems, and select Task Sequences.

2. Select the build-and-capture task sequence, and click Deploy on the Home tab of the Ribbon.

3. Specify the collection where the reference computer resides, and select the distribution point(s) where the content needs to be deployed to, as shown in Figure 9.18.

FIGURE 9.18
Specify deployment information

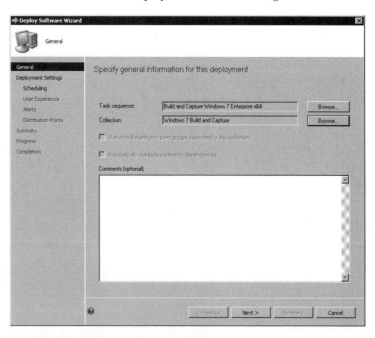

Be sure that you create a special collection for building and capturing operating systems.

4. Click Next to proceed in the wizard.

Now you need to configure the deployment settings; for Purpose you can select either Available or Required. If you choose Available, you need to press F12 to enter the PXE boot procedure and select the task sequence in the WinPE environment. If you choose Required, the machine will boot into WinPE during the PXE boot procedure. Click Next.

5. Select the option Make Available To Boot Media And PXE, as shown in Figure 9.19, and click Next to configure the deployment settings.

FIGURE 9.19

Specify the deployment settings

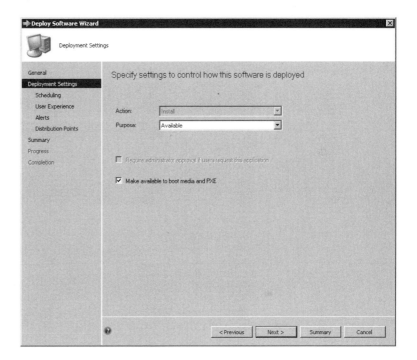

6. Configure the scheduling settings, and click Next.

7. Since you are configuring a deployment for a build-and-capture task sequence, no user experience options need to be configured, so click Next.

8. Configure Alerts options for failed deployments; you are able to set a threshold for alerts to be sent when the threshold is higher than percentage of failed deployments. Click Next to proceed.

9. Configure the distribution point settings, and click Next to review the summary.

10. After reviewing the summary, click Next and then Close.

After making the build-and-capture task sequence available for deployment, you can go into action and build and capture the image. To begin, shut down your reference computer and be sure that you can boot from the network. To cause less overhead on drivers, building and capturing images is often done with virtual machines. To use the following procedure, be sure that your computer object in Configuration Manager is added to the collection where the task sequence is deployed to.

1. Start your computer or virtual machine and boot into PXE.

2. At the Welcome To This Task Sequence screen, click Next.

3. Select the build-and-capture Windows 7 Enterprise x64 Task sequence, as shown in Figure 9.20, and click Next.

FIGURE 9.20
Select the task sequence

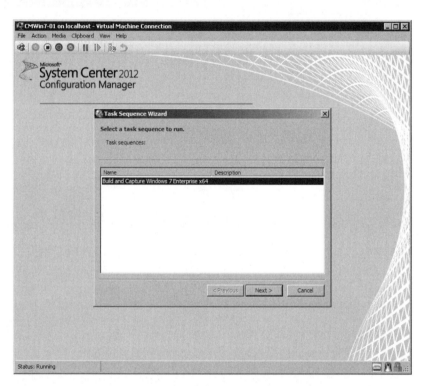

After the build-and-capture process, described earlier, has finished, you will have your captured Windows image. The computer will restart in Windows.

The captured WIM image can be used for deployment to the computers in your environment. Be sure to always test your deployment in a test environment.

Capturing a Reference Computer

When creating an image of a reference computer, you need to be aware of a few issues. First, ensure that the computer is a member of a workgroup instead of a member of the domain. This is a required step; if the reference computer is a member of the domain, you will be required to remove it from the domain to create the image of the operating system of the computer. Second, we recommend removing the Configuration Manager client from the machine. This is not a requirement, just a recommendation. Another item that is recommended is to blank the local administrator password.

1. To begin creating an image of the reference computer, insert the CD that was created from the ISO file you created earlier.

2. Run TSMBAutorun.exe located in the SMS\Bin\i386 or SMS\Bin\x64 folder on the CD. This opens the Image Capture Wizard.

3. Click Next to open the Image Destination page, shown in Figure 9.21, which allows you to specify where to copy the image when the capture is completed.

FIGURE 9.21
Image Capture Wizard—
Image Destination page

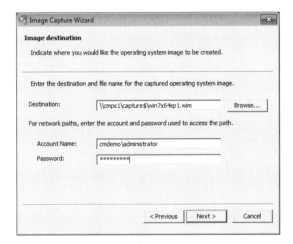

4. Fill in the correct information, and click Next.

As you can see, we copy the WIM file to our site server.

You will now be able to add some information about the image on the Image Information page. You can fill in the Created By, Version, and Description fields for the WIM file.

5. Fill in this information with as much detail as you can; then click Next.

6. On the Summary page, click Finish to begin the capture phase.

An Installation Progress window appears, telling you that the Image Capture Wizard is working and running in the background. When the image capture is complete, a System Restart message will appear, and the system will reboot. When the system reboots, it will boot into WinPE and begin capturing the system. This process can be a lengthy one, so be patient while the operating system is being captured.

Once the image capture is complete, you will see the Image Capture Wizard success message, shown in Figure 9.22.

FIGURE 9.22
Image capture
success message

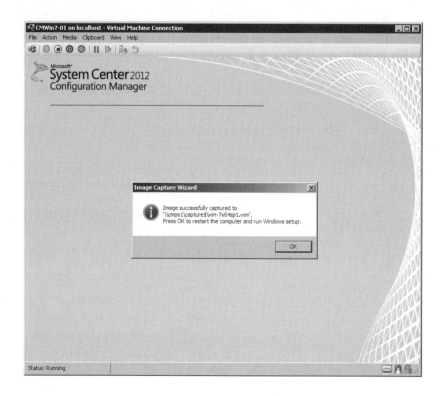

7. Clicking OK will allow the machine to reboot and return to the operating system.

Deploying an Image

Since you've now successfully captured an image, you need to add this operating system image to Configuration Manager. Then you need to deploy this image by creating a task sequence and deploy this task sequence to the computers in your environment. Always be sure to thoroughly test the image in a separate test environment before deploying it into production.

Adding a Captured Image

The WIM file that you just created needs to be added as an available operating system for Configuration Manager 2012. To deploy this image, follow this procedure:

1. From within the Configuration Manager console, select the Software Library workspace, expand Overview ➢ Operating Systems, and select Operating System Images.

2. Click Add Operating System Image on the Home tab of the Ribbon.

   This opens the Add Operating System Image Wizard's Data Source page.

3. Ensure that the (UNC) Path field points to the location where the WIM file was created, and click Next.

   The General page allows you to customize the Name, Version, and Comments fields for the image file.

4. Fill in the appropriate information, and click Next.

5. The Summary page will be displayed; review the information and click Next.

6. Finally the Wizard Completed screen will appear. On this page, click Close.

Distributing and Deploying the Image

Next, you need to configure a distribution point in order to distribute this image. This step is a little different from the steps for assigning distribution points for packages that we discussed elsewhere in this book:

1. From within the Configuration Manager console, choose the Software Library workspace, expand Overview ➤ Operating Systems, and select Operating System Images.

2. Select the image that you added, and click Distribute Content on the Home tab of the Ribbon.

3. In the Distribute Content Wizard click Next.

4. Click Add and select Distribution Point or Distribution Point Group.

5. Select in the Add Distribution Points or Add Distribution Point Groups dialog the distribution points or groups that you want to distribute the WIM image to, and click OK.

6. Click Next to review the summary.

7. After reviewing the summary, click Next and then Close.

Developing a Task Sequence for Deployment

Now you will need to create a task sequence for deploying the Windows operating system image. Creating a task sequence will give Configuration Manager 2012 a series of steps to perform on the new installation of the workstation:

1. From within the Configuration Manager console, select the Software Library workspace, expand Overview ➤ Operating Systems, and select Task Sequences.

2. Select Create Task Sequence on the Home tab of the Ribbon.

   This will open the New Task Sequence Wizard's Create A New Task Sequence page.

3. Because you have already built an image of a Windows client, select Install An Existing Image Package, and then click Next.

   This opens the New Task Sequence Wizard's Task Sequence Information page.

4. Specify the task sequence name and a comment, and specify the boot image to use during the installation of the image. Click on Next after supplying the information.

   The Install Windows page, shown in Figure 9.23, allows you to specify the Configuration Manager 2012 image package containing the operating system you want to install.

FIGURE 9.23
Create Task Sequence
Wizard—Install
Windows page

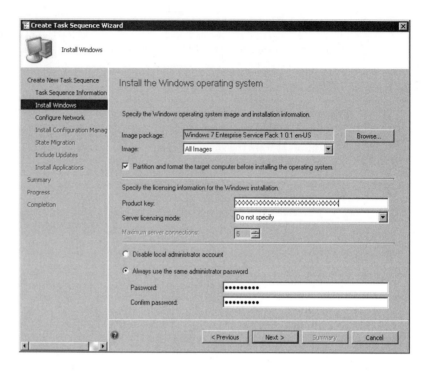

5. Click the Browse button to find the image of the operating system you want to install, and click OK.

6. If you want to partition and format the target computer before installing the operating system, leave the Partition box selected, and format the target computer before installing the operating system.

7. Enter the licensing information for the version of Windows you are installing in the Product Key field, and click Next.

8. On the Configure The Network page, select the domain or workgroup to join.

   If you select to join a domain, you can specify which OU to put the computer in once it joins the domain. If you select to join a domain, you will need to specify the account that has permission to join computers to a domain. The Configuration Manager Network Access account is often used to join the computer to the domain. You need to delegate this access to the user account.

9. Click Next to continue.

   Now all the work you did earlier will finally be put to use.

10. On the Install Configuration Manager Client page, specify any additional packages you want to install once the operating system has been installed on the workstation.

   This will allow you to use the Microsoft Configuration Manager client upgrade package you configured earlier in this chapter.

11. Click the Browse button, select Microsoft Configuration Manager Client Upgrade, and click OK.

    This brings you back to the Install Configuration Manager Client page, where you can specify additional installation properties.

12. Then click Next to continue.

    The Create Task Sequence Wizard page that appears is State Migration, shown in Figure 9.24, which allows you to configure the user state migration capture.

FIGURE 9.24

Create Task Sequence Wizard— State Migration page

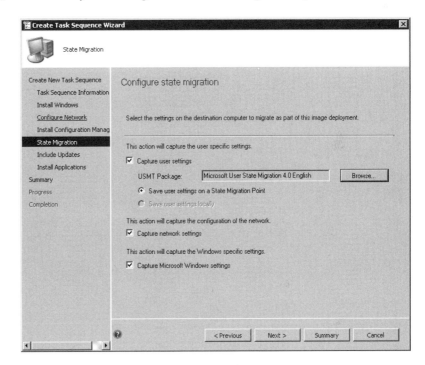

13. Select or deselect whether you want to capture network and Microsoft Windows settings.

14. Click Browse, select the USMT package created earlier in this chapter, and then click Next.

    After you've configured the state migration, the Include Updates In Image page will appear, which allows you to specify whether the client will get mandatory, all, or no software updates after the image has been installed.

15. Configure the installation of software updates, and click Next.

    Now you have the option to install additional applications by adding the configured applications to the task sequence. This is extremely useful if you have a large number of applications you want installed on each system after the operating system has been installed. Figure 9.25 shows the Install Applications page, where you can specify the additional applications.

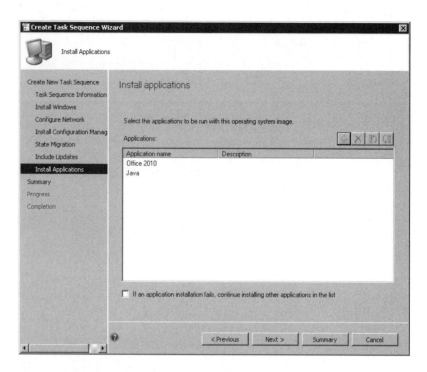

16. Select the option If An Application Installation Fails, Continue Installing Other Applications In The List, if you want to let the task sequence proceed with its tasks.

17. Select Next once you have the additional applications specified.

18. Click Next on the Summary page, and Configuration Manager 2012 will complete the Create Task Sequence Wizard.

19. Click Close.

Deploying the Task Sequence

You have successfully created a new task sequence to install a new operating system on a machine, join the system to the domain, and install the Configuration Manager 2012 client on the machine once it comes online. However, the task sequence won't do you any good unless you deploy it to a collection. Take the following steps:

1. From within the Configuration Manager console, choose the Software Library workspace, expand Overview ➤ Operating Systems, and select Task Sequences.

2. Select the task sequence you want to deploy, and click Deploy on the Home tab of the Ribbon.

3. Click Deploy to open the General page of the Deploy Software Wizard.

4. Click Browse to find the collection where you want to install this operating system package, and then click Next to continue.

The next wizard page is Deployment Settings, shown in Figure 9.26.

FIGURE 9.26
Deploy Software
Wizard—Deployment
Settings page

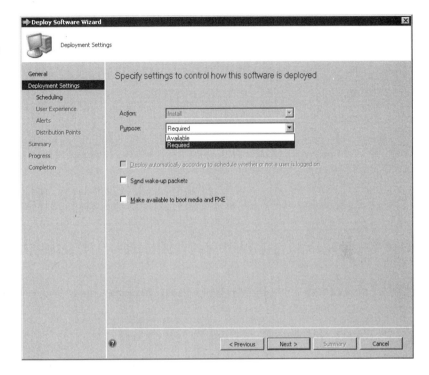

5. Supply the purpose of the deployment.

   ◆ If you want to let your users choose to reinstall their operating system, choose the Available option.

   ◆ If you want the installation to start automatically, choose the Required option.

   Choosing the Required option enables you to send wake-up packets to the computers in the collection. Of course, you need to first configure Wake On LAN support in Configuration Manager 2012. At this time you do not need to enable the option for PXE support; the task sequence we are creating is used to refresh your Windows installation.

6. Click Next to continue.

   The next step is to configure the scheduling options for the deployment.

7. Configure the availability of the deployment and when the deployment will expire.

8. Define the assignment schedule, and be sure to set the rerun behavior to Rerun if the previous attempt failed.

   If you do not set this option, the deployment will rerun as soon the deployment is finished, thereby creating a deployment loop.

9. Click Next to proceed.

10. On the User Experience page, specify how users are notified about the deployment and how they interact with the deployment.

    We prefer to show the task sequence progress to let the end user know that the computer is being reloaded.

11. Click Next to proceed and configure the Alerts options for this deployment.

12. Click Next and configure how to run the content for this deployment on the Distribution Points page, and click Next.

13. Review the summary, click Next, and click Close when the wizard has finished processing the deployment.

Now you have advertised the operating system deployment, and any system in the collection you specified will get the new advertisement during the next policy refresh. Once the policy refresh takes place, the workstation will receive the Assigned Program About To Run notification. Once the installation begins, you will see the Installation Progress message box in Windows, as shown in Figure 9.27.

FIGURE 9.27
Installation
Progress
message box

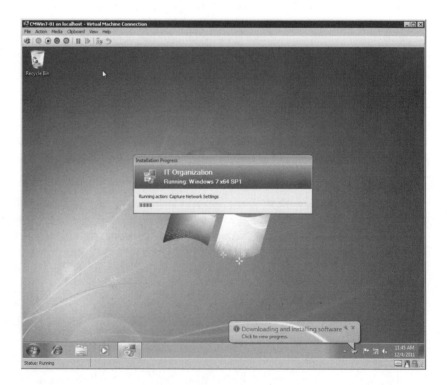

The system will automatically reboot and then begin the boot to WinPE, as shown in Figure 9.28.

FIGURE 9.28

Booting to WinPE

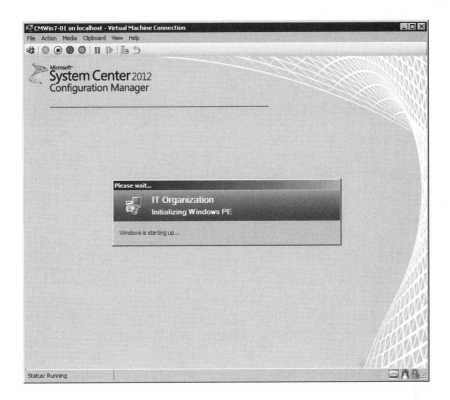

The installation will take some time to complete. During this install, Configuration Manager is gathering the user state and saving the date in the USMT folder on the site server, which you configured earlier in this chapter. You can monitor the `<drive>:\USMTData` folder on the site server to see the user state migration data being copied to the server.

Configuration Manager will push the new operating system down to the new machine and then join it to the domain, install the Configuration Manger client, and finally copy back all the user data on the client.

You can monitor the progress of the operating system deployment in the Deployment Status window, shown in Figure 9.29.

FIGURE 9.29
Monitoring the
OSD advertisement
status

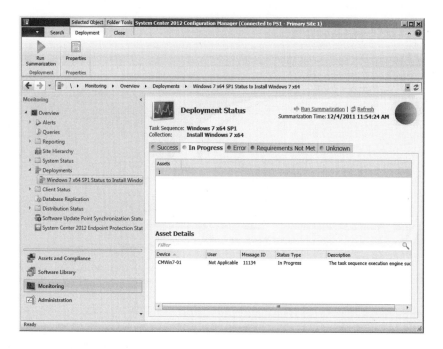

1. From within the Configuration Manager console, choose the Monitoring workspace, expand Overview ➤ Deployments, and select the deployment that you want to monitor.

2. After selecting the deployment, click Run Summarization on the Home tab of the Ribbon.

3. After the summarization is updated, click View Status on the Home tab of the Ribbon to see the status of the deployment, as shown in Figure 9.29.

4. While viewing the status, you can refresh the status by clicking Run Summarization or Refresh.

Deploying the Operating System on Bare Metal

After deploying an operating system in a refresh scenario, you also need to create a task sequence and deployment to be able to deploy an operating system to bare-metal computers. Bare-metal computers are computers without any operating system present.

To deploy an operating system to a bare-metal computer, you can use a CD or DVD to start into WinPE, but you can also boot into PXE to start the WinPE image from the network. Let's see how this works with PXE. To be able to deploy an operating system to a bare-metal computer, you need to perform the following tasks:

◆ Import information about a computer.

◆ Create a task sequence.

◆ Deploy the task sequence.

Importing Computer Information

Now you are ready to set up a computer association so that Configuration Manager can identify the bare-metal machines that will receive a fresh install. To specify the computer association, you will need to open the Configuration Manager console and proceed as follows:

1. From within the Configuration Manager console, choose the Assets and Compliance workspace and expand Overview ➤ Devices.

2. Click Import Computer Information on the Home tab of the Ribbon.

    This will allow you to import a single computer or import many systems from a comma-separated values (CSV) file.

3. Select the option Import Single Computer, and click Next.

    This will bring up the Single Computer page, as shown in Figure 9.30.

FIGURE 9.30
Import Computer Information Wizard—Single Computer page

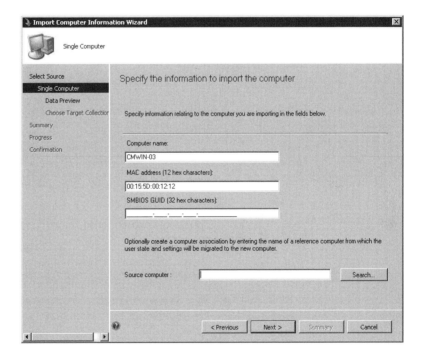

You must enter the computer name along with either the MAC address or the SMBIOS GUID. The computer name is just how the machine will appear in the collections, not what the actual computer will be named.

4. Fill in the appropriate information, and then click Next.

5. This sends you to the Data Preview page; check the information and click Next.

    You'll then see the Choose Target Collection page.

6. Here, specify which collection you want to add to this new machine.

   It is extremely important to put all the bare-metal installs into the same collection, used only for bare-metal deployment.

7. Click Next.

8. After specifying the collection, you will see the Summary page. Click Next, and then click Close on the Finish page.

Creating a Task Sequence for the Bare-Metal OSD

When you deploy a bare-metal machine, it is wise to create a dedicated task sequence for this purpose. Once you create this special task sequence, you need to deploy it to a special collection in which you can place the bare-metal computers.

Creating a task sequence for deploying an image to a new machine is very straightforward:

1. From within the Configuration Manager console, choose the Software Library workspace, expand Overview ➢ Operating Systems, and select Task Sequences.

2. From there, click New Task Sequence on the Home tab of the Ribbon of the Configuration Manager console.

   This opens the Create A New Task Sequence page of the New Task Sequence Wizard.

3. Select the Install An Existing Image Package option, and click Next.

4. On the Task Sequence Information page, fill in the name, optionally add a comment, and select the boot image you want to use for the operating system deployment and click Next.

5. On the Install The Windows Operating System page, select the image package by browsing to the correct image.

6. Because this example is deploying Windows to a bare-metal machine, enable the option to partition and format the target computer.

   The next options you can configure are the network settings.

7. On the Configure The Network page, specify whether you want to join the new machine to the domain or join a workgroup, click Next after configuring the network settings.

   A Configuration Manager task sequence will allow you to install the Configuration Manager client during an operating system deployment.

8. On the Install The Configuration Manager Client page, select the client installation package you created earlier in this chapter, and click Next.

9. Since you are deploying Windows to a bare-metal machine, on the State Migration page, shown in Figure 9.31, deselect all the options because you do not need to worry about

capturing any data from these machines. Click Next to configure the installation of software updates.

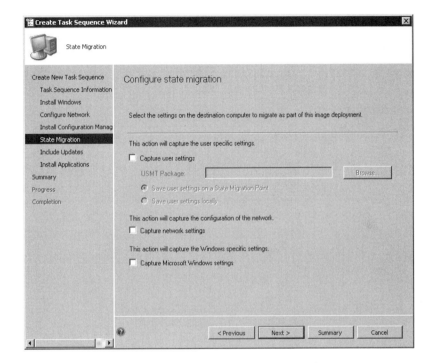

On the Include Updates In Image page, you can now allow Configuration Manager to include software updates during the install.

10. Make the selections you desire, and click Next.

If you have any additional applications you want to deploy, such as Microsoft Office or anything else, on the Install Applications page, you can add any applications to install on the machine after the operating system has been deployed.

11. Click Next to view the Summary page.

12. After viewing the summary, click Next and then Close to complete the wizard.

Deploying the Bare-Metal Task Sequence

After creating the task sequence for bare-metal deployment, you need to deploy this task sequence, as discussed earlier. Be sure to enable the option that allows booting into available boot media and PXE.

USING THE UNKNOWN COMPUTER COLLECTION

You can enable support for unknown computers. Unknown computers is a feature in Configuration Manager 2012 that will allow unmanaged systems to be managed with Configuration Manager 2012 during an OS deployment. To do so, open the Configuration Manager console, select the Administration workspace, and expand Overview ➢ Site Configuration ➢ Servers And Site System Roles. Select the server with the distribution point where PXE is enabled, and click Role Properties in the Site Role section of the Ribbon. Browse to the PXE tab in the Distribution Point Properties dialog box, shown here, and select the box Enable Unknown Computer Support.

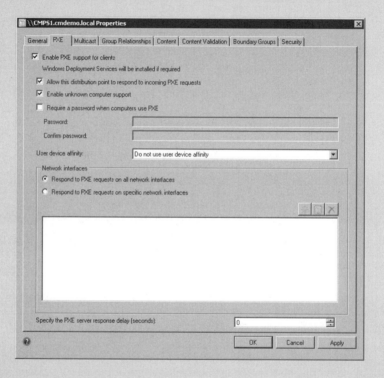

When you enable this option, you will be prompted with the caution message shown next. Assuming you are ready to proceed, click OK.

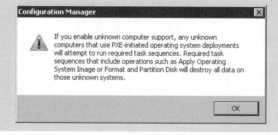

To create a task sequence for bootable media, open the Configuration Manager console, choose the Software Library workspace, and expand Overview ➤ Operating System ➤ Task Sequences. Click Create Task Sequence Media on the Home tab of the Ribbon. This opens the Create Task Sequence Media Wizard's Select Media Type page.

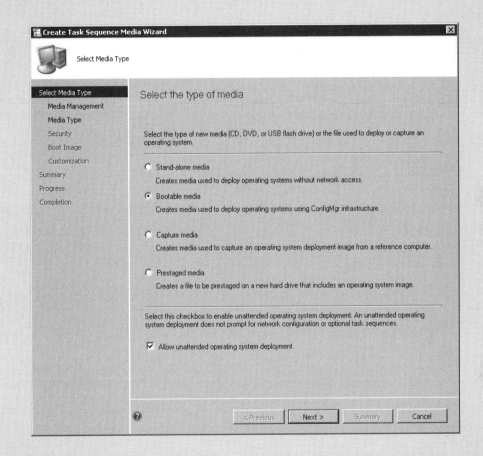

Select Bootable Media, and click Next. Choose Dynamic Media when the media contacts a management point, which redirects the client to a different management point based on the client location in the site boundaries, or choose site-based media when you want to specify a management point. Click next to configure the media type. On the Media Type page, select the type of media you will be using, either a USB flash drive or a CD/DVD set, and then click Next. The Security page offers the Enable Unknown Computer Support option. Selecting this will allow you to target the unknown computer collection with the operating system deployment.

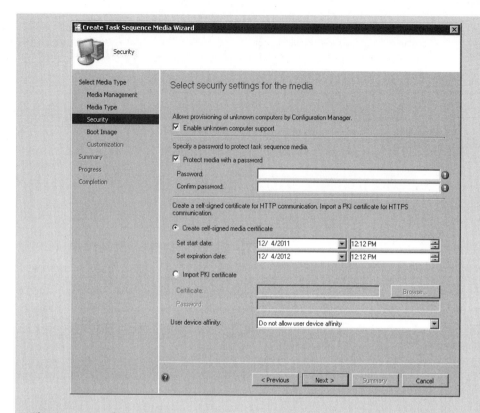

The next step, after configuring unknown computer support, is configuring the boot image, distribution point, associated management points, and customizations.

After creating the boot media you can create a deployment to this collection for the OSD task sequence, and Configuration Manager will process the task sequence for the unknown computers. Be sure to enable your deployment to be accessible for boot media and PXE.

Installing Device Drivers into OSD

Now you have configured one package to perform Windows upgrades and another package to install that same Windows install package onto a bare-metal system. But what happens if you get a new system with a completely new setup, including device drivers that are not installed within the current package, so that when the machine comes online it will not be able to attach to the network?

Microsoft has provided the ability to import device drivers into Configuration Manager 2012 and add them to the boot images or driver packages so they can be installed as part of the operating system deployment task. To import Windows device drivers, take the following steps:

1. From within the Configuration Manager console, choose the Software Library workspace, expand Overview ➤ Operating Systems, and select Drivers.

2. Click Import Driver on the Home tab of the Ribbon of the Configuration Manager console.

   This opens the Locate Driver page, shown in Figure 9.32.

FIGURE 9.32
Import
New Driver
Wizard—
Locate
Driver page

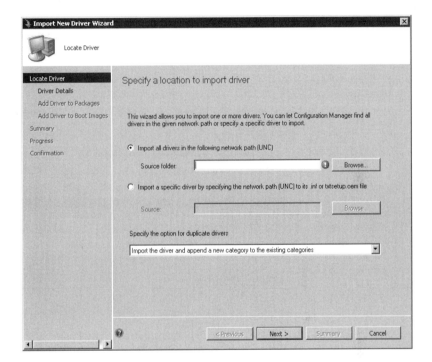

3. You can specify to import all drivers or just a single device driver. When importing drivers you could run into the fact that there are duplicate drivers. Next you should configure the import behavior when duplicate drivers are detected; you can configure the following options.

   ◆ Import the drivers and append a new category to the existing categories.

   ◆ Import the driver and keep the existing categories.

   ◆ Import the driver and overwrite the existing categories.

   ◆ Do not import the driver.

4. Click Next after picking the correct driver(s), and then you will be presented with the Driver Details page. Next you should assign the driver(s) to one or more categories.

> **WORKING WITH CATEGORIES ENABLES YOU TO MANAGE DRIVERS**
>
> If you add categories to drivers, you can manage your drivers in the store more easily. By adding the category to the search criteria, you can easily select the drivers and delete them by clicking Delete on the Home tab of the Ribbon in the Configuration Manager console.

5. On the Add Driver To Packages page, shown in Figure 9.33, specify the package(s) you want to add this driver to, or specify a new package. If you need to create a new driver package, do the following:

A. Click New Package.

B. Supply a name and a UNC path for the source of the package.

C. Click OK.

D. If desired, select Update Distribution Points When Finished so the driver will be available as soon as possible to your site.

FIGURE 9.33
Import
New Driver
Wizard—Add
Driver To
Packages page

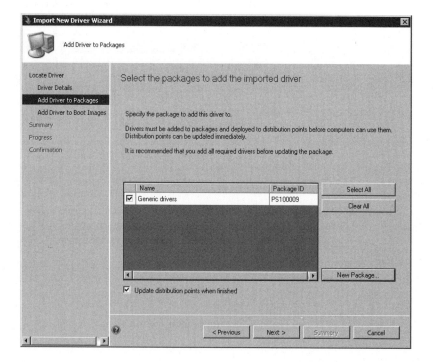

6. Click Next to continue.

7. Next select which boot images you want to add the driver to, as shown in Figure 9.34.

FIGURE 9.34
Adding drivers
to boot images

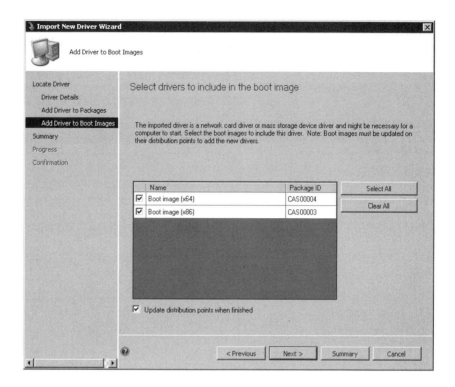

8. Clicking Next opens the Summary page. Review the configuration, click Next, and then click Close.

Now Configuration Manager will inject that driver package into the packages and boot images you selected. This could take some time to process.

Servicing Your Operating System Images Offline

In Configuration Manager 2007 you needed a tool called Deployment Imaging Servicing and Management (DISM)—a command-line tool used to maintain and update your images offline. Configuration Manager 2012 comes with the ability to update your operating system images from the console. This feature uses the software update point and software update deployments that you configured earlier. Follow the next steps if you want to update a WIM image:

1. From within the Configuration Manager console, select the Software Library workspace, expand Overview ➢ Operating Systems, and select Operating System Images.

2. Select the operating system you want to update, and click Schedule Updates on the Home tab of the Ribbon.

3. Select the updates that you want to install in the Windows image, as shown in Figure 9.35, and click Next.

FIGURE 9.35
Select the updates that you want to install

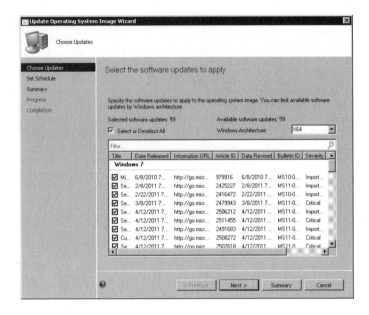

4. Select the schedule (as soon as possible or a custom schedule) for the update process, and click Next.

5. Review the summary, and click Next. Click Close when the process of scheduling the updates is finished.

The process of updating the Windows image can take a while; you can view the status of the process in the Schedule Update Status column in the Configuration Manager console. Once the update is finished, you can view the installed updates in the console, as shown in Figure 9.36.

FIGURE 9.36
View the installed updates in the Windows image

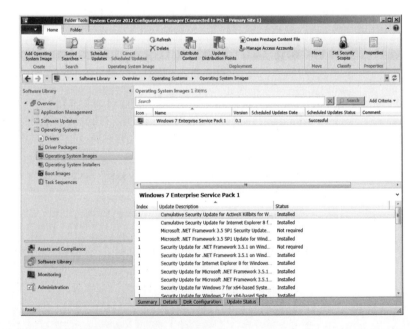

MONITOR AND TROUBLESHOOTING OFFLINE SERVICING

You can use the OfflineServicingMgr.log file in the logs folder of the Configuration Manager 2012 installation folder to monitor or troubleshoot while offline servicing your images.

You are also able to monitor the offline servicing by accessing the properties of the WIM image and viewing the servicing tab, as shown in the following image. You are also able to change the schedule if you have scheduled the offline servicing.

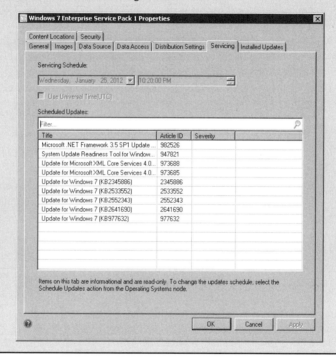

Using User Device Affinity

As discussed earlier, user device affinity enables you to deploy user-targeted applications during the operating system deployment process. There are several ways to configure user device affinity. Let's look at the following options:

- ◆ Manually configure a primary user for a device.
- ◆ Manually configure a primary device for a user.
- ◆ Configure a site to automatically create user device affinities.
- ◆ Import user device affinities.
- ◆ Enable users to configure their primary device.

Manually Configure a Primary User for a Device

To manually configure a primary user for a device, follow this procedure:

1. From within the Configuration Manager console, choose the Assets and Compliance workspace, expand Overview, and select Devices.

2. Select a device, and click Edit Primary Users on the Home tab of the Ribbon. Search for the user, as shown in Figure 9.37, select the user, and click Add and then OK to set the primary user for the device.

FIGURE 9.37
Search for
and select the
primary user

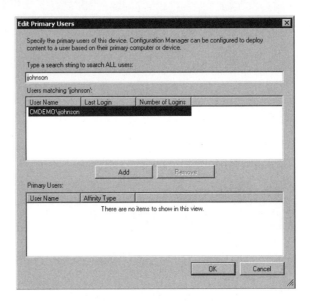

Manually Configure a Primary Device for a User

To manually configure a primary device for a user, follow these steps:

1. From within the Configuration Manager console, select the Assets and Compliance workspace, expand Overview, and select Users.

2. Select a user, and click Edit Primary Devices on the Home tab of the Ribbon. Search for the device, select the device, and click Add and then OK to set the primary device for the user.

Configure a Site to Automatically Create User Device Affinities

With Configuration Manager 2012 you can also create the user device affinity automatically. Creating the affinity automatically is based on thresholds configured in the client settings. Configuring the client settings to create user device affinities is described here:

1. From within the Configuration Manager console, choose the Administration workspace, expand Overview, and select Client Settings.

2. Select the default client agent settings package or create a new client device agent settings package, and click Properties on the Home tab of the Ribbon.

3. Select User And Device Affinity, as shown in Figure 9.38, and configure the following options:

    User Device Affinity Usage Threshold (Minutes)   Configure the number of minutes of usage by a user before a user device affinity is created.

    User Device Affinity Usage Threshold (Days)   Configure the number of days over which the configured minutes that the device is used are measured. For example, if User Device Affinity Usage Threshold (Minutes) is configured with a value of 120 minutes and User Device Affinity Usage Threshold (Days) is set to 14 days, the user must use the device for 120 minutes over a period of 14 days before the user device affinity is created.

    Automatically Configure Used Device Affinity From Usage Data   Enable the feature by setting the value to True, or disable the feature by setting the value to False.

FIGURE 9.38
Configure client
device settings

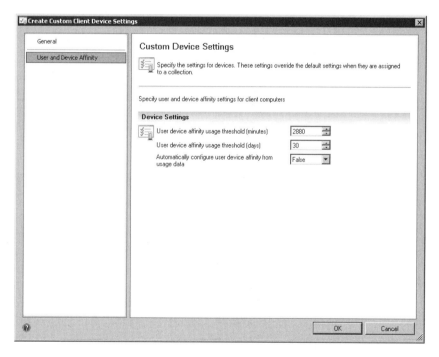

Import User Device Affinities

If you have the information from your client computers and primary users in a CSV file, you can import the user device affinity information to Configuration Manager 2012.

1. From within the Configuration Manager console, select the Assets and Compliance workspace, expand Overview, and select Devices Or Users.

2. On the Home tab of the Ribbon select Import User Device Affinity.

3. Browse and select the CSV file containing the information that you want to import, and click Open. The format of the CSV file must be <user name>,<domain name \device name>.

4. Check in the File Preview section of the Choose Mapping page of the wizard to see if the column mapping is configured correctly, as shown in Figure 9.39, and click Next twice. Click Close after reviewing the results.

FIGURE 9.39
Check the column mapping

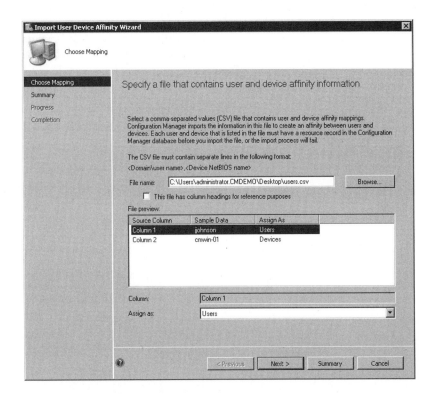

Enable Users To Configure Their Primary Device

Another option is to configure the Configuration Manager 2012 site to let the users define their own user device affinities. This is done as follows:

1. From within the Configuration Manager console, select the Administration workspace, expand Overview, and select Client Settings.

2. Select the default client agent settings package or create a new client device agent settings package. Then click Properties on the Home tab of the Ribbon.

3. Select User And Device Affinity, and set the option Allow Users To Define Their Primary Devices to True. Setting the option to False will disable the feature.

From now on, the users can configure their user device affinity by selecting the I Regularly Use This Computer To Do My Work option in the My Systems tab of the Application Catalog website.

Pre-deploy User Applications

After configuring user device affinity for a client computer, the pre-deploy of user targeted applications that are targeted to the primary user are pre-deployed automatically during deployment of the OS. Be sure to configure, while deploying the application to a user, the option to enable the Deploy Automatically According To Schedule With Or Without User Login, and set the Purpose to Required, as shown in Figure 9.40. You will find more information about deploying applications in Chapter 6, "Client Installation."

FIGURE 9.40
Configure deployment settings

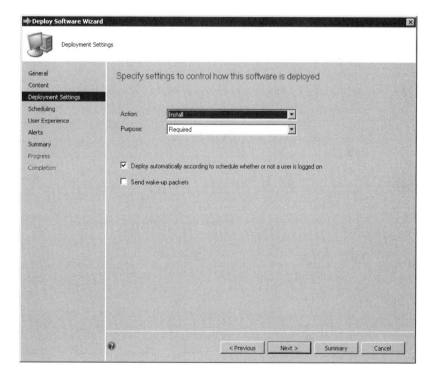

Microsoft Deployment Toolkit 2012

The Microsoft Deployment Toolkit 2012 is a solution accelerator that can be integrated with Configuration Manager 2012. The integration gives you the ability to smooth your deployment process with the scripts that come with the Deployment Toolkit. Let's configure the Microsoft Deployment Toolkit integration and see what it offers us when deploying operating systems.

The Microsoft Deployment Toolkit includes extra deployment scenarios that are built with a Task Sequence Wizard, such as the following:

Replace Hardware Scenario This scenario enables you to capture the user state from an old client computer and place it while deploying the new operating system on the new client computer.

Server Deployment Scenario This scenario allows you to deploy Windows-based servers and their roles.

User-Driven Installation Scenario This scenario allows your users to use a simple User Driven Installation (UDI) Wizard to initiate and customize an OS deployment on their PCs that's tailored to their individual needs.

The wizard uses existing supporting packages like the boot image, the Microsoft Deployment Toolkit, or the User State Migration Package or allows you to create new packages while configuring the task sequence.

Installing Microsoft Deployment Toolkit 2012

The Microsoft Deployment Toolkit is a free tool that you can download from the Microsoft Download site. Install the `MicrosoftDeploymentToolkit2012_x64.msi` or `MicrosoftDeploymentToolkit2012_x86.msi` file on your site system. It's a straightforward Next, Next, Finish installation. You need to install the Microsoft Deployment Toolkit on every site server that you want to integrate with.

Integrating the Deployment Toolkit

To be able to use the deployment intelligence of the Microsoft Deployment Toolkit in Configuration Manager 2012, you need to integrate the Deployment Toolkit with Configuration Manager. This is done by following these steps.

1. After installing the Microsoft Deployment Toolkit 2012 on your site system, choose Start ➢ All Programs ➢ Microsoft Deployment Toolkit.

2. Click Configure ConfigMgr Integration to start the integration tool.

3. Configure the integration as shown in Figure 9.41.

FIGURE 9.41
Configure the integration

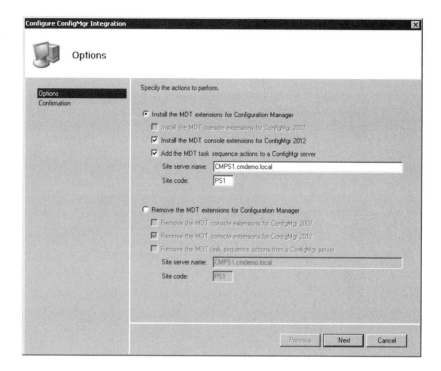

4. Select the Install The MDT Console Extensions For ConfigMgr 2012 and Add The MDT Task Sequence Actions To A ConfigMgr Server. Next, configure the Site Server Name, Site Code, and click Next.

5. Review the summary, and click Finish.

Creating a New Boot Image

To add scripting, WMI, XML, and ADO support to your boot images, you need to re-create the boot images for your deployment. Follow the next steps to re-create the Microsoft Deployment Toolkit boot images. You can also create a boot image with the Microsoft Deployment Toolkit integration features while creating a new Microsoft Deployment Toolkit task sequence.

1. From within the Configuration Manager console, choose the Software Library workspace, expand Overview ➤ Operating Systems, and select Boot Images.

2. Click Create Boot Image Using MDT on the Home tab of the Ribbon, and supply the UNC path to the location where you want to store the boot image; click Next.

3. Supply a name, version, and comments, and click Next.

4. Select the platform, Scratch Space, as shown in Figure 9.42, and click Next. The Scratch Space is a RAM drive that is used during OSD.

FIGURE 9.42
Configure the platform and Scratch Space

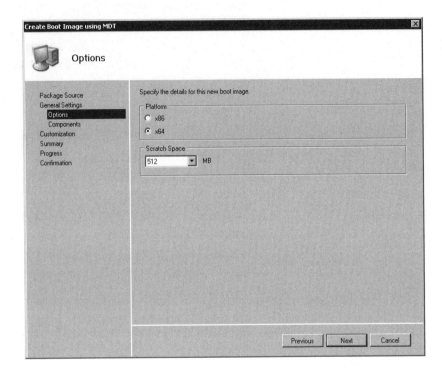

5. Configure the optional languages and components like MDAC/AO support and PPPoE support and click on Next.

6. Configure the customizations, such as the pre-execution hook, custom background image, and command support.

7. Click Next to review the summary.

8. Click Next after reviewing the summary, and click Finish after creating the custom boot image; this process can take awhile.

9. Be sure to enable the boot image for PXE support and the deployment of the boot image to the distribution points.

Creating a Deployment Toolkit Task Sequence

After creating the Microsoft Deployment Toolkit boot images, you need to create a task sequence that you can use to deploy the operating system. In this example we will use the client replace scenario, which consists of two task sequences: the Client Replace task sequence and one based on the New Computer scenario. The New Computer scenario is like the bare-metal scenario, but we also use the User State Migration Toolkit to bring back the user state.

1. From within the Configuration Manager console, choose the Software Library workspace, expand Overview ➤ Operating Systems, and select Task Sequences.

2. Click Create MDT Task Sequence on the Home tab of the Ribbon, and select the Client Replace Task Sequence option. Then click Next.

3. Give the task sequence a name, supply comments, and click Next.

4. Select the boot image that you just created, or create a new boot image using the Create A New Boot Image Package option. Click Next.

    The first time you create a Microsoft Deployment Toolkit task sequence, you will need to create a Microsoft Deployment Toolkit Files package.

5. Select this option and supply a package source folder, as shown in Figure 9.43.

FIGURE 9.43
Create a new Microsoft Deployment Toolkit Files package

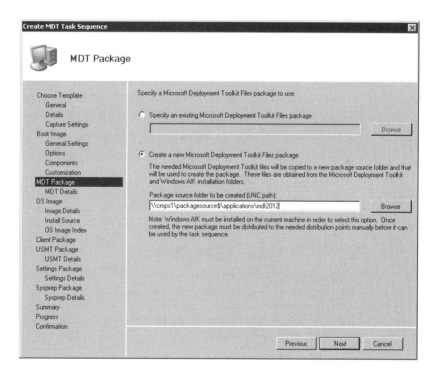

The next time you create a Microsoft Deployment Toolkit task sequence, you can select the Microsoft Deployment Toolkit 2012 package.

6. Click Next.

7. Now you need to supply information about the package. Fill in the name, version language, and manufacturer, and click Next to proceed.

8. Select the User State Migration Toolkit package, and click Next.

9. Select Create A New Settings Package For This Operating System Deployment, supply the UNC path, and click Next.

10. Supply information about the package. Fill in the name, version language, and manufacturer, and click Next to proceed.

11. Review the summary and click Next. Click Finish after you've finished creating the packages and the task sequence.

After creating the Client Replace task sequence, you will need to create a task sequence based on the New Computer scenario.

1. From within the Configuration Manager console, select the Software Library workspace, expand Overview ➢ Operating Systems, and select Task Sequences.

2. Click Create MDT Task Sequence on the Home tab of the Ribbon, and select the Client Task Sequence option. Then click Next.

3. Give the task sequence a name, supply comments, and click Next.

4. Supply the domain information, the account that has permissions to join the domain, and the Windows settings, and then click Next.

5. Select This Task Sequence Will Never Be Used To Capture An Image, and click Next.

6. Select the boot image that you just created, or create a new boot image using the Create A New Boot Image Package option. Click Next.

7. Select the Microsoft Deployment Toolkit 2012 package that you created earlier, and click Next.

8. Select the operating system image you want to deploy, as shown in Figure 9.44, and click Next.

9. Select the Configuration Manager Client 2012 package, and click Next.

10. Select the User State Migration Toolkit package, and click Next.

11. Select Create A New Settings Package For This Operating System Deployment, supply the UNC path, and click Next.

12. Supply information about the package. Fill in the name, version language, and manufacturer, and click Next to proceed.

FIGURE 9.44

Select or create the operating system image you want to deploy

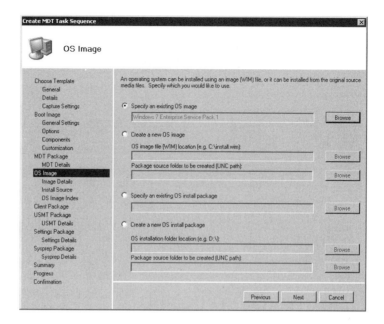

13. Select No Sysprep Package Is Required, and click Next.

14. Review the summary, and click Next.

15. After the task sequence has been created, click Finish.

Using a Replace Scenario

The next step in creating a replace scenario for a computer is creating a computer association. This way the User State Migration Toolkit knows where to place the user state after installing the new computer.

1. From within the Configuration Manager console, select the Assets and Compliance workspace, and expand Overview ➤ Devices.

2. Click Import Computer Information on the Home tab of the Ribbon.

This will allow you to enter a single computer or import many systems from a comma-separated values (CSV) file.

3. Select the option Import Single Computer and click Next. This will bring up the Single Computer page.

You must enter the computer name along with either the MAC address or the SMBIOS GUID. The computer name is just how the machine will appear in the collections, not what the actual computer will be named.

4. Fill in the appropriate information, and select the source computer.

This creates an association with the old computer, and the User State Migration Toolkit knows where to get the user state.

5. After configuring, click Next.

6. On the Data Preview page, check the information and click Next.

7. Next you'll see the Choose Target Collection page. Here specify which collection you want to add to this new machine.

   It is extremely valuable to put all the new computer installs into the same collection, which is used exclusively for new computer deployment.

8. Click Next.

9. After specifying the collection, you will see the Summary page. Review the information, click Next, and then click Close on the Finish page.

Next you need to deploy the task sequences you just have created. The Client Replace task sequence must be deployed to a collection that is especially created for the old client computers. Then you need to deploy the New Computer task sequence to the collection that was specially created for the new computers. The deployment must support booting from PXE, as you learned in the "Deploying the Task Sequence" section earlier in this chapter.

Maintaining the User State

When you browse to the User State Migration node in the Assets and Compliance workspace, as shown in Figure 9.45, you can manage computer associations. In this workspace you can create new computer associations, as mentioned earlier, and see recovery information, find information about the user state migration, or specify the user accounts.

FIGURE 9.45
Managing the user state

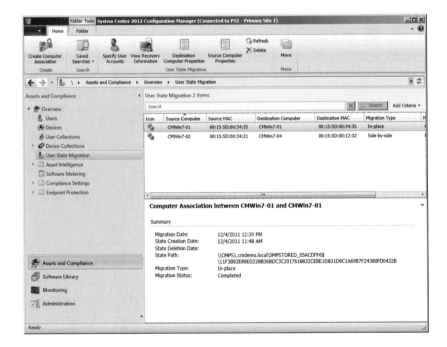

Specifying the user accounts is done as follows:

1. From within the Configuration Manager console, choose the Assets and Compliance workspace and expand Overview ➢ User State Migration.

2. Select the User State Migration item, and click Specify User Accounts to add user accounts for which data needs to be migrated.

3. Click the starburst icon, and on the Add User Account screen click Browse. Search for the user and click OK twice.

4. Click OK to set the user account to migrate.

From this view you are also able to create Computer Associations when, for instance, migrating user state data from one computer to an existing computer that is being reinstalled.

 **Real World Scenario**

ASSIGNING MANY COMPUTERS TO THE BARE-METAL DEPLOYMENT

George T. Management sends an email to the help desk stating that his department just ordered 10 new machines with no operating system and that he wants them all configured by the end of the day with the same image that was used on his machine. The list of 10 machines was included in the email.

You meet with your Configuration Manager team and decide that the best way to do this would be to use Configuration Manager to push the image out using the PXE service point that has already been used in the environment.

So, you open the Configuration Manager console, choose the Assets and Compliance workspace, expand Overview ➢ Devices, and click Import Computer Information on the Home tab of the Ribbon. On the Import Computer Information page, you select Import Computers Using A File, and click Next. On the Choose Mappings page, you click Browse to browse the comma-separated file that Mr. Management sent you containing the list of computers on which you need to deploy the new operating system.

After you import the file and assign the data mappings, you click Next. Then you verify that the data is correct on the Data Preview page and add these systems into the bare-metal collection created earlier with the Windows 7 build already assigned. Finally, you click Finish to add the members to the collection. Configuration Manager will then deploy the new operating system when the machines are powered on and booted up in PXE boot.

The Bottom Line

Specify a Network Access account. The Network Access account is the account Configuration Manager will use to access the system while running WinPE.

> **Master It** How do you specify the Network Access account?

Enable PXE support. PXE support in Configuration Manager is used to begin the operating system deployment process. The PXE feature responds to Configuration Manager clients making PXE boot requests.

Master It How do you set up PXE support?

Update the driver catalog package. The driver catalog allows you to add drivers to the already created packages and images you have within your organization so you are not constantly re-creating your images when you get a new machine in your environment.

Master It How do you update the driver catalog package?

Update an image from the console. In the past it was a big issue to keep your images up to date; no easy procedure existed. In Configuration Manager 2012 a feature called Schedule Updates exists to update your Windows images.

Master It How do you update your Windows images?

Chapter 10

Asset Intelligence

System Center 2012 Configuration Manager gives organizations better control over their information technology infrastructure and assets through Asset Intelligence technologies by enabling IT professionals to see what hardware and software assets they have, who is using them, and where they are. Asset Intelligence translates inventory data into information; this gives the IT professionals the ability to build reports to understand how these assets are being used in their environment.

ConfigMgr tracks nearly all the software assets on a network, providing comprehensive details about both physical and virtual applications installed across an enterprise. Asset intelligence lets IT professionals define, track, and proactively manage conformity to configuration standards. Metering and reporting the deployment and the use of both physical and virtual applications help organizations make better business decisions about software licensing and maintenance of licensing agreements. In this chapter we will cover the aspects of Asset Intelligence in ConfigMgr 2012 and show you how to enable it to take full advantage of this information.

In this chapter you will learn to

◆ Enable Asset Intelligence.

◆ Configure the Asset Intelligence synchronization point.

◆ Import the Microsoft Volume License Statement.

Requirements for Asset Intelligence

The Asset Intelligence feature in ConfigMgr 2012 has both external and internal dependencies that you will need to consider when using this feature. Those requirements include the following:

◆ Client agent requirements

◆ Site maintenance task requirements

◆ Windows event log requirements

Client Agent Prerequisites

The Asset Intelligence reports are based on information gathered through hardware and software inventory. To get the necessary information from clients for all Asset Intelligence reports, you must enable these client agents:

◆ Hardware Inventory Client Agent

◆ Software Metering Client Agent

HARDWARE INVENTORY CLIENT AGENT REQUIREMENT

To be able to collect inventory data required for some Asset Intelligence reports, you must enable the Hardware Inventory Client Agent. In addition, some hardware inventory reporting classes that Asset Intelligence reports depend on must be enabled on primary site server computers. You'll see how to do this in Chapter 11, "Inventory and Software Metering."

REPORTS THAT REQUIRE SOFTWARE METERING

Six reports require the Software Metering Client Agent to be enabled before they can provide any data:

Software 07A   Recently Used Executables by Number of Computers

Software 07B   Computers That Recently Used a Specified Executable

Software 07C   Recently Used Executables on a Specific Computer

Software 08A   Recently Used Executables by Number of Users

Software 08B   Users That Recently Used a Specified Executable

Software 08C   Recently Used Executables by a Specified User

Maintenance Tasks

The following maintenance tasks are associated with Asset Intelligence. By default, both maintenance tasks are enabled and configured by default.

Check Application Title with Inventory Information   This maintenance task checks to see if the software title that is reported in software inventory is reconciled with the software title in the Asset Intelligence Catalog. Basically it compares software hash from inventory to software code in the catalog to ensure accuracy and completeness. By default, this maintenance task is scheduled to run on Saturday after 12:00 a.m. and before 5:00 a.m.

Summarize Installed Software Data   This maintenance task provides the information that is displayed in the Inventoried Software node under the Asset Intelligence node in the Assets and Compliance workspace. When the task runs, Configuration Manager gathers a count of all inventoried software titles at the primary site. This task is available only on primary sites. By default, this maintenance task is scheduled to run on Saturday after 12:00 a.m. and before 5:00 a.m.

To configure these maintenance tasks, do the following:

1. In the ConfigMgr console, click Administration. See Figure 10.1.

2. In the Administration workspace, expand Site Configuration, and then click Sites.

3. Select the site on which to configure the Asset Intelligence maintenance task.

4. On the Home tab of the Ribbon, in the Settings group, click Site Maintenance.

   A list of all available maintenance tasks will appear.

5. Choose the desired maintenance task, and then click Edit to modify the settings.

6. Enable and configure the maintenance task.

7. Click Apply to save your settings.

FIGURE 10.1

Site Maintenance Ribbon

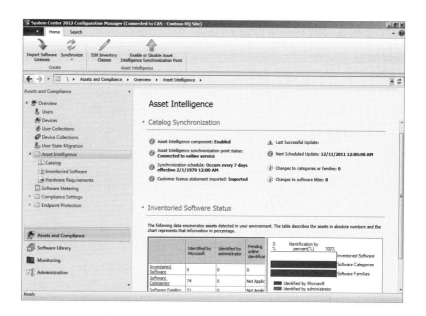

The task will now run according to its schedule. If you want to know more about this maintenance task, check Chapter 15, "Troubleshooting."

Windows Event Log Settings

Four Asset Intelligence reports display data gathered from the Windows security event logs on client computers. If the security event log is not set up properly, these reports will be empty even if the appropriate hardware inventory class has been enabled. We will discuss configuring these settings later in the chapter. The following reports require these collected events:

Hardware 3A   Primary Computer Users

Hardware 3B   Computers for a Specific Console User

Hardware 4A   Shared (Multi-user) Computers

Hardware 5A   Console Users on a Specific Computer

To enable auditing of success logon events, follow these steps:

1. On a domain controller computer, navigate to Administrative Tools ➢ Domain Security Policy.

2. Navigate to Security Settings ➢ Local Policies ➢ Audit Policy.

3. In the results pane, double-click Audit Logon Events, and ensure that Success is selected.

Elements of Asset Intelligence

Asset Intelligence enhances the inventory capabilities of ConfigMgr 2012 by extending hardware and software inventory. The Asset Intelligence category now contains more than 60 reports that present this information in an easy-to-use format. Most reports link to more detailed reports that allow the administrator to query for general information and drill down to more detailed information as needed.

Asset Intelligence Catalog

The ConfigMgr 2012 Asset Intelligence Catalog is a set of tables stored in the ConfigMgr database containing categorization and identification data for more than 300,000 software titles and versions that are divided into almost 100 families and almost 2,000 specific categories. These database tables are also used to manage hardware requirements for specific software titles and catalogued CPU properties information.

With ConfigMgr 2012, the Asset Intelligence Catalog was enhanced to allow software titles in use (both Microsoft and general software) to be manually imported. In addition, it now includes a large collection of known CPU properties, and the hardware requirements for software titles stored in the Asset Intelligence Catalog have been updated. Also, it is now possible to edit the local Asset Intelligence Catalog and to upload software title information to System Center Online (SCO) for categorization.

WHAT IS SYSTEM CENTER ONLINE?

Hosted by Microsoft, System Center Online is "software as a service," an online management service aimed at the IT community. Some of the services that will be eventually hosted are antivirus, anti-spyware, system monitoring, backup/restore, policy management, and, in the case of ConfigMgr, asset inventory monitoring.

Asset Intelligence Catalog updates containing newly released software and hardware definitions will be available for download periodically for bulk catalog updates, or the catalog can be dynamically updated by Microsoft Software Assurance (SA) customers using the Asset Intelligence synchronization point site system role.

SOFTWARE CATEGORIES

Administrators can view available software category information stored in the Asset Intelligence Catalog by using the Asset Intelligence ➤ Catalog ➤ Software Categories node in the ConfigMgr console.

These software categories are used to give broad listings of inventoried software titles and are also used as high-level groupings of more detailed software families. The Asset Intelligence Catalog has many predefined software categories, and you can create user-defined categories to continue to define inventoried software as needed. For example, the predefined E-mail and Collaboration category includes applications such as Microsoft Outlook and Outlook Express. The validation state for software categories already defined is always validated, while custom category information added to the Asset Intelligence catalog is user-defined. Note that predefined software category information is read-only and can't be changed. User-defined software categories can be added, modified, or deleted by administrators. We will cover managing software categories later in the chapter in the section "Asset Intelligence Validation States."

SOFTWARE FAMILIES

Administrators can view available software family information stored in the Asset Intelligence Catalog by using the Asset Intelligence ➤ Catalog ➤ Software Families node in the ConfigMgr console.

Software families in Asset Intelligence are used to define inventoried software even further within software categories. For example, the Security software family is defined by the Security and Security Threat labels. Like software categories, predefined software families always have a validation state of validated, while custom software family information has a state of user-defined. Also like software categories, predefined software family information can't be modified.

SOFTWARE LABELS

You can create custom software labels to even further categorize inventoried software titles that are in the Asset Intelligence Catalog. Administrators can use custom labels to create user-defined groups of software titles that share a common attribute. For example, a custom label could be called *bank software*, and that label would be used to identify inventoried bank software titles, which in turn could be used in a report to show all software that has that label. Custom labels have no validation state since they are always created locally.

In the ConfigMgr console, you can view all the custom labels that you or another administrator has made in the Asset Intelligence Catalog by choosing Asset Intelligence ➤ Catalog ➤ Software Labels.

INVENTORIED SOFTWARE TITLES

The Inventoried Software Titles node is located under Asset Intelligence ➤ Inventoried Software in the ConfigMgr console. Administrators can look at inventoried software title information collected from ConfigMgr clients in this node and can even create up to three custom labels per inventoried software item to further utilize user-defined categorization.

Each software title shows the following information:

- Name of the software title

- Name of the software vendor

- Product version

- Assigned software category

- Assigned software family

All of this information except for software category and software family is read-only and can't be changed.

PROCESSOR PROPERTIES

You can use the Asset Intelligence ➤ Hardware Requirements ➤ Processor Properties node to view processor property information about CPU types that are stored in the Asset Intelligence Catalog. These processor properties are preloaded into the Asset Intelligence Catalog and are not based on hardware inventory data. The following information is shown for each CPU that is listed:

- Name of the CPU

- Date of manufacture of the CPU

- Manufacturer of the CPU

- CPU brand ID

- CPU processing speed (in MHz)
- Whether the CPU is designed for mobile devices
- Amount of cache memory available for the CPU

HARDWARE REQUIREMENTS

With the Asset Intelligence ➢ Hardware Requirements node, you can manage software title hardware requirements data that is stored in the Asset Intelligence Catalog. The hardware requirements that are preloaded into the Asset Intelligence Catalog are not based on inventoried software information but are included as part of the Asset Intelligence Catalog. In addition to the default hardware requirements listed in this node, administrators can add new software title hardware requirements as needed to meet custom report requirements. The information that is displayed in this node includes the following:

- Name of the software title that hardware requirement is for
- Validation state for the hardware requirement (System Center Online requirements are always validated; custom hardware requirements are always user-defined.)
- Minimum processor speed, in MHz, that the software title requires
- Minimum RAM, in KB, that the software title requires
- Minimum free disk space, in KB, that the software title requires
- Minimum hard disk size, in KB, that the software title requires

As in other parts of the Asset Intelligence Catalog, custom hardware requirements for software titles that aren't stored in the catalog can be modified, but the predefined information is read-only and can't be changed or deleted.

Asset Intelligence Validation States

Asset Intelligence validation states show the source and current validation status of Asset Intelligence Catalog information. They are outlined in Table 10.1, which is reproduced from the ConfigMgr documentation.

TABLE 10.1:   Asset Intelligence validation states

STATE	DEFINITION	ADMINISTRATOR ACTION	COMMENT
Validated	Catalog item has been defined by System Center Online (SCO) researchers.	None	This is the best state.
User-defined	Catalog item has not been defined by SCO researchers.	Customized the local catalog information	This state will be shown in Asset Intelligence reports.

STATE	DEFINITION	ADMINISTRATOR ACTION	COMMENT
Pending	Catalog item has not been defined by SCO researchers but has been submitted for categorization.	Requested categorization from SCO	The catalog item will remain in this state until SCO categorizes the item and the Asset Intelligence Catalog is synchronized.
Updateable	A user-defined catalog item has been categorized differently by SCO.	Customized the local Asset Intelligence Catalog to categorize an item as user-defined	The administrator can use the Software Details Conflict Resolution dialog box to choose which category to use.
Uncategorized	Catalog item has not been defined by SCO; the item has not been submitted to SCO and has not been categorized by admin.	None	Request categorization or customize local catalog. This is the base state of all unknown software.

Asset Intelligence Synchronization Point

ConfigMgr has a site system role for Asset Intelligence called the Asset Intelligence synchronization point. This site system role is used to connect to System Center Online over TCP port 443 so dynamic Asset Intelligence Catalog updates can be managed.

This site role can be installed only on the ConfigMgr 2012 Central Administration Site (CAS), and all of your Asset Intelligence Catalog customization must be done on a ConfigMgr console that is connected to your CAS. You must configure all the updates at the central site, but all Asset Intelligence Catalog information is replicated to all child primary sites using ConfigMgr SQL Replication. If a CAS doesn't exist on the environment, this can be done on the stand-alone primary site server.

Using the Asset Intelligence synchronization point, SA license customers can also request on-demand catalog synchronization with System Center Online or schedule automatic catalog synchronization, and they can upload uncategorized software titles to System Center Online for identification.

The Asset Intelligence Home Page

With ConfigMgr 2012, an Asset Intelligence home page was added to the ConfigMgr console; it's similar to home pages in some of the other features, such as Software Updates.

To display the Asset Intelligence home page, do the following in the ConfigMgr console: select Assets and Compliance ➤ Asset Intelligence. Figure 10.2 shows an example of the Asset Intelligence home page.

FIGURE 10.2

Asset Intelligence
home page

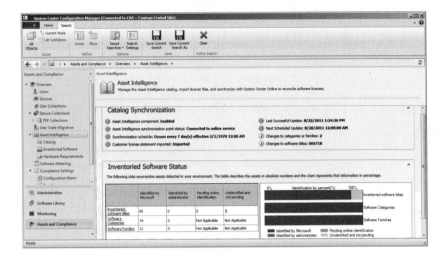

The Asset Intelligence home page is divided into the following sections:

◆ Catalog Synchronization

◆ Inventoried Software Status

ASSET INTELLIGENCE CATALOG SYNCHRONIZATION

This section display the following information:

Asset Intelligence Component Status   This section displays the status of the component as either Enabled or Disabled.

Asset Intelligence Synchronization Point Status   This section displays the online status of the synchronization point or any failure that happened during this synchronization.

Synchronization Schedule   This section matches the configured schedule of the catalog; by default, this is set for every 7 days, but you can change this on the Assets and Compliance ➤ Asset Intelligence node. Right-click the node, choose Synchronize ➤ Schedule Synchronization, and choose the desired schedule.

Customer License Statement Imported   This section shows whether the Microsoft volume license has been imported into the ConfigMgr database.

Last Successful Update   This section shows the last time Configuration Manager was able to synchronize the catalog. If it was not able to synchronize, a warning icon will show and will display a Not Applicable status.

Next Scheduled Update   This displays the next date and time when the catalog will synchronize.

Changes To Categories Or Families   This displays the number of changes or updates in categories that occurred on the database during the last synchronization with System Center Online.

Changes To Software Titles   This displays the number of changes or updates in software titles that occurred during the last synchronization with System Center Online.

INVENTORIED SOFTWARE STATUS

The following data enumerates assets detected in the ConfigMgr environment. The table describes the assets in absolute numbers, and the chart represents that information in percentages.

Inventoried Software Status Table   This displays the assets of the Asset Intelligence Catalog in summary table format with the following information:

- Inventoried Software Titles
- Software Categories
- Software Families

Each of these are shown in one of the following states:

- Identified By Microsoft
- Identified By Administrator
- Pending Online Identification
- Unidentified And Not Pending

Identification By Percent Chart   This displays an Asset Catalog summary in bar chart format, including the following information as percentages:

- Inventoried Software Titles
- Software Categories
- Software Families

These in turn are shown color coded for easier identification:

- Identified By Microsoft
- Identified By Administrator
- Pending Online Identification
- Unidentified And Not Pending Online Identification

Asset Intelligence Reports

To see the real power behind the Asset Intelligence feature, you have to examine the various Asset Intelligence reports that are provided with ConfigMgr right out of the box.

You can find the Asset Intelligence reports in the ConfigMgr console by choosing Monitoring ➢ Reporting. Expand Reports and click Asset Intelligence. The numbers in the installed software and license information shown in Asset Intelligence reports may not be accurate; they may vary from the true number of software products installed or licenses in use on your network because of complex dependencies and limitations in inventorying software license information for software titles installed in an enterprise environment. Therefore, you should not use Asset Intelligence reports as the sole source of deciding how many software licenses to purchase for compliance.

The following are example dependencies that are involved in inventorying installed software and licenses in an enterprise using Asset Intelligence that might affect the accuracy of the data:

Client Hardware Inventory Dependency Asset Intelligence–installed software reports are based on data collected from ConfigMgr clients by extending hardware inventory to enable Asset Intelligence reporting. Because of this, Asset Intelligence reports will report data only from ConfigMgr clients that have completed a hardware inventory scan successfully and have the required Asset Intelligence WMI reporting class enabled. Also, since hardware inventory runs on a schedule that is set by the administrator, there may be a delay in data being reported that might affect the accuracy of Asset Intelligence reports at any given time.

Software Packaging Dependencies Because Asset Intelligence reports are based on installed software title data using standard ConfigMgr client hardware inventory processes, some of that data might not be collected properly if the software executables don't conform to standard installation processes or have been modified prior to installation.

Server Role Dependencies When you're using CAL reporting, it is important to remember that these reports were designed to provide visibility into the specific usage of products in specific scenarios, such as a Windows server hosting only one server role. In cases where a Windows server is hosting more than one role, this might cause inaccurate Asset Intelligence reports.

Location And Usage Remember that Asset Intelligence reports were designed to report license usage, not how many licenses have been actually bought and for what purpose they are allowed to be used.

HARDWARE REPORTS

Asset Intelligence hardware reports provide information about hardware assets in your organization, such as a computer's age and its ability to handle a software upgrade. Some reports are based on information collected from the System Security Event Log, so you should clear that log if a computer is assigned to another user. The following hardware Asset Intelligence reports are available:

Hardware 01A Summary of Computers in a Specific Collection

Hardware 03A Primary Computer Users

Hardware 03B Computers for a Specific Primary Console User

Hardware 04A Shared (Multi-user) Computers

Hardware 05A Console Users on a Specific Computer

Hardware 06A Computers for Which Console Users Could Not Be Determined

Hardware 07A USB Devices by Manufacturer

Hardware 07B USB Devices by Manufacturer and Description

Hardware 07C Computers with a Specific USB Device

Hardware 07D USB Devices on a Specific Computer

Hardware 08A   Hardware That Is Not Ready for a Software Upgrade

Hardware 09A   Search for Computers

Hardware 10A   Computers That Have Changed Within a Specified Collection

Hardware 10B   Changes on a Specified Computer Within a Time Range

---

 **Real World Scenario**

PLANNING FOR A SOFTWARE UPGRADE

You get word from your manager that the department responsible for all the company training manuals is working on updating many of the manuals because of some new federal regulations. They are making these updates with a new version of the Adobe Acrobat software, and there is a possibility that you might have to deploy Acrobat Reader X so that employees will be able to read the updated manuals properly.

The company is also in the middle of a hardware refresh, so your manager is concerned that there may be computers on the network that do not have the necessary hardware requirements to run Acrobat Reader X properly, so she wants to use ConfigMgr to generate a list of those computers if there are any.

Hearing this, you are glad that you have already enabled Asset Intelligence, because there is a specific report for just this scenario. To meet your manager's request, just go to the report Hardware 08A: Hardware That Is Not Ready for a Software Upgrade. Since you are concerned with user computers in this instance, select the desired collection in the Collection field. The Asset Intelligence knowledge base, which is part of the ConfigMgr database, already has information about Acrobat Reader X, so select that for the Product field.

After you run the report, you can provide that link to your manager so she can either print it or export it into Excel for her own use.

SOFTWARE REPORTS

Software Asset Intelligence reports provide information about software families, categories, and specific software titles installed on computers within your organization. The following software Asset Intelligence reports are available:

Software 01A   Summary of Installed Software in a Specific Collection

Software 02A   Software Families

Software 02B   Software Categories with a Family

Software 02C   Software by Category and Family

Software 02D   Computers with a Specific Software Product

Software 02E   Installed Software on a Specific Computer

Software 03A   Uncategorized Software

Software 04A   Auto-start Software

Software 04B   Computers with a Specific Auto-start Software

Software 04C   Auto-start Software on a Specific Computer

Software 05A   Browser Helper Objects

Software 05B   Computers with a Specific Browser Helper Object

Software 05C   Browser Helper Objects on a Specific Computer

Software 06A   Search for Installed Software

Software 07A   Recently Used Executables by Number of Computers

Software 07B   Computers That Recently Used a Specified Executable

Software 07C   Recently Used Executables on a Specific Computer

Software 08A   Recently Used Executables by Number of Users

Software 08B   Users That Recently Used a Specified Executable

Software 08C   Recently Used Executables by a Specified User

Software 09A   Infrequently Used Software

Software 09B   Computers with Infrequently Used Software Installed

Software 10A   Software Titles with Specific, Multiple Custom Labels Defined

Software 10B   Computers with a Specific Custom Label Software Title Installed

Software 11A   Software Titles with a Specific Custom Label Defined

Software 12A   Software Titles Without a Custom Label

License Management Reports

The following license management Asset Intelligence reports are available:

License 01A   Microsoft License Ledger for Microsoft License Statements

License 01B   Microsoft License Ledger Item by Sales Channel

License 01C   Computers with a Specific Microsoft License Ledger Item and Sales Channel

License 01D   Microsoft License Ledger Products on a Specific Computer

License 02A   Count of Licenses Nearing Expiration by Time Ranges

License 02B   Computers with Licenses Nearing Expiration

License 02C   License Information on a Specific Computer

License 03A   Count of Licenses by License Status

License 03B   Computers with a Specific License Status

License 04A   Count of Products Managed by Software Licensing Service

License 04B   Computers with a Specific Product Managed by Software Licensing Service

License 05A   Computers Providing Key Management Service

License 06A   Processor Counts for Per-Processor Licensed Products

License 14A   Microsoft Volume Licensing Reconciliation Report

License 14B   List of Microsoft Software Inventory Not Found in MVLS

License 15B   Third Party Reconciliation Report

Configuring Asset Intelligence

ConfigMgr Asset Intelligence is enabled by default. Depending on what data you want information on, you will have to do the following:

1. Choose the Assets And Compliance node in the ConfigMgr console.

2. Right-click Asset Intelligence, and click Edit Inventory Classes.

3. Choose to enable only the desired Asset Intelligence reporting class.

4. Make sure that certain client agents are enabled, which we will go over in the following sections.

Enabling Asset Intelligence

To successfully collect data for the hardware and software reports in Asset Intelligence, you first need to enable the Hardware Inventory Client Agent.

The classes that are used for the hardware and software inventory reports include the following:

SMS_SystemConsoleUsage

SMS_SystemConsoleUser

SMS_InstalledSoftware

SMS_AutoStartSoftware

SMS_BrowserHelperObject

SoftwareLicensingService

SoftwareLicensingProduct

Win32_USBDevice

To enable one or all of these classes in ConfigMgr, you have to follow these steps:

1. Choose Assets And Compliance ➤ Asset Intelligence.

2. Right-click, and choose Edit Inventory Classes. Figure 10.3 shows the dialog box that opens.

3. Choose the inventory classes that need to be enabled, and click OK.

FIGURE 10.3
Asset Intelligence
Reporting Class
Settings dialog box

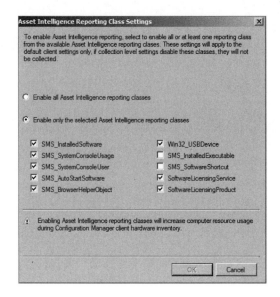

After you do that, it could take up to a few days for these changes to take full effect, depending on your ConfigMgr hierarchy and how often you have the Hardware Inventory Client Agent set to run inventory.

INSTALLING AN ASSET INTELLIGENCE SYNCHRONIZATION POINT

As discussed earlier in the chapter, the Asset Intelligence synchronization point role is used to connect ConfigMgr sites to System Center Online to synchronize Asset Intelligence catalog information. You can install this role only on a site system located in the CAS of a ConfigMgr hierarchy, and you'll require Internet access to synchronize with System Center Online on TCP port 443. The Asset Intelligence synchronization point can also upload custom software title information to System Center Online for categorization. All information uploaded to System Center Online will be treated as public information by Microsoft, so you should be sure that your custom information does not contain any sensitive information.

To install the Asset Intelligence synchronization point and have it be secure, you can acquire an optional System Center Online authentication certificate (*.pfx), which can be acquired only by SA license customers. (For more information on Software Assurance, check out the SA website at www.microsoft.com/licensing/sa/default.mspx.) Before you begin the installation of the Asset Intelligence synchronization point, make sure that all of the following are true:

◆ You have a valid SCO authentication certificate. If you don't have one, do not put any certificate information in the field since this certificate is optional.

◆ The Asset Intelligence synchronization point will be available on a shared network folder accessible to the server where you will be running the New Site Role Wizard.

◆ The Asset Intelligence synchronization point will stay in that location until the Asset Intelligence synchronization point has done its first synchronization with System Center Online.

To install an Asset Intelligence synchronization point, follow these steps:

1. In the ConfigMgr console, select Administration ➤ Site Configuration ➤ Sites.

2. Select CAS Site Server Name. Choose the Home tab of the Ribbon, and click Add Site System Role to start the Create Roles Wizard.

3. As you have done with other ConfigMgr wizards covered in this book, verify the site system settings on the General page, and click Next.

4. On the System Role Selection page, select the Asset Intelligence Synchronization Point check box, and then click Next.

5. On the Asset Intelligence Synchronization Point Connection Settings page, you can set up an optional certificate. If you choose to do so, then set the path to the SCO authentication certificate (*.pfx) file, as shown in Figure 10.4, and click Next.

FIGURE 10.4
Asset Intelligence
Synchronization
Point Connection
Settings page

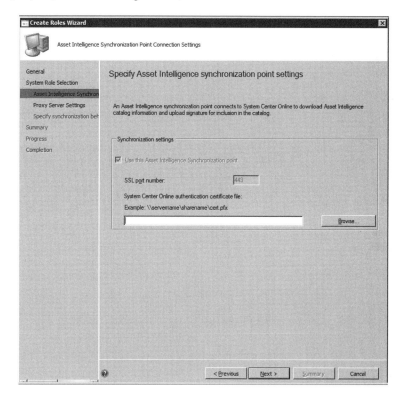

6. On the Proxy Server Settings page, configure the settings for the proxy server if needed.

7. On the Synchronization Point Schedule page, you can choose whether to set up synchronization on a simple or custom schedule, as you've seen in other ConfigMgr options.

8. On the Summary page of the wizard, review the settings you have specified to make sure they are correct. If you need to make any changes, click the Previous button. Otherwise, click Next to finish the rest of the configuration.

Import Software License into Asset Intelligence

One of the most important pieces of Asset Intelligence is the availability to import the current Microsoft Volume License Summary into the database for better reporting of this license count. Also you can import a non-Microsoft product license count into the database by selecting the option to upload a General License Statement File.

As shown in Figure 10.5, you can now import the Microsoft Volume License Statement or General License Statement in one easy wizard. First, select the type of file you are going to import. This will be either an .xml or .csv file for the Microsoft Volume License Statement or a .csv file for the Non Microsoft License Statement. Once you have chosen the file you are going to upload, this information will be imported into the ConfigMgr database. On the next hardware and software inventory the data will be analyzed, and the new imported license count will be available for the IT administrator's analysis. You can upload the license information as many times as needed to update the license or when the enterprise agreement of the Microsoft product gets updated. You'll need to follow the same process for the non-Microsoft product when you want to review the license count.

FIGURE 10.5
Import Software License Wizard

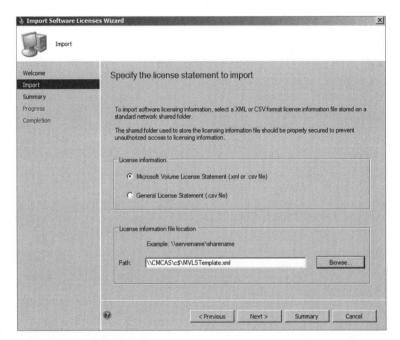

Importing Software License Information

The following sections describe the procedures necessary to import both Microsoft and general software licensing information into the ConfigMgr 2012 site database using the Import Software License Wizard. When you import software licenses from license information files into the site database, the site server computer account requires Full Control NTFS permissions to the file share that will be used to import software license information. When this license information gets imported into the site, the existing software license information file used with the Import Software License Wizard contains a complete list of all necessary software license information.

Follow these steps to import the software license:

1. In the Assets and Compliance workspace, click Asset Intelligence.

2. On the Home tab of the Ribbon, in the Asset Intelligence Group, click Import Software Licenses.

   The Import Software License Wizard opens, as shown in Figure 10.5.

3. On the Welcome page, click Next.

4. On the Import page, specify whether you are importing a Microsoft Volume License Statement (.xml or .csv) or a general license statement (.csv).

5. Enter the UNC path to the license information file, or click Browse to select a network shared folder and file.

6. On the Summary page, review the information you have specified to ensure that it is correct before continuing.

   If you need to make changes, click Previous to return to the Import page. Otherwise click Next.

7. Once completed click Close.

Perform the following steps for the General License Statement as well; just make sure to select this in step 4.

Creating the Microsoft Volume License Statement

Before we start the process of creating the Microsoft Volume License Statement, make sure you have access to http://licensing.microsoft.com/" \o "http://licensing.microsoft.com. If you don't have access, please talk to your Microsoft Account Manager or Microsoft Technical Account Manager and ask them to send you your License Summary. Once you have the proper access, select the License Summary from the licensing site, and export it to Excel. When you have it in Excel, make sure the following fields and values are selected:

PRODUCT POOL	LICENSE PRODUCT FAMILY	LICENSE VERSION	EFFECTIVE QUANTITY	UNRESOLVED QUANTITY
Applications	Access	2010	70	0

Once you have imported the Microsoft Volume License Statement, you can run any of the reports with the title "License."

Creating the General License Statement

Now let's look at an example of the General License Statement. To create this file you need to manually create a .csv file with the fields you need and the software for which you want ConfigMgr to keep track of the license count. Once you finish creating the file, follow the same steps as you did to import the software license, but now use the example shown in Figure 10.6.

FIGURE 10.6
General License
Statement Import

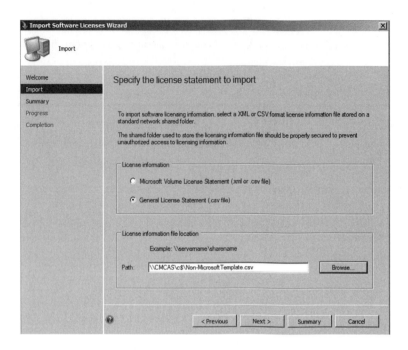

As you can see in Figure 10.7, all you need to do is create the file with the example title names and the 3rd party software that it needs to keep track of the license count.

The following is a list of reports that you can run:

License 14A   Microsoft Volume Licensing Reconciliation Report

License 14B   List of Microsoft Software Inventory Not Found in MVLS

License 15B   Third Party Reconciliation Report

FIGURE 10.7
General License
Statement

Name	Publisher	Version	Language	EffectiveQuantity	PONumber	ResellerName	DateOfPurchase	SupportPurchased	SupportExpirationDate	Comments
Software Title 1	Software Publisher	1.01	English	1	Purchase number	Reseller name	License purchase date	0	8/4/2008	Comment
Software title 2	Software publisher	1.02	English	1	Purchase number	Reseller name	License purchase date	0	8/4/2008	Comment
Software title 3	Software publisher	1.03	English	1	Purchase number	Reseller name	License purchase date	0	8/4/2008	Comment
Software title 4	Software publisher	1.04	English	1	Purchase number	Reseller name	License purchase date	0	8/4/2008	Comment
Software title 5	Software publisher	1.05	English	1	Purchase number	Reseller name	License purchase date	0	8/4/2008	Comment
Software title 6	Software publisher	1.06	English	1	Purchase number	Reseller name	License purchase date	0	8/4/2008	Comment
Software title 7	Software publisher	1.07	English	1	Purchase number	Reseller name	License purchase date	0	8/4/2008	Comment
Software title 8	Software publisher	1.08	English	1	Purchase number	Reseller name	License purchase date	0	8/4/2008	Comment
Software title 9	Software publisher	1.09	English	1	Purchase number	Reseller name	License purchase date	0	8/4/2008	Comment
Software title 10	Software publisher	1.1	English	1	Purchase number	Reseller name	License purchase date	0	8/4/2008	Comment

This is how the General License Statement should look in the `.csv` file before you import the file. When you import the file, it should look like it does in Figure 10.6.

VIEW THE 3RD PARTY LICENSE INFORMATION

Viewing 3rd party licenses, or general licenses as they are called in ConfigMgr 2012, requires that you import the 3rd party license data into ConfigMgr 2012. This can be done by either creating a `.csv` file that you see on the Creating General License Statement in Figure 10.6 with the appropriate license information, or by integrating a freeware tool from CoreTech.

Importing 3rd Party License Information Using a Tool

There are several freeware tools for Configuration Manager, one being the Asset Intelligence License Wizard (AILW) from CoreTech. The benefit of the tool is that it offers you a GUI to import and create the 3rd party license information. The tool is available for download from `http://blog.coretech.dk/kea/asset-intelligence-3rd-party-software-utility/`.

To configure the AILW tool:

1. Download the AILW and extract the files to a folder, e.g., C:\Tools\AILW.

2. Copy `C:\Tools\AILW\AILW\CT-AILW.exe` to `C:\Program Files\Coretech\AILW\` (you need to create the CoreTech and AILW folders manually).

3. Copy the content of `C:\Tools\AILW\AILW 2012 Console Extensions\` to `C:\Program Files\Microsoft Configuration Manager\Admin Console\XmlStorage\Extensions\Actions\` (notice, you may need to create the `Extensions` and `Actions` folder manually).

4. Restart the Configuration Manager Administrator console and navigate to the Assets and Compliance workspace; select Asset Intelligence.

5. Click Edit 3rd Party Licenses on the Ribbon (Figure 10.8).

FIGURE 10.8
Edit 3rd Party
Licenses Ribbon

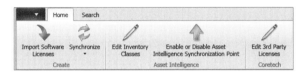

6. Click Run and Connect to Database.

7. Make sure you are on the Edit tab. Scroll down to the end and enter a new product (notice the tool also allows you to copy application information already found in SQL):

   ◆ Product: Adobe Reader 9.3

   ◆ Vendor: Adobe Systems Incorporated

   ◆ Version: 9.3.0

   ◆ Licenses: 100

   ◆ Select the Commit tab and click Commit to SCCM.

8. Run the report License 15A – General License Reconciliation Report against All Systems. You should have a new entry showing Adobe Reader 9.3 with the number of available licenses.

The Bottom Line

Enable Asset Intelligence.   If you installed ConfigMgr from scratch, you will find that Asset Intelligence is not enabled by default. Depending on the data that you want information on, you will have to select the ConfigMgr Asset Intelligence Reporting Class Settings and make sure that client agents are enabled.

Master It   Which classes in the Asset Intelligence Reporting Class Settings do you have to enable to use Asset Intelligence?

Configure the Asset Intelligence synchronization point.   The Asset Intelligence synchronization point is used to connect to System Center Online to synchronize Asset Intelligence Catalog information and get periodic updates.

Master It   What do you need to do in order to configure the Asset Intelligence synchronization point?

Import the Microsoft Volume License Statement.   In ConfigMgr you can import the Microsoft Volume License Statement and the General License Statement so that the software inventory and Asset Intelligence can count the number of licenses currently in use on the environment.

Master It   What file types does ConfigMgr 2012 support for the License Statements?

Chapter 11

Inventory and Software Metering

Out of all of the capabilities of Configuration Manager 2012, inventory is still considered a core feature; it is one that, by itself, has made Configuration Manager and its predecessors a very useful product since the early days of SMS 1.0.

Configuration Manager has the ability to inventory the hardware and software in client computers. Hardware inventory can gather information from your systems such as the processor, computer manufacturer, and amount of installed memory. Software inventory can gather lists of file types and their versions installed on your computers. Combine this with the extensive information in the Asset Intelligence knowledge base covered in Chapter 10, "Asset Intelligence," and you can use Configuration Manager to really get a handle on what kind of software is being used in your environment. Inventory can be considered the backbone of Configuration Manager. You can run it without enabling inventory, but you really wouldn't be able to do much, since other features, such as software metering, require it.

Software metering, the second major topic in this chapter, allows you to collect information on software usage to assist in managing software purchases and licensing. With this feature, you can report on the software that is being used in your environment and which users are running particular programs. You can also find software that is installed but isn't being used, and you can report on software license requirements and other items related to license management.

In this chapter, you will learn to

- ◆ Configure and manage Software Inventory.
- ◆ Configure and manage Hardware Inventory.
- ◆ Configure and manage Software Metering.

Inventory in Configuration Manager 2012

Gathering inventory data is considered one of the most important features of any system management system. With Configuration Manager 2012, the default settings will perform hardware and software inventory scanning immediately after the Configuration Manager client agent is installed.

Hardware inventory scanning will give you such information as disk space, video card type, memory installed, and much more. Configuration Manager 2012 uses WMI to gather the needed data, and once you have learned the basics of WMI, you will find it fairly easy to modify the default hardware inventory settings.

Software inventory scanning will give you such information as the software installed, file types, and the versions of software. Unlike previous versions of Configuration Manager, in Configuration Manager 2012 the client is not configured to scan for any special files. The software inventory process can also collect files and store them on the primary site server. Collection files are very rarely used because they can flood the network and consume lots of disk space on the site server.

The data inventory that is gathered is often used to create reports, queries, and collections. One thing that is very important to know is that data is not life data; it is based on the latest inventory scanning and can potentially be several days or weeks old. When a Configuration Manager client performs an inventory scan, data is send to the client's management point. The management point will verify the data and send it to a Configuration Manager site server. At the site server, data is imported into the site database. You can use several methods in Configuration Manager to use that information in your organization:

◆ You can create queries that target computers based on their hardware configuration or installed software. You can use these queries to be proactive in preventing problems such as low hard disk space. Using inventory data for this proactive step is not as important in Configuration Manager 2012 as it used to be in the previous versions of the software because you can now achieve the real-time check using global conditions.

◆ You can create queries that show computers that don't have your organization's standard antivirus program installed in order to make a collection that can be a target for deploying that software to the computers that have the hardware to support it.

◆ You can create reports showing hardware configuration and software installations that management can use to improve the current computer environment.

◆ You can provide Resource Explorer with reports on individual computers that your PC support department can use to remotely troubleshoot problems.

The first inventory-scanning process will always send a full report from the client on all of the hardware and software resources. After that, subsequent scans will only send *delta* inventory information, identifying what has changed.

Delta inventory reports, for both inventory agents, are processed in the order in which they are received at the Configuration Manager site server. If for some reason a delta inventory is received from a client that is not in the database (such as a reimaged or new client, for example), the site server will delete the delta inventory and ask for a full inventory from that client the next time a scheduled scan is run.

Configuration Manager provides only limited support for computers that can boot up two or more operating systems. Configuration Manager clients can be discovered in multiple boot states, and the clients can be installed on each boot state. Inventory that is collected from these computers, however, will be from only the operating system that was running when the inventory scan was run.

Collecting Hardware Inventory

Hardware Inventory collects data from clients by querying several data stores of information that are on computers, such as the registry and Windows Management Instrumentation (WMI). The Hardware Inventory Client Agent doesn't query all WMI classes; it only pulls the information that is defined in the client settings assigned to the client. As you learned in Chapter 6, "Client Installation," you can have multiple client settings and assign them to different collections. Inventory scans are done on the schedule you configure in the client settings. Unless there is a problem with the client, only delta inventories will be collected after the first inventory. This greatly decreases the network traffic required by client inventory reporting because deltas are usually only a small percentage of the size of a full inventory from a client. With every hardware inventory collection done on a client, Configuration Manager updates the site database with the current inventory while keeping a history of the previous information. You can view the current and historical inventory information in queries, reports, and Resource Explorer.

Hardware Inventory will also collect certain basic information about a client's installed software. This information is gathered from the registry, most notably from Add Or Remove Programs. By using the software inventory, however, you can get a larger amount of and much more detailed information about the software that is present on client computers.

WHAT DEFINES HARDWARE INVENTORY?

Configuration Manager gathers information about clients based on the settings defined in the client settings and the content of the `Configuration.mof` (managed object format) file stored on the primary site server in the `<Folder where Configuration Manager is installed>\ inboxes\clifiles.src\hinv` folder.

The configuration.mof File

The `configuration.mof` file defines the data classes to be inventoried by the Hardware Inventory Client Agent. Data classes can be created to inventory existing or custom WMI repository data classes or registry keys found on clients.

This file also defines and registers the WMI providers used to access computer information during hardware inventory. Registering providers defines the type of provider to be used and the classes that the provider will support. WMI can access only registered providers, so that applies to the Hardware Inventory Client Agent as well. The `configuration.mof` file can't be used to register new providers for clients. New or custom providers must be sent to clients to be compiled manually before they can be added to hardware inventory.

When Configuration Manager clients request computer policies as part of their policy polling interval, the `configuration.mof` file is part of the policy that clients download and compile. When you add, modify, or delete data classes from the `configuration.mof` file, clients will automatically compile those changes the next time the client compiles a computer policy that it receives.

Later in the chapter you'll get hands-on practice in modifying `configuration.mof` to extend the information collected in hardware inventory.

The Client Settings

Unlike in previous versions of Configuration Manager, you now have a GUI, as shown in Figure 11.1, to edit the reporting classes used by the inventory process. In Configuration Manager 2007 and previous SMS versions, you would modify the `sms_def.mof` file to define whether specific client data class information is reported. In Configuration Manager 2012, you either use the default client settings or create custom client settings to enable and disable reporting classes. The reporting classes are based on the WMI data classes that are on clients by default or have been added after the `configuration.mof` file has been modified.

This reporting class information in the client settings is converted to a reporting policy that is downloaded to clients as part of their computer policy polling download. After the client has finished compiling the new reporting policy, the reporting information is stored in the client WMI repository in the `InventoryDataItem` class of the `Root\CCM\Policy\Machine` WMI namespace. Unlike the `configuration.mof` file, the inventory client settings file is never sent to clients directly. Only the policy generated by the client settings is actually compiled by Configuration Manager clients.

Later in the chapter you will see several examples on how to extend hardware inventory.

FIGURE 11.1
Default hardware
inventory settings

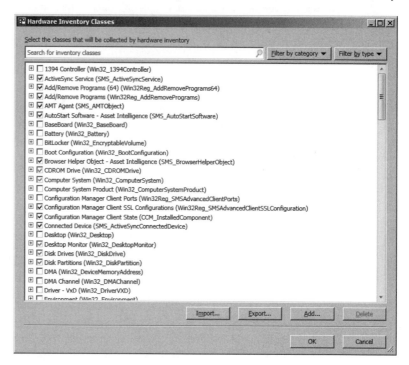

The Default Hardware Inventory Reporting Classes

The default client settings have some reporting classes enabled. These default classes might change depending on what version of Configuration Manager and which service pack you have installed and on whether you have enabled classes for Asset Intelligence. Here is an example of the hardware inventory data classes that are enabled by default in Configuration Manager 2012 RTM with Asset Intelligence classes enabled:

ActiveSync Service	CDROM Drive	Connected Device
Add/Remove Programs	Computer System	Desktop Monitor
AMT Agent	Configuration Manager Client SSL Configurations	Disk Drives
AutoStart Software		Disk Partitions
Browser Helper Object	Configuration Manager Client State	IDE Controller

Installed Software - Asset Intelligence

Logical Disk

Memory

Mobile Device Client Agent Version

Mobile Device Computer System

Mobile Device Display

Mobile Device Installed Applications

Mobile Device Installed Applications

Mobile Device Memory

Mobile Device OS Information

Mobile Device Password

Mobile Device Power

Motherboard

NAP Client

NAP System Health Agent

Network Adapter

Network Adapter Configuration

Network Client

Operating System

Parallel Port

PC BIOS

Physical Memory

PNP Device Driver

Power Capabilities

Power Configuration

Power Insomnia Reasons

Power Management Daily Data

Power Management Exclusion Settings

Power Management Monthly Data

Power Settings

Processor

Recently Used Applications

SCSI Controller

Server Feature

Services

Software Licensing Product - Asset Intelligence

Software Licensing Service - Asset Intelligence

System Console Usage - Asset Intelligence

System Console User - Asset Intelligence

Sound Devices

System Devices

System Enclosure

Tape Drive

TS Issued License

TS License Key Pack

USB Controller

USB Device

Video Controller

Virtual Application Packages

Virtual Applications

Virtual Machine

Virtual Machine Details

Windows Update Agent Version

Each one of these reporting classes has certain criteria enabled; these represent the actual data classes that are being collected. Some reporting classes might have all their data classes being captured or only some of them. The best way to get a handle on what is being actually collected by hardware inventory is to browse through the individual classes in the GUI.

THE ROLE OF MIF FILES IN HARDWARE INVENTORY

Management information format (MIF) files can be used to extend hardware inventory information that is collected from clients. The type of information that can be collected by MIF files can be just about anything, depending on how the MIF file is structured. During a hardware inventory cycle, the information in a MIF file is added to the client inventory report and stored in the Configuration Manager site database, where it can be used just like default client inventory data. The two types of MIF files that can be used to extend hardware inventory in this way are NOIDMIF and IDMIF.

By default, NOIDMIF and IDMIF file information is not inventoried by Configuration Manager. For this information to be added to hardware inventory, you must enable one or both file types in the Hardware Inventory settings. When you do, Configuration Manager creates new tables or modifies existing tables in the site database to add the properties in NOIDMIF and IDMIF files. NOIDMIF and IDMIF files are not validated, so they can be used to alter tables that you don't want altered. Doing this runs the risk that valid data could be overwritten by invalid data or large amounts of data could be imported into the Configuration Manager database, which would cause delays in all Configuration Manager functions. To lower the risk of this happening, use MIF collection only when it is absolutely necessary. Later in the chapter, you'll see how to change the location of MIF files from the default.

More on NOIDMIF Files

NOIDMIF files are the standard MIF files that are used in Configuration Manager hardware inventory. NOIDMIF files do not contain a unique identifier for the data they contain, and hardware inventory automatically associates the NOIDMIF information with the client that it was found on. NOIDMIF files are not sent to the site server during a client hardware inventory cycle, but their data is added to the client inventory report itself.

If the classes in the NOIDMIF file don't exist in the Configuration Manager database, the new inventory class tables are created in the Configuration Manager site database to store the new inventory information. As long as the NOIDMIF file is present on the client, the inventoried data from the NOIDMIF file will be updated in the Configuration Manager database. If the NOIDMIF file is removed, all the classes and properties relating to it are removed from the inventory of that client in the database. For NOIDMIF information to be pulled from a client, the NOIDMIF file must be stored here: `%WINDIR%\ \CCM\Inventory\Noidmifs`.

More on IDMIF Files

IDMIF files are custom MIF files that contain a unique ID and are not attached to the client that they are collected from. IDMIF files can be used to collect inventory data about devices that are not Configuration Manager clients, such as a shared network printer, an external hard drive, a copy machine, or other equipment that may not be attached to a client computer.

When you enable the IDMIF collection on your Configuration Manager site, IDMIF files are collected only if they are within the size limit that you set in the Hardware Inventory Client Agent properties. Depending on the maximum custom MIF size that you set for each site, IDMIF collection may cause increased network bandwidth usage during client inventory, which you should consider before you enable IDMIF collection.

Differences between NOIDMIF and IDMIF Files

IDMIF files are in most ways the same as NOIDMIF files. Both types have key properties that must be unique. Any class that has more than one instance must at least have one key property defined, or instances will overwrite previous instances. They differ in the following ways:

◆ IDMIF files must have a delta header that lists the architecture and a unique ID. NOIDMIF files are given a delta header automatically when processed by the client.

◆ IDMIF files must have a top-level group with the same class as the architecture being added or changed, and the class must have at least one property.

◆ Removing an IDMIF file from a client doesn't cause any data to be deleted from the Configuration Manager database.

◆ IDMIF files aren't added to a client's inventory, and the files themselves are sent across the network to be processed by a site server.

Collecting Software Inventory

When you enable Software Inventory in Configuration Manager, the software inventory process collects software inventory data directly from files by gathering data from the file's header information. Unknown files (files that don't have any detailed information in their file headers) can also be inventoried. You can also have Configuration Manager actually collect files you configure under a certain size. Both software inventory and collected file information can be viewed in Resource Explorer, which we will discuss later in the chapter.

You can also inventory encrypted and compressed files. This will usually cause Software Inventory to run much more slowly because of the extra processing imposed on the client computer. When you inventory an encrypted file, an unencrypted copy of the file must be made so its information can be scanned. If antivirus software is running at the same time, it will show that the software inventory process is opening the files that are being scanned and then scanning them again to make sure they aren't infected by a virus.

Software Inventory can use a considerable amount of network capacity and also increase disk activity along with CPU usage locally on the computer while running, depending on the number of Configuration Manager clients, how frequently you schedule software inventory, and the size of the files you collect (if any, which we wouldn't recommend anyway). If you think that software inventory will cause problems with your network, schedule it to run after business hours. Figure 11.2 shows the default software inventory settings; notice that no file types are selected by default.

FIGURE 11.2
Default software inventory settings

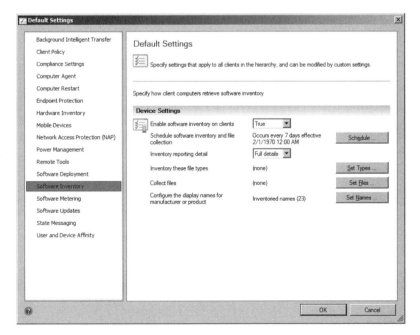

MORE ABOUT FILE COLLECTION

When a file is selected for collection, the Software Inventory Client Agent will search for that file when a software inventory scan runs on each client in the Configuration Management site. If the software inventory client agent finds a file that should be collected, then the file is attached to the inventory report and sent to the site server.

The site server keeps the five most recently changed versions of the collected files and stores them in the *<Configuration Manager installation directory>*\Inboxes\Sinv.box\ Filecol directory. If a file has not changed since the last software inventory was collected, the file will not be collected again. Files larger than 20 MB are not collected by Configuration Manager software inventory file collection even if they are defined in the file collection settings.

This feature of Configuration Manager can greatly affect network bandwidth, as well as cause other problems. With this in mind, we recommend not using it in any circumstance.

DISPLAY NAMES FOR SOFTWARE INVENTORIED PRODUCTS

During a software inventory cycle, the Configuration Manager 2012 software inventory process gets information from the file headers of files installed on clients. That information, including the names of the companies that made the files and the names of the files (or software products) themselves, is also inventoried. After the data is collected, you can view the information with Resource Explorer.

Because company and product names are retrieved from the file header information, any mismatches in the way these names are entered in the header information will also appear in the Configuration Manager database. These mismatches make it difficult to read and query against software inventory information since the data will appear to be under multiple company or software product names instead of a single name.

To help with this issue, you can set display names for inventoried products on the Inventoried Names tab of the Software Inventory Client Agent tab. For example, you can do the following:

1. Change variations of a company name to a single display name.

2. Refresh the view of software inventory in Resource Explorer.

You will see the changes. You will also see them when you make and run queries.

Doing this doesn't actually change the names in the file header information of the files installed on clients; it changes the names in the Configuration Manager site database.

Using Resource Explorer to View Inventory

When hardware and software inventory is collected from clients, it can be viewed by Resource Explorer. When you start Resource Explorer, a new console opens, as shown in Figure 11.3.

FIGURE 11.3
Resource Explorer

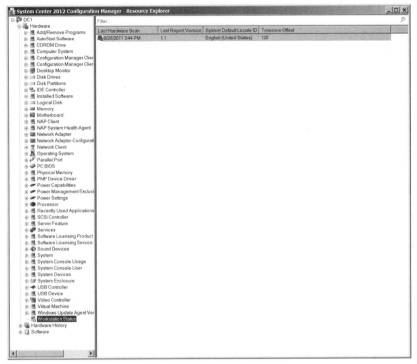

This displays the information collected from clients by hardware inventory and software inventory. The contents of the Resource Explorer details pane on the right will vary depending on what node is selected on the left pane in the console tree. You can use Resource Explorer to view client hardware, hardware history, and software inventory.

If a resource is a Configuration Manager client and if you are collecting hardware inventory at your site, the information displayed for that resource will be a list of the hardware installed on the client and other details. If you are collecting software inventory, then you will see a list of installed software on the client. If the resource isn't a Configuration Manager client, then no information will be displayed, since no inventory will be collected from that client.

You can start Resource Explorer to view a single client's inventory from the Configuration Manager console.

To open Resource Explorer from the Configuration Manager console, follow these steps:

1. In the Configuration Manager console, select the Asset and Intelligence workspace and click Devices.

2. Find the client that you want to view.

3. Once you have selected the client you want, click Start ➢ Resource Explorer on the Ribbon.

Scheduling Inventory

The hardware inventory and software inventory processes each collect inventory according to a schedule that is set in the client settings. Table 11.1 gives a simple rundown of scheduling options for each inventory process.

TABLE 11.1:   Inventory scheduling options

TYPE	DESCRIPTION
Simple schedule	An interval between inventory cycles, such as every six hours or daily
Custom schedule	A start time and an interval for inventory collection, such as every Monday or the first Tuesday of every month

By default, both hardware and software inventory schedules are set to run every seven days. If a client is not running when an inventory is schedule to run, it will run the inventory the next time the client is started.

The simple schedule doesn't give you as much flexibility as custom scheduling does; however, the simple schedule usually causes less network traffic because the time interval between each client's inventory cycle is based on the time that the Configuration Manager client was installed and when the first policies are retrieved, for every client. When you use a custom schedule, all the clients will begin inventory cycles at exactly the same time.

Since software inventory is more resource intensive on clients than hardware inventory, you might consider not running software inventory as often as you do hardware inventory, depending on your organization's needs. For example, if your organization has locked down user rights on workstations, then the software that is installed on them should not change frequently, so you can set software inventory cycles for every few days or once a week.

When you change an inventory collection schedule on the Configuration Manager site server, this will update the client computer policies downloaded and compiled by clients according to their regular client policy polling interval. When the client inventory agent detects a change in schedule, it will make a delta inventory file. The next inventory cycle will run according to the new schedule.

Configuration Manager also keeps historical inventory records for the number of days set in the Delete Aged Inventory History site maintenance task, which has a default setting of 90 days.

SCHEDULING INVENTORY

Even if all installations are unique, it is often considered best practice to have a daily hardware inventory schedule and a weekly software inventory schedule. For servers it is often considered good practice to have a custom schedule for both inventory processes. That way you can schedule when inventory will run and not put a load on the hardware during peak hours.

Configuring Inventory

Now that we have discussed the inventory process, its components, and its capabilities, you are ready to configure the inventory function to fit your company's needs.

CONFIGURING HARDWARE INVENTORY FOR A CONFIGURATION MANAGER SITE

Before you configure Hardware Inventory, you need to know what kind of information you are gathering. In essence you have three different scenarios, as explained in Table 11.2.

TABLE 11.2: Inventory scenarios

SCENARIO	HOW TO GATHER THE INVENTORY
Data class already exists in the default client settings.	All you have to do is enable the class in either the default client settings or in custom client settings as explained later in this chapter.
Data class does not exist in the default client settings but exists locally in WMI on each client.	On the Central Administration Site, open the default client settings. Connect to a remote host containing the data class, and import the data class.
Data class does not exist in the default client settings or on any of the local clients.	On one of the clients add the information to WMI. On the Central Administration Site open the default client settings. Connect to a remote host containing the data class and import the data class.

Configuring the Default Hardware Inventory Client Settings

To configure the default hardware inventory, select Client Settings in the Administration workspace. Open the default client agent settings properties, select hardware Inventory, and click Set Classes, as shown in Figure 11.4. You can configure the following properties:

FIGURE 11.4
Configuring Hardware Inventory

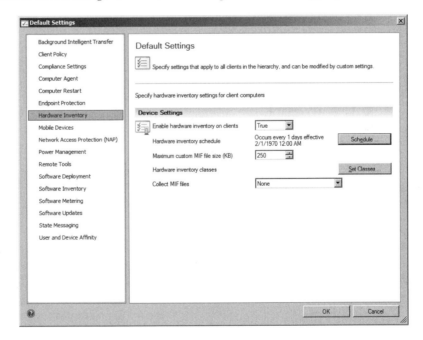

Enable Hardware Inventory On Clients   Configure this to True to enable (the default) or False to disable hardware inventory.

Hardware Inventory Schedule Click Schedule and select a simple schedule or define a custom schedule:

Simple Schedule This schedules hardware inventory to run at a single, specific interval for all clients that read the client settings. By default, this option is enabled and set for 7 days. For any other setting, use the Run Every field, and enter the number and type of time units (minutes, hours, days) in the simple schedule. This setting can be from 1 to 60 minutes, from 1 to 24 hours, or from 1 to 31 days.

Custom Schedule Click Customize to open the Custom Schedule dialog box and set the hardware inventory schedule. This gives you the ability to schedule the first start date and time for inventory to run on clients. Once the start time for inventory has passed, all future inventories will recur on the schedule that you set on all clients at the same time. The custom schedule can be set to run weekly, to run monthly, or to run on a custom interval, with the following criteria:

◆ Custom weekly schedules can run from 1 to 4 weeks on the day of the week you set.

◆ Custom monthly schedules can run from 1 to 12 months on either a specific day of the month from 1 to 31; the last day of each month; or the first, second, third, fourth, or last selected day of the week for each month.

◆ Custom schedules can also be set on a custom interval of either 1 to 31 days, 1 to 23 hours, or 1 to 59 minutes.

Collect MIF Files From the drop-down box select whether you want to collect IDMIF, NOIDMIF, both types, or none of them (default setting).

Maximum Custom MIF File Size (KB) This is the maximum size, in kilobytes, allowed for each custom MIF file that will be collected from a client during a hardware inventory cycle. You can set the size from 1 KB to 5,120 KB; the default value is 250 KB. If a custom MIF is larger than the maximum size, the Hardware Inventory Client Agent will move the IDMIF to the \Badmifs folder, and the IDMIF file will not be sent to the site server to be processed.

Collect IDMIF files Adds a new architecture, and attributes and classes, to the Configuration Manager database.

Collect NOIDMIF files Extends the hardware inventory by adding attributes and classes to existing architectures on a client. They are used to extend, or add, new information about existing Configuration Manager clients to the site database.

Changing the Default MIF Storage Location on a Client

You can change the MIF storage location after the client is installed by modifying the registry keys for the IDMIF and MOIDMIF files.

To change the default location for IDMIF files, follow these steps:

1. On the client for which you want to change the MIF location settings, select Start ➤ Run, type **regedit**, and then press Enter to start the Registry Editor.

2. Go to the following registry key: HKEY_LOCAL_MACHINE\SOFTWARE\Microsoft\SMS\Client\Configuration\Client Properties\IDMIF Directory.

3. Right-click IDMIF Directory, and click Modify.

4. Enter the path to which you want to change.

5. Close the Registry Editor.

To change the default storage location for NOIDMIF files, follow these steps:

1. On the client that you want to change the MIF location settings, select Start ➤ Run, type **regedit**, and then press Enter to start the Registry Editor.

2. Go to the following registry key: HKEY_LOCAL_MACHINE\SOFTWARE\Microsoft\SMS\ Client\Configuration\Client Properties\NOIDMIF Directory.

3. Right-click NOIDMIF Directory, and click Modify.

4. Enter the path to which you want to change.

5. Close the Registry Editor.

Note that this procedure will change the MIF storage location on only the client that you worked on. If you want to make this a sitewide client change, you can use the remediation feature in Settings Management.

 Real World Scenario

CONFIGURE CUSTOM HARDWARE INVENTORY CHANGES FOR ALL LAPTOPS

As the Configuration Manager administrator, you have been requested to ensure that portable battery information is inventoried for all laptops.

1. Open the Configuration Manager 2012 administrative console.

2. Select the Administration workspace and browse to Client Settings.

3. On the Ribbon, click Create Custom Client Settings and select Create Custom Client Device Settings.

4. Type **Hardware Settings for laptops** in the Name column.

5. From the list of custom settings, select Hardware Inventory.

6. In the left column, select Hardware Inventory and click Set Classes.

7. Find Portable Battery (Win32_Portable) and enable the data class.

8. Click OK.

9. Click OK to save the custom client settings.

10. Back in the administrative console, select the newly created custom settings and click Deploy on the Ribbon.

11. Select the All Laptop device collection and click OK.

EXTENDING HARDWARE INVENTORY

As described in Table 11.2, you can also customize Hardware Inventory to collect information that is not reported by default or add totally new information that you want to be collected that you configure yourself.

You can extend Hardware Inventory by inventorying additional WMI classes, additional WMI class attributes, registry keys, and other customizations to fit your company's needs. If you need to, you can also modify Hardware Inventory to reduce the amount of information reported by clients.

Before you start modifying the `configuration.mof` file, you should make sure you have a good idea of what you are doing and make backups of the file before you edit it. There are some great blog posts on how to edit MOF files and even a complete MOF guide. Here are some of the resources that are available:

```
http://technet.microsoft.com/en-us/library/gg712290.aspx
```

```
http://www.sccmexpert.com/MOF_guide.aspx
```

```
http://www.myitforum.com/myitwiki/SCCMINV.ashx
```

```
http://myitforum.com/cs2/files/folders/proddocs/entry152945.aspx
```

The MOF guide might need to be revised to work exactly with Configuration Manager 2012, but it will give you a good basis on just what is involved in editing MOF files to get the information you need out of hardware inventory. The RegKeyToMof tool written by Mark Cochrane is a free GUI that can be used to create most entries in the `Configuration.mof` file. The latest version of the tool has been updated to support Configuration Manager 2012.

Providers Used in Hardware Inventory

When you extend hardware inventory that is collected by Configuration Manager clients, the `configuration.mof` file is modified to inventory client information by leveraging a registered inventory data provider. Providers used during client hardware inventory are listed at the top of the `configuration.mof` file and are registered on clients when they first get a computer policy, and then they compile the `configuration.mof` file after the Configuration Manager client is installed.

Extending Hardware Inventory Using the configuration.mof File

The `configuration.mof` file is used to modify data class information inventoried by clients with hardware inventory.

To modify the `configuration.mof` file, follow these steps:

1. Make a backup copy of the `configuration.mof` file, and put it in a safe location.
2. On the primary site server, go to the `<Configuration Manager install folder>/inboxes/clifiles.src/hinv` folder.
3. Using Notepad, open the `configuration.mof` file, and make any necessary changes.

   Figure 11.5 shows part of the `configuration.mof` file.

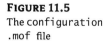

FIGURE 11.5
The configuration
.mof file

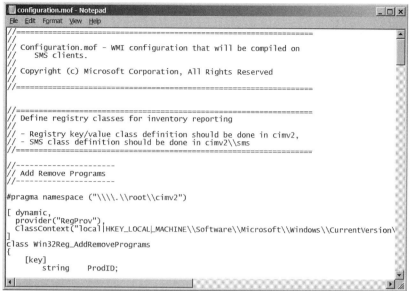

4. Close the configuration.mof file, and save the changes.

5. Copy the configuration.mof file to the same location that is listed in step 2 and to all the primary sites in your hierarchy to propagate the changes to the other sites.

Extending Hardware Inventory Using the Default Client Settings

The default client settings are used to modify reporting class information inventoried by clients during hardware inventory. The default client settings contain a list of classes and attributes that relate to data classes stored in the WMI repository of Configuration Manager clients.

Classes and properties that have the reporting checkmark enabled are collected, and those without a checkmark are not. You must always modify the default classes in the default client settings at the Central Administration Site; you will not be able to enable or disable these settings in any custom client settings.

To modify the default client settings, follow these steps:

1. Navigate to the Administration workspace, select Client Settings, and open the Default Client Settings properties.

2. Select Hardware Inventory and click Set Classes.

3. Use the GUI to enable or disable any of the existing inventory data classes.

4. Choose OK to save the changes.

5. Close the Default Client Settings.

Adding Custom Registry Settings to the Hardware Inventory

You will most likely be able to work with the default inventory settings for a long time without having to change them. But at some point, you will run into a situation where you must inventory custom registry information. An example of useful information would be information about the image version installed on the desktops. Often companies have different image versions installed and use a naming standard to distinguish between the different versions. One of the many features of the Microsoft Deployment Toolkit (MDT) is the ability to write information to the registry during the operating system deployment process. To gather this information you must first add the registry information to WMI on the client and add the data class to become part of the inventory process.

In this example you will see how you can combine free community tools (the RegKeyToMof tool developed by Mark Cochrane) with Configuration Manager 2012 to ease your daily work. The example will take the custom registry information from HKLM\Software\CM2012\ and add it to the inventory process.

1. Log on to the reference PC with administrative permissions.

2. Make sure you have a copy of RegKeyToMofV3.exe (or a later version). See Figure 11.6.

3. Open RegKeyToMofV3.exe and navigate to HKLM\Software\CM2012.

FIGURE 11.6
Using RegKeyToMof .exe to extend hardware information

4. Select the configuration.mof tab and copy everything from `#pragma namespace` (`"\\\\.\\root\\cimv2"`).

5. Open the `configuration.mof` file and paste the information into the end of the file.

6. Save the `configuration.mof` file.

You can monitor the process of adding the new data class by reading the `<Installation directory>`\Program files\Microsoft Configuration Manager\logs\dataldr.log file on the site server using CMTrace.exe (Figure 11.7).

FIGURE 11.7
Verifying the MOF process in
dataldr.log

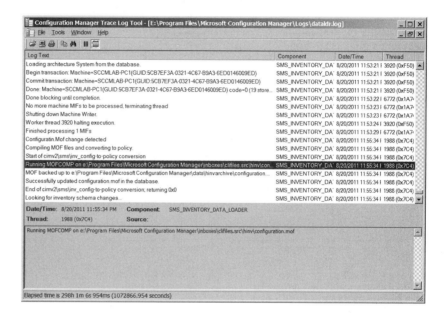

Now where the data class is added to the `configuration.mof` file all you need to do is enable the reporting class. You can do that by creating a MOF file and importing the file to the default client settings or from the client settings connect to WMI on a reference computer and import the reporting class. In this example a MOF file is created and imported into the default client settings.

7. In `RegKeyToMof.Exe` select the To Import in Admin/AgentSetting/HardwareInventory/SetClasses/Import tab, and copy all text from `#pragma namespace` (`"\\\\.\\root\\cimv2\\SMS"`).

8. Open Notepad and paste the information into a text file.

9. Save the file as `ImageVersion.mof` (Figure 11.8).

FIGURE 11.8
Custom MOF file

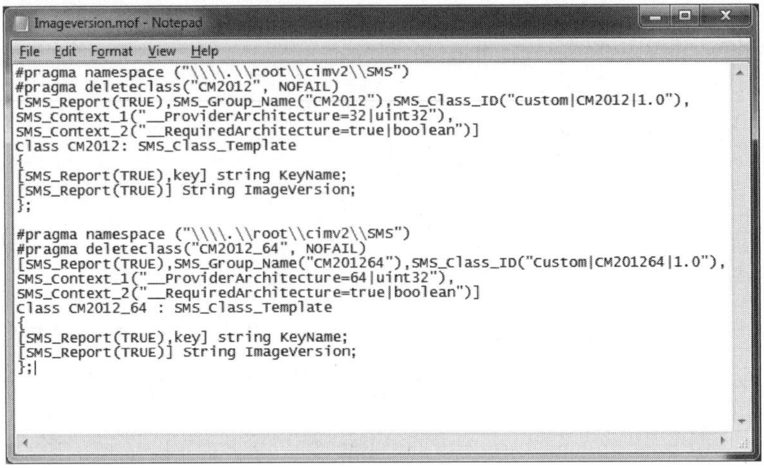

```
Imageversion.mof - Notepad
File  Edit  Format  View  Help
#pragma namespace ("\\\\.\\root\\cimv2\\SMS")
#pragma deleteclass("CM2012", NOFAIL)
[SMS_Report(TRUE),SMS_Group_Name("CM2012"),SMS_Class_ID("Custom|CM2012|1.0"),
SMS_Context_1("__ProviderArchitecture=32|uint32"),
SMS_Context_2("__RequiredArchitecture=true|boolean")]
Class CM2012: SMS_Class_Template
{
[SMS_Report(TRUE),key] string KeyName;
[SMS_Report(TRUE)] String ImageVersion;
};

#pragma namespace ("\\\\.\\root\\cimv2\\SMS")
#pragma deleteclass("CM2012_64", NOFAIL)
[SMS_Report(TRUE),SMS_Group_Name("CM201264"),SMS_Class_ID("Custom|CM201264|1.0"),
SMS_Context_1("__ProviderArchitecture=64|uint32"),
SMS_Context_2("__RequiredArchitecture=true|boolean")]
Class CM2012_64 : SMS_Class_Template
{
[SMS_Report(TRUE),key] string KeyName;
[SMS_Report(TRUE)] String ImageVersion;
};
```

10. Open the Configuration Manager administrative console, navigate to the Administration workspace, and select Client Settings.

11. Select the Default Client Agent Settings and open the properties.

12. Select Hardware Inventory and click Set Classes.

13. Click Import, select the `ImageVersion.mof` file, and click Open.

14. Click Import, and the MOF entries will be imported. Figure 11.9 shows the Import Summary screen.

FIGURE 11.9
Successfully imported custom MOF file

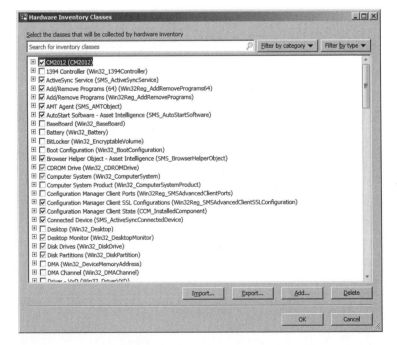

Configuring Software Inventory for a Configuration Manager Site

Software Inventory is enabled by default when you install Configuration Manager, but unlike previous versions, ConfigMgr 2012 will not inventory any files by default. To configure Software Inventory to scan for EXE files, follow these steps:

1. Navigate to the Administration workspace, select Client Settings, and open the Default Client Settings properties.

2. Select Software Inventory.

   The first thing you will see is the default settings, as shown in Figure 11.10.

FIGURE 11.10
Default Software
Inventory settings

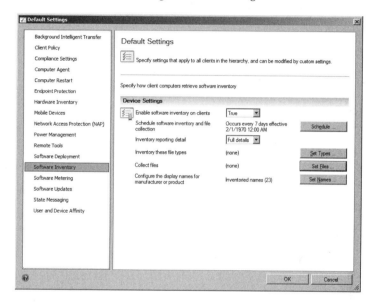

3. Click Set Types.

4. Click the yellow starburst icon to create a new entry.

5. Type *.exe, as shown in Figure 11.11, and click OK twice.

FIGURE 11.11
Scanning for EXE files

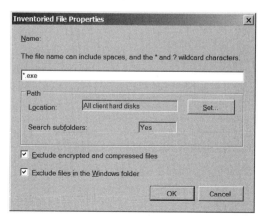

This will search for EXE files on the entire hard disk, excluding the `Windows` folder and compressed files. If you want to, you can specify which folders to include in the scanning; likewise you can specify a filename instead of a file type.

Inventory Reporting Detail is by default set to Full Details. This will ensure that you gather information about the file regardless of whether the file has a product mentioned in the file header or not. Selecting Product Only will not gather information from unknown files.

Collect Files allows you to copy a file from the client and store a copy on the site server. When you enable this feature, the site server will keep up to five versions of each file in `<Configuration Manager installation directory>\Inboxes\Sinv.box\Filecol`. Even though it sounds tempting to collect files, you should think twice before enabling this feature. It can generate a substantial amount of network traffic and cause your site server to run low on disk space. As shown in Figure 11.12, you can collect a single file or all files of a certain file type.

FIGURE 11.12
Collecting files

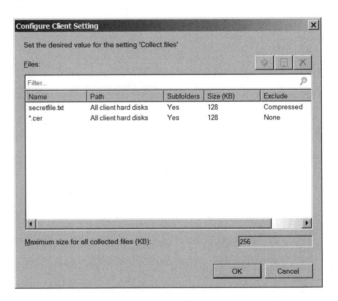

6. To specify a file, click the yellow New icon, and type a filename or use a wildcard to specify a given type.

7. Click Set to narrow the search to a given location; this will speed up the process.

   Figure 11.13 shows how you can search for all `*.sus` files in the `%programfiles%\MySoftware` folder.

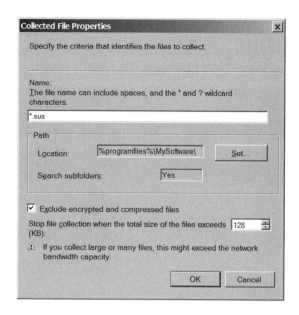

Configuring the display names for manufacturer or product allows you to group files according to the correct vendor and application. As mentioned earlier in this chapter, the names are derived from the file header, which often contains alternative ways to spell the manufacturer's name.

8. Click Set Names, and click the yellow New icon to configure a new display name.

Figure 11.14 shows a new display name for Adobe applications.

FIGURE 11.14
Configure a
new display name

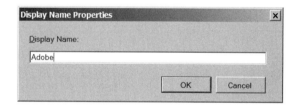

9. Once the display name is created, select the display name and click the yellow New icon to the right of Inventoried Names.

When you specify an entry in the Inventoried Names section, you can use these wildcard variables:

%	Any string of zero or more characters
_ (underscore)	Any single character
[ ] (brackets)	Any single character within a range
[^]	Any single character *not* with a range

10. When you have typed a name, click OK.

Figure 11.15 shows an example where all inventory names starting with "Adobe" will be grouped below the Adobe manufacturer.

FIGURE 11.15
A custom display name

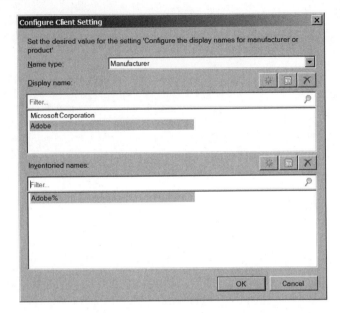

VIEWING SOFTWARE INVENTORY DATA

Software inventory information is often used in queries and reports. In the Configuration Manager administrative console, you can use Resource Explorer to view information from a single client (Figure 11.16). You will be able to read file information including File Name, File Path, File Size, File Version, and File Modified Date. The information is divided into four sections, as described here:

Collected Files   List all files collected from the client.

File Details   List all inventoried files that are not associated with any vendor.

Last Software Scan   Lists the last file collection and software inventory scanning data.

Products Details   List all inventoried files that are associated with a vendor. You can modify the list of vendors by customizing the display name in the Software Inventory Client Settings.

FIGURE 11.16

Software information in Resource Explorer

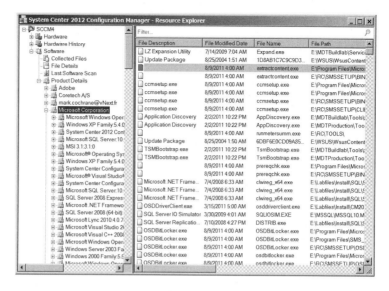

MISCELLANEOUS INVENTORY CONFIGURATIONS AND OPTIONS

The following sections cover some configuration options for inventory that don't neatly fit into other categories.

Encrypting Client Inventory Reports

Configuration Manager can be configured to sign and encrypt data sent between the client and the management point. To enhance security for inventory, you can enable inventory encryption.
To enable inventory encryption, follow these steps:

1. In the Configuration Manager console, select the Administration workspace ➤ Site Configuration ➤ Sites.

2. Right-click the site and click Properties.

3. Click the Signing And Encryption tab.

4. Select Use Encryption.

5. Click OK to finish.

Excluding Files from Software Inventory

To exclude folders or entire drives from the software inventory process, create a file called skpswi.dat and save it to the root of the area you want to exclude. You can skip the entire C: partition by storing the file in C:\ or a folder (and subfolders) by saving the file in the root of the folder.

You can ensure that folders and drivers are excluded by reading the FileSystemFile.log file on the client. Figure 11.17 shows how you can verify that the skpswi.dat file is working.

FIGURE 11.17
FileSystem-
File.log

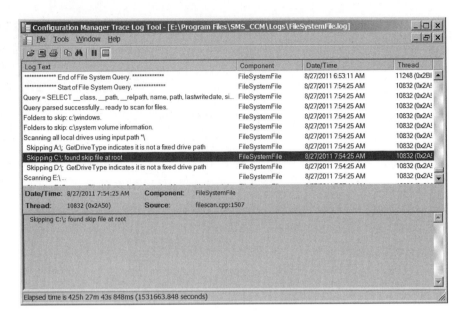

To exclude files from software inventory, follow these steps:

1. Using Notepad, make an empty file named skpswi.dat.

2. Right-click that file, and click Properties.

3. In the file properties for skpswi.dat, select the Hidden attribute.

4. Place the skpswi.dat file at the root of the drive or folder where you don't want to collect software inventory.

Monitoring the File and Size Being Sent to the Management Point

One of the questions you often hear before enabling any inventory process is how much network utilization is generated by running this process? The Configuration Manager client will send Heartbeat Discovery data, hardware inventory data, and software inventory data on a regular basis. The three files generated by each of these processes will be temporarily stored in %systemroot%\ccm\inventory\temp\ before being sent to the management point. After files are sent to the management point, they will automatically be deleted from the temp folder. You can create a file called archive_reports.sms, discussed next, and save it to the same folder. This will prevent the Configuration Manager client from deleting the XML files after they are sent to the management point.

Figure 11.18 shows three files generated: one for hardware inventory, one for software inventory, and one for Heartbeat Discovery.

FIGURE 11.18
Files generated by the inventory and discovery processes

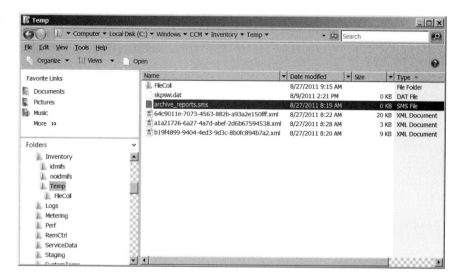

To prevent XML files from being deleted, follow these steps:

1. Using Notepad, create an empty file named `archive_reports.sms` (make sure that it's not a `.txt` file).

2. Save the file in the `%systemroot%\ccm\inventory\temp\` folder.

3. Initiate a hardware, software, and/or discovery inventory cycle on the client, and monitor the `%systemroot%\ ccm\inventory\temp\` folder.

   You should be able to see one XML file for each process that contains data.

4. Remember to delete the `archive_reports.sms` file from the client once you have enough information to estimate the average file size for each of the three processes.

Viewing Collected Files

You can view collected files by opening the `<:\>Program Files\Microsoft Configuration Manager\inboxes\sinv.box\FileCol\` folder on the site server or through Resource Explorer. Using Resource Explorer is by far the best tool because it will link the collected files and computer together. As shown in Figure 11.19, you can open and read each collected file.

FIGURE 11.19

Reading a collected file in Resource Explorer

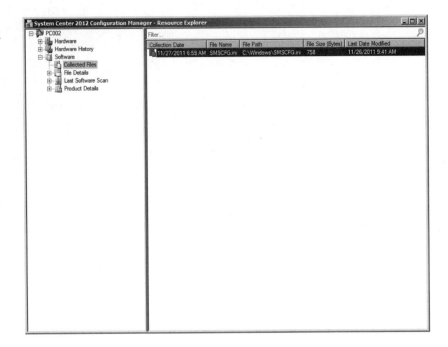

To view the collected files of a particular client, follow these steps:

1. In the Configuration Manager console, select the Asset and Compliance workspace ➤ Overview ➤ Devices.

2. In the Search area of the Ribbon, type the name of the client you wish to find and click Search.

3. Once you have found the client you want, right-click it.

4. Then click All Tasks ➤ Start Resource Explorer.

5. In the left pane, select Software Collected Files.

   You will see a list of all the files that have been collected from that client in the right pane.

6. To view a file, you have two options:

   ◆ Right-click a file, and select View File.

   ◆ Right-click a file, and select Save.

Troubleshooting Inventory

The following sections cover some basic information that will help you troubleshoot specific problems. In order to troubleshoot and fully understand what's going on behind the scenes, you need to have information about the log files in the process.

HARDWARE INVENTORY

When you troubleshoot hardware inventory, you need to know how data travels from the client to the SQL database. Inventory data will be sent from the client to the management point and then to the site server before being added to the database.

CLIENT-SIDE PROCESSING

All client-side hardware inventory processes are recorded in the `InventoryAgent.log` file. The log file will contain several lines that are important for you to understand.

The following line tells you what kind of inventory report will be sent from the client to the management point. It can be a full, delta, or resync report.

```
Inventory: Action=Hardware ReportType=Delta
```

The following line queries for data:

```
Collection: Namespace = \\localhost\root\Microsoft\appvirt\client; Query = SELECT
__CLASS, __PATH, __RELPATH, LastLaunchOnSystem, Name, PackageGUID, Version FROM
Application; Timeout = 600 secs
```

The following line gives information about the number of classes that the client is searching for and the number of classes found. The information in this line is worth checking whenever you make changes to the data classes. When you enable an extra data class, the last number should increase by one.

```
Collection: 55/64 inventory data items successfully inventoried.
```

The following line basically informs you that the client-side processing has completed successfully and information has been sent to the management point.

```
Inventory: Successfully sent report. Destination:mp:MP_HinvEndpoint, ID:
{D886D5C8-59E4-4C9C-B9CD-08D7DA40BA20}, Timeout: 80640 minutes MsgMode: Signed,
Not Encrypted
```

MANAGEMENT POINT PROCESSING

At the management point the client data will be converted from an XML file to an MIF file and sent to the site server. You can monitor the process by reading the `MP_HINV.log` file.

SITE SERVER PROCESSING

At the site server the client data will be added to the SQL database by the Inventory Data Loader process. In the `Dataldr.log` file you will see entries similar to these:

```
Thread: 10368 will use GUID GUID:1E8A9DD4-C572-48F9-BEDB-B33D8E0F07F4
SMS_INVENTORY_DATA_LOADER   8/27/2011 11:34:04 AM   10368 (0x2880)
Processing Inventory for Machine: DC1   Version 1.7  Generated: 08/27/2011
11:33:27   SMS_INVENTORY_DATA_LOADER   8/27/2011 11:34:04 AM   10368 (0x2880)
Begin transaction: Machine=DC1(GUID:1E8A9DD4-C572-48F9-BEDB-B33D8E0F07F4)
SMS_INVENTORY_DATA_LOADER   8/27/2011 11:34:04 AM   10368 (0x2880)
Commit transaction: Machine=DC1(GUID:1E8A9DD4-C572-48F9-BEDB-B33D8E0F07F4)
SMS_INVENTORY_DATA_LOADER   8/27/2011 11:34:04 AM   10368 (0x2880)
```

```
Done: Machine=DC1(GUID:1E8A9DD4-C572-48F9-BEDB-B33D8E0F07F4) code=0 (20 stored
procs in XH3JZIA70.MIF)   SMS_INVENTORY_DATA_LOADER   8/27/2011 11:34:04 AM
10368 (0x2880)
```

The MIF file is added to the SQL database from

```
<:>\Program Files\Microsoft Configuration Manager\inboxes\auth\dataldr.box\
Process
```

If you see a large number of MIF files in one of the dataldr.box folders, it's normally a clear indication of a backlog.

When Clients Are Deleted from the Database but Not Uninstalled

A commonly seen issue occurs when an administrator accidently deletes all client computers from a collection. This will remove client data from the database, but the Configuration Manager Client Agent is not aware of that. In the following sequence you can see that the client is still sending delta inventory information to the site server, but since the site server does not have any existing records, it will not be able to process that delta data and asks the client to perform a resync.

In the InventoryAgent.log file on the client, notice that the first report type is delta.

```
<![LOG[Inventory: Action=Hardware ReportType=Delta]LOG]!><time="12:38:31.453-120"
date="08-27-2011" component="InventoryAgent" context="" type="1" thread="212"
file="agentstate.cpp:1563">
```

The data loader component receives the delta information and tries to add it to an existing record in the database. The record does not exist in the database, which is why the MIF file is discarded and moved to the Badmifs folder. Furthermore, the data loader component will initiate a resync, which instructs the client to send up a full inventory report.

```
ERROR - attempt to update non-existent row. Invalid command:  exec dbo
.pWorkstationStatus_DATA 1,16777222,'08/27/2011 12:49:49',1,'8/27/2011 12
:49:42',N'4294967305',1033,120  $$<SMS_INVENTORY_DATA_LOADER><08-27-2011
12:49:49.740-120><thread=2720 (0xAA0)>
Rollback transaction: Machine=DC1(GUID:1E8A9DD4-C572-48F9-BEDB-B33D8E0F07F4)
$$<SMS_INVENTORY_DATA_LOADER><08-27-2011 12:49:49.744-120><thread=2720 (0xAA0)>
Remote client hardware inventory resync generated for client GUID:1E8A9DD4-
C572-48F9-BEDB-B33D8E0F07F4; update/insert result = 2  $$<SMS_INVENTORY_DATA_
LOADER><08-27-2011 12:49:49.825-120><thread=2720 (0xAA0)>
~Send resync command to local site for machine GUID:1E8A9DD4-C572-
48F9-BEDB-B33D8E0F07F4.   $$<SMS_INVENTORY_DATA_LOADER><08-27-2011
12:49:49.830-120><thread=2720 (0xAA0)>
STATMSG: ID=2722 SEV=I LEV=M SOURCE="SMS Server" COMP="SMS_INVENTORY_DATA_
LOADER" SYS=SCCM4.sccmlab.local SITE=RC1 PID=9052 TID=2720 GMTDATE=Sat Aug
27 10:49:49.833 2011 ISTR0="DC1" ISTR1="" ISTR2="" ISTR3="" ISTR4="" ISTR5=""
ISTR6="" ISTR7="" ISTR8="" ISTR9="" NUMATTRS=0  $$<SMS_INVENTORY_DATA_
LOADER><08-27-2011 12:49:49.835-120><thread=2720 (0xAA0)>
~Cannot process MIF XHIJ3F4L2.MIF, moving it to e:\Program Files\Microsoft
Configuration Manager\inboxes\auth\dataldr.box\BADMIFS\44p7g21x.MIF  $$<SMS_
INVENTORY_DATA_LOADER><08-27-2011 12:49:49.843-120><thread=2720 (0xAA0)>
```

On the client, the next hardware inventory will send a full hardware report to the management point. Notice the ReportType=Resync notation:

```
![LOG[Inventory: Opening store for action {00000000-0000-0000-0000-000000000001}
...]LOG]!><time="13:03:21.391-120" date="08-27-2011" component="InventoryAgent"
context="" type="1" thread="2668" file="datastore.cpp:176">
<![LOG[Inventory: Action=Hardware ReportType=ReSync]
LOG]!><time="13:03:37.734-120" date="08-27-2011" component="InventoryAgent"
context="" type="1" thread="2668" file="agentstate.cpp:1563">
```

Once the resync report is processed, the client will be added to the database and will show up in the Configuration Manager administrative console.

When Clients Try to Inventory Data Classes That Don't Exist

As we have already discussed, the Hardware Inventory Client Agent gets information about a computer's hardware from the WMI data classes. Sometimes not all of the WMI data classes that Configuration Manager is set up to inventory are present on a client.

Clients with different operating systems are a good example. The default client settings are configured to inventory certain new WMI classes in Windows 2008 R2 that aren't available on other operating systems. The hardware inventory process will still try to inventory those classes on a Windows 7 or Windows Vista client since they also read the settings in the default client settings.

When a client tries to inventory a class that doesn't exist, you will see an entry only in the InventoryAgent.log file, because no status message will be sent to the site server. If you need to figure out whether a client is trying to inventory nonexistent data classes, you will see entries similar to Collection: Class "<Class Name>" does not exist in the InventoryAgent.log file.

Software Metering in Configuration Manager 2012

Software Metering is used to track usage of administrator-defined applications using software-metering rules. It is not used to prevent users from running an application (this is a job for the Software Restriction Group Policy). By default Configuration Manager will automatically create disabled software-metering rules based on the recently used inventory data. Often you will find yourself disabling the feature and creating your own software-metering rules.

Overview of Software Metering

Software Metering in Configuration Manager 2012 allows you to monitor and collect information about software usage on Configuration Manager clients. The information collected is based on the software metering rules that can be configured in the Configuration Manager console or created automatically based on usage data collected by inventory.

The Software Metering Client Agent on each client evaluates these rules, collects the requested data, and then reports it to the Configuration Manager database. The software metering process will continue to collect usage data even if it can't connect to its management point and will send the collected data on to the site server after it connects to the network. By default clients will send the software metering usage report every seven days.

Software metering data is held on the site server until it is summarized. The summarization schedule is defined in the Site Maintenance tasks for the site. By default the process will begin every night at 00:00.

You will be able to see the software metering data in the reports once the software metering report data has been received on the site server and summarized. By default this process can take up to eight days from client activity to seeing information in reports. This might sound like a long delay, but often you will only use the reports once a month or so when evaluating licenses. Combined with software inventory, software metering gives administrators a powerful tool to help answer questions that come up in every IT organization. Examples of these questions include the following:

◆ What is the relationship between how many instances of a software program are installed on clients and how many actually use that software?

◆ Do you need to buy more licenses when renewing your license agreement with a software vendor?

◆ What users are still using an obsolete program?

Configuring Software Metering

The Software Metering feature is enabled by default when you install Configuration Manager. You can enabled or disable the feature by editing the default Client Agent settings or creating a custom client setting.

CONFIGURING THE SOFTWARE METERING FEATURE

Take these steps to configure the Software Metering feature:

1. Navigate to the Administration workspace, select Client Settings, and open the Default Client Settings properties.

2. Select Software Metering, and notice the default setting, as shown in Figure 11.20.

   By default, Enable Software Metering On Clients is set to True.

FIGURE 11.20
Default Software
Metering settings

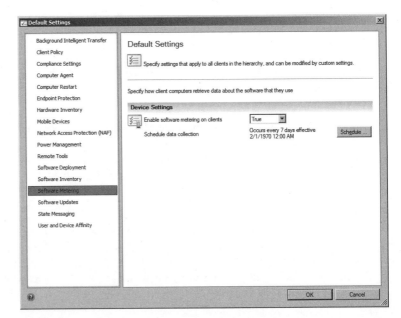

3. To disable the feature, select False in the drop-down box.

   Schedule Data Collection defines how often the Configuration Manager client will send
   software metering data from WMI to the site server.

Configuring Automatic Software Metering Rule Generation

As discussed earlier in the chapter, Configuration Manager will automatically create disabled
software metering rules based on recently gathered inventory data. You can configure or disable
the feature from the Assets and Compliance workspace.

To configure automatic rule generation, follow these steps:

1. Navigate to the Assets and Compliance workspace, select Software Metering, and click
   Software Metering Properties on the Ribbon.

   This opens the Software Metering Properties dialog box, as shown in Figure 11.21.

FIGURE 11.21

Software Metering
Properties dialog box

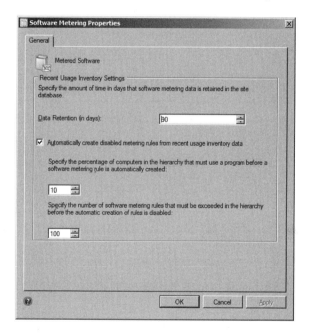

2. You can set the following options:

   ◆ You can specify the amount of time in Data Detention (In Days) that data generated
   by software rules will be held in the site database. The default setting is 90 days.

   ◆ You can select the Automatically Create Disabled Metering Rules From Recent Usage
   Inventory Data check box.

◆ You can set the percentage of computers in a Configuration Manager site that must use an executable before a software metering rule for that executable is automatically created. The default setting is 10 percent.

◆ You can set the maximum number of rules that software metering will automatically generate. The default setting is 100 rules.

3. When you have finished setting these options, click OK.

Enabling and Disabling Software Metering Rules

You don't have to delete a rule if you don't want to use it; instead, you can enable it or disable it as needed if you want to keep it.

To enable or disable a software metering rule, follow these steps. Figure 11.22 shows automatically generated software metering rules in the Configuration Manager console.

FIGURE 11.22
Software Metering node with software metering rules

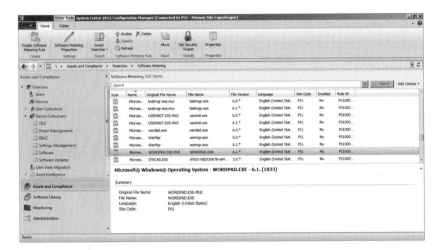

1. Navigate to the Assets and Compliance workspace, and select Software Metering.

2. Right-click one or more rules that you want to configure, and then click either Enable or Disable.

The option that is available will depend on what state the rule is already in.

Adding a Software Metering Rule

If the automatically generated rules aren't what you need, then you can manually make your own to meet your organization's needs. To make your own software metering rules, follow these steps:

1. Navigate to the Assets and Compliance workspace, and select Software Metering.

2. Click Create Software Metering Rule on the Ribbon.

This opens the General page of the Create Software Metering Rule Wizard, shown in Figure 11.23.

FIGURE 11.23
General page of
the Create Software
Metering Rule
Wizard

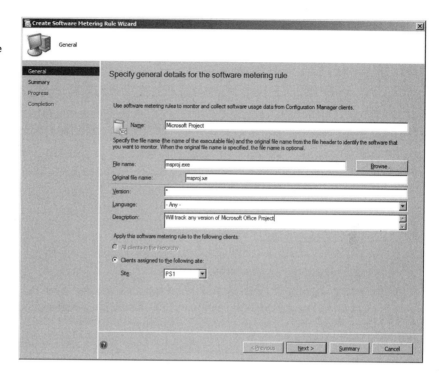

This page has the following options:

Name   The name of the software metering rule, which should be unique. You can have rules with the same name, as long as the filenames are different. This way you can track suites of applications like the Adobe Creative Suite or Microsoft Office.

File Name   The name of the executable file you want to meter. You can click Browse to display the Open dialog box, where you can select the file that you want to meter. You can manually type in this filename, but when you do that, no checks are made to determine whether the file exists or whether it contains the needed file header information. For the best results, always use the Browse button if possible. Wildcard characters can't be used in this field, and selecting the Original File Name field is optional.

Original File Name   The name of the executable file that you want to meter. This name is matched to the information in the file header, not the filename itself, so you still meter it if the file is renamed. Wildcard characters can't be used in this field, and selecting the File Name field is optional.

Version   The version of the executable file that you want to meter. If you use the Browse button to select your file, this field will be filled out automatically from the file's header information (as shown in Figure 11.19). You can use the wildcard character (*) to represent any string of characters or the wildcard character (?) to represent any single character. If you want to meter all versions of the file, you can use the default value (*).

Language   The language of the file that you want to meter. The default value is English (United States). If you use the Browse button to select your file, then this is filled out automatically from the file's header information. If you want to meter all language versions of this file, then select Any from the drop-down list.

Comment   A description that you want for the rule. This is an optional field.

Apply This Software Metering Rule To The Following Clients: Your options are All Clients In The Hierarchy or Clients Assigned To The Following Site.

3. Fill in the information and click Next.

4. Review the information on the Summary page and click Next.

5. Click Close.

The rule is now created and will be downloaded to clients during the next machine policy cycle.

DELETING SOFTWARE METERING RULES

When you delete a software metering rule, the change will be downloaded to clients during their next policy polling interval, just like when you create rules.

To delete a software metering rule, follow these steps:

1. Navigate to the Assets and Compliance workspace, and select Software Metering.

2. Find the metering rule that you want to delete, right-click it, and click Delete.

You will then see a Confirm Object Delete dialog box.

3. If you are sure that you want to delete this rule, then click Yes.

SOFTWARE METERING MAINTENANCE TASKS

Depending on how you configure software metering, you could end up with a lot of data collected in the Configuration Manager database. To help you manage that data, several maintenance tasks are included in the Configuration Manager console. There are four tasks in total in two categories—two tasks for deleting aged software metering data and two tasks for summarizing software metering data. All of these tasks are enabled by default.

To find them in the Configuration Manager console, navigate to the Administration workspace and choose Site Configuration ➤ Sites. From the Ribbon click Site Maintenance.

Figure 11.24 shows the four software metering site maintenance settings. To edit, just double-click the task you want to configure.

FIGURE 11.24
Software metering
maintenance task

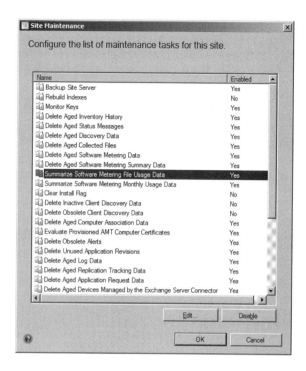

These tasks summarize software metering usage data to compress the amount that is stored in the Configuration Manager database. Summarization runs daily by default and will run only against data that is at least 12 hours old. This is required for all software metering reports to produce any meaningful data. To get an idea of what is in the most current set of summarized data, you have to know when that last summarization took place.

The Software Metering Summarization Progress report, as shown in Figure 11.25, will provide you with information about the last summarization process.

FIGURE 11.25
Software Metering
Summarization
Progress report

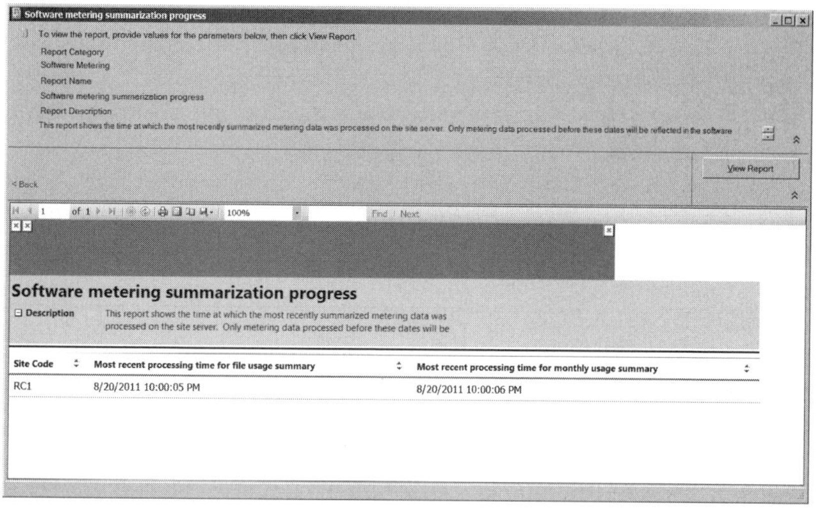

The Summarize Software Metering File Usage Data task summarizes software metering file usage data from several records into one record. This record gives information about the program name, version, language, and number of distinct users over intervals of 15 minutes to 1 hour. This process compresses and optimizes the amount of data stored in the Configuration Manager database.

For every hour and every 15-minute time frame within the hour, this task will calculate the total number of distinct user/computer combinations that are running the programs that are being metered. Within 15-minute intervals, this will give an approximate number of concurrent users of a metered program.

When software summary data is sent up the Configuration Manager hierarchy, data from each site is kept separate from the data from the other sites. When the data reaches a parent site, each record is marked with the site code of the site it came from.

The Summarize Software Metering Monthly Usage Data task summarizes detailed software metering usage data from many records into one record. This record gives information on the program name, program version, language, program running times, number of times used, last time used, username, and computer name. This summarization compresses the amount of data that is stored in the Configuration Manager database and is sent to the central site.

The summary data also includes the number of times each matching metered piece of software was run on a specific computer by a specific user during that month. This task is set to run every day by default, and the summary is done for a period of one month.

 Real World Scenario

MANUALLY SUMMARIZE SOFTWARE METERING DATA

As the Configuration Manager administrator, you have been requested to demonstrate the Software Metering feature. You need to ensure that all the latest data is summarized and part of the reports. To do so, follow these steps:

1. Log on to the site server.

2. From the Configuration Manager DVD, copy `runmetersumm.exe` (found in the Tools folder) to `<:>\Program Files\Microsoft Configuration Manager\bin\x64`.

3. Open a command prompt as administrator, and navigate to `<:>\Program Files\Microsoft Configuration Manager\bin\x64`.

4. Type **`runmetersumm.exe CM_<Configuration Manager site code>`**, for example, **`runmetersumm.exe CM_S01`**.

5. Press Enter, and notice the number of records that have been summarized.

MONITOR CLIENT ACTIVITY

Whenever a client runs a program, it will be registered in the `mtrmgr.log` file on the client. If the program has a matching software metering rule, the client agent will start tracking the process associated with the program, as shown in Figure 11.26.

FIGURE 11.26

Reading the `mtrmgr`
`.log` file on the client

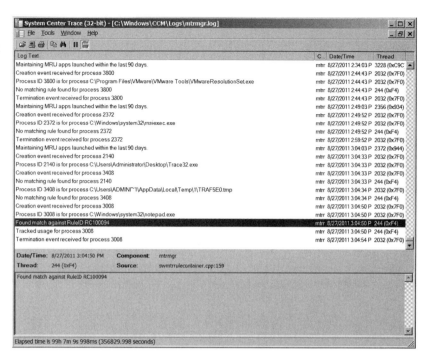

Each client will generate a software metering usage report and send the report to the management point. You can initiate the action manually by running the Software Metering Usage Report Cycle in the Configuration Manager Properties on the client, as shown in Figure 11.27.

FIGURE 11.27

Running the
Software Metering
Usage Report Cycle
on the client

Activity from this process is written to the SWMTRReportGen.log file on the client. The data will be sent to the site server and recorded in the swmproc.log file on the site server.

DEFAULT SOFTWARE METERING REPORTS

Configuration Manager 2012 ships with several canned software metering reports:

◆ All Software Metering Rules At This Site

◆ Computers That Have A Metered Program Installed But Have Not Run The Program Since A Specified Date

◆ Computers That Have Run A Specific Metered Software Program

◆ Concurrent Usage For All Metered Software Programs

◆ Concurrent Usage Trend Analysis Of A Specific Metered Software Program

◆ Install Base For All Metered Software Programs

◆ Time Of Day Usage Summary For A Specific Metered Software Program

◆ Total Usage For All Metered Software Programs

◆ Total Usage For All Metered Software Programs On Windows Terminal Servers

◆ Total Usage Trend Analysis For A Specific Metered Software Program

◆ Total Usage Trend Analysis For A Specific Metered Software Program On Windows Terminal Servers

◆ Users That Have Run A Specific Metered Software Program

◆ Software Metering Summarization Progress

One of the disadvantages of having a large number of disabled software metering rules is that all rules will be shown in the Install Base For All Metered Software Programs report. This might clutter the picture a little bit because you will see programs that you might not be interested in seeing.

By combining the values from the Install Base For All Metered Software Programs report with the report Computers That Have A Metered Program Installed But Have Not Run The Program Since A Specified Date, you can easily see how many installed instances you have and measure that against how many times the application has been used in a specific period. This will give the names of computers where you can uninstall the application and that way save money on the software budget.

The Bottom Line

Configure and manage Software Inventory.   Configuring Software Inventory has changed in Configuration Manager 2012, although the client-processing part is almost the same as in Configuration Manager 2007.

Master It   By default, Configuration Manager does not scan for any file types. Where would you go to do that?

Configure and manage Hardware Inventory.   Hardware Inventory provides a wealth of information on the hardware resources in your organization. That information is vital when planning for things such as updating standard business software or upgrading the standard operating system your organization uses. If the standard hardware inventory collected is not enough for your needs, then you have many options to extend the hardware inventory to get that vital information.

Master It   Where do you enable or disable data classes in Hardware Inventory?

Configure and manage Software Metering.   Keeping track of software that is installed and actually being used is a large part of being able to manage software licenses effectively. By pairing Software Metering in Configuration Manager with Software Inventory, you can get detailed information on just what software is out there and who is or is not using it. This goes a long way to help keep your software licensing in compliance.

Master It   How long do you have to wait, at the very least, after you configure Software Metering before you can expect to see any data returned?

Chapter 12

Reporting

Reporting in Configuration Manager has grown from being a feature mainly used to view inventory information to become one of the primary features. Reporting helps you to gather, organize, and present information like the following:

- Inventory information
- Software update compliance data
- Migration information
- Audit information
- Power management information
- Alert information
- User data

In Configuration Manager 2012, the Reporting feature has changed compared to any earlier releases of the product. Gone are the ASP web reports, and the only supported reporting solution left is SQL Server Reporting Services (SSRS). Using SQL Server Reporting Services gives you as an administrator several benefits compared to the classic web reports, such as these:

- Schedule reports to render during non-business hours.
- Execute reports from a cache.
- Create snapshots.
- Subscribe to reports and have them mailed to you based on a schedule.
- More easily modify existing reports with custom logos, text, and chart objects.
- No 10,000-row limitations.
- Standard reporting engine used by other Microsoft applications like SharePoint and the other Microsoft System Center applications.

Another great feature of using reports is that you can allow users outside the IT department to view part of the rich information that is being gathered through Configuration Manager 2012. Viewing reports does not require access to the Configuration Manager administrative console, only membership in the appropriate groups. With that in mind, in this chapter you will learn skills that will help you install and manage Reporting Services as well as modify and create reports.

In this chapter, you will learn to

◆ Install the Reporting Services point.

◆ Manage reporting security.

◆ Create and manage report subscriptions.

◆ Create custom reports.

Installing SQL Server Reporting Services

Prior to installing the SQL Server reporting services role you need to ensure that you have installed SQL Server Reporting Services. SQL Server Reporting Services can be found on the SQL DVD media you used to install the SQL Server.

Before you install SQL Server Reporting Services you need to make sure that the server meets the minimum requirements:

◆ SQL Server 2008 with Service Pack 1 (SP1) Reporting Services

◆ .NET Framework 4

For a list of recommended hardware and software requirements for SQL Server 2008, see

```
http://technet.microsoft.com/en-us/library/ms143506(SQL.100).aspx#SEx64
```

Considerations for Installing SQL Server Reporting Services

There are several considerations prior to installing SQL Server Reporting Services, such as which extra tools to install, security, where to place the site system role, and SQL instance support. This section will try to answer what are considered to be the most common considerations.

With the installation of SQL Server Reporting Services you not only install a reporting engine, but you also install the following:

◆ The report server web service

◆ Report Builder

◆ Reporting Services configuration tool

◆ Command-line utilities, such as `rsconfig.exe`, `rs.exe`, and `rskeymgmt.exe`.

Besides the core tools and services, you should also consider these features:

Business Intelligence Development Studio   When you select to install Business Intelligence Development Studio (BIDS) using the SQL media, it will install Visual Studio and provide you reporting and report model design tools. This tool comes in very handy for creating more advanced reports and report models.

SQL Server Management Studio   The client tools feature on the SQL media gives you SQL Server Management Studio, which is another tool often used in the report-creation process. SQL Server Management Studio is also used to configure SQL maintenance jobs, configure SQL security, and provide a GUI for maintaining the databases.

You also chose modes and instances:

Installation Mode During setup you can choose between Native mode or SharePoint mode. Configuration Manager 2012 supports only Native mode.

Instance You can install SQL Server Reporting Services in either the default instance or a named instance.

WHERE TO INSTALL THE REPORTING SERVICES

The Reporting site system can be installed on any primary site or the Central Administration Site. It is considered best practice to install the site system on the Central Administration Site. At the Central Administration Site you will have access to all global data and all site data. Installing the site system on a primary site will only allow you to display global data and site data that are local to the corresponding site. Installing the site system on a secondary site is not supported.

You can install the site system on the site server or on a remote server. For performance reasons it is often best to have a specific server acting as a reporting server. However, this all depends on several factors such as hardware and number of resources. Some IT professionals claim that splitting SQL services from the Central Administration Site leaves a server with very little work to do.

SECURITY

Unlike SQL Server Reporting Services integration in Configuration Manager 2007 R2, Configuration Manager 2012 will connect to SQL and set the necessary permissions in Reporting Services. This eliminates the need to go into Reporting Services Configuration Manager and manually configure security. The security settings will be Credentials Stored Securely In The Report Server and Use As Windows Credentials When Connecting To The Data Source.

Installation of the Reporting Services Site System

The reporting site system role is one of the first roles you should install. Prior to installing the site system, you should verify that SQL Server Reporting Services is installed correctly and works as expected. For detailed information about SQL Server Reporting Services, read this TechNet article: `http://technet.microsoft.com/en-us/library/ms159106.aspx`.

The account that you use to install the site system role must have Read access to the database. To retrieve information about named instances, the user must also have Read access to WMI on the site system. To install a SQL Server reporting services point, take the following steps:

1. In the Configuration Manager administrative console, select the Administration workspace and navigate to Site Configuration ➤ Servers And Site System Roles.

2. Select the server where you want to install the role:

   ◆ From the Ribbon click Add Site System Roles to start the Add Site System Roles Wizard.

   ◆ If you want to install the role on a new server, click Create Site System Server.

3. On the General page click Next.

4. On the System Role Selection page, select Reporting Services Point from the list of available roles, and click Next.

5. On the Reporting Services Point page, you must create the data source.

A data source (or database connection) includes the data source type, connection information, and authentication settings used when connecting. The wizard will automatically create the data source based on the information you configure on this page in the wizard.

6. The wizard will discover the name of the site database server and the Configuration Manager database. To specify a named instance, type **<Server Name>\<Instance Name>**.

7. To verify the settings in the Site Database and Database Name fields, click the Verify button.

8. The folder name will default to ConfigMgr_<Sitecode>; you can change the folder name if you want.

9. In the Authentication Settings area, click Set and choose an existing Configuration Manager account or select a new account.

It is considered best practice to have a specific low-rights user account for Authentication settings.

10. Once all settings are configured as shown in Figure 12.1, click Next.

11. On the Summary page, verify the settings and click Next.

12. On the Completion page, click Close.

FIGURE 12.1
Creating the data source

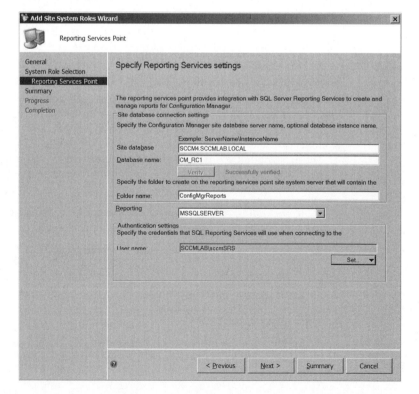

A FEW NOTES ABOUT THE DATA SOURCE AUTHENTICATION ACCOUNT

The data source authentication account is used when Reporting Services retrieves the data for reports from the site database. When you specify the account in the wizard, the installation process will take the account and do the following:

◆ Assign it the proper SQL permissions.

◆ Display it as the ConfigMgr SRS reporting point in the Administration workspace, Accounts folder.

◆ Store the account and password encrypted in the Reporting Services database.

WHAT HAPPENS DURING THE INSTALLATION?

When the installation begins, Configuration Manager will perform these steps:

1. Create the data source with the specified data source authentication account.

2. Create a folder for all Configuration Manager reports.

3. Add the ConfigMgr report users and ConfigMgr report administrators security roles in Reporting Services.

4. Create folders and files in %programfiles%\SMS_SRSRP.

5. Deploy all reports in the %programfiles%\SMS_SRSRP\Reports folder.

6. Assign all user accounts in Configuration Manager the ConfigMgr Report Reader rights on root folders and the Configuration Manager folder.

7. Assign all user accounts with Site Modify rights in Configuration Manager the ConfigMgr Report Administrator rights on root folders and the Configuration Manager folder.

8. Read the current permissions in Configuration Manager, and map those to the newly created reporting folders.

9. Assign users who have Run Report permission for any object ConfigMgr Report Reader rights to the associated report folder.

10. Assign users who have Report Modify rights in Configuration Manager ConfigMgr Report Administrator rights on the associated report folder.

VERIFYING THE INSTALLATION

You can verify the Reporting Services installation by monitoring these log files:

sitecomp.log   The sitecomp.log file will have an entry like this:

```
Starting service SMS_SERVER_BOOTSTRAP_Server with command-line arguments
"SiteCode e:\Program Files\Microsoft Configuration Manager /install E:\Program
Files\Microsoft Configuration Manager\bin\x64\rolesetup.exe SMSSRSRP"
```

srsrpMSI.log srsrpMSI.log is the main log file for the installation. You can monitor this for detailed information. Most likely you will only find this log file interesting when troubleshooting a failed installation.

srsrp.log Once the site system is installed, you can monitor the srsrp.log file. It gives you detailed information about the folders and reports as they are published to the reporting site.

You can also monitor the folders created in %ProgramFiles%\SMS_SRSRP:

Reports Contains all the default RDL files. The reports are imported during the original installation process. You can use the RDL files to import one or multiple reports again.

Resources Contains various DLL files.

Style Contains the three graphical elements used in most reports. You can replace these files with a custom company logo, for example.

The final test is to connect to the reporting site and verify that you can view all of the reports. Open a browser and type **http://reportingserver/reports**. Figure 12.2 shows the items in ConfigMgrReports.

FIGURE 12.2
Viewing the default reports

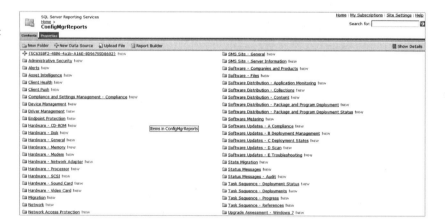

Default Reports

By default almost 400 canned reports are added during the installation. The reports are organized in several different folders. You can move the reports between the folders as you like and also create new folders. The following folders are available:

Administrative Security Contains information about role-based security, scopes, and audit information.

Alerts Contains information about alerts, such as who closed the alerts.

Asset Intelligence Contains inventory and software license information.

Client Status Contains information about the overall client health and status the clients installed.

Client Push   Contains information about current and past client push installation attempts.

Compliance and Settings Management - Deployment   Allows administrators and others to report on Settings Management assignment for a computer or collection.

Compliance and Settings Management - Compliance   Contain information about the compliance states for computers and collections along with detailed information on configuration items.

Device Management - Exchange Connector   Contains information about device information collected using the Exchange mobile connector and from natively managed mobile devices.

Driver Management   Contains information about drivers imported into the drivers repository.

Endpoint Protection   Provides detailed information about malware and virus activities. These reports will provide the Security department with up-to-date information about the overall security threat level in the organization.

Hardware - CD-ROM   Contains information about CD-ROMs.

Hardware - Disk   Contains physical and logical disk information.

Hardware - General   Contains a very useful hardware report along with information about the various inventory classes assigned.

Hardware - Memory   Contains memory information. You will find information for a specific computer and a count of each unique memory configuration.

Hardware - Modem   Contains modem information.

Hardware - Network Adapter   Contains network adapter information like IP address, MAC address, and adapter information.

Hardware - Processor   Contain processor information.

Hardware - SCSI   Contains SCSI information.

Hardware - Sound Card   Contains sound card information.

Hardware - Video Card   Contains video card information.

Migration   Contains information about the migration process from Configuration Manager 2007 to Configuration Manager 2012.

Network   Provides information about IP addresses and IP subnets. These reports will give you the number of IP subnets in the network and how many IP addresses you have in each subnet.

Network Access Protection   Provides information about NAP rules and computers that have been affected by one or more NAP policies.

Operating System   Provides information about operating systems and service packs in the organization.

Power Management   Provides power management information like computer activity, energy cost by day, and energy consumption. The information provides the organization with valuable data about the overall power consumption and also how new client power settings have lowered the environmental impact.

SMS Site - Client Information   Provides information about Configuration Manager client versions, deployments, assignments, communication settings, and out-of-band management configurations.

SMS Site - Discovery and Inventory Information   Provides information about client discovery and inventory information. These reports can be very useful when determining the overall client health of the sites.

SMS Site - General   Lists computers belonging to a specific Configuration Manager site, and shows when the site status was last updated.

SMS Site - Server Information   Lists all site servers and site system roles for a specific site.

Software - Companies and Products   One of the primary folders when searching for installed software applications.

Software - Files   Provides information based on the software inventory processes.

Software Distribution - Application Monitoring   Provides basic and detailed information about application deployment. These reports will provide you with information about computers where requirements or dependencies have not been met.

Software Distribution - Collections   Contains information about collections, maintenance windows, and resources belonging to specific collections.

Software Distribution - Content   Contains information about distribution points, distribution groups, and content.

Software Distribution - Package and Program Deployment   Contains information about package deployments.

Software Distribution - Package and Program Deployment Status   Contains information about statuses for package deployments.

Software Metering   When software is enabled you will use the reports as the primary information source to find information about the applications you monitor, when they were last started and by whom, and where they are installed but not used. The reports will enable you to determine which applications you can uninstall and that way cut down on the license costs.

Software Updates - A Compliance   Provides overall compliance information about the software updates released from Windows Updates and also third-party software updates authored and published using the System Center Update Publisher tool.

Software Updates - B Deployment Management   Provides information about the software update deployments created in the organization and updates that are required but not yet deployed. You can use the reports in this category to assist you when troubleshooting software update deployments.

Software Updates - C Deployment States   This category contains some of the most used reports whenever you work with software update deployment. The single-most important report (in my opinion) is States 1 - Enforcement States for a Deployment. This report can be used to track down the deployment processes of any given software update deployment along with compliance information.

Software Updates - D Scan Reports in this category provide you with information about which clients are able to perform a scan against the WSUS server. The report Scan 1 - Last Scan States by Collection is the very first report you should run whenever you want to troubleshoot software update problems. If clients are unable to perform a scan, they will not be able to upload compliance information or install required software updates.

Software Updates - E Troubleshooting Contains a few reports that can assist you when troubleshooting client scans and update deployments.

State Migration Provides operating system state migration information for a specific site or state migration site system point.

Status Messages Allows you to see all status messages received by the site server.

Status Messages - Audit Allows you to see audit status messages for a specific site or user.

Task Sequence - Deployment Status Provides you with detailed information about the status of running and historical task sequence deployments.

Task Sequence - Deployments Provides you with detailed information about running and historical task sequence deployments.

Task Sequence - Progress Provides you with detailed information about the progress of task sequences.

Task Sequence - References Provides information about the objects referenced by a specific task sequence.

Upgrade Assessment - Windows 7 Provides you with an overview of computers that meet the system requirements for a Windows 7 deployment and those computers that are not capable of being upgraded.

User - Device Affinity Provides you with UDA information, such as UDA associations per collection and UDA statistics.

Users Provides you with information about users in a specific domain, a count of users, and computers used by specific users.

Virtual Applications Provides information about virtual applications installed in the environment and information about virtual application packages.

Wake On LAN Provides information about the Wake On LAN activity and configurations.

As you can see, Microsoft has done a good job of providing some key reports that are ready to use out of the box.

Running a Report

There are two ways to run a report. The first is to use the Configuration Manager administrative console, and the second is to use the web-based Report Manager. From a management perspective it seems nicer to run the reports from the web-based Report Manager. From here you can also manage and customize the reports.

Viewing Available Reports

You can view the list of available reports from within the Configuration Manager administrative console or through the web-based Report Manager created during the configuration of the Reporting Services site system role. Both Report Manager and Configuration Manager group reports in folders. If needed, you can always move a report from one folder to another folder or even create your own folders.

Running a Report from the Administrative Console

To run a report using the Configuration Manager administrative console, follow these simple steps:

1. Open the Configuration Manager administrative console and select the Monitoring workspace.

2. Expand Reporting, select Reports, and choose the reporting category, for example, Client Push.

3. Select the report you want to run, and click Run on the Ribbon.

   For example (Figure 12.3), I ran Client Push Installation Status Summary.

FIGURE 12.3
The Client Push status report opened from the console

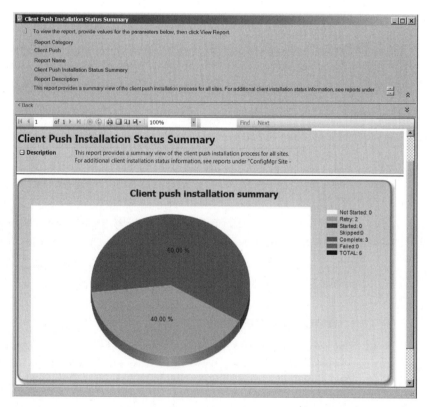

4. Many of the reports require that you select additional information, such as a collection to narrow the search.

In this example, I clicked Values and selected a value from the Parameter Value window.

5. Click View Report.

This will open the report in a new window. You can choose to print or export the report. If you choose to export the report, you can select a file format like Word, Excel, PDF, TIFF, MHTLM, CSV, or XML. A sample report is shown in Figure 12.3, demonstrating some of the available options once you have the report open.

Running a Report from Report Manager

To run a report using the web-based SQL Server Reporting Services, follow these simple steps:

1. Open your web browser to the URL (the default is `http://ReportServer/Reports`) for Report Manager.

As described earlier in the chapter, this URL is the location you specified when setting up the reporting site system role.

2. Open the folder to the category of the report you want to run.

In this example, I selected Software Distribution - Application Monitoring.

3. Click the Display icon in the Report Information area to display the report contents.

4. Select the report you want to run.

I selected All Application Deployments (Advanced).

5. Again, you will be required to select some criteria from the drop-down boxes.

6. Once you have selected the criteria, click View Report.

This will display a report, as shown in Figure 12.4.

FIGURE 12.4
Contents of the Software Distribution - Application Monitoring report

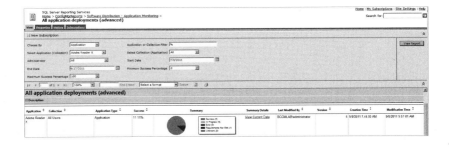

Real World Scenario

MODIFYING THE STANDARD LOGO FOR ALL REPORTS

You have been asked by your boss to make sure that canned SQL reports are branded with the company logo in the right corner. In most canned reports you will find three standard images. You want to replace the Report_Header_Right.png file with the custom company logo. To achieve that, you'll use your knowledge of the Style folder and make a change in the registry.

1. Log on to the Reporting server.

2. Open the %ProgramFiles%\SMS_SRSRP\style folder.

3. Make a backup of the existing Report_Header_Right.png file.

4. Copy the file of your company's logo to the Style folder and rename it **Report_Header_Right.png**.

5. Open the registry by clicking Start ➢ Run, and type **regedit**.

6. Navigate to HKEY_Local_Machine\Software\Microsoft\SMS\SRSRP\SRSInitializeState.

7. Change the value to **0**, as shown in the following graphic:

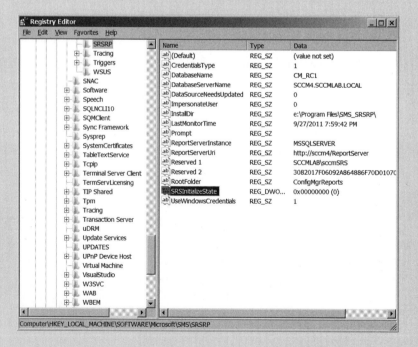

This will restart the deployment of the canned reports. Note that *all* existing changes to the reports will be overwritten.

It can take a little while for the changes to take effect; you can monitor the srsrp.log file on the site server for progress.

Working with Reporting Security

Working with security for reports is not that different from working with security for other objects in Configuration Manager. Configuration Manager will automatically synchronize the security settings configured using the Configuration Manager administrative console to SSRS. In theory you can configure security in both the Configuration Manager administrative console and in Report Manager. The preferred method is using the Configuration Manager administrative console because all changes applied here will automatically be synchronized to SQL Server Reporting Services. If you configure security directly in Report Manager, you will find that all your custom settings will be overwritten by the security settings in Configuration Manager. By default Configuration Manager will connect to SQL Server Reporting Services every 10 minutes and verify that security settings are correctly configured.

Permissions Required to Run Reports

Configuration Manager will create two new Reporting security groups in SQL Server Reporting Services:

ConfigMgr Report Administrators   Offers full administrative permissions to all tasks related to working with reports.

ConfigMgr Report Users   Allows users to read reports and create subscriptions.

When you assign the Read permission to a user or group in the Configuration Manager console, that group will automatically be granted the ConfigMgr Report Users role in SQL Server Reporting Services.

Most, but not all, objects will be assigned either Run Report or Modify Report or both, as shown in Figure 12.5, for the Asset Manager. To read reports not associated with a specific role, you must have Read permission to the site. When security is granted, Configuration Manager will automatically assign the appropriate group or user permissions to the reports.

FIGURE 12.5
Report options for built-in security roles

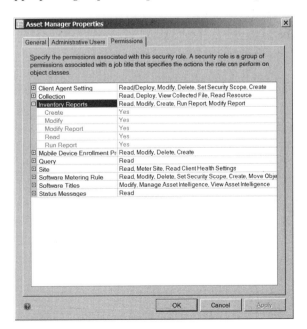

The following list shows the built-in roles and the report folders they can access:

Application Administrator:

- Alerts
- Device Management
- Endpoint Protection
- Software Distribution - Application Monitoring
- Software Distribution - Collections
- Software Distribution - Content
- Software Distribution - Package and Program Deployment
- Software Distribution - Package and Program Deployment Status
- User - Device Affinity
- Virtual Applications

Application Author:

- Alerts
- Endpoint Protection
- Software Distribution - Application Monitoring
- Software Distribution - Collections
- Software Distribution - Content
- Software Distribution - Package and Program Deployment
- Software Distribution - Package and Program Deployment Status
- Virtual Applications

Application Deployment Manager:

- Alerts
- Endpoint Protection
- Software Distribution - Application Monitoring
- Software Distribution - Collections
- Software Distribution - Content
- Software Distribution - Package and Program Deployment
- Software Distribution - Package and Program Deployment Status
- User - Device Affinity
- Virtual Applications

Asset Manager:

- ◆ Asset Intelligence
- ◆ Endpoint Protection
- ◆ Hardware - CD-ROM
- ◆ Hardware - Disk
- ◆ Hardware - General
- ◆ Hardware - Memory
- ◆ Hardware - Modem
- ◆ Hardware - Network Adapter
- ◆ Hardware - Processor
- ◆ Hardware - SCSI
- ◆ Hardware - Sound Card
- ◆ Hardware - Video Card
- ◆ Operating System
- ◆ SMS Site - Discovery and Inventory Information
- ◆ Software - Companies and Products
- ◆ Software - Files
- ◆ Upgrade Assessment - Windows 7
- ◆ Users

Compliance Settings Manager:

- ◆ Alerts
- ◆ Compliance and Settings Management - Compliance
- ◆ Endpoint Protection

Endpoint Protection Manager:

- ◆ Alerts
- ◆ Endpoint Protection

Full Administrator: All folders

Infrastructure Administrator:

- ◆ Alerts
- ◆ Asset Intelligence
- ◆ Client Health

- Client Push
- Endpoint Protection
- Hardware - CD-ROM
- Hardware - Disk
- Hardware - General
- Hardware - Memory
- Hardware - Modem
- Hardware - Network Adapter
- Hardware - Processor
- Hardware - SCSI
- Hardware - Sound Card
- Hardware - Video Card
- Migration
- Network
- Network Access Protection
- Operating System
- Power Management
- SMS Site - Client Information
- SMS Site - Discovery and Inventory Information
- SMS Site - General
- SMS Site - Server Information
- Software - Companies and Products
- Software - Files
- Status Messages
- Status Messages - Audit
- Upgrade Assessment - Windows 7
- Users
- Wake On LAN

Operating System Deployment Manager:

- ◆ Alerts
- ◆ Driver Management
- ◆ Endpoint Protection
- ◆ Software Distribution - Application Monitoring
- ◆ Software Distribution - Collections
- ◆ Software Distribution - Content
- ◆ Software Distribution - Package and Program Deployment
- ◆ Software Distribution - Package and Program Deployment Status
- ◆ State Migration
- ◆ Task Sequence - Deployment Status
- ◆ Task Sequence - Deployments
- ◆ Task Sequence - Progress
- ◆ Task Sequence - References
- ◆ Virtual Applications

Operations Administrator: All folders

Read-only Analyst: All folders

Remote Tools Operator: Endpoint Protection

Security Administrator:

- ◆ Administrative Security
- ◆ Endpoint Protection

Software Update Manager:

- ◆ Alerts
- ◆ Endpoint Protection
- ◆ Software Updates - A Compliance
- ◆ Software Updates - B Deployment Management
- ◆ Software Updates - C Deployment States
- ◆ Software Updates - D Scan
- ◆ Software Updates - E Troubleshooting

> ### Real World Scenario
>
> #### ASSIGN A GROUP PERMISSION TO VIEW ALL REPORTS
>
> In your organization you have an Active Directory group named CM_Reporting_Viewers that requires read access to all reports in Configuration Manager. As a Configuration Manager administrator you have been assigned the task of assigning the appropriate permissions using the least administrative effort possible.
>
> 1. Open the Configuration Manager administrative console.
> 2. Navigate to the Administration workspace and select Security ➢ Administrative Users.
> 3. From the Ribbon click Add User Or Group.
>   This will launch the Add User Or Group dialog.
> 4. In User Or Group Name field, click Browse, type **CM_Reporting_Viewers**, and click OK.
> 5. In the Associated Security Roles dialog, click Add, select the Read-only Analyst security role, and click OK.
> 6. Click OK to close the Add User Or Group dialog.

Managing Reports

One of the main benefits of using SQL Server Reporting Services is the ability to manage reports. Once a report is published, you will be able to use the Report Manager to modify some of the reporting properties. Properties control security, parameter values, the data source, when the report runs (scheduled or on demand), caching options, and more.

To manage the properties for a report, follow these simple steps:

1. Open your web browser to the URL (the default is `http://ReportServer/Reports`) for the Report Viewer.
2. Open the folder to the category of the report you want to manage, for example, Software Distribution - Application.
3. Click the drop-down arrow for the report you want to manage.
4. From the list of options, click Manage.

The first properties you will see are the General properties for the report. You will find a list of report properties in Tables 12.1 through 12.9. Table 12.1 lists the General properties.

TABLE 12.1:   General properties

PROPERTY	DESCRIPTION
Delete	Allows you to delete the report.
Move	Lets you move the report to another folder. This is especially useful if you want to create your own folder with a mix of canned reports from different folders. You should always consider creating custom folders like Servicedesk, Software, or License and move the reports you use the most to those folders.
Create Linked Report	Allows you to create a link to another report. You will find more information on this property later in this chapter.
Download	Allows you to save the report as an RDL file.
Replace	Allows you to import a new version of the report.
Name	Lets you specify the name of the report.
Description	Lets you provide the report description.
Hide In Tile View	Enable this to hide the report from the Report Manager tile view mode. Tile view mode is the default view when users browse for reports.

SHOWING HIDDEN REPORTS IN REPORT MANAGER

To view a report that is configured to be hidden in List view, do the following:

1. Open the Report Manager website.
2. Click Details View.
3. Open the folder containing the report you want to view.
4. In Details view all reports and data sources are visible. You can now open the specific report's properties and remove the check mark from Hide In Tile View on the General properties page.

REIMPORT A CANNED REPORT

As you start working with reports, you might find yourself modifying reports and later regretting it. All canned reports that are installed with Configuration Manager are located in a folder on the reporting site system. In this example we will reimport the Client Status Summary report from the Client Health folder. To manually import this report, do the following.

1. Open the Report Manager website.
2. Open the Client Health folder.
3. Open the Client Summary report properties, and make sure you are on the General properties page.
4. Click Replace.

5. Click Browse and navigate to `E:\Program Files\SMS_SRSRP\Reports\Client_Health`, where `E:\` is the partition where you have installed the reporting site system role.

6. Select `CH_Report_ClientSummaryCurrent.rdl` and click Open.

7. Back in Report Manager, click OK.

8. Click Apply and close the report properties.

Using prompts (or parameters) in reports is very common. It is an easy way for the report user to specify what data to view without having to have deep knowledge of the underlying dataset or SQL reporting skills. You as the administrator can customize the parameters and configure settings such as the default parameter values described in Table 12.2.

TABLE 12.2: Parameter properties

PROPERTY	DESCRIPTION
Parameter Name	The name of the parameter.
Data Type	Specification of the data type.
Has Default	Allows you to specify a default value, thus saving time whenever you run the report. With this selected you can specify the value in Default Value and/or use the Null property.
Default Value	A default value can originate from the report definition, can be query based, or can be a value you type in. The value you enter must adhere to the data type; the use of wildcards is also determined in the report itself.
Null	Allows you to specify that the report will run even if the user does not select any prompted value. This does require that the report allows the use of Null values.
Hide	Allows you to hide the parameters in the Report Manager from users when they run a report. The parameter value will still be visible if the user starts the subscription wizard.
Prompt User	With this selected, users will be prompted for a parameter. Deselect the check box if you want to control the parameters to be used in the report.
Display Text	Text that will be displayed with the parameter value.

As part of the SQL Server Reporting Services point installation, a shared data source is created. The data source is used to specify what data to access and which security credentials to use. Table 12.3 describes the values you can specify for the created data source. Notice that it is highly unlikely that you will need to change the data source from the Report Manager.

TABLE 12.3: Data Source properties

PROPERTY	DESCRIPTION
A Shared Data Source	Specifies the shared data source.
A Custom Data Source	Allows you to specify a custom data source.
Connection String	Specifies the connection string used to connect to the data source.
Connect Using	Defines how you connect to the data source. For all the canned reports, the connection settings are already defined in the connection string.
Connect Using Credentials Supplied By The User Running The Report	Defines that each user must provide a username and password.
Use As Windows Credentials When Connecting To The Data Source	Configure this option if the credentials supplied by the user are Windows Authentication credentials.
Credentials Stored Securely In The Report Server	Encrypts and stores the credentials in the report server. This will allow you to run a report unattended, which is a requirement for scheduled reports.
Impersonate The Authenticated User After A Connection Has Been Made To The Data Source	Used only in rare occasions to allow delegation of credentials if supported by the data source.
Windows Integrated Security	Uses the credentials of the logged-on user to access the data source.
Credentials Are Not Required	Does not prompt for credentials when running the report. This works only if the data source does not require a user logon.
Test Connection	Performs a test to the data source using the supplied credentials.

One of the advantages of using SQL Server Reporting Services is that you can configure automatic delivery of specified reports by either email or storing the report to a file share. You can create subscriptions in the Report Manager or using the Create Subscription Wizard in the Configuration Manager administrative console. Table 12.4 explains the subscription options available when you are using the Report Manager.

TABLE 12.4: Subscription options

PROPERTY	DESCRIPTION
New Subscription	Allows you to create a new report subscription.
Delete	Lets you delete the selected subscription.
Edit	Allows you to edit the subscription properties.
Report Delivery Options (Email Selected)	Can be delivered by email or can be file based. Following are the properties for an email-based subscription.
To	Fill in the recipient email address; it can be a group or a list of individual email addresses separated by a semicolon (;). Note that the reporting server will not validate any of the email addresses.
Cc	Fill in the email address of any recipients who will receive the email as Cc. Can be a group or a list of individual email addresses separated by a semicolon.
Bcc	Fill in the email address of any recipients who will receive the email as Bcc. Can be a group or a list of individual email addresses separated by a semicolon.
Reply-To	Fill in the Reply To email address.
Subject	The email subject; you can use these variables combined with custom text: @ExecutionTime—The run time for the report @ReportName—The name of the report
Include Report	Includes the report in the email as an attachment.
Render Format	Reports can be delivered in different formats: XML CSV (comma delimited) TIFF Acrobat (PDF) HTML 4.0 MHTML (MIME HTML) RPL Renderer (RPL) Excel Word
Include Link	Includes a URL in the email body.

PROPERTY	DESCRIPTION
Priority	Choose from these email priorities:
	Low
	Medium
	High
Comment	Text entered in the comment will be added to the email body.
Report Delivery Options (Windows File Share)	Following are the properties for Windows file share subscription.
File Name	Type in the filename of the report.
Add A File Extension When The File Is Created	By default the file type will not be appended to the filename unless you enable this setting.
Path	A UNC to an existing folder on the network. The specified user account must have Write permissions to the share.
Render Format	Same as the email rendering formats.
Credentials Used To Access The File Share	Specify the user account that will be used to save the file.
Overwrite Options	Choose from these options:
	Overwrite An Existing File With A Newer Version.
	Do Not Overwrite An Existing File.
	Increment File Names As Newer Versions Are Added. This will place a number at the end of the filename and increment the number as new reports are saved.

When reports are executed, they will be transformed from the reporting database into a viewable format. The defined query in the dataset will be executed and will return data to the reporting server, where the selected rendering extension will create the report. The performance impact of running a report depends very much on the amount of data retrieved and the rendering format selected. By default when users run a report, that report is generated on demand. Most of the data in Configuration Manager is either inventory data or state messages, which are very rarely real-time data. By knowing the processing options described in Table 12.5 and the report content, you will quickly learn how to speed up the processing for reports.

When you cache a report, the first time the report is executed the process is similar to running an on-demand report. However, the intermediate format is stored in the ReportServerTempDB (cache) for a configured period. If any other users request the same data, the server will take the intermediate format and render the report much more quickly.

TABLE 12.5: Processing options

PROPERTY	DESCRIPTION
Always Run The Report With The Most Recent Data.	Always shows the latest data in the report.
Cache A Temporary Copy Of The Report. Expire The Copy Of Report A Number Of Minutes:	Specifies the number of minutes the intermediate format will be available in the cache.
Cache A Temporary Copy Of The Report. Expire The Copy Of Report On The Following Schedule.	You can specify when the intermediate format will be removed from the cache based on a custom specific schedule or by using a shared schedule.
Render This Report From A Snapshot.	This option allows you to create the intermediate format prior to running the report the first time. The intermediate format can be created on a custom specific schedule or by using a shared schedule. Note that cached reports will be added as permanent storage to the ReportServer database, unlike cached reports, which will be removed. This feature is closely related to the values you specify on the Snapshot Options page.
Create A Report Snapshot When You Click The Apply Button On This Page.	Creates a snapshot of the report as soon as possible without using the specified schedule.
Report Timeout	Controls the report processing timeout value. The default timeout value is specified in the Site Settings page.

You can preload the cache with temporary copies of the report by creating a refresh plan with the parameters described in Table 12.6. Creating a cache refresh plan requires that the cache options have been defined.

TABLE 12.6: Cache Refresh options

PROPERTY	DESCRIPTION
New Cache Refresh Plan	Lets you create a new plan.
Description	You can provide a meaningful description for the plan.
Refresh The Cache According To The Following Schedule	The cache can be refreshed on a custom specific schedule or by using a shared schedule.

As snapshots are generated, you will be able to view the reports in the Report History page. On this page you can also create a manual snapshot of the report. The options are shown in Table 12.7.

TABLE 12.7: Report History options

PROPERTY	DESCRIPTION
Delete	Deletes the selected report snapshot.
New Snapshot	Creates a new snapshot. This option is available only if Allow Report History To Be Created Manually has been selected on the Snapshot Options page.

Report history is stored in the Report Server database. The Snapshot options, shown in Table 12.8, will assist you in controlling how many items are stored and when the snapshot is generated.

TABLE 12.8: Snapshot options

PROPERTY	DESCRIPTION
Allow Report History To Be Created Manually	Enables the New Snapshot button on the Report History page.
Store All Report Execution Snapshots In Report History	With this feature, reports that are created based on the execution settings on the Processing Options page will be added to the Report History page.
Select The Number Of Snapshots To Keep	Controls how many snapshots are added to the history. You can select from three different values: Use Default Unlimited Snapshots Limit To A Specific Number

As described earlier in this chapter, Configuration Manager will apply default security settings when the Reporting Services point is installed and will check those security settings every 10 minutes. Table 12.9 describes the Security setting applied to a report.

TABLE 12.9: Security option

PROPERTY	DESCRIPTION
Edit Item Security	Allows you to customize the default Security settings. Notice that Configuration Manager will overwrite any custom settings you configure.

CREATING A SHARED SCHEDULE

To lower the performance on the server when running reports, you have been asked to control when reports are rendered. Prior to configuring the execution options, you decide to create a shared schedule that can be selected for all reports. You follow these steps to create a shared schedule:

1. Open the Report Manager website.

2. Click Site Settings.

3. Click the Schedules link.

4. Click New Schedule.

5. Type in a schedule name and configure the schedule details.

6. Click OK to save the shared schedule.

Working with Subscriptions

One of the many features of using SQL Server Reporting Services is working with subscriptions. You can subscribe to reports and have them delivered via mail or as a file on a network share. A standard user can create and customize their own subscriptions with the options described in Table 12.4. You can create a subscription in Report Manager or use the Create Subscription Wizard in the Configuration Manager administrative console.

CREATING A FILE-BASED REPORT SUBSCRIPTION

Prior to creating a file-based subscription, you need to ensure that you have an account with write permissions to a predefined server share. In this example we'll create a subscription for the Client Push Status Summary report.

To create a file-based report subscription using the Configuration Manager administrative console, follow these steps:

1. Open the Configuration Manager console and select the Monitoring workspace.

2. Click Reporting, and select the report from the `Reporting` folder.

3. With the report selected, click Add To The Subscription on the Ribbon.

4. In the Report Delivered By field, ensure that Windows File Share is selected.

5. In File Name field, type in the name of the file without any extension, for example, `ClientPushSummary`.

6. Enable Add File Extension When Created.

7. In the Path field, type in the UNC to an existing share.

8. Select the rendering format; in the example I have selected Acrobat (PDF) File.

9. In the User Name field, specify an account with Read access to the report and Write permissions to the specified UNC.

10. Configure the needed Overwrite Option, and click Next.

Figure 12.6 shows how the delivery options can be specified.

FIGURE 12.6
Creating a Windows file-based report subscription

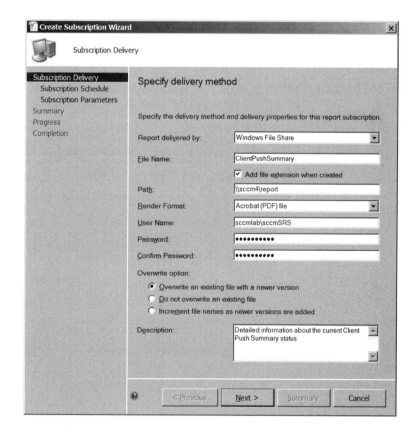

11. On the Subscription Schedule page, select a shared schedule or create a new schedule, and click Next.

This report is a prompted report, and it requires that you select the prompted value. In this example you must click Values and select the number of days.

12. Select All, click OK, and click Next.

13. Read the summary information and click Next.

14. Click Close; the subscription is now created.

You can view information and edit the scheduled report by clicking Reporting ➤ Subscriptions in the Monitoring workspace. You can also open the Report Manager and open the properties for the report. Select Subscriptions; here you will find detailed information about when the subscription is about to run or when it was executed the last time.

CREATING AN EMAIL-BASED REPORT SUBSCRIPTION

Prior to creating an email-based subscription, you need to configure the email options in the Reporting Services Configuration Manager. In this example you will configure the required mail options and use Report Manager to create a subscription for the Client Push Status Summary report.

To configure email support in the Reporting Services Configuration Manager and create an email-based subscription in Report Manager, follow these steps:

1. From the Start menu, choose All Programs ➤ Microsoft SQL Server 2008 R2 ➤ Configuration Tools ➤ Reporting Services Configuration Manager.

2. You will be prompted to connect to a reporting server. Make sure the correct reporting server and instance are selected and click Connect.

3. Click E-Mail Settings.

4. In Sender Address, type the email address that will be used to send the mail.

5. In Current SMTP Delivery Method, ensure that USE SMPT Server is selected.

6. In SMTP Server, type the name of the SMTP server and click Apply to store the settings.

7. Click Exit to close Reporting Services Configuration Manager.

8. Open the SQL Report Manager and connect to the Configuration Manager report by typing `http://reportingserver/reports`.

9. Open the `Configuration Manager` folder and the `Client Push` folder.

10. Hover the mouse over the report, and select Subscribe from the drop-down list.

11. In Delivered By, ensure that E-Mail is selected.

12. In To, type the recipient email addresses.

    Note that there will be no validation of the addresses; you need to make sure that what you type is correct. You can type multiple addresses by separating them with a semicolon (;).

13. Fill in any other CC, BCC, and Reply-To email addresses.

14. Type a subject using the variables explained in Table 12.4.

15. Choose from among the following options:

    ◆ Send A Link

    ◆ Include The Report As Attachment

    ◆ Embed The Report In The Mail

If the recipients support HTLM 4.0 and MHTML 5.0, you can select the Render format MHTML; this will embed the report in the mail.

16. In the Comment field, type in any information that you want to include in the mail body.

17. Configure the processing options, and click OK to create the subscription.

You can create the subscription in Report Manager as explained previously or in the Configuration Manager administrative console as explained for file-based subscription. The difference between the two methods is that subscriptions created in the administrative console will be listed in the administrative console as well as in Report Manager, unlike subscriptions created in Report Manager, which will be listed only in Report Manager.

Creating Reports

Even though Configuration Manager 2012 ships with almost 400 canned reports, at some point you will need to modify an existing report or create a new one. Creating reports requires that you have a basic understanding of SQL and that you are familiar with the different tools available to customize reports. In essence you can create a new report in the following ways:

◆ From scratch using the Report Builder or BIDS

◆ By copying and modifying an existing report

◆ By creating a new report based on a report model

When you create reports, you will use data stored in the site server database through SQL *views*. SQL views are essentially virtual tables that do not themselves contain any data but are based on tables that contain data. The data is dynamically compiled from source tables when the view is referenced. It is not recommended to query tables directly because tables can be changed, for example, by installing a Configuration Manager service pack. Once you know the basics of the naming standard used for views, they actually start to make sense:

◆ V_GS_Name—Contains current inventory data

◆ V_HS_Name—Contains history inventory data

◆ V_R_Name—Contains discovery data

◆ V_RA_Name—Contains array (multivalue) discovery data

Basic SQL Commands

So far in the chapter you've seen how to create a new report using SQL Report Builder and how to import a report. The other option is to define the report using SQL scripting. This, of course, requires you to know the relevant SQL commands. In general, an understanding of SQL syntax is a huge asset for a Configuration Manager administrator but not a requirement. However, within the scope of this book, we cannot cover SQL commands in depth. We suggest that you read up on basic SQL commands so you can create rich and powerful reports. Another way to learn is by simply opening existing reports and seeing how they are written.

Although we cannot cover every topic within SQL programming, such as how to define queries to achieve rich reports within Configuration Manager, it will be useful to cover basics such as ORDER BY, sorting with DESC and ASC, COUNT, and setting header names using AS.

For all the examples we will be using the same report statement, shown here:

```
SELECT count(mode()) as Count, Model(), Manufacture() from v_gs_Computer_system
GROUP BY Model(), Manufacturer() ORDER BY count DESC
```

One way to make the presentation of reports look professional is to sort the items in some fashion. Within SQL you can use a command such as the following to sort your reports:

```
ORDER BY count DESC
```

ORDER BY is the command that tells SQL to sort based on the column COUNT in this example. The order in which the items will be sorted is DESC, or descending. You can use ASC to sort in ascending order.

If you want to sort on multiple items, just add them to the list in the order in which you want to sort, for example:

```
ORDER BY count, Model() DESC
```

Many times you will be tasked with showing very concise reports in which the end user just wants to know, "How many units of model X do we have in our organization?" This is easily achieved by using the COUNT command:

```
SELECT count(model())
```

This will show the count of the item Model() in your report.

Many times, you will not want to have a report with column headings such as Model(), Manufacturer(), and so on. You will want to display meaningful header names. So the following example shows how to achieve this naming.

```
SELECT count(model()) as Count, Model() as 'Computer Model', Manufacture() as
'Manufacturer'
```

By adding the word AS into your SQL statement, you can specify the name of the column header. If the name contains a space, then you have to use a single quote.

Report Models

A report model contains predefined views and fields logically grouped together. By using report models you can assist users in building reports that expose only the needed views and fields. This shortens the learning curve for building reports and also speeds up the process because only the selected views and fields will be presented to the report builder. Later in this chapter you will learn how to build your own report model and create reports based on the canned Configuration Manager report models. Some of the benefits of using report models are these:

◆ You can assign reporting model logical names.

◆ The underlying database structure can be hidden from the person creating the report.

♦ The report model can contain multiple tables and views yet still list the model as a single object.

♦ Time saved is money saved. By creating reporting models, not every person creating reports needs to have deep SQL knowledge.

Creating a Report Using Report Builder

Configuration Manager 2012 uses Microsoft SQL Server 2008 Reporting Services Report Builder 2.0 as the authoring and editing tool for both model and SQL-based reports. SQL Server 2008 R2 ships with a new version of SQL Reporting Builder 3.0, which is an updated version of the version that ships with SQL Server 2008. Report Builder will automatically be installed on your computer when you create or modify a report for the first time. Report Builder has a lower learning curve than BIDS and is often used by non-SQL experts to create custom reports. The tool is not a full-blown developer tool but still offers the support needed by many, such as the following:

♦ Developing one report at a time in a Microsoft Office lookalike environment

♦ Creating charts and gauges

♦ Creating rich SQL

♦ Rich formatting capabilities

♦ Exporting to reports in other formats

 Real World Scenario

CHANGE REGISTRY TO LAUNCH REPORTING BUILDER 3.0 INSTEAD OF REPORTING BUILDER 2.0

You have been asked to modify some of the canned reports using Reporting Builder 3.0. By default ConfigMgr 2012 will launch Reporting Builder 2.0 unless you modify registry.

1. Log on to the computer where you have the ConfigMgr 2012 Administrator installed.

2. Click Start, Run and type Regedit to launch the registry editor.

3. Navigate to HKEY_LOCAL_MACHINE\SOFTWARE\Wow6432Node\Microsoft\ConfigMgr10\ AdminUI\Reporting.

4. Modify the ReportBuilderApplicationManifestName key and change the string to ReportBuilder_3_0_0_0.application, as shown in Figure 12.7.

5. Click OK and close the registry editor.

FIGURE 12.7:
Modifying registry
to launch Report
Builder 3.0

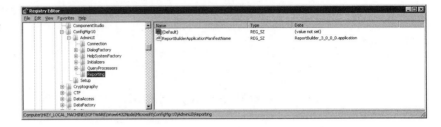

Next you will see how to create a report using Report Builder 3.0. The report will be created in the report folder called hardware - General. Use the following steps to create a basic SQL report that will show and count all the different hardware models you have in the database:

1. Open the Configuration Manager console and select the Monitoring workspace.

2. Expand Reporting and right-click Reports.

3. From the drop down menu click Create Report.

4. Select **SQL-based Report**.

5. In Name type **Count Hardware Models**.

6. In Description type **Group and count all hardware models**.

7. In Path, click Browse, select the Hardware - General folder, and click **OK**.

8. Click Next.

9. On the Summary page click **Next** (this will create the report).

10. Click **Close**.

    Report Builder will launch automatically. If this is the first time you launched the wizard, you will be prompted to install Report Builder.

11. In Report Builder click **Table Or Matrix**.

    This will launch the New Table Or Matrix Wizard.

12. Click **Create a dataset** and click **Next**.

13. In **Data Source Connections**, verify that the Configuration Manager data source is selected, and click **Next**.

13. Expand dbo ➢ Views ➢ v_GS_COMPUTER_SYSTEM.

14. Select Manufacturer() and Model(), as shown in Figure 12.8, and click Next.

FIGURE 12.8:
Creating a report
using Report
Builder 3.0

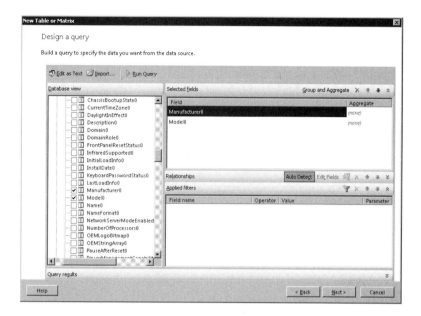

15. Drag Manufacturer() and Model() to Row Groups and Model() to Values.

16. In Values, right-click Model() and select Count; click Next when finished.

17. In Choose The Layout, select Stepped Subtotals Above, and click Next.

18. Select a style and click Finish.

    The report is now open in Design view, allowing you to customize colors, fonts, and much more.

19. To view the report, click Run from the Ribbon.

20. Click Save to save the report.

21. Exit Report Builder.

22. When prompted to publish the report, click Yes.

ADDING A CUSTOM LOGO TO AN EXISTING REPORT

You have been asked by your boss to modify the canned report Enforcement States for a deployment from the Software Updates folder.

1. Open the Configuration Manager console and select the Monitoring workspace.

2. Expand Reporting ➢ Reports ➢ Software Updates - C Deployment States.

3. Select States 1 - Enforcement States for a deployment, and click Edit on the Ribbon. This will launch the SQL Server Report Builder.

4. From the Report Data column, right-click Images, and select Add Image.

5. Locate the image file and click Open.

6. Drag and drop the image object into the report header.

7. Click OK in the Image Properties dialog.

Creating a Report Using Business Intelligence Development Studio

Business Intelligence Development Studio, or BIDS, is often used by developers when creating more advanced reports. BIDS is a component that ships with SQL Server and is in essence Microsoft Visual Studio 2008 with prebuilt project types used in SQL-like reporting services. BIDS can be installed on SQL Server as well as on a workstation operating system like Windows 7. The following example demonstrates how you can create and publish a report using BIDS. The report will list and count Adobe applications installed on all workstations.

1. Click Start ➢ All Programs ➢ Microsoft SQL Server 2008 R2 ➢ SQL Server Business Intelligence Studio.

2. Select File ➢ New ➢ Project.

3. Select Report Project ➢ Server Project.

4. Save the project as **Mastering CM2012**, and click OK.

   This will start a wizard to take you through the process of creating the report.

5. In the Welcome To The Report Wizard dialog, click Next.

6. In Select The Data Source under Name, type **CM2012** and click Edit.

7. In Connection Properties, type the name of the SQL Server in Server Name, and select the Configuration Manager database from the Connect To A Database drop-down list.

8. Click OK to save the connection properties.

9. Click Make This A Shared Data Source, and click Next.

   In the design query step you can either paste an existing SQL statement or click Query Builder and create your own statement. In this example you will build the statement yourself.

10. Click Query Builder.

11. Click the Add Table icon in the toolbar.

12. Select the Views tab, navigate to V_R_System, and click Add.

13. Select V_GS_ADD_REMOVE_PROGRAMS, click Add, and click Close.

14. Back in Query Designer, arrange the two views so you can see both.

15. From V_R_SYSTEM, drag ResourceID and drop the field on ResourceID in the V_GS_
ADD_REMOVE_PROGRAMS view.

By doing so, you are creating an inner join between the two views. You should see a SQL
statement like this:

```
SELECT FROM  v_GS_ADD_REMOVE_PROGRAMS INNER JOIN
              v_R_System ON v_GS_ADD_REMOVE_PROGRAMS.ResourceID = v_R_System
.ResourceID
```

16. From V_GS_ADD_REMOVE_PROGRAMS, select DisplayName(), Publisher(), and
Version().

17. In Publisher() Filter, type **Like Adobe%**.

This will ensure that you see only the application from a specific vendor.

18. From V_R_System, select Operating_System_Name_and0.

19. In Filter, type **like %workstation%**, and remove the check mark in Output.

This will query for all workstations but not show the operating system information in the
report.

20. From V_GS_ADD_REMOVE_PROGRAMS, drag DisplayName() down to the fourth field
in your query.

21. In Alias, type **Total**.

You can use the Alias column to type a more descriptive title for each of the fields.

22. To calculate the number of applications installed, click the Use Group By icon on the
toolbar.

Notice that this will add an extra column named Group By.

23. In the last column with DisplayName(), change Group By to Count.

24. Click the red exclamation mark to run the query.

Your query should look like this (notice that I have used some aliases not mentioned in
the previous steps):

```
SELECT v_GS_ADD_REMOVE_PROGRAMS.DisplayName0 AS Application, v_GS_ADD_REMOVE_
PROGRAMS.Publisher0 AS Publisher,
              v_GS_ADD_REMOVE_PROGRAMS.Version0 AS Version, COUNT(v_GS_ADD_
REMOVE_PROGRAMS.DisplayName0) AS Total
FROM  v_GS_ADD_REMOVE_PROGRAMS INNER JOIN
              v_R_System ON v_GS_ADD_REMOVE_PROGRAMS.ResourceID = v_R_System
.ResourceID
GROUP BY v_GS_ADD_REMOVE_PROGRAMS.DisplayName0, v_GS_ADD_REMOVE_PROGRAMS
.Publisher0, v_GS_ADD_REMOVE_PROGRAMS.Version0,
              v_R_System.Operating_System_Name_and0
HAVING (v_R_System.Operating_System_Name_and0 LIKE '%workstation%') AND (v_GS_
ADD_REMOVE_PROGRAMS.Publisher0 LIKE 'Adobe%')
```

25. Click OK to close Query Designer.

26. In the Report Wizard, the Design The Query screen, click Next.

27. In Select The Report Type, ensure Tabular is selected and click Next.

28. In Design The Table, move all available fields to the Details section and click Next.

29. In Choose The Table Style, select Corporate and click Next.

30. In Choose The Deployment Location, verify that the correct SQL report server version and report server are selected.

The `Deployment` folder will be the location where SQL Server Reporting Services will publish the report. It is often a good idea to publish reports to a "sandbox" folder before adding the report to the same folder as the canned Configuration Manager reports.

31. Click Next.

32. On the Completing The Wizard page, type **Number of Adobe applications installed**.

33. Click Finish.

Your report is now ready to be customized. You will find many of the features in BIDS that you have in Report Builder to create a fancy report.

Once you have finished modifying the report, you can deploy the report to the sandbox folder.

34. From the Build menu, select Deploy Mastering CM2012.

Moving Reports

When you are satisfied with the newly created report, you can move it from the sandbox folder to the folder where you have the canned Configuration Manager reports, as follows:

1. Open a browser and connect to `http://reportingserver/reports`.

2. Open the sandbox folder.

3. Click Show Details from the toolbar.

4. Select the report and click Move from the toolbar.

5. Browse to the destination folder containing the canned Configuration Manager reports.

6. Click OK, and the report will be moved to the new location.

7. Open the report properties and select Data Source.

8. Browse to the folder containing the canned Configuration Manager reports, and select the shared data source.

9. Click OK.

10. Click Apply.

Linked Reports

A linked report is something you can create when you want to have several versions of the same report with different data. You can look at linked reports as you would cloning an existing report with the exception that a linked report inherits the layout and data source properties of the original report. Properties like parameters, subscriptions, and schedules can be changed in the linked report.

 Real World Scenario

PROVIDING DIFFERENT TEAMS WITH THE SAME REPORT BUT DIFFERENT DATA

You need to provide managers from the desktop and server team with a monthly third-party software license reconciliation report in their mailbox. The managers need the same report but with data from different collections. From time to time, you have modified the layout of the report, and you do not want to do that on multiple reports. To meet the challenge you decide to create two linked reports derived from the canned report License 15A - General License Reconciliation Report. Here's how you create the first linked report:

1. Open a browser and connect to http://reportingserver/reports.

2. Open the Asset Intelligence folder.

3. Click the drop-down arrow for the report License 15A - General License Reconciliation.

4. Select Create Linked Report; notice that you can also do the same thing by opening the report properties.

5. Type a descriptive name for the linked report like **License 15A - Server License Reconciliation Report**.

6. Click OK.

7. Open the properties for the new linked report (notice that by default you still have the properties for the original report open).

8. Select Parameters.

9. Check Has Default, and type the Collection ID in Default Value. You can find the Collection ID by viewing the collection properties in the Configuration Manager administrative console.

10. Check Hide, and remove the check mark from Prompt User.

11. Click Apply, and run the report.

Importing and Exporting Reports

One of the fastest and easiest ways to build reports into your Configuration Manager console is to import them from others who have already created the report you want. This technique allows administrators to share reports quickly and easily. Here is a list of some sites where you can download examples:

http://blog.coretech.dk/category/confmgr/config-mgr-inventory-and-reporting/   Contains ready-made reports to download and import. Offers step-by-step descriptions of how to create and modify reports.

`http://support.enhansoft.com/blogs/` Offers free reports ready to download from Enhansoft. They publish a new report every month.

`http://myitforum.com/cs2/blogs/sthompson/default.aspx` Personal blog of Steve Thompson, long-time Configuration Manager and SQL MVP. Steve publishes full reports as well as useful troubleshooting tips.

`http://www.myitforum.com` Large online System Center community where you will find several community leaders and contributors posting reporting solutions.

Importing Reports

Unlike in previous versions of Configuration Manager, you will not be able to import reports using the Configuration Manager console. Instead you will use Report Manager and upload an RDL file as described here:

1. Open a browser and connect to `http://reportingserver/reports`.

2. Open the `Configuration Manager 2012` folder.

3. Click New Folder, and type a descriptive name like **Mastering Configuration Manager 2012**. Click OK when finished.

4. Open the newly created folder and click Upload File.

5. Click Browse, select the report file, and click Open.

6. You can type a new name for the report; click OK when finished.

   It is very likely that the data source specified in the report is not valid and needs to be changed after the import.

7. Open the report properties.

8. Select Data Sources.

9. Select A Shared Data Source and click Browse.

10. Navigate to the Configuration Manager site folder, and select the data source.

11. Click OK.

12. Back in Data Sources, click Apply.

The newly imported report is now ready for use and will also be imported into the Configuration Manager administrative console.

Exporting Reports

Exporting reports also requires that you use Report Manager and download the report as described here:

1. Open a browser and connect to `http://reportingserver/reports`.

2. Open the `Configuration Manager 2012` folder.

3. Navigate to the report you want to export.

4. Open the report properties as explained previously in this chapter.

5. Select Properties and click Download.

6. Click Save, and save the RDL file to a location of your choice.

The Bottom Line

Install the Reporting Services point.   Installing a Reporting Services site system within Configuration Manager allows not only administrators but everyone to view reports in some fashion either via different file formats or a direct link within the Web Reporting Manager.

Master It   What is the procedure to enable Reporting with Configuration Manager?

Manage reporting security.   Reporting security is an integrated part of the built-in security. You provide users with access to reports by adding them to a predefined security role or by creating a custom role with permissions to run or modify reports.

Master It   Add users to a built-in security role.

Create and manage report subscriptions.   Creating subscriptions can be very helpful in many scenarios. You can configure subscriptions from Report Manager or in the Configuration Manager console.

Master It   Create an email-based subscription.

Create custom reports.   Creating custom reports can be helpful in many scenarios. You will quickly find that the canned reports are very useful but may be limited for all your needs.

Master It   Create a custom report.

Chapter 13

Compliance Settings

Compliance Settings in Configuration Manager 2012 allow you to assess the compliance of client devices with regard to a number of configurations, such as whether the correct operating system version is installed and configured appropriately, whether all required applications are installed and configured correctly, whether optional applications are configured appropriately, and whether prohibited applications are installed on your clients. Additionally, you can check for compliance with software updates, security settings, and mobile devices. Configuration item settings for the Windows Management Instrumentation (WMI), registry, and script in ConfigMgr 2012 allow you to automatically remediate noncompliant settings when they are found.

Compliance Settings is the new name for ConfigMgr 2007 *Desired Configuration Management* (DCM). With the new name come changes to the UI by simplifying the process of creating compliance settings, which ensures that IT professionals can remediate those noncompliant settings.

In this chapter you will learn to

◆ Enable the client settings.

◆ Create configuration items.

◆ Define a configuration baseline.

Overview of Compliance Settings

Compliance settings are evaluated by defining a configuration baseline that contains the configuration items you want to monitor and rules that define the required compliance. This configuration data can be imported from http://pinpoint.microsoft.com in Microsoft System Center Configuration Manager configuration packs, defined as best practices by Microsoft and other vendors, defined within Configuration Manager, or defined externally and then imported into Configuration Manager.

After a configuration baseline is defined, it can be deployed to devices through collections and evaluated on a schedule. Client devices can have multiple configuration baselines assigned to them, which provide the administrator with a high level of control.

Client devices evaluate their compliance against each configuration baseline they are assigned and immediately report back the results to the site using state messages and status messages. If a client is not currently connected to the network but has downloaded the configuration items referenced in its assigned configuration baselines, the compliance information will be sent on reconnection.

You can monitor the results of the configuration baseline evaluation compliance from the Deployments node of the Monitoring workspace in the Configuration Manager console. You can also run a number of compliance settings reports to drill down into details, such as which devices are compliant or noncompliant and which element of the configuration baseline is causing a computer to be noncompliant. You can also view compliance evaluation results from Windows clients on the Configurations tab of Configuration Manager in the Windows Control Panel.

What's New in Configuration Manager 2012?

The following Compliance Settings features are new or have been changed since Configuration Manager 2007 (see Figure 13.1).

◆ Configuration Manager 2007 Desired Configuration Management is now called Compliance Settings in Configuration Manager 2012.

◆ The process of creating configuration baselines has been simplified.

◆ Settings can be reused for multiple configuration items.

◆ Remediation is supported for WMI, registry, and script settings that are noncompliant.

◆ The new monitoring features of Configuration Manager 2012 can be used to monitor compliance settings.

◆ Configuration baselines can be deployed to users and devices.

◆ Compliance Settings can be used to manage mobile devices in the enterprise.

◆ Unlike Configuration Manager 2007, Configuration Manager 2012 does not support uninterpreted configuration items.

An uninterpreted configuration item is one that is imported into Compliance Settings and that cannot be interpreted by the Configuration Manager console. Consequently this configuration item's properties cannot be viewed or edited in the console. Before you import configuration packs or configuration baselines into Configuration Manager 2012, you must remove uninterpreted configuration items from Configuration Manager 2007.

FIGURE 13.1
Compliance Settings home page

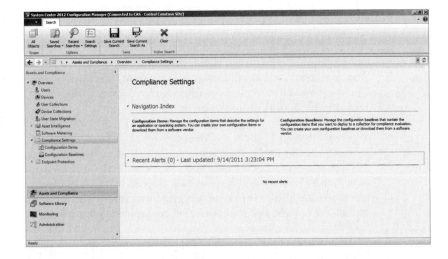

What Can You Do with Compliance Settings?

The best answer is that with Compliance Settings you can automatically check the compliance of your Configuration Manager clients against standards that you choose. Those standards can be company policies regarding how a computer is configured, policies for compliance with regulations such as Sarbanes-Oxley (SOX), or best practices defined by a vendor or based on your internal IT department's experience. They can be settings that a department manager has decided all the computers within the department must meet or a means to identify computers that need more memory as defined by the IT manager in charge of desktops.

Given that range of potential applications, the next question is, what settings can you check with Compliance Settings? This seems like an easy question to answer, but of course it isn't. So, let's explore what you can and cannot do with Compliance Settings. First, Compliance Settings cannot allow you to get an extra hour of sleep every day. However, it can help you create a baseline for your environment.

Let's examine this from a different perspective, and then it will be clear what exactly you can and cannot check for using Compliance Settings.

Configuration Items

Configuration items (CIs) are the standards that you assemble to create a configuration baseline, which is then applied to Configuration Manager clients. You can choose from specific types of configuration items to create these checks:

- Application CIs
- Operating system CIs
- Software update CIs
- General CIs

These checks are keys to understanding the limits of what you can do with Compliance Settings. When you choose the type of configuration items using the wizard in the Configuration Manager console, it will determine what types of checks you are allowed to include as part of a CI. Table 13.1 summarizes the four CI types.

TABLE 13.1:   Configuration item types

TYPE	DEFINITION	EXAMPLE
Application	Used to check an application's settings for compliance	Checking Microsoft Office Word for the latest Normal.dot file
Operating system	Used to check a particular operating system's version or settings for compliance	Checking to ensure that Configuration Manager clients have the latest service pack for Microsoft Windows Vista installed
Software update	Used to check Configuration Manager clients for software update compliance	Checking the status of approved software updates on Configuration Manager clients
General	Used to check settings of objects that do not fall under the other categories	Checking the hosts file to ensure that spyware has not modified the file or that the system has the latest hosts file installed

As you would expect, not all of these configuration item types offer the same properties. For example, the operating system type contains a property to check for the exact build of the operating system that is running on the Configuration Manager client being evaluated; this option is not available in the other configuration types. As mentioned earlier, a configuration baseline can (and almost always will) contain multiple configuration items of all configuration types. The properties available to each configuration item type are listed in Table 13.2.

TABLE 13.2:   Properties of configuration item types

TYPE	AVAILABLE	NOT AVAILABLE
Application	General, Objects, Settings, Detection Method, Applicable, Security	Windows Version
Operating system	Windows Version, Objects, Settings, Security	Detection Method, Applicable
Software update	General, Security	Windows Version, Objects, Settings, Detection Method, Applicable
General	General, Objects, Settings, Applicable, Security	Windows Version, Detection Method

The reason for restricting configuration item types to specific properties, instead of having a single type with all properties available, is to keep the configuration items as small as possible. Defining configuration items as specific types allows you to reuse them when you create configuration baselines. For example, you can create an operating system configuration item that checks for Microsoft Windows 7.

Additional objects and settings are available when you create this configuration item type. You can also check for the presence of a specific file and its attributes. You can run validation against an assembly that is present, and you can even check the string value of a registry key and report on noncompliance for any of these objects or settings, all within the same configuration item. But if you design your configuration items with the idea of being able to reuse them in multiple configuration baselines, they should be as lean and specific as possible. If you need the configuration item to validate something else for a particular scenario, you can simply create a child configuration item. This configuration item will inherit all the original settings of the configuration item and allow you to add additional validations, leaving the original configuration item intact and not affecting any of the configuration baselines that are using that configuration item.

Configuring Compliance Settings Client Settings

Configuring the Compliance Settings client settings is as easy as selecting True or False on the Enable Compliance Evaluation On Clients option and determining the appropriate schedule for clients to evaluate their compliance. This is located on the Administration workspace ➢ Client Settings ➢ Default Client Agent Settings. Then right-click and select Properties. This will open the properties window for the client settings (see Figure 13.2). By setting the Enable Compliance Evaluation On Clients option to True, you enable this option on the default settings. The default schedule for evaluation is set to a simple schedule of every seven days. You can adjust this schedule as necessary for your environment, including using a custom schedule that will allow you more control over when it runs, but the default schedule will typically be adequate for most environments. You can also modify the default client settings, create new custom client settings, or modify existing custom client settings. You create or modify custom client settings when you want to apply a group of client settings to specific collections on the client settings.

FIGURE 13.2
The default client settings

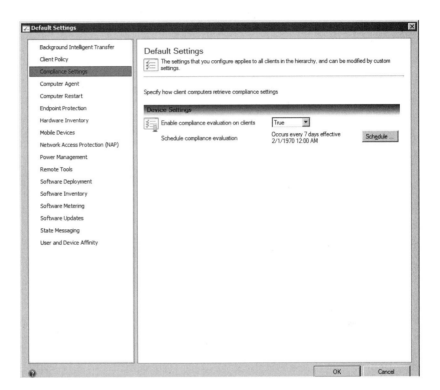

Creating Configuration Items

Configuration items are pieces of the configuration baseline that, when assembled, will allow you to monitor configuration drift from what you have specified. To demonstrate the processes of creating configuration items and a configuration baseline, we'll use a utility called Microsoft Calculator Plus, described in the accompanying sidebar. Because there are so many ways to configure this product and use it, we'll demonstrate its use throughout this chapter so you can gain a better understanding of Compliance Settings. You can then take these examples and apply them to any product you choose.

CALCULATOR PLUS

This application is a mathematical calculator that allows you to complete many different types of conversions; it also includes all the mathematical functions offered in Microsoft Calculator. This is a very small application, which is why we selected it to use in this example.

To download this application, go to

    http://www.microsoft.com/download/en/details.aspx?displaylang=en&id=21622

You will need to install this application on your ConfigMgr client.

Start by opening the Configuration Manager console, if necessary. From the Asset and Compliance workspace expand Compliance Settings, right-click Configuration Items, and click Create Configuration Item. You should be on the General page of the Create Configuration Item Wizard, as shown in Figure 13.3.

FIGURE 13.3
The Create Configuration Item Wizard - General page

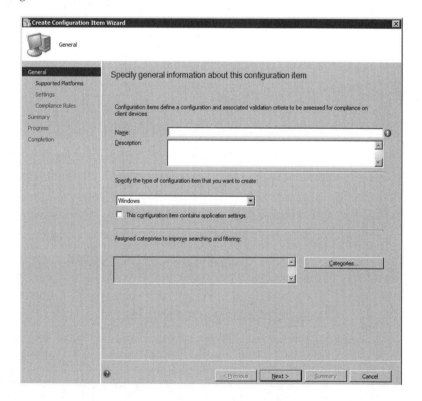

To create a new configuration item, follow the instructions in the wizard. As part of this chapter you will be guided through the steps to create your first configuration item and apply this to any collection for evaluation. In this example we will validate that Microsoft Calculator Plus is installed. You could also use any of the applications used in Chapter 7, "Application Deployment."

Name, Description, and Category

In the Create Configuration Item Wizard, you begin on the General tab. Fill in the Name and Description fields and then create a category before moving to the next tab.

1. In the Name field, type **Microsoft Calculator Plus - Installed**.

2. In the Description field, type **This configuration item validates that the Microsoft Calculator is installed**.

3. Then, still in the Description field, press Ctrl+Enter to simulate a carriage return and add something descriptive stating when and by whom this item was created or changed.

   You could use your initials or the current date or a combination; it just needs to be something that will help you later know who created or changed the item and when, so that if anyone has a question about your configuration item, they know who to contact.

4. Click the Categories button to open the categories list.

   The list is populated with a few default categories, and the top section allows you to add your own custom categories.

 Real World Scenario

WHAT IS A GOOD CATEGORY?

This will depend on your own administration style to a certain degree as well as the number of configuration items you will be creating. If you plan to check only Exchange servers for configuration drift, then you may not need any additional categories or just a few more. If you plan to check clients for application settings, Internet Explorer for configuration drift, different operating systems, files for the correct security settings, and so on, you would probably be wise to set up a standard for determining when new category types are needed and when you can use existing ones.

We have seen administrators who set up categories for every possible difference and others who set up none. If you are going to use the categories and build a large number of configuration items and baselines, then you should set up custom categories, but don't go overboard. Remember that categories are used to sort and search, so if you have too many, you get little or no benefit; too few is the same as none. It's best to use simple rules to create a standard: Does this configuration item fit into a category that exists already? Does that category generally and easily define this configuration item's purpose? If the answer is no to either, then you probably need a new category.

For this example we are going to create a new category.

5. In the Add A New Category section, type **Microsoft** and click the Add button.

   This should add it to the Administrative Available Categories section and select it.

6. Before you click OK, verify that your categories look like those in Figure 13.4.

FIGURE 13.4
The Create
Configuration Item
Wizard's Manage
Administrative
Categories dialog box

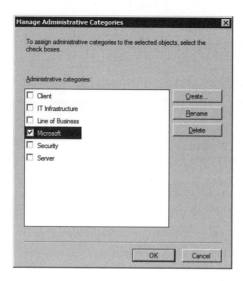

7. Click OK to return to the General tab in the Create Configuration Item Wizard, which should now contain the name, a description, and your newly created category.

8. Verify that your dialog looks the same as Figure 13.5, and then click Next.

FIGURE 13.5
Create Configuration
Item Wizard - General
page completed

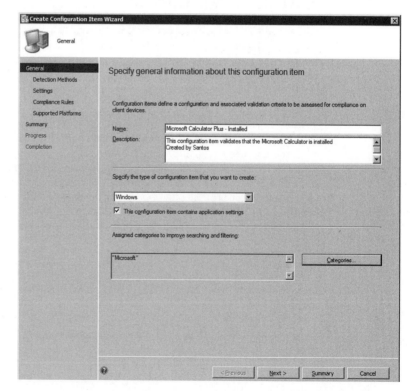

Choosing a Detection Method

The next tab in the wizard is Detection Methods, which is unique to the Application configuration item type; it is not offered with the other types. The purpose of this tab is to specify the method used to verify that the application being checked for is installed on the client.

Three options are available:

◆ The first is Always Assume Application Is Installed.

This will skip any verification check, which sounds great; you're essentially telling the system to check the application for just the settings you're about to specify. But if you do this while using certain rules in creating your configuration baseline, you will run into problems.

BASELINE RULES

Which baseline rules cause problems? You will need to decide which if any of the following are problematic:

◆ If these optional application configuration items are detected, they must be properly configured.

◆ These application configuration items must not be present.

◆ If another baseline is dependent on these configuration items, it may invalidate your dependency.

◆ The second option, Use Windows Installer Detection, is used to verify the product code the application vendor included with the MSI installer and the version.

◆ The final option is Use A Custom Script To Detect This Application; you can use VBScript, JScript, or PowerShell.

In the following procedure, you'll use the second option:

1. Select the Use Windows Installer Detection radio button.

   This will require you to have access to the installation files, but if you downloaded the Microsoft Calculator Plus application from the Microsoft Downloads site, you should already have this file. If not, please download it now.

2. Assuming you have the Microsoft Calculator Plus files downloaded and extracted, click the Open button on the Detection Methods page, and browse to the folder where you extracted the files.

3. Find and click the `calcplus.msi` file, and it will populate the Product Code and Version fields on the Detection Methods page.

   If this application is installed on a per-user basis, you may also need to check the corresponding box for it to be properly detected. If it was installed for all users, that is not necessary.

4. Before moving on to the next step, creating and validating an object, verify that your wizard settings look similar to those in Figure 13.6. (Your product code and version number may be different.)

FIGURE 13.6
CI application
Detection
Methods page

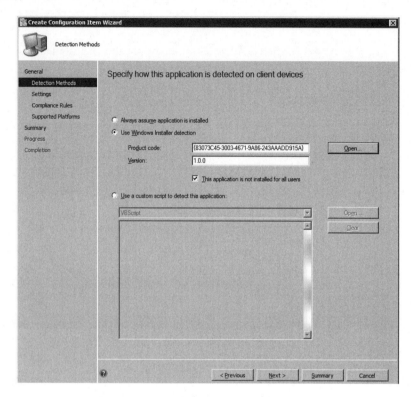

5. If everything is in order, click Next to proceed to the Settings tab.

Creating and Validating a Setting

On the Settings page, you tell the Create Configuration Item Wizard what type of setting to look for and where that setting is found.

CREATING A SETTING

In the empty window there are four columns—Name, Setting Type, Inherited, and User Setting—and a New button.

1. Click New (see Figure 13.7); once clicked a Create Setting Window will show.

FIGURE 13.7
CI application
Settings page

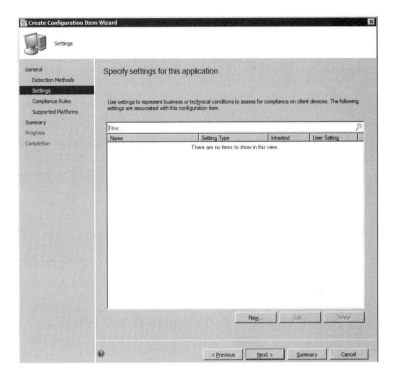

FIGURE 13.7
CI application
Settings page

This opens the Create Setting window, shown in Figure 13.8. The General tab has several fields and drop-down menus. The red circles with exclamation points indicate that the blank fields require input before you can create the configuration item.

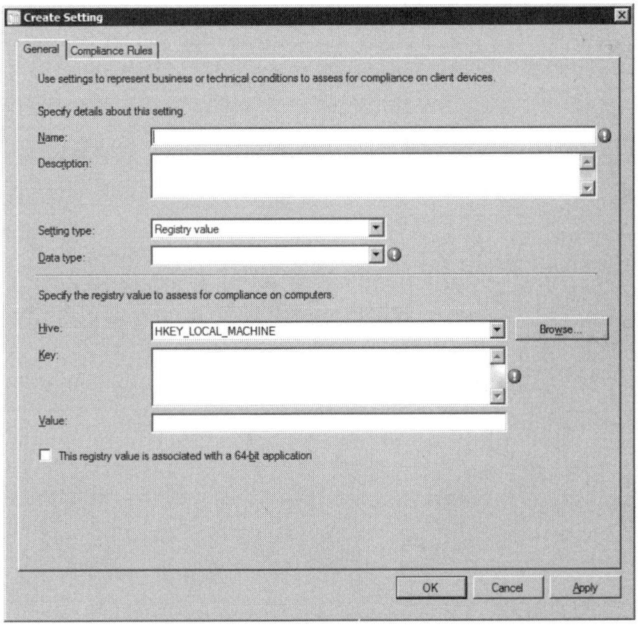

FIGURE 13.8
Create Setting
dialog box

2. From the Setting Type Drop Down menu, select File System.

3. In the Path field, enter **C:\Program Files (x86)\Microsoft Calculator Plus**, and in the File Or Folder Name field, enter **calcplus.exe**.

WILDCARDS AND ENVIRONMENT VARIABLES WITH COMPLIANCE SETTINGS

The use of wildcards is allowed and actually required for the Specify File or Folder to Assess for compliance on the computer Section in the path field. Path The ? and * characters are the permitted wildcards, but they should be considered and used carefully. Using wildcards can produce additional overhead when you're trying to find a file or folder, because the search will work exactly as instructed. Specifying the Windows directory, for example, and then telling it to search all subdirectories is not ideal. You can also make use of environment variables such as %ProgramFiles% or %AllUsersProfile%. The result may be that you get more than one return result if the users all have the file or folder you are looking for in the search path.

---

4. In the Description field, enter **This configuration item locates the file calcplus.exe and validates that it is the latest version of this file**.

5. You can leave the Is This File Or Folder From A 64-Bit Application check box disable for Microsoft Calculator Plus.

64-BIT APPLICATIONS AND THE REGISTRY

Readers who have 64-bit applications should be aware of a possible issue with the registry and configuration baselines. Because of the registry reflector that mirrors certain registry keys for interpretability, it is possible that you could detect the presence of two registry keys with a single configuration baseline. If you are running 64-bit applications, you will need to check for this before deploying a configuration baseline containing a configuration item that involves checking for a registry key associated with a 64-bit application.

You have finished creating the object's details by telling Compliance Settings what you are looking for and where you want it to look for it. The next step is to validate the setting by telling Compliance Settings the specifics of the setting to validate.

6. Before you click OK to move to the Compliance Rule tab, make sure your General page looks like the one in Figure 13.9.

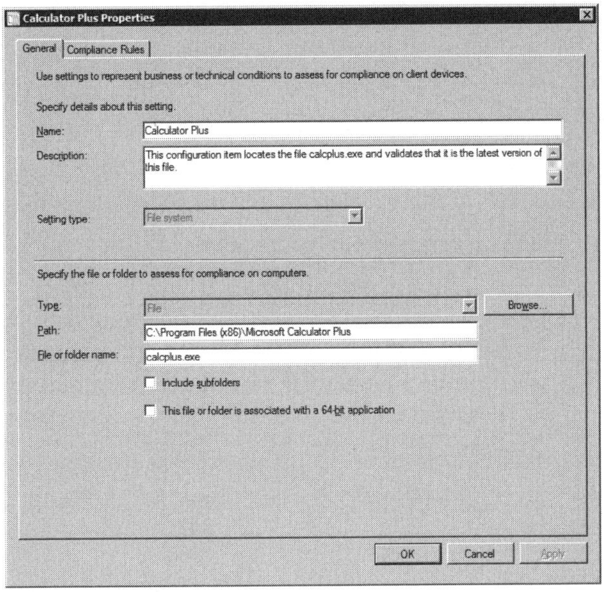

FIGURE 13.9
General page of the
Create Setting dialog
box completed

VALIDATING A SETTING

Now that you have created your setting, you are going to tell Compliance Settings how you
want this CI to validate the file.

1. As you did when creating a new setting, click the New button, shown in Figure 13.10, to
get started.

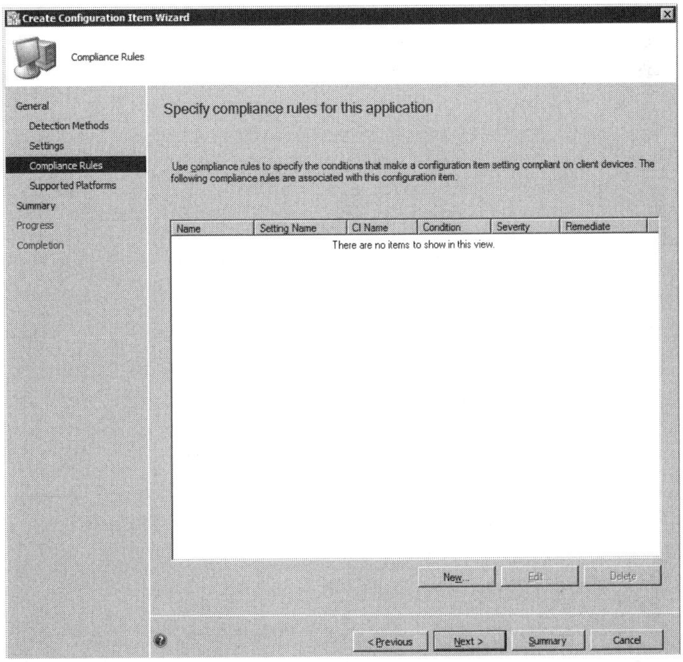

FIGURE 13.10
The Compliance
Rules page's
New button

The top field of the Create Rule dialog box is the name of the compliance rule. This is a required field, and a value will be supplied by default.

2. Just remove _New_Rule from the end of the default text, resulting in a rule name of `File_calcplus.exe_Date Modified`.

3. In the Description text box, enter the following or something similar, but make sure you also put your initials and the date in the event someone else reviewing this rule has questions:

`Validates that the calcplus.exe file in the Microsoft Calulcator Plus folder has the latest version of the file approved and distributed by IT. 9/16/2011`

In the Create Rule dialog box, you tell Compliance Settings exactly how to validate this file. The Setting field on the lower part of the page is grayed out and unavailable because you have already selected the type of setting you are going to validate against. Next to that is a drop-down menu, where you have nine operators to choose from:

◆ Between

◆ Equals

◆ Greater Than

◆ Greater Than Or Equal To

◆ Less Than

◆ Less Than Or Equal To

◆ None Of

◆ Not Equals

◆ One Of

If you choose Between as the operator, you get the option to specify a range.

4. In this example, choose the Greater Than Or Equal To operator, and in The Following Values field, enter the current date and time to which you want the rule to be applied.

Obviously, because you are going to use this as a test, you should make a change to the file so that the modified date is not its original date, or input your validation date and time.

In the bottom section of the Create Rule dialog, you choose the level of noncompliance severity should this check fail on one of your Configuration Manager clients. There are four levels to choose from:

◆ Information—No Windows Event Message

◆ Information

◆ Warning

◆ Error

All four levels report back to Configuration Manager, but the first one does not write an event to the application event log in Windows as the other three do. This was made an option to prevent Compliance Settings rules from filling up the event logs on clients if a check comes back as invalid too many times. This might happen if, for example, you input the wrong validation data or if something out of your control occurs, such as an upgrade or service pack installation.

5. In this exercise, select Information if you don't already have it selected, and then verify that your window looks like Figure 13.11 before clicking OK to continue.

FIGURE 13.11

The Compliance Rules Create Rule dialog box

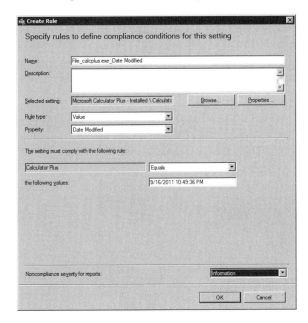

6. Return to the Compliance Rules window, where in the formerly empty section you'll now see the new compliance rule for this file.

   You now have to tell Compliance Settings if you want it to report on a noncompliant event and, if so, the details of when and how it should report.

   The Report A Non-Compliant Event When This Instance Count Fails check box should already be selected. This option turns on and off the reporting of a noncompliant client and allows you to set the severity of noncompliance as well as at what point it should report. Next to Instance Count Operator, you have the same drop-down menu selections as in the Create Rule, and these same nine options are available with other configuration item types.

7. You are going to use the Greater Than operator in this case. Leave Value and Severity at their defaults as well, which results in a compliance rule that will report when a compliance rule check fails at least once and will report as an Information severity.

   In this example, we have left the Severity settings at their defaults. Later in this chapter, you will see how different severity levels combine with other settings during the reporting.

8. You have now created your first compliance item. After reviewing all information and verifying that it is correct, click Next to validate the supported operating systems.

This is the only object you are going to create in this first example, but we'll cover other tabs and their options in the following examples or in later examples.

9. Because you are not going to make changes to this configuration item, you can click through to the end using the Next button at the bottom of the window.

   Eventually you should reach the Summary tab, shown in Figure 13.12, which will give you a list of all the options and settings selected while creating this configuration item.

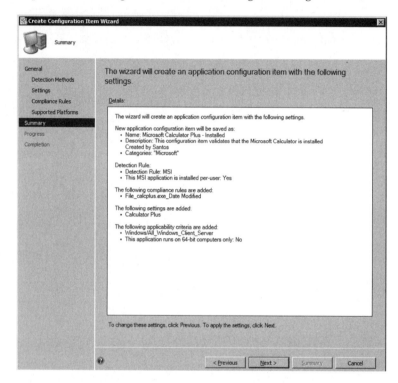

FIGURE 13.12
Application CI
Summary page

10. Verify that these are as you expect them to be; if any are not, use the Previous button or the tabs to make any modifications.

11. Once you have checked to ensure that everything is in order, click the Next button or the Progress tab to start the process of building the configuration item.

After a short period, the progress indicator and window should disappear and you should see the Completion window, which says

```
Success: You have successfully completed the Create Configuration Item Wizard
with the following settings
```

It also shows a list of the settings you chose. Verify again that everything is listed as expected. You can now click the Close button to complete the wizard and return to the Configuration Manager console.

Building a Configuration Baseline

You have built a configuration item to make your configuration baseline, which is what you assign to your clients to check for drift.

Briefly, you have a configuration item that validates that your Microsoft Calculator Plus application is installed and the file is the latest file you deployed. In order to deploy this compliance setting and rule, you need to create a baseline and apply this baseline to a specific collection to validate its compliance.

Configuration baselines in Configuration Manager 2012 contain predefined configuration items and optionally other configuration baselines. After a configuration baseline is created, you can deploy it to a collection so that devices in that collection will download the configuration baseline and assess their compliance with it.

Configuration baselines in Configuration Manager 2012 can contain specific revisions of configuration items or can be configured to always use the latest version of a configuration item.

Creating the Initial Baseline

As it does with most tasks, Configuration Manager provides a wizard to guide you in creating a configuration baseline.

1. In the ConfigMgr 2012 console choose the Asset and Compliance workspace ➤ Compliance Settings ➤ Configuration Baselines and right-click Create Configuration Baseline.

   You should now see the Create Configuration Baseline Wizard, shown in Figure 13.13. Here you select the categories and input the name, description, and configuration data.

FIGURE 13.13
Create Configuration
Baseline Wizard -
Identification tab

2. Fill in the following details.

Name: **Microsoft Calculator Plus - Check**

Description: **This configuration baseline validates the Microsoft Calculator Plus settings to make sure that there has been no configuration drift and that the latest copy of the calcplus.exe script has been distributed to the client**

3. To select Microsoft as the category, click the Categories button to display a list. This section is a the bottom of the window.

The Configuration Data list displays all the configuration items or configuration baselines that are included in the configuration baseline.

4. Click Add to add a new configuration item or configuration baseline to the list. You can choose from the following:

Configuration items

Software updates

Configuration baselines

5. Once the Add Configuration Items window checks for available configuration items, choose Microsoft Calculator Plus - Installed.

6. Click Add, and then click OK.

7. Verify that your settings match those shown in Figure 13.13 and click OK.

You can now click the Close button and return to the Configuration Manager console where you will next assign your new configuration baseline to clients that will be evaluated for compliance.

Baseline Rules

The process of creating rules is similar to the way you build rules in Outlook. Or you can think of it as telling Compliance Settings a story or writing a recipe to build your baseline. The available rules include those that reference which operating system you want to check for; in this option you will be able to see all the different operating systems and service pack levels. If you have not built a configuration item to check for a specific operating system, when you click the link in the rule there will be no configuration items to choose from and nothing to put into this rule. Although our example doesn't include them, Figure 13.14 illustrates the additional selections available when you have also created one or more CIs.

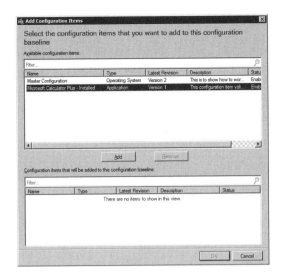

FIGURE 13.14
Add Configuration
Items

Another available rule is Checking For Software Updates. Earlier in the chapter we mentioned that you cannot create CIs for software updates in the same location as the other CI types and you must specify them when creating your configuration baseline; this is exactly where you would specify the software updates to check for. If you click the link in the software update rule, this option will show up on step 4 of Creating a Baseline. It will spawn a new window called Add Software Updates (see Figure 13.15) where you will see the same folder display as in the Configuration Manager console, and you will have all the updates that you set to download to your server available to choose from. It is important to understand that you will not see software updates that you may have already added to the baseline. You can see the software updates that are included in the configuration baseline by viewing its properties in the Configuration Manager console.

FIGURE 13.15
Add Software Updates
window

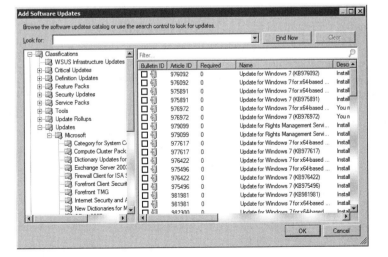

Another rule that you can build is Configuration Baselines. This is how you would reuse other configuration baselines that you have created and thus save quite a few steps. Clicking this rule opens another window that lists the configuration baselines previously created and available to select, much like Figure 13.14.

We have saved the other three rules for last because they are all related to application CI types, differing in the way that they build the rules of your baseline:

♦ Applications And General CIs That Are Required And Must Be Properly Configured

♦ Optional Application CIs That If Detected Must Be Properly Configured

♦ Application CIs That Must Not Be Present

Let's consider how each of these might be used when building a configuration baseline.

APPLICATIONS AND GENERAL CIS THAT ARE REQUIRED AND MUST BE PROPERLY CONFIGURED

This rule means that if you select an application CI, it will use the detection method specified to ensure that the application is installed. We used two different detection methods when we built the application CIs for Microsoft Calculator Plus:

♦ For the first one, we pointed it at the MSI file and got the version and GUID.

♦ For the last set of parent and child CIs, we told it to always assume the application was installed.

When we build an application CI and use the "always assume installed" detection method, we are simply skipping the detection method. Thus, there is no chance that the detection method will fail, and the next step in our application CI will do its check. Once a CI fails a check, the remainder of the CI checks to see if settings or objects are not validated against the client. The actual status returned can vary depending on these settings as well; if the detection method is specified and it fails, it will return Not Detected compliance.

You would use this to add general CIs to your list of rules but also for applications that you want to ensure are installed, or at least to detect that they are installed and that they are configured correctly. Going back to the CIs we created for Microsoft Calculator Plus, if we specified the CIs that detect if the latest calcplus.exe file is on the client, the CI for Microsoft Calculator Plus would first have to pass the detection method we specified, so if the version or GUID returned Noncompliant, then the rest of the CI validation would be skipped and we would get a status message indicating that the application was not detected.

IF OPTIONAL APPLICATION CIS ARE DETECTED THEY MUST BE PROPERLY CONFIGURED

The rule that if optional application CIs are detected, they must be properly configured means that if you make application CIs part of the baseline and they fail to be detected, then the validation checks that are part of that CI will be skipped; if the application is detected, it will then validate the objects or settings specified in the CI and report compliance or noncompliance. A typical use for this type of rule might be a situation in which you are not sure an application is installed on the client, but in the event that it is, you want to make sure that the application is configured correctly.

SELECTED APPLICATION CIS MUST NOT BE PRESENT

The last application CI rule specifies that selected application CIs must *not* be present. This type of rule could be used to make sure that an application is not present on a system. For instance, if you are checking the configuration of Microsoft Calculator Plus 5.*x*, you might want to make sure that Microsoft Calculator Plus 4.*x* was properly removed. Assuming you had a baseline that you used to check the configuration of Microsoft Calculator Plus 4.*x*, you could select one of these rules and run it to validate that the application had been previously uninstalled.

Assigning the Configuration Baseline to Clients

Now that you have all the baselines configured, you need to assign them to the clients or all your hard work won't be used. Assigning the configuration baselines to the clients will allow Configuration Manager to monitor the clients and ensure the baselines are met.

1. Back in the Configuration Manager console, you should still see the configuration baselines. If you highlight the newly created baseline, you will see its details at the bottom of your console.

2. To assign this configuration baseline to clients for validation, right-click the baseline and choose Deploy.

   This will start the Deploy Configuration Baselines Wizard, shown in Figure 13.16.

FIGURE 13.16
Deploy Configuration
Baselines Wizard

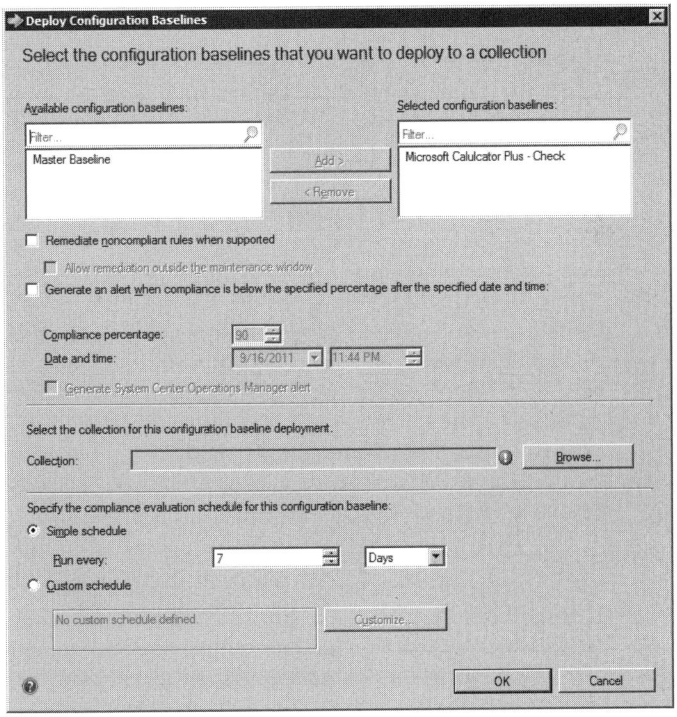

This should prepopulate the selected configuration baseline that you used to launch the wizard; as you can see, you can add or remove configuration baselines by clicking the Add or Remove button on the center.

3. At this time if you see the correct configuration baseline, select the baseline and click Add to move it to the list on the right.

4. In the Select The Collection For This Configuration Baseline Deployment section, indicate the collection you are going to assign this baseline to. Do that now by clicking the Browse button.

   Be sure to select a collection that includes the clients where you have installed and configured the Microsoft Calculator Plus client.

5. After you have selected the appropriate collection, click OK to go back to the deployment baseline window.

   Next you set the schedule. Here you set the compliance evaluation schedule, much as you do with a deployment. You can create a simple schedule such as Run Every 7 Days or create a custom schedule for more flexibility.

6. For the example, choose Custom Schedule and set it to reoccur every four hours; this ensures that the validation will run and return data so you can examine the reports.

7. After reviewing the settings, proceed to assigning the baseline by clicking OK.

Additional Configuration Baseline Options

Within the Configuration Manager console, some additional options are available when you view the configuration baseline folder. If you have the Actions pane visible, you should see the option Import Configuration Data. This option allows you to import a CAB file that could have been created by a vendor, using an external tool such as CP Studio 2008, or it could come from another Configuration Manager site. If you have a baseline currently selected, you should also see some additional options, including the ability to export configuration data. This will allow you to export your data so that you can import it to another site or edit it with an external tool.

You also have the ability to disable the baseline; if you select this option it will stop the clients from evaluating this baseline. Once a baseline is disabled, the option changes to allow you to reenable it from the same location on the Actions pane. You can also view the XML that defines this baseline by clicking the View XML Definition button. The Manage Categories option should be self-evident at this point; you can add or remove categories from the baseline using this button. Finally, there is an Add button, which allows you to add a new rule to the baseline. Going back to the Duplicate button, you can see how much of a timesaver these two buttons can be if used together.

Client Validation of Compliance Baseline Rules

Once you have deployed the compliance baseline to a collection, you should log on to a client and validate that this rule has been applied and what its current state is; this will help you to understand better if the rule has been applied correctly or not and if the compliance state is the desired one.

1. Log on to the Windows 7 client or any resource on the collection deployed.

2. Click Start ➤ Control Panel ➤ All Control Panel Items, and locate Configuration Manager.

3. Choose Configuration Manager ➤ Properties ➤ Configurations.

4. Select the Microsoft Calculator Plus baseline and click Evaluate.

   As shown in Figure 13.17, the Compliance State field now shows Compliant.

FIGURE 13.17
Configuration
Manager client
configurations

5. Now click View Report and wait for Internet Explorer to show the results. You can see the results in Figure 13.18.

FIGURE 13.18
Compliance
Report

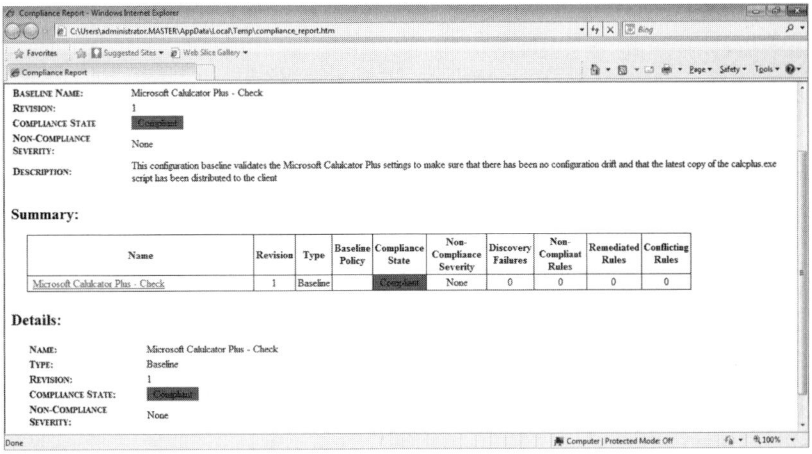

Once you have finished reviewing the compliance setting results, you can also look at the client log files to see more details about the compliance state; two of these log files are as follows:

`dcmagent.log`   Provides high-level information about the evaluation of assigned configuration baselines and desired configuration management processes

`ciagent.log`   Provides information about downloading, storing, and accessing assigned configuration baselines

Open these log files using `CMTrace.exe` and you will see more details. Now that you have been able to successful apply a configuration baseline, you may want to try this again using a production application for which you may need to confirm its compliance state.

COMPLIANCE SETTINGS ALERTS

As part of the new alert and notification system, once the compliance baseline is deployed you can decide if you need to get alerts when the compliance check falls below a specific percentage. To do this you must perform the following task:

1. Choose the Assets and Compliance workspace.

2. Expand Compliance Settings.

3. Select Configuration Baselines.

4. In the right section select Microsoft Calculator Plus - Check; right-click and select Properties.

5. Click the Deployment tab.

6. Select the deployed collection and click Edit.

7. Click Generate An Alert When Compliance Is Below The Specified Percentage After The Specific Date And Time, as shown in Figure 13.16.

8. Set Compliance Percentage to 95.

9. Click OK twice.

This will generate the alert configuration on the Monitoring workspace.

Compliance Settings Reporting

After a short period of time you should be able to run several of the reports included with Configuration Manager for compliance and setting management. These reports can be customized to suit your needs, or you can build your own reports if they don't provide the level of detail you require. Reports are located in the Monitoring workspace ➢ Reporting ➢ Reports, and on the search criteria look for Compliance And Settings Management. The current list of reports is as follows:

◆ Compliance history of a configuration baseline

◆ Compliance history of a configuration item

- ◆ Details of compliance rules of configuration items in a configuration baseline for an asset

- ◆ Details of conflicting rules of configuration items in a configuration baseline for an asset

- ◆ Details of errors of configuration items in a configuration baseline for an asset

- ◆ Details of non-compliance rules of configuration items in a configuration baseline for an asset

- ◆ Details of remediated rules of configuration items in a configuration baseline for an asset

- ◆ List of assets by compliance state for a configuration baseline

- ◆ List of assets by compliance state for a configuration item in a configuration baseline

- ◆ List of rules conflicting with a specified rule for an asset

- ◆ List of unknown assets for a configuration baseline

- ◆ Rules and errors summary of configuration items in a configuration baseline for an asset

- ◆ Summary compliance by configuration baseline

- ◆ Summary compliance by configuration items for a configuration baseline

- ◆ Summary compliance of a configuration baseline for a collection

Importing Configuration Packs

In this section you will learn how to implement a configuration pack from the Security Compliance Manager tool. This tool has different baselines, and each of the baselines can be exported to ConfigMgr and later on imported as Compliance Settings data.

WHAT IS SECURITY COMPLIANCE MANAGER?

Microsoft Security Compliance Manager provides security configuration recommendations from Microsoft, centralized security baseline management features, a baseline portfolio, customization capabilities, and security baseline export flexibility to accelerate your organization's ability to efficiently manage the security and compliance process for the most widely used Microsoft products.

To download this tool, go to

    http://www.microsoft.com/download/en/details.aspx?displayLang=en&id=16776

To learn more about this tool, go to

    http://technet.microsoft.com/en-us/library/cc677002.aspx

Figure 13.19 shows the Security Compliance Console focused on Internet Explorer 9 Computer Security Compliance. As an example, to import the Internet Explorer 9 configuration pack, perform the following procedure:

1. Download Security Compliance Manager from the Microsoft Download site.

2. Install Security Compliance Manager.

3. Confirm that the product has been installed and all the baselines have downloaded it.

4. Launch the Security Compliance Manager tool.

5. For the Microsoft baseline select Internet Explorer 9.

6. For Internet Explorer 9 select IE 9 Computer Security Compliance.

7. In the right section the Export option will be enabled; click SCCM DCM 2007 (.cab), as shown in Figure 13.20.

   The Export to SCCM DCM 2007 dialog box will open.

   Note: Even though it says SCCM DCM 2007, this works great with ConfigMgr 2012. On the new version of Security Compliance Manager, this should be updated.

FIGURE 13.19
Security
Compliance
Manager

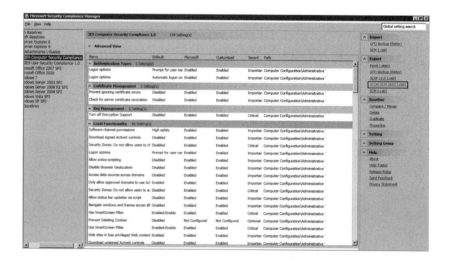

8. Save the .cab file to a known location.

9. Open the Configuration Manager console.

10. Choose the Assets and Compliance workspace.

11. In the navigation pane, expand Compliance Settings, and then click Configuration Items.

12. In the navigation pane, right-click Configuration Baselines.

13. Choose Import Configuration Data.

The Import Configuration Data Wizard will appear.

14. Click Add.

15. The Open dialog box will appear; locate the file saved in step 8 and click Open.

Your screen should look like the one in Figure 13.20. ← Changed this to correct Figure.

FIGURE 13.20
Import Configuration
Data Wizard - Select
Files page

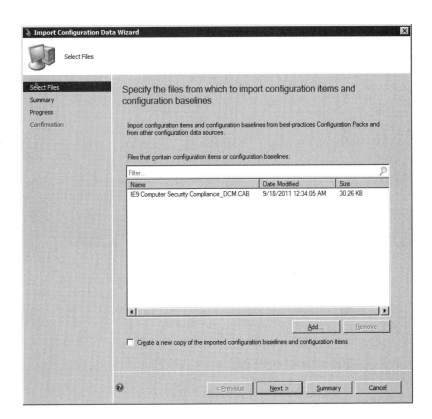

16. Click Next. The import will analyze the .cab file.

The Import Configuration Data Wizard Summary page will label one configuration baseline and six configuration items.

17. Click Next.

The Import Configuration Data Wizard will complete at this point. Your Confirmation screen should look like the one in Figure 13.21. You can close the wizard.

FIGURE 13.21
Import Configuration
Data Wizard -
Confirmation page

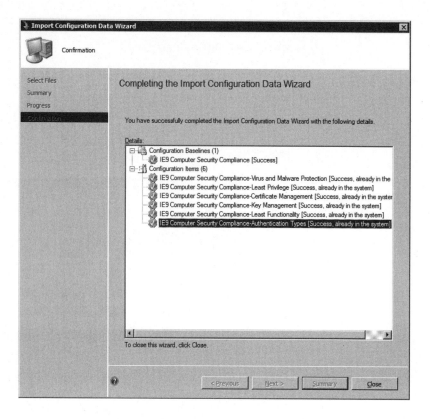

Now that you have imported the configuration data to Configuration Manager's Compliance Settings, you can deploy this baseline to any collection and evaluate the current compliance state for Internet Explorer 9. This will also give you a better idea of how to use Compliance Settings and the configuration items.

The Bottom Line

Enable the client settings. Until the client settings are enabled for your Configuration Manager clients, your clients will not evaluate any of the configuration baselines. This is the first step in using Compliance Settings to validate client settings.

Master It   Enable Compliance Settings for the Configuration Manager clients.

Create configuration items.   Configuration items are the pieces that make up a configuration baseline. There are a number of different configuration item types in Configuration Manager, and depending on the type you choose to create, you are presented with certain options when creating your configuration item. The steps to create configuration items were covered in the first part of this chapter and they included several examples of how to create the different types of configuration items.

Master It   Create a configuration item for an application that checks a registry string value.

Define a configuration baseline.   This is where you take one or more of the CIs and put them into a package that the Configuration Manager client downloads and at the scheduled time validates by checking the CIs against the computer. The Configuration Manager client then reports the outcome of those checks back to Configuration Manager, where you can then run reports to see if your clients are within the specified configuration or not. These steps were covered in the last section of the chapter.

Master It   Assemble a configuration baseline with one or more configuration items you have created.

Chapter 14

Mobile Device Management

The power of the mobile device as a computing platform has grown significantly in recent years. The number of mobile devices is increasing all the time. The devices are a favorite among the user community and are definitely here to stay. Having a mechanism to manage these devices effectively is crucial to IT.

These devices are now a significant part of the computing landscape and are only accelerating in relevance. As a result, organizations of all sizes are tasked with finding the best way to handle these devices, allowing users the flexibility inherit with these devices while balancing the needs of corporate security and management when these devices are used in an enterprise setting.

A further challenge is the sheer number of device types and operating systems in use, including devices running the Windows Phone or upcoming Windows 8 operating systems (which are both *really* cool, and you should check them out), devices from Apple such as the iPhone or iPad, devices running the Android or BlackBerry platforms, and others. Each device type and operating system allows for different management capabilities—and these capabilities will continue to evolve over time. Being able to manage these devices consistently, regardless of the type of device, is important for organizations and is exactly what Configuration Manager 2012 is designed to do.

This chapter will detail the mobile device management options available in Configuration Manager 2012. In this chapter you will learn to

- ◆ Detail the differences between lite and depth management.

- ◆ Understand how to configure mobile device management.

- ◆ Understand the depth-management enrollment process.

What's New in Mobile Device Management

The mobile devices world has changed at an amazing pace since the last full release of Configuration Manager, version 2007. A variety of device and operating system manufacturers are in the market, and the number of users with mobile devices has grown significantly. Mobile devices have become center stage for many users, and such devices are often the single computing device where users spend the bulk of their time. These devices often blur the lines between the individual user environment where music and photographs are important and the business environment used for apps, business email, and documents. Enterprises may choose to allow employees to use their own devices for business purposes, or there may be a requirement that IT procure and configure devices that will be used for business purposes. In either case, management of these devices is important to protect IT and corporate resources.

Configuration Manager 2012 has also changed in a significant way with the addition of support for non-Windows devices. There are two support models for devices in Configuration Manager 2012—lite management and depth management:

Lite Management Lite management is the mechanism used to manage Microsoft's own Windows Phone 7/7.5 platform and is also the management mode that supports any other device capable of working with an Exchange Active Sync connection. This includes BlackBerry, iPhone, and Android. Lite management requires Exchange 2010 either on premise or in the cloud.

There is no client software installed on the device in a lite-management scenario. The management capabilities available are dependent on the capabilities of the device and what is offered via the Exchange ActiveSync connector available in Configuration Manager 2012.

Depth Management Depth management is available for traditional Windows phone platforms, Windows CE, Windows Mobile, and Nokia phones running Symbian. Depth management does install client software on the device and affords more capabilities than lite management alone.

Both will be discussed in detail later in the chapter. For now, it's sufficient to know that lite management will allow any device capable of communicating with Exchange Server 2010 through ActiveSync to be managed.

MOBILE DEVICE MANAGER

It's also worth mentioning that Configuration Manager 2012 is the mobile device management product going forward. Mobile Device Manager, a product specifically designed to handle management of mobile devices, is now restructured into the Configuration Manager 2012 product.

Requirements for Mobile Device Management

The requirements for mobile device management differ depending on whether devices are being managed using lite-management or depth-management options.

Lite Management

There are a few components required for lite management of mobile devices:

♦ A device capable of establishing an ActiveSync connection with an Exchange Server

♦ An Exchange 2010 Server providing ActiveSync services, either on premise or in the cloud.

♦ A properly configured ActiveSync connector in Configuration Manager 2012

CONFIGURING REQUIRED COMPONENTS

The first requirement is totally dependent on the capability of the device being used—a device is either able to communicate via an ActiveSync connection or it isn't. Fortunately, most modern devices have this capability. The process of configuring the ActiveSync connection on a device may vary depending on the type of device in use. Thus, discussing specifics on how to configure the ActiveSync connection from a device perspective is beyond the scope of discussion for this chapter.

Configuring an Exchange 2010 Server to deliver ActiveSync services, the second requirement, is specifically an Exchange 2010 activity. There are no specific Configuration Manager requirements that need to be considered when setting up Exchange 2010 ActiveSync. Once ActiveSync is configured and working in an Exchange 2010 environment, Configuration Manager can be configured to make use of it. Discussion of how to enable ActiveSync for Exchange 2010 is beyond the scope of discussion for this chapter. Details on how to configure the Exchange 2010 ActiveSync component can be found with a quick Bing search. The following URLs are a good starting point to understand the setup requirements and process:

`http://technet.microsoft.com/en-us/library/aa998357.aspx`

`http://technet.microsoft.com/en-us/library/bb124234.aspx`

This leaves the third option for discussion—configuring the ActiveSync connector in Configuration Manager 2012. The ActiveSync connector option is configured from the Administration node of the console, as shown in Figure 14.1. In the console the connector is labeled Exchange Server Connectors. Note that the options available in the wizard are the only ones configurable for lite device management in Configuration Manager 2012. There may be other options for ActiveSync management available directly in Exchange beyond what are listed in the wizard.

FIGURE 14.1
Exchange Server Connectors location in the Configuration Manager console

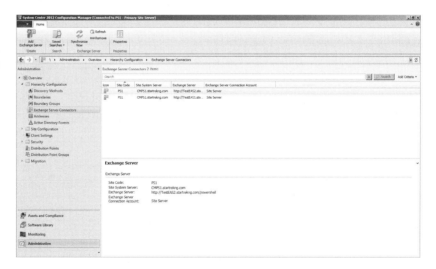

As shown, it's possible to have multiple connectors configured per site depending on need.

You configure a connector by right-clicking Exchange Server Connectors and selecting Add Exchange Server. This will launch the General page of the Add Exchange Server Wizard, as shown in Figure 14.2.

FIGURE 14.2
Add Exchange
Server Wizard—
General page

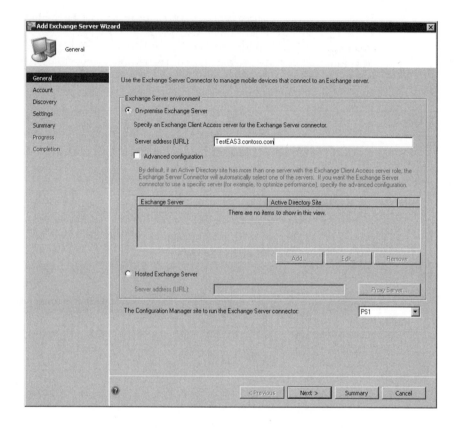

The first choice to make is whether the Exchange Server being configured is an On-premise Exchange Server or a Hosted Exchange Server. The connector works fine with either. In either case you must specify an FQDN for the Exchange Server. When you specify an On-premise Exchange Server, you can also specify Advanced Configuration options. Selecting the Advanced Configuration check box allows you to specify a specific Client Access Server (CAS) that should be used by the connector when more than a single CAS is available. If the advanced option is not specified, then Configuration Manager will simply choose a CAS to use based on information published in Active Directory.

The last option on the General page allows you to select which Configuration Manager site the connector should be associated with. Once the configurations on this page are complete, click Next to continue to the Account page, shown in Figure 14.3.

FIGURE 14.3

Add Exchange Server Wizard—Account page

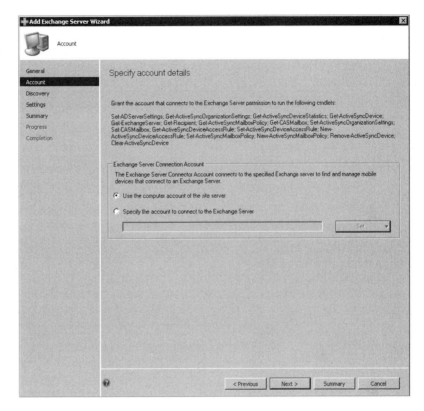

The Account page allows administers to configure whether the Exchange Server Connection Account should be configured to use the computer account of the site server or a specific account. Regardless of the configuration you choose here, ensure that the configured account has proper rights to access the Exchange Client Access Server(s) chosen. Once configurations on this page are complete, click Next to continue to the Discovery page, shown in Figure 14.4.

FIGURE 14.4

Add Exchange Server
Wizard—Discovery page

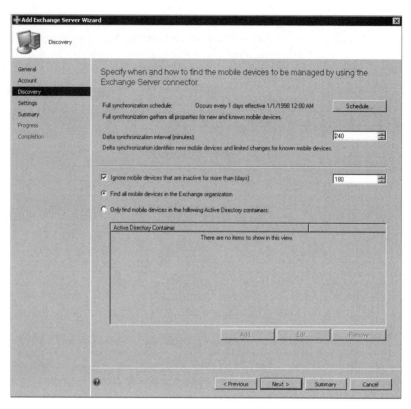

The Discovery page allows administrators to determine how device discovery takes place in the environment.

Full Synchronization Schedule This option configures the schedule and frequency for full synchronization in the environment. Full synchronization gathers all properties for new and existing mobile devices. The default option is for full synchronization to run daily at midnight.

Delta Synchronization Interval This option configures the schedule and frequency for delta synchronization in the environment. Delta synchronization identifies new mobile devices and gathers limited changes for known mobile devices. The default option is for delta synchronization to run every four hours.

FULL VS. DELTA

Full versus delta synchronization is similar in concept to full versus delta discovery or full versus delta collection updates.

Ignore mobile devices that are inactive for more than (days). This option indicates that devices that have been inactive for the configured number of days, by default 180 days, should be ignored from further management attempts.

Find all mobile devices in the exchange organization; only find mobile devices in the following active directory containers. The choice you make for the first setting determines whether to attempt management of all mobile devices connecting with Exchange ActiveSync or only those belonging to a specific container. If you select to limit management, individual containers with mobile devices that should be managed must be configured.

Note that if settings are not specifically configured on this page, existing settings configured in Exchange ActiveSync will be persisted as noted by the Status column. If settings are configured through the connector, the Status column will change to indicate Configured by Configuration Manager. Once configurations on this page are complete, click Next to continue to the Settings page, shown in Figure 14.5.

FIGURE 14.5
Add Exchange Server
Wizard—Settings page

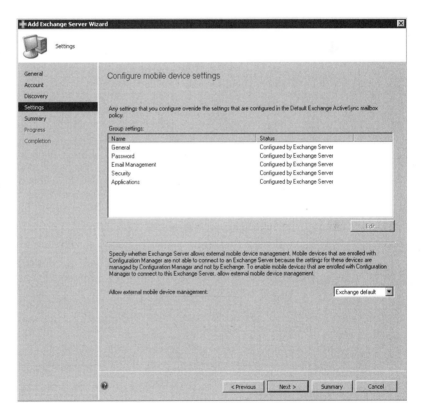

The Settings page is where the action is! This page is the launch point for configuring all options that are available for lite management. The categories for configurable settings are General, Password, Email Management, Security, and Application. Further discussion on these categories follows. From this page, administrators are also able to choose whether to allow external mobile device management.

General Settings

Selecting to edit the General settings will reveal available choices for this category, as shown in Figure 14.6.

FIGURE 14.6
Add Exchange Server
Wizard—Settings
page—General Settings

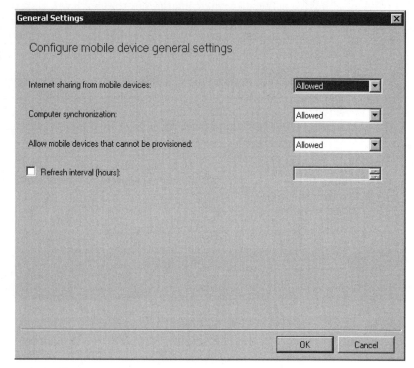

Internet Sharing From Mobile Devices   This option allows administers to either allow or prohibit Internet sharing on managed mobile devices.

Computer Synchronization   This option allows administers to either allow or prohibit synchronization of the mobile device with computers.

Allow Mobile Devices That Cannot Be Provisioned   This option allows administrators to either allow or prohibit mobile devices that cannot be provisioned from being visible in Configuration Manager.

Refresh Interval (Hours)   This option allows administrators to specify a specific refresh interval, if desired.

Password Settings

Selecting to edit the Password settings will reveal available choices for this category, as shown in Figure 14.7.

FIGURE 14.7
Add Exchange Server
Wizard—Settings
page—Password
Settings

FIGURE 14.7
Add Exchange Server
Wizard—Settings
page—Password
Settings

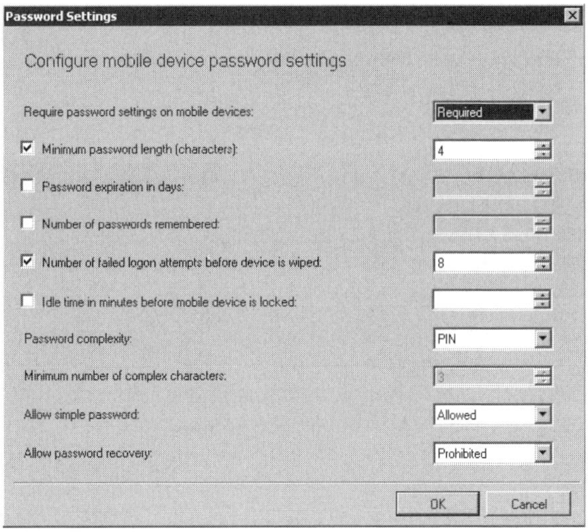

Require Password Settings On Mobile Devices   This option allows administrators to decide whether or not to enforce password settings on the mobile device. If it's set to Optional, additional settings on this page will not be configurable.

Minimum Password Length (Characters)   This option allows administrators to specify a minimum password length for the mobile device. The default length is 4 characters with a maximum length of 16 characters.

Password Expiration In Days   This option allows administrators to configure how frequently the configured password will expire and need to be reset.

Number Of Passwords Remembered   This option allows administrators to configure how many passwords are stored, thus preventing reuse of the same password again and again.

Number Of Failed Logon Attempts Before Device Is Wiped   This option allows administrators to specify the number of bad logon attempts before the device is wiped. The default is eight invalid password attempts allowed. After the configured number of failed password attempts, the device is wiped. This is a good option to use for ensuring device security, but with the result being a complete device wipe, you must carefully evaluate the final settings you choose for this option.

Idle Time In Minutes Before Mobile Device Is Locked   This option allows administrators to specify the length of idle time allowed before the device will lock itself, requiring a password to regain access.

Password Complexity   This option allows administrators to specify how complex the device password should be. The default option is to specify a PIN. The other option is to specify a strong password. If a strong password is selected, the option to specify a minimum number of complex characters becomes available. The default number of strong characters is three.

Allow Simple Password   This option specifies whether simple passwords, such as 1234, are allowed on a device. The default option allows a simple password.

Allow Password Recovery   This option allows administrators to configure whether it is possible to recover passwords on a device. The default option prohibits this action.

Email Management Settings

Selecting to edit the Email Management settings reveals available choices for this category, as shown in Figure 14.8.

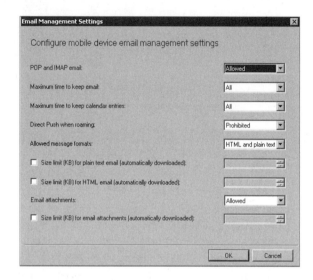

POP And IMAP Email   This option allows administrators to specify whether both POP and IMAP email are allowed or prohibited. There is no option to specify that one or the other is available.

Maximum Time To Keep Email   This option allows administrators to specify the length of time email will be retained on the device. The default option is All, which indicates that all email should be retained indefinitely. Other available options are One Day, Three Days, One Week, Two Weeks, and One Month.

Maximum Time To Keep Calendar Entries   This option allows administrators to specify the length of time calendar entries should be retained on the device. The default option is All, which indicates that all calendar items should be retained indefinitely. Other available options are Two Weeks, One Month, Three Months, and Six Months.

Direct Push When Roaming   This option allows administrators to determine whether email can be directly pushed while a device is in roaming status. The default option is Prohibited to help avoid additional expense in such situations.

Allowed Message Formats   This option allows administrators to define what email formats are acceptable. The default option is HTML And Plain Text. The only other choice is Plain Text Only.

Size Limit (KB) For Plain Text Email (Automatically Downloaded)   If specified, this option allows administrators to specify the maximum size for a plain text email that will be automatically downloaded to devices.

Size Limit (KB) For HTML Email (Automatically Downloaded)   This option, not specified by default, allows administrators to specify the maximum size for an HTML-formatted email that will be automatically downloaded to devices.

Email Attachments   This option allows administrators to specify whether email attachments are allowed on connected devices. The default option is Allowed.

Size Limit (KB) For Email Attachments (Automatically Downloaded)   This option, not specified by default, allows administrators to specify the maximum size for an attachment that will be automatically downloaded to devices.

Security Settings

Selecting to edit the Security settings will reveal available choices for this category, shown in Figure 14.9.

FIGURE 14.9

Add Exchange Server Wizard—Settings page—Security Settings

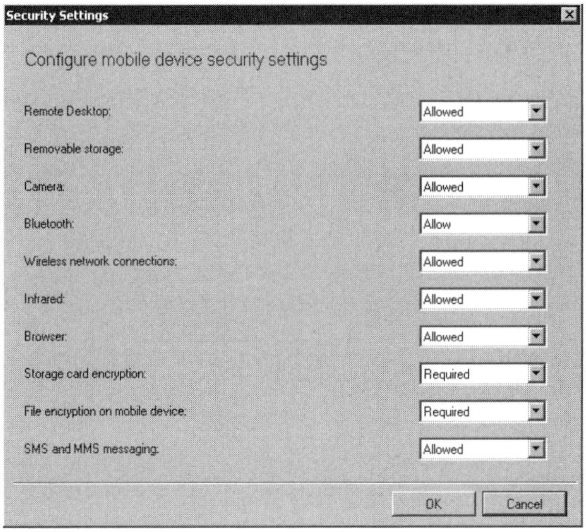

Remote Desktop   This option allows administrators to specify whether Remote Desktop to the device is allowed.

Removable Storage   This option allows administrators to specify whether removable storage is allowed on the device.

Camera   This option allows administrators to specify whether the use of the camera is allowed on the device.

Bluetooth   This option allows administrators to specify whether the use of Bluetooth is allowed on the device. An option is included in this setting to allow configuring hands-free operation only for Bluetooth.

Wireless Network Connections   This option allows administrators to specify whether the use of wireless network connections is allowed on the device.

Infrared   This option allows administrators to specify whether the use of infrared capabilities for a device is allowed.

Browser   This option allows administrators to specify whether the use of a browser is permitted for a device.

Storage Card Encryption   This option allows administrators to configure whether encryption of device storage cards is required or optional.

File Encryption On Mobile Devices   This option allows administrators to configure whether file encryption on mobile devices is required or optional.

SMS And MMS Messaging   This option allows administrators to configure whether messaging is allowed on devices.

Applications Settings

Selecting to edit the Applications settings will reveal available choices for this category, shown in Figure 14.10.

FIGURE 14.10
Add Exchange Server
Wizard—Settings
page—Application
Settings

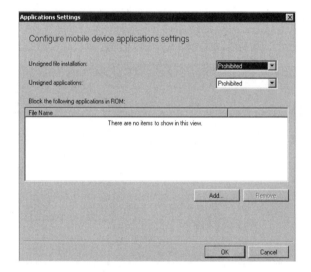

Unsigned File Installation   This option allows administrators to specify whether installation of unsigned files is allowed on devices.

Unsigned Applications   This option allows administrators to specify whether installation of unsigned applications is allowed on devices.

Block The Following Applications In ROM   This option allows administrators to specify a list of applications that should be blocked from being installed on the device.

RESULTS OF LITE-MANAGEMENT CONFIGURATION

Once all settings are configured as required on these pages, click Next and continue through the wizard, verifying that all options chosen are appropriate on the Summary page. This action implements the settings as required on the Exchange Server and, from this point, devices connecting to Exchange through ActiveSync will receive and implement the configured settings, or at least the ones the device is capable of implementing.

After a few devices have synchronized using the ActiveSync connector, they will be visible and available for management in the Devices collections, as shown in Figure 14.11.

FIGURE 14.11
Lite-managed devices

Now that devices are in collections, is it possible to do any management directly at this level? Mostly *no*. Remember, these devices are lite managed, which means almost all management is done through the ActiveSync connector. There are a couple of things that you can do, though. Right-clicking a lite-managed device will show the options available. Specifically there are options to wipe the device and also to decide whether to block the device. This is also the location to set the primary device user, to open Resource Explorer for the device to view hardware inventory that has been collected, and also to view device properties. These options are shown in Figure 14.12.

FIGURE 14.12
Device context menu
options

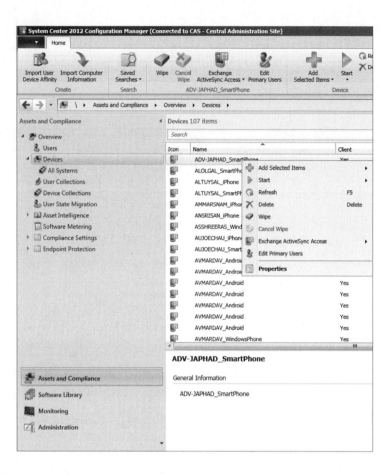

Depth Management

Several components are used for depth management of mobile devices. Some components are required and others optional but likely needed.

Required roles

◆ Enrollment proxy point site system role

◆ Enrollment service point site system role

◆ Management point configured for HTTPS communication

◆ Microsoft enterprise certification authority

Optional roles—depending on services being provided

◆ Distribution point configured for HTTPS communication

◆ Application Catalog web service point

We describe configuring both the required and optional roles in detail in the following sections and end with discussions of depth-management device enrollment and device-settings management.

ENROLLMENT PROXY POINT SITE SYSTEM ROLE

This site system role is used by devices during initial enrollment and client installation. This is also the site system role contacted to initially download the client for depth-managed devices.

This role is configured in the DMZ and must be configured with a web server certificate from the certification authority. Installing the enrollment proxy point site system role is straightforward; simply select the server that will host the role in the Administration ➤ Site Configuration ➤ Servers and Site System Roles node of the console, choose to add a new site system role, and select Enrollment Proxy Point from the list. The only configurations needed for this role are shown in Figure 14.13.

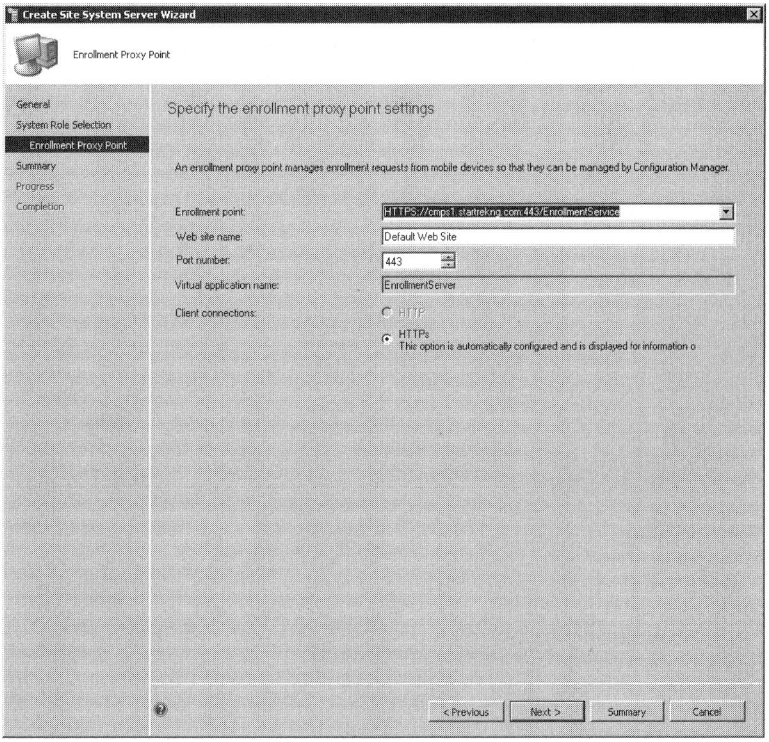

FIGURE 14.13
Enrollment proxy point site system role settings

Enrollment Point   This setting allows administrators to configure the URL for the enroll-ment point. Typically this should be left at the default value.

Web Site Name   This setting allows administrators to configure the website where the enrollment proxy point should be installed. The default is to use the default website. Often, organizations will require a website other than the default website, particularly in the DMZ. If this is the case, specify which website should host the enrollment proxy point.

Port Number   This setting allows administrators to specify the port that should be used to connect with the enrollment proxy point. Using port 443 is typical, but this is user configurable if needed.

The remaining options on this page, Virtual Application Name and Client Connections, are displayed but are not user configurable.

ENROLLMENT POINT SITE SYSTEM ROLE

This site system role resides on the internal network, receives information from the enrollment proxy point, and interacts with the primary site server, Active Directory, and the certification authority to orchestrate the device-provisioning process. The server hosting this role must be provisioned with a web server certificate from the internal certification authority.

Installing the enrollment point site system role is straightforward; simply select the server that will host the role in the Administration ➤ Site Configuration ➤ Servers and Site System Roles node of the console, choose to add a new site system role, and select Enrollment Point from the list. The only configurations needed for this role are shown in Figure 14.14.

FIGURE 14.14
Enrollment point site system role settings

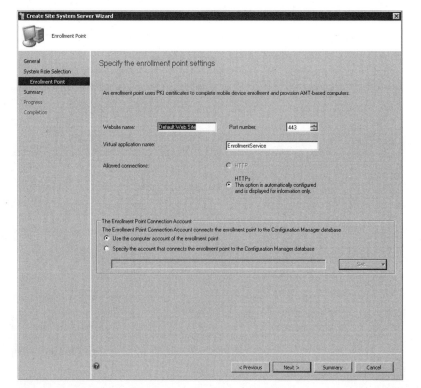

Website Name/Port Number   This option allows administrators to configure the website name to be used for installing the enrollment point. The default is to use the default website. Some organizations disable the default website as a matter of policy. If this is the case in your organization, choose an appropriate alternative. The port number is also listed as an option and defaults to port 443. This setting will be unchanged in most environments but is user configurable if needed.

Virtual Application Name   This option allows administrators to specify the virtual application name if different from the default.

The Enrollment Point Connection Account   This option allows administrators to specify which account should be used to facilitate communication from the enrollment point to the primary site server. If the enrollment point is collocated on the primary site server, it is typical to allow the computer account to be used for communication. If the site system is remote, it's possible to use the computer account of the remote site system, provided appropriate rights are granted on the primary site server. In the remote scenario it's often easier to specify an account to use. One key deciding factor might be account password maintenance requirements. In the case of the computer account, the password is managed automatically. For user accounts, password management is manual.

The remaining option on this page, Allowed Connections, is displayed but is not user configurable.

MANAGEMENT POINT

A management point is required for any primary site that will host clients. Managing devices also requires a management point configured to allow mobile devices to connect as well. Figure 14.15 shows the Properties page for the management point. You'll need to adjust a couple of items if the management point will support device clients.

FIGURE 14.15
Management Point
Properties page

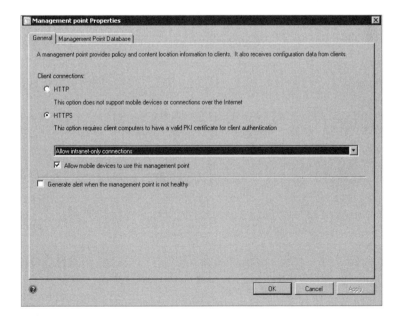

Management points purposed for device management must be configured for HTTPS communication and, accordingly, must have a web server certificate from the configured certification authority installed. Further, the check box Allow Mobile Devices To Use This Management Point must be selected.

When you decide on the placement and configuration of management points, you should consider the available configuration options:

HTTP Connected Computer Devices   These devices are typically located on the internal network. A management point purposed to support this type of device cannot be also configured to support mobile devices unless all connected computers are reconfigured to use HTTPS communication and the management point configuration is updated accordingly.

HTTPS Connected Computer Devices   Any management point can be configured to communicate with clients using HTTPS, whether the computer devices are on the internal or external network. In fact, using HTTPS communication is the most secure way to configure client/management point interaction. If a management point is configured in this way and mobile devices are also available that need to be managed, simply check the box to allow the management point to also serve mobile devices.

Microsoft Enterprise Certification Authority

Mobile devices require certificates to communicate and be approved in the environment. Certificates are a topic that seems to bring hesitation and uncertainty for many Configuration Manager administrators—often either because the topic of certificates isn't familiar or the use of certificates might involve dependency on another operational team in the organization. Oftentimes it seems easier to just do it yourself than involve other teams! Don't let either of these prevent you from using certificates—it's really not difficult to do, and the added security and flexibility it brings is worth the time.

Discussing configuration of a certification authority is beyond the scope of this chapter—not to mention the fact that any discussion may or may not line up with specific organizational requirements. Documentation that walks through the process of deploying required certificates in a lab environment to afford testing of mobile device management is available at the following link:

```
http://technet.microsoft.com/en-us/library/gg682023.aspx
```

Figure 14.16 shows a screenshot of a certification authority configured to deploy the needed certificates for mobile device management.

FIGURE 14.16
Certification
authority

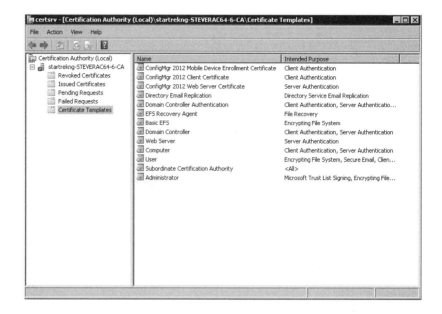

DISTRIBUTION POINT

Distribution points purposed for device management must be configured for HTTPS communication and, accordingly, must have a web server certificate from the configured certification authority installed. Making distribution points available for access by mobile devices means placing the distribution point in the DMZ. Because of this requirement and the different content required by devices, distribution points for access by mobile devices may be kept separate from those accessed by computer devices. Figure 14.17 shows distribution point properties used to enable HTTPS communication.

FIGURE 14.17
Distribution Point
Properties page

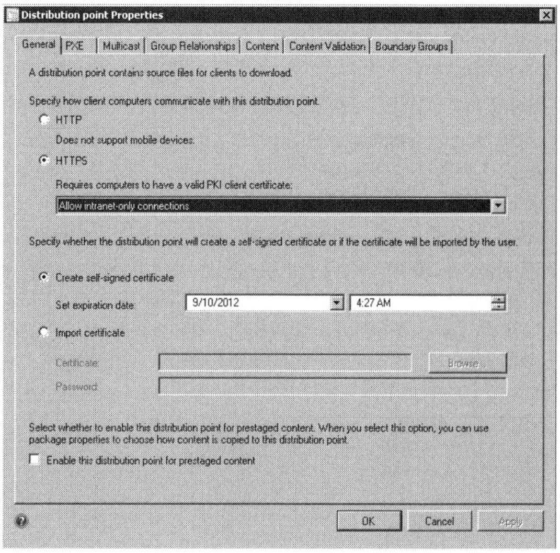

APPLICATION CATALOG WEB SERVICE POINT

The Application Catalog web service point is an optional site system role for use by mobile devices but is required to provide the mobile device user with the ability to wipe their own device. Like other roles, configuring the Application Catalog point for use by mobile devices requires the use of HTTPS communication, which requires that a web server certificate from the local certification authority be configured. Figure 14.18 shows the HTTPS configuration option for the Application Catalog web service point.

FIGURE 14.18
Application Catalog
Web Service Point
Properties page

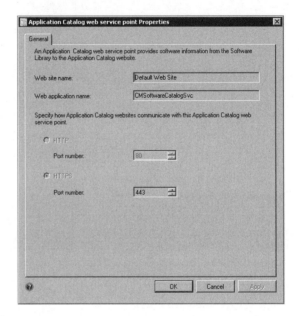

DEPTH-MANAGEMENT DEVICE ENROLLMENT

The enrollment process and provisioning process require action from both the device user and the ConfigMgr administrator. The administrator portion of the configuration must be in place prior to user involvement, so our discussion will focus there first.

Administrator Configuration

The administrator must decide which users are able to participate in device enrollment and provisioning. This is done through client settings configuration. The option to enable mobile device enrollment is a user setting that is available either by configuring the Default Client Agent Settings, which combine both default user and device settings for the site, or by choosing to configure a custom settings profile for users. The Default Client Agent Settings should be used when device enrollment should be enabled for all users, while the custom settings profile should be used where enrollments rights should be granted only to select users. The example will demonstrate the latter option:

1. To configure user-specific enrollment options, create custom user settings and enable enrollment, as shown in Figure 14.19.

FIGURE 14.19
Custom user settings to enable enrollment

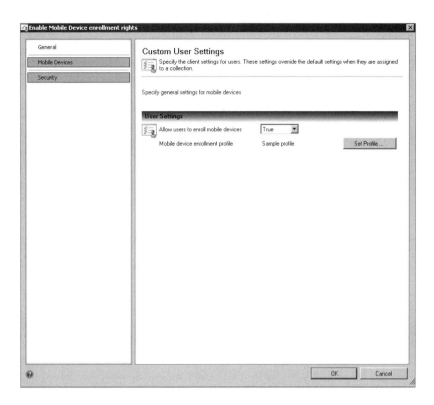

2. Configure a user collection that contains all users who should be granted the right of device enrollment.

   This collection can consist of either individual users or groups of users. The example uses individual users, as shown in Figure 14.20.

FIGURE 14.20
Collection of users where device enrollment should be enabled

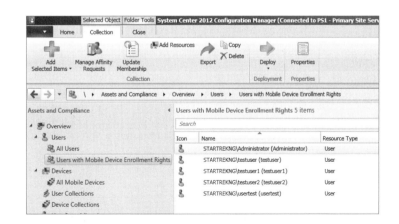

3. With both of these items created, it's a matter of linking the two. Simply go back to the custom user settings and assign them to the collection just created, as shown in Figure 14.21.

FIGURE 14.21

Custom user settings assigned to device enrollment collection

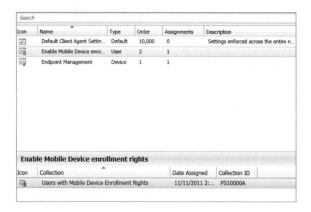

Complete the assignment process by right-clicking the custom setting and selecting Assign. It is also possible to link custom settings to more than a single collection.

This configuration of appropriate site systems and appropriate client settings is all that is required in order to enroll and provision devices. There is more work for the administrator to do in terms of configuring settings that should be in place on the various devices, but we'll cover that later.

User Configuration

Actions required from the device user's perspective are straightforward. The actual enrollment process behind the scenes is a bit more involved.

The device user will need to do only two things: install some software and enter credentials.

You can obtain the Enterprise Enrollment software from the enrollment web proxy site system by directing the device's web browser to the URL for this site system. The default URL is

```
https://<enrollmentwebproxyservername>/EnrollmentService
```

It's also possible that the Enterprise Enrollment software could be made available through another means, such as an email link. Regardless of the mechanism used to deliver the Enterprise Enrollment software to the device, it must be installed. In the example scenario, we obtain the software by browsing to the enrollment web proxy site system. Figure 14.22 shows the user being prompted for what action to take when presented with the enrollment software.

FIGURE 14.22
User prompted for
action regarding
enrollment software

For the example, we save the software to the device before running it. This is shown in
Figure 14.23 and Figure 14.24.

FIGURE 14.23
Select a location for the
enrollment software

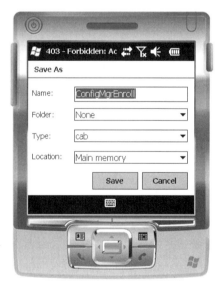

FIGURE 14.24
Enrollment software
download in progress

Once you've downloaded the software, you can find it in the root folder when viewing
File Explorer on the device. For the example, do the following:

1. Locate the software and select it to begin the installation process. Figure 14.25 and
   Figure 14.26 show the process.

FIGURE 14.25
Enrollment software
seen in File Explorer

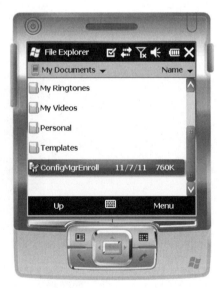

FIGURE 14.26
Enrollment software
installing to the device

Once it is installed, the enrollment software should automatically launch. If it doesn't, you can initiate it from the Start menu, as shown in Figure 14.27.

FIGURE 14.27
Enrollment software
installed and available
on the Start menu

2. Once it is launched, review the text and click Enroll, as shown in Figure 14.28.

FIGURE 14.28
Beginning the enroll-
ment process

3. Figure 14.29 shows the credentials screen. Provide an email address, password, and server address.

By default the option Use The Default Enrollment Server is selected. In the example scenario, the default configuration was inaccurate. Once you've provided the details, click Next.

A FEW WORDS ABOUT EMAIL LOOKUP AND USER ACCOUNTS

The email address is used to look up the proper domain account. Once looked up, the actual account in domain\user format is used for verifying credentials. You can see this in the enrollment logs, discussed later.

FIGURE 14.29
Credentials screen of
the enrollment wizard

From here, it's possible the user will see a warning screen regarding the site's certificate.

4. If so, verify that the certificate is OK, and click Yes to continue. This is shown in Figure 14.30.

FIGURE 14.30
Enrollment certificate
warning screen

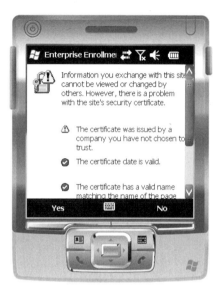

The enrollment process begins. To the device user, the process is fairly boring, as shown in Figure 14.31.

FIGURE 14.31
Enrollment in progress

In reality, there is a lot going on behind the scenes. In brief, the process is as follows:

1. The enrollment web proxy point takes the information supplied and passes it to the enrollment service point.

2. The enrollment service point forwards the information to the primary site for evaluation. This evaluation confirms the user has been granted rights to enroll their device in the site.

3. Assuming the user is approved, the enrollment service point will contact the enterprise certification authority to retrieve the needed certificate and send that back to the device through the enrollment web proxy point.

After this process completes, the device is enrolled and ready to be provisioned and managed. This is shown in Figure 14.32.

FIGURE 14.32
Enrollment process complete

Once the enrollment process is complete, there will be a delay before the device will be fully managed by the site—sometimes as long as eight hours. After this period the device should show up in the All Mobile Device collection as Active, as shown in Figure 14.33.

FIGURE 14.33
Device in Active status after enrollment and provisioning

The device should also have inventory information associated with it. This is another sign that it is properly configured and is shown in Figure 14.34.

FIGURE 14.34
Device inventory

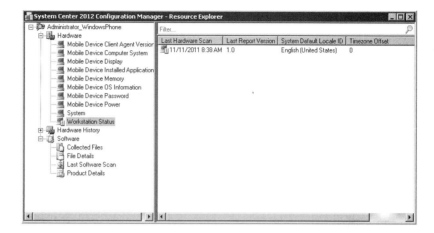

Previous versions of Configuration Manager separated device client settings from computer client settings. Configuration Manager 2012 unifies these settings so that, where applicable, the same values apply equally to all device types. Just remember that not all of the available settings are applicable to mobile devices. As an example, mobile devices are able to participate in hardware inventory as well as software distribution, but mobile devices do not submit software inventory. It is also possible to extend the hardware inventory for devices by modifying the SMS_DEF.MOF and Configuration.MOF files.

DEVICE SETTINGS MANAGEMENT

Settings management options are available for depth devices in addition to the standard client operations. You configure these settings through Compliance Settings. Configuring settings for mobile devices requires creating one or more configuration items and then delivering them to the mobile devices by associating them with configuration baselines, which are then assigned to a given collection. Since the number of configuration items and baselines needed will depend on individual configurations, the example will use a unified approach where a single configuration item and baseline are used for all devices:

1. Start configuring the configuration item by selecting Compliance Settings ➢ Configuration Items.

2. Right-click Configuration Items and select Create Configuration Item.

3. On the General page of the Create Configuration Item Wizard, shown in Figure 14.35, supply a Name and Description and then specify that the configuration item is targeted for a mobile device.

4. Optionally, select any categories that should be used for this configuration item. Click Next.

FIGURE 14.35
Create Configuration
Item Wizard—
General page

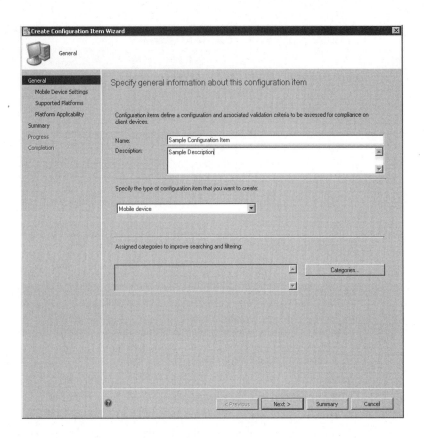

5. On the Mobile Device Settings page, determine which settings should be managed by this configuration item.

For the example, select all settings and choose to configure additional settings, as shown in Figure 14.36. This will allow you to review all potential settings that might be enforced on a device. Click Next.

FIGURE 14.36
Create Configuration
Item Wizard—Mobile
Device Settings page

SETTINGS VS. DEVICE CAPABILITY

Not all devices are capable of implementing all settings. It's fine to configure a setting in general, but the settings will be implemented only on capable devices.

6. After selecting the additional settings that will be defined by this configuration item, click Next.

7. Configure the appropriate device password options.

   The password settings are shown in Figure 14.37. Password settings are not configured by default.

FIGURE 14.37
Create Configuration
Item Wizard—
Password page

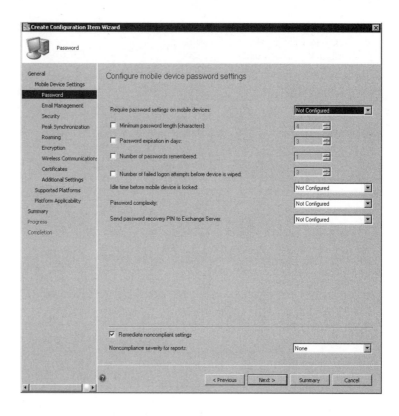

Require Password Settings On Mobile Devices   This option allows administrators to determine whether password settings should be enforced. Assuming this option is enabled, a few specific password configurations are possible:

- ◆ Minimum Password Length (Characters): This option allows administrators to specify the minimum number of characters that should be supplied as part of the password.

- ◆ Password Expiration In Days: This option allows administrators to specify the number of days that are allowed to elapse before requiring a password change.

- ◆ Number Of Passwords Remembered: This option allows administrators to configure how many passwords are retained. This setting is useful to prevent the reuse of passwords.

- ◆ Number Of Failed Logon Attempts Before Device Is Wiped: This option allows administrators to specify how many incorrect passwords can be supplied before the device is automatically wiped.

Idle Time Before Mobile Device Is Locked   This option, not enabled by default, allows administrators control over how long a device might be left unlocked when idle.

Password Complexity   This option allows administrators to specify the required password complexity level, in this case allowing either a PIN or a strong password.

Send Password Recovery PIN To Exchange Server   This option allows administrators to configure where the password recovery PIN is stored on the Exchange Server.

DEVICE COMPLIANCE REMEDIATION

If a device is not compliant with all required settings, it will be updated to the required state by default as a result of selecting Remediate Noncompliant Settings on the Password page. When device settings are remediated, it is possible to configure that a noncompliance indication should be logged in reports. This is disabled by default.

8. After all password options are configured, click Next.

9. Configure email options for the device in the Email Management settings, shown in Figure 14.38.

FIGURE 14.38
Create Configuration
Item Wizard—Email
Management page

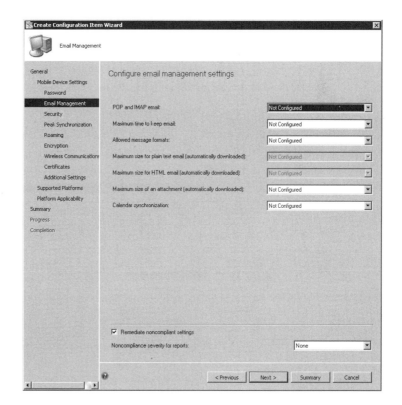

PDP And IMAP Email   This option allows administrators to define whether PDP and IMAP email are allowed. This is not an either/or setting; either both are allowed or both are prohibited.

Maximum Time To Keep Email   This option allows administrators to specify how long email should be retained on the device.

Allowed Message Formats This option allows administrators to specify the format allowed for email, either plain text only or both plain text and HTML. If this option is configured, up to two additional options become available for configuration.

Maximum Size For Plain Text Email (Automatically Downloaded) This option allows administrators to define the size of a plain text email that is allowed to be automatically downloaded to the device. Incremental sizes are configurable up to allowing the entire email to be downloaded.

Maximum Size For HTML Email (Automatically Downloaded) This option allows administrators to define the size of an HTML email that is allowed to be automatically downloaded to the device. Incremental sizes are configurable up to allowing the entire email to be downloaded.

Maximum Size Of An Attachment (Automatically Downloaded) This option allows administrators to define the size of an attachment that is allowed to be automatically downloaded to the device. Incremental sizes are configurable up to allowing the entire email to be downloaded.

Calendar Synchronization This option allows administrators to specify whether calendar synchronization to the device is allowed.

10. After all email options are configured, click Next.

11. Configure the security options for the device. The security management settings are shown in Figure 14.39.

FIGURE 14.39
Create Configuration
Item Wizard—
Security page

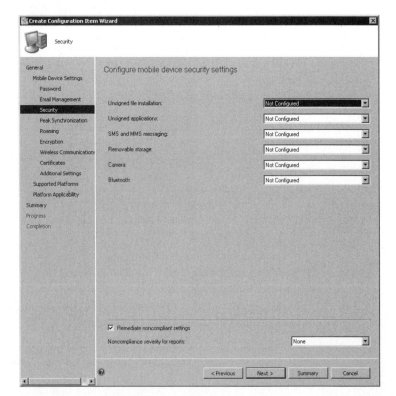

Unsigned File Installation   This option allows administrators to specify whether the installation of unsigned files is allowed or not allowed. If they are allowed, administrators then choose what parties are allowed this right. Available options are Mobile Operator, Manager, User Authenticated, IT Administrator, User Unauthenticated, and Trusted Provisioning Server.

Unsigned Applications   This option allows administrators to specify whether the installation of unsigned applications is allowed or prohibited.

SMS And MMS Messaging   This option allows administrators to configure whether SMS and MMS messaging are allowed or prohibited on the device.

Removable Storage   This option allows administrators to configure whether removable storage is allowed or prohibited on the device.

Camera   This option allows administrators to configure whether the camera is allowed or prohibited on the device.

Bluetooth   This option allows administrators to configure whether Bluetooth is allowed or prohibited on the device.

12. After all security options are configured, click Next.

13. Configure the synchronization options for the device in the Peak Synchronization settings, shown in Figure 14.40.

FIGURE 14.40
Create Configuration
Item Wizard—Peak
Synchronization page

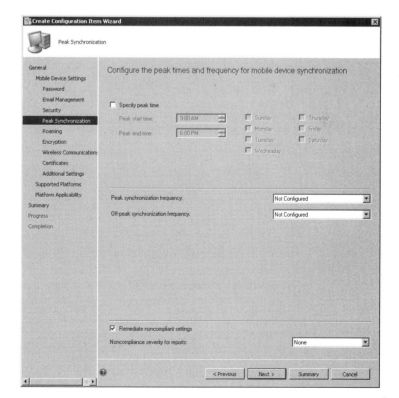

Specify Peak Time   This option allows administrators to define the specific time considered to be peak on devices.

Peak Synchronization Frequency   This option allows administrators to specify how often the device will synchronize during the defined peak time.

Off-Peak Synchronization Frequency   This option allows administrators to specify how often the device will synchronize outside the defined peak time.

14. After all Peak Synchronization options are configured, click Next.

15. Configure the roaming options for the device in the Roaming settings, shown in Figure 14.41.

FIGURE 14.41
Create Configuration
Item Wizard—
Roaming page

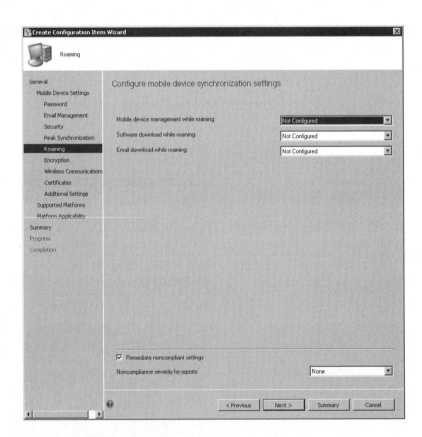

Mobile Device Management While Roaming   This option allows administrators to configure whether a device should be actively managed when roaming.

Software Download While Roaming   This option allows administrators to specify whether software downloads should be allowed when a device is roaming.

Email Download While Roaming   This option allows administrators to control whether email is downloaded while a device is roaming.

16. After all the Roaming options are configured, click Next.

17. Configure the encryption options for devices in the Encryption settings, shown in Figure 14.42.

FIGURE 14.42

Create Configuration
Item Wizard—
Encryption page

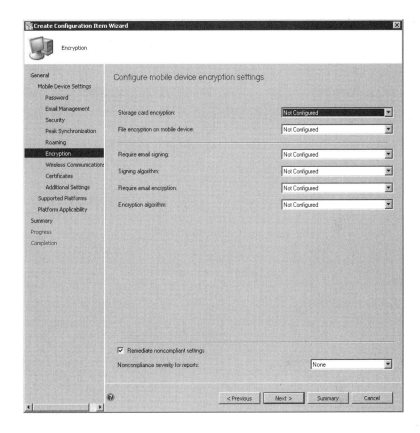

Storage Card Encryption   This option allows administrators to specify whether encryption is on or off for a device's storage card.

File Encryption On Mobile Device   This option allows administrators to configure whether file encryption is on or off for a device.

Require Email Signing/Signing Algorithm   This option allows administrators to specify whether email signing is enabled or disabled. If email signing is enabled, the Signing Algorithm option allows administrators to specify whether SHA, MD5, or the default signing algorithm should be used.

Require Email Encryption/Encryption Algorithm   This option allows administrators to configure whether email encryption is on or off for a device. If email encryption is enabled, the Encryption Algorithm option allows administrators to specify which encryption algorithm should be used. Available choices are Triple DES, DES, RC2 128-bit, RC2 64-bit, RC2 40-bit, or the default algorithm.

18. After all Encryption options are configured, click Next.

19. Configure the wireless communication options for devices in the Wireless Communication settings, shown in Figure 14.43.

FIGURE 14.43
Create Configuration Item Wizard—Wireless Communications page

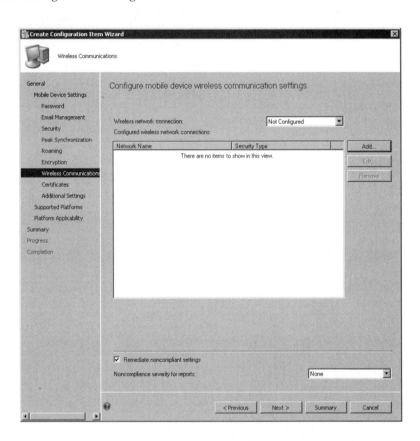

20. Configure whether wireless network connections are allowed or prohibited on the device.

If they are allowed, administrators can click the Add button to specify one or more networks and associated network configuration. Available network configuration options include Proxy, 802.1X, Authentication, Data Encryption, and more. A blank Wireless Network Connection configuration page is shown in Figure 14.44.

FIGURE 14.44
Wireless Network
Connection page

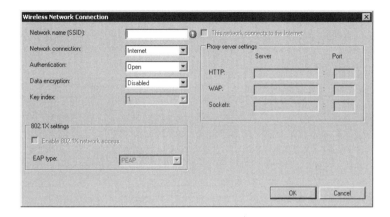

21. After all Wireless Network Connection options are configured, click Next.

22. Configure the certificate options for devices in the Certificates settings, shown in Figure 14.45.

FIGURE 14.45
Create Configuration
Item Wizard—
Certificates page

The Certificates To Install On Mobile Devices option allows administrators to specify certificates that should be installed on mobile devices. Clicking the Import button brings up the Import Certificate page, shown in Figure 14.46, which allows certificates to be imported from the filesystem and allows administrators to specify in which certificate store the certificate should be placed on the device.

FIGURE 14.46
Import Certificate page

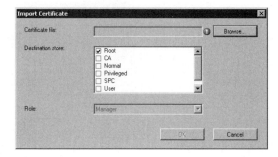

23. After all Certificate options are configured, click Next.

24. Configure any additional settings, either predefined or custom for the device, in the Additional Settings page, shown in Figure 14.47.

FIGURE 14.47
Create Configuration
Item Wizard—
Additional
Settings page

Clicking the Add button will display a list of all predefined additional settings that can be applied to a device, as shown in Figure 14.48.

FIGURE 14.48
Browse Settings page

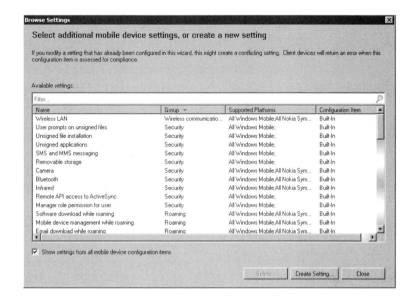

The list will include items already discussed and additional ones that are available but less common. Specific supported platforms are also listed for each item. Selecting the Show Settings From All Mobile Device Configuration Items option will add even more settings to the list. If a specific configuration is possible but not in the list of options, you can create custom settings by clicking Create Setting. The setting type to be created can be either an OMA-URI or a registry value.

Adding a setting from the list requires clicking the setting and then clicking Select. This action opens the setting to allow you to review the setting values. In some cases, a value must be supplied for a given setting. Once the setting is configured properly, click OK. Figure 14.49 shows an example of the Rule For Desktop PIM Sync setting.

FIGURE 14.49
Rule For Desktop PIM
Sync setting

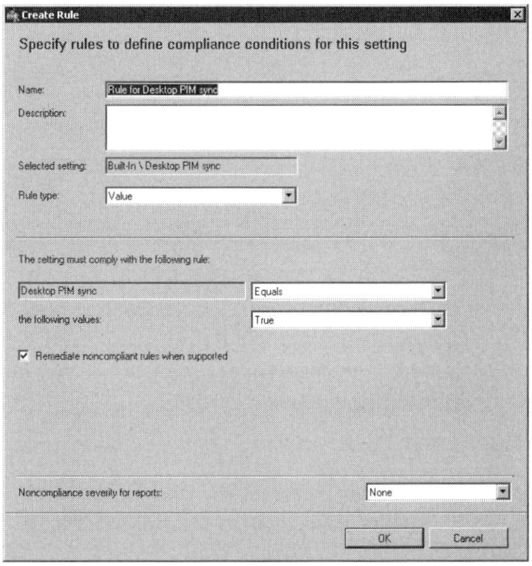

In the case of additional settings, the choice of whether to remediate or to report is specified individually. Using individual settings it would be possible to configure all settings options. When you specify individual settings, just ensure that there is no overlap between settings configured here and settings configured elsewhere.

25. Once any additional or custom settings are added to the Available Settings list, click Edit to review the settings. When you've complete your review, click Next.

The ability to review the details behind each setting exposes how each setting is implemented.

26. Specify which platforms should be targeted with the configurations just defined in the Supported Platforms page, shown in Figure 14.50, and click Next.

FIGURE 14.50
Create Configuration
Item Wizard—
Supported
Platforms page

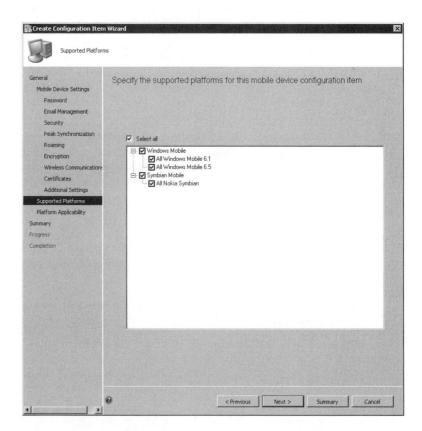

As already mentioned, not all settings apply to all device types. The Platform Applicability page of the wizard, shown in Figure 14.51, displays any settings that have been chosen but are not supported by a selected target platform. There is no configuration available here.

FIGURE 14.51
Create Configuration
Item Wizard—Platform
Applicability page

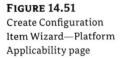

FIGURE 14.51
Create Configuration
Item Wizard—Platform
Applicability page

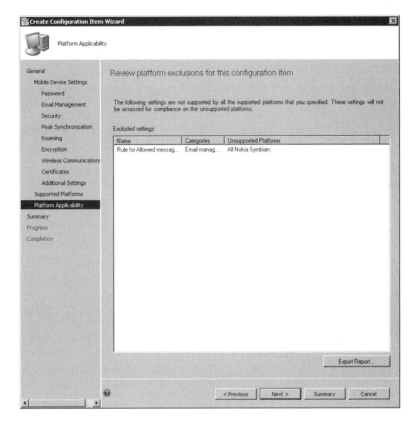

27. From here, simply complete the wizard to save the configuration item.

Defining the configuration item is not sufficient. Implementing the baseline requires attaching it to a baseline and assigning that baseline to a collection. This is a general task for compliance setting management and is discussed in Chapter 13, "Compliance Settings."

Troubleshooting

The method of troubleshooting problems with mobile devices depends on the management mode chosen. For lite management, troubleshooting will be mostly focused on Exchange—both in terms of ensuring that the Exchange ActiveSync connector is running properly and ensuring that the ConfigMgr 2012 Exchange ActiveSync connector is properly configured and operational.

When it comes to depth management, there are a few more places to check when you run into problems. Depth-managed devices require enrollment before management can begin. The enrollment process is not difficult, but there are a number of moving parts that must be configured properly, not the least of which is certificates. When enrollment fails, it's clear on the device that there was a problem, but it's not always easy to collect diagnostic information from the device to understand why enrollment failed. Fortunately, there is excellent logging around the enrollment process to help. The `EnrollmentService.log` and `EnrollmentWeb.log` may contain errors that might occur as the enrollment process progresses. These logs are located in the SMS_CCM folder, under the `EnrollmentService\logs` and `EnrollmentProxyPoint\logs` folders, respectively.

The depth-managed mobile device client has similarities to the computer device client in that client health data is provided. Simply reviewing a device in the collections to ensure client health evaluations are current and successful, along with checking the Client Status data from the Monitoring node, is a good indicator of whether the client is behaving properly.

The Bottom Line

Detail the differences between lite and depth management.   The various management options and settings available for mobile devices will vary depending on whether lite- or depth-management options are in place.

Master It   List mobile device management capabilities for lite versus depth management.

Understand how to configure mobile device management.   Properly configuring mobile device management requires addressing several potential scenarios. From a Configuration Manager 2012 perspective, though, the choice is simple: lite or depth management.

Master It   List the items that need to be configured for both lite and depth management.

Understand the depth-management enrollment process.   From the user perspective the enrollment process for depth management is straightforward. Behind the scenes, there are a number of moving parts. Each of these components is critical to the enrollment process.

Master It   List the components required to enroll depth-managed devices.

Chapter 15

Troubleshooting

So far you have read about various aspects of Configuration Manager 2012, and in each chapter we have explained different aspects of the product and have assumed that every component will work correctly. However, everyone knows that situations may occur with the product that require troubleshooting, and every IT professional needs to know how to identify the problem and find a possible solution. There are many resources online that can assist you in this process; some of these places are Microsoft TechNet, Bing, and MVP blogs.

In this chapter, we will cover the basics of troubleshooting a ConfigMgr 2012 infrastructure and determining which log file you should look at first when a problem arises.

In this chapter, you will learn to

- ◆ Create a basic maintenance plan.
- ◆ View log files using CMTrace.
- ◆ Troubleshoot DRS replication.

Creating the Maintenance Plan

The best way to prevent issues from arising in Configuration Manager 2012 is to create and follow a standard maintenance plan. A well-executed maintenance plan allows administrators to be actively aware of their ConfigMgr 2012 hierarchy, offering a better chance of finding possible concerns before they become issues. Proactively watching the environment can reduce the number of major issues and thus keep your environment healthier.

ConfigMgr 2012 has some predefined site maintenance tasks that are enabled by default and some that need to be enabled. To view and modify the site maintenance tasks, take the following steps:

1. Open the ConfigMgr console, and choose the Administration workspace.

2. Expand Site Configuration ➢ Sites, and select Site Name.

3. Right-click, browse to Site Maintenance, and click it to open the Site Maintenance window.

   By default, Microsoft has 10 predefined tasks for the CAS server and 31 predefined tasks for primary sites. (There are no predefined tasks for secondary sites.) Some of these predefined tasks are enabled, while others are disabled by default.

4. To enable a task, select its name and click Edit to display the task's Properties dialog box.

   Figure 15.1 shows the Properties dialog box for the Backup Site Server task.

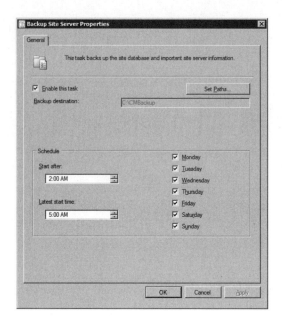

FIGURE 15.1
Enabling the Backup
Site Server task in its
Properties dialog box

5. Select Enable This Task.

SECONDARY SITES

You can back up a Central Administration Site and primary site, but there is no backup support for secondary sites or site system servers.

To ensure the proper health of the site, you should enable some of the predefined site maintenance tasks provided by Microsoft, and you'll need to modify the schedule of other tasks. Table 15.1 lists how the tasks should be configured in a typical maintenance plan; this might not be appropriate for all environments, but you can use the table as a guide.

TABLE 15.1: Site maintenance tasks

TASK NAME	ENABLED BY DEFAULT?	SCHEDULE	SITE LEVEL
Backup Site Server	No	Daily	CAS/Primary
Rebuild Indexes	No/Yes	Weekly	CAS/Primary
Monitor Keys	Yes	Weekly	CAS/Primary
Delete Aged Inventory History	Yes	Weekly	Primary
Delete Aged Status Messages	Yes	Daily	CAS/Primary

TASK NAME	ENABLED BY DEFAULT?	SCHEDULE	SITE LEVEL
Delete Aged Discovery Data	Yes	Weekly	Primary
Delete Aged Collected Files	Yes	Weekly	Primary
Delete Aged Software Metering Data	Yes	Daily	Primary
Delete Aged Software Metering Summary Data	Yes	Weekly	Primary
Summarize Software Metering File Usage Data	Yes	Daily	Primary
Summarize Software Metering Monthly Usage Data	Yes	Daily	Primary
Clear Install Flag	No	Weekly	Primary
Delete Inactive Client Discovery Data	Yes	Weekly	Primary
Delete Obsolete Client Discovery Data	Yes	Weekly	Primary
Delete Aged Computer Association Data	Yes	Weekly	Primary
Evaluate Provisioned AMT Computer Certificates	Yes	Weekly	Primary
Check Application Title with Inventory Information	Yes	Weekly	CAS/Primary
Delete Aged Client Operations	Yes	Daily	CAS/Primary
Delete Aged Log Data	Yes	Daily	CAS/Primary
Delete Aged Replication Tracking Data	Yes	Daily	CAS/Primary
Delete Obsolete Alerts	Yes	Daily	CAS/Primary
Delete Obsolete Forest Discovery Sites and Subnets	Yes	Weekly	CAS/Primary
Delete Unused Applications Revisions	Yes	Daily	Primary
Delete Aged Exchange Partnership	Yes	Weekly	Primary
Summarize Installed Software Data	Yes	Weekly	Primary
Delete Aged Threat Data	Yes	Weekly	Primary
Delete Aged Application Request Data	Yes	Daily	Primary
Delete Aged Device Wipe Record	Yes	Weekly	Primary

TABLE 15.1: Site maintenance tasks *(CONTINUED)*

TASK NAME	ENABLED BY DEFAULT?	SCHEDULE	SITE LEVEL
Delete Aged Enrolled Devices	Yes	Weekly	Primary
Evaluate Collection Members	Yes	Intervals	Primary
Update Application Catalog Tables	Yes	Intervals	Primary

Some tasks do not need to be performed as frequently as others, but it's important to develop a maintenance plan for them to ensure the proper health of the site.

Table 15.2 summarizes what a typical maintenance plan should be for ConfigMgr 2012. Again, these recommendations might not be appropriate for organizations of all sizes; the table is meant to be used only as a guide.

TABLE 15.2: Maintenance plan

TASK	INTERVAL	COMMENTS
Check status messages.	Daily	Check for warnings and errors. They are available in either a web report or within the administrative console.
Check event log on site server for warnings or errors.	Daily	This is the Windows event log.
Check log folders for crash dumps.	Daily	This will help you know whether the site system failed.
Monitor site system's inbox folder(s).	Daily	Check this for possible backlogs of files.
Clean out old machines and user accounts.	Daily	Remove old resources.
Check client status.	Daily	
Back up site server to removable media.	Daily	Ensure that the copy of the site backup is moved to removable media such as tape.
Delete unnecessary objects.	Weekly	Remove unneeded collections, packages, programs, advertisements, and queries.
Delete unnecessary files from site systems.	Weekly	Delete unneeded files.
Check disk space on all site systems.	Weekly	
Defragment all site systems.	Monthly	This can improve site performance.

TASK	INTERVAL	COMMENTS
Review site boundaries.	Quarterly	Ensure that your site boundaries are still valid.
Perform DR test.	Biannually	Ensure that backups actually work.
Review documentation.	Biannually	Confirm that documentation is updated and complete.
Review maintenance plan.	Biannually	Modify the maintenance plan if anything has changed or needs to be added or removed.

Getting an approved maintenance plan for your hierarchy is your first step to developing a solid ConfigMgr infrastructure. The next step is to automate as many of the tasks as possible so they can be done in the most efficient manner without sacrificing the results. A maintenance plan is only as strong as the people implementing the plan.

Using Troubleshooting Tools

The most important troubleshooting tools are log files and status messages. Getting to know the most common log files for ConfigMgr is the first step in identifying a potential situation on your site servers; you can also use this proactively to monitor your site server activity and to know what is being processed in your environment. That being said, let's take a look at the most common log files.

Log Files

For the majority of troubleshooting, administrators will focus on the log (.log) files on either the client or the server and in some cases both. The client stores the log files in the folder C:\Windows\ccm\logs, while the site server stores the log files in the folder <installation Directory>\Microsoft Configuration Manager\Logs. Table 15.3 lists the site server log files, Table 15.4 lists the management point log files, and Table 15.5 lists the client log files.

The default location for the management point log files is Program Files\SMS_CCM\Logs on the management point.

TABLE 15.3:   Site server and site system server log files

LOG FILE	PURPOSE
Ccm	Records client ConfigMgr tasks
Cidm	Records changes to the client settings by the Client Install Data Manager (CIDM)
Colleval	Logs when collections are created, changed, and deleted by the Collection Evaluator
Compsumm	Records Component Status Summarizer tasks
Csnfsvc	Records Courier Sender information between sites

TABLE 15.3:   Site server and site system server log files   *(CONTINUED)*

LOG FILE	PURPOSE
Dataldr	Processes management information format (MIF) files and hardware inventory in the ConfigMgr 2012 database
Ddm	Saves Discovery Data Record (DDR) information to the ConfigMgr 2012 database by the Discovery Data Manager
Despool	Records incoming site-to-site communication transfers
Distmgr	Records package creation, compression, delta replication, and information updates
Hman	Records site configuration changes and publishes site information in Active Directory Domain Services
Inboxast	Records files that are moved from the management point to the corresponding INBOXES folder
Inboxmgr	Records file maintenance
Invproc	Records the processing of delta MIF files for the Dataloader component for client inventory files
Mpcontrol	Records the registration of the management point with WINS and records the availability of the management point every 10 minutes
Mpfdm	Management point component that moves client files to the corresponding INBOXES folder
Mpmsi	Management point .msi installation log
Mpsetup	Records the management point installation wrapper process
Offermgr	Records advertisement updates
Offersum	Records summarization of advertisement status messages
Policypv	Records updates to the client policies to reflect changes to client settings or advertisements
Replmgr	Records the replication of files between the site server components and the scheduler component
Sched	Records files that are sent to other child and parent sites
Sender	Records the files that transfer by file-based replication between sites
Sinvproc	Records client software inventory data processing to the site database in Microsoft SQL Server

Log File	Purpose
Sitecomp	Records maintenance of the installed site components
Sitectrl	Records site setting changes to the Sitectrl.ct0 file
Sitestat	Records the monitoring process of all site systems
Smsdbmon	Records database changes
Smsexec	Records processing of all site server component threads
Smsprov	Records WMI provider access to the site database
Srvacct	Records the maintenance of accounts when the site uses standard security
Statmgr	Writes all status messages to the database
Swmproc	Processes metering files and maintains settings
Adctr	Records enrollment processing activity
ADForestDisc	Records Active Directory Forest Discovery actions
ADService	Records account creating and security group detail in Active Directory
Adsgdis	Records Active Directory Security Group Discovery actions
Adsysdis	Records Active Directory System Discovery actions
Adusrdis	Records Active Directory User Discovery actions
CertMgr	Records the certificate activities for intra-site communications
Chmgr	Records activities of the client health manager
Compmon	Records the status of component threads monitored for the site server
ComReqSetup	Records the initial installation of COM registration results for a site server
ConfigMgrPrereq	Records prerequisite component evaluation and installation activities
EPCtrlMgr	Records information about the synchronization of malware threat information from the endpoint protection site system role into the ConfigMgr database
EPMgr	Records the status of the endpoint protection site system role
EnrollSrv	Records activities of the enrollment service process
EnrollWeb	Records activities of the enrollment website process
Migmctrl	Records information for migration actions involving migration jobs, shared distribution points, and distribution point upgrades

TABLE 15.4:   Management point log files

MANAGEMENT POINT LOG FILE	PURPOSE
MP_Ddr	Records the conversion of XML .ddr records from clients and copies them to the site server
MP_GetAuth	Records the status of the site management points
MP_GetPolicy	Records policy information
MP_Hinv	Converts XML hardware inventory records from clients and copies the files to the site server
MP_Location	Records Location Manager tasks
MP_Policy	Records policy communication
MP_Relay	Copies files that are collected from the client
MP_Retry	Records the hardware inventory retry processes
MP_Sinv	Converts XML hardware inventory records from clients and copies them to the site server
MP_Status	Converts XML .svf status message files from clients and copies them to the site server
MP_CliReq	Records the client registration activity processed by the management point
MP_Framework	Records the activities of the core management point and client framework components
MP_OOBMgr	Records the management point activities related to receiving
MP_SinvCollFile	Records details about file collection

TABLE 15.5:   Client log files

CLIENT LOG FILE	PURPOSE
CAS	Content Access Service for the local machine's package cache
CcmExec	Tracks the clients activities and SMS agent host service information

CLIENT LOG FILE	PURPOSE
CertificateMaintenance	Records Active Directory certificates for the directory service and management points
ClientIDManagerStartup	Used for the maintenance of the resource's GUID
ClientLocation	Tracks the resource's site assignments
ContentTransferManager	Records scheduling information for the Background Intelligence Transfer Service (BITS) or Server Message Block (SMB) to download or to access ConfigMgr packages
DataTransferService	Records all BITS communication for policy or package access
Execmgr	Records advertisement information as advertisements execute
FileBITS	Records SMB package access tasks
Fsinvprovider	Windows Management Instrumentation (WMI) provider for software inventory and file collection tasks
InventoryAgent	Creates DDRs and hardware and software inventory records
LocationServices	Identifies located management points and distribution points
MIFProvider	Identifies the MIF WMI provider
Mtrmgr	Tracks software metering processes
PolicyAgent	Requests policies by using the data transfer service
PolicyAgentProvider	Records any policy changes
PolicyEvaluator	Records any new policy settings
RemCtrl	Logs when the remote control component starts
Scheduler	Records schedule tasks for all client operations
SMSCliui	Records usage of the Systems Management tool in Control Panel
StatusAgent	Logs status messages that are created by the client components
SWMTRReportGen	Generates a usage data report that is collected by the metering agent
EndpointProtectionAgent	Records details about the installation of the Endpoint Protection client and the application of antimalware policy to that client

There are also log files outside ConfigMgr 2012 that you will need to be aware of when troubleshooting issues within Configuration Manager; Table 15.6 lists them.

TABLE 15.6: Additional log files

NAME OR CATEGORY	LOCATION	DESCRIPTION
IIS log files	`%windir%\system32\Logsfiles`	Log file for Internet Information Services (IIS). Logs HTTP transactions.
SQL log files	`SQL Enterprise Manager`	Logs SQL activities.
WMI	`%windir%\system32\wbem\logs`	The WMI repository is the key to the hardware inventory of the clients. Become very familiar with these logs.

There are many more log files for each ConfigMgr component. To learn more about the rest of the log files you can check out the ConfigMgr 2012 Library at `http://technet.microsoft.com/en-us/library/hh427342.aspx`. Here you can find details including the log file location and descriptions. Since ConfigMgr has many log files, we point out only the most common ones in this chapter.

The best tool for reading log files we have seen is CMTrace, a log viewer that constantly monitors the opened file for updates. You can find CMTrace in the `SMSSETUP\Tools` folder on the ConfigMgr 2012 source media. It provides real-time updates of any log file, allowing administrators to see exactly what is happening on a client or site system. If that isn't enough to win you over, CMTrace includes the capability to highlight and filter features to allow at-a-glance log viewing. Finally, the tool includes an error code dictionary, shown in Figure 15.2, so that you can quickly translate most of Microsoft's decimal error codes into useful information right within the tool. For example, entering 5 in the Error Lookup window returns "Access Denied." This feature is available by selecting Tools ➢ Lookup in the CMTrace utility. CMTrace will highlight errors, as shown in Figure 15.3, so they stand out.

FIGURE 15.2
CMTrace Error Lookup window

FIGURE 15.3

Highlighted error in CMTrace

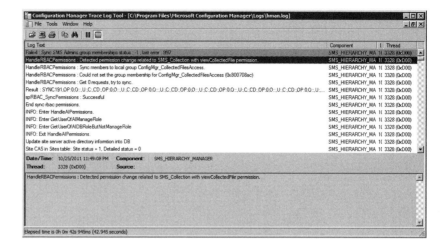

The other tool you need is a reference to all the log files. We covered the log files and their locations earlier in this chapter, and this information is a great reference. So now you are well equipped to troubleshoot a ConfigMgr 2012 site using the log files from the client or site systems, using the status messages in Configuration Manager, or using the web reporting feature of Configuration Manager.

Status Messages

Now that you have seen where the log files reside on both the client and servers, we will cover the troubleshooting components in the Configuration Manager 2012 console. Microsoft has continued to provide status messages within the console.

LIMITATIONS OF STATUS MESSAGES

Status messages do have some limitations. The first limitation is that site systems must be able to communicate in order for status messages to be transferred back; if a site system component cannot report back because of a failed network connection, it might still be showing that it is available. Another limitation is that most client messages are transferred as low priority by default, and during high utilizations these messages might be delayed.

Although status messages have some limitations, they can still be vital weapons in the troubleshooting arsenal of a ConfigMgr administrator. They just shouldn't be the only source for troubleshooting, however.

Status messages reside in one location, which is why they provide some benefit when troubleshooting. They are arranged in one place so you can quickly see the health of the site at a glance. To view the site status, in the ConfigMgr console choose Monitoring ➢ System Status ➢ Site Status.

The System Status dashboard is a summarized collection of the status of all the reported sites for easy viewing, and it has drill-down capability for each message. The System Status dashboard is organized into two categories, Component Status and Site Status, as shown in Figure 15.4.

FIGURE 15.4
The Site Status dashboard

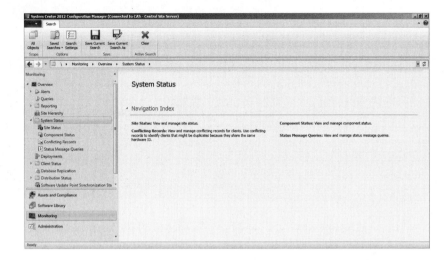

FIGURE 15.4
The Site Status dashboard

To dig deeper into a Component Status message to see details about a problem, follow these steps:

1. In the ConfigMgr console, choose Monitoring ➢ System Status ➢ Component Status.

2. Select the component you want to investigate.

   In this example, we will select the component SMS_DATABASE_NOTIFICATION_MONITOR.

3. Right-click the component, and select Show Messages ➢ All, as shown in Figure 15.5.

FIGURE 15.5
The Show Messages menu

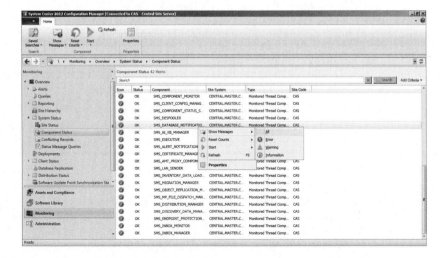

This opens the Configuration Manager Status Message Viewer for *<Site Code> <Site Name>* window, as shown in Figure 15.6.

Note that you can filter the returned messages by selecting All, Info, Warning, or Error messages.

FIGURE 15.6
The Configuration
Manager Status
Message
Viewer window

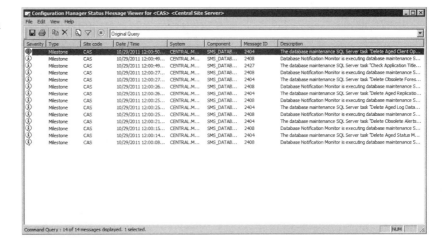

4. Within the Configuration Manager Status Message Viewer window, double-click any of the messages to get a detailed view of the message, as shown in Figure 15.7.

FIGURE 15.7
The Status
Message Details
dialog box

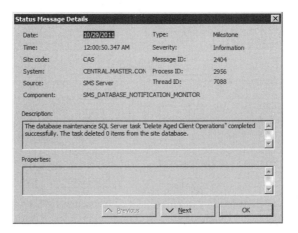

USING WEB REPORTS TO VIEW STATUS MESSAGES

You can view status messages from the Web Reports tool within Configuration Manager 2012. This is beneficial in case you are not able to access the ConfigMgr console or you have limited access to it. In either case, you can browse to your reporting point web console and view the status messages within a browser.

As discussed in Chapter 12, "Reporting," web reports allow administrators to provide focused views of a ConfigMgr 2012 site database via a web browser and can be set up within a dashboard to give managers an at-a-glance overview of the hierarchy. Table 15.7 lists the reports available in the Status Messages category.

TABLE 15.7:   Status Messages reports

NAME	DESCRIPTION
All Messages for a Specific Message ID	Lists the messages with a single message ID
Clients Reporting Errors in the Last 12 Hours for a Specific Site	Lists the computers and components reporting errors in the last 12 hours and the number of errors reported
Component Messages for the Last 12 Hours	Lists the component messages for the last 12 hours for a specific site code, computer, and component
Component Messages for the Last Hour (for a Specific Site, Computer, and Component)	Lists the status messages created in the last hour by a specified component on a specified computer in a specified SMS site
Count Component Messages for the Last Hour for a Specific Site	Displays the number of status messages by component and severity reported in the last hour at a single specified site
Count Errors in the Last 12 Hours	Displays the number of server component error status messages in the last 12 hours
Fatal Errors (by Component)	Lists the computers reporting fatal errors by component
Fatal Errors (by Computer Name)	Lists the computers reporting fatal errors by computer name
Last 1,000 Messages for a Specific Computer (Errors and Warnings)	Summarizes the last 1,000 error and warning component status messages for a single specified computer
Last 1,000 Messages for a Specific Computer (Errors)	Summarizes the last 1,000 error server component status messages for a single specified computer
Last 1,000 Messages for a Specific Computer (Errors, Warnings, and Information)	Summarizes the last 1,000 error, warning, and informational component status messages for a single specified computer
Last 1,000 Messages for a Specific Server Component	Summarizes the most recent 1,000 status messages for a single specified server component

As you can see, Microsoft has provided some nice reports out of the box for status messages. Of course, you can create your own report or modify any of the existing reports to fit your needs.

Deployment Status

Configuration Manager 2012 offer deployment status via the Monitoring workspace in the ConfigMgr console; you can monitor the deployment of all software (software updates, compliance settings, applications, task sequences, packages, and programs). To view this section of the console, do the following:

1. In the Configuration Manager console, choose Monitoring.

2. In the Monitoring workspace, choose Deployments.

3. To review general status information about an application deployment, select a deployment, and then choose the Summary tab of the Selected Deployment window.

4. To review deployment details for a compliance state and the devices in that state, select a deployment, and then, on the Home tab of the deployment group, click View Status.

5. To review information about the application's deployment type, select a deployment, and then click the Deployment Types tab of the Selected Deployment window.

Applications in Configuration Manager support state-based monitoring, which allows you to track the last application deployment state for users and devices. These state messages display information about individual devices. As you can see in Table 15.8, you can review the different states within the deployment.

TABLE 15.8:   Application deployment state

COLUMN NAME	DESCRIPTION
Success	The application deployment succeeded.
In Progress	The application deployment is in progress.
Unknown	The state of the application deployment could not be determined.
Requirements Not Met	The application was not deployed because it was not compliant with a dependency or a requirement rule.
Error	The application failed to deploy because of an error.

You can view additional information for each compliance state, which includes subcategories within the compliance state and the number of users and devices in this category. For example, the Error compliance state contains three subcategories:

◆ Error Evaluating Policy

◆ Content Related Errors

◆ Installation Errors

When more than one compliance state applies for an application deployment to a user who has more than one device, you will see the aggregate state that represents the lowest compliance. For example, if a user logs into two devices, and the application is successfully installed on one device but fails to install on the second device, the aggregate deployment state of the application for that user is Error.

Use these subcategories to help you to quickly identify any important issues with an application deployment. You can also view additional information about which devices fall into a particular subcategory of a compliance state.

DISTRIBUTION STATUS

The Configuration Manager 2012 console provides improved content monitoring, including the status for all package types in relation to the associated distribution points, including the content validation status for the content in the package, the status of content assigned to a specific distribution point group, the state of content assigned to a distribution point, and the status of optional features for each distribution point.

The console provides a Content Status node in the Monitoring workspace (see Table 15.9). Inside this workspace you can review the information of the different packages and how many distribution points have been targeted. This is very similar to the old package status on Configuration Manager 2007. To monitor the content status and view the status, follow these steps:

1. In the Configuration Manager console, choose Monitoring.

2. In the Monitoring workspace, expand Distribution Status, and then choose Content Status. The packages are displayed.

3. Select the package for which you want detailed status information.

4. On the Home tab, click View Status. Detailed status information for the package is displayed.

TABLE 15.9: Content status monitoring

COLUMN NAME	DESCRIPTION
Name	Displays the name of the package
Type	Displays the type of content
Source Version	Displays the version number of the source files
Version Date	Displays the time and date the package was last changed
Targeted	Displays the total number of distribution points that have a copy of this package
Installed	Displays the total number of distribution points that have a copy of the current version
Retrying	Displays the total number of distribution points that have had a failure in copying the package but have not exceeded the number of retries allowed and are currently retrying to copy the package or are in the state of removing the old package

Column Name	Description
Failed	Displays the total number of distribution points that have exceeded the number of retries and were unsuccessful at copying the package
Source Site	Displays the site where the package was created
Size	Displays the size of the package source folder
Compressed Size	Displays the size of the compressed version of the package source folder
Package ID	Displays the package ID

DISTRIBUTION POINT GROUP STATUS

This node can be found in the Monitoring workspace in the Configuration Manager 2012 console; here you can review information such as the distribution point group name, description, how many distribution points are members of the distribution point group, how many packages have been assigned to the group, distribution point group status, and compliance rate. You can also identify errors for the distribution point group, how many distributions are in progress, and how many have been successfully distributed. To perform this action, take the following steps:

1. In the Configuration Manager console, choose Monitoring.

2. In the Monitoring workspace, expand Distribution Status, and then choose Distribution Point Group Status. The distribution point groups are displayed.

3. Select the distribution point group for which you want detailed status information.

4. On the Home tab, click View Status.

   Detailed status information for the distribution point group is displayed.

DISTRIBUTION POINT CONFIGURATION STATUS

On this node you can review what attributes are enabled for the distribution point, such as PXE, multicast, and content validation, as well as the distribution status for the distribution point. To view this information, perform the following steps.

1. In the Configuration Manager console, choose Monitoring.

2. In the Monitoring workspace, expand Distribution Status, and then choose Distribution Point Configuration Status. The distribution points are displayed.

3. Select the distribution point for which you want distribution point status information.

4. In the results pane, click the Details tab.

   Status information for the distribution point is displayed.

System Status

The System Status home page will highlight all the site systems within your Configuration Manager infrastructure and show a summary of the systems. Table 15.10 displays the information shown when you browse to the System Status home page by choosing the Monitoring workspace ➢ System Status in the Configuration Manager console.

TABLE 15.10:   System status

COLUMN NAME	DESCRIPTION
Status	Displays the status of the ConfigMgr 2012 site and any child site. The status will be OK, Warning, or Critical.
Site System	Displays the NetBIOS name of the site system.
Role	Displays the role assigned to the site system.
Storage Object	Displays the name and location of the storage unit.
Total	Displays the total available disk space.
Free	Displays the total available free space.
% Free	Displays the percentage of available free space.
Down Since	Displays the time when the site system could not be contacted.
Availability	Displays whether the site system is currently online or offline.

Because of the slow replication speed of status messages, most ConfigMgr administrators will focus on the log files of the client, the server, and often a combination of both. Because there are so many log files, to keep track of which log file contains the information you need for troubleshooting, every ConfigMgr administrator needs two tools:

CMTrace   With this tool you can view the logfile in real time.

Flowcharts   This usually explains how each process works and their flow.

Troubleshooting Configuration Manager Deployment

If you experience issues deploying ConfigMgr 2012, you should first look into the following areas to see whether the issue is related to permissions, disk space, network connectivity, or timing:

Permissions   Permissions are extremely important to ConfigMgr deployment. If ConfigMgr does not have appropriate rights to make the connection, then the operation will fail. Admins using the ConfigMgr console will need the appropriate permissions for WMI, for DCOM, for NTFS, and within ConfigMgr itself.

Disk Space   Disk space is used to store the site database, packages, software updates, inventory, and collected files; all of these can use up a lot of disk space. How much space is used depends on your environment, but you should always verify that you have sufficient disk space to store all the data within Configuration Manager.

Network Connectivity   Network connectivity is a key requirement of Configuration Manager. The site system must be able to communicate with other site systems and clients. As stated earlier, sometimes the network connectivity might be down but the status messages have not updated, so you need to ensure the clients and servers can connect to each other.

Timing   Patience is not always a trait of ConfigMgr administrators, but it is an important one to develop. Some tasks within Configuration Manager, Active Directory, and Windows in general take some time to complete. That is why examining the log files is so important.

Troubleshooting Configuration Manager Database Replication

Database Replication in Configuration Manager 2012 (shown in Figure 15.8) is based on Data Replication Service (DRS). This depends on two SQL features: SQL Server Service Broker and Change Tracking; these have nothing to do with transactional replication. This replication is very important in ConfigMgr and for this reason you need to ensure that this replication is working at all times. SQL Server Service Broker manages internal and external processes that can send and receive guaranteed async messages by using a data manipulation language (DML). Messages can be sent to a queue in the same database as the sender, to another database in the same SQL instance, or to another SQL instance on a remote server. To better understand this concept you can visit the following site:

```
http://msdn.microsoft.com/en-US/library/ms345108(v=SQL.90).aspx
```

FIGURE 15.8
The Database
Replication node

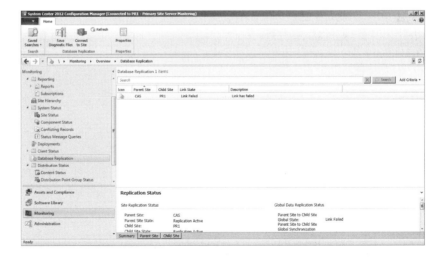

To look at the status of the current database replication, choose the Monitoring workspace ➢ Database Replication.

A SQL communication link is a logical entity that is used to reflect the overall status of SQL communication between two sites. The link reflects the overall status of global and site data being replicated between two sites.

Each global and site data replication link will have one of the following states:

Link Active   This state implies that data is being replicated as per schedule.

Link Failed   This state implies that data is not being replicated because of errors. This state can also be caused when communication does not occur for more than 25 minutes.

Link Degraded   This state implies that no communication has occurred for approximately 15 minutes. Regular replication intervals are approximately every 2 minutes, so a 15-minute delay in communication could indicate a degraded link.

Link Error   This state implies the replication data has synced but with errors; these errors could be due to failed data validation or conflicts.

Data Types

There are various data types in Configuration Manager. Objects that will be replicated in Configuration Manager are based on these types.

The type of data generated at the Central Administration Site and primary sites and replicated across the hierarchy is called *global data*. Since this data is globally available, it can be modified or deleted from the Central Administration Site or any primary site, regardless of where it was created, provided proper role-based access control (RBAC) permissions are configured.

The following elements are part of global data:

◆ Collections

◆ Packages

◆ Programs

◆ Deployments

◆ Configuration Items

◆ Software Updates

◆ Task Sequences

◆ OS Images (boot images, driver packages, and the like)

◆ Site Control File

◆ System Resource List (site servers)

◆ Site Security Objects (roles, scopes, and so on)

◆ Client Authentication

◆ Client Discovery

Global data replication is built on the Service Broker infrastructure provided by SQL Server.
Primary sites generate *site data*; it is potentially replicated to the Central Administration Site
but never replicated between primary sites. You can view this process in Figure 15.9. Since this
data is visible only at the Central Administration Site and the primary site where the data origi-
nated, it cannot be modified or deleted from other primary sites. If the data needs to be modified, it can be modified only at the originating site.

FIGURE 15.9
Replication flow

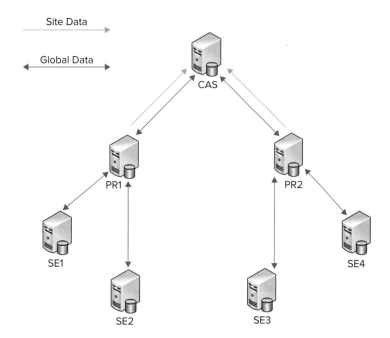

The following elements are part of site data:

◆ Collection Membership

◆ Alerts

◆ Hardware Inventory

◆ Software Inventory & Metering

◆ Status Messages

◆ General Site Data

◆ Asset Intelligence CAL Track Data

◆ Software Distribution Status Details

◆ Software Updates Replicated Site Data

◆ Software Updates Non-Replicated Site Data

◆ Status Summary Data

- ◆ Component and Site Status Summarizers
- ◆ Client Health Data
- ◆ Client Health History
- ◆ Wake On LAN
- ◆ Quarantine Client Restriction History

DRS Initialization

The process of DRS initialization is as follows:

1. A receiving site sends an `init` request to the sending site for the required replication group.

2. The sending site uses `bcp` (Bulk Copy Program) to export all the data from the tables in the replication group. During this phase, you can open the `RCMCtrl.log` file, as shown in Figure 15.10.

3. Hierarchy Replication copies the BCP files and sends a count of each row for each table to the receiving site inbox via the senders. To view the details about this process, see Figure 15.11.

By default ConfigMgr starts with the Replication Configuration Data group, which contains the data about other groups to be replicated.

To evaluate this process you can then open the `RCMCtrl.log` at the primary site or CAS (Figure 15.10).

FIGURE 15.10

`RCMCtrl.log` viewed in `CMTrace.exe`

You can also open SQL Server Management Studio and expand the Configuration Manager database ➢ Programmability and locate the `spDiagDRS` stored procedure. Executing this stored procedure will show the different statuses of the data types and the link status between sites.

FIGURE 15.11
Replication process

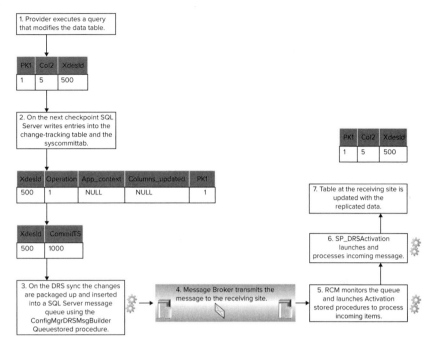

1. Provider executes a query that modifies the data table.

PK1	Col2	Xdesid
1	5	500

2. On the next checkpoint SQL Server writes entries into the change-tracking table and the syscommittab.

Xdesid	Operation	App_context	Columns_updated	PK1
500	1	NULL	NULL	1

Xdesid	CommitTS
500	1000

3. On the DRS sync the changes are packaged up and inserted into a SQL Server message queue using the ConfigMgrDRSMsgBuilder Queuestored procedure.

4. Message Broker transmits the message to the receiving site.

5. RCM monitors the queue and launches Activation stored procedures to process incoming items.

6. SP_DRSActivation launches and processes incoming message.

7. Table at the receiving site is updated with the replicated data.

PK1	Col2	Xdesid
1	5	500

Understanding these processes is key to troubleshooting DRS replication in Configuration Manager. Be sure to review this process and learn how the DRS and stored procedures are executed in this process for a successful replication.

 **Real World Scenario**

TROUBLESHOOTING CONTOSO

In this scenario you have been asked to go onsite to troubleshoot a problem with a Contoso hierarchy. Contoso is a financial institution that has a Tier 3 Level Configuration Manager Hierarchy. As an engineer you will review the Contoso's environment for potential issues.

THE SITUATION

The hierarchy is not replicating changes to a specific package.

TROUBLESHOOTING STEPS

As an engineer, the first thing you have to do is understand the Consoto's issues and their goals. It's important to follow a process to resolve the problem. I always use the following process—seven steps of problem solving:

1. Define and identify the problem.

2. Analyze the situation.

3. Identify possible solutions.

4. Select the best solution.

5. Evaluate the solution.

6. Develop an action plan.

7. Implement the solution.

If you follow these steps, you will be able to resolve most Configuration Manager issues or any problems that may arise.

1. Define and identify the problem.

   One package is not replicating to a primary site.

2. Analyze the situation.

   Find this package on the Configuration Manager 2012 console and note the Package ID. Then validate the current state of the database replication. In the Monitoring workspace you can validate the content by using Content Monitoring.

   At this point you know the Package ID, the distribution points this package is currently deployed to, and the potential issues this package may have. But the problem is still not fixed because you have only identified potential issues.

3. Identifying possible solutions.

   During the review of Database Replication you found out that the current state is link degraded. In this chapter you learned that this state indicates that SQL has not been able to communicate with the server in the past 15 minutes. To continue troubleshooting this issue you must open RCMCtrl.log using CMTrace.exe and find out the last time the package was replicated to this site. If the replication hasn't occurred in the past 15 minutes, you must try to resolve other potential issues related to communication.

4. Select the best solution.

   You have determined that the issue identified in step 3 is related to communication with the primary site. You contact the network administrator and explain the communication problems you are having on the site. The administrator promises to resolve the issue within a couple of hours. To solve the problem you decide you will reinitiate database replication, resend the package to the primary site, and review the log files for confirmation that the package has replicated.

5. Evaluate the solution.

   The solution provided in step 4 was to reinitiate database replication. You also need to review the replication process as described in Figure 15.11. If this solution is the one that makes the most sense to implement in this environment, then it is the one you will execute. It's very important to evaluate the solution in detail before implementing it.

6. Develop an action plan.

   To be able to accomplish this, you need to understand what you need to solve this problem:

   ◆ You need to determine what people need to be involved and what tasks they need to perform.

   ◆ Since the solution provided is related to communication, you must explain your action plan to the network administrator, who will evaluate the communication.

◆ You will execute a new database replication on the Configuration Manager 2012 environment; it's a good idea to have the database administrator involved just in case you need to back out your plan or have them help you understand the process involved in resolving the situation.

◆ Once all the tasks are outlined and everyone understands what is needed to solve the problem on the site, you can execute the plan on the environment.

You should always have a backout plan just in case your solution doesn't solve the problem. If that happens, you'll need to go back to step 1.

7. Implement the solution.

Now that you have all the tasks figured out, go ahead and execute the plan to solve this problem:

a. Get the database replication in place again.

b. Resend the package to the distribution point.

c. Evaluate the log files to confirm the package was sent out to the distribution point.

d. Validate that the content is on the primary site where you were having the problem.

After executing each task, you should solve the problem on the primary site and the package should be replicated. If the problem is still not fixed at this point, go back to steps 5 and 6, and make sure you understand the situation correctly.

Solving a problem can take from minutes to hours in a Configuration Manager environment; it will depend on the complexity of the hierarchy you are working on and the type of problem. In all my years of experience, I have used this method for all my problem solving at a customer's site. This is my quick guide to resolving issues in a structured way. Always make sure you understand the problem correctly before attempting to solve it.

The Bottom Line

Create a basic maintenance plan. Setting up a basic maintenance plan is a vital step to ensure the proper health of your Configuration Manager 2012 hierarchy.

Master It How do you create a basic maintenance plan?

View log files using CMTrace. Although using CMTrace is not a requirement for viewing log files, it is highly recommended because CMTrace constantly monitors the opened file for updates.

Master It Use CMTrace to view log files.

Troubleshoot DRS replication. To view the current status of the ConfigMgr DRS replication and to know the latest information about the changes being requested on the site, it's important to be familiar with the log file and the replication process.

Master It To view the latest changes on the replication process, what log file do you need to open to view this information?

Chapter 16

Disaster Recovery

No matter what kind of hardware you are using for your Configuration Manager sites, there is always the possibility that hardware or some other failure will bring a site down. The only thing you can really do to prepare for something like this is to back up Configuration Manager the best you can so that you can get your site back up and running as soon as possible. Fortunately, Microsoft continues to provide the options that are present in earlier versions of Configuration Manager, and it provides a specialized set of backup and recovery options that you will need to recover your sites.

A Configuration Manager site stores information in the site server's registry, the system files, and the SQL site database. A site will operate properly only if all of these sources of data are synchronized.

To make sure that you are getting a complete backup of your Configuration Manager sites, you need to configure the Backup ConfigMgr Site Server maintenance task. This task creates a complete backup snapshot of the data sources that are needed to perform a restore. You will need the Backup ConfigMgr Site Server maintenance task even if you have a SQL backup procedure that also includes the Configuration Manager site database.

In this chapter, you learn to

◆ Configure backups for Configuration Manager sites.

◆ Recover Configuration Manager sites.

◆ Archive backup snapshots to another location.

◆ Reinstall the site components and reset file and registry permissions to their default settings.

Planning for Disaster Recovery

Planning for disaster recovery in Configuration Manager 2012 is not complicated, but as you'll see in the section "Recovering Configuration Manager," it is different than it was in Configuration Manager 2007 and previous versions of System Management Server (SMS). With that in mind, you should consider the following when you are planning to set up your backup and recovery plans for your Configuration Manager hierarchy.

◆ The Configuration Manager backup task uses the Volume Shadow Copy Service (VSS), which is a part of Windows Server 2008 R2 and is configured during the installation of Configuration Manager, to make its backup snapshots.

Microsoft describes VSS as "a framework which facilitates communication between applications, storage subsystems, and storage management applications (including backup applications) in order to define point-in-time copies of storage data." The shadow copies that are made from VSS of the site server and the site database information are used to back up and restore Configuration Manager. By using VSS, the Backup ConfigMgr Site Server maintenance task can keep server downtime for backups to a minimum.

◆ A complete backup of a Configuration Manager site server includes the following:

   ◆ The Configuration Manager site database (SQL)

   ◆ `<ConfigurationManager installation dir>\Bin`

   ◆ `<ConfigurationManager installation dir>\Inboxes`

   ◆ `<ConfigurationManager installation dir>\Logs`

   ◆ `<ConfigurationManager installation dir>\Data`

   ◆ `<ConfigurationManager installation dir>\srvacct`

   ◆ `<ConfigurationManager installation dir>\install.map`

   ◆ `HKLM\Software\Microsoft\SMS` registry keys on the site server

◆ Unlike most other SQL applications, the master SQL database isn't needed to restore a Configuration Manager site, so it isn't backed up with the Configuration Manager database when the Backup ConfigMgr Site Server maintenance task is run.

◆ If you have a site hierarchy with a Central Administration Site and multiple primary sites, a newly installed primary site will automatically receive all global data when the site is reinstalled.

What Is Not Included in the Backup

When planning for a backup, it is also very important to know what is *not* part of the backup maintenance task. As a rule of thumb, only the site server and the site database are included. You must also plan for the backup of remote site systems, add-on products, and the like.

The Content Library

The content library contains all packages (software updates, applications, and images). You will find a content library on the site server and all distribution points. As a consequence of not backing up the content library, you will need to add several hours to the restore process because all files must be processed from the original source folders and inserted into the content library. With that in mind, also consider where you place source folders for any package. Organizations often host source files on the site server. This is not a recommended strategy; instead you should host all source folders on a separate file server.

Site Systems

The consequence of having a remote site system that fails is often a reinstallation of the specific site system. It is no big issue because most site systems cannot contain data and can be reinstalled quickly. Add to that the fact that you can have multiple instances of the same site system in the environment.

Clients

No client will be backed up during the backup maintenance task. In the event of a client failure, the new built-in client remediation task will be able to fix the error and perform a client reinstallation if needed.

SQL Reporting Services

Any customizations made to the default reports and custom reports will be lost in the event of a failure. All default reports will be recovered during the reinstallation of the site system.

When planning for a SQL Reporting Services backup you need to consider the following:

- Use the full recovery model in SQL to back up the reportserver database.

- Use the simple recovery model in SQL backup to back up the reportservertempdb database.

- Back up the encryption keys, using the rskeymgmt utility or the Reporting Services Configuration Manager.

- Back up these configuration files:

  - `Rsreportserver.config`

  - `Rssvrpolicy.config`

  - `Rsmgrpolicy.config`

  - `Reportingservicesservice.exe.config`

  - `Web.config` for both the Report Server and Report Manager ASP.NET applications

  - `Machine.config` for ASP.NET

- Back up any custom reports, models, and custom projects.

For more detailed information about backing up SQL Reporting Services, check `http://msdn.microsoft.com/en-us/library/ms155814.aspx`.

WSUS Database

Windows Server Update Services is not part of the backup, and you should consider performing a regular backup using SQL, as described in this article:

`http://technet.microsoft.com/en-us/library/ms187510.aspx`

System Center Updates Publisher

System Center Updates Publisher (SCUP) is a stand-alone product installed with a single database stored in the user profile. You either need to perform a backup of the database from the user profile or configure SCUP 2011 to use a database from a shared network location.

To configure SCUP 2011 to use a database in `E:\SCUPDB`, follow these simple steps:

1. Open Explorer and navigate to `C:\Users\Installation account\AppData\Local\Microsoft\System Center Updates Publisher 2011\5.00.1727.0000\`.

2. Copy the database file to a shared location.

3. Navigate to the SCUP 2011 installation folder and edit the `scup2011.exe.config` file.

4. Find `<setting name="SSCEDataFile" serializeAs="String">`.

5. Add this line:

<value>E:\SCUPDB\scupdb.sdf</value>

6. Save and close the file.

With the database file on the network, all you need is a backup of the file.

MICROSOFT DEPLOYMENT TOOLKIT

Microsoft Deployment Toolkit (MDT) is a free stand-alone tool from Microsoft that is often used with Configuration Manager 2012. MDT can contain a SQL database that you need to include in the normal SQL backup routines. Furthermore, you need to make sure that you have a backup of any custom scripts.

Backing Up Configuration Manager

The first thing to know about backing up Configuration Manager sites is that you can automate the procedure by scheduling the Backup ConfigMgr Site Server maintenance task. We will cover this maintenance task in more detail later in the chapter.

When the Configuration Manager backup service (SMS_SITE_BACKUP) starts, it uses instructions in the backup control file, located at

<ConfigMgr Install Location>\Inboxes\smsbkup.box\smsbkup.ctl

You can modify this file in Notepad to change what the backup service takes a snapshot of, but it isn't usually necessary.

Information on the site backup process is written to the smsbkup.log file, which can be found in the default location for log files and in the location that is designated in the Backup ConfigMgr Site Server maintenance task when the task is run. You can customize the smsbkup.ctl file as long as you do not modify any of the default settings. Customizations that might be valuable to add are other registry keys or file locations. Figure 16.1 shows the default smsbkup.ctl file.

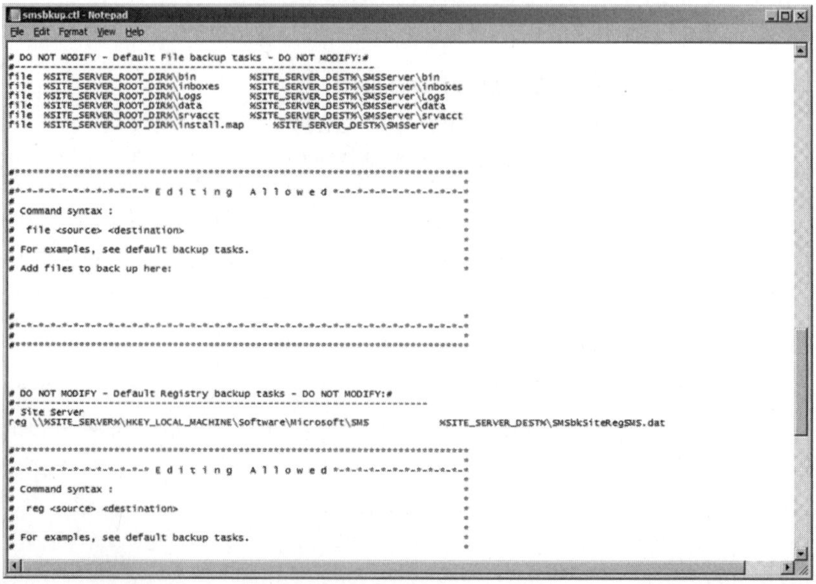

FIGURE 16.1
The smsbkup
.ctl file

Backup Considerations for the Central Administration Site

The process of backing up and recovering a central site is pretty much the same as with any primary site (discussed shortly), but there are special considerations to keep in mind when you back up and restore the Central Administration Site that make it different than other primary sites when you set up backups of the central site and when you recover them:

- The Central Administration Site is the busiest site in your hierarchy, which gives you a smaller time frame for scheduling a backup. Configuration changes are made on a constant basis, and you will probably not be able to recover them all.

- The Central Administration Site has the largest amount of data, because it is the only site that contains all global and site data. It will take longer to back up than your primary sites.

These combined factors might make you consider backing it up less frequently than your primary sites. But this is not a good idea, because the Central Administration Site is the most important site in your Configuration Manager hierarchy. If one of your primary sites fails, and for some reason your backups for that site are corrupted, you can always install a new primary site and replicate the most current global data from the Central Administration Site. That's not the case with the Central Administration Site. With this in mind, we recommend scheduling the backup of your Central Administration Site to run every day.

A couple of steps will enable you to recover as much of your central site as possible in the event of data loss:

- Back up the Central Administration Site every day.

- Have a reference site for the central site so that the restore process will be able to recover global data that is created after the site is backed up.

With these steps, you should be able to recover most of the Central Administration Site without too much trouble. You will be able to recover global and site data from the reference site.

Copying Site Backups to Another Location

The first time the Backup ConfigMgr Site Server task runs, it creates a backup snapshot, which can be used to recover a Configuration Manager site system when it fails. The next time the backup task runs, it makes a new backup snapshot that will overwrite the one that was made during the last snapshot. This could be a problem if the current backup snapshot becomes corrupt for some reason, because there will not be another backup to restore from.

For that reason, Microsoft recommends that you archive the backup to another location off the site server itself. As a best practice, it also recommends having multiple backup archives, for the following reasons:

- It is common for backup media to fail, get misplaced, or contain only a partial backup. Recovering a failed site from an older backup is better than recovering with no backup at all.

- A corruption in a site can go undetected for several backup cycles. You may need to go back several cycles to the backup snapshot from before the site became corrupted.

- The site might have no backup at all if, for example, the Backup ConfigMgr Site Server task fails. Because the backup task removes the previous backup snapshot before it starts to back up the current data, there will not be a valid backup snapshot.

Archiving the Backup Snapshot to Another Server with *AfterBackup.bat*

Microsoft has included support for a batch file appropriately called AfterBackup.bat to run tasks on the site server after the backup task is complete. After you successfully run the Backup ConfigMgr Site Server maintenance task, ConfigMgr will try to run this batch file. This batch file is not installed during site setup and will have to be created manually by an administrator after a site server is configured and stored in \Microsoft Configuration Manager\inboxes\smsbkup.box.

If the AfterBackup.bat file exists and is stored in the correct folder on the site server, the batch file will run automatically once the backup task is complete. You can include commands in the AfterBackup.bat file that will archive the backup snapshot to a location off the server at the end of the backup operation and perform other post-backup tasks. The AfterBackup.bat file integrates the archive and backup operations, thus ensuring that every new backup is archived. If the batch file does not exist, it has no effect on the backup success, but in order to archive the backup snapshot, you must use another method.

Although the AfterBackup.bat file is intended to archive backup snapshots, you can include commands in that batch file that will run after every backup. As noted, the AfterBackup.bat file isn't created for you when ConfigMgr is installed, and the ConfigMgr documentation does not explain how to set up the AfterBackup.bat file to be able to accomplish this task.

There are several ways to do this (including using third-party tools), some more complicated than others, but probably the simplest way is to use the Windows command robocopy. As illustrated in Figure 16.2, a robocopy command will copy all files from D:\CM2012.bck to a network share called \\File01\backup\CM01.

FIGURE 16.2
A sample
Afterbackup.bat file

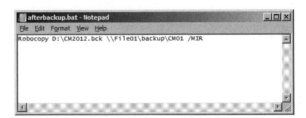

To create the Afterbackup.bat file, follow these simple steps:

1. Open Explorer and navigate to \Microsoft Configuration Manager\inboxes\smsbkup.box.

2. Create a new ASCII file and name it **AfterBackup.bat**.

3. Type **Robocopy D:\CM2012.bck \\File01\backup\CM01 /MIR**.

4. Save and close the file.

5. Upon the next backup, open the smsbkup.log file and search for the text Afterbackup.bat to verify that the file has been executed.

This isn't the perfect solution, but it will get the job done. One of the drawbacks of archiving this way is that the files will be copied over the network uncompressed to your remote file location. Depending on the size of your ConfigMgr database, archiving may take a long time and might use up a lot of bandwidth if your remote location is on a slow link. With that in mind, you can also add commands to the `AfterBackup.bat` file to use file compression software such as WinZip to compress the backup files before they are copied to the remote archive location.

Windows Application Log Entries Created by the Backup Process

The Backup ConfigMgr Site Server task will write backup status messages to the Application log in Windows event viewer. Table 16.1 shows a list of the events and their event IDs that are written to the Application Log, as described in the Microsoft documentation. You will be able to intercept the events using a monitoring system like Microsoft System Center Operations Manager.

TABLE 16.1:   Configuration Manager Backup Application Log entries

EVENT ID NUMBER	MESSAGE
5055	Component SMS_SITE_BACKUP on computer site server reported: Site Backup task is starting. This task will interact with the Windows VSS services and the appropriate writers to create a volume snapshot and then back up the required files to the specified destination.
6829	Component SMS_SITE_VSS_WRITER on computer CM03 reported: SMS Writer is about to stop the ConfigMgr Services as part of the preparation for the site backup.
3197	I/O is frozen on database CM_SiteCode. No user action is required. However, if I/O is not resumed promptly, you could cancel the backup.
3198	I/O was resumed on database CM_SiteCode. No user action is required.
18264	Database backed up. Database: CM_SiteCode, creation date(time): 2011/10/30(17:24:17), pages dumped: 76829, first LSN: 1388:858:3, last LSN: 1388:2253:1, number of dump devices: 1, device information: (FILE=1, TYPE=VIRTUAL_DEVICE: {'{776CCC64-70CC-4C6E-ABEC-976F9626B36B}1'}). This is an informational message only. No user action is required.
6830	Component SMS_SITE_VSS_WRITER on computer site server reported: The snapshots of the volumes required for the Site Backup have been successfully created.
6831	Component SMS_SITE_VSS_WRITER on computer site server reported: SMS Writer has started the ConfigMgr Services successfully.
5056	Component SMS_SITE_BACKUP on computer site server reported: Site Backup is starting to copy the files from the snapshot.
5057	Component SMS_SITE_BACKUP on computer site server reported: Site Backup has successfully completed copying the files from the snapshot.
6833	Component SMS_SITE_BACKUP on computer site server reported: Site Backup has successfully completed copying the files from the snapshot.

Configuring the Backup ConfigMgr Site Server Maintenance Task

The Backup ConfigMgr Site Server maintenance task backs up a Configuration Manager site, including the site database, files, registry keys, and system configuration data. The site-recovery process does not support using third-party tools to back up your Configuration Manager site; it will only use backups made by the Backup ConfigMgr Site Server maintenance task. If you are running Configuration Manager in a virtual environment, please note that taking snapshots of the site server is not a supported backup method and cannot replace using the site maintenance backup task.

BACKING UP A SITE SERVER

To configure a daily backup do the following:

1. In the Configuration Manager console, navigate to the Administration workspace ➤ Site Configuration ➤ Sites.

2. Select the site and choose Settings ➤ Site Maintenance from the Ribbon.

3. Select the Backup Site Server task, and click Edit.

4. Select Enable This Task.

5. Click Set Paths and type the path for the backup folder.

   If you are logged on locally to the site server, you can click Browse and select a location; otherwise, you will have to manually type a path. Depending on the location of the SQL database, you will be given three choices for where to save the database and the backup files:

   ◆ Local Drive On Site Server For Site Data And Database

      This option is available if the SQL database is hosted locally on the site server.

   ◆ Network Path (UNC Name) For Site Data And Database

      This option will allow you to specify a network share to store the backup files.

   ◆ Local Drives On Site Server And SQL Server

      This option is available only if you have SQL running on a remote server. The SQL database will be stored locally on the SQL Server separately from the site data.

   Regardless of what location you select, you need to ensure that the site server computer account has write access to the folder or share that is used to store the backup files. It is recommended to create the folder prior to running the backup task.

6. You can also modify the Start After and Latest Start Time if the default schedule interferes with other maintenance routines.

7. Select Enable Alerts For Backup Task Failures, and click OK, as shown in Figure 16.3.

This will ensure a daily backup. The duration of the backup will vary from site to site, but by reading the smsbkup.log file or monitoring the events created in the viewer as described in Table 16.1, you will be able to tell the exact duration in your environment.

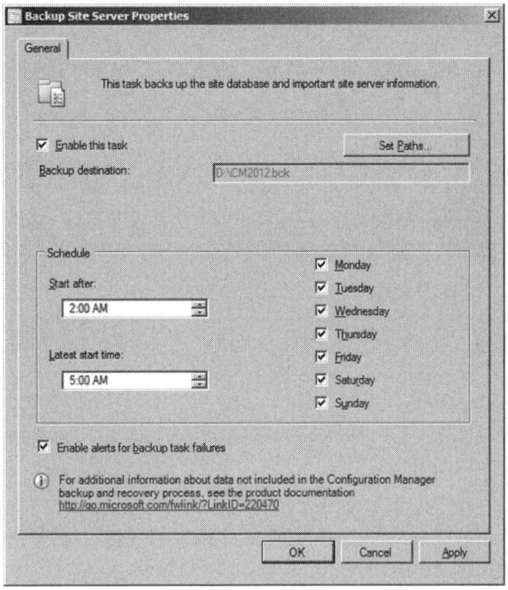

FIGURE 16.3
The Backup Site
Server task

TESTING THE SITE BACKUP

As soon as you set up the backup maintenance task on a site, you should let it run and verify that it is running. That way, you won't be surprised to find yourself without a good backup if you have to restore one of your site servers.

To do this, follow these steps:

1. Log on to the site server.

2. Open a command prompt as administrator.

3. Type **net start sms_site_backup**, as shown in Figure 16.4; this will start the backup service and perform the first backup.

FIGURE 16.4
Manually starting
the Backup Site
Server task

4. Open CMtrace (formerly known as SMS Trace or Trace32) and monitor the smsbkup.log file from the Logs folder on the site server.

   The backup log file will give you valuable information about the process. By reading the log file you can calculate the backup duration, troubleshoot errors related to the process, and see if the Afterbackup.bat file started successfully.

COMMON BACKUP TROUBLESHOOTING METHODS

If the previous tests don't help you figure out what is causing the problem with the backup, you can look for errors in a few additional places:

- Look in the Event Viewer logs for any account and/or access violations.

- The SMS_SITE_BACKUP runs under the local system account. Make sure that this account has access to any remote locations in the SMS Backup control file, and that this account has the rights to perform the tasks in the control file's [Tasks] section.

- Check the smsbkup.log for errors.

   You should be able to see a status message with the ID 5035 to indicate a successful backup. It can be found at <Configuration Manager installation directory>\ Logs\smsbkup.log.

SECONDARY SITES

There are no recovery or backup options for secondary sites. In order to recover a failed secondary site, you need to reinstall the site. The biggest concern of recovering a remote site, which is a remote distribution point or secondary site, is the number of packages that need to be redistributed to the remote location. Configuration Manager 2012 allows you to prestage content by creating prestaged packages in the Configuration Manager console. You can distribute the compressed packages using USB or similar media to the remote location. At the remote distribution point run ExtractContent .exe found in the SMS_DP$\SMS\Tools folder on the remote distribution point.

Restoring Configuration Manager

Besides getting a failed site up and running again, recovery of a Configuration Manager site is also required if that site is installed with a site code or site server name that has already been used in the hierarchy. Repairing and resynchronizing data is what site recovery is designed for, and it is required in order to avoid interruption of operations and corruption of data.

Configuration Manager provides recovery and reset tools to help you quickly and consistently complete the tasks that are essential to restoring Configuration Manager site operations. These tools allow you to run recovery and reset commands that will override existing configuration settings without having to directly access low-level data, as well as to start operations that are not available through other methods.

Understanding the Effects of a Site Failure

Configuration Manager is made up of various site systems and clients. Each site has at least one site system—namely, the site server. The site server will monitor and manage the Configuration Manager site. Each Configuration Manager site also has a site system that is the site database server and at least one site system that acts as a management point. As already established in previous chapters, the management point is the site system that allows the site server and the site's clients to communicate properly.

Along with these important site systems, a site can have any number of additional site systems that perform different roles for a site hierarchy. If the site server or any of its site systems fail, then they would not be able to provide the services they normally do. If more than one site role is installed on the same server and it fails, then all the services provided by that server will become unavailable. Table 16.2 shows the results of various site systems going offline or otherwise becoming unavailable.

TABLE 16.2:   Results of Configuration Manager site failure

SITE SERVER	SITE DATABASE *	MANAGEMENT POINT *	DISTRIBUTION POINT *	RESULT
Offline	Online	Online	Online	No site administration will be possible, including creation of new deployments. The management point will collect client information and cache it until the site server is back online. Existing deployments will run, and clients can find distribution points.
Online	Offline	Online	Online	No site administration will be possible, including creation of new deployments. If the Configuration Manager 2012 client already has a policy assignment with new policies and if the management point has cached the policy body, the client can make a policy body request and receive the policy body reply. No new policy assignments requests can be serviced. Clients will be able to run programs only if they have already been detected and the associated source files are already cached locally at the client.
Online	Online	Offline	Online	Although new deployments can be created, the clients will not receive them until a management point is online again. Clients will still collect inventory, software metering, and status information and store it locally until the management point is available. Clients will be able to run programs only if they have already been detected and the associated source files are already cached locally at the client.
Online	Online	Online	Offline	Configuration Manager 2012 clients will be able to run deployments only if the associated source files have already been downloaded locally.

* Note that you configure multiple management points and distribution points and cluster the SQL database. By doing so, you will minimize the risk of service breakdown in the event that one site system is unavailable.

Recovering a Configuration Manager Site

Before starting a site restore you will need to know why you are performing the restore and what you are trying to achieve. If you experience data loss or a complete hardware failure, you will need to perform a site restore. But if you experience problems with some of the site server components, you might want to start with a site reset.

Unlike previous versions of Configuration Manager and SMS, there is no longer a specific Site Repair Wizard. Instead, the recovery process is offered as part of the standard installation process. When you start a Configuration Manager site installation, you will be given the option to recover a site, as shown in Figure 16.5.

FIGURE 16.5
Starting the site recovery process

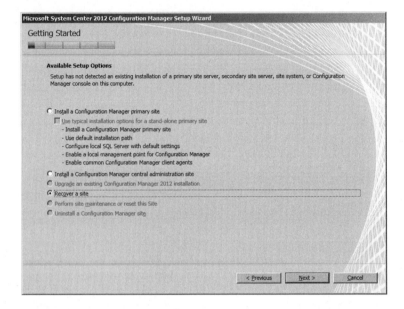

If you do not see the Recover A Site option, first uninstall the site. Uninstalling a site is a straightforward process for a single site. If you want to uninstall a parent site in a multisite hierarchy, you will need to manually delete the site database first.

 **Real World Scenario**

PREPARING FOR A SITE RESTORE ON A CENTRAL ADMINISTRATION SITE

As a Configuration Manager administrator for YNWA Inc., you have been asked to perform a complete site restore for the Central Administration Site, named CAS. You run the setup utility but notice that you do not have the option to recover the site. You then try running the site uninstall option but it fails because the site has multiple child sites. You realize that you first need to delete the database. To do so, you follow these steps:

1. Log on to the SQL Server.

2. From the Start menu, select All Programs ➢ Microsoft SQL Server.

3. Start SQL Server Management Studio.

4. Click New Query and enter the following query:

```
ALTER DATABASE CM_CAS
SET SINGLE_USER WITH ROLLBACK IMMEDIATE
Drop Database CM_CAS
```

5. Highlight the query statement and click Execute in the toolbar.

6. Close SQL Server Management Studio and start the setup utility again.

When you start the recovery process you will be given two site server recovery choices and four database recovery choices, as explained in Table 16.3.

TABLE 16.3:   Recovery options

OPTION	USED WHEN
Recover This Site Server Using An Existing Backup	You have the backup files created using Configuration Manager. This offers you a complete recovery scenario, as described later in this chapter.
Reinstall The Site Server	You do not have a backup of the site server. All site settings will be lost, and you will have to manually reconfigure the site.
Recover The Site Database Using A Backup Set At The Following Location	You have a backup of the Configuration Manager site database. This offers you a complete recovery scenario, as described later in this chapter.
Create A New Database For This Site	You are recovering a site that is part of a hierarchy, and you want to replicate data from the Central Administration Site or from another reference site. Note that this option is available only in multisite environments. Depending on the size of the site database, this will generate a lot of WAN traffic.
Use A Site Database That Has Been Manually Recovered	You already have recovered the site database using a tool other than the one provided by Configuration Manager 2012.
Skip Database Recovery	You haven't experienced any data loss and the existing database is intact.

Recovering Configuration Manager

As mentioned earlier in this chapter, there are major differences between recovering a ConfigMgr 2012 site and a Configuration Manager 2007 site. Gone is the Site Repair Wizard; instead, you initiate the recovery process by running the site setup process. The process can be divided into two phases:

1. Reading the `ConfigMgrBackup.ini` file from the backup source

2. Running the setup process based on the information in the `ConfigMgrBackup.ini` file combined with user input in the recovery phase

Unlike previous versions of Configuration Manager and SMS, there is no need to run a site reset process manually after recovering the site because that is an integrated part of the recovery process.

How to Start a Recovery Process

The site recovery process is designed to make recovering a Configuration Manager site as easy as possible.

Before you start the recovery process, ensure that you have the following:

◆ The SQL installation media

◆ The Configuration Manager 2012 prerequisites

◆ The Configuration Manager 2012 installation media

◆ Access to the Configuration Manager 2012 backup set

Furthermore, ensure that you use the following:

◆ Same site server name (it can be a different operating system)

◆ Same SQL Server name (it can be a different SQL version)

◆ Same site code

◆ Same database name

◆ Same Configuration Manager major version

To recover from a failed site you are given two options to start the process:

◆ Run `<Installation source>\SMSSETUP\BIN\X64\Setup.exe`, and select the Recover A Site Server option.

◆ Run an unattended installation of Configuration Manager using the `setup.exe /script` option.

Recovering a Central Administration Site

To restore the Central Administration Site using the setup process, do the following:

1. On the site server, open a command prompt with administrative privileges.

2. Navigate to `.\SMSSetup\BIN\X64\` in the Configuration Manager installation source and run `Setup.exe`.

3. Click Next in the Before You Begin page.

4. Select Recover A Site.

5. On the Site Server and Database Recovery Options page, click Browse, and select the location of the Configuration Manager backup files.

6. Select Recover This Site Server Using An Existing Backup.

7. Click Browse, and navigate to the location of the backup folder.

8. In the site database option, select Recover The Site Database Using The Backup Set At The Following Location.

9. Click Browse and navigate to the location of the backup folder.

10. Once you have selected the recovery options for the site and the database (see Figure 16.6), click Next.

FIGURE 16.6
The Site Server and
Database Recovery
Options page

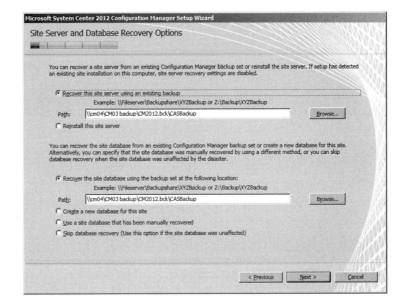

11. On the Site Recovery Information page, shown in Figure 16.7, type the name of the site to reference and click Next.

The reference site will be used as the authoritative source in the recovery process. Data changes from other non-reference primary sites will be lost.

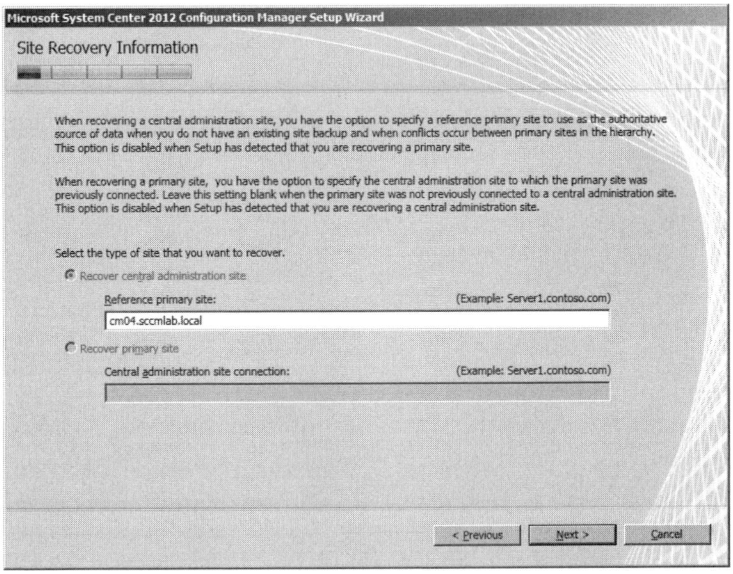

FIGURE 16.7
The Site Recovery
Information page

12. Accept the license terms and click Next.

13. On the Updated Prerequisite Components page, shown in Figure 16.8, select Use Previously Downloaded Updates From The Following Location.

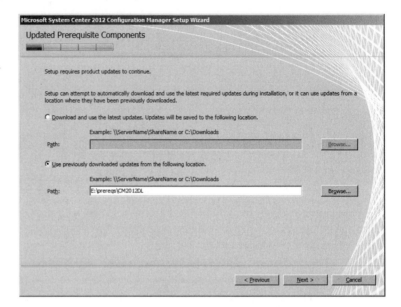

FIGURE 16.8
The Updated
Prerequisite
Components page

14. Click Browse, and select the location where you have the stored prerequisites.

15. On the Site and Installation Settings page, shown in Figure 16.9, modify the installation folder to reflect where you want to install Configuration Manager, and click Next.

FIGURE 16.9
Site and Installation
Settings page

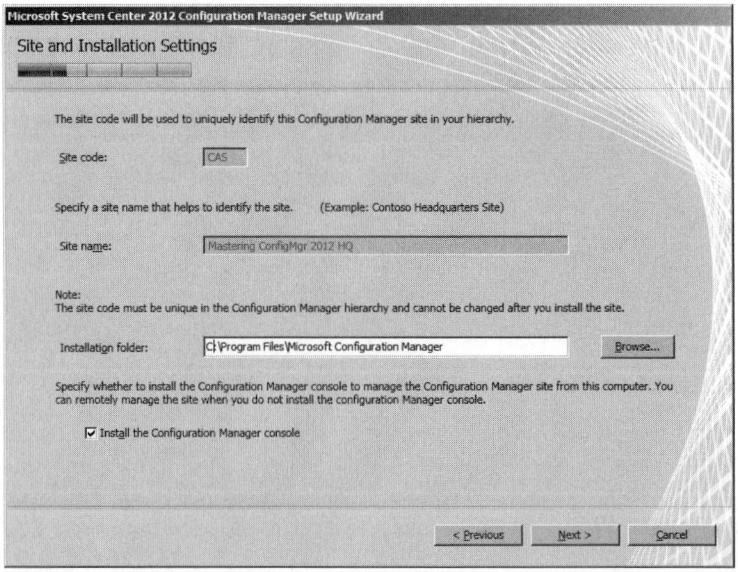

16. On the Database Information page, shown in Figure 16.10, verify that the SQL Server Service Broker port is correct, and click Next.

FIGURE 16.10
Database
Information page

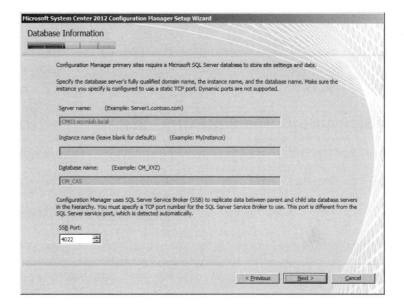

17. On the Settings Summary page, shown in Figure 16.11, review the information, and click Next if everything is correct.

FIGURE 16.11
Settings Summary page

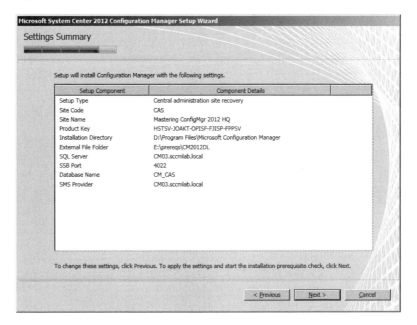

18. On the Prerequisite Check page, shown in Figure 16.12, ensure that all the prerequisites are met, and click Begin Install.

FIGURE 16.12

Prerequisite Check page

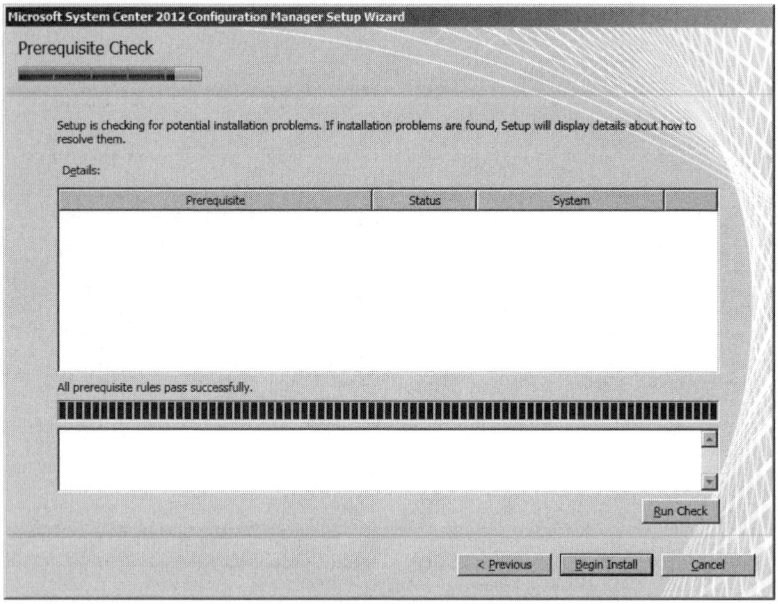

The installation and recovery process will require some time to finish. Once the process is finished, you will see the Install page, as shown in Figure 16.13.

FIGURE 16.13

Install page

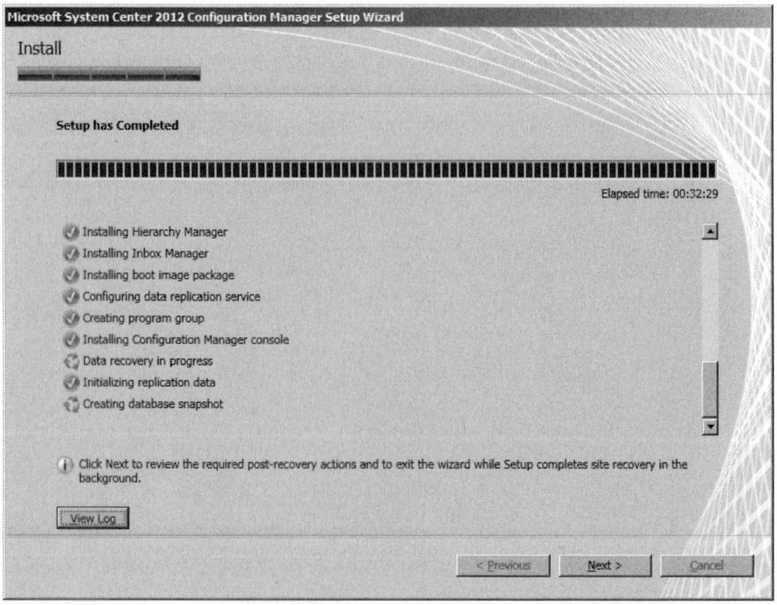

19. Review the page, and click Next.

The Finished page is the last page and explains the post-recovery tasks that you must perform.

20. Read the information and click Close.

After the recovery process and the global data has been replicated from the reference site, the CAS will go through these steps:

1. IDs are recalculated.

2. Identity keys are reseeded.

3. A site reset is initialized to reinstall the site components.

4. Public keys are generated for child sites.

MONITORING THE RECOVERY PROCESS

You can monitor the process by following the Setup Wizard as it moves through the different setup steps. For a deeper dive into what's going on behind the scenes, you should open these log files:

ConfigMgrSetupWizard.log In this log file you will see how the backup process starts by reading the ConfigMgrBackup.ini file from the Configuration Manager backup folder. The information from the .ini file is used to configure some of the mandatory settings presented on the Site and Installation Settings page.

ConfigMgrSetup.log This is the main log file where you can find information about verifying the reference site and running the actual installation. Figure 16.14 illustrates that you can use the ConfigMgrSetup.log file to verify the recovery process.

FIGURE 16.14
Verifying the recovery process

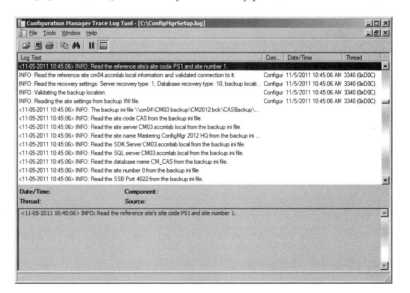

Recovering a Primary Child Site

Recovering a primary child site is almost identical to recovering a Central Administration Site, except that the wizard automatically will configure the Central Administration Site as the reference site.

Recovering a Primary Standalone Site

Recovering a primary standalone site is almost identical to recovering a Central Administration Site, except that the wizard will not allow you to configure any reference sites during the setup process.

Recovery Scenarios for Multisite Environments

In a multisite environment you might come across different recovery scenarios where data might be recovered from another site in the hierarchy or might be lost. Let's look at three different scenarios. Common for all three scenarios is that you create an application with a single revision, perform a backup, and after that modify that same application with revision 2. That way the current backup contains only revision 1.

ENVIRONMENT	SCENARIO	REVISION AFTER RECOVERY
One primary site with a secondary child site	Global data about the application with revision 1 being replicated to the secondary site.	1
One CAS with two primary sites (PS1 and PS2)	You create revision 2 on PS1, after which revision 2 is replicated to the CAS and PS2. PS1 fails and is recovered from backup.	2 PS1 will recover revision 1 from backup but will update to revision 2 after synchronizing with the CAS.
One CAS with two primary sites (PS1 and PS2)	You create revision 2 on PS1, after which PS1 fails before synchronizing any global data and is recovered from backup.	1 PS1 will recover revision 1 from backup and revision 2 will be lost.

Other Site Maintenance Options

Besides doing a full recovery you can start other maintenance options by running Configuration Manager Setup from the Start menu. Those options are explained in Table 16.4.

TABLE 16.4:   Site reset and maintenance options

OPTION	USED WHEN
Reset Site With No Configuration Changes	You want to perform a site reset. During the site reset, all site components are reinstalled, and permissions and registry keys are restored to their default settings.

OPTION	USED WHEN
Modify SQL Server Configuration	You want to move the site database to another SQL Server. Note that this process requires that you have already copied the SQL database to the new SQL Server. The process will not detach the database from the old location or attach it to the new server. The process also allows you to modify the SQL Service broker port.
Modify SMS Provider Information	You want to install the SMS provider on another server.
Modify Language Configurations	You want to add new server and client languages to the installation.

The Hierarchy Maintenance Tool

The Hierarchy Maintenance tool (`preinst.exe`) is a command-line tool that you may need to use to diagnose problems with a site system, help repair a site, shut down site systems, or do other maintenance tasks that, for whatever reason, can't be performed using the Configuration Manager console. This tool must be run locally on the site server computer.

To use the Hierarchy Maintenance tool, do the following:

1. Open a command prompt window with administrative privileges.

2. Navigate to the location of `preinst.exe`, which by default is

   `<drive where ConfigMgr is installed>`\Microsoft Configuration Manager\bin\ x64\`<language code>`

   The language code for English is 00000409.

3. Once you are there, just type **preinst.exe** to get a list of command-line options.

4. Then use `preinst.exe` with its command-line options, listed in Table 16.5 (adapted from Microsoft documentation), to complete your task.

TABLE 16.5:   Hierarchy Maintenance tool syntax

COMMAND	DESCRIPTION
/dump `<site code>`	This command writes site control images to the root of the folder of the drive where the site is installed. /dump `<site code>` writes the site control file of only the site specified. /dump writes the site control files for all sites.
/deljob `<site code>`	This command deletes all jobs targeted to the site you specify in the command line.
/delsite `<site code>`	This command deletes child sites that were not previously removed successfully from the site database of its parent site.

TABLE 16.5: Hierarchy Maintenance tool syntax *(CONTINUED)*

COMMAND	DESCRIPTION
/stopsite	This command shuts down the Configuration Manager 2012 Site Component Manager service, which will partially reset the site. When this shutdown is finished, ConfigMgr services on a site server and its remote systems are stopped. These services are flagged for reinstall, and some passwords are automatically changed when these services are reinstalled. When the shutdown cycle is started, it automatically runs and skips any computers or components that are not responding. If the Site Component Manager service can't access a remote site system during this process, the components on the remote site system will be reinstalled when the Site Component Manager service is restarted. This will continue until the Site Component Manager succeeds in reinstalling all services that are marked for reinstallation. You can restart the Site Component Manager service using Service Manager just like other Windows services. After you use the /stopsite command to start a shutdown cycle, there is nothing you can do to stop the subsequent reinstall cycles when the Site Component Manager service is restarted. You can monitor the effect of the process by reading the sitecomp.log file on the site server.
/keyforparent	This command is run on sites that you are trying to recover after failure and is used to distribute the new public key to a parent site of the failed site. The /keyforparent command places the public key of the failed site in the file *<site code>*.CT4 at the root of the drive from where the command is run. After the file is made, you will have to manually copy the file to the parent site's hman.box inbox (not in the pubkey folder).
/keyforchild	This command is run on sites that you are trying to recover after failure and is used to distribute the new public key to a child site of the failed site. The /keyforchild command places the public key of the failed site in the file *<site code>*.CT6 at the root of the drive from where the command is run. After the file is made, you will have to manually copy the file to the child site's hman.box inbox (not in the pubkey folder).
/childkeys	This command is run on the recovering site's child sites and is used to distribute public keys from all child sites to the recovering site. The /childkeys command places this and all child site public keys into the file *<site code>*.CT6 at the root of the drive from where the command is run. After the file is made, you will have to manually copy the file to the parent site's hman.box inbox.
/parentkeys	This command is run on the recovering site's parent site and is used to distribute public keys from all parent sites to the recovering site. The /parentkeys command places this and all parent site public keys into the file *<site code>*.CT7 at the root of the drive from where the command is run. After the file is made, you will have to manually copy the file to the child site's hman.box inbox.

Post-Recovery Tasks

After you recover a site, there are tasks that you should perform to make sure that the site has been properly repaired and is functioning correctly:

◆ Monitor site processes.

◆ Verify site setting configuration.

◆ Re-enter user passwords.

All user passwords will be reset during the recovery process. You can find a list of affected user accounts in the C:\ConfigMgrPostRecoveryActions.html file, as shown in Figure 16.15.

FIGURE 16.15

The
C:\ConfigMgrPost
RecoveryActions
.html file

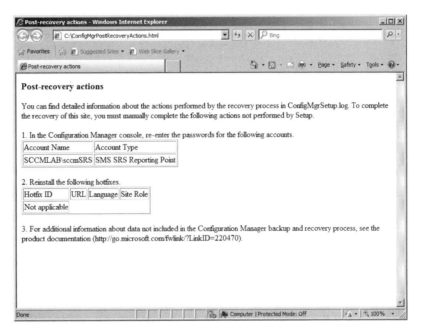

◆ Reinstall previously applied hotfixes.

You can find a list of installed hotfixes in the C:\ConfigMgrPostRecoveryActions.html file.

◆ Verify that the content library is fully rebuilt from the original data sources.

◆ Recover any custom reports.

◆ Recover the SCUP 2011 database if that was affected. This is done by copying the database file.

◆ Reprovision previously provisioned Intel AMT computers.

This requires that you request the AMT provisioning certificate again and reconfigure the passwords for the MEBx, AMT Provisioning Removal, and AMT Provisioning and Discovery accounts.

◆ Recover the MDT.

 Real World Scenario

MOVING THE SITE DATABASE

As a Configuration Manager administrator for YNWA Inc., you have been asked to move the site database and log files named CM_PS1 stored in D:\SQLDB and E:\SQLLogs from SQL1 to a new SQL Server on SQL2. Configuration Manager 2012 is installed on CM01. The new SQL Server is installed and is using the same collation order as the old server and the same disk layout. To move the database and log files, follow these steps:

1. Log on to CM01.

2. Open a command prompt with administrative privileges and navigate to *<configuration manager install dir>*\ SMS\bin\x64*<language code>*.

3. Run preinst.exe /stopsite, and wait until all components and services have been successfully stopped.

4. Still in the command prompt, type **Net stop ccmexec** to stop the management point service.

5. Log on to the old SQL Server, Server1.

6. From the Start menu, select All Programs ➢ Microsoft SQL Server.

7. Start SQL Server Management Studio.

8. Click New Query, and type

   ```
   use master
   go
   sp_detach_db 'CM_PS1'
   go
   ```

9. Highlight the query statement, and click Execute in the toolbar.

10. Copy the database and log files to the new SQL Server.

11. Log on to the new SQL Server, Server2.

12. From Start, select All Programs ➢ Microsoft SQL Server.

13. Start SQL Server Management Studio.

14. Click New Query, and type

   ```
   use master
   go
   sp_attach_db 'CM_PS1','D:\SQLDB\CM_PS1.MDF','E:\SQLlogs\CM_PS1_Log.LDF'
   go
   ```

15. Log on to CM01, and open a command prompt with administrative privileges.

16. Navigate to `<configuration manager install dir>\` Microsoft Configuration Manager\bin\x64 and run Setup.exe.

17. Select Perform Site Maintenance Or Reset This Site, as shown in the following graphic, and click Next.

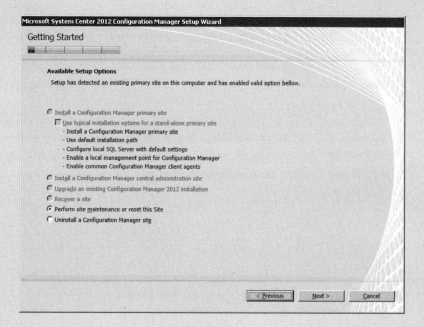

18. Select Modify SQL Configuration, and click Next.

19. In the Server Name field type **Server2** and click Next.

20. Once the SQL process is finished, close the wizard by clicking Close.

21. Restart the CM01 server.

The Bottom Line

Configure backups for Configuration Manager sites.   Backing up Configuration Manager sites can be automated by scheduling the Backup ConfigMgr Site Server maintenance task. When the Configuration Manager backup service (SMS_SITE_BACKUP) starts, it uses instructions in the backup control file, located at

`[ConfigMgr Install Location]Microsoft Configuration Manager\Inboxes\smsbkup.box\smsbkup.ctl`

Master It   Recovering Configuration Manager sites is only supported with site backups from what source?

Recover Configuration Manager sites. Recovery of a Configuration Manager site requires that you do not have a Configuration Manager site installed when starting the `Setup.exe` process. The recovery process will recover data from the backup files and from a reference site provided you have a multisite hierarchy.

Master It What is Site Recovery designed for?

Archive backup snapshots to another location. The first time the Backup ConfigMgr Site Server task runs, it creates a backup snapshot, which can be used to recover a Configuration Manager site system when it fails. The next time the backup task runs, it makes a new backup snapshot that will overwrite the one that was made during the last snapshot. This could be a problem if the current backup snapshot becomes corrupt for some reason, because there is no other backup to restore from.

Master It What script can you use to copy backup snapshots from the site server to a new location but is not created when ConfigMgr is installed?

Reinstall the site components and reset file and registry permissions to their default settings. From time to time other administrators mess around with the default permissions that are configured on the different folders and shares created by Configuration Manager.

Master It How can you restore the file and registry permissions without performing a complete restore?

Chapter 17

System Center Endpoint Protection

System Center Configuration Manager 2007 provided the ability to integrate with Microsoft Forefront Endpoint Protection 2010. Forefront Endpoint Protection, or FEP, is Microsoft's industry-leading security and antimalware product, and the integration with Configuration Manager 2007 allowed administrators to easily manage and control its configuration.

The Forefront Endpoint Protection product has been updated for 2012, and the new version is called System Center 2012 Endpoint Protection, or SCEP. As you will see in this chapter, the integration between Endpoint Protection and Configuration Manager is carried forward and greatly enhanced in the System Center 2012 versions of the products.

In this chapter, you will learn to

- ◆ Differentiate between FEP and SCEP.

- ◆ Deploy and configure the System Center 2012 Endpoint Protection site system and client.

- ◆ Create and assign an SCEP policy.

Differences between FEP and SCEP

Before taking a closer look at System Center 2012 Endpoint Protection, let's take a moment to review some of the key differences between Forefront Endpoint Protection 2010 and System Center 2012 Endpoint Protection:

- ◆ FEP used two separate databases to store data, FEP_DB and FEP_DW. SCEP uses the ConfigMgr site database to store all data.

- ◆ FEP required a separate client to be deployed and installed on each managed computer.

- ◆ SCEP includes the endpoint client software as part of the ConfigMgr 2012 client install media, and the SCEP client is enabled and configured in the ConfigMgr 2012 console.

- ◆ FEP had a delay between when a malware event occurred at a client, such as virus detection, and when that information was made available to the ConfigMgr 2007 administrator. ConfigMgr 2012 has new internal processes that work to greatly reduce the time that elapses between the event and the alerting and reporting.

- ◆ Delegating the administration of FEP was a challenge in ConfigMgr 2007. In ConfigMgr 2012, the role-based security model allows the ConfigMgr administrator to easily delegate the SCEP-related functions to a specific person or group without providing those users with access to other areas of ConfigMgr.

WHAT IS MALWARE?

We will use the term *malware* a great deal in this chapter, so it's probably a good idea to define that word.

Malware is short for *malicious software*, which is basically software, code, or scripts that are typically designed to perform invasive, destructive actions on a computer. Some malware attempts to delete files or corrupt the operating system, while others may attempt to steal personal or corporate data. Malware includes items such as computer viruses, worms, Trojan horses, adware, and some rootkits. Antimalware software (such as SCEP) is software designed to detect, block, and remove malware.

Additional Benefits of SCEP

Now that we have identified some of the key differences between the FEP 2010 and SCEP products, let's take a look at some of the additional benefits of the SCEP product. We will expand on these in the remainder of the chapter.

Deployment

The deployment and configuration of SCEP are managed in the ConfigMgr 2012 console. Because of the tight integration with ConfigMgr 2012, SCEP is easily deployable to environments of any size. The ConfigMgr administrator enables SCEP in ConfigMgr 2012 by deploying the new Endpoint Protection Point site system role, enabling the Endpoint Protection client, and then configuring the antimalware policies. SCEP also includes several policy templates that provide recommended antimalware configurations for standard workloads. These templates are generally ready to deploy but can be customized to meet the specific needs of the organization if needed. You can also export policies that were created in FEP 2010 and import them into SCEP.

Protection

SCEP provides ConfigMgr administrators with the ability to ensure that their computer infrastructure is safe and secure from malware attacks. The SCEP product protects the computer infrastructure by detecting and blocking malware and also by providing management of Windows Firewall. SCEP ensures that the computers are protected from many known exploits and vulnerabilities, and SCEP is backed by the Microsoft Security Response Center and the Microsoft SpyNet community. For more information on the Microsoft Security Response Center visit

```
http://www.microsoft.com/security/msrc
```

SPYNET IS NOW MAPS

Before moving on, we should discuss the Microsoft Active Protection Service. In FEP 2010 this feature was referred to as Microsoft SpyNet but is now referred to as the Microsoft Active Protection Service, or MAPS.

MAPS is a cloud-based service that allows the Endpoint client on a computer to report data about programs that exhibit suspicious behavior to the Microsoft Malware Protection Center (MMPC). Once the data is submitted to the MMPC, it can be analyzed and researched by engineers. Once the data has been analyzed, information about the behavior can be included in a new definition update and deployed to computers around the world via FEP or SCEP. This feature is sometimes referred to as the Dynamic Signature Service.

When you configure the Endpoint Protection site system you will need to define how MAPS should be configured for your environment.

As you can see in the following illustration, there are three available choices for the Microsoft Active Protection Service:

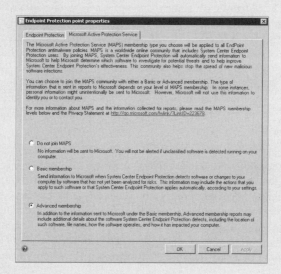

◆ Do not join MAPS

If you choose this option, it means that information will not be sent from the managed computers to Microsoft. You will not be alerted if software that is currently unclassified is detected in the environment.

◆ Basic Membership

If you choose the Basic Membership option, SCEP will submit information to Microsoft about potentially unsafe software or software that has not yet been analyzed for risks.

◆ Advanced Membership

If you choose the Advanced Membership option, SCEP will submit more detailed information about detected software and will also alert you if software has been detected that has not yet been analyzed for issues or risks. This option also collects additional information from the computers, including IP address and operating system.

You can change the membership setting at any time by making the change in the Forefront Endpoint Protection site system properties. You can also override this sitewide setting with a custom antimalware policy if needed.

Monitoring

ConfigMgr 2012 includes several enhancements around the monitoring and the reporting of the health and status of the environment. This is especially true for the Endpoint Protection feature of ConfigMgr 2012.

One key improvement is the manner and speed in which endpoint protection activity (such as a malware event on a workstation) is sent to the site servers for monitoring purposes. In FEP 2010 there was some delay before malware outbreaks were made visible to the ConfigMgr administrator. The extent of that delay varied, depending on how FEP and ConfigMgr 2007 were configured, but with some scenarios it might have taken 30 minutes or more before the ConfigMgr administrator was aware of the malware activity.

In ConfigMgr 2012 a new mechanism has been implemented that greatly reduces the delay in getting endpoint malware activity data from the client to the site servers. This mechanism, called the high-speed data channel, uses state messages to deliver malware activity information to the site server in almost real time. As a result, the ConfigMgr 2012 administrator will typically become aware of malware activity within just a few minutes of it taking place.

Security

The role-based security model in ConfigMgr 2012 greatly simplifies the process of defining access for administrative users. The ConfigMgr 2012 security role that is related to the SCEP feature is the Endpoint Protection Manager. This security role provides the administrative user with the ability to create, modify, and delete security policies. Administrative users with this security role can also manage the security policies that are assigned to collections, monitor the status of SCEP, and also execute remediation tasks on managed computers.

One possible use of this role is to assign it to the corporate IT security department and allow them to manage the configuration of SCEP without giving them access to other areas of ConfigMgr.

Now that you understand some of the features of System Center 2012 Endpoint Protection, let's take a closer look at the product.

Endpoint Protection Site System Role

System Center 2012 Configuration Manager introduces a new site system role, the Endpoint Protection Point site system role. This role must be installed and configured before you can use Endpoint Protection in ConfigMgr 2012. Also, the role must be installed at the top of the ConfigMgr 2012 hierarchy, which will be the Central Administration Site (CAS) if one exists. If the environment does not have a CAS, then the role will be installed on the standalone primary site.

CAN SCEP BE USED IN AN UNMANAGED SCENARIO?

Since you are reading this book, it is likely that you plan to use SCEP with ConfigMgr 2012 in a managed scenario and receive the many benefits of the integration between the two products.

However, SCEP can also be used in an *unmanaged* scenario, where ConfigMgr 2012 is not used to centrally administer, maintain, and monitor the configuration of SCEP. This scenario has some limitations but may be useful in environments where either ConfigMgr 2012 is not installed or the ConfigMgr client cannot be installed on computers.

In the unmanaged scenario, ConfigMgr 2012 is not available to deploy the SCEP clients and policies or update the SCEP definition files. An alternative is to use Active Directory Group Policy objects (GPOs) to deploy the SCEP client and policies and use Microsoft Update, Windows Server Update Services (WSUS), or the Microsoft Malware Protection Center (MMPC) to update the definition files. This same approach was available for FEP 2010, and Microsoft released a set of tools called Forefront Endpoint Protection 2010 Tools to assist with the configuration. It is possible that Microsoft will release a similar toolset for SCEP. One advantage of the GPO approach over the integrated ConfigMgr scenario is that group policies are dynamically merged when applied at the computer and allow the administrator to maintain fewer group policies.

Another limitation of the unmanaged SCEP scenario is that you have no ability to receive real-time notification in the event of a malware outbreak in the environment, and you also have no ability to determine whether the SCEP clients are using outdated definition files. One possible exception is if the environment uses System Center Operations Manager (SCOM). If SCOM is in place, and the affected computers have the SCOM agent installed, the administrator may receive malware activity and outdated definition file status as SCOM alerts via an Endpoint Protection security management pack. A management pack was provided for FEP 2010 (Forefront Endpoint Protection 2010 Security Management Pack), and it's likely that Microsoft will provide a management pack for SCEP. However, SCOM is typically only used to monitor servers, and it's likely that your desktops and laptops will not have the SCOM agent installed.

As you can see, in some scenarios using SCEP in an unmanaged configuration may be useful but the approach has some limitations. Also, you will need to contact your Microsoft account team or software reseller to determine the SCEP licensing requirements for this scenario.

The installation and configuration of the role is fairly straightforward:

1. In the Configuration Manager console, select Administration ➢ Site Configuration ➢ Servers and Site System Roles.

2. Select the Central Administration Server (or the standalone primary site server), right-click, and select Add Site System Roles. The Add Site System Roles Wizard opens.

3. On the General page, specify the settings for the site system server. Click Next.

4. On the next screen, select Endpoint Protection Point from the list of available roles and click Next. See Figure 17.1.

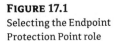

FIGURE 17.1

Selecting the Endpoint Protection Point role

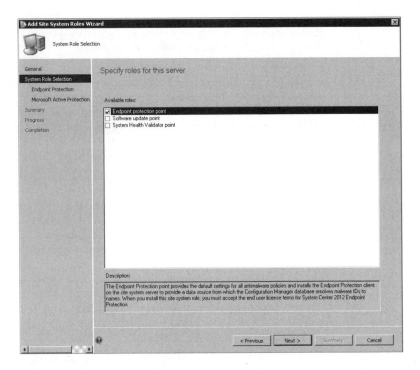

5. On the Specify Endpoint Protection License Page, accept the Endpoint Protection license terms and click Next.

THE ENDPOINT PROTECTION CLIENT LICENSE

Note that you must accept the license agreement in order to install the Endpoint Protection Point role. As with FEP 2010, the Endpoint Protection client license is part of the Microsoft core Client Access License (CAL). However, the license for the Endpoint Protection site server is not part of the core CAL and has specific licensing requirements. Contact your Microsoft account team or software reseller for additional information on the licensing requirements for SCEP.

---

6. Choose the Print License Terms option if you would like to review the license terms before agreeing to them. Click Next.

7. On the Specify Microsoft Active Protection Service membership type window, choose the membership option you require for your environment and click Next.

8. On the Confirm Settings page, click Next and then click Close once the role has been successfully installed.

9. You can monitor the status of the installation of the role in the EPMgr.log file on the site server.

SHOW ME THE LOGS!

The SMS and ConfigMgr products have always had detailed, informative logs, and ConfigMgr 2012 is no different. The relevant logs for SCEP are discussed here:

On the SCEP Site System

The SCEP site system log files are in the standard location for ConfigMgr 2012 site server logs (\Program Files\Microsoft Configuration Manager\Logs), and there are three logs related to SCEP:

♦ EPCtrlMgr.log records information about the sync of malware threat data from the SCEP site system role to the ConfigMgr database.

♦ EPMgr.log monitors the status of the SCEP role.

♦ EPSetup.log records information about the installation of the SCEP role on the site server.

On the SCEP Clients

The SCEP client log files are located in \Program Files\SMS_CCM\Logs on the ConfigMgr 2012 site servers and in \Windows\CCM\Logs for ConfigMgr clients. There is one log related specifically to SCEP: EndpointProtectionAgent.log. This logs details the installation of the SCEP client and the application of antimalware policy.

Endpoint Protection Client Agent

Once the Endpoint Protection Point site system role has been enabled and configured, you need to enable and configure the System Center 2012 Endpoint Protection client agent. The installation media for the endpoint client is distributed to the managed devices as part of the ConfigMgr 2012 client install media. The name of the file is SCEPInstall.exe, and it can be found in the CCMSETUP folder (C:\Windows\CCMSETUP) on the client. Although the SCEP client install media is copied to the CCMSETUP folder during the ConfigMgr 2012 client install, SCEP won't actually be installed on managed devices until the Endpoint Protection client is enabled and configured in an assigned client settings policy. Also note that the Endpoint Protection client cannot be enabled until the Endpoint Protection site system role is enabled.

You have two choices on how to enable and configure the SCEP client.

♦ You can make changes to the default client settings policy and enable and configure SCEP there.

♦ You can create a new, separate settings policy that enables and configures SCEP.

If you wanted every ConfigMgr 2012 client to be configured with the same settings, then you might modify the default client settings, but it's possible that you may want different client setting configurations for different types of devices. For example, you may want any required reboots as a result of the SCEP client install to be suppressed on servers but not be suppressed for desktop devices. So, you may need multiple client settings policies in order to handle certain scenarios.

If you decide to modify the default client settings for the SCEP configuration, you will need to do the following:

1. Open the ConfigMgr 2012 console and choose Administration ➢ Overview ➢ Client Settings.

2. Select the Default Client Settings entry and choose Properties from the Ribbon.

3. Select the Endpoint Protection setting and set the required configuration. See Figure 17.2.

FIGURE 17.2
Endpoint Protection default settings

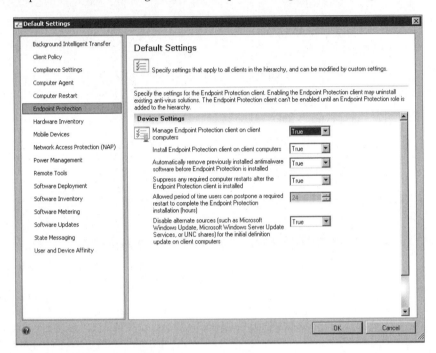

If you want to create a separate client settings policy for SCEP, follow these steps:

1. Open the ConfigMgr 2012 console and choose Administration ➢ Overview ➢ Client Settings.

2. Click Create Custom Client Device Settings in the Ribbon.

3. Give the custom device settings a name and description.

4. Select Endpoint Protection as the custom setting to be enforced on the client devices. See Figure 17.3.

FIGURE 17.3
Selecting the Endpoint Protection custom setting

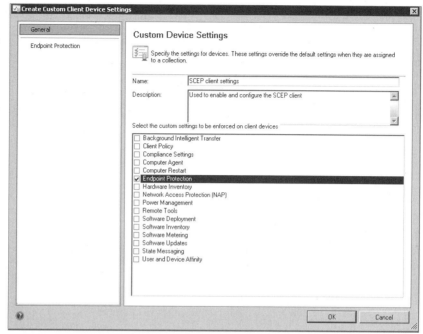

5. Click the Endpoint Protection option on the left side of the window. This will open the Endpoint Protection configuration settings. See Figure 17.4.

6. Set the required configuration settings, and click OK.

7. Deploy the new client settings policy to a collection.

After creating the client settings policy for SCEP, don't forget to assign the policy to a collection:

1. Select the policy you created.

2. Choose Deploy from the Ribbon.

3. Select the appropriate collection.

FIGURE 17.4
Configuring Endpoint
Protection settings

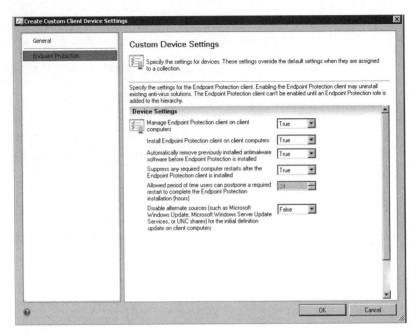

Regardless of whether you modify the default client settings or create a new client setting for SCEP, the options that can be configured are the same. As an administrator, you can do the following:

◆ Define whether the SCEP client should be installed and also if it should be managed.

◆ Determine if previously installed antimalware software should be automatically removed (see the following list).

◆ Define if any required reboots after enabling SCEP will be suppressed.

◆ Disable alternate sources for the initial definition update.

The list of products that can be replaced by SCEP may change somewhat, but the following were the supported titles for removal at the time this book was written:

◆ All current Microsoft antimalware products (except for Windows Intune and Microsoft Security Essentials)

◆ Symantec AntiVirus Corporate Edition version 10

◆ Symantec Endpoint Protection version 11

◆ Symantec Endpoint Protection Small Business Edition version 12

◆ McAfee VirusScan Enterprise version 8

◆ Trend Micro OfficeScan

Use this link to obtain an updated list of products that can be removed:

`http://technet.microsoft.com/en-us/library/gg682067.aspx`

If you have an antimalware product installed in the environment that is not on this list, you may need to deploy a removal package for that product. In that scenario, make sure you coordinate the removal of the old product and the enabling and deployment of the SCEP client and minimize the amount of time that the computer is not protected by antimalware software.

Endpoint Protection Policies

SCEP has two policy types:

Antimalware   The antimalware policy is used to define the antimalware settings that will be applied to the endpoint client.

Windows Firewall   The Windows Firewall policy can be used to control the configuration of Windows Firewall on managed computers.

Both types of Endpoint Protection policies can be created and modified in the ConfigMgr 2012 console.

Antimalware Policy

ConfigMgr 2012 includes a default antimalware policy (Default Client Malware Policy) that can be modified. However, you should understand that changes made to that policy will be applied to all managed computers in the environment. Instead, the ConfigMgr administrator may decide to create a custom policy (or policies), and those policy settings would override the default client policy.

The following configuration changes can be made in the antimalware policy:

Scheduled Scans   This option defines various information about the antimalware scan, including when the scan should occur, when the definition files should be updated, and if CPU usage should be limited. See Figure 17.5.

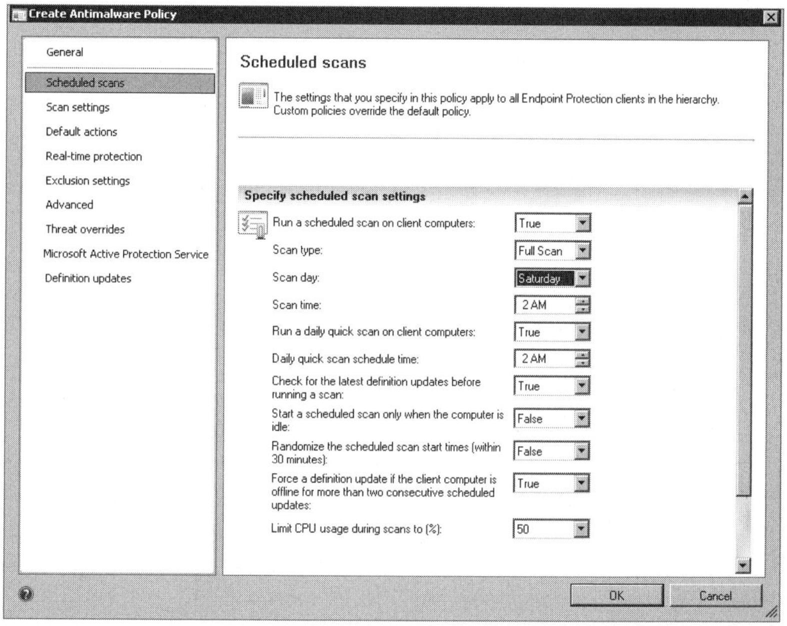

FIGURE 17.5
Configuring the Scheduled Scans settings

QUICK SCAN OR FULL SCAN?

The Scheduled Scans option allows you to configure when quick and full scans occur. But what is the difference between a quick scan and a full scan?

A quick scan does a check on locations where malware likes to hide in memory and on the hard drive. A quick scan should take only a few minutes, and performing the quick scan daily is a good practice.

A full scan checks all of the files on the hard disk and also checks memory and all programs that are currently active. This scan is more intensive and uses more resources on the computer, so performance on the computer may be impacted somewhat. This scan should typically be performed weekly and at a time when the computer will be on but not in use.

In the event of an active malware outbreak you can trigger a quick or a full scan or a definition file download from the ConfigMgr 2012 console. The specified action will be taken after the next client policy polling interval. To trigger the scan or definition file download action, follow these steps:

1. Select Assets and Compliance ➤ Overview ➤ Device Collections.

2. Right-click the appropriate collection.

3. Select Endpoint Protection, and choose the appropriate action (Full Scan, Quick Scan, or Download Definition), as shown in the following illustration.

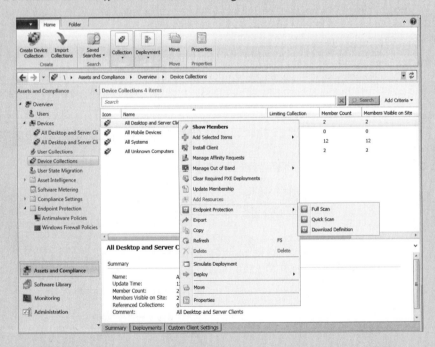

This will initiate an antimalware scan or definition download against the member computers of the collection.

Scan Settings   This option defines what types of items should be scanned and also defines whether the end user can change the scan settings (Figure 17.6).

FIGURE 17.6

Configuring the Scan Settings

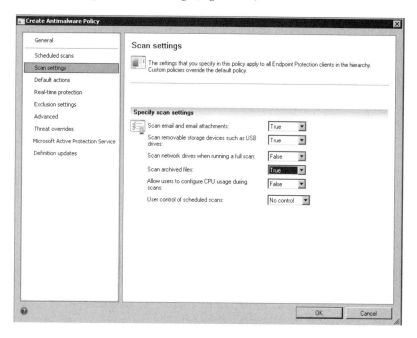

Default Actions   This option defines the action that will be taken on threats based on their classification (Figure 17.7).

FIGURE 17.7

Configuring the Default Actions settings

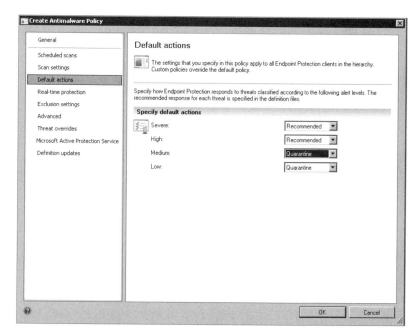

Real-Time Protection This option defines the configuration of real-time protection and scanning (Figure 17.8).

FIGURE 17.8
Configuring the
Real-Time Protection
settings

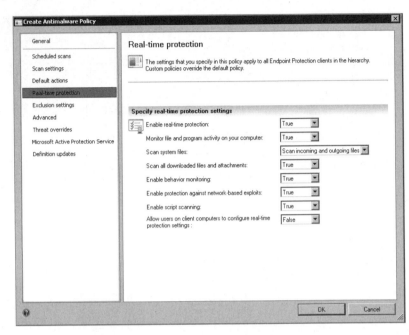

Exclusion Settings This option defines any files, folders, file types, or processes that should be excluded from malware scanning (Figure 17.9). Note that excluding items may increase the risk of malware not being detected on a computer.

FIGURE 17.9
Configuring the
Exclusion Settings

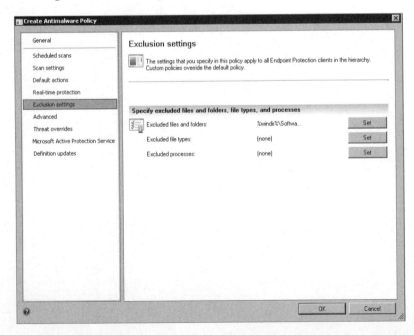

Advanced   This option provides the ability to customize advanced settings, including interaction with users, how long quarantined files should be retained, and so on (Figure 17.10).

FIGURE 17.10
Configuring the
Advanced settings

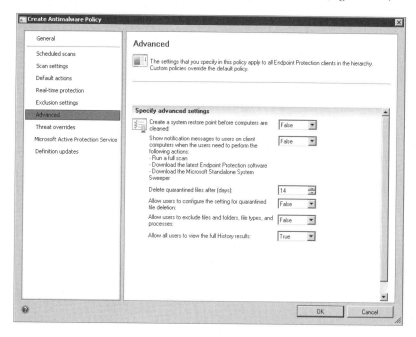

Threat Overrides   This option allows you to add threat names to the threat list (Figure 17.11).

FIGURE 17.11
Configuring the
Threat Overrides
settings

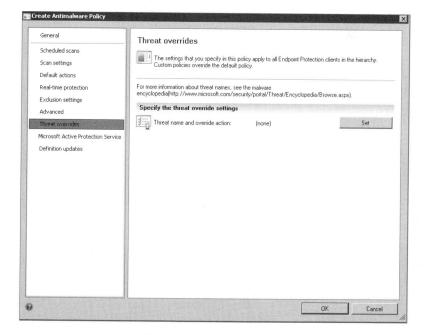

Microsoft Active Protection Service   This option allows you to configure MAPS (Figure 17.12).

FIGURE 17.12
Configuring the
MAPS settings

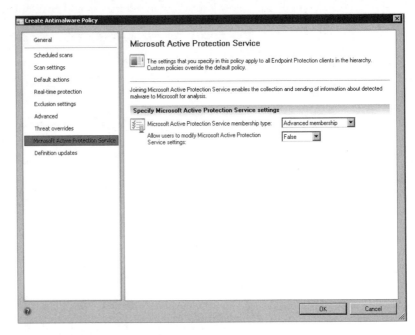

Definition Updates   This option allows you to configure how Endpoint Protection clients will receive definition updates (Figure 17.13).

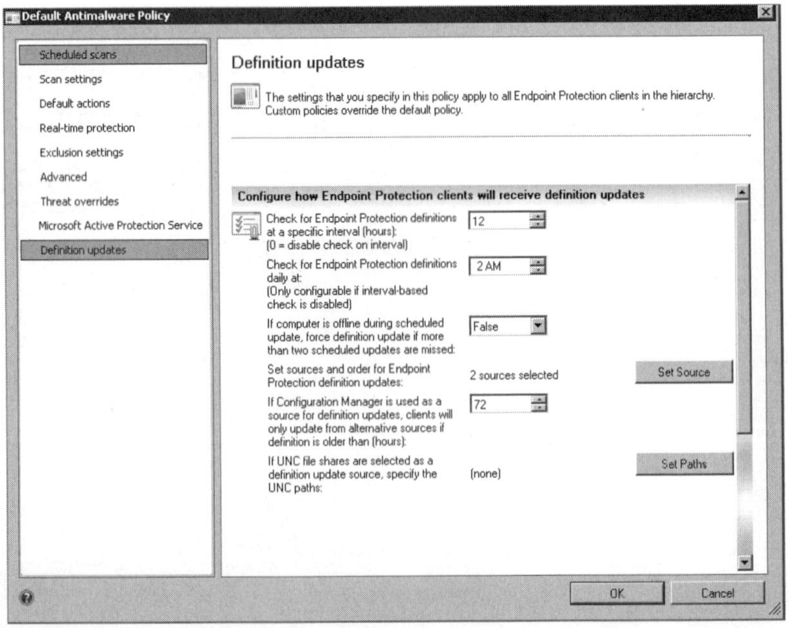

FIGURE 17.13
Configuring the
Definition Updates
settings

ConfigMgr 2012 includes a number of predefined antimalware policy templates for several Microsoft products, including ConfigMgr 2007 and 2012, SQL 2005 and 2008, Exchange, and Windows. The complete list of policies that are provided with ConfigMgr 2012 can be viewed in the following folder on the ConfigMgr 2012 site server:

```
\Program Files (x86)\Microsoft Configuration Manager\AdminConsole\XmlStorage\
EPTemplates
```

These policies apply settings that are optimized for a particular product or feature and can easily be imported and used in the environment. You can also import antimalware policies that were created in FEP 2010.

In ConfigMgr 2012 you can also merge policies by taking a default policy and merging it with another policy. This scenario may be useful if you want to use the default client policy but apply some specific file or folder exclusions that were included in one of the policies that was imported.

Windows Firewall Policy

The SCEP feature of ConfigMgr 2012 can also be used to manage the Windows Firewall policies for managed computers. ConfigMgr 2012 does not include a default Windows Firewall policy, and there is no ability to import or export a policy, but you can easily create a new policy in the ConfigMgr 2012 console.

As you can see in Figure 17.14, the Windows Firewall policy configuration is straightforward. You can create a new Windows Firewall policy in the ConfigMgr 2012 console and configure the policy to enable/disable the firewall, to block incoming connections, and also to define user communication. Once you have configured the policy you can then deploy it to a collection.

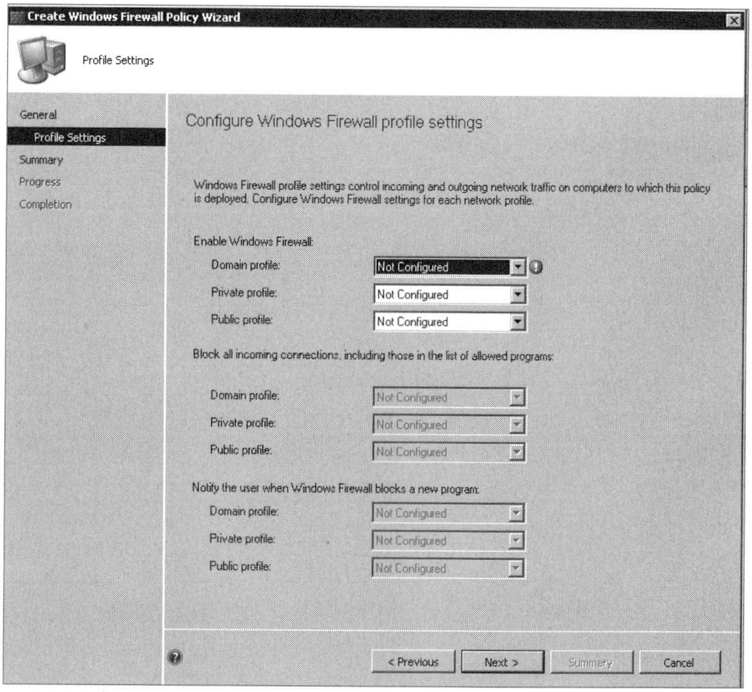

FIGURE 17.14
Configuring Windows Firewall policy

You may notice that there are three profile types: domain, public, and private. These profiles are related to the network that the user or computer is connected to.

Domain The domain profile will be applied if the connection is authenticated to a domain controller for the domain of which the user or computer is a member. By default, all other network connections are initially classified as public networks, and Windows asks the user to identify the network as either public or private.

Public The public profile is intended for use in public locations (such as airports and coffee shops).

Private The private network location is typically intended for use in a home or office.

Assigning Policy

The Default Client Malware Policy is automatically applied to all of the computers managed by ConfigMgr 2012. If you create a custom policy and assign it to a collection, the settings in the custom policy will override the settings that are defined in the default policy.

Use the following steps to assign a custom antimalware policy to a collection:

1. Open the ConfigMgr 2012 console and choose Assets and Compliance ➢ Overview ➢ Endpoint Protection ➢ Antimalware Policies.

2. Select the custom policy and choose Deploy from the Ribbon.

3. Select the collection, and click OK.

The next time the ConfigMgr 2012 clients in the targeted collection retrieve policy (every 60 minutes by default), they will apply the SCEP client settings that were established in the policy. If two custom policies have different values configured for the same settings, the policy with the highest order will be applied. You can adjust the order in the ConfigMgr console by right-clicking the custom policy and selecting Increase Priority or Decrease Priority. See Figure 17.15.

FIGURE 17.15
Increasing policy priority

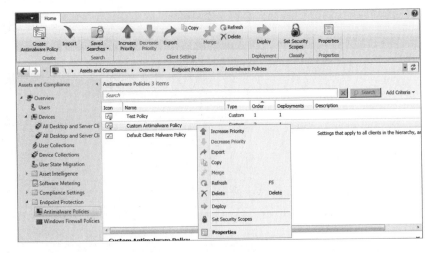

> **DEFAULT ORDER VALUE**
>
> The order for the Default Client Malware Policy has a default value of 10,000 and cannot be changed.

Definition Files

As discussed in Chapter 8, "Software Updates," ConfigMgr 2012 provides the ability to automatically download and deploy security updates to managed computers using a feature called Automatic Deployment Rules (ADR). These rules can be used for monthly security updates (Patch Tuesday, for example), and they can also be used for SCEP definition file updates. The SCEP definition files are updated several times a day, and you need an automated solution like ADR to handle the download and deployment of the updated files as they become available. For more information on how to create automatic deployment rules, refer to the software updates chapter.

Once the automatic deployment rules for SCEP have been configured, you may want to verify that the automatic deployment rules are working properly for the SCEP definition updates. The following process will ensure that the clients have the latest definition files.

The first question is what is the latest version of the Endpoint Protection definition files? Checking the Microsoft Malware Protection Center website

```
http://www.microsoft.com/security/portal/Definitions/HowToForeFront.aspx
```

is one quick method to provide that answer.

As you can see in Figure 17.16, the latest Forefront definition update that was available at the time this image was captured is 1.117.5450. So you now know which version of the definition file the environment should be using.

FIGURE 17.16
Obtaining the definition update version

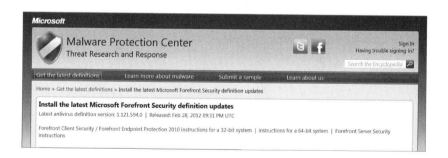

If you open the ConfigMgr 2012 console and choose Software Library ➢ Overview ➢ Software Updates ➢ All Software Updates, you can view the list of software updates in the catalog. If you search for "endpoint," you can look for software updates that have a matching title and focus on the SCEP definition files.

Expect to see several definition files listed, but only one should typically be current and active (the green arrow indicates the current definition file). As you can see in Figure 17.17, the version of that file is 1.121.594.0, so all of your clients should be using that version of the definition file. Note that superseded updates have yellow arrows, and the expired definition files have a black X, as shown in the figure.

FIGURE 17.17
Definition update status

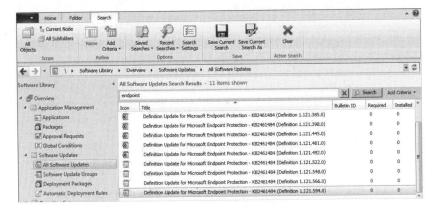

You now know that the Endpoint clients should be using version 1.121.594.0 of the definition file. If you open the SCEP client on a managed workstation, you can check the definition file that is currently being used by the client. See Figure 17.18.

FIGURE 17.18
Verifying SCEP client definition version

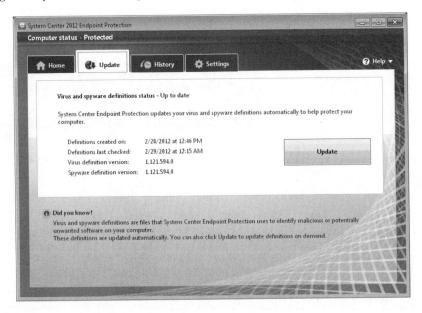

As you can see, this client is using the correct version of the definition file. If the definition file was an older version, it's possible that the client hasn't triggered the process yet to get the latest definition file. You could click Update and force the client to obtain the latest file. If the client still does not have the latest definition file, then you may need to troubleshoot the issue further and determine why the client is unable to retrieve the updated content.

Alerts

The ability to create alerts is new in ConfigMgr 2012. Alerts can be used to notify a ConfigMgr administrative user when specific events (such as a malware outbreak) have occurred in the environment. The administrator can view alerts in the ConfigMgr 2012 console, in reports, and also via email subscriptions. The ability to display alerts in the console or via email is especially important for SCEP-related events because it allows the administrator to quickly become aware of a malware event.

ConfigMgr 2012 Alerts vs. SCOM Alerts

The alert feature in ConfigMgr 2012 should not be confused with the alerting that is provided in the System Center Operations Manager product.

SCEP alerts are configured in the device collection properties. You cannot configure user collections for alerts. ConfigMgr 2012 has alerts for various issues and conditions and includes four alerts related specifically to malware:

Malware Detection   An alert is generated if a managed computer in the specified collection has malware.

Malware Outbreak   An alert is generated when a certain percentage of managed computers in the specified collection have malware detected.

Repeated Malware Detection   An alert is generated if specific malware is detected more than a certain number of times over a certain number of hours in a specified collection.

Multiple Malware Detection   An alert is generated if more than a specified number of malware types are detected over a given period for a specified collection.

In order to receive alerts you must enable a device collection to send alerts. The following is the process:

1. In the ConfigMgr 2012 console, select the device collection that should be configured to send alerts, and select Properties from the Ribbon.

    We will select the built-in All Desktop and Server Clients device collection for this scenario.

2. In the collection properties window, select the Alerts tab. See Figure 17.19.

FIGURE 17.19

Alerts tab in the collection properties

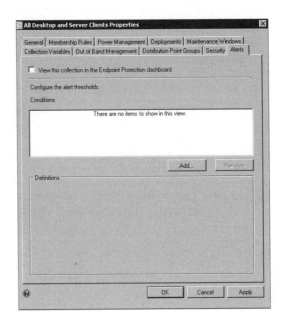

3. Enable the View This Collection In The Endpoint Protection Dashboard option, and click Add to specify alert thresholds.

ENABLING A COLLECTION

Until you enable a collection to be viewed, the System Center 2012 Endpoint Protection Status node in the Monitoring workspace of the ConfigMgr 2012 console will be blank, and a message will appear: "No collections have been configured to display in Endpoint Protection status."

When you click Add to specify alert thresholds, the Add New Collection Alerts window will appear, and all of the items will be unchecked by default. The needs of the administrative users may vary, but we will assume for this scenario that all of the alert conditions are needed in the environment.

4. Select each option and click OK (Figure 17.20).

FIGURE 17.20

Enabling collection alerts

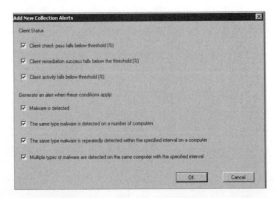

5. If you want to customize the thresholds you can, but for now use the default settings and click OK (Figure 17.21).

FIGURE 17.21
Setting alert thresholds

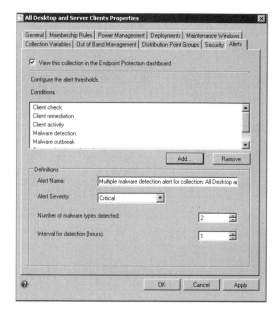

At this point you have configured the devices in a collection to generate alerts if the alert conditions are met. Those alerts can be viewed in the console, viewed in reports, and also sent via email subscriptions.

CONFIGMGR CAN SEND YOU EMAIL

In ConfigMgr 2012 you can configure an SMTP server that will be used to email Endpoint Protection alerts to administrative users. Follow these steps:

1. In the ConfigMgr 2012 console, choose Administration ➤ Overview ➤ Site Configuration ➤ Sites.

2. Select the CAS (or standalone primary site server) and click Settings ➤ Configure Site Components ➤ Email Notification.

3. Enable the email notification option, as shown in the following illustration, enter the required email settings for your environment, and click Apply.

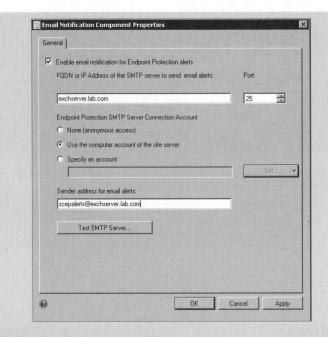

You also have the option to test the SMTP server and verify that the configuration is set properly.

4. Configure alert email subscriptions in the Monitoring workspace by choosing Monitoring ➢ Overview ➢ Alerts ➢ Subscriptions, as shown in the following example.

Reporting

ConfigMgr 2012 has several reports related to the Endpoint Protection products. There are currently four reports in the Endpoint Protection category:

Top Users By Threats   This report lists the users with the highest number of detected threats.

User Threat List   This report shows the list of threats found under a particular user account.

Antimalware Activity Report   This report shows an overview of antimalware activity and is shown in Figure 17.22.

FIGURE 17.22
Antimalware
Activity Report

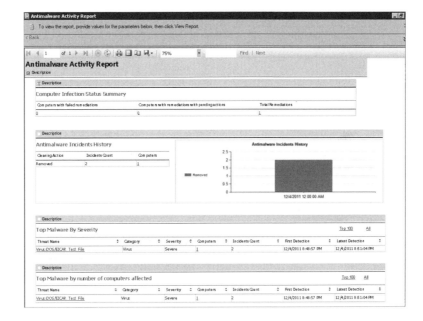

Infected Computers   This report shows a list of computers with a particular threat detected. We will use the remainder of this chapter to work through a real-world scenario.

 Real World Scenario

LET'S DEPLOY SOME MALWARE!

You are the ConfigMgr 2012 administrator at a company, and you have been telling your fellow IT department personnel about all of the great features that have been added to the ConfigMgr product. You are especially excited about the Endpoint Protection feature and the security that it provides.

Your manager has asked you to demonstrate to the team how the SCEP feature works. You decide it would be a great demo to actually deploy malware to the environment and have ConfigMgr 2012 identify the outbreak and remediate it. Seems a bit risky, right? And where do you get a virus so that you can prove SCEP works? Download some questionable files from the Internet or click on that email attachment from an unknown person? Not likely. It would be much safer to use a test virus, a piece of software that *looks* like malware but doesn't actually cause any damage.

One possible option is to use the antimalware test file that was created by the IT security research organization called EICAR (you can read more about them at www.eicar.org). The EICAR test file that they provide on their website looks like a virus or malware to antimalware software, but it is completely safe and benign. The test file simulates a malware attack but does not harm the computer in any way. However, just to be safe, you decide to perform this demo in your ConfigMgr 2012 test environment that is separated from the production network.

Using the EICAR test file, in a *test* ConfigMgr 2012 environment that is *not* connected to the production network, you can safely simulate the occurrence of a malware event on a managed computer without actually damaging the computer or causing a malware outbreak.

Note: Before using this tool visit the EICAR website and make sure you read through all of the documentation and disclaimers for the use of the tool.

RUN THE TEST!

You are now ready to run the demo for your team.

1. Log onto the Windows 7 computer that will become your "infected" workstation, launch the EICAR malware test file, and then monitor the results.

   First, you see by the red monitor icon that SCEP on the Windows 7 computer detected the EICAR test file as a potential threat and suspended the file.

The antimalware policy for this environment was configured to automatically remove threats, so the EICAR test malware was immediately removed.

2. Look at the SCEP client again, and see that the monitor icon is now green and the threat has been removed.

3. Choose the History tab of the SCEP client, and you'll see the action taken against the EICAR simulated virus.

The threat was removed, and the computer is now clean and malware free.

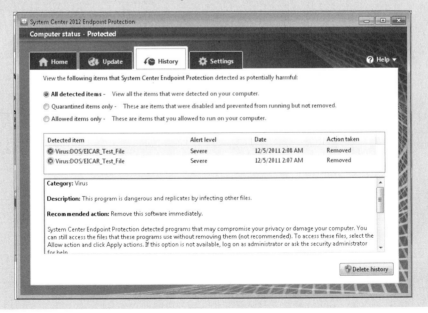

BUT WHAT HAPPENED ON THE SITE SERVER?

You saw SCEP on the Windows 7 computer flag the EICAR test file as malware and immediately remove the malware. But what would you see at the site server level? How would the built-in monitoring make you aware of the issue? Follow these steps to find out:

1. Open System Center 2012 Endpoint Protection Status in the ConfigMgr 2012 console (Monitoring ➤ Overview ➤ System Center 2012 Endpoint Protection Status).

2. Select the collection (All Desktop and Server Clients in this case) to see the overall status for the environment, including the number and percentage of clients that were affected by malware (one computer in this test).

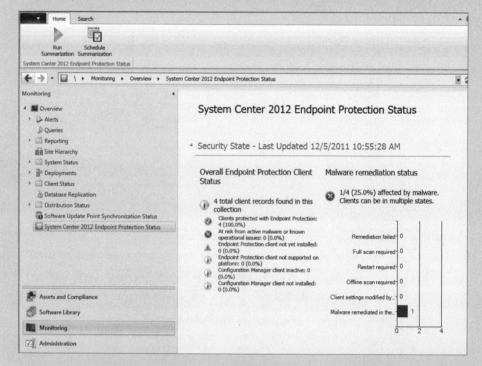

3. By scrolling down the Endpoint Protection Status window you can view the top five malware types that have been identified in the environment and also the operational and definition status on the managed computers.

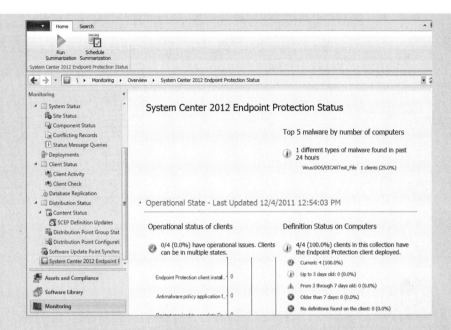

4. Open the Alerts section of the Monitoring workspace to view the alerts that were generated as a result of the EICAR malware test being executed on the Windows 7 client.

If you had configured email subscriptions, you would also have gotten those alerts as emails sent via the SMTP server you configured on the ConfigMgr site server.

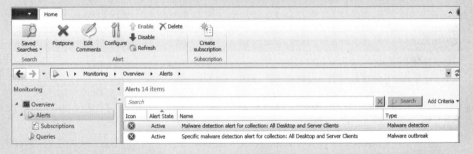

5. View the Antimalware Activity Report to see the status of the environment there.

You can clearly see the total number of remediations, the number of antimalware incidents, and so on.

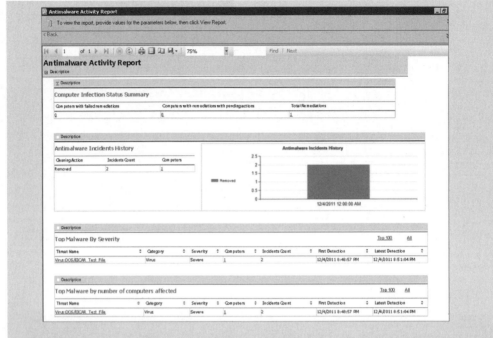

SUMMARY

You were able to demonstrate the effectiveness of the System Center 2012 Endpoint Protection feature of ConfigMgr 2012 to your peers, and they gave you a standing ovation. And bought you lunch.

The Bottom Line

Differentiate between FEP and SCEP. There are several differences between FEP and SCEP, including the architecture and the deployment process.

Master It Where does SCEP store its data?

Deploy and configure the System Center 2012 Endpoint protection site system and client. The three main components of enabling SCEP are as follows:

◆ Install and configure the Endpoint Protection site system.

◆ Enable and configure the SCEP client.

◆ Configure the antimalware policies.

Master It Do you need to create a package or application to deploy the SCEP client?

Create and assign a SCEP policy. SCEP has two types of policy:

◆ Antimalware

◆ Windows Firewall

The antimalware policy is used to define the antimalware settings, while the Windows Firewall policy can be used to control the configuration of Windows Firewall on managed computers. Both types of Endpoint Protection policies are created and modified in the ConfigMgr 2012 console.

Master It If you modify the default client antimalware policy and also create a custom antimalware policy with different values for the settings and apply it to a collection, which settings will be applied?

Chapter 18

Client Health

Maintaining healthy Configuration Manager clients is critical for delivering Configuration Manager services and meeting required service-level agreements. When clients in the environment are not healthy, the accuracy and dependability of Configuration Manager services are degraded, resulting in systems that are either completely or partially unmanaged.

Client health has been a challenge historically with Configuration Manager, and many tools or processes have been developed to help identify and repair broken clients. The most recent offering from Microsoft was the Client Status Reporting tool, which arrived in Configuration Manager 2007 R2. While good, many of these tools fall short in that client health problems must be managed manually, and automatic remediation is not generally part of the process. Configuration Manager 2012 changes the game in a dramatic way by not only detecting health problems through a thorough set of diagnostics but automatically remediating the problems as well. Before continuing, we must point out that no solution is 100 percent effective, and there will be problems that can't be resolved automatically. However, the majority of client problems that happen now are anticipated to be those that happen because of external issues not related to Configuration Manager specifically. The inclusion of client health evaluation/remediation by default in Configuration Manager 2012 will significantly enhance the stability of deployments. While this solution won't address every potential issue, it goes a long way to reducing administrator workload in keeping systems active and healthy.

This chapter details the client health mechanism in Configuration Manager 2012. In this chapter you will learn to

- ◆ Detail client health evaluations in Configuration Manager 2012.

- ◆ Review client health results in the Configuration Manager console.

Understanding the Client Health Mechanism

Managing client health issues involves detecting potential issues and fixing problems as they arise. Configuration Manager clients can become unhealthy for any number of reasons, often because of external issues such as WMI failure, DCOM permissions, service failures, and more. Configuration Manager 2012 introduces an automated mechanism to detect the most common client health issues and automates the process of fixing the problem. While this mechanism will go a long way toward helping maintain healthy clients, there will likely still be situations where manual intervention is required, but those situations should be greatly minimized.

Any tool to effectively validate and potentially repair client health issues, by definition, must be able to execute independently without relying on a healthy client to operate. Further, such a tool must execute locally to mitigate any potential network issues. The client health tool in Configuration Manager 2012 addresses this requirement nicely by running as a scheduled task—set apart from the client itself. The next section reviews the elements of this scheduled task for implementing the client health scanning.

Scheduled Task

The client health tool in Configuration Manager 2012 operates as a scheduled task. The required scheduled task is automatically created when the Configuration Manager 2012 client is installed and set to run daily or a bit past midnight. Figure 18.1 shows the scheduled task created on a client system.

DIFFERENCES BETWEEN PLATFORMS

All platforms supported for use with the Configuration Manager client also support the client health scheduled task, but there are differences in the way various configurations may appear between platforms. The example discussion focuses on a Windows 7 workstation.

FIGURE 18.1
Scheduled task created by a client installation

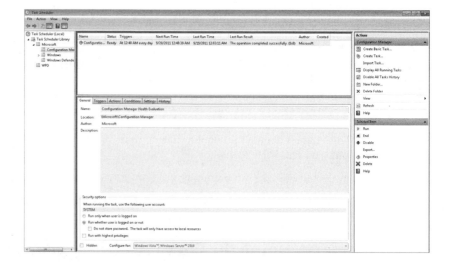

The overview of the scheduled task shown in Figure 18.1 provides helpful information, including the last run time and next run time for the task and whether the task was successful.

CLIENT HEALTH VS. PROBLEM-FREE EXECUTION

A successful task doesn't necessarily mean that the Configuration Manager client is healthy; it simply means that the client evaluation tool was able to execute without encountering a problem.

Notice that this view also provides various tabs that allow you to view the underlying configuration for the scheduled task. In order to make any changes to the task, you must select the properties for the task, which will present the same information but in an editable format, as shown in Figure 18.2 and described in the following sections.

FIGURE 18.2
Properties window
for the scheduled task

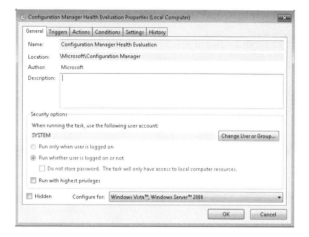

TRIGGERS TAB

The Triggers tab of the scheduled task shown in Figure 18.3 is the place where you might adjust the run schedule for the scheduled task. The default setting is that this task should be run just after midnight. If Configuration Manager client systems are not powered on and able to run the task on schedule, it might be helpful to change the default schedule to something that matches when systems are anticipated to be running in the environment. Before making the change, though, it is also worth considering the power management options available in Configuration Manager that allow you to wake up systems at a scheduled time to handle any pending tasks.

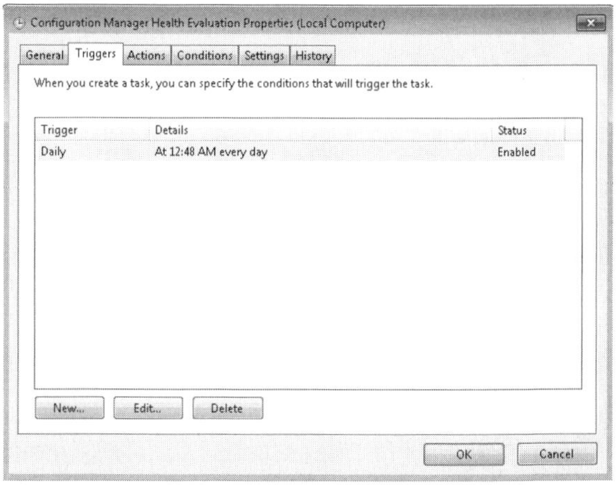

FIGURE 18.3
Triggers tab for the
scheduled task

ACTIONS TAB

The Actions tab of the scheduled task, shown in Figure 18.4, shows the command line that is to be executed when the scheduled task runs. As you can see from the figure, the task executes `CCMEval.exe`, which is in the `Windows\CCM` directory. We'll discuss CCMEval in more detail shortly. No command-line parameters are needed for this executable.

FIGURE 18.4

Actions tab for the scheduled task

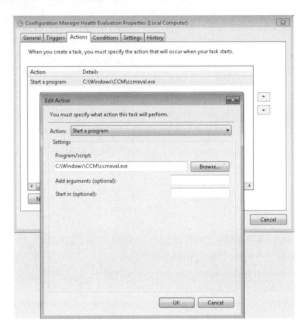

CONDITIONS TAB

The Conditions tab, shown in Figure 18.5, allows administrators to specify specific conditions that must be met before starting the task. There are no conditions set on this tab by default.

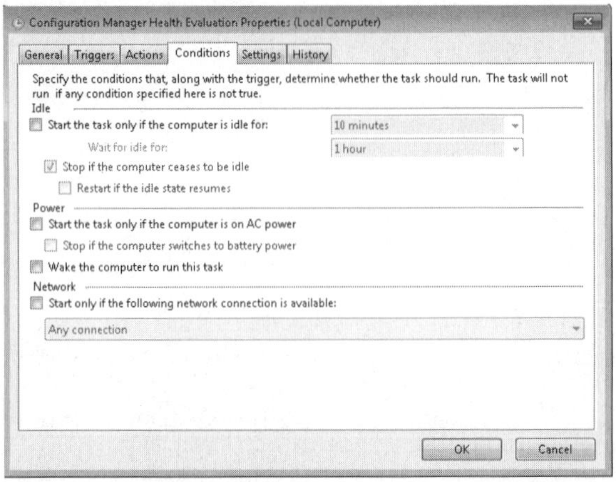

FIGURE 18.5

Conditions tab for the scheduled task

SETTINGS TAB

The Settings tab, shown in Figure 18.6, specifies various settings for the task. The default values configured are as follows:

FIGURE 18.6
Settings tab for the scheduled task

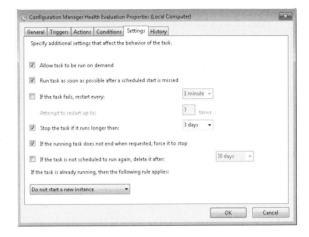

Allow Task To Be Run On Demand   This setting specifies that the task can be started by administrators as needed, such as in troubleshooting scenarios, outside the scheduled start time.

Run Task As Soon As Possible After A Scheduled Start Is Missed   This setting specifies the run behavior for the task if the system isn't able to run it on the defined schedule. As an example, if the system is powered off overnight and cannot run the task at the assigned time, then the task will be initiated the next time the system is started. The CCMEval process is lightweight but in this scenario is just one more thing for a system to do during startup, a process already loaded with significant activity. To avoid additional system load during startup caused by running this task, it may be worth considering rescheduling the start time for the task so that it takes place when the system is anticipated to be available.

Stop The Task If It Runs Longer Than   This setting ensures that a hung task doesn't continue to run long term. The default setting for this is 3 days, and it's unlikely that the CCMEval task will run into issues causing the process to hang. Having this set as a failsafe, though, is a good idea.

If The Running Task Does Not End When Requested, Force It To Stop   This setting works with the previous setting and will force the CCMEval thread to terminate if it remains in a hung state even after termination is requested.

The last setting, Do Not Start A New Instance, prevents multiple instances of CCMEval from spinning up.

HISTORY TAB

The History tab, shown in Figure 18.7, allows administrators to review the execution history for the task. There are no configurable settings on this tab.

FIGURE 18.7
History tab for the scheduled task

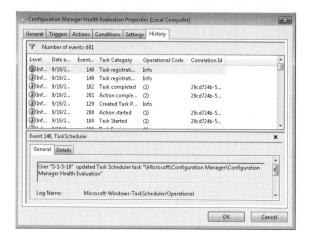

CCMEval Process

The task to execute CCMEval runs on a daily schedule by default. It is fully possible to change this schedule, but it's not recommended. If needed, the task can be run manually for trouble-shooting or other purposes, as previously alluded to.

With the understanding that client health checking and remediation for Configuration Manager 2012 clients is handled by CCMEval, it's natural to wonder what this process actually does. That's the next part of the discussion.

CCMEval is an executable that exists in the `Windows\CCM` folder on all Configuration Manager 2012 clients, as shown in Figure 18.8.

FIGURE 18.8
CCMEval executable in the `Windows\CCM` folder

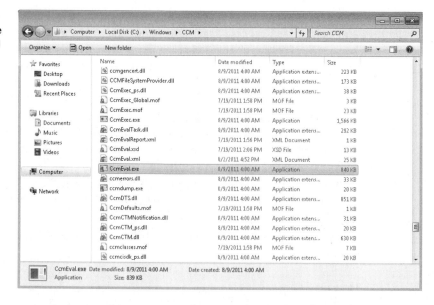

Note that in addition to CCMEval.exe there are also CCMEval.xml, CCMEval.xsd, CCMEvalReports.xml, and CCMEval.log. These are support files for the CCMEval process and are used as follows:

CCMEval.exe This is the executable file used to drive the health evaluation and remediation process on Configuration Manager 2012 clients.

CCMEval.xml This is the control file that defines the tests and remediation actions that will be taken as a result of test conditions. This file will be discussed in some detail shortly.

CCMEval.xsd This file defines the schema used to validate client health evaluation and report data.

CCMEvalReports.xml This is a header file used for building reporting information forwarded to Configuration Manager 2012 servers.

CCMEval.dll This is a library file for use with CCMEval.exe.

CCMEval.log This file records the progress of health check and remediation activities and is located in the Windows\CCM\logs folder.

Understanding the health check and remediation mechanism provided by CCMEval requires reviewing the work that is done during a CCMEval cycle along with the various checks that are performed. You can mine this information by reviewing CCMEval.xml along with CCMEval.log, and it will help you understand what is happening behind the scenes. Table 18.1 lists the checks and potential remediation outcomes that take place when problems are found during evaluation.

TABLE 18.1: CCMEval evaluation tasks and potential remediation actions

EVALUATION TASK	POTENTIAL REMEDIATION ACTION
Verify WMI service exists	No remediation
Verify/Remediate WMI service startup type	Reset service startup to Automatic
Verify/Remediate WMI service status	Reset service status to Running
WMI Repository Integrity Test	Reinstall Configuration Manager client
WMI Repository Read/Write Test	Reset WMI repository and reinstall Configuration Manager client
Verify BITS exists	No remediation
Verify/Remediate BITS startup type	Reset service startup to Automatic
Verify/Remediate client and client prerequisite installation	Install ConfigMgr prerequisites
Verify SMS Agent Host service exists	No remediation
Verify/Remediate SMS Agent Host service startup type	Reset service startup to Automatic

TABLE 18.1:   CCMEval evaluation tasks and potential remediation actions   *(CONTINUED)*

EVALUATION TASK	POTENTIAL REMEDIATION ACTION
Evaluation Task	Potential Remediation Action
Verify/Remediate SMS Agent Host Service	Reset service status to Active
	Restart SMS Agent Host Service
Verify/Remediate Lantern service startup type (Lantern = Microsoft policy platform processor service)	Reset service status to Manual
Verify/Remediate Antimalware service startup type	Reset service startup type to Manual
Verify/Remediate Antimalware service status	Reset service status to Running
Verify/Remediate Inspection service startup type	Reset service startup type to Manual if installed
Verify/Remediate Windows Update service startup type	Reset service startup type to Automatic
Verify/Remediate Windows Update Service status	Reset service status to Active
Verify/Remediate Configuration Manager Remote Control service	Reset service startup type to Automatic
Verify/Remediate Configuration Manager Remote Control service status	Reset service status to Active
Verify/Remdiate SQL CDE database health	Validate CCMStore.sdf

Figure 18.9 is a portion of the CCMEval.xml file that contains the rules that are used during the client health/remediation evaluation cycle.

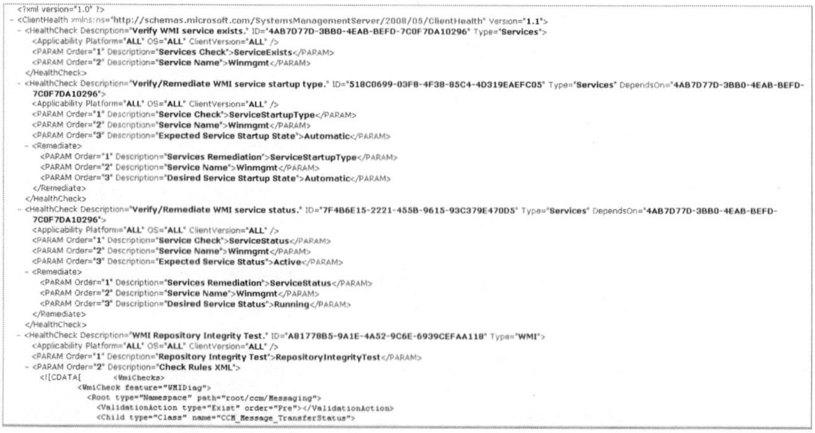

FIGURE 18.9
CCMEval.xml
example

Figure 18.10 is an example of the CCMEval.log file after an evaluation cycle is complete. Experienced administrators may notice that after the health-checking cycle is complete, the report is sent back to the site in the form of a state message. We mentioned earlier that an effective client health tool must function independently and not rely on a client function for any of its operation. State messages are commonly sent by the Configuration Manager client, so you might question whether the health evaluation tools simply offload the resulting state report to the client or handle it independently. The latter is true; client health forwards the state message directly to the clients management point using its own mechanism. This is also noted in the log snip below.

FIGURE 18.10
CCMEval.log
sample

```
==========[ ccmeval started in process 4084 ]==========
Loading manifest file: C:\Windows\CCM\CcmEval.xml
Successfully loaded ccmeval manifest file.
Begin evaluating client health rules.
Successfully retrieved all client health checks.
Evaluating health check rule {4A87D7D-3BB0-4EA8-BEFD-7C0F7DA10296} : Verify WMI service exists.
Evaluating health check rule {51BC0699-03F8-4F38-B5C4-4D319EAEFC05} : Verify/Remediate WMI service startup type.
Evaluating health check rule {7F4B6E15-2221-455B-96C1-93C379E47D05} : Verify/Remediate WMI service status.
Evaluating health check rule {A8177BB5-9A1E-4A52-9C6E-6939CEFAA118} : WMI Repository Integrity Test.
Evaluating health check rule {14E6774A-1795-4E09-B17D-B6F36A12420S} : WMI Repository Read/Write Test.
Evaluating health check rule {5CC6C949-5001-4765-8484-DD4FDC1E6940} : Verify BITS exists.
Evaluating health check rule {C6E29CF5-F9B2-4508-AE61-C4B256A75023} : Verify/Remediate BITS startup type.
Evaluating health check rule {CF4EFD8F-9A1E-4A89-8B35-7021D5176D08} : Verify/Remediate client and client prerequisites installation.
Evaluating health check rule {8883C683-04C8-422B-8B76-2EDD666BA781} : Verify SMS Agent Host service exists.
Evaluating health check rule {13F46523-5B82-417d-A363-A644E80CAD76} : Verify/Remediate SMS Agent Host service startup type.
Evaluating health check rule {70BECB51-44A1-4b46-8A23-6EA3D3458677} : Verify/Remediate SMS Agent Host service status.
Evaluating health check rule {C35E79OD-4C05-40A8-8B46-A6857896DD19} : WMI Event Sink Test.
Evaluating health check rule {D9D024SD-0617-4C2F-8837-84A197AC5B22} : Verify/Remediate Microsoft Policy Platform service startup type.
Evaluating health check rule {09886643-8E8B-431F-BC00-7D917632E22C} : Verify/Remediate Antimalware service startup type.
Result: Not Applicable, ResultCode: 0, ResultType: 0, ResultDetail:
Evaluating health check rule {5B5056GC-363E-4F1C-8A7D-6F2D2A51B142} : Verify/Remediate Antimalware service status.
Result: Not Applicable, ResultCode: 0, ResultType: 0, ResultDetail:
Evaluating health check rule {6BC824B4-8D8C-4779-8B10-ABD8CDSAFAEB} : Verify/Remediate Network Inspection service startup type.
Result: Not Applicable, ResultCode: 0, ResultType: 0, ResultDetail:
Evaluating health check rule {D6CB32EA-423D-44CB-9C58-97CE55D2148E} : Verify/Remediate Windows Update service startup type.
Evaluating health check rule {D3E01C5F-CE42-4022-B51D-68DADFA1CCD4} : Verify/Remediate Windows Update service status.
Evaluating health check rule {9040BA8C-580D-4FCA-8846-88D5F5BB1597} : Verify/Remediate Configuration Manager Remote Control service startup type.
Result: Not Applicable, ResultCode: 0, ResultType: 0, ResultDetail:
Evaluating health check rule {9DCD49EF-E021-46FF-A777-492108S18527} : Verify/Remediate Configuration Manager Remote Control service status.
Result: Not Applicable, ResultCode: 0, ResultType: 0, ResultDetail:
Evaluating health check rule {7B9F8FF6-EDF7-42CA-A67F-073A2E161C19} : Verify/Remediate SQL CE database is healthy.
Successfully evaluated all client health rules.
Fail to get integer from registry
Fail to get MPFailCount from registry, restart counting from 0
Client is set to use HTTPS when available. The current state is 480.
Client is set to use HTTPS when available. The current state is 480.
Raising event:

instance of CCM_CcmHttp_Status
{
        ClientID = "GUID:0CDS8D52-D98D-4D0C-B0AF-DAC54966D594";
        DateTime = "20120205081438.268000+000";
        HostName = "cmss1.contoso.com";
        HRESULT = "0x00000000";
        ProcessID = 4084;
        StatusCode = 0;
        ThreadID = 4760;
};

Client's current MP is http://cmss1.contoso.com and is accessible
MP check succeeded
Send previous report if needed.
Fail to get time from registry
Can't determine whether previous sent succeed, assume sent failed
Fail to get string from registry
There is no previous report sent
Fail to get time from registry
Can't determine whether previous sent succeed, assume sent failed
Previous send is not complete, need to send report this time.
Begin to send client health status report
Successfully sent client health status as a state message.
```

Client Health Evaluation: Results

Client health evaluation results are accessible in the Configuration Manager console in several areas. First, client health is reported on a device level by reviewing collection membership. Any collection in which the device is a member will provide the same health information. To view health results for a device, simply select it in the console, and the bottom of the screen will reveal five tabs: Summary, Client Activity Detail, Client Check Detail, Endpoint Protection, and Malware Detail. All of these tabs contain useful health information but for client health evaluation the first three are the main ones to review.

Summary   The Summary tab, shown in Figure 18.11, reports the latest client health information as Pass or Fail and also reports whether the last remediation attempt was successful.

FIGURE 18.11
Summary tab
for specific device

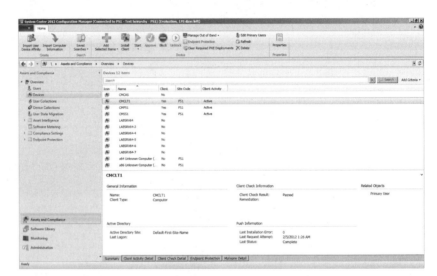

Client Activity Detail   The Client Activity Detail tab, shown in Figure 18.12, reports the last time the client requested policy, sent a heartbeat, reported hardware or software inventory, and sent a status message. The Days Since Last Communication field reflects how long the site has gone without hearing from the client. All of this information taken together gives a good idea about client health, but it's important to also factor in systems that may be powered are off for extended periods or are offline because of network or other issues. The Last Management Point field documents the last management point in use by the client. This information can help identify potential issues with boundaries, roaming, and the like.

FIGURE 18.12
Client Activity
Detail tab for
specific device

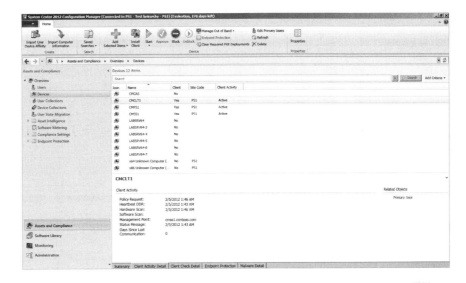

Client Health Detail   The Client Health Detail tab, shown in Figure 18.13, provides summary information about the device's last health evaluation scan. The specific evaluation rules and remediation status are reflected in the summary.

FIGURE 18.13
Client Health
Detail tab for
specific device

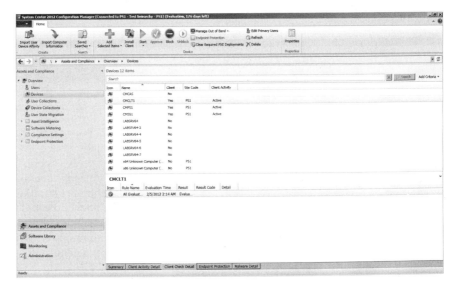

Monitoring: Client Health

The Monitoring workspace of the Configuration Manager console is the place to view Client Health and Client Activity information summarized for all clients in the hierarchy. This information is located under the Client Status node.

The Client Health node shown in Figure 18.14 shows a collective view of client health in the hierarchy. The number of devices that have passed or failed or are in an unknown status for health evaluation are reflected in a pie chart, and the accompanying bar chart details issues that have been found for those systems failing health evaluation. There is also a line graph showing trending information for client health. For more detail simply click the section of interest from the pie chart, the pie chart legend, or the bar chart, which will open a view of all devices in the selected category.

FIGURE 18.14
Client Health node
in the Monitoring
workspace of the
Configuration
Manager console

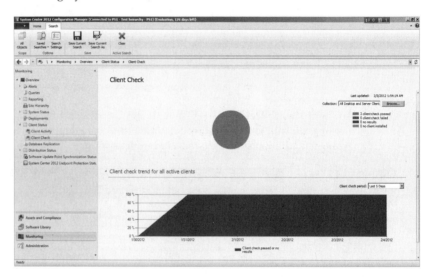

Monitoring: Client Activity   The Client Activity node shown in Figure 18.15 shows a collective view of client activity in the hierarchy. Device are represented in a pie chart as either active or inactive. In the example, all clients are active. Having 100 percent active clients would be a *great* result in a production environment but likely will not often be achieved because of environmental issues, systems being powered off for extended periods, network issues, and the like. This view also provides a line chart for trend analysis. To view specific systems that are in an active or inactive state, simply click the area of the pie chart or pie chart legend of interest to drill down for additional detail.

FIGURE 18.15
Client Activity node
in the Monitoring
workspace of the
Configuration
Manager console

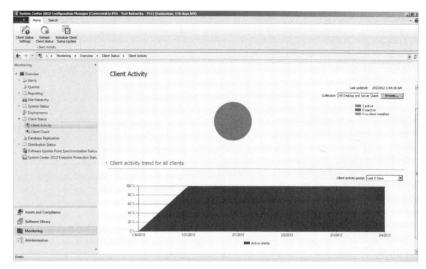

Reporting: Client Health   Configuration Manager 2012 provides a wealth of information through the reports available in the console. Reports are grouped by category and, as shown in Figure 18.16, there are five reports specifically geared to client health information. Combining the reports with the ability to create report subscriptions, as detailed in Chapter 12, "Reporting," gives administrators significant flexibility to pick reports that best serve their needs and render or deliver automatically.

FIGURE 18.16
Client health
reports

The Bottom Line

Detail client health evaluations in Configuration Manager 2012.   Health evaluations and remediations take place daily on every Configuration Manager 2012 client in the hierarchy. This information is updated at the site and is available for review on every client and also summarized for every client across the hierarchy.

> **Master It**   List the health evaluations and remediations that take place on Configuration Manager clients.

Review client health results in the Configuration Manager console.   Client health data is available in several locations of the console to allow access to health for individual devices and summarized data for all clients in the hierarchy.

> **Master It**   List the locations in the console where individual client health and summarized client health data are accessible.

Appendix

The Bottom Line

Each of The Bottom Line sections in the chapters suggest exercises to deepen skills and understanding. Sometimes there is only one possible solution, but often you are encouraged to use your skills and creativity to create something that builds on what you know and lets you explore one of many possible solutions.

Chapter 2: Planning a Configuration Manager Infrastructure

Plan and design a central administration site. One of the first questions you will ask yourself while starting to design and plan a new Configuration Manager 2012 hierarchy is "Do I need a central administration site?" The answer to this question is essential for your final design.

Master It Determine when a central administration site is needed.

Solution When there is a need for more than one primary site in your Configuration Manager infrastructure, you also need a central administration site. Adding a central administration site to the Configuration Manager 2012 hierarchy is not possible, so be sure to plan your Configuration Manager 2012 hierarchy correctly.

Plan and design an effective Configuration Manager 2012 infrastructure. When planning and designing a new Configuration Manager 2012 infrastructure, it is important to plan your primary sites appropriately. The design rules for primary sites have changed from how they were in Configuration Manager 2007.

Master It Understand the reasons for *not* needing a primary site implementation.

Solution You don't need to implement a primary site for the following reasons:

- ◆ Decentralized administration
- ◆ Logical data segmentation
- ◆ Client settings
- ◆ Languages
- ◆ Content routing for deep hierarchies

Identify the enhancements to the distribution point site system role. Distribution points in older versions were used to provide local points for accessing content and later also for App-V streaming. In Configuration Manager 2012 distribution points do a lot more.

Master It Distribution points have been enhanced. What roles and components are merged with the new distribution point, and what's new?

Solution Tricky question; not only are the PXE enabled distribution points and the multicast enabled distribution points merged with the new distribution point, but also the old branch distribution point and the distribution share are merged. The distribution point can be installed on Windows versions for servers and computers. Some new features of the distribution point are

- Bandwidth control
- Scheduling and throttling data synchronization
- Ability to specify drives for content
- Content validation on the distribution point
- Support for content prestaging

Prepare your current Configuration Manager 2007 environment for migration to Configuration Manager 2012. An in-place upgrade of Configuration Manager 2007 to Configuration Manager 2012 is not supported. Configuration Manager 2012 has a migration feature within the feature set to enable side-by-side migration.

Master It How can you as a Configuration Manager administrator or consultant prepare a current Configuration Manager 2007 environment for migration to Configuration Manager 2012?

Solution Steps you can take to prepare for the migration to Configuration Manager 2012 include the following:

- Flatten your hierarchy where possible.
- Plan for Windows Server 2008 R2, SQL 2008, and 64-bit.
- Start with the implementation of BranchCache with Configuration Manager 2007.
- Move from web reporting to SQL Reporting Services.
- Avoid mixing user and device-collection definitions.
- Use the UNC path in your packages instead of local paths.

Chapter 3: Migrating from Configuration Manager 2007

Determine what you are able to migrate with the migration feature. The new migration feature in Configuration Manager 2012 allows you to migrate the old Configuration Manager 2007 investments to Configuration Manager 2012 side by side. In earlier versions you were able to migrate the server in place or side by side by replicating data, but no real manageable migration feature was available.

Master It   With the migration feature you cannot migrate things like the following:

♦ Queries

♦ Security rights for the site and objects

♦ Configuration Manager 2007 reports from SQL Server Reporting Services

♦ Configuration Manager 2007 web reports

♦ Client inventory and history data

♦ AMT client-provisioning information

♦ Files in the client cache

To keep it positive, identify what objects you are able to migrate with the migration feature of Configuration Manager 2012.

Solution   Almost every investment you made in Configuration Manager 2007 you are able to migrate to Configuration Manager 2012. The following list includes all the objects that can be migrated:

♦ Advertisements

♦ Software distribution packages

♦ Virtual application packages

♦ Software update deployments

♦ Software update deployment packages

♦ Operating system deployment boot images

♦ Operating system deployment driver packages

♦ Operating system deployment images

♦ Operating system deployment packages

♦ Boundaries

♦ Software update lists

♦ Task sequences

♦ Configuration baselines

♦ Configuration items

♦ Asset Intelligence Catalog

♦ Asset Intelligence hardware requirements

♦ Asset Intelligence software list

♦ Software metering rules

Discover which migration approach is supported. Configuration Manager 2012 provides migration features that can be used for your migration of Configuration Manager 2007 to Configuration Manager 2012.

Master It With the earlier upgrades or migrations of Configuration Manager in your mind, what migration approaches are supported when migrating from Configuration Manager 2007 to Configuration Manager 2012?

Solution Configuration Manager 2012 officially supports only one migration approach, the side-by-side migration approach, when using the migration feature. The wipe-and-load approach is used only if you do not need to migrate anything from your old Configuration Manager 2007 environment.

Ascertain what kind of interoperability is supported during the migration. Interoperability like that supported in earlier versions is no longer supported; nevertheless, the migration feature of Configuration Manager 2012 supports some kinds of interoperability during the migration process. Depending on the size of your Configuration Manager 2007 source hierarchy, this can take some time.

Master It Interoperability like you were used to in SMS 2003 and Configuration Manager 2007 is no longer supported. Give two examples of interoperability features in Configuration Manager 2012.

Solution For interoperability purposes you are able to use shared distribution points in the process of migrating objects from Configuration Manager 2007 to Configuration Manager 2012. Another interoperability feature is the ability to re-migrate update objects. In other words, you can re-migrate objects that have been updated in Configuration Manager 2007 while migrating other objects.

Migrate packages and programs to the new application model. The classic packages just migrated to Configuration Manager 2012 can be used and targeted to collections of users and computers, but Configuration Manager is built around a new application model that allows you to implement user-centricity in your Configuration Manager 2012 environment.

Master It Converting classic packages to the application model is not a feature of Configuration Manager, but with extra software it can be done from the Configuration Manager 2012 console in a couple of different ways. What is the name of the tool that you use to convert the classic packages, and what are the steps to convert a classic package?

Solution The tool that is used for converting classic packages is Package Conversion Manager. Package Conversion Manager fully integrates with the Configuration Manager 2012 console.

The steps you need to take to convert a classic package are as follows:

1. Analyze the classic packages for their readiness state.

2. Convert classic packages that have a readiness state of Automatic.

3. Fix and convert the packages that have a Manual readiness state.

4. Test the applications before deploying them.

Chapter 4: Installation and Site Role Configuration

Understand Configuration Manager 2012 sites and the new approach to hierarchy design. Configuration Manager 2012 has three types of sites: the Central Administration Site, which is new, and the primary and secondary sites, which are familiar. Although two of the three site types are familiar, their use and approach to hierarchy design—or whether a hierarchy is needed at all—are quite different now.

Master It Describe the purpose of each site type and map each to specific management needs.

Solution

◆ Central Administration Site: Only present if a hierarchy is being configured. Provides centralized administration for the hierarchy but no direct client management.

◆ Primary site: Clients are assigned to primary sites, and this is where they receive management instruction, regardless of where in the hierarchy the client might be located.

◆ Secondary site: This type of site is of use only in situations where bandwidth conditions are so slow or unstable as to require a site server to throttle even small traffic, such as discovery and inventory information.

Construct a Configuration Manager 2012 hierarchy. The site hierarchy in Configuration Manager 2012 consists of the site types just described. The approach to design is very different from the previous version, with the number of primary sites being limited to a single tier. The chapter walked through configuring a hierarchy with all three site types.

Master It Describe a Configuration Manager 2012 site hierarchy. Detail components needed for site-to-site communication and security settings.

Solution

◆ Hierarchies always consist of a CAS and at least one primary child site. Additional primary child sites might be in place as well. Secondary sites should rarely be used but may be added if needed.

◆ Site-to-site communication requires site servers to have proper addresses and senders configured and correct credentials assigned where applicable.

◆ ConfigMgr 2012 installations create several local security groups that are used to grant access to site resources and facilitate site-to-site communication.

Determine when to expand a hierarchy and when to simply add a site system role for additional service. A major design goal of Configuration Manager 2012 is simplified hierarchy design. Administrators familiar with previous versions of Configuration Manager may be tempted to retain old hierarchy approaches when designing Configuration Manager 2012. Taking such an approach will often lead to inefficient designs and additional server cost and in some cases simply won't work.

Master It Understand the changes in sites and site components that lend themselves to hierarchy simplification and enable parity management with fewer site servers.

Solution

◆ Distribution point modifications include the ability to throttle content directly to remote distribution points. In addition, it is now possible to install distribution points on workstation systems directly where needed.

◆ Boundary groups simplify hierarchy configurations by allowing administrators to strictly define which distribution points are used to service specific client content requests.

◆ The updated security model in Configuration Manager 2012 allows administrators to scale out a single site while still maintaining logical separation of user role and function. There is no longer a technical need to have separate primary sites for servers and workstations. When managed properly, a single primary site is able to manage both seamlessly while protecting resources from access by unauthorized users.

Deploy and configure the various site system roles available per site. There are many roles available to enable management at a site. Understanding each role and the service it delivers is critical to getting the most out of an investment in Configuration Manager 2012.

Master It Review critical system roles and understand the services that are enabled through each.

Solution

◆ Critical site system roles are those that are required for basic ConfigMgr functionality at most sites. These include the management point and distribution point roles.

◆ Management points facilitate client-to-site server communication.

◆ Distribution points store content that may be needed by clients of the site.

Chapter 5: Role-Based Administration

Understand the role-based administration model in ConfigMgr 2012. SMS and ConfigMgr 2007 used a class and instance security model, which could be confusing at times. ConfigMgr 2012 adopts the RBAC model, thereby making the administration of security in ConfigMgr 2012 a less-daunting task.

Master It What does the acronym RBAC stand for? And what does role-based administration mean?

Solution RBAC is an acronym for Role-Based Access Control and is the security model used in many products in the System Center suite, including ConfigMgr 2012.

Role-based administration means that the ConfigMgr 2012 administrator can use a combination of security roles, security scopes, and collections to define what the ConfigMgr administrative users can view and manage.

Distinguish security roles from security scopes. Security roles and security scopes are important components of the role-based security model in ConfigMgr 2012.

Master It Can you identify the key differences between a security role and a security scope?

Solution   The primary difference between the two is that a security role is used to organize tasks or functions, while a security scope is used to define access to objects. The security role is the action (or lack thereof if trying to block access), while the security scope is what is acted upon (or lack thereof if trying to block access).

Understand which objects in ConfigMgr 2012 define an administrative user.   The administrative user consists of the security role, the security scope, and collections. In this chapter you learned the differences between a security role and a security scope, and you know that collections can be used to control the objects that an administrative user can access.

Master It   As the ConfigMgr 2012 administrator, do you need to create a custom ConfigMgr 2012 console so that the administrative user can see only what you want them to see?

Solution   No. The beauty of the role-based administration model is that the user will see only what they have access to in the ConfigMgr 2012 console. You do not need to provide a modified console for them. They simply log onto the environment with their administrative user account and open the ConfigMgr 2012 console, and they will see only the objects they have access to. Objects that they do not have access to will be hidden.

Chapter 6: Client Installation

Configure boundaries and boundary groups.   Before starting any client installation, verify that you have configured a boundary group for site assignment.

Master It   Let Configuration Manager Forest Discovery automatically create the boundaries and add them to the correct boundary groups.

Solution   Once you have configured Forest Discovery, add the automatically created IP subnets to a new or existing discovery group.

Select the relevant discovery methods.   You configure discovery methods in the Configuration Manager console. The Active Directory discovery methods all require a schedule and an LDAP path. There are schedules for delta and full discovery. In Configuration Manager 2012, delta discovery will also find changes to existing objects; this eliminates the need to run a full discovery more than once a week.

Master It   Always know what you want to discover and where. Based on that knowledge, configure the needed discovery methods.

Solution   The correct discovery method depends on how you want to deploy clients and work with features like application deployment. For a client push installation to work, it is a good idea to configure Active Directory Computer Discovery. On the other hand, if you want to deploy applications to end users, you also need to configure Active Directory Users Discovery.

Employ the correct client installation methods.   When configuring the client installation methods, make sure you know the pros and cons for each method. Some require firewall settings; others require local administrative permissions. You need to make sure that all the required settings are in place. Do not start any installation until you have the needed site systems, boundary groups, and command lines specified.

Master It Configure the correct command-line properties and ensure they will work for all environments (local forest, workgroup, and DMZ). Create multiple client push installation accounts, and ensure that you have a good understanding of the three phases (preinstallation, installation, and post-installation).

Solution Configure the command-line properties in the properties for the client push installation method. That way you ensure that the properties are always replicated to Active Directory and can be read during the client installation.

Furthermore you should add the command-line properties that will also work in another forest and workgroup in the client push properties.

Ensure client health. Client Status might not be the first task you think about when implementing a system like Configuration Manager. But it is crucial to the daily administration that you can trust the numbers you see in the reports and in the console. One way to ensure that is by making certain that all clients are healthy and are providing the server with up-to-date status messages and discovery information.

Master It Discuss the different environment that exists in your organization, and use that information when configuring client health alerts. Make sure that you know the client activity during a normal period and that you have a set of defined SLAs for each of the environments (laptops, road warriors, servers, call center, and so on).

Solution Create unique collections corresponding to each computer role type that you have. In the properties for every collection, configure the unique client Status values.

Chapter 7: Application Deployment

Explain the options available for Application Deployment. The new Application Deployment model is a significant and welcome change for deploying software in the enterprise. There are many new components including a rules-based Requirements engine, the ability to detect whether the application is already installed, the option to configure application dependencies and relationships, and more.

Master It List several configuration options available for applications and deployment types.

Solution Applications: The ability to publish in the Software Catalog, define supersedence, and reference information.

Deployment types: The ability to set dependency information, specify criteria defining whether an application is already installed, configure requirements, and set return codes.

Detail the various components required for Application Deployment. Success with Application Deployment requires that several other Configuration Manager 2012 components be available and properly configured. The list includes management point(s), distribution point(s), IIS, BITS, the client itself, and possibly more.

Master It List the components required for configuring an application deployment.

Solution The application and at least one deployment type and deployment content must be staged on at least one available distribution point. Clients must receive the deployment and pass any configured requirements, allowing the deployment to be initiated.

Understand the role of and manage distribution points.   The role of distribution points has not changed significantly in that this is the role that makes content available to Configuration Manager 2012 devices and users. The options available for implementing the role have changed significantly with the inclusion of throttling control content flow from site server to remote distribution points, the single-instance storage approach for placing content on distribution points, the ability to detect content corruption, and the requirement that all distribution points be BITS enabled.

> **Master It**   Discuss the differences between implementing a distribution point role on the site server locally and remotely.
>
> **Solution**   Local distribution point: Content is transferred by local file copy; there is no ability to throttle a local distribution point.
>
> Remote distribution point: Content is transferred by network file copy without compression. The ability to throttle content is available, but content is not compressed.

Chapter 8: Software Updates

Plan to use Software Updates.   You can use the same method of deployment intelligence that was used in Chapter 2 to gather information for planning to implement Software Updates. This will be very helpful in making sure that you get the most out of the Software Updates feature for your organization.

> **Master It**   What is the first step in gathering deployment intelligence for planning to implement Software Updates?
>
> **Solution**   You must determine what needs to be accomplished with Software Updates.

Configure Software Updates.   Before you can utilize Software Updates in your environment, you must set up and configure the various components of this feature.

> **Master It**   What is the first thing you have to install before you can use Software Updates?
>
> **Solution**   You must install Windows Server Update Services (WSUS) 3.0 SP2. You can use either the full install or the WSUS Administrative Console, depending on what you are setting up.

Use the Software Updates feature to manage software updates.   The hardest thing to do in SMS 2003 relating to patch management was to programmatically prioritize software updates that are critical so they can be deployed with a higher priority than other updates.

> **Master It**   What does Configuration Manager provide that can help with prioritizing software updates?
>
> **Solution**   Configuration Manager now includes the severity of all of the updates that are synchronized into the Configuration Manager database. With that data you can sort updates by that category and create search criteria and update groups based on their severity level so that you can use them as a source for your software update components.

Use automatic update deployment to deploy software updates.   When you deployed software in Configuration Manager 2007, you deployed software updates through a procedure that consumed a lot of time.

Master It   Configuration Manager has a new feature called Automatic Deployment Rules. What kinds of updates are suitable to deploy via the automatic deployment rules?

Solution   Patch Tuesday software updates and definition files for Forefront Endpoint Protection can be deployed via the automatic deployment rules. Be sure to always test the updates to see if they have any impact on your environment.

Chapter 9: Operating System Deployment

Specify a Network Access account.   The Network Access account is the account Configuration Manager will use to access the system while running WinPE.

Master It   How do you specify the Network Access account?

Solution   Open the Configuration Manager 2012 console, and do the following:

a. Choose the Administration workspace and expand Overview ➤ Site Configuration ➤ Site.

b. Select one of the sites for which you want to configure the Network Access account, and click Configure Site Components on the Home tab of the Ribbon.

c. Select Software Distribution.

d. Select the Network Access Account tab, set the Network Access account to the account created earlier, and click OK.

Enable PXE support.   PXE support in Configuration Manager is used to begin the operating system deployment process. The PXE feature responds to Configuration Manager clients making PXE boot requests.

Master It   How do you set up PXE support?

Solution   Open the Configuration Manager 2012 console, and do the following:

a. Choose the Administration workspace and expand Overview ➤ Distribution Points.

b. Select the site server on which the distribution point resides, and click Properties on the Site Role area of the Ribbon.

c. Select the PXE tab and click Enable PXE Service Point.

Update the driver catalog package.   The driver catalog allows you to add drivers to the already created packages and images you have within your organization so you are not constantly re-creating your images when you get a new machine in your environment.

Master It   How do you update the driver catalog package?

Solution   From within the Configuration Manager console, do the following:

a. Choose the Software Library workspace, expand Overview ➤ Operating Systems, and select Drivers.

b. Click Import Driver on the Home tab of the Ribbon of the Configuration Manager console.

c. Browse to the network location of the drivers you want to import.

d. Specify which package and boot images you want to import the specific drivers into.

Update an image from the console. In the past it was a big issue to keep your images up to date; no easy procedure existed. In Configuration Manager 2012 a feature called Schedule Updates exists to update your Windows images.

> **Master It** How do you update your Windows images?
>
> **Solution** From within the Configuration Manager console, do the following:
>
> **a.** Choose the Software Library workspace, expand Overview ➢ Operating Systems, and select Operating System Images.
>
> **b.** From there select a Windows image and click Schedule Updates in the Home tab of the Ribbon of the Configuration Manager console.
>
> The process of updating the images is scheduled; after finishing, the wizard and the update will start automatically.

Chapter 10: Asset Intelligence

Enable Asset Intelligence. If you installed ConfigMgr from scratch, you will find that Asset Intelligence is not enabled by default. Depending on the data that you want information on, you will have to select the ConfigMgr Asset Intelligence Reporting Class Settings and make sure that client agents are enabled.

> **Master It** Which classes in the Asset Intelligence Reporting Class Settings do you have to enable to use Asset Intelligence?
>
> **Solution** You need to enable the following classes in the Asset Intelligence Reporting Class Settings to use Asset Intelligence:
>
> SMS_SystemConsoleUsage
>
> SMS_SystemConsoleUser
>
> SMS_InstalledSoftware
>
> SMS_AutoStartSoftware
>
> SMS_BrowserHelperObject
>
> SoftwareLicensingService
>
> SoftwareLicensingProduct
>
> Win32_USBDevice

Configure the Asset Intelligence synchronization point. The Asset Intelligence synchronization point is used to connect to System Center Online to synchronize Asset Intelligence Catalog information and get periodic updates.

> **Master It** What do you need to do in order to configure the Asset Intelligence synchronization point?

Solution

◆ You need to configure it on only the CAS or stand-alone primary site.

◆ You may want to obtain an optional System Center Online authentication certificate.

◆ If no valid certificate is issued, you can install the Asset Intelligence synchronization point without a certificate.

Import the Microsoft Volume License Statement.   In ConfigMgr you can import the Microsoft Volume License Statement and the General License Statement so that the software inventory and Asset Intelligence can count the number of licenses currently in use on the environment.

Master It   What file types does ConfigMgr 2012 support for the License Statements?

Solution   It will be a `.csv` file if the file to be imported is a General License Statement. If you are going to import a Microsoft Volume License Statement, it will be an `.xml` or `.csv` file. You can obtain this file by logging into the following website: `http://licensing.microsoft.com`. Or you can request this file from your Microsoft Technical Account Manager or Account Manager.

Chapter 11: Inventory and Software Metering

Configure and manage Software Inventory.   Configuring Software Inventory has changed in Configuration Manager 2012, although the client-processing part is almost the same as in Configuration Manager 2007.

Master It   By default, Configuration Manager does not scan for any file types. Where would you go to do that?

Solution   Take the following steps:

1. Navigate to the Administration workspace, select Client Settings, and open the Default Client Settings properties.

2. Select Software Inventory.

3. Click Set Types.

4. Click the New button, and configure the files or file types you want to include in the software-scanning process.

Configure and manage Hardware Inventory.   Hardware Inventory provides a wealth of information on the hardware resources in your organization. That information is vital when planning for things such as updating standard business software or upgrading the standard operating system your organization uses. If the standard hardware inventory collected is not enough for your needs, then you have many options to extend the hardware inventory to get that vital information.

Master It   Where do you enable or disable data classes in Hardware Inventory?

Solution   You need to open the default client agent settings or create a custom client setting. Custom client settings can only be used when you want to enable data classes that already exist in Configuration Manager. For custom classes (or to delete classes) you need to modify the default client settings.

Configure and manage Software Metering. Keeping track of software that is installed and actually being used is a large part of being able to manage software licenses effectively. By pairing Software Metering in Configuration Manager with Software Inventory, you can get detailed information on just what software is out there and who is or is not using it. This goes a long way to help keep your software licensing in compliance.

Master It How long do you have to wait, at the very least, after you configure Software Metering before you can expect to see any data returned?

Solution You must wait at least 12 hours. Software Metering Data Summarization runs daily by default and will run only against data that is at least 12 hours old. This is required for all software metering reports to produce any meaningful data.

Chapter 12: Reporting

Install the Reporting Services point. Installing a Reporting Services site system within Configuration Manager allows not only administrators but everyone to view reports in some fashion either via different file formats or a direct link within the Web Reporting Manager.

Master It What is the procedure to enable Reporting with Configuration Manager?

Solution Open the Configuration Manager 2012 console, and do the following:

1. Navigate to the Administration workspace.
2. Expand Site Configuration ➤ Servers And Site System.
3. Right-click the server and select Add Site System Roles.

Manage reporting security. Reporting security is an integrated part of the built-in security. You provide users with access to reports by adding them to a predefined security role or by creating a custom role with permissions to run or modify reports.

Master It Add users to a built-in security role.

Solution Open the Configuration Manager 2012 console, and do the following:

1. Navigate to the Administration workspace ➤ Security ➤ Administrative Users.
2. Click Add User Or Group from the Ribbon.

Create and manage report subscriptions. Creating subscriptions can be very helpful in many scenarios. You can configure subscriptions from Report Manager or in the Configuration Manager console.

Master It Create an email-based subscription.

Solution Open the Configuration Manager 2012 console, and do the following:

1. Navigate to the Monitoring workspace.
2. Expand Reports.
3. Select the report, and click Create Subscription from the Ribbon.

Create custom reports. Creating custom reports can be helpful in many scenarios. You will quickly find that the canned reports are very useful but may be limited for all your needs.

Master It Create a custom report.

Solution Open the Configuration Manager 2012 console, and do the following:

1. Navigate to the Monitoring workspace.

2. Expand Reports, and select the appropriate folder.

3. Click Create Report from the Ribbon to start the process in Report Builder.

Chapter 13: Compliance Settings

Enable the client settings. Until the client settings are enabled for your Configuration Manager clients, your clients will not evaluate any of the configuration baselines. This is the first step in using Compliance Settings to validate client settings.

Master It Enable Compliance Settings for the Configuration Manager clients.

Solution In the Compliance Settings section of the client settings, set Enable Compliance Evaluation On Clients to True.

Create configuration items. Configuration items are the pieces that make up a configuration baseline. There are a number of different configuration item types in Configuration Manager, and depending on the type you choose to create, you are presented with certain options when creating your configuration item. The steps to create configuration items were covered in the first part of this chapter and they included several examples of how to create the different types of configuration items.

Master It Create a configuration item for an application that checks a registry string value.

Solution Start the wizard from the Assets and Compliance workspace, Compliance Settings node; make sure you have Configuration Items selected, and right-click it. Choose Create Configuration Item. In the wizard, complete the following settings:

1. On the General tab, enter appropriate information for these fields:

   Name: Application name and value description

   Description: Configuration item for …

   Categories: Add categories

2. On the Settings tab, choose New Settings ➤ Registry Key from the menu and set the following options:

   Hive: HKEY_LOCAL_MACHINE

   Key: SOFTWARE\ …

   Is This Registry Key Associated With A 64-Bit Application: No

   Report A Noncompliance Event When This Instance Count Fails: Yes/Checked

Instance Operator: Greater Than

Values: 0

Severity: Warning

3. On the Settings tab, choose New Registry from the menu.

4. On the General tab of the new registry validation, enter the following information:

   Display Name: User-friendly name

   Description: Description of what you are checking for

   Hive: `HKEY_LOCAL_MACHINE`

   Key: `SOFTWARE\` …

   Value Name: Registry key value name

   Is This Registry Key Associated With A 64-Bit Application: No

5. On the Compliance Rule tab of the new registry compliance, set Data Type to String.

6. Click New on the menu in the details pane and, in the Configure Settings window that appears, configure these settings:

   Name: User-friendly name

   Description: Description of the value you are going to check for

   Operator: Equals or Other operator

   Value: Value to check the registry key for

   Severity: Warning

7. Click OK to return to the Validation tab of the new registry validation and set the following:

   Is This Registry Key Associated With A 64-Bit Application: No

   Report A Noncompliance Event When This Instance Count Fails: Yes/Checked

   Instance Operator: Greater Than

   Values: 0

   Severity: Warning

8. Click OK to save your changes to the Settings tab and move on.

9. On the Detection Method tab, select the radio button Always Assume Application Is Installed.

Define a configuration baseline. This is where you take one or more of the CIs and put them into a package that the Configuration Manager client downloads and at the scheduled time validates by checking the CIs against the computer. The Configuration Manager client then reports the outcome of those checks back to Configuration Manager, where you can then run reports to see if your clients are within the specified configuration or not. These steps were covered in the last section of the chapter.

Master It   Assemble a configuration baseline with one or more configuration items you have created.

Solution   Follow these steps:

1. In the Assets and Compliance workspace, expand Compliance Settings, and then choose Configuration Baselines.

2. Right-click and choose Create Configuration Baseline.

3. Enter an appropriate name for this baseline and a description, and select or create any categories necessary.

   The Configuration Data list displays all the configuration items or configuration baselines that are included in the configuration baseline.

4. Click Add to add a new configuration item, and choose the configuration items you have created.

5. Click OK and Apply, and you will have your baseline created.

6. Deploy the configuration baseline to a collection.

Chapter 14: Mobile Device Management

Detail the differences between lite and depth management.   The various management options and settings available for mobile devices will vary depending on whether lite- or depth-management options are in place.

Master It   List mobile device management capabilities for lite versus depth management.

Solution   Lite management of devices allows for limited device inventory, settings management, and remote wipe.

Depth management of devices allows for over-the-air enrollment, full inventory, more complete settings management, software distribution, and remote wipe.

Understand how to configure mobile device management.   Properly configuring mobile device management requires addressing several potential scenarios. From a Configuration Manager 2012 perspective, though, the choice is simple: lite or depth management.

Master It   List the items that need to be configured for both lite and depth management.

Solution   Lite management requires a properly configured ActiveSync connection between the Exchange Server and managed devices and also proper configuration of the ConfigMgr 2012 Exchange ActiveSync connector.

Depth management requires proper configuration of an enterprise certification authority, Active Directory, and several different site system roles. The site system roles include the enrollment point, enrollment proxy point, device management point, and distribution point.

Understand the depth-management enrollment process.   From the user perspective the enrollment process for depth management is straightforward. Behind the scenes, there are a number of moving parts. Each of these components is critical to the enrollment process.

Master It   List the components required to enroll depth-managed devices.

Solution

◆ Enrollment web proxy site system role

◆ Enrollment service point site system role

◆ Mobile device management point

◆ Enterprise Microsoft certification authority

◆ Active Directory services

Chapter 15: Troubleshooting

Create a basic maintenance plan.   Setting up a basic maintenance plan is a vital step to ensure the proper health of your Configuration Manager 2012 hierarchy.

Master It   How do you create a basic maintenance plan?

Solution   Develop a plan, similar to the guidelines discussed earlier in Chapter 15 in the section "Creating the Maintenance Plan." Review and modify the plan on a biannual basis, and update it throughout the year to ensure nothing gets overlooked and the documentation is up to date with the current design of the Configuration Manager site.

View log files using CMTrace.   Although using CMTrace is not a requirement for viewing log files, it is highly recommended because CMTrace constantly monitors the opened file for updates.

Master It   Use CMTrace to view log files.

Solution   ConfigMgr CMTrace is located on your installation media in SMSSETUP\ Tools\cmtrace.exe. Click File, browse to the log file you want to review, and open it.

Troubleshoot DRS replication.   To view the current status of the ConfigMgr DRS replication and to know the latest information about the changes being requested on the site, it's important to be familiar with the log file and the replication process.

Master It   To view the latest changes on the replication process, what log file do you need to open to view this information?

Solution   Locate the RCMCtrl.log file and open it using CMTrace. Locate the DRS initiation and RCM changes.

Other solutions might include executing the spDiagDRS stored procedure to view the current replication status and details about the data that is being replicated. You can find more details about the RCMCtrl.log at the beginning of this chapter.

Chapter 16: Disaster Recovery

Configure backups for Configuration Manager sites.   Backing up Configuration Manager sites can be automated by scheduling the Backup ConfigMgr Site Server maintenance task. When the Configuration Manager backup service (SMS_SITE_BACKUP) starts, it uses instructions in the backup control file, located at

`[ConfigMgr Install Location]Microsoft Configuration Manager\Inboxes\smsbkup`
`.box\smsbkup.ctl`

Master It   Recovering Configuration Manager sites is only supported with site backups from what source?

Solution   The backups must be created by the Backup ConfigMgr Site Server maintenance task.

Recover Configuration Manager sites.   Recovery of a Configuration Manager site requires that you do not have a Configuration Manager site installed when starting the `Setup.exe` process. The recovery process will recover data from the backup files and from a reference site provided you have a multisite hierarchy.

Master It   What is Site Recovery designed for?

Solution   It is used for repairing and resynchronizing ConfigMgr data.

Archive backup snapshots to another location.   The first time the Backup ConfigMgr Site Server task runs, it creates a backup snapshot, which can be used to recover a Configuration Manager site system when it fails. The next time the backup task runs, it makes a new backup snapshot that will overwrite the one that was made during the last snapshot. This could be a problem if the current backup snapshot becomes corrupt for some reason, because there is no other backup to restore from.

Master It   What script can you use to copy backup snapshots from the site server to a new location but is not created when ConfigMgr is installed?

Solution   You can use `AfterBackup.bat`.

Reinstall the site components and reset file and registry permissions to their default settings.   From time to time other administrators mess around with the default permissions that are configured on the different folders and shares created by Configuration Manager.

Master It   How can you restore the file and registry permissions without performing a complete restore?

Solution   Run `setup.exe` from the Start menu or from the `<Configuration Manager installation directory>`\Microsoft Configuration Manager\bin\x64 folder. Select Perform Site Maintenance Or Reset This Site and click Next. On the Site Maintenance page select Reset Site With No Configuration Changes and finish the wizard.

Chapter 17: System Center Endpoint Protection

Differentiate between FEP and SCEP.   There are several differences between FEP and SCEP, including the architecture and the deployment process.

Master It   Where does SCEP store its data?

Solution   Remember that FEP used two databases to store data: FEP_DB and FEP_DW. SCEP uses the ConfigMgr 2012 database to store SCEP-related data.

Deploy and configure the System Center 2012 Endpoint protection site system and client. The three main components of enabling SCEP are as follows:

◆ Install and configure the Endpoint Protection site system.

◆ Enable and configure the SCEP client.

◆ Configure the antimalware policies.

Master It   Do you need to create a package or application to deploy the SCEP client?

Solution   No. The installation media for the System Center 2012 Endpoint Protection client (SCEPInstall.exe) is distributed to the managed devices as part of the ConfigMgr 2012 client install media. Remember that the SCEP client won't actually be installed on managed devices until the Endpoint Protection client is enabled and configured in an assigned client settings policy. Also remember that the Endpoint Protection client cannot be enabled until the Endpoint Protection site system role is enabled.

Create and assign a SCEP policy.   SCEP has two types of policy:

◆ Antimalware

◆ Windows Firewall

The antimalware policy is used to define the antimalware settings, while the Windows Firewall policy can be used to control the configuration of Windows Firewall on managed computers. Both types of Endpoint Protection policies are created and modified in the ConfigMgr 2012 console.

Master It   If you modify the default client antimalware policy and also create a custom antimalware policy with different values for the settings and apply it to a collection, which settings will be applied?

Solution   Changes made to the default policy will be applied to all managed computers in the environment. However, the custom policy will override any settings that are in conflict with the default policy.

Chapter 18: Client Health

Detail client health evaluations in Configuration Manager 2012.   Health evaluations and remediations take place daily on every Configuration Manager 2012 client in the hierarchy. This information is updated at the site and is available for review on every client and also summarized for every client across the hierarchy.

Master It   List the health evaluations and remediations that take place on Configuration Manager clients.

Solution

◆ Review the CCMEval.log file to see all evaluations and remediations that are taking place on clients.

◆ Review the CCMEval.xml file to understand the details behind each evaluation.

Review client health results in the Configuration Manager console.   Client health data is available in several locations of the console to allow access to health for individual devices and summarized data for all clients in the hierarchy.

Master It   List the locations in the console where individual client health and summarized client health data are accessible.

Solution

- Individual client health data is available by viewing devices individually in collections.

- Summarized client health data is available in the Monitoring workspace of the Configuration Manager console by choosing the Client Status node and then the Client Activity and Client Health nodes.

- Configuration Manager 2012 reports also offer a view into client health data.

Index

Note to the Reader: Throughout this index **boldfaced** page numbers indicate primary discussions of a topic. *Italicized* page numbers indicate illustrations.